D0982935

SPECIAL EDUCATION INTERNATIONAL PERSPECTIVES: PRACTICES ACROSS THE GLOBE

ADVANCES IN SPECIAL EDUCATION

Series Editor: Anthony F. Rotatori

Recent Volumes:

ADVANCES IN SPECIAL EDUCATION   VOLUME 28

SPECIAL EDUCATION INTERNATIONAL PERSPECTIVES: PRACTICES ACROSS THE GLOBE

EDITED BY

ANTHONY F. ROTATORI
Saint Xavier University, Chicago, IL, USA

JEFFREY P. BAKKEN
Bradley University, Peoria, IL, USA

SANDRA BURKHARDT
Saint Xavier University, Chicago, IL, USA

FESTUS E. OBIAKOR
Valdosta State University, Valdosta, GA, USA

UMESH SHARMA
Monash University, Victoria, Australia

United Kingdom – North America – Japan
India – Malaysia – China

Emerald group publishing limited
Howard House, Wagon Lane, Bingley BD16 1WA, UK

First edition 2014

Copyright © 2014 Emerald Group Publishing Limited

Reprints and permission service
Contact: permissions@emeraldinsight.com

British Library Cataloguing in Publication Data
A catalogue record for this book is available from the British Library

ISBN: 978-1-78441-096-4
ISSN: 0270-4013 (Series)

ISOQAR certified
Management System,
awarded to Emerald
for adherence to
Environmental
standard
ISO 14001:2004.

ISOQAR
REGISTERED
Certificate Number 1985
ISO 14001

INVESTOR IN PEOPLE

CONTENTS

PART III: AFRICA

LIST OF CONTRIBUTORS

Turki A. Alquraini	Department of Special Education, King Saudi University, Riyadh, Kingdom of Saudi Arabia
John Anderson	School of Education, Queen's University Belfast, Belfast, UK
Hagit Ari-Am	Department of Special Education, The Hebrew University of Jerusalem, Jerusalem, Israel
Jeanmarie Badar	Department of Curriculum, Instruction, and Special Education, University of Virginia, Charlottesville, VA, USA
Brian R. Barber	Department of Special Education, Kent State University, Kent, OH, USA
Girma Berhanu	Department of Education and Special Education, University of Gothenburg, Gothenburg, Sweden
Dóra S. Bjarnason	Department of Inclusive Education, Iceland University, Reykjavik, Iceland
Cristina M. Cardona	Department of Health Psychology, University of Alicante, Alicante, Spain
Esther Chiner	Department of Health Psychology, University of Alicante, Alicante, Spain
Elyana Danilavichute	Institute of Special Pedagogy of the National Academy of Pedagogical Sciences of Ukraine, Kyiv, Ukraine
Ajay Das	Department of Special Education, Murray State University, Murray, KY, USA

C. Jonah Eleweke	Department of World Languages and Literatures, Portland State University, Portland, OR, USA
Rocio Espinosa de Gaitan	Ministry of Education, Guatemala City, Guatemala
Yajing Feng	Department of Education, Beijing Normal University, Beijing, China
Todd V. Fletcher	Department of Education, University of Arizona, Tucson, AZ, USA
Lani Florian	Moray House School of Education, University of Edinburgh, Edinburgh, UK
Ismael García-Cedillo	Graduate School of Psychology, Universidad Autónoma de San Luis Potosí, México
Thomas P. Gumpel	Department of Special Education, The Hebrew University of Jerusalem, Jerusalem, Israel
Rune Sarrormaa Hausstatter	Department of Education and Social Work, Lillehammer University College, Lillehammer, Norway
Shanna Eisner Hirsch	Department of Curriculum, Instruction, and Special Education, University of Virginia, Charlottesville, VA, USA
Judith Hollenweger	Department of Research and Continuing Education, Zurich University of Teacher Education, Zurich, Switzerland
Garry Hornby	Department of Education, University of Canterbury, Christchurch, New Zealand
James M. Kauffman	Department of Curriculum, Instruction, and Special Education, University of Virginia, Charlottesville, VA, USA
Alla Kolupayeva	Institute of Special Pedagogy of the National Academy of Pedagogical Sciences of Ukraine, Kyiv, Ukraine

Iuliia Korolkova Department of Psychology and Pedagogy, Altai State Pedagogical Academy, Barnaul, Russia

Kullaya Kosuwan Special Education Program, Songkhla Rajabhat University, Songkhla, Thailand

Ahmed Bawa Kuyini University of New England, Armidale, Australia

Tim Loreman Faculty of Education, Concordia University College of Alberta, Edmonton, Canada

Kenneth J. Luterbach Department of Education, East Carolina University, Greenville, NC, USA

Md. Saiful Malak Department of Special Education, Institute of Education and Research, University of Dhaka, Dhaka, Bangladesh

Gretar L. Marinósson Department of Special Needs Education, Iceland University, Reykjavik, Iceland

Macid Ayhan Melekoğlu Department of Special Education, Eskişehir Osmangazi University, Eskişehir, Turkey

Sigamoney Naicker Division of Curriculum and Development, West Cape Education Department, Cape Town, South Africa

Festus E. Obiakor Department of Early Childhood and Special Education, Valdosta State University, Valdosta, GA, USA

Shaila Rao Department of Special Education and Literacy Studies, Western Michigan University, Kalamazoo, MI, USA

Diane Rodriguez Department of Education, Fordham University, New York, NY, USA

Silvia Romero-Contreras Graduate School of Psychology, Universidad Autónoma de San Luis Potosí, México

Anthony F. Rotatori	Psychology Department, Saint Xavier University, Chicago, IL, USA
Martyn Rouse	School of Education, The University of Aberdeen, Aberdeen, UK
Rina Shah	LearningLinks Educare, Mumbai, India
Umesh Sharma	Department of Special Education and Psychology, Monash University, Clayton, Australia
Ron Smith	School of Education, Queen's University, Belfast, UK
Mark E. Swerdlik	Department of Psychology, Illinois State University, Normal, IL, USA
Oksana Taranchenko	Institute of Special Pedagogy of the National Academy of Pedagogical Sciences of Ukraine, Kyiv, Ukraine
Harald Thuen	Department of Education and Social Work, Lillehammer University College, Lillehammer, Norway
Yuwadee Viriyangkura	Special Education Program, Chiang Mai University, Chiang Mai, Thailand
Mian Wang	Department of Education, University of California Santa Barbara, Santa Barbara, CA, USA
Andrew L. Wiley	Department of Special Education, Kent State University, Kent, OH, USA

PREFACE

Special Education International Perspectives is divided into two volumes;
Volume 27, Biopsychosocial, Cultural, and Disability Aspects and Volume
28, Practices Across the Globe. There is limited literature examining the origins, practices, and challenges in special education from an international perspective as such these volumes add considerably to the knowledge base across
the globe. While an analysis and direct comparisons of the development of
special education across different countries are extremely complex and
beyond the scope of these volumes, there are common themes about meeting
the special needs of students with disabilities across the globe. First, an examination of the origins of special education in different countries illustrates the
society's general concern, support, assistance, and welfare for persons with
disabilities such as those with significant sensory and intellectual deficits.
Secondly, the practice of special education within countries evolved and was
influenced by religious, cultural, and political contexts as well as citizens
with philanthropic, humanitarian, and parental concerns. Thirdly, while the
philosophy of identifying and educating students with disabilities has taken
different routes (e.g., medical, environmental, segregation, and inclusion),
there appears to be a prevailing societal belief that students with disabilities
have a fundamental right to access education to enhance the quality of their
life. Fourthly, to ensure and protect this right, it was necessary to put into
place governmental protective legislation, policies, and monetary funding.
Lastly, while there is no single global association that evaluates and monitors
special education internationally, there are a number of agencies, organizations, and councils that have been extremely influential in providing countries
with best practices related to special education policies, standards, guidelines
and educational interventions such as the United Nations Children's
Fund (UNICEF), the United Nations Educational, Scientific and Cultural
Organizations (UNESCO), the Organization for Economic Cooperation and
Development (OECD), the World Health Organization (WHO), the
European Agency for Special Needs and Inclusive Education (EASIE), and
the Council for Exceptional Children (CEC). The purpose of *Special
Education International Perspectives* is to examine in detail these themes
across countries and exceptionality areas.

Volume 27 is divided into three parts. Part I presents an overview on disability that focuses on two major themes, namely, the biopsychosocial approaches to disability and diversity and disability. This overview is followed by Part II which examines five main high incidence exceptionalities: cognitive impairment, learning disabilities and attention deficit hyperactivity disorders, autism spectrum disorders, behavioral/emotional disabilities, and speech and language disorders. The examination of each exceptionality domain includes international perspectives from major global regions, research and intervention issues, information from national and international organizations, and a detailed introduction and summary by an expert in that exceptionality area. Part III delineates technological advances and research endeavors in special education.

Volume 28 provides a comprehensive discussion of special education across the globe that includes chapters from countries in the following geographic areas: North and Central America (the United States, Canada, Mexico, and Guatemala), Europe (the United Kingdom, Norway, Sweden, Switzerland, Spain, Iceland, Ukraine, and Russia), Africa (Nigeria, South Africa, and Ghana), the Middle East (Israel, Saudi Arabia, and Turkey), South Asia (India and Bangladesh), the Far East (China and Thailand) and Australasia (Australia and New Zealand). Discussions related to these countries includes information on the following: origins and early beginnings of special education specific to that country, prevalence rates, trends in legislation and litigation, educational interventions, working with families, teacher preparation, perspectives on the progress of special education and challenges that remain.

Anthony F. Rotatori
Series Editor

PART I
NORTH AND CENTRAL AMERICA

SPECIAL EDUCATION TODAY IN THE UNITED STATES OF AMERICA

James M. Kauffman, Shanna Eisner Hirsch, Jeanmarie Badar, Andrew L. Wiley and Brian R. Barber

ABSTRACT

Special education in the USA is, in most respects, a 20th century phenomenon and is now governed primarily by federal legislation first enacted in 1975. The federal law in its most recent reauthorization (2004) continues to require a free appropriate public education (FAPE) for all students with disabilities, a full continuum of alternative placements (CAP) ranging from residential or hospital care to inclusion in general education, an individual education plan or program (IEP) for each student identified as needing special education, and placement in the least restrictive environment (LRE) that is thought best for implementing the IEP. Parents must be involved in the special education process. Approximately 14 percent of public school students were identified for special education in 2004–2005, but the number and percentage of students identified in most high-incidence categories as needing special education have declined in recent years (the total for all categories was about 8.5 percent of public school students in 2010). A variety of evidence-based

Special Education International Perspectives: Practices Across the Globe
Advances in Special Education, Volume 28, 3–31
Copyright © 2014 by Emerald Group Publishing Limited
ISSN: 0270-4013/doi:10.1108/S0270-401320140000028001

interventions can be used to address the wide range of instructional and behavioral needs of students with disabilities and their families, including transition to further education or work, family services, and teacher education. Special education in the USA may find new sources of support and thrive or may become less common or be abandoned entirely due to criticism and withdrawal of support for social welfare programs of government.

ORIGINS

Precisely when and where special education began in the USA is somewhat unclear, but it was initiated through the action and advocacy of physicians and ministers who often imitated or adapted what they had observed in Europe in the mid-19th century. Special education first involved individuals who were blind, deaf, or mentally retarded (i.e., had intellectual disabilities, in 2014 terminology), and was implemented primarily in special schools (see Kauffman, 1976, 1981, 2008; Kauffman & Landrum, 2006; Sarason & Doris, 1979; Seguin, 1866). Besides physicians and ministers, psychologists played an important role in early special education. Although it existed in some public schools in major cities in the late 19th century, special education is considered primarily a 20th century phenomenon (Gerber, 2011). Gerber also observed correctly that special education must be seen in the context of social, scientific, and political movements.

Naming pioneers in special education is questionable, as anyone who does so is certain to leave out important people. Elizabeth Farrell and many other women pioneers worked in partnership with men (see Gerber, 2011). Farrell was instrumental in establishing special education in New York City in the early 20th century and in founding the international Council for Exceptional Children (CEC). Certainly, Samuel Kirk, Lloyd Dunn, William Cruickshank, James Gallagher, and Edwin Martin are among USA pioneers, though there are many others. Kirk, Dunn, and Cruickshank are known for their early textbooks (beginning in the 1950s) and their other publications (including tests), although the first special education textbook was likely Horn's (1924). Kirk, Dunn, and Cruickshank effectively described the variety of disabilities leading to most of the federal definitions and categories included in federal legislation. These categories (and common abbreviations of some of them) now include mental retardation or intellectual and developmental disability (MR, ID, or IDD), specific learning disability (SLD or LD), emotional disturbance (ED or EBD for emotional and behavioral disorders), communication (speech or language) disorders, deafness and impaired hearing, blindness and impaired vision, physical disability or other health impairment (OHI), and severe or multiple disabilities (e.g., deaf-blindness). In the late 20th century, other categories were added: autism spectrum disorders (ASD) and traumatic brain injury (TBI). Controversy continues around defining some disabilities (especially LD and ED) and whether some problems (e.g., attention deficit-hyperactivity disorder or ADHD) should be defined as separate categories or be included in an existing category.

Martin's (2013) memoir about the enactment of the federal special education law in the USA in 1975 (first known as Public Law 94-142, later as the *Individuals with Disabilities Education Act* or IDEA) details the law's political and social contexts as well as its basic requirements. IDEA requires an individualized education program (IEP) for all students with disabilities and placement of those with disabilities in the least restrictive environment (LRE) chosen from a continuum of alternative placements (CAP) (see Bateman, 2011).

Early special educators assumed that students with disabilities needed special *instruction* and that the primary reason for identifying them and providing special programs was that the *teaching* provided in general education was not appropriate for them. Many children with disabilities received no schooling at all in the first 75 years of the 20th century, and many who did go to school languished in classes that did not meet their needs. The two primary problems to be solved were, first, access to education of any kind and, second, access to *appropriate* education. Appropriate education for *all* children with disabilities was assumed to be possible only if instruction could be provided in a continuum of placements or CAP, ranging from regular public school classes to special schools and including such alternatives as resource rooms and special classes in public schools (see Hallahan, Kauffman, & Pullen, 2012). Unfortunately, the focus on appropriate and effective schooling and the attendant CAP was lost to the idea that *all* education (both general and special) could and should occur in the same place (see Kauffman, 2014; Kauffman & Badar, 2014; Kauffman & Hung, 2009; Zigmond, 2003; Zigmond, Kloo, & Volonino, 2009). This loss of focus also occurred in other nations (see Warnock, 2005).

Beginning in the 1980s, placement of students in the LRE came to dominate special education issues, and the idea of *inclusion* (sometimes referred to as inclusive education) led to a loss of focus on effective instruction and to preoccupation with the placement of students in regular public schools and general education classes (see Crockett & Kauffman, 1999;

Hallahan & Pullen, 2015; Kauffman, 2008; Kauffman & Badar, 2014; Kauffman, Nelson, Simpson, & Mock, 2011; Kauffman, Ward, & Badar, in press; Zigmond & Kloo, 2011). Unfortunately, some assumed that placement should be decided *before* appropriate education was designed (see Bateman & Linden, 2006), that appropriate education could occur *only* in so-called inclusive settings, that disability of any kind carried the same implications for education as other differences (e.g., color, parentage, social status, national origin, religion, and sexual preference; see Kauffman & Landrum, 2009), and that *all* students, regardless of ability, could be taught appropriately in the same venue (see Kauffman & Badar, 2014; Kauffman & Hallahan, 2005a, 2005b).

Considerable misunderstanding of special education law, special education as a social project, and the continuing need for special education still exists in the USA and, perhaps, many other nations of the world (Kauffman, 2015; Kauffman & Badar, 2014; Kauffman & Hallahan, 2005a). Many issues about disability, the law, and the implications of disability for schooling remain controversial (see Hallahan et al., 2012).

Finally, we note that although giftedness (extraordinarily advanced abilities) has been recognized as an exceptionality for over a century in the USA, current federal legislation (IDEA) does not include any provision for gifted students unless they also have a disability. In that case, it is disability, not giftedness, that makes the student eligible for special education. Most students with disabilities do not also have abilities resulting in their classification as gifted. Thus, "twice exceptional" students, as those with a combination of disabilities and giftedness are sometimes called, are a relative rarity.

PREVALENCE

For about four decades after enactment of PL 94-142 in 1975, the number and percentage of students receiving special education school-aged (ages 6–21 years) increased. However, special education participation peaked in the 2004–2005 school year, when students with disabilities comprised 13.8 percent of all students (Scull & Winkler, 2011). Since 2005, the numbers and percentages have steadily declined, with the most recently reported federal child count data indicating that approximately 8.5 percent of the school-age population receives special education (U.S. Department of Education, 2010).

The drop in special education enrollment after 2005 appears to be primarily attributable to a decrease in the numbers of students identified in the high-incidence (i.e., most often identified) disability categories of LD, ED, and ID. LD identification fell from a high of around 4.4 percent (ages 6–21) in 2000 to just over 3.4 percent in 2010. Students identified as having ID decreased from approximately 2.2 percent to 0.8 percent of all students. Identification of ED has also declined, and in recent years has been well under 1.0 percent of the school population, although prevalence estimates based on mental health surveys are at least five times higher (Forness, Freeman, Paparella, Kauffman, & Walker, 2012). The decrease in ED identification is particularly worrisome, as students with ED have historically been under-identified and under-served in special education (Forness et al., 2012; Kauffman, Mock, & Simpson, 2009).

Counter to the decline of high-incidence disabilities sharp increases occurred in the prevalence of students with autism. The number of students with autism has risen steadily and at an accelerated rate, more than quadrupling from 1.5 to 7 percent of the total *special education* population and constituting 0.8 percent of the total *student* population. Similarly, the number of OHI students more than doubled from 4.8 percent in 1999–2000 to 10.6 percent of the special education population, constituting about 2.0 percent of the total student population. The sharp increase in OHI enrollment is attributable to the fact that, in 1999, Attention Deficit Disorder (ADD) and Attention Deficit-Hyperactivity Disorder (ADHD) were added to the list of conditions under OHI in IDEA. Prior to 1999, many of these students with autism and OHI potentially were identified under the LD category (Cortiella, 2011). The prevalence of developmental delay, often considered a general disability category for younger students (3–5 or 3–9 years of age) increased from 0.4 percent 1999–2000 to 0.7 percent of all students. The remaining disability types, comprising a small fraction of the total number of students with disabilities, have remained relatively stable or decreased only slightly from the time of their categorical formalization.

Although it is beyond the scope of this chapter to provide a review of potential causes for the shifting prevalence of specific disability categories, researchers have provided some important hypotheses regarding the declines in high-incidence, as well as the declines in overall prevalence of students with disabilities enrolled in special education. One hypothesis is that identification practices for special education have improved, resulting in a decrease of "false positives" (students identified for special education who do not need such services). An alternative hypothesis is that schools in the United States are practicing better prevention of learning and behavior problems, thus reducing the number of students requiring special education (Cortiella, 2011). Still another possibility is that economic pressures (i.e., decreases in federal and state funds for public schools), perhaps in combination with persistent claims by some that special education is unnecessary, wasteful, or even harmful, have contributed to fewer students being identified for services (see Kauffman, 2009; Samuels, 2010; Zirkel, 2013).

In addition to the lack of recognition of factors that contribute causally to trends in growth or decline of disabilities, many issues cloud the accurate identification of students with disabilities and thus contribute to potentially unreliable estimates of prevalence for the various disabilities. Specifically, minority, as well as gender and socio-economic disproportionality (i.e., over-identification and/or under-identification) continue to plague special education (e.g., Coutinho, Oswald, & Best, 2002; Skiba, Poloni-Staudinger, Simmons, Feggins, & Chung, 2005; Wiley, Brigham, Kauffman, & Bogan, 2013). Under the 2004 reauthorization of IDEA, the U.S. Department of Education placed an increased emphasis on addressing the challenge of disproportionate representation of students from culturally and linguistically diverse backgrounds in special education. These difficulties continue, however, due to a variety of potential issues including flawed assessment practices or inadequate instruction (Skiba, Middelberg, & McClain, 2014; Skiba et al., 2008).

TRENDS IN LEGISLATION AND LITIGATION

Until the federal law now known as IDEA was enacted in 1975, special education was left to state or local governments for all exceptionalities (see Martin, 2013). The law has been renamed and revised several times since 1975, with the most recent revision as of this writing being in 2004, which is sometimes referred to as Individuals with Disabilities Education Improvement Act of 2004 (IDEIA, but IDEA, or IDEA, 2004, is nevertheless used to refer to the federal law in general; see Huefner, 2006; Yell, 2012). The federal law was enacted primarily because of the demands of parents of children with disabilities. IDEA requires both appropriate education and related services such as transportation and physical therapy. Parents must also have the opportunity to be involved in decisions about their children's special education. Free appropriate public education

(FAPE) remains the central requirement of the law, but supplementary and transition services are required as well. Related federal law extends services to preschool children.

Only the central requirements of IDEA are mentioned here, as the legislation and the regulations related to it are quite detailed. Moreover, IDEA is not the only law addressing disabilities and special education. In general, the trend in all federal legislation related to education in the USA is to include students with disabilities in general education as much as possible. Until this century, students receiving special education often were not expected to take state-mandated tests, so their progress often could not be compared to that of students without disabilities. Now, most students with disabilities must take the same tests as their nondisabled peers. Proponents of this requirement argue that most students with disabilities who receive appropriate instruction should be expected to pass the same tests as nondisabled students. People who question this expectation point out that it is unreasonable and unfair, and that although students with disabilities should be expected to achieve all they can, the average for those with disabilities will always be lower than the average for those without disabilities, even if both groups receive the best possible instruction (see Kauffman, 2010, 2011).

Much controversy has accompanied trends in legislation and litigation, and some would like to see the law changed or interpreted to correspond to their views. Since the 1970s, an increasingly popular argument is that general and special education should be merged, such that the differences between them become increasingly imperceptible. A common suggestion has been that general and special education should not be separate but a single system serving *all* students. People who question the demand for a single, integrated system point out that special and general education are both part of public education and, therefore, already are part of a single system of education in the USA. They argue that any effective subpart of a system must have its own identity, authority, budget, and personnel. This is true in government generally (e.g., a government department is not merged with another if it is believed to be very important and has a unique mission). Special education must have these (identity, authority, budget, and personnel) if it is to have integrity, just as various other subunits of the public schools must have them (e.g., athletics and music; see Kauffman & Hallahan, 1993; Singer, 1988).

Another decade-old line of argument is that special education should develop and give to general education those ways of working with exceptional children that have been found successful, such that special education will gradually become superfluous (i.e., "work itself out of business"). Those questioning this have pointed out that the realities of mathematics preclude the elimination of low achievement and that special education will always be necessary to serve the extremes, regardless of how good general education becomes (see Kauffman, 2010; Kauffman & Hallahan, 2005a; Kauffman & Landrum, 2007; Kauffman & Lloyd, 2011).

A popular idea of the late 20th and early 21st centuries is that general and special education teachers should work together, should collaborate and consult with each other to discover what is best for the student or co-teach classes in which some of the students have disabilities and the general education curriculum is taught. Access to the general education curriculum is thought to be the key idea. Although collaboration, consultation, and co-teaching capture the imagination of many, research has not shown that these are better than instruction from a special education teacher in meeting the special needs of exceptional children. Those who question collaboration, consulting, and co-teaching of the general education curriculum point to the necessity of individualized, focused, intensive, persistent, and specialized instruction that only a well-trained special education teacher can provide, arguing that students with disabilities need the heart of special education – *special instruction*, and not just be in the general education curriculum (Kauffman & Badar, 2014; Zigmond, 2007; Zigmond & Kloo, 2011; see also other chapters in section III of Kauffman & Hallahan, 2011).

Trends in legislation, regulation, and litigation in the USA since 1975 have been more interpretative than legal or substantive. The core requirements of the initial legislation (Public Law 94-142) remain in IDEIA. FAPE is the centerpiece; IEPs are required; and placement in the LRE *after* consideration of the CAP remain legal requirements (see Bateman, 2011; Bateman & Linden, 2006). It is illegal under IDEA for any school to eliminate any option in the CAP. Someone who states or intimates – for whatever reason – that their schools simply do not support placement in one of the options in the CAP violates both the letter and the spirit or intent of IDEA (see Yell, 2012 and Section II of Kauffman & Hallahan, 2011).

PROMINENT EDUCATIONAL INTERVENTIONS

Mandates such as IDEA (2004) have prompted schools to embrace proactive approaches to preventing and reducing educational risk (academic, behavioral, or social). Multi-tiered models of education are currently used to identify students for targeted academic (Response to Intervention [RtI], Fuchs & Fuchs, 2006) and behavioral (School-Wide Positive Behavior Support [SWPBS], Sugai & Horner, 2002) interventions. A Comprehensive, integrated, three-tiered model of support (CI3T; Lane, Kalberg, & Menzies, 2009) is another comprehensive model that blends the RtI and SWPBS framework and incorporates a social skills component. Multi-tiered models (e.g., RtI, SWPBS, and CI3T) have similar structures. Specifically, each model strives to provide every student (regardless if they are eligible for special education) with scientifically based instruction (O'Connor & Sanchez, 2011), whether it is academic or social/behavioral instruction, making sure all students have every opportunity to learn.

In addition to ensuring that effective instruction is provided, another common component of multi-tiered models is reliable detection of at-risk students through systematic screenings. Once identified, students are pro-vided with small-group or targeted interventions (for children birth through age three this is called early intervention). Thus these models offer a conti-nuum of support that increases in intensity in response to the individual student's need. Student progress is monitored consistently throughout the process to determine the interventions' effectiveness. For some students the targeted interventions (Tier II and Tier III) remediate learning or social-behavioral needs. If adequate progress is not made, a student could be referred for a special education evaluation to determine whether he or she qualifies for special education services. Students with disabilities receive special education services when their disability affects their ability to learn and they require specialized instruction. Once a student is found eligible for special education under the guidelines set forth in IDEA (2004), educators work with the parents to develop a plan. Children under three years of age typically receive an individualized family service plan (IFSP). School-aged students receive an IEP. In addition to an IEP, adolescents with disabilities receive a transition plan to help prepare them for adulthood.

Individual Family Service Plan

Infants and toddlers in the USA who are identified as having a disability are legally required to receive early intervention services through an IFSP. Early intervention reduces the number of children who require special education later in life by improved developmental functioning (Guralnick, 1997, 1998). Services include medical diagnosis, special education, applied behavior analysis, speech language therapy, and physical therapy

(Hallahan et al., 2012). The IFSP also requires that the child's family participate in developing the plan with the care manager and service providers.
The IFSP outlines the child's present level of development along with
family factors related to the child's development such as strengths,
resources, concerns, and priorities. Expected outcomes, service delivery
information, and the steps to transition the child to preschool are also
noted in the IFSP (Hallahan et al., 2012). Once children transition to preschool, they are to be reassessed for special education eligibility.

Individualized Education Programs

It is common for children with disabilities starting at age three to receive
interventions, services, accommodations, necessary assistive technologies
and supports that are prescribed in their IEP. The IEP goals are developed
by a team that often includes the following members: the student with the
disability (when appropriate), the parents of the student with a disability,
teachers (both special and general education teachers), a representative
from the local education agency, an individual who can interpret evaluation results, and other individuals who have expertise regarding the child,
such as a speech-language pathologist or occupational therapist (Hallahan
et al., 2012). The team works together to develop annual goals for the student in his or her deficit area(s). These goals contain information regarding
the instructional approach, accommodations, and assistive technology
required for the student to meet the goals. Examples of assistive technology
include low-tech devices (e.g., calculators, graph paper, and spell-checkers)
and high-tech devices (e.g., assistive communication devices and Kurzweil
readers; see Bausch & Ault, 2008; Berekely & Lindstrom, 2011 for additional information). The specific intervention domains, along with secondary transition plans, featured in the IEP depend on the student's need and
age level and may include interventions in academic, behavior, and social
skills domains.

Academic
Techniques for teaching students with high-incidence (e.g., SLD) and low-
incidence (e.g., autism) disabilities include using explicit instruction
(Brophy & Good, 1986). For example, Direct Instruction (DI) is a
research-supported program that provides students with explicit and systematic instruction (Adams & Engelmann, 1996; Becker & Carnine, 1981).
Stein, Carnine, and Dixon (1998) described the model as an "integration of

effective teaching practices with curriculum design" (p. 227). These design features (e.g., organization of instructional content; teaching of explicit, generalizable strategies; scaffolded instruction, skills and concepts integration; and providing a review of material) have been studied and tested to ensure that learners master a skill (Carnine, 1980; Engelmann, 1979; Gersten, White, Falco, & Carnine, 1982). Engelmann (1970) identified DI as an effective intervention for students at risk; research continues to build on Engelmann's foundational work. DI has been effective for students with autism (Flores & Ganz, 2007; Ganz & Flores, 2009), LD (Glover, McLaughlin, Derby, & Gower, 2010), and ID (Horner & Albin, 1988) as well as English Language Learners (Viel-Ruma, Houchins, Jolivette, Fredrick, & Gama, 2010). It has been effective in general education classrooms (Kamps et al., 2008), special education settings (Miao, Darch, & Rabren, 2002), and in the community (Horner & Albin, 1988). Other common research-based academic interventions for students with high and low-incidence disabilities include explicit instruction in math (Kroesbergen & Van Luit, 2003), repeated readings to promote oral reading fluency (Rasinski, 1990), and self-regulated strategy development (Harris, Graham, Mason, & Friedlander, 2008) for persuasive and narrative writing (Ennis & Jolivette, 2014; Lane et al., 2011).

Behavior

In the USA, schools also address student behavior when it impedes their learning or the learning of peers. One way to mitigate the challenging behavior is through proactive behavioral interventions such as the use of Functional Behavior Assessments (FBA) and Functional Assessment-Based Interventions (FABI; Umbreit, Ferro, Liaupsin, & Lane, 2007), which is based in applied behavior analysis. FBAs can also be used to identify and address skill and performance deficits (Umbreit et al., 2007). Unlike traditional assessments that use norm-based criteria to determine behavioral deficits, an FBA evaluates the student within a setting using multiple methods to hone in on the student's target behavior(s). In addition, norm-referenced interventions typically are based on the behavior's topography (what the behavior *looks* like) instead of on the behavior's function (*why* the it occurs). Targeted function-based interventions (FABIs) can teach replacement behaviors and adjust contingencies to set the stage for a replacement behavior (Umbreit et al., 2007). However, current special education law does not specify the procedures that should be employed when developing a FABI. Moreover, neither Congress nor the Department of Education delineates what components should be included in a FABI. This poses a threat to the integrity of the programs that are being developed and implemented for all students, including those with EBD. Consequently, studies have identified vast differences between conducting an FBA and implementing a FABI (Blood & Neel, 2007; Conroy, Alter, & Scott, 2009; Gable, 1999; Scott, McIntyre, Liaupsin, Nelson, & Conroy, 2004). Katsiyannis, Conroy, and Zharg (2008) argue that researchers and practitioners lack consensus on this important topic.

However, FBAs have long been a practical and efficient means of enacting meaningful changes in problem behaviors across diverse individuals and settings (Baer, Wolf, & Risley, 1968, 1987). Historically, function-based assessment and interventions have largely been restricted to individuals with severe disabilities and primarily in clinical settings (Dunlap, Kern-Dunlap, Clarke, & Robbins, 1991; Sasso, Conroy, Stichter, & Fox, 2001). In recent years, they have been shown to be effective for students with diverse demographic backgrounds and across a range of target behaviors, disability categories, and academic placements. For example, function-based interventions have been used with students who have ADHD (Ervin, DuPaul, Kern, & Friman, 1998) and students at risk for EBD (Lewis & Sugai, 1996). Further, studies have shown the effectiveness of FBA in self-contained classrooms (Kern, Dunlap, Clarke, & Childs, 1994; Umbreit & Blair, 1997), general education classrooms (Umbreit, Lane, & Dejud, 2004), and job-share classrooms (Lane et al., 2009).

Social Skills
Good social skills are critical to success both in school and later in life for students with disabilities. Social skills are a group of behaviors that allow students to: (a) initiate and maintain positive social relationships, (b) contribute to peer acceptance and to a satisfactory school adjustment, and (c) cope effectively and adaptively with large social environments (Walker, Colvin, & Ramsey, 1995). This also includes nonverbal communication, including gestures and affect. These nonverbal skills may include imitative behavior, turn-taking, and appropriate body language (Brown, Odom, & McConnell, 2008). Students with positive social and communication skills have been shown to be more successful academically (Caprara, Barbaranelli, Pastorelli, Bandura, & Zimbardo, 2000). Moreover, research suggests that students with poor social skills have a difficult time forming and maintaining relationships and have lower academic achievement (Caprara et al., 2000; Lane, Menzies, Oakes, & Kalberg, 2012). This could be due to a lack of skills or knowledge of how to produce the behavior, which signals a skill deficit. On the contrary a student could possess

the skill but they lack the motivation to produce the socially appropriate behavior, which signals a performance deficit.

One framework with a growing evidence base is Social and Emotional Learning programs (SEL; Collaborative for Academic, Social, and Emotional Learning, 2003; Elias et al., 1997). SEL promotes social-emotional development through self-awareness, self-management, social awareness, relationship skills, and responsible decision-making through teaching students skills that help them (Mart, Dusenbury, & Weissberg, 2011). This occurs when social and emotional skills are explicitly taught in a caring environment that provides opportunities for students to practice the skills (Collaborative for Academic Social, and Emotional Learning, 2003; Mart et al., 2011). SEL has proven to help students across the K-12 continuum demonstrate the following outcomes: superior academic performance, improved attitudes and behaviors, fewer negative behaviors, and decreased emotional stress (Durlak, Weissberg, Dymnicki, Taylor, & Schellinger, 2011).

Postsecondary Transition

By the time students are 16 years old, schools are required to add a transition section to a student's IEP (this section can also be added earlier based on the student's need). The purpose is to support a successful transition of students with disabilities to postsecondary education, independent living, employment, and community engagement (Hallahan et al., 2012). Postsecondary goals are derived from age-appropriate assessments and may be related to education, training, employment, and independent living skills, when they are appropriate for the student (Hallahan et al., 2012; IDEA, 2004). In addition to postsecondary goals, the IEP must outline transition services that are required to facilitate the student meeting those goals. These services may include academic courses, training, or independent living skills (Madaus, Banerjee, & Merchant, 2011). In addition, promoting self-determination is critical for a successful transition to postsecondary education (Fielder & Danneker, 2007).

As students prepare for the transition to adulthood, self-determination is considered one of the most critical skills. Self-determination was described by Field, Martin, Miller, Ward, and Wehmeyer (1998) as:

> a combination of skills, knowledge, and beliefs that enable a person to engage in goal-directed, self-regulated, autonomous behavior. An understanding of one's strengths and

limitations together with a belief in oneself as capable and effective, are essential. When acting on the basis of these skills and attitudes, individuals have greater ability to take control of their lives and assume the role of successful adults. (p. 2)

Self-determination has been highlighted in the IDEA (2004) and in research. Carter, Lane, Pierson, and Glaeser (2006) noted that self-determination may improve secondary student outcomes, such as academic performance (Martin et al., 2003), employability (Wehmeyer & Palmer, 2003), independence (Sowers & Powers, 1995), and quality of life (Wehmeyer & Schwartz, 1997). For additional information on self-determination research see Carter, Lane, Crnobori, Bruhn, and Oakes (2011).

WORK WITH FAMILIES

Parent involvement in special education is legally mandated in the United States and is considered critical to meeting the educational needs of students with disabilities. Parents and families are viewed as *equal partners* with the schools in making important educational decisions and supporting positive educational and developmental outcomes (Turnbull, Turnbull, Erwin, Soodak, & Shogren, 2011). Before IDEA, parents were typically viewed as lacking the professional training necessary to participate in decision-making related to special education services for their own children (Yell, Rogers, & Rogers, 1998). Both the spirit and the letter of IDEA make it clear that parents and families are to be full and equal partners in all decision-making aspects of the special education process (Shepherd, Giangreco, & Cook, 2013). This does not mean that parents actually teach their children in school. Rather, it means that parents are allowed and encouraged to contribute as members of the IEP team to the development, implementation, and monitoring of special education services (Christle & Yell, 2012).

There are two major reasons for the emphasis on parent participation in special education. The first is the role for parents envisioned by IDEA. Many provisions of IDEA are based on the assumption that parents are best suited to advocate for their children's education, and to *hold schools accountable* for providing timely and appropriate services. In this regard, IDEA grants considerable power to parents. Parental consent is required for many aspects of the special education process, and parents have a right to impartial due process if they disagree with school actions or decisions. The main vehicle for parent involvement in their child's special education is through the various stages of the IEP process (e.g., eligibility; goal-setting; developing and evaluating the effectiveness of the IEP; see Bateman & Linden, 2006).

The second major reason for the emphasis on parent and family participation is substantial research indicating that active, meaningful parent involvement can enhance educational outcomes for students with disabilities (Turnbull et al., 2011). Parents and family members can provide the school and the IEP team with information and insights that are essential for developing effective IEPs, and they can support the educational progress of the student in numerous other ways. Building on the parent participation principle in IDEA, some special education researchers and advocates have called for even greater family participation in providing special education to students with disabilities (Shepherd et al., 2013). *Family-centered* approaches place family's needs and wants at the center of special education (Bruder, 2000) and work to incorporate family involvement beyond the IEP process.

Unfortunately, the vision of active parent participation leading to better services and more positive student outcomes does not always reflect what actually happens in schools. It is important to note that parents differ in their desire to play an active role in their child's education. Some parents wish to be fully involved, while other parents want to be less involved, and schools are expected to honor and accommodate these differences among parents (Bruder, 2000). When parents do wish to participate in their child's special education, several barriers can hinder active and productive family–school partnerships For example, family members may feel unprepared to participate, can be intimidated by schools and educational jargon, and may have difficulty expressing their ideas and desires in formal meetings (Turnbull et al., 2011). Language and cultural differences can also inhibit effective collaboration between families and schools (Harry, 2008). Furthermore, educator attitudes can be barriers to parent participation and involvement. Despite legal requirements, some educators continue to believe that parents should not play an active role in special education decision-making (Gerber, Banbury, Miller, & Griffin, 1986). Finally, IEP teams may lack the skills, tools, and knowledge needed to initiate, build, and sustain productive family–school partnerships (Turnbull et al., 2011). Overcoming barriers to parent participation requires thoughtful and deliberate action by both schools and families.

Numerous strategies exist for improving collaboration between families and schools. Shepherd et al. (2013) overview several approaches that have at least some research support for their effectiveness. One example is

COACH, which stands for Choosing Outcomes and Accommodations for Children (Giangreco, Cloninger, & Iverson, 2011). COACH provides a collaborative decision-making framework for families and schools that enables families to make informed decisions and helps all stakeholders develop IEPs for students with severe disabilities. Through a structured interview process, families and schools identify high priority instructional goals and develop an educational plan for pursuing those goals. Shepherd and colleagues describe several other practices and strategies for encouraging and enabling meaningful collaboration between schools and the families of students with disabilities.

TEACHER TRAINING

Students with disabilities in the USA are sometimes instructed by both general education teachers and special education teachers (SETs). The two groups of teachers are often expected to share the responsibility of educating students with disabilities (Hallahan et al., 2012). Their joint responsibilities should include: (a) providing evidenced-based instruction that is differentiated to meet the individual student's needs, (b) assessing student performance across academic areas, (c) documenting intervention efforts prior to referring for special education, (d) participating in special education eligibility meetings, (e) participating in the development of the IEP, (f) communicating with parents during an evaluation process, (g) attending due process hearings if a family is dissatisfied with the school, and (h) collaborating with each other and other professionals (Hallahan et al., 2012). In addition to the previously stated joint responsibilities, Hallahan and colleagues (2012) outlined additional responsibilities for SETs, who are expected to: (a) provide direct instruction to students with disabilities, (b) address behavior problems, (c) evaluate and integrate technology to support students with disabilities, and (d) have a firm understanding of special education law. SETs gain these skills through traditional and alternative certification programs.

Traditional Training

In the USA, teacher licensure rules and regulations vary by state. It is common for states to require SETs to complete a state-approved educator program. Accreditation programs such as the National Council for

Accreditation of Teacher Education (NCATE) help establish high-quality teacher preparation programs. There are currently 656 accredited programs in the USA. Together with the Council for Exceptional Children (the USA's largest special education advocacy group), NCATE outlined standards that are designed to unify the coursework and experiences (e.g., semester long student teaching placement) across the accredited institutions. NCATE/CEC (2002) emphasize that SETs have an understanding of special education history, law, evidenced-based practices, and procedures. SETs typically possess an understanding the characteristics of learners, understanding of curriculum content and goals, and an understanding of and skills for teaching in addition to completing a supervised student teaching (Darling-Hammond & Baratz-Snowden, 2005). In addition to completing an accredited program, the SET must hold a bachelor's degree in education to teach at a public school and complete a series of teaching exams.

Alternative Certification

In the 1980s, there was a decline in the number of candidates completing traditional teaching programs. Researchers reported a need for 74,000 teachers across the country (Boe, Sunderland, & Cook, 2006; Mastropieri, Scruggs, & Mills, 2011). Moreover 98 percent of schools reported a shortage of SETs (ERIC Clearinghouse on Disabilities and Gifted Education, 2001). This shortage of teachers was addressed through alternative teacher certification programs along with provisional and emergency licenses (Mastropieri et al., 2011). These programs recruit individuals who already have a bachelor's degree but lack the education courses and experience required for certification. The alternative certification teachers (ACTs) complete an intensive teacher training, often during the summer, prior to fall school year. Examples of training topics include teaching methods, classroom management, and child development. Throughout the school year the ACTs participate in on-going professional development and receive coaching from a mentor teacher with special education experience. During this time ACTs may also enroll in graduate school to earn a master's degree in education.

Licensure

In the USA, laws specify that "highly qualified" teachers are defined as demonstrating mastery in all subjects they teach (Mastropieri et al., 2011).

Both traditional teachers and alternative certification teachers must complete the state licensure. In order to be licensed applicants must hold a bachelor's degree, complete the necessary coursework (or be enrolled in an alternative certification program), pass the state exams, and apply for a teaching license through the state's Department of Education.

Teaching licenses are issued for a specific period of time and must be renewed. Teachers must demonstrate that they are engaging in professional development by earning continuing education units (CEUs). Attending educational workshops and enrolling in a graduate level course could count as CEUs. Each state has different renewal periods and requirements.

If an applicant moves to another state, he or she may apply for reciprocity, which is the process of the new state acknowledging the previous state's teaching license. The teacher must review the requirements for the new state and submit a formal application to have the license transferred. However, reciprocity does not guarantee that the license will be recognized.

PROGRESS

The most significant progress has depended on the foundational, legal guarantee that IDEA makes to students with disabilities and their families to provide a FAPE in the LRE. Before IDEA, the vast majority of students with disabilities were denied the right to an education, and in fact many states had laws that expressly forbade students with certain disabilities from attending public schools. For the few attending public schools, the instruction and related services were often inadequate (Gerber, 2011). We highlight three areas in which significant change has occurred in (a) inclusion of students with disabilities in general education, (b) evidence-based instructional practices, and (c) early childhood education and transition. Much of this change has depended on federal subsidies. Whether the change represents progress is an open question in particular instances.

Inclusion of Students with Disabilities

The expectation that all students attend school and that students with disabilities receive special education in their LRE highlighted issues surrounding special classes and schools for students with disabilities and the need for closer working relationships between general and special educators. According to IDEA, educating students in special classes should only occur when the nature or severity of the disability is such that education in general classes, with the use of supplementary aids and services, cannot be satisfactorily achieved.

Interpretations vary regarding the legal determination of the LRE for students with disabilities, but there is little doubt that the law has led to their greater inclusion in the regular education classroom. During the last 30 years there has been a dramatic decrease in the percentage of students with disabilities who are served in separate educational environments. Today, over 95 percent of students with disabilities are educated in their local neighborhood schools, and over 55 percent of these students spend 80 percent or more of their school day in general education classrooms, with another 24 percent spending 40−79 percent of the day in general education classrooms (see McLeskey, Landers, Williamson, & Hoppey, 2012; West & Whitby, 2008). Many will automatically view this trend toward inclusion in neighborhood schools and general education classrooms as progress. However, without additional information about the appropriateness and effectiveness of services, it is impossible to say whether, and for whom, a change from one educational environment to another represents improvement (Kauffman & Badar, 2014; Zigmond & Kloo, 2011; Zigmond & Volonino, 2009).

Research-Based Instructional Practices

There is growing emphasis on identifying and using evidence-based educational practices. Federal mandates (e.g., IDEA, 2004) support the idea that the academic and behavioral interventions should be supported by sound scientific research documenting their effectiveness. Practices that meet a threshold of support from high-quality research studies are referred to as *evidence-based practices*.

There are numerous challenges associated with identifying and implementing evidence-based practices in special education; however, the increased focus on scientific evidence (as opposed to popular opinion, ideology, or other non-scientific sources of information) as the primary basis for educating students with disabilities represents progress and has the potential to greatly improve services and outcomes for students with disabilities (see Cook & Odom, 2013; Cook & Tankersley, 2013; Walker & Gresham, 2014).

Early Childhood Special Education and Transition Services

Progress has also been made in the areas of *early intervention* and *early childhood special education*, as well as at the other end of the childhood-age continuum with stipulation of and improvements in *transition services* (i.e., preparing students with disabilities for life after school). In 1986, IDEA was extended to require special education services for children with disabilities ages 3–5 years old, with additional incentives for states to develop and implement early intervention programs for infants with disabilities from birth to 36 months. Early childhood special education includes not only services available to students with known disabilities but those children judged to be at risk for poor developmental outcomes (Ramey & Ramey, 1998). Whether due to the inclusion of students determined to be "at-risk" for poor development or other reasons, the number of children ages birth to five receiving early childhood special education, either at home or in preschool, increased dramatically after 1995 (Diamond, Justice, Siegler, & Snyder, 2013). For approximately 16 percent of these children, early intervention served as successful primary prevention (i.e., their functioning improved to the point that they no longer needed services). Features of early childhood education, including qualities of teacher–student relationships, peer experiences, and instructional foci and use of specific instructional strategies continue to be critically associated with positive outcomes of children with disabilities (e.g., Mashburn & Pianta, 2010).

Transition services have also improved for students with disabilities, in large part because of amendments to IDEA and related research initiatives to develop more effective transition programs. An important advance in transition services has been preparing students with disabilities (particularly students with moderate to severe disabilities) for supported competitive employment (as opposed to working in special or "sheltered" work environments; Wehman, 2012). From 1987 to 2005, the percentage of students with disabilities enrolled in postsecondary education increased from 14 percent to almost 32 percent, and some indicators suggest positive trends in post-school employment (U.S. Department of Education, 2010). Post-school outcomes and quality of life indicators vary widely for different disability groups (Newman et al., 2011) and, despite significant advances in transition services, it is clear that there is need for more effective approaches.

CHALLENGES

Precisely what will become of special education in the USA in the coming decades is unknown. In part, what happens will depend on how the differences we call disabilities are perceived, whether they are related to education in ways that other differences (e.g., height, weight, wealth, color, nationality, religion, and sexual orientation) are not. In part, what happens will depend on economic and political circumstances – whether the public finds it appropriate to spend the money necessary to fund special education for given groups of students. In part, what happens will depend on public notions of fairness and social justice and on how disabilities are viewed philosophically (see Anastasiou & Kauffman, 2011, 2012, 2013).

One possibility is the obliteration of public special education under the assumption that it will be an invisible service subsumed completely under general education. This scenario seems most likely if it is assumed that whatever is good for students in general is good for all students regardless of their differences, that all students should receive the same instruction (or at least not instruction labeled special education or not provided in settings other than general education classrooms), and that all students should have the same academic goals and meet the same academic standards.

A second possibility is that special education will be offered only to those with the most obvious and severe disabilities, simply because these students so clearly cannot be expected to meet the same expectations as average students. This scenario seems most likely if it becomes politically infeasible to fund special education for a substantial percentage of the school-age population and funding is thought feasible for only the most extreme cases.

A third possibility is that special education will be seen as a good idea that needs to be maintained at its current level but improved. This scenario seems most likely if instruction becomes the central focus of special education and its teachers are trained to use practices based on sound scientific evidence after having been successful teachers in general education (see Kauffman, 2011; Kauffman & Landrum, 2007).

Special education in the USA faces unusual if not unique challenges in coming decades. One of the clearest challenges is providing special education fairly to a student population that is extraordinarily diverse. Another is fitting special education into an education system that has no clearly defined national curriculum and that for the most part is left to the control of extremely diverse states and localities. Still another is the argument that special education is broken, often ineffective and undesirable, a second-rate, stigmatizing, and wasteful way of dealing with difference. Because no way of dealing with the differences we call disabilities in schooling is flawless, educators will be greatly tempted to abandon special education as conceptualized in IDEA for a newer but equally flawed concept. Finally, special education may face the same challenges as other social welfare programs of government, the charge that it was a misguided attempt to address intransigent social problems through federal over reach and largess.

REFERENCES

Adams, G. L., & Engelmann, S. (1996). *Research in direct instruction: 25 years beyond DISTAR*. Seattle, WA: Educational Achievement Systems.
Anastasiou, D., & Kauffman, J. M. (2011). A social constructionist approach to disability: Implications for special education. *Exceptional Children, 77*, 367–384.
Anastasiou, D., & Kauffman, J. M. (2012). Disability as cultural difference: Implications for special education. *Remedial and Special Education, 33*, 139–149.
Anastasiou, D., & Kauffman, J. M. (2013). The social model of disability: Dichotomy between impairment and disability. *Journal of Medicine and Philosophy, 38*, 441–459.
Baer, D. M., Wolf, M. M., & Risley, T. R. (1968). Some current dimensions of applied behavior analysis. *Journal of Applied Behavior Analysis, 1*, 91–97.
Baer, D. M., Wolf, M. M., & Risley, T. R. (1987). Some still-current dimensions of applied behavior analysis. *Journal of Applied Behavior Analysis, 20*, 313–327.
Bateman, B. D. (2011). Individual education programs for children with disabilities. In J. M. Kauffman & D. P. Hallahan (Eds.), *Handbook of special education* (pp. 91–106). New York, NY: Taylor & Francis.
Bateman, B. D., & Linden, M. A. (2006). *Better IEPs: How to develop legally correct and educationally useful programs* (4th ed.). Longmont, CO: Sopris West.
Bausch, M. E., & Ault, M. J. (2008). Assistive technology implementation plan: A tool for improving outcomes. *Teaching Exceptional Children, 41*, 5–14.
Becker, W. C., & Carnine, D. W. (1981). Direct instruction: A behavior theory model for comprehensive intervention with the disadvantaged. In S. W. Bijou & R. Ruiz (Eds.), *Behavior modification: Contributions to education* (pp. 145–210). Hillsdale, NJ: Erlbaum.
Berekely, S., & Lindstrom, J. H. (2011). Technology for the struggling reader: Free and easily accessible resources. *Teaching Exceptional Children, 43*, 48–55.
Blood, E., & Neel, R. S. (2007). From FBA to implementation: A look at what is actually being delivered. *Education and Treatment of Children, 30*(4), 67–80.
Boe, E. E., Sunderland, B., & Cook, L. (2006, November). *Special education teachers: Supply and demand*. Paper presented at the meeting of the Teacher Education Division of the Council of Exceptional Children, San Diego, CA.
Brophy, J., & Good, T. L. (1986). Teacher behavior and student achievement. In M. C. Whittrock (Ed.), *Handbook of research on teaching* (3rd ed.). New York, NY: Macmillan.

Brown, W. H., Odom, S. L., & McConnell, S. R. (2008). *Social competence of young children: Risk, disability, and evidenced-based practices* (2nd ed.). Baltimore, MD: Brookes.

Bruder, M. B. (2000). Family-centered early intervention: Clarifying our values for the new millennium. *Topics in Early Childhood Special Education, 20,* 105–116.

Caprara, G. V., Barbaranelli, C., Pastorelli, C., Bandura, A., & Zimbardo, P. G. (2000). Prosocial foundations of children's academic achievement. *Psychological Science, 11,* 302–306.

Carnine, D. (1980). Relationships between stimulus variation and the formation of misconceptions. *Journal of Educational Research, 74,* 106–110.

Carter, E., Lane, K. L., Pierson, M., & Glaeser, B. (2006). Self-determination skills and opportunities of transition-age youth with emotional disturbances and learning disabilities. *Exceptional Children, 72,* 333–346.

Carter, E. W., Lane, K. L., Crnobori, M. E., Bruhn, A. L., & Oakes, W. P. (2011). Self-determination interventions for students with and at risk for emotional and behavioral disorders: Mapping the knowledge base. *Behavioral Disorders, 36,* 100–116.

Christle, C. A., & Yell, M. L. (2012). Individualized education programs: Legal requirements and research findings. *Exceptionality, 18*(3), 109–123.

Collaborative for Academic, Social, and Emotional Learning. (2003). *Safe and sound: An educational leader's guide to evidence-based social and emotional learning programs.* Chicago, IL: Author.

Conroy, M. A., Alter, P. J., & Scott, T. M. (2009). Functional behavior assessment and students with emotional/behavioral disorders: When research, policy, and practice collide. In T. E. Scruggs & M. A. Mastropieri (Eds.), *Policy and practice* (Vol. 22, pp. 133–167). Advances in Learning and Behavior Disabilities. Bingley, UK: Emerald Group Publishing Limited.

Cook, B. G., & Odom, S. L. (2013). Evidence-based practices and implementation science in special education. *Exceptional Children, 79,* 135–144.

Cook, B. G., & Tankersley, M. G. (Eds.). (2013). *Research-based practices in special education.* Upper Saddle River, NJ: Pearson Education.

Cortiella, C. (2011). *The state of learning disabilities.* New York, NY: National Center for Learning Disabilities.

Coutinho, M. J., Oswald, D. P., & Best, A. M. (2002). The influence of socio-demographics and gender on the disproportionate identification of minority students as learning disabled. *Remedial and Special Education, 23,* 49–59.

Crockett, J. B., & Kauffman, J. M. (1999). *The least restrictive environment: Its origins and interpretations in special education.* Mahwah, NJ: Lawrence Erlbaum Associates.

Darling-Hammond, L., & Baratz-Snowden, J. (Eds.). (2005). *A good teacher in every classroom: Preparing the highly qualified teachers our children deserve.* San Francisco, CA: Jossey-Bass.

Diamond, K. E., Justice, L. M., Siegler, R. S., & Snyder, P. A. (2013). *Synthesis of IES research on early intervention and early childhood education (NCSER 2013–3001).* Washington, DC: National Center for Special Education Research, Institute of Education Sciences, U. S. Department of Education.

Dunlap, G., Kern-Dunlap, L., Clarke, S., & Robbins, F. R. (1991). Functional assessment, curricular revision, and severe behavior problems. *Journal of Applied Behavior Analysis, 24,* 387–397.

Durlak, J. A., Weissberg, R. P., Dymnicki, A. B., Taylor, R. D., & Schellinger, K. B. (2011). The impact of enhancing students' social and emotional learning: A meta-analysis of school-based universal interventions. *Child Development, 82,* 405–432.

Elias, M. J., Zins, J. E., Weissberg, R. P., Frey, K. S., Greenberg, M. T., Haynes, N. M. ... Shriver, T. P. (1997). *Promoting social and emotional learning: Guidelines for educators.* Alexandria, VA: Association for Supervision and Curriculum Development.

Engelmann, S. (1970). The effectiveness of direct instruction on IQ performance and achievement in reading and arithmetic. In Helmuth, J. (Ed.), *Compensatory education: A national debate.* New York, NY: Brunner/Mazel Publishers.

Engelmann, S. (1979). Theory of mastery and acceleration. In J. W. Lloyd, E. J. Kameenui, & D. Chard (Eds.), *Issues in educating students with disabilities* (pp. 177−195). Mahwah, NJ: Lawrence Erlbaum Associates.

Ennis, R. P., & Jolivette, K. (2014). Existing research and future directions for self-regulated strategy development with students with and at-risk for E/BD. *Journal of Special Education, 48,* 32−45.

ERIC Clearinghouse on Disabilities and Gifted Education. (2001). *Educating exceptional children: A statistical profile.* Arlington, CA: The Council for Exceptional Children.

Ervin, R. A., DuPaul, G. J., Kern, L., & Friman, P. C. (1998). Classroom-based functional and adjunctive assessments: Proactive approaches to intervention selection for adolescents with attention deficit hyperactivity disorder. *Journal of Applied Behavior Analysis, 31,* 65−78.

Field, S. S., Martin, J. E., Miller, R. J., Ward, M., & Wehmeyer, M. L. (1998). Self-determination in secondary transition assessment. *Assessment for Effective Intervention, 32,* 181−190.

Fielder, C. R., & Danneker, J. E. (2007). Self-advocacy instruction: Bridging the research to practice gap. *Focus on Exceptional Children, 39*(8), 1−20.

Flores, M. M., & Ganz, J. B. (2007). Effectiveness of direct instruction for teaching statement inference, use of facts, and analogies to students with developmental disabilities and reading delays. *Focus on Autism and Other Developmental Disabilities, 22,* 224−251.

Forness, S. R., Freeman, S. F. N., Paparella, T., Kauffman, J. M., & Walker, H. M. (2012). Special education implications of point and cumulative prevalence for children with emotional or behavioral disorders. *Journal of Emotional and Behavioral Disorders, 20,* 1−14.

Fuchs, D., & Fuchs, L. S. (2006). Introduction to responsiveness-to-intervention: What, why, and how valid is it? *Reading Research Quarterly, 41,* 92−99.

Gable, R. A. (1999). Functional assessment in school settings. *Behavioral Disorders, 24,* 246−248.

Ganz, J. B., & Flores, M. M. (2009). The effectiveness of direct instruction for teaching language to children with autism spectrum disorders: Identifying materials. *Journal of Autism and Developmental Disorders, 39,* 75−83.

Gerber, M. M. (2011). A history of special education. In J. M. Kauffman & D. P. Hallahan (Eds.), *Handbook of special education* (pp. 3−14). New York, NY: Taylor & Francis.

Gerber, P. J., Banbury, M. M., Miller, J. H., & Griffin, H. D. (1986). Special educators' perceptions of parental participation in the individual education plan process. *Psychology in the Schools, 23*(2), 158−163.

Gersten, R. M., White, W. A., Falco, R., & Carnine, D. (1982). Teaching basic discriminations to handicapped and non-handicapped individuals through a dynamic presentation of instructional stimuli. *Analysis and Intervention in Developmental Disabilities, 2,* 305−317.

Giangreco, M. F., Cloninger, C. J., & Iverson, V. S. (2011). *Choosing outcomes and accommodations for children (COACH): A guide to educational planning for students with disabilities* (3rd ed.). Baltimore, MD: Brookes.

Glover, P., McLaughlin, T., Derby, K., & Gower, J. (2010). Using a direct instruction flash-card system with two students with learning disabilities. *Electronic Journal of Research in Educational Psychology, 8*, 457–472.

Guralnick, M. J. (Ed.). (1997). *The effectiveness of early intervention.* Baltimore, MD: Brookes.

Guralnick, M. J. (1998). Effectiveness of early intervention for vulnerable children: A developmental perspective. *American Journal of Mental Retardation, 102*, 319–345.

Hallahan, D. P., Kauffman, J. M., & Pullen, P. C. (2012). *Exceptional learners: An introduction to special education* (12th ed.). Upper Saddle River, NJ: Pearson Education.

Hallahan, D. P., & Pullen, P. C. (2015). What is special education instruction? In B. D. Bteman, J. W. Lloyd, & M. M. Tankersley (Eds.), *Understanding special education issues: Who, where, what, when, how and why.* New York, NY: Routledge.

Harris, K. R., Graham, S., Mason, L. H., & Friedlander, B. (2008). *Powerful writing strategies for all students.* Baltimore, MD: Brookes.

Harry, B. (2008). Collaboration with culturally and linguistically diverse families: Ideal versus reality. *Exceptional Children, 74*, 372–388.

Horn, J. S. (1924). *The education of exceptional children: A consideration of public school problems and policies in the field of differentiated education.* New York, NY: Century.

Horner, R. H., & Albin, R. W. (1988). Research on general procedures for learners with severe disabilities. *Education and Treatment of Children, 11*, 375–388.

Huefner, D. S. (2006). *Getting comfortable with special education law: A framework for working with children with disabilities* (2nd ed.). Norwood, MA: Christopher Gordon.

Individuals with Disabilities Education Improvement Act of 2004. 20 U.S.C., 1415 et seq. (2004).

Kamps, D., Abbott, M., Greenwood, C., Wills, H., Veerkamp, M., & Kaufman, J. (2008). Effects of small-group reading instruction and curriculum differences for students most at risk in kindergarten two-year results for secondary- and tertiary-level interventions. *Journal of Learning Disabilities, 41*, 101–114.

Katsiyannis, A., Conroy, M., & Zharg, D. (2008). District-level administrators' perspectives on implementation of functional behavior assessments in schools. *Behavioral Disorders, 34*, 14–26.

Kauffman, J. M. (1976). Nineteenth century views of children's behavior disorders: Historical contributions and continuing issues. *Journal of Special Education, 10*, 335–349.

Kauffman, J. M. (1981). Introduction: Historical trends and contemporary issues in special education in the United States. In J. M. Kauffman & D. P. Hallahan (Eds.), *Handbook of special education* (pp. 3–23). Englewood Cliffs, NJ: Prentice-Hall.

Kauffman, J. M. (2008). Special education. In T. L. Good (Ed.), *21st century education: A reference handbook* (Vol. 1, pp. 405–413). Thousand Oaks, CA: Sage.

Kauffman, J. M. (2009). Attributions of malice to special education policy and practice. In T. E. Scruggs & M. A. Mastropieri (Eds.), *Policy and practice* (Vol. 22, pp. 33–66). Advances in Learning and Behavioral Disabilities. Bingley, UK: Emerald Group Publishing Limited.

Kauffman, J. M. (2010). *The tragicomedy of public education: Laughing and crying, thinking and fixing.* Verona, WI: Attainment.

Kauffman, J. M. (2011). *Toward a science of education: The battle between rogue and real science.* Verona, WI: Attainment.

Kauffman, J. M. (2014). Past, present, and future in EBD and special education. In B. G. Cook, M. Tankersley, & T. J. Landrum (Eds.), *Special education past, present, and future: Perspectives from the field* (Vol. 27, pp. 63–88). Advances in Learning and Behavioral Disabilities. Bingley, UK: Emerald Group Publishing Limited.

Kauffman, J. M. (2015). Why should we have special education? In B. Bateman, J. Lloyd, & M. Tankersley (Eds.), *Enduring issues in special education: Personal perspectives.* New York, NY: Routledge.

Kauffman, J. M., & Badar, J. (2014). Instruction, not inclusion, should be the central issue in special education: An alternative view from the USA. *Journal of International Special Needs Education, 17,* 13–20.

Kauffman, J. M., & Hallahan, D. P. (1993). Toward a comprehensive delivery system for special education. In J. I. Goodlad & T. C. Lovitt (Eds.), *Integrating general and special education* (pp. 73–102). Columbus, OH: Merrill/Macmillan.

Kauffman, J. M., & Hallahan, D. P. (2005a). *Special education: What it is and why we need it.* Boston, MA: Allyn & Bacon.

Kauffman, J. M., & Hallahan, D. P. (Eds.). (2005b). *The illusion of full inclusion: A comprehensive critique of a current special education bandwagon* (2nd ed.). Austin, TX: Pro-Ed.

Kauffman, J. M., & Hallahan, D. P. (Eds.). (2011). *Handbook of special education.* New York, NY: Taylor & Francis.

Kauffman, J. M., & Hung, L. Y. (2009). Special education for intellectual disability: Current trends and perspectives. *Current Opinion in Psychiatry, 22,* 452–456.

Kauffman, J. M., & Landrum, T. J. (2006). *Children and youth with emotional and behavioral disorders: A history of their education.* Austin, TX: Pro-Ed.

Kauffman, J. M., & Landrum, T. J. (2007). Educational service interventions and reforms. In J. W. Jacobson, J. A. Mulick, & J. Rojahn (Eds.), *Handbook of intellectual and developmental disabilities* (pp. 173–188). New York, NY: Springer.

Kauffman, J. M., & Landrum, T. J. (2009). Politics, civil rights, and disproportional identification of students with emotional and behavioral disorders. *Exceptionality, 17,* 177–188.

Kauffman, J. M., & Lloyd, J. W. (2011). Statistics, data, and special education decisions: Basic links to realities. In J. M. Kauffman & D. P. Hallahan (Eds.), *Handbook of special education* (pp. 27–36). New York, NY: Taylor & Francis.

Kauffman, J. M., Mock, D. R., & Simpson, R. L. (2009). Problems related to underservice of students with emotional or behavioral disorders. *Behavioral Disorders, 33,* 43–57.

Kauffman, J. M., Nelson, C. M., Simpson, R. L., & Mock, D. R. (2011). Contemporary issues. In J. M. Kauffman & D. P. Hallahan (Eds.), *Handbook of special education* (pp. 15–26). New York, NY: Taylor & Francis.

Kauffman, J. M., Ward, D. M., & Badar, J. (in press). The delusion of full inclusion. In R. M. Foxx & J. A. Mulick (Eds.), *Controversial therapies for autism and intellectual disabilities* (2nd ed.). New York, NY: Taylor & Francis.

Kern, L., Dunlap, G., Clarke, S., & Childs, K. E. (1994). Student-assisted functional assessment interview. *Diagnostique, 19,* 20–39.

Kroesbergen, E. H., & Van Luit, J. E. H. (2003). Mathematics interventions for children with special needs: A meta-analysis. *Remedial and Special Education, 24,* 97–114.

Lane, K., Harris, K., Graham, S., Driscoll, S., Sandmel, K., Morphy, P., & Schatschneider, C. (2011). Self-Regulated strategy development at tier 2 for second-grade students with writing and behavioral difficulties: A randomized controlled trial. *Journal of Research on Educational Effectiveness, 4,* 322–353.

Lane, K. L., Eisner, S. L., Kretzer, J. M., Bruhn, A. L., Crnobori, M. E., Funke, L. M. … Casey, A. M. (2009). Outcomes of functional assessment-based interventions for students with and at risk for emotional and behavioral disorders in a job-share setting. *Education and Treatment of Children, 32,* 573–604.

Lane, K. L., Kalberg, J. R., & Menzies, H. M. (2009). *Developing schoolwide programs to prevent and manage problem behaviors: A step-by-step approach.* New York, NY: Guilford Press.

Lane, K. L., Menzies, H. M., Oakes, W. P., & Kalberg, J. R. (2012). *Systematic screenings of behavior to support instruction: From preschool to high school.* New York, NY: Guilford Press.

Lewis, T., & Sugai, G. (1996). Functional assessment of problem behavior: A pilot investigation on the comparative and interactive effects of teacher and peer social attention on students in general education settings. *School Psychology Quarterly, 11,* 1–19.

Madaus, J. W., Banerjee, M., & Merchant, D. (2011). Transition to postsecondary education. In J. M. Kauffman & D. P. Hallahan (Eds.), *Handbook of special education* (pp. 571–583). New York, NY: Taylor & Francis.

Mart, A., Dusenbury, L., & Weissberg, R. P. (2011). Social, emotional, and academic learning: Complementary goals for school-family partnerships. In S. Redding, M. Murphy, & P. Sheley (Eds.), *Handbook of family and community engagement* (pp. 38–42). Charlotte, NC: Information Age Publishing.

Martin, E. W. Jr. (2013). *Breakthrough: Federal special education legislation 1965–1981.* Sarasota, FL: Bardolf.

Martin, J. E., Mithaug, D. E., Cox, P., Peterson, L. Y., Van Dycke, J. L., & Cash, M. E. (2003). Increasing self-determination: Teaching students to plan, work, evaluate, and adjust. *Exceptional Children, 69,* 431–447.

Mashburn, A., & Pianta, R. (2010). Opportunity in early education: Improving teacher-child interactions and child outcomes. In A. Reynolds, A. Rolnick, M. Englund, & J. Temple (Eds.), *Childhood programs and practices in the first decade of life: A human capital integration* (pp. 243–265). New York, NY: Cambridge University Press.

Mastropieri, M. A., Scruggs, T. E., & Mills, S. (2011). Special education teacher preparation. In J. M. Kauffman & D. P. Hallahan (Eds.), *Handbook of special education* (pp. 47–58). New York, NY: Taylor & Francis.

McLeskey, J., Landers, E., Williamson, P., & Hoppey, D. (2012). Are we moving toward educating student with disabilities in less restrictive settings? *Journal of Special Education, 46,* 131–140.

Miao, Y., Darch, C., & Rabren, K. (2002). Use of precorrection strategies to enhance reading performance of students with learning and behavior problems. *Journal of Instructional Psychology, 29,* 162–174.

Newman, L., Wagner, M., Knokey, A. M., Marder, C., Nagle, K., Shaver, D., & Wei, X. (2011). *The post-high school outcomes of young adults with disabilities up to 8 years after high school: A report from the national longitudinal transition study-2 (NLTS2).* (NCSER 2011–3005). Menlo Park, CA: SRI International.

O'Connor, R. E., & Sanchez, V. (2011). Responsiveness to intervention models for reducing reading disabilities and identifying learning disability. In J. M. Kauffman & D. P. Hallahan (Eds.), *Handbook of special education* (pp. 123–133). New York, NY: Taylor & Francis.

Ramey, C. T., & Ramey, S. L. (1998). Early intervention and early experience. *American Psychologist, 53,* 109–120.

Rasinski, T. V. (1990). Effects of repeated reading and listening while reading on reading fluency. *The Journal of Educational Research, 83,* 147–150.

Samuels, C. A. (2010, September 15). Boom in learning-disabled enrollments ends. *Education Week*, 1–15.

Sarason, S. B., & Doris, J. (1979). *Educational handicap, public policy, and social history*. New York, NY: Macmillan.

Sasso, G. M., Conroy, M. A., Stichter, J. P., & Fox, J. J. (2001). Slowing down the bandwagon: The misapplication of functional assessment for students with emotional or behavioral disorders. *Behavioral Disorders, 26*, 282–296.

Scott, T. M., McIntyre, J., Liaupsin, C., Nelson, C. M., & Conroy, M. (2004). An examination of team-based functional behavior assessment in public school settings: Collaborative teams, experts, and technology. *Behavioral Disorders, 29*, 384–395.

Scull, J., & Winkler, A. (2011). *Shifting trends in special education*. Washington, DC: Thomas E. Fordham Institute.

Seguin, E. O. (1866). *Idiocy and its treatment by the physiological method*. New York, NY: W. Wood.

Shepherd, K. G., Giangreco, M. F., & Cook, B. G. (2013). Parent participation in assessment and in development of individualized education programs. In B. G. Cook & M. Tankersley (Eds.), *Research-based practices in special education* (pp. 260–272). Upper Saddle River, NJ: Pearson Education.

Singer, J. D. (1988). Should special education merge with regular education? *Educational Policy, 2*, 409–424.

Skiba, R. J., Middelberg, L., & McClain, M. (2014). Multicultural issues for schools and EBD students: Disproportionality in discipline and special education. In H. M. Walker & F. M. Gresham (Eds.), *Handbook of evidence-based practices for emotional and behavioral disorders: Applications in schools* (pp. 54–70). New York, NY: Guilford.

Skiba, R. J., Poloni-Staudinger, L., Simmons, A. B., Feggins, L. R., & Chung, C. G. (2005). Unproven links: Can poverty explain ethnic disproportionality in special education. *Journal of Special Education, 39*, 130–144.

Skiba, R. J., Simmons, A. B., Ritter, S., Gibb, A. C., Karega Rausch, M., Cuadrado, J., & Chung, C. G. (2008). Achieving equity in special education: History, status, and current challenges. *Exceptional Children, 74*(3), 264–288.

Sowers, J., & Powers, L. (1995). Enhancing the participation and independence of students with severe physical and multiple disabilities in performing community activities. *Mental Retardation, 33*, 209–220.

Stein, M., Carnine, D., & Dixon, R. (1998). Direct instruction: Integrating curriculum design and effective teaching practice. *Intervention in School and Clinic, 33*, 227–234.

Sugai, G., & Horner, R. H. (2002). Introduction to the special series on positive behavior supports in schools. *Journal of Emotional and Behavioral Disorders, 10*, 130–135.

Turnbull, A., Turnbull, R., Erwin, E. J., Soodak, L. C., & Shogren, K. A. (2011). *Families, professionals, and exceptionality: Positive outcomes through partnerships and trust* (6th ed.). Upper Saddle River, NJ: Pearson.

Umbreit, J., & Blair, K. (1997). Using structural analysis to facilitate treatment of aggression and noncompliance in a young child at-risk for behavioral disorders. *Behavioral Disorders, 22*, 75–86.

Umbreit, J., Ferro, J. B., Liaupsin, C. J., & Lane, K. L. (2007). *Functional behavioral assessment and function-based intervention: An effective, practical approach*. Upper Saddle River, NJ: Prentice-Hall.

Umbreit, J., Lane, K. L., & Dejud, C. (2004). Improving classroom behavior by modifying task difficulty: Effects of increasing the difficulty of too easy tasks. *Journal of Positive Behavior Interventions, 6*, 13−20.

U.S. Department of Education, Office of Special Education and Rehabilitative Services. (2010). *Thirty-five years of progress in educating children with disabilities through IDEA.* Washington, DC: Office of Special Education and Rehabilitative Services.

Viel-Ruma, K., Houchins, D. E., Jolivette, K., Fredrick, L. D., & Gama, R. (2010). Direct instruction in written expression: The effects on English speakers and English language learners with disabilities. *Learning Disabilities Research & Practice, 25*(2), 97−108.

Walker, H. M., Colvin, G., & Ramsey, E. (1995). *Antisocial behavior in schools: Strategies and best practices.* Pacific Grove, CA: Brooks/Cole.

Walker, H. M., & Gresham, F. M. (Eds.). (2014). *Handbook of evidence-based practices for emotional and behavioral disorders: Applications in schools.* New York, NY: Guilford.

Warnock, M. (2005). *Special educational needs: A new look.* Impact No. 11. London: Philosophy of Education Society of Great Britain.

Wehman, P. (2012). Supported employment: What is it? *Journal of Vocational Rehabilitation, 37*, 139−142.

Wehmeyer, M. L., & Palmer, S. B. (2003). Adult outcomes for students with cognitive disabilities three years after high school: The impact of self-determination. *Education and Training in Developmental Disabilities, 38*, 131−144.

Wehmeyer, M. L., & Schwartz, M. (1997). Self-determination and positive adult outcomes: A follow-up study of youth with mental retardation or learning disabilities. *Exceptional Children, 63*, 245−255.

West, J. E., & Whitby, P. J. S. (2008). Federal policy and the education of students with disabilities: Progress and the path forward. *Focus on Exceptional Children, 41*(3), 1−16.

Wiley, A. L., Brigham, F. J., Kauffman, J. M., & Bogan, J. E. (2013). Disproportionate poverty, conservatism, and the disproportionate identification of minority students with emotional and behavioral disorders. *Education and Treatment of Children, 36*(4), 29−50.

Yell, M. (2012). *The law and special education* (3rd ed.). Upper Saddle River, NJ: Pearson.

Yell, M. L., Rogers, D., & Rogers, E. L. (1998). The legal history of special education: What a long, strange trip it's been! *Remedial & Special Education, 19*, 219−238.

Zigmond, N. (2003). Where should students with disabilities receive special education services? Is one place better than another? *The Journal of Special Education, 37*, 193−199.

Zigmond, N. (2007). Delivering special education is a two-person job: A call for unconventional thinking. In J. B. Crockett, M. M., Gerber, & T. J. Landrum (Eds.), *Achieving the radical reform of special education: Essays in honor of James M. Kauffman* (pp. 115−137). Mahwah, NJ: Lawrence Erlbaum Associates.

Zigmond, N., & Kloo, A. (2011). General and special education are (and should be) different. In J. M. Kauffman & D. P. Hallahan (Eds.), *Handbook of special education* (pp. 160−172). New York, NY: Taylor & Francis.

Zigmond, N., Kloo, A., & Volonino, V. (2009). What, where, and how? Special education in the climate of full inclusion. *Exceptionality, 17*, 189−204.

Zirkel, P. A. (2013). The trend in SLD enrollments and the role of RTI. *Journal of Learning Disabilities, 46*, 473−479.

SPECIAL EDUCATION TODAY IN CANADA

Tim Loreman

ABSTRACT

This chapter provides an overview of special education in Canada, with specific reference to historical and modern trends and practices. Information regarding demographic trends, legislation and policy, contentious issues, Provincial differences, school and classroom practices, teacher education and professional development, and family involvement are outlined. The chapter concludes with a discussion of the ongoing challenges faced by education jurisdictions in Canada with respect to special education.

INTRODUCTION

Canada, with a total population nearing 35 million (Statistics Canada, 2012), is the second largest country in the world in terms of area, consisting of 10 provinces and three territories in the north. It is a French–English bilingual constitutional monarchy with popularly elected federal and provincial governments based on the Westminster parliamentary system, along with elected local governments.

Special Education International Perspectives: Practices Across the Globe
Advances in Special Education, Volume 28, 33–60
ISSN: 0270-4013/doi:10.1108/S0270-401320140000028008

As a nation, Canada developed gradually beginning as a confederation of a few east-central provinces in 1867. This new nation accumulated provinces to the west, north, and east throughout the 19th and 20th centuries, by degrees resembling the nation it is today. Responsibility for the provision of education has always rested with the provinces. This responsibility is delegated to the extent that no Canadian federal Ministry of Education currently exists, although matters concerning education at the federal level are sometimes addressed in other ministries (such as through Aboriginal Affairs). Each Canadian province is composed of a number of different school districts that ultimately answer to the government of the province in which they are located. These school districts typically consist of an elected board of trustees who set local education policy, and a board appointed Superintendent of Schools who assumes responsibility for leading the day-to-day operations and management.

Education in Canada spans a diverse range of historical, political, social, language, religious, and geographical contexts that are so varied that it is not possible to make definitive statements that are true for the entire country. Although governed by international and federal laws and charters, because education in Canada is largely a provincial matter a high degree of difference between regions is evident. Special education provisions in New Brunswick, for example, are vastly different to special education provisions in Alberta. Therefore, it is not possible in a single chapter to provide a comprehensive overview of special education for the nation. Rather, this chapter will attempt to outline key points and representative markers from different areas of the country in order to provide a rough evidence-based sketch of trends, history, law, policy, and practice in various Canadian school jurisdictions.

ORIGINS

Education in Canada has a long history dating back to the foundation of a school by the Jesuits in Quebec in 1640 (Abbott, 1990), however, like many other Western countries formal education was initially intended only for a select portion of the population. Children with disabilities were in most cases excluded from school (Andrews & Lupart, 2000).

Consistent with the history of the institutionalization of people with disabilities and mental illness examined by Foucault (1965), the "Age of Reason" bought with it the large-scale institutionalization of people with disabilities in Canada. People with disabilities were included in the same residential institutions as people living in poverty, the mentally ill, and at times orphans (Winzer, 2008). It has been argued that this trend was bought about by increasing industrialization and capitalist economies where people were valued more on what they could produce in economic terms rather than on their inherent value as people (Scull, 1979). People who could not produce economic benefits were cared for in paternalistic residential care (not education) systems initiated by the church but quickly adopted by the medical profession that restricted freedoms and left a segment of the population powerless and disenfranchised, mirroring the situation in Europe at the time (Foucault, 1965). Thinking and educational philosophies that came out of the French Enlightenment were very much in evidence in North American education systems (Winzer, 1986). In addition, the first school for the deaf opened in Quebec in 1831 with additional schools for this segment of the population, some residential and some not, opening throughout what would become Canada over the course of the 19th and 20th centuries (Clarke & Winzer, 1983). What special education did exist at this time typically had a vocational or "life skills" tone to it, and some special education principles that would be recognized today such as individualized instruction, task analysis, multi-sensory teaching, environmental manipulation, and behavioral techniques were in use (Andrews & Lupart, 2000; Hallahan, Kauffman, & Pullen, 2009).

The legacy of exclusion that was more firmly established in the 19th century continued into the 20th century, with the first half of that century being distinguished by a rapid increase in the number and size of newly formed residential schools and separate classrooms in response to the growing number of laws requiring compulsory education for all children. The difference between residential schools and the institutions of the previous century was an emphasis on education, rather than only care (Andrews & Lupart, 2000). While faltering steps to provide education earlier were apparent, segregated classes and schools for children with disabilities were first available in 1910, proliferating through to the 1960s and beyond to become the standard mode of education for these children (Winzer, 2008). This coincided with a shameful period in Canadian history (extending into the 1970s) during which large numbers of people with disabilities were forcibly sterilized as the result of a eugenic view of eliminating what were seen as impurities from the population (Winzer, 2006). People with disabilities were increasingly institutionalized socially, psychologically, physically, and even reproductively.

Polloway, Patton, Smith, and Smith (1996) identified four paradigms of special education in the 20th century, and each of these paradigms was evident in Canada during this period. The model they presented includes relative isolation (early to mid-20th century), integration, inclusion, and finally empowerment and self-determination. This final paradigm is still in development today, and it can be easily argued that to various degrees each of the paradigms is still in existence concurrently. For example, residential institutions for children with disabilities still exist, along with educational models that closely resemble integration, inclusion, and those promoting empowerment.

Andrews and Lupart (2000) divide the history of special education in Canada into six periods: Institutionalization (1800s), segregation (1900–1950), categorization (1950s–1960s), integration (1970s), mainstreaming (1980s), and inclusion (1990s). However, as is the case with the model proposed by Polloway et al. (1996) some of these periods are still in evidence concurrent with others, and many of the periods overlap. A model reflecting the history and current practice in special education in Canada is presented in Fig. 1, with the various periods overlapping. For example, segregation has been evident since the beginning of the 20th century and is still

Fig. 1. Tracing the Development of Special Education in Canada.

a very common model of special education in many parts of the country. It has continued to operate alongside the more recent developments of integration, mainstreaming, and inclusion.

The 1950s saw a move by parents and advocacy associations to advocate for the provision of education for their children in special schools or special classes in regular schools based on the type of disability. This had the effect of bringing special education into closer alignment with the regular education system, although students still received their education in almost total isolation from their non-disabled peers (Andrews & Lupart, 2000). Special classes for various categories of children with disabilities, such as children deemed to be "Trainable Mentally Handicapped" or "Dependent Handicapped" became commonplace, with medical and psychological assessments such as IQ tests being the basis for classification and classroom placement. In the 1960s Canadian educators, like those in other parts of the world, began reassessing a segregated system of education based on categorization based on ideas of normalization developed by Wolfensberger (1972), parent and advocate group pressure, and the dubious educational effectiveness of segregated placements (Hutchinson, 2010; Winzer, 2008). This was not the end of segregated education based on categories of disability, which is still very much in evidence today. Edmonton Public Schools in Alberta, for example, has roughly the same number of special programs for children with significant individual differences as it does schools, with many of them being self-contained segregated placements. Rather, in the spirit of deinstitutionalization that was gaining momentum in Canada (Hutchinson, 2010), new ways of educating children with disabilities in regular schools developed alongside this educational paradigm.

The 1970s was the period during which integration began to be practiced, where children with disabilities began to be placed in regular schools and expected to work to meet the demands of that setting, possibly with some adjustments being made on the part of the school. The 1980s saw a further influx of children with high incidence disabilities into regular schools in an effort to help them fit in with mainstream models of education (mainstreaming) (Andrews & Lupart, 2000). Individual Education Plans became commonplace ways of providing curriculum that attempted to meet the needs of children who it was felt would not benefit from the regular curriculum. These individual plans are still widely used today.

Efforts at integration and mainstreaming morphed, with considerable modifications in philosophy and practice, into what has become the dominant paradigm for educating children with disabilities today – *inclusion*. Inclusive education, represented by a broad range of practices, was increasingly adopted throughout Canada during the 1990s, but to varying degrees. In essence, inclusion involves schools and teachers modifying the ways in which they work so as to cater to the needs of a wide variety of learners within the context of a regular school and classroom (Loreman, Deppeler, & Harvey, 2010). Some eastern Canadian provinces operate under policies of virtually full inclusion for every child, while others advocate for a dual segregated-inclusive system approach. Inclusive education has become increasingly accepted throughout Canada. For example, initially many Canadian teachers' associations were reticent to support the approach, however, over time their stances became more conciliatory and in some cases even positive with respect to inclusion, engaging in dialogue around implementation, funding and supports, professional development, and other issues (Winzer & Mazurek, 2011).

Since the 1960s, there has been a marked rise in the number of students with disabilities in school systems throughout Canada. For example, between the early-1960s and 2007 the percentage of children with disabilities being educated in the school system in Alberta rose from below 1% of the total school population to approximately 11% (Jahnukainen, 2011). Although Alberta has had compulsory schooling since 1910, this increase in children with disabilities in schools coincides roughly with Alberta raising the school leaving age to 16 years in 1966 and lowering school entry age to 6 years in 1970. The school leaving age was again raised to 17 years in 2001 (Oreopoulos, 2005). This increased focus on compulsory education was also extended to children with disabilities at that time, and continues through to the present day. The "inclusive education system" Alberta is currently working toward implementing acknowledges that some children with disabilities are still not being served by the education system and that this system needs to change to ensure that they are (Alberta Education, n.d.). In addition to this, refinements in the identification of disabilities and the expansion of disability categories funded in school jurisdictions has meant that children who were probably always present in schools but with unidentified disabilities are now included in these statistics (Jahnukainen, 2011).

This system of categorization (or coding) children on the basis of their disability has served in Canada as both a mechanism for providing funding, along with a mechanism for grouping students into segregated special education classrooms in some regions. Table 1 shows the broad categories into which children with disabilities are grouped in Canada. Northwest Territories, Nunavut, and the Yukon are missing from this table as the extant information is dated or available only from dubious sources. It

Table 1.   Formal Categories of Disability by Canadian Province Grades K-12 Based on Information Found on Provincial Government Websites.

	Behavior/Emotional Disorder	Autism/PDDs	Substance Related (Pre-natal Included)	Hearing Impairment	Visual Impairment	Cognitive Disability	Physical/Medical Disability	Learning Disability	Communication Disorder	Severe/Multiple Disability
British Columbia	✓	✓		✓	✓	✓	✓	✓		✓
Alberta	✓	✓		✓	✓	✓	✓	✓	✓	✓
Saskatchewan	✓	✓	✓	✓	✓	✓	✓		✓	✓
Manitoba	✓	✓		✓	✓		✓		✓	✓
Ontario	✓	✓		✓	✓	✓	✓	✓	✓	✓
Quebec	✓	✓		✓	✓	✓	✓		✓	✓
Newfoundland and Labrador	✓	✓	✓	✓	✓	✓	✓	✓	✓	✓
New Brunswick	✓			✓	✓	✓	✓		✓	
Nova Scotia	✓	✓		✓	✓	✓	✓	✓	✓	✓
Prince Edward Island				✓	✓		✓	✓		✓

should be noted that within many of these categories different degrees of disability are often sub-categorized (e.g., severe, moderate, mild). A degree of consistency between Canadian provinces is evident in this regard. It also needs to be noted that in some provinces certain disabilities are funded by different mechanisms or within different categories, so the lack of a check mark in one of the categories below does not necessarily mean that this issue is not addressed through funding in a different category. This is the case, for example, in some of the Atlantic provinces, particularly Prince Edward Island. The overall point of the information provided in Table 1 is that there are a wide number of recognized categories of disability throughout Canadian education systems. Indeed, it can be said that each category of disability is identified to some degree in each province.

Also instructive are the governance levels at which the requirement for the identification of students with special needs is found. Some provinces such as Alberta, Manitoba, Ontario, and Saskatchewan tackle the issue at many levels, possibly demonstrating a heightened commitment to categorization. Others, such as British Columbia and the Atlantic provinces, approach the issue from only one or two types of framework. Table 2 provides information on identification by jurisdiction, legislation, regulation, policy, and guideline.

Such identification is a clear demonstration that, notwithstanding talk about inclusive education and the social model, the medical model of disability in which identification, categorization, prescription, and treatment of the individual is important (Mittler, 2013) still exists across Canada to

Table 2. Identification of Students with Special Needs (McBride, 2008).

Jurisdiction	Legislation	Regulation	Policy	Guideline
Alberta	X	X		X
British Columbia				X
Manitoba	X	X	X	
New Brunswick				X
Newfoundland and Labrador				X
Northwest Territories				X
Nova Scotia			X	X
Nunavut				X
Ontario	X	X		X
Prince Edward Island		X		
Quebec				X
Saskatchewan	X		X	X
Yukon				X

greater or lesser degrees. This is evidenced in the continued need for formal psychological and other forms of assessment in order to attain the various levels of funding, with possibly the most salient exemplar of this being in Alberta. For example, according to the *Special education coding criteria 2012–2013* document:

> A student/ECS child identified as having a moderate cognitive disability should have:
>
> - an intelligence quotient (IQ) in the range of approximately 30 to 50 ± 5 as measured on an individual intelligence test,
> - an adaptive behaviour score equivalent to the moderately delayed level on an adaptive behaviour scale such as AAMR Adaptive Behaviour Scale – School: Second Edition (ABS-S:2) or Vineland Adaptive Behaviour Scale, and
> - programming that reflects significant modifications to basic curriculum and instruction in literacy, numeracy and living/vocational skills. (Alberta Education, 2012, p. 3)

Funding in instances such as these is distributed less on the basis of identified needs and more on the basis of individual psychological and cognitive characteristics, failing to take into account the social context of the child (except perhaps in the instance of adaptive behavior measures and programming modifications) which, according to Mittler (2013), might be considered not only inappropriate, but to some degree unethical.

DISABILITY PREVALENCE AND INCIDENCE RATES

At the time of writing the most recent national data with respect to the prevalence of disability in the child and youth population comes from 2006, the last year in which the government agency charged with this task, Statistics Canada, attempted to measure this though the 2006 Participation and Activity Limitation Survey (PALS). PALS was a post-census survey that collected information about persons with disabilities whose everyday activities were limited because of a health-related condition or problem (Statistics Canada, 2008). The following descriptors were provided by Statistics Canada (2008) for each category of disability examined.

- *Hearing*: Difficulty hearing.
- *Seeing*: Difficulty seeing.
- *Speech*: Difficulty speaking and/or being understood (applicable only to children aged 5–14 years).

- *Mobility*: Difficulty walking. This means walking on a flat firm surface, such as a sidewalk or floor (applicable only to children aged 5–14 years).
- *Agility*: Difficulty using hands or fingers to grasp or hold small objects, such as a pencil or scissors (applicable only to children aged 5–14 years).
- *Learning*: Difficulty learning due to the presence of a condition, such as attention problems, hyperactivity or dyslexia, whether or not the condition was diagnosed by a teacher, doctor or other health professional (applicable only to children aged 5–14 years).
- *Developmental delay*: Child has a delay in his/her development; a physical, intellectual or another type of delay (applicable only to children under 5 years).
- *Developmental disability or disorder*: Cognitive limitations due to the presence of a developmental disability or disorder, such as Down syndrome, autism or mental impairment caused by a lack of oxygen at birth (applicable only to children aged 5–14 years).
- *Psychological*: Limited in the amount or kind of activities that one can do due to the presence of an emotional, psychological or behavioral condition (applicable only to children aged 5–14 years).
- *Chronic condition*: Limited in the amount or kind of activities that one can do due to the presence of one or more chronic health conditions that have lasted or are expected to last six months or more and that have been diagnosed by a health professional. Examples of chronic conditions are asthma or severe allergies, heart condition or disease, kidney condition or disease, cancer, epilepsy, cerebral palsy, Spina Bifida, Cystic Fibrosis, Muscular Dystrophy, Fetal Alcohol Syndrome, etc.
- *Other*: The type of disability is "other" if the respondent answered YES to the general questions on activity limitations, but did not provide any YES to the questions about type of disability that followed.

Table 3 shows the various categories measured along with the number of identified Canadian residents in each category. This table indicates that for children aged 0–4 years the most widespread conditions were chronic health problems and developmental delay. Amongst school-aged children learning disabilities and chronic health conditions were the most prevalent forms of disability, and most school-aged children with disabilities have multiple disabilities. Fig. 2 shows that in all areas (with the exception of mobility) boys are impacted to a significantly higher degree than are girls. The unanswered question with regard to this is why is this the case? From the perspective of the social model of disability, what is it about Canadian society that results in higher incidences of identified disability in boys?

Table 3. Canadian Child and Youth Disability Prevalence and Incidence Rates.

Types of Disability	Age Groups					
	0–4 years		5–14 years		Total	
	Number	%	Number	%	Number	%
All categories	27,540	100	174,810	100	202,350	100
Hearing[a]	3,270	11.9	20,020	11.5	23,290	11.5
Seeing[a]	3,030	11.0	16,680	9.5	19,710	9.7
Speech[b]	–	–	78,240	44.8	78,240	44.8
Mobility[b]	–	–	23,160	13.2	23,160	13.2
Agility[b]	–	–	37,240	21.3	37,240	21.3
Learning[b]	–	–	121,080	69.3	121,080	69.3
Developmental[b]	–	–	53,740	30.7	53,740	30.7
Psychological[b]	–	–	60,310	34.5	60,310	34.5
Delay[c]	17,090	62.1	–	–	17,090	62.1
Chronic[a]	19,230	69.8	116,340	66.6	135,570	67.0
Other[a]	1,810	6.6	6,290	3.6	8,100	4.0

Source: Statistics Canada, Participation and Activity Limitation Survey, 2006. http://www.stat-can.gc.ca/pub/89-628-x/2007002/t/4125014-eng.htm
Note: The sum of the categories is greater than the population with disabilities because persons could report more than one type of disability.
[a]Applies to all children under 15 years.
[b]Applies to children aged 5–14 years.
[c]Applies to children aged 0–4 years.

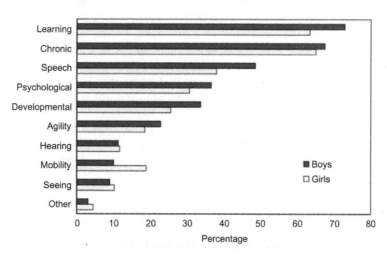

Fig. 2. Disability Rates in Canada by Gender. *Source*: Statistics Canada, Participation and Activity Limitation Survey, 2006. http://www.statcan.gc.ca/pub/89-628-x/2007002/c-g/4124994-eng.htm

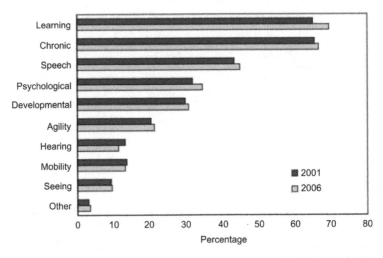

Fig. 3. 2001–2006 Comparison of Child and Youth Disability Rates in Canada. *Source*: Statistics Canada, Participation and Activity Limitation Survey (2001, 2006). http://www.statcan.gc.ca/pub/89-628-x/2007002/c-g/4124995-eng.htm

The overall disability rate in 5–14-year-olds between 2001 and 2006 increased from 4.0% to 4.6%. While small increases in disability rates between 2001 and 2006 were noted in most areas except hearing and mobility, Fig. 3 shows that disability rates increased the most in learning and psychological-related disabilities from 2.6% to 3.2% (Statistics Canada, 2008). This begs questions as to whether there are simply more children with disabilities in Canadian schools, or if identification has improved, or if identification has not improved and more children are being identified as having disabilities when they do not actually have them.

With respect to severity the PALS survey found that 1.5% of Canadian children have a severe disability, and that severity of disability is impacted by the presence of multiple disabilities (Statistics Canada, 2008).

LEGISLATIVE AND LEGAL TRENDS IN CANADIAN SPECIAL EDUCATION

The 1960s was a period of significant change in Canadian special education, and this change was reflected in the legislation that developed during that period. According to Winzer (2006) "Parents, consumers, and advocates used the period's increased sensitivity to human and civil rights to promote the normalization philosophy, the 'handicappism' movement, and to mount a case against special education as it was practiced at that time" (p. 30). The first review of existing Canadian special education legislation took place in 1969, finding that only Nova Scotia had mandatory legislation. Mandatory provisions for special education were introduced in Saskatchewan in 1971, with such provisions being similar to yet predating later US law that has been seen as influential, including the Education for All Handicapped Children Act, 1975 (PL 94-142) (Treherne & Rawlyk, 1979). Winzer (2008), for example, notes that Canadian legislative and administrative issues have been directly impacted by ideas in the United States such as PL 94-142 and the Individuals with Disabilities Education Act (1990, PL 101-476). The major way the legal system differs, though, is that in Canada there is no national office or ministry that directly governs education as is the case in the United States. In Canada, legislation governing education is passed by each Province and Territory, typically through what is called an Education Act or a School Act. These tend to be omnibus pieces of legislation addressing all areas of education, including special education. Typically, the legislation is amended over time to reflect changing circumstances and political views, with full re-authoring done only rarely. It is from this legislation that policy and regulations are devised at various levels, down to individual school district and school level.

Legislation and policy in Canada could be said to follow a cascade model (see Fig. 4). Canada is signatory to various international conventions and statements at the international level from the UN or UNESCO. At the Federal level provincial legislation and policy must not contravene the 1982 Canadian Charter of Rights and Freedoms. Section 15 of the Charter guarantees all Canadians, including children, the right to equal treatment before the law, particularly those with individual differences such as disability (Government of Canada, 2002). Taking into account the international commitments along with the Canadian Charter of Rights and Freedoms each Province passes its own legislation and, usually, policy to accompany that legislation. Further policy is devised at the school district level and the school level, but this policy must not contradict policy at any of the levels above.

Throughout Canada a clear preference for inclusive education is expressed in law and policy, with even those Provinces with a well-established segregated system of education recommending it as a first

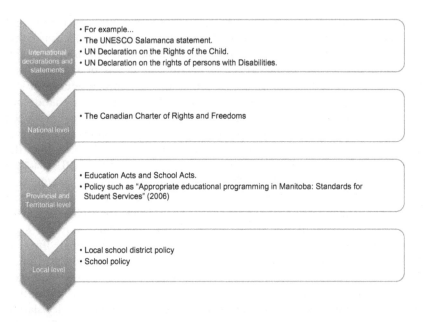

Fig. 4.   Cascade Model of Canadian Special Needs Law and Policy.

option. One example of this preference comes from the Government of New Brunswick (2012) where all children are required to attend inclusive schools by law. A government report states that:

> Every child, no matter his/her differences, has the right to learn with his/her peers to his/her potential and feel safe, secure and respected while doing so. Children and students of all backgrounds, including those new to Canada, First Nations, those with socio-economic challenges, struggling learners, those with behaviour issues, and those with disabilities benefit from inclusive, positive learning environments. Inclusion is based on values and beliefs that support each child while promoting social cohesion, belonging, and active participation in learning, a complete school experience, and positive interactions with peers and others in the school community. (p. 4)

This preference, however, has been challenged in Canada. In 1997 the Supreme Court in Canada ruled in favor of retaining segregated classrooms in a "continuum of services" model in the Eaton v. Brant County Board of Education case, finding that such a placement was in the best interests of the 12-year-old child who had a disability (Kohen, Uppal, Kahn, & Visentin, 2010). While litigation in Canada is not as common as in the United States as Canada arguably lacks the tradition of corrective legal action (Treherne & Rawlyk, 1979), where it does occur it is typically around issues of inclusive education, advocacy groups supporting parents, and interpretations of the Canadian Charter of Rights and Freedoms (Winzer, 2008). Other landmark cases in Canadian litigation in the area of special education and disability include:

- The 1978 Carriere case in Alberta where it was ruled that local school districts must provide education for all children within their geographical boundaries.
- The 1982 Clark v. Clark case saw Justin Clark win his rights to an equitable education.
- The 1997 Eldridge v. The Attorney General of British Columbia ruled that services for people who are deaf and hard of hearing can include an interpreter provided free of charge.

One of the more significant continuing legal controversies in Canadian special education is connected to an evidence-based treatment for autism spectrum disorder called Applied Behavior Analysis (ABA, Boutot & Dukes, 2011). In the 2004 Auton case, the parents of a child with autism challenged the decision of the Government of British Columbia not to fund ABA for their child. The case was heard by the Supreme Court of Canada after initial victories by the family in lower courts. The parents argued that not funding ABA was discrimination under the Canadian Charter of Rights and Freedoms in that a medically necessary treatment was not being provided. Ultimately, the Supreme Court concluded that British Columbia was not required to provide this controversial therapy (Law Clerks of the Court of Appeal for Ontario, n.d.). The decision has stimulated significant discussion around the provision of ABA throughout the country since that time, with some provinces such as Alberta deciding to fund it, at least partially under some circumstances, and others deciding not to fund it.

PROMINENT EDUCATIONAL INTERVENTIONS

Early Intervention

Early intervention programs are common throughout Canada, both through private and semi-private associations such as Head Start, along with fully government funded programs provided through school jurisdictions or health agencies. Many jurisdictions, aware of research demonstrating the value of early intervention in ameliorating challenges later in life, provide a significant focus on this area and devote considerable resources to it (Willms, 2002). According to Statistics Canada (2008) in 2006, 69.8% of children aged 0–4 years surveyed by the PALS with one or more disabilities had a chronic health condition-related disability. This accounted for 1.2% of all Canadian children under the age of 5 years. In all, a total 1.4% of all boys and 0.9% of all girls within this age group experienced a chronic health condition-related disability such as asthma or severe allergies, attention deficit disorder with or without hyperactivity (Attention Deficit Disorder or Attention Deficit Hyperactivity Disorder), and autism.

The approach to early intervention in Canada is inconsistent between provinces and territories, and even internally within provinces and territories as the result of an absence of federal government legislation and/or direction in this area. As an example, Underwood (2012) noted that in that "Early intervention in Ontario is provided through a fragmented system of services and varied organizations in the province. Many of these services are funded through the provincial government" (p. 128). This is broadly true for other Canadian Provinces and Territories. Underwood found that in Ontario services for young children tended to be more often delivered in clinical and center-based settings rather than natural settings (such as the home), although the outcomes were not necessarily any better as a result of these more intensive types of interventions. The types of disabilities catered to in early intervention programs in Ontario included intellectual/developmental disability, communication, behavioral/psychosocial, medical conditions, social conditions targeted for developmental support, multiple disabilities, and physical disabilities. While this is largely unsurprising, what is noteworthy are the number of different types of intervention offered according to geographic location. These include a rather large laundry-list of 15 interventions as follows: social work services, residential placement services, ABA and behavioral services, communication therapies, school/childcare support, segregated school/preschool, referral services, recreational/social, professional consultation and education, physical and sensory rehabilitation, parent support/training, case management, developmental assessment, and medical treatment and diagnosis.

Inclusive Education

All Canadian provinces and territories recognize the value of inclusive education, although in practice commitment to it varies considerably across the country. The Maritime Provinces, for example, have well-developed systems of inclusive education and a stated philosophical preference for it (see, e.g., Government of New Brunswick, 2012). Other provinces such as Alberta provide a wide variety of entrenched segregated options alongside inclusive education under the banner of "choice." This choice, however, is heavily undermined by the ability of the school district superintendents to direct students to segregated placement options if they deem it necessary and the proliferation of these programs. Indeed, the Government of Alberta's (Alberta Education, n.d.) own initiative on inclusive education, known as Action on Inclusion, "... no longer exists as a project or initiative" (para. 4) despite having received considerable high-profile attention from the previous Minister of Education over a number of years, and having cost considerable sums of money in extensive public consultations and bureaucratic time and expertise.

That being said, the most recent data available indicates that in Canada the majority of children with disabilities, 64%, attend what might be characterized as inclusive schools with 61% attending regular classes only (Kohen et al., 2010).

Continuum of Services

As mentioned in the section above, the most recent data available indicates that in Canada the majority of children with disabilities attend what might be characterized as inclusive schools. However, nationally a further 26% attend segregated classrooms within regular schools, and 6% attend segregated special education schools (Kohen et al., 2010). Presumably the remainder receive no educational services, or services that do not fit into these categories, as educational services are available in homes, hospitals, youth correctional facilities, or medical-style residential institutional settings. Therefore, in Canada a "continuum of services" model exists with what are viewed by some as "least restrictive placements" of inclusive education being at one end of the continuum, and "most restrictive" institutional placements at the other end (see Fuchs, Fuchs, & Stecker, 2010, for a discussion of the continuum of services model). The continuum of services model, however, still fails to provide adequate access to services for children with disabilities in Canada, with 31% reporting having had difficulty accessing services as a result of inadequate resources, difficulties in having assessments conducted, communication difficulties with the school, and the unavailability of local services (Kohen et al., 2010).

Table 4. School Placement in 10 Canadian Provinces.

Province	Regular School	Attends Only Regular Classes	Regular School, Special Class	Attends Regular and Special Class	Special School
British Columbia	68%	55%	26%	34%	NA
Alberta	67%	64%	23%	24%	NA
Saskatchewan	68%	60%	26%	35%	NA
Manitoba	72%	65%	21%	29%	NA
Ontario	63%	59%	31%	31%	NA
Quebec	51%	65%	21%	18%	22%
New Brunswick	84%	76%	N/A	19%	NA
Nova Scotia	80%	71%	15%	24%	NA
PEI	87%	79%	NA	NA	NA
Newfoundland	65%	56%	31%	39%	NA

Where a child is placed on the continuum is influenced by geographic location as demonstrated in Table 4 using data from Kohen et al. (2010). Table 4 shows that children with disabilities in Quebec are most likely to receive segregated special education services, with those in the Maritime Provinces being the least likely. While it would appear that Quebec is the only province with segregated special schools, this is in fact misleading. Other provinces do maintain segregated special schools but these are apparently hidden in or omitted from the data. One example is that while Alberta lists no segregated special schools, L.Y. Cairns School located in Edmonton is clearly a special school specifically for children with learning disabilities, but is for some reason not recognized as such in this data (see http://lyc.epsb.ca/).

Home Schooling

Home schooling has for some time been a popular means of educating children with and without disabilities in Canada (Luffman, 1997). While on the face of it home schooling results from parent choice, many families elect to home school as a result of what they see as being a lack of choice. According to an anonymous Canadian parent (2007) "I started to home-school because the school environment was hurting my children. After seven years in the system, they were sinking deeper and deeper emotionally, behaviourally, and academically" (p. 38). Arai (2000) found that parents choosing to home school their children in Canada did so for a mixture of ideological and pedagogical reasons, believing that home was a better environment and that they could do a better job in terms of meeting the instructional needs of their children. The Ontario Federation of Teaching Parents (1996) estimates that in Canada approximately 60,000 children are homeschooled (1–2% of the school-aged population).

Support for home schooling is offered throughout Canada through the provision of some funding and curricular supervision and consulting provided by school jurisdictions. However, not all provinces require parents to register their children with a school jurisdiction if they intend to educate them at home. Further, not all provinces, for example Alberta, require parents who home school to follow the curriculum (in the case of Alberta the term "home educated" is typically used in this circumstance).

Transition to Work

According to Johnson, McGrew, Bloomberg, Bruininks, and Lin (1997) young adults with disabilities, particularly severe disabilities, have difficulties with respect to their transition to work, specifically with respect to limited job options, disadvantages in workplace competition, lower earnings, and reduced social interactions with co-workers. Transition to work, then, is an important area of focus and one to which some attention has been devoted in Canada.

As in all other areas relating to education in Canada, the provinces and territories assume the responsibility for transition to work programs while students are still of a school age. After that point Non-Government Organizations (NGOs) such as the Canadian Association for Community Living and various regional autonomous "branches" provide support. Sometimes there are collaborative initiatives between government agencies and NGOs such as the Ontario "Passport Mentoring Initiative" (PMI). The PMI promotes a mentoring approach to transition out of school for youth with developmental disabilities aged 14–21 years (Community Living Ontario, 2013). Support from community associations, while of great value, is however tenuous as it relies on the various non-profit NGOs capacity to raise adequate funds to support this activity. These programs tend to approach transition through attempts to build independence via support provided in the workplace along with providing support in areas of life outside of the workplace as required (Community Living Research Project, 2006).

Canada has also been an international leader in facilitating inclusive post-secondary education. This is becoming popular across the country, but was largely spearheaded and developed first in Alberta where a number of universities, small and large, public and private, participate in the program supported by the Alberta Association for Community Living. This program supports people with disabilities in attending universities with their peers, typically as auditors of courses, although some expectations for assignments are negotiated. Graduates attend convocation and are recognized during the ceremony during the conferring of degrees.

TEACHER EDUCATION

An Outcomes-Based Approach

Teacher education in Canada typically follows an outcomes-based approach. In this approach required traits for teacher certification are outlined by the certifying body; typically provincial governments, although in British Columbia and Ontario this role is undertaken by the relevant professional associations. Teacher education institutions then construct their programs in order to assist students in meeting those outcomes. There are a number of pathways to teacher certification. A prospective teacher can engage in a 4-year Bachelor of Education degree directly after completion of secondary schooling, or complete an initial degree in another discipline before embarking on a two-year after-degree program in Education that will lead to teacher certification. This is true except in Ontario, where a 1-year after degree has been deemed adequate (Ontario Ministry of Education, 2013). Notably 1-year educated teachers are not eligible for certification in other areas of the country including but not limited to British Columbia and Alberta. While universities across Canada offer courses in special education areas (often of a categorical nature) the only province that requires extra qualifications for special education teachers is Ontario. This is unusual given that 63% of children with disabilities attend inclusive schools in that province. Thus, it is almost as likely that regular teachers will encounter children with disabilities in their work as qualified special education teachers. Other provinces note that such qualifications are desirable but not necessarily required for teaching in segregated special education settings (McBride, 2008).

Given the outcomes-based approach, provincial and territorial governments shy away from prescribing specific courses in areas related to special needs education, although Saskatchewan comes close with respect to practicing teachers. Instead, there is generally an outcome required for certification that requires teachers to be able to teach to a diverse range of learner needs. Teacher education programs may or may not mandate courses in this area as a pre-requisite for graduation. Further significant variation exists with respect to the amount of special needs education content a student may encounter over the course of a teacher education program (McBride, 2008). Some jurisdictions argue that teacher preparedness in this area is inadequate; however, in a previous publication I argued that graduates of teacher education programs are by definition novices and that it is unrealistic to expect newly minted teachers in Canada to have proficiency in anything other than the fundamentals in this area (Loreman, 2010b). True expertise, it is argued, comes with professional learning during teaching practice (Loreman, 2010a).

Models of Diversity Education for Pre-Service Teachers

In-service teachers can gain the knowledge, skills, and attributes they require for teacher certification in two ways, or through a combination of these ways at the discretion of the teacher education institution. The first way is the traditional course-based model of teacher education for diversity. Under this model pre-service teachers engage in one or more mandated or elective courses addressing areas such as inclusive education, differentiating instruction, or more categorical approaches to special needs education. While this approach can be effective (Sharma, Forlin, & Loreman, 2008) another model, content infusion, has also shown promise.

A content infused approach is also used in teacher education in Canada. This approach involves infusing content about special needs education, and particularly about inclusive education, throughout various courses in a teacher education program (Loreman, 2010b). The approach has been found to be effective in preparing teachers in this area although it does require significant coordination and cooperation from instructors. At Concordia University College of Alberta in Edmonton a dual approach is currently employed. Inclusive education content is infused at various key points in the program, with students also receiving more targeted instruction in a course on inclusive education.

Professional Development for Practicing Teachers

Canadian teachers are generally required to use Professional Growth Plans. These are normally required by professional associations, governments, local school jurisdictions, or possibly all three. Various templates exist for professional growth plans, but in essence they require teachers to set goals, devise plans to achieve those goals, and then evaluate their progress at the conclusion of the plan. Often these goals are based on professional standards for practice required for the maintenance of teacher certification, and therefore may include areas pertinent to special needs education and/or inclusive education. Teachers, then, assume in large part responsibility for engaging in their own professional learning, although in reality these pursuits are often supported through the provision of funds at the school level to help defray the costs of professional learning.

Practicing teachers may select from a wide range of mandatory and elective professional development activities. These activities may be provided by the provincial governments (in Manitoba, Northwest Territories, and Ontario), local school jurisdictions, or third-party professional development providers and may include organized presentations, conferences, university programs and courses, specialist professional council meetings, train-the-trainer models, mentorships, action research programs, or similar activities. Those activities for which resources are provided (such as time off or financial support) are typically regarded as mandatory, while other activities may be seen as being more elective, notwithstanding the professional requirement to maintain skills at an acceptable level (McBride, 2008). Taking all this into account a practicing teacher's learning with respect to inclusive and special education is often at their own discretion, producing an uneven patchwork of knowledge, attributes, and skills in this area in the teaching profession across the country.

ONGOING CHALLENGES

Poor Education Outcomes for Students with Disabilities

The education outcomes for children with disabilities in Canadian schools lag behind that of their counterparts without disabilities. Kohen et al. (2010) noted that with respect to respondents included in their study:

- 43% reported that health conditions contributed to their taking longer to achieve their present level of education compared to peers without health conditions.
- 4% of students with disabilities had to take a lighter course load.
- 15% of students with disabilities had their education interrupted for long periods of time as a result of their condition or health problem.
- 14% of children with disabilities or health issues had to leave their home community in order to attend school as a result of their disability.

One finding from the 2006 PALS survey was that "parents were asked to rate their child's academic performance during the 2005 and 2006 school year on a scale ranging from very well to very poorly. On average, children in special education were reported by their parents as underperforming compared to their regular education counterparts" and further "a large portion of children who had unmet needs for special education performed poorly or very poorly (45.8%) compared to their classmates with disabilities who did not require special education (7.3%) and to children participating in special education (31.8%). This contributed to an average performance that was weaker than both these latter groups" (Statistics Canada, 2008).

Special Education/Inclusive Education Dichotomy

One challenge for special education in Canada is the maintenance of two approaches to education that lack alignment both philosophically and also in practice. This has produced a dichotomy between segregated types of education found on the continuum of services on one side and inclusive education on the other. Supporters of segregated education options for children with disabilities do so under the banner of choice, arguing that they want the right to choose the sort of education they think is best for their children (see Gordon & Morton, 2008). Supporters of inclusive education argue that it is a superior way of educating children and more socially just and defensible (Specht, 2013). The maintenance of both systems is expensive and inefficient. In fact, Samuels (2011) reported that in the United States there is a shift away from supporting so many segregated classrooms toward inclusive education in some areas simply to try to better streamline costs.

The resolution of this seemingly intractable binary may lie in Slee's (2011) "irregular school." The irregular school is one in which barriers to

inclusion are removed and in doing so we don't need to worry about inclusive and non-inclusive education. We just get back to having appropriate
education for all in settings that look different according to context and
that do not exclude and marginalize individuals or groups. This idea while
compelling is yet to be developed to the point where it can be operationalized, leaving the dichotomy unresolved.

Evidence-Based Practice

The dilemma for advocates of inclusive education in Canada is summed up
by Specht (2013) who notes that "Settings that promote inclusion are more
successful in achieving learning for all, the ultimate goal of education.
Despite research and provincial/territorial legislation stating that inclusive
education is the preferred system ... a large percentage of students
with exceptionalities continue to be excluded from the regular classroom"
(p. 16). Further, she adds that "The question is not whether inclusive education is effective, but rather why it is not done well everywhere" (p. 17). In
support of this notion Timmons and Wagner (2009) found that in Canada:

> The analysis of data revealed that parents were more likely to report that their children
> with disabilities are in better general health, progress very well/well at school, interact
> very well/well with their peers, and more frequently look forward to going to school in
> higher inclusive educational settings than in mid-range or lower inclusion settings. This
> positive association was consistent, regardless of severity and type of disability. (p. 2)

International evidence on the outcomes of inclusive education seems to
demonstrate that at the very least it is not less effective than segregated
forms of education. Lindsay (2007) in his analysis of studies on inclusive
education concluded that this work did not produce a clear endorsement
for inclusive education as there were many areas in which the research was
still unclear. However, notably, his study did not find that it was less effective. This is an important point. Those who argue for the retention of the
continuum of services model expect that supporters of inclusive education
provide evidence for its efficacy. However, what is almost absent from the
discourse in this area is the expectation that supporters of the continuum
of services respond in kind and produce efficacy evidence supporting the
continuance of that model. Significant effort is currently being dedicated
across Canada to research inclusive education (see, e.g., the Canadian
Research Centre on Inclusive Education http://www.edu.uwo.ca/inclusive_
education/), yet Sobsey (2005) observed that in truth very little research

evidence exists and has ever existed for the efficacy of segregated education for children with disabilities. Despite this, segregated options for the education of children with disabilities exist throughout Canada, almost by default. It is hard to imagine the maintenance of other forms of costly education in the Canadian education system (such as segregated education is; see Samuels, 2011) when the evidence for the effectiveness of that approach as documented in research cannot be produced.

CONCLUSION

This chapter has traced the history of special education in Canada from its inception to the present day. Information with respect to prevalence and types of disabilities has been presented, along with information on the varied means of educating children with disabilities ranging from segregated to inclusive options. The data is indicative of significant differences in practice across the country with varying philosophical positions being taken toward inclusion depending on the provincial context. Special education legislation and policy has been addressed along with a select description of key legal cases in Canada with respect to special education. The most prominent educational interventions such as early intervention, inclusive education, the continuum of services model, home schooling, and post-school transition programs have been described. Teacher education has been addressed, noting that Canadian teacher education programs typically engage in backwards design of content based on a set of outcomes determined by teacher certification bodies. The chapter concludes with some of the ongoing challenges for special education in Canada which include poor educational outcomes for students with disabilities, the yet to be resolved dichotomy between special and inclusive education, and the maintenance of a continuum of services segregated education model in the face of compelling evidence in favor of inclusive education in Canada.

REFERENCES

Abbott, E. (Ed.). (1990). *Chronicle of Canada*. Montreal, Canada: Chronicle Publications.
Alberta Education. (n.d.). *About an inclusive education system*. Edmonton, Canada: Alberta Education. Retrieved from http://education.alberta.ca/department/ipr/inclusion/about. aspx. Accessed on May 28, 2013.

Alberta Education. (2012). *Special education coding criteria 2012–2013*. Edmonton, Canada: Alberta Education.

Andrews, J., & Lupart, J. (2000). *The inclusive classroom: Educating exceptional children*. Ontario, Canada: Nelson Thomson Learning.

Anonymous. (2007). Giving up on school: One family's story. *Education Canada, 47*(3), 38–42.

Arai, A. (2000). Reasons for home schooling in Canada. *Canadian Journal of Education, 25*(3), 204–217.

Boutot, E. A., & Dukes, C. (2011). Evidence-based practices for educating students with autism spectrum disorder. In E. Boutot & B. S. Myles (Eds.), *Autism spectrum disorders: Foundations, characteristics, and effective strategies* (pp. 68–92). Upper Saddle River, NJ: Pearson.

Clarke, B. R., & Winzer, M. A. (1983). A concise history of education of the deaf in Canada. *Association of Canadian Educators of the Hearing Impaired Journal, 9*(1), 36–51.

Community Living Ontario. (2013). *Passport mentoring*. Retrieved from http://www.communitylivingontario.ca/families-individuals/passport-mentoring. Accessed on June 14, 2013.

Community Living Research Project. (2006). *Young adults with developmental disabilities: Transition from high school to adult life. Literature and initial program review*. Vancouver, Canada: Community Living Research Project.

Education for All Handicapped Children Act of 1975. P.L. 94-142.

Foucault, M. (1965). *Madness and civilization: A history of insanity in the age of reason*. New York, NY: Vintage.

Fuchs, D., Fuchs, L. S., & Stecker, P. M. (2010). The "blurring" of special education in a new continuum of general education placements and services. *Exceptional Children, 76*(3), 301–323.

Gordon, L., & Morton, M. (2008). Inclusive education and school choice: Democratic rights in a devolved system. In S. L. Gabel & S. Danforth (Eds.), *Disability and the politics of education: An international reader* (pp. 237–250). New York, NY: Peter Lang Publishing, Inc.

Government of Canada. (2002). *Your guide to the Canadian charter of rights and freedoms: Special edition*. Ottawa, Canada: Government Services Canada.

Government of New Brunswick. (2012). *Government's response to the recommendations of: Strengthening inclusion, strengthening schools. An action plan for 2012–13*. Fredericton, NB: Government of New Brunswick.

Hallahan, D. P., Kauffman, J. M., & Pullen, P. C. (2009). *Exceptional learners: An introduction to special education*. Boston, MA: Allyn & Bacon.

Hutchinson, N. L. (2010). *Inclusion of exceptional learners in Canadian schools: A practical handbook for teachers* (3rd ed.). Toronto, Canada: Pearson Prentice Hall.

Individuals with Disabilities Education Act of 1990. Pub. L. No. 101-476, Stat. 1142.

Jahnukainen, M. (2011). Different strategies, different outcomes? The history and trends of the inclusive and special education in Alberta (Canada) and in Finland. *Scandinavian Journal of Educational Research, 55*(5), 489–502. doi:10.1080/00313831.2010.537689

Johnson, D. R., Mc Grew, K. S., Bloomberg, L., Bruininks, R. H., & Lin, H. (1997). Results of a national follow-up study of young adults with severe disabilities. *Journal of Vocational Rehabilitation, 8*(2), 119–133.

Kohen, D., Uppal, S., Kahn, S., & Visentin, L. (2010). *Access and barriers to educational services for Canadian children with disabilities*. Ottawa, Canada: Canadian Council on Learning.

Law Clerks of the Court of Appeal for Ontario. (n.d.). *Landmark case: Equality rights and access to health care. Auston vs. BC (A.G.).* Ontario, Canada: Ontario Justice Education Network.

Lindsay, G. (2007). Annual review: Educational psychology and the effectiveness of inclusive education/mainstreaming. *British Journal of Educational Psychology, 77*(1), 1–24.

Loreman, T. (2010a). Essential inclusive education-related outcomes for Alberta pre-service teachers. *Alberta Journal of Educational Research, 56*(2), 124–142.

Loreman, T. (2010b). A content-infused approach to pre-service teacher preparation for inclusive education. In C. Forlin (Ed.), *Teacher education for inclusion: Changing paradigms and innovative approaches* (pp. 56–64). Abingdon, UK: Routledge.

Loreman, T., Deppeler, J., & Harvey, D. H. P. (2010). *Inclusive education: Supporting diversity in the classroom.* Abingdon, UK: Routledge.

Luffman, J. (1997). A profile of home schooling in Canada. *Education Quarterly Review, 4*(4), 30–47.

McBride, S. (2008). *A cross-Canada review of selected issues in special education.* Victoria, Canada: McBride Management.

Mittler, P. (2013). *Overcoming exclusion.* London: Routledge.

Ontario Federation of Teaching Parents. (1996). *Homeschooling FAQs.* Retrieved from http://ontariohomeschool.org/. Accessed on June 14, 2013.

Ontario Ministry of Education. (2013). *The teaching profession.* Ontario, Canada: Queens Printer of Ontario. Retrieved from http://www.edu.gov.on.ca/eng/teacher/employ.html. Accessed on June 14, 2013.

Oreopoulos, P. (2005). *Canadian compulsory school laws and their impact on educational attainment and future earnings.* Ottawa, Canada: Statistics Canada.

Polloway, E. A., Patton, J. R., Smith, J. D., & Smith, T. E. C. (1996). Historic changes in mental retardation and developmental disabilities. *Education & Training in Mental Retardation, 31*(1), 3–12.

Samuels, C. A. (2011). Finding efficiencies in special education programs. *Education Week, 30*(16), 32–34.

Scull, A. (1979). *Museums of madness: The social organization of insanity in nineteenth-century England* (2nd ed.). London, UK: Penguin Education.

Sharma, U., Forlin, C., & Loreman, T. (2008). Impact of training on pre-service teachers' attitudes and concerns about inclusive education and sentiments about persons with disabilities. *Disability & Society, 23*(7), 773–785.

Slee, R. (2011). *The irregular school: Exclusion, schooling, and inclusive education.* London, UK: Routledge.

Sobsey, R. (2005, April). Inclusive education research. Paper presented at the Whole Schooling Conference 2005, Edmonton, Canada.

Specht, J. (2013). School inclusion: Are we getting it right? *Education Canada, 53*(2), 16–19.

Statistics Canada. (2008). *Participation and activity limitation survey 2006: Analytical report.* Ottawa, Canada: Government of Canada. Retrieved from http://www.statcan.gc.ca/pub/89-628-x/89-628-x2007002-eng.htm

Statistics Canada. (2012). *Canada at a glance.* Ottawa, Canada: Government of Canada. Retrieved from http://www.statcan.gc.ca/pub/12-581-x/2012000/pop-eng.htm

Timmons, V., & Wagner, M. (2009). *Inclusive education knowledge exchange initiative: An analysis of the statistics Canada participation and activity limitation survey.* Retrieved from www.ccl-cca.ca/CCL/Research/FundedResearch/201009TimmonsInclusiveEducation.html. Accessed on June 20, 2013.

Treherne, D., & Rawlyk, S. (1979). Canadian legislative processes: Special education. *McGill Journal of Education, 14*(3), 265–273.

Underwood, K. (2012). Mapping the early intervention system in Ontario, Canada. *International Journal of Special Education, 27*(2), 126–135.

Willms, J. D. (Ed.). (2002). *Vulnerable children: Findings from Canada's national longitudinal survey of children and youth.* Edmonton, Canada: University of Alberta Press.

Winzer, M., & Mazurek, K. (2011). Canadian teachers' associations and the inclusive movement for students with special needs. *Canadian Journal of Educational Administration and Policy, 117*, 1–24.

Winzer, M. A. (1986). Early developments in special education: Some aspects of enlightenment thought. *Remedial and Special Education: RASE, 7*(5), 42–49.

Winzer, M. A. (2006). Confronting difference: An excursion through the history of special education. In L. Florian (Ed.), *The Sage handbook of special education* (pp. 21–33). New York, NY: Sage.

Winzer, M. A. (2008). *Children with exceptionalities in Canadian classrooms* (8th ed.). Toronto, Canada: Pearson Prentice Hall.

Wolfensberger, W. (1972). *The principles of normalization in human services.* Toronto, Canada: National Institute on Mental Retardation.

SPECIAL EDUCATION TODAY IN MEXICO

Ismael García-Cedillo, Silvia Romero-Contreras and Todd V. Fletcher

ABSTRACT

This chapter is a presentation of Mexico's efforts in advancing inclusive education as a vehicle to provide children with special needs a quality and equitable education. It provides a detailed description of the development, realignment of educational practices, and polices necessary to allow inclusive education to succeed. The chapter begins with the origins of special education in Mexico via four stages. Next, the chapter provides a comprehensive classification of disability and the prevalence rates in Mexico. Then, the chapter delineates legislation and public policy that are essential components in providing a quality and equitable special education system. Next, a comprehensive description of special education intervention models follows along with how these models are incorporated in current teacher preparation endeavors. The chapter concludes with a summary of the progress that Mexico has attained in moving toward inclusive education as well as challenges to inclusive education.

Special Education International Perspectives: Practices Across the Globe
Advances in Special Education, Volume 28, 61–89
Copyright © 2014 by Emerald Group Publishing Limited
All rights of reproduction in any form reserved
ISSN: 0270-4013/doi:10.1108/S0270-401320140000028009

INTRODUCTION

As we gaze over the historical panorama of special education, it is important to take pause and reflect on the "state of the state" of educational
services and programs for students with disabilities 20 years after the 1994
World Conference on Special Educational Needs in Salamanca, Spain
(UNESCO, 1994). The Declaration of Salamanca adopted at the conference declared that it was the right of individuals with special educational
needs (SEN) to study in general schools and proposed a child-oriented
pedagogy. The course charted by the Declaration outlined principles underlying inclusive education, discussed the political implications of the initiative, and provided an action plan for the successful implementation of
inclusive education in schools. It set in motion a series of pronouncement
and initiatives that has become the "tipping point" for the integration and
inclusion of students with SEN in regular schools and classes on an international scale. The adoption of this policy in nation states such as Mexico
has created tension and resistance in the educational system; challenging
educational systems to change, transform, re-align, and redesign as school
systems wrestle with the complex processes of including students with SEN.
In this chapter, we document the development, advancement, and realignment of educational practice and policies in Mexico toward providing a
quality and equitable education through the vehicle of inclusive education.

ORIGINS OF SPECIAL EDUCATION

Special education in Mexico evolved into four stages. The first one, from
1867 to 1970, was based on an welfare model with a medical perspective;
the second stage, during the 1970s characterized by the emergence of public
institutions still with a medical and rehabilitation approach; the third stage,
during the 1980s, was characterized by a psychogenetic and psychoeducational model; and the fourth stage, which began in the 1990s is based on
the integration/inclusive model (Dirección de Educación Especial del
Distrito Federal [DEE-DF, Direction of Special Education-Federal
District], 2010).

The beginning of special education is marked by the creation in 1867 of
the National School for Deaf and Mute and in 1870 of the National School
for Blind, during the presidency of Benito Juárez. These schools were
financed by public and private welfare and provided services to the specific

group of disability and also functioned as teacher-training centers. Students were trained to have a non-skilled job. In the school for the deaf, students were taught to use sign language and to communicate orally (DEE-DF, 2010).

Ignacio Trigueros, a Mexican philanthropist who was the mayor of the capital, played an important role in the creation of these schools. Trigueros opened up the schools with his own resources and was the principal of the school for the blind, which he started in a two-room house with only three students (DEE-DF, 2010). The School for the Deaf was a boarding school, while the School for the Blind was an all-day school where students attended from 8 am to 9 pm. In 1905, the Children's Hospice was converted into a school to serve abandoned children. These three schools were the backbone of special education in Mexico (Padilla, 2010).

The concept of special education was very broad and not only included the provision of services for students with disabilities but a series of schools, which did not offer general basic education. Nevertheless, during the 19th and the mid-20th centuries two types of schools for children were identified: general and special. General schools served school-age students with typical development for their age and special education schools for children with auditory, visual, physical, mental, or intellectual impairments (Padilla, 2010).

The emergence of special education in the sense of educating *abnormal* students emerged during the first stage and is closely related to the principle of mandatory education. By the end of the 19th and the beginning of the 20th centuries the idea of mandatory and universal elementary education gained momentum in Mexico. The implementation of such education revealed that there were many *abnormal* children who required a special pedagogy. It is at this time that the government took charge of the institutions where children with mental, visual, and auditory impairments had been rehabilitated and treated with the support of private and public welfare and transformed them into educational environments. According to Padilla (2010), special education emerged as a consequence of mandatory education in the country.

As a result of the implementation of mandatory education, in 1896 the General Direction of Elementary Instruction for the Federal District and Territories was created to enforce through the medical-hygienic inspection of schools the Regulations for Mandatory Instruction. Four physicians were hired to inspect the schools and to examine and diagnose students referred by teachers for not learning at the expected pace without apparent cause (DEE-DF, 2010).

Rodolfo Menéndez published the first known classification of students with disabilities in the press in 1906 (DEE-DF, 2010). This classification included five types of *abnormalities*: (1) physical (i.e., hunchback); (2) sensory (i.e., deaf); (3) intellectual (i.e., so called "imbeciles"); (4) neurological (i.e., epileptic); and (5) educational (i.e., abandoned and neglected) (DEE-DF, 2010).

The idea of special education as remedial and transitory was also present since the beginning of the 20th century. Justo Sierra a prominent Mexican educator (1848–1912) who was head of the Secretariat of Public Instruction and Fine Arts (1905–1911), proposed the creation of special education schools for students with disabilities to attend and receive the necessary supports to attain normal-level abilities so that they could study afterward in general schools (DEE-DF, 2010).

Some principles of inclusive education were in the thoughts of Mexican scholars as early as the 19th century. For example, Enrique Rébsamen (1857–1904), a Mexican–Swiss educator considered that students' school achievement was a poor indicator of their future as adults; all children, he believed, have different skills and capabilities; therefore, parents and teachers must identify their capacities in order to advance them (DEE-DF, 2010).

The idea of special education as a different or specific form of pedagogy in Mexico, which characterized the second stage, emerged as a consequence of various international congresses where it was argued that children with disabilities could learn. The educational approaches first embraced had a strong medical influence, as physicians were involved in diagnosing and defining, along with teachers, the abilities that children had to learn. Several national congresses were organized where it was argued that special education schools were necessary to serve students with other types of disabilities, such as the so called "imbeciles" and "juvenile delinquents" (DEE-DF, 2010).

Another important trait of the second stage was the institutionalization of special education. While in its origins, special education schools were sustained by private and public welfare institutions and individuals actively involved in supporting people with disabilities, during the second stage, a series of public schools were founded in order to serve the wide range of special education populations identified.

The First Mexican Congress for the Child organized in 1921, which gathered 55 medical doctors and 16 teachers, marked the beginning of the institutionalization of special education, as specific diagnostic tools were presented to classify students (DEE-DF, 2010). The following year the

School Hygienic Service later called the Department of Psychopedagogy and School Hygiene became part of the Secretariat of Education, and it was established that students with disabilities would be educated by teachers and physicians (DEE-DF, 2010). During the next few years, this institution adapted several tests to assess students (i.e., Binet–Simon Intelligence Scale) and in 1935 the Organic Education Law was modified to include four types of disabilities to be served by the State: "I. Mentally retarded, II. Physically or mentally abnormal, III. Socially disadvantaged minors or juvenile delinquents, IV. Adult delinquents" (DEE-DF, 2010, p. 58).

Some of the most important schools created during this phase, which are still functioning, are the Behavior Clinic (Clínica de la Conducta) founded in 1937 to serve students with behavioral problems, the Ortholalia Clinic (Clínica de Ortolalia) founded in 1952 to serve students with speech and language problems, and the Institute for the Rehabilitation of Blind and Short-sighted Children (Instituto para la Rehabilitación de los Niños Ciegos y Débiles Visuales) founded in 1952 (DEE-DF, 2010; Secretaría de Educación Pública [SEP, Secretariat of Public Education], 2004).

As a result of the creation in 1959 of the Office for the Coordination of Special Education headed by Odalmira Mayagoitia, a prominent special education teacher who received in 2003, a year before her passing, the medal Adolfo Ruiz Cortines for her outstanding 40-year long professional trajectory (Orizaba Noticias [Orizaba News], 2003), 22 special education schools were founded (DEE-DF, 2010). Odalmira Mayagoitia also was the first head of the General Direction of Special Education, created in 1970. During her administration (1970–1976), the national system of special education was installed and services to students with disabilities expanded rapidly (Martínez, 2009); 256 special education schools were created throughout the country and new forms of service emerged (DEE-DF, 2010). In 1972, the Psychopedagogical Centers (Centros Psicopedagógicos) emerged in order to offer out-of-school diagnostic and therapeutic services to students with language and learning problems. Other services created during this period include the integrated groups and the Centers for Rehabilitation and Special Education (CREE, Centros de Rehabilitación y Educación Especial). The integrated groups gathered students with physical, intellectual, and hearing disabilities to offer them education and rehabilitation services in a classroom within regular schools. The integrated groups are precursors of educational integration in the country as students with disabilities studied in the same building as non-disabled children. These groups disappeared by the end of the 20th century when children with SEN were incorporated into general education classrooms. The CREE are rehabilitation centers offering preventive and remedial medical and therapeutic services to children, youth and adults with disabilities to promote educational, social, and labor integration (Sistema Nacional para el Desarrollo Integral de la Familia [SNDIF, National System for the Integral Development of Families], 2012). These centers emerged as a coordinated effort between the educational and the medical sectors (DEE-DF, 2010), and later became part of the social public sector. In 1973, the Federal Education Law (Diario Oficial de la Federación [DOF, Official Gazette of the Federation], 1973) in Article 15 incorporated, for the first time, special education into the national educational system. By 1976, 23,000 atypical children were being served by special education services in the country (DEE-DF, 2010).

Second Stage

Between 1976 and 1978, when Guadalupe Méndez Grácida took office as General Director of Special Education, the integrated groups and the Centers for Rehabilitation and Special Education (CREE, Centros de Rehabilitación y Educación Especial) expanded (DEE-DF, 2010).

The work of Binet and Simon was influential during this second stage in setting the standards and procedures for diagnosis. The typology created for the Mexican population by José de Jesús González, M. D., based on Binet and Simon classified intellectually abnormal students in two categories: "(1) *idiotic children*, those who at the age of two or beyond were unable to comprehend nor speak, without proved hearing or phonic limitation; (2) *imbecilic children*, those who even though were able to comprehend and speak, were unable to learn how to read and write, without a clear explanation for this disability" (Padilla, 2010, p. 15).

In 1978, Margarita Gómez-Palacio took office as head of the General Direction of Special Education. She was a disciple of Jean Piaget and received her doctoral degree in Geneva Switzerland. As she came back to Mexico, she conducted research in the state of Nuevo Leon on children's learning processes with a psychogenetic perspective (DEE-DF, 2010).

Third Stage

During the 1980s the nature and objectives special education services in the country were transformed, marking a new era (third phase). The work of

Gómez-Palacio and the work she promoted from her position were very influential in general education to prevent children's educational failure and support the recovery of students experiencing educational lag. During the third phase, special education services adopted a psychoeducational and research-based perspective. Several research projects and pilot experiences were conducted to learn about children's learning and the effect of intervention and teaching practices. These experiences were systematically documented and translated into diagnostic and teaching tools to help general and special educators distinguish between students with learning difficulties due to inequality and ineffective teaching methods and students with learning disabilities and offer each student the support he/she required making every effort to reduce school segregation practices. Special education services also expanded to serve gifted and talented students (DEE-DF, 2010).

Special education services reorganized into indispensible and complementary. The former were aimed at students with marked and permanent disabilities and the latter at students with mild, transitory, or surmountable difficulties in learning, achievement, language, or behavior (Martínez, 2009).

Fourth Stage

Following UNESCO's declarations presented at Jomtien (UNESCO, 1990) and Salamanca (UNESCO, 1994) regarding the rights of students with SEN to be educated in general schools, Mexico initiated the process of educational integration and thus the fourth stage of special education. In the early 1990s, the purpose of special education was redefined in Article 41 of the General Education Law (DOF, 1993) which mandated that special education served students with SEN within general schools and in special education school whenever students' conditions prevented them from attending general classrooms, providing the necessary supports for them and their families to achieve social integration.

Special education services were reorganized into two main modalities, still functioning: (1) General Education Support Units (USAER, Unidades de Servicios de Apoyo a la Educación Regular) and (2) Multiple Attention Centers (CAM, Centros de Atención Múltiple). USAER are new type of service which consists of groups of special education professionals (head of unit, psychologist, communication specialist, social worker, and special education support teacher) who serve one or more schools (five on average) providing support for students with SEN, general teachers, and parents, in order to assure adequate educational services within the general schools. The old special education schools organized by disability were transformed into CAM, to serve students with SEN with disability (grouped by age) offering access to the general curriculum (SEP, 2006). The purpose and functioning of CAM were unfortunately poorly defined allowing the enrollment of students with and without disability and the co-existence, in the same classroom, of students with varied educational needs, academic competencies, and disabilities (García, Romero-Contreras, Motilla, & Martínez, 2009). In order to offer information about these new services, information centers (Unidades de Orientación al Público) were created; these later became Resource and Information Centers for Educational Integration (CRIIE, Centros de Recursos e Información para la Integración Educativa) (SEP, 2006).

In 1995, the under secretariat of Basic and Normal Education (Subsecretaría de Educación Básica y Normal, SEBN, in charge of general education) organized a team of researchers to investigate how educational integration had advanced in the country. The public opinion had shown a strong rejection toward educational integration. Parents, general teachers, and special education professionals were not satisfied with the changes in special education procedures and structures. The study conducted by the appointed team revealed that in most states few actions had been taken to implement educational integration mainly due to confusion, lack of training, and poor or non-existent coordination between general and special education authorities and personnel (García et al., 2003).

As a result, the appointed team designed a National Project for Educational Integration which consisted of four articulated programs: (1) Training, (2) Pilot experiences of educational integration, (3) Follow up and (4) Educational materials. This project started in 1998 in three states with 46 schools where 159 students were integrated. The scope of the project grew every year. By 2002, 24 states were involved with a total of 642 schools where 2,827 students were being integrated and 19,478 teachers had been trained. The successful actions of the project then became the bases for National Program for the Strengthening of Special Education and Educational Integration (García et al., 2009; SEP, 2002).

Transitioning from the medical to the psychoeducational model and now toward a more educational model of special education in the country requires the transformation of legal, social, academic, and educational perceptions and structures. These transformations have not been completely achieved. While the legislation is aligned with international trends, the medical approach still prevails in many instances. Currently, the country is undergoing a transitional stage. In the sections that follow, we will discuss some of the main tensions that have played an important role in the evolution and current state of special education in the country.

CLASSIFICATION OF DISABILITY

In the previous section, we presented some of the classifications that have been used in Mexico to classify people with disabilities. The first classifications referred to terms that emphasized the disability such as mute and deaf, blind, abnormal, atypical; classifications then were modified incorporating more relative terms, such as people with special needs, and later on, this was substituted by the concept of people or students with SEN.

Although several classifications co-exist, generally speaking when referring to people with SEN associated to a disability, four types are recognized: sensory (visual and hearing), physical (motor), intellectual, and multiple. Some official documents issued by the Secretariat of Education also recognize a fifth type; mental or psychosocial disability, which includes mental problems such as depression or schizophrenia, as well as developmental impairments such as autism or Asperger syndrome (Comisión de Política Gubernamental en Materia de Derechos Humanos [Commission on Government Policy on Human Rights], n.d.). In the special education glossary, various specific conditions are also described such as: behavioral problems, attention deficit disorder with or without hyperactivity, learning disability, pervasive developmental disorder, outstanding capacities, and aptitudes (SEP, 2012). Another document, classifies autism and attention deficit disorder with our without hyperactivity as two distinct types of disability (SEP, 2002).

In an effort to comply with UNESCO's recommendation to participate in a regional information center to gather accurate, objective and up-to-date information about children with disability, the Secretariat of Education is recently following this agency's criteria to classify disability from a socio interactive and human rights perspective. The Regional System of Educational Information on Students with Disability considers the following types: motor disability, intellectual disability, auditory sensory disability (hard of hearing and deafness), visual sensory disability (low vision and blindness), multiple disabilities, pervasive developmental disorder, and other disabilities (OREALC-UNESCO, 2010).

It should be pointed out that in Mexico there is not a great deal of discussion or controversy among teachers, special education personnel, or researchers on the classification of disability. The reason being that the category for the student's placement is of little relevance as the supports provided for students with disabilities are not clearly differentiated and tend to be minimal. Even though the General Law for the Inclusion of People with Disabilities and its corresponding Regulations (DOF, 2011, 2012) mandate the delivery of all necessary supports for people with disabilities, in practice, these supports are not defined by disability and are seldom provided. Generally, it is the responsibility of parents to seek and provide for the necessary supports in order for students with disabilities to grow, develop, and benefit from the education they receive. For example, when a student with SEN enters a school that has a USAER, the personnel of this unit will conduct a psychoeducational evaluation, identify the needs of the student, design the educational plan with the corresponding curricular adaptations, support general teachers in the implementation of such plan, and very often offer the student educational support in the resource room. When as a result of the evaluation conducted a very specific personal support is required (hearing aid, Perkins machine, etc.) then the USAER personnel will inform the parents so that they seek the support to get the specific device and all the expenses associated with it.

PREVALENCE

In Mexico, reliable statistical data is very scarce. Regarding the prevalence of disability, the National Record of Minors with Some Sign of Disability published in 1995 indicated that there were a total of 2,700,000 children in such condition (Instituto Nacional de Estadística y Geografía [INEGI, National Institute of Statistics and Geography], 2001). In contrast, the National Census of Population and Housing, which for the first time in the year 2000 included the identification of people with some type of disability, reported that there were 1,795,300 people with disabilities (INEGI, 2000). The next Census was conducted in 2010, in this edition, the number of people with disability reported was 5,739,000 (INEGI, 2013). This seems to be a more reliable data. The 2010 considered people with disability as having difficulty in one or more of the following areas: mobility, vision, hearing, intellectual, language and communication, self-care, and attention or learning (INEGI, 2013).

One of the main problems to obtain reliable data regarding the number of people with special needs is the variation in the definitions used for their identification and classification. Prior to 1997, data were reported in ten groups: intellectual disability, visual impairment, hearing impairment, motor disability, gifted and talented, behavioral problems, learning disability, language impairment, and early intervention and autism. From 1997, a new classification was used to identify students with SEN without disability; also students served in early intervention were counted by area of attention and not as a separate category. In 1998, the classification of students with SEN without disability was redefined to include those with behavioral problems, learning disability, language impairment, autism, and students served in early intervention services.

The Secretariat of Education published statistics with data of students with SEN diagnosed and served between 1995 and 2009. The historic statistics are shown in Fig. 1. As can be seen in Fig. 1, the changes in classification make it difficult to compare data across time. The new classification used since 1998, moreover, collapses together all students considered without disability, leaving a large group of students under classified; this new category of students (light gray bar) represents the largest group.

Attention centers for students with SEN, as mentioned earlier, were transformed. The major change was the emergence of USAER (General Education Support Units) and the gradual disappearance of Special Education Schools. Some of these schools became Centers for Multiple Attention (CAM), which now serve children with various kinds of conditions or disability. Fig. 2 shows the number of attention centers from 1995 to 2009. As can be seen, USAER and CAM have considerably grown in number, while Special Education Schools and Centers for Gifted and Talented students have drastically diminished their presence.

The distribution of disability and of services for this population, as revealed by the Census conducted in 2010 (INEGI, 2013), is related to issues of poverty and underdevelopment. The proportion of people with disability is higher in rural areas (6.1%) where access to health services is limited and physical and social barriers to achieve a fuller development are more frequent, than in urban areas (4.8%). Moreover, the proportion of people with disabilities in the age range 3–29 years in rural areas attending school is lower (40.2%) compared to people with disabilities in the urban areas (47.3%) in the same age group. On average, people with disability in rural areas have completed 2.8 years of schooling while people with disability in urban area have completed 5.8 years.

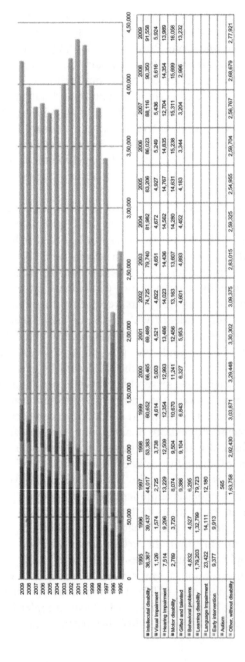

	1995	1996	1997	1998	1999	2000	2001	2002	2003	2004	2005	2006	2007	2008	2009
Intellectual disability	36,367	39,437	44,017	53,383	60,652	66,465	69,489	74,725	79,740	81,982	83,206	86,023	88,116	90,350	91,558
Visual Impairment	1,126	1,574	2,725	3,738	4,614	5,003	4,521	4,822	4,651	4,672	4,927	5,249	5,436	5,616	5,924
Hearing Impairment	7,514	9,296	13,229	12,509	12,354	12,983	13,486	14,023	14,436	14,562	14,767	14,835	12,704	14,354	13,989
Motor disability	2,789	3,720	8,074	9,504	10,670	11,241	12,456	13,163	13,607	14,280	14,631	15,238	15,311	15,699	16,056
Gifted and talented			9,386	9,104	6,843	6,327	5,953	4,601	4,893	4,452	4,183	3,344	3,204	2,996	13,232
Behavioral problems	4,832	4,527	6,295												
Learning disability	1,79,203	1,32,799	79,723												
Language Impairment	23,422	14,111	12,160												
Early intervention	9,377	9,913													
Autism			565												
Other, without disability			1,63,758	2,92,430	3,03,871	3,29,448	3,30,302	3,09,375	2,83,015	2,59,325	2,54,955	2,59,704	2,56,767	2,68,679	2,77,921

Fig. 1. Students Served in Special Education Services by Condition from 1995 to 2009 (SEP, 2010).

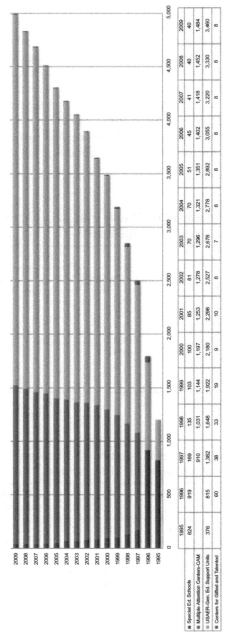

	1995	1996	1997	1998	1999	2000	2001	2002	2003	2004	2005	2006	2007	2008	2009
▪ Special Ed. Schools	824	919	169	135	103	100	85	81	70	70	51	45	41	40	40
▦ Multiple Attention Centers–CAM			910	1,031	1,144	1,197	1,253	1,278	1,296	1,321	1,351	1,402	1,418	1,452	1,484
▨ USAER–Gen. Ed. Support Units	376	815	1,382	1,648	1,922	2,180	2,298	2,527	2,678	2,778	2,892	3,055	3,220	3,330	3,460
▪ Centers for Gifted and Talented	376	60	38	33	19	9	10	8	7	8	8	8	8	8	8

Fig. 2. Attention Service Centers for Students with Special Needs (SEP, 2010).

Educational services for people with disability concentrate in early childhood and elementary education. Overall, only 45% of the people with disability in the age range 3–29 years attend school, while 56% of the population without disability in the same age range does so. School attendance is lower for people with disability when compared to people without disability in the same age range. This difference becomes more evident after the age of 11 years, indicating that education beyond the elementary grades is less accessible for people with disabilities (see Table 1).

Consequently, attained educational levels are less favorable for people with disability than for people without disability, as can be seen in Table 2.

Table 1. Access to Education for People with and without Disability by Sex and Age Range.

Sex and Age Group	Condition	
	Without Disability	With Disability
Men	56.8	44.9
Women	55.1	46.1
3–5 years	52.3	48.2
6–11 years	96.3	81.4
12–14 years	91.7	72.4
15–18 years	61.9	45.6
19–29 years	17.3	11.6

Source: INEGI (2013).

Table 2. Educational Level for Population 15 Years and Older with and without Disability (Percentages).

Educational Level	Without Disability	With Disability
None or preschool only	5.9	27.9
Complete or incomplete elementary (1st–6th grades)	27.3	45.4
Complete or incomplete secondary (7th–9th grades)	28.5	13.3
Complete or incomplete high school or equivalent (10th–12th grades)	21.7	7.3
Complete or incomplete undergraduate or graduate university degree	15.7	5.2

Source: INEGI (2013).

LEGISLATION AND PUBLIC POLICY

The Mexican legislation is advanced regarding the rights and services granted for people with disabilities. The laws and regulations grant the rights of people with disabilities to a quality education, and mandate the provision of specialists and material supports to achieve this goal. As will be seen in the following sections, the Mexican legislation is well aligned to *avant-garde* international policies. Nevertheless, most of these laws and regulations are not regularly enforced.

Inclusive education in Mexico is mandated in Article 3 of the Constitution (DOF, 2014) which grants free public basic education (preschool–high school) for all individuals. This article indicates that educational services should tend to "promote the harmonic development of all of the individuals' capacities" (p. 4). Inclusive education is specifically defined in Article 41 of the General Educational Law, previously discussed.

In particular the General Law for the Inclusion of People with Disabilities (DOF, 2011) protects the rights of students with disabilities and of other vulnerable groups. Article 4 of this law establishes that "People with disabilities will have all the rights granted by the Mexican judicial system without distinction of ethnical or national origin, gender, age, social, economical or health condition, religion, personal opinions, marital status, sexual preferences, pregnancy condition, political identity, language, migratory situation or any other characteristic of the human condition or that may put at risk their dignity" (DOF, 2011). In the section on Education, this law asserts that the Secretariat of Education shall promote the inclusion of people with disabilities at all levels of the educational system. In section VI of Article 12, the law establishes that the Secretariat of Education must:

> ... provide students with disabilities with all the materials and technological supports necessary to support their academic achievement, making efforts to provide schools and educational centers with texts in Braille, didactic materials, interpreters in Mexican sign language or specialists in Braille system, computer equipment with technology for blind people and all those supports that are identified as necessary to offer quality education. (DOF, 2011)

In order to implement these measures, the Regulations for the General Law for the Inclusion of People with Disabilities (DOF, 2012) mentions that the Secretariat of Public Education will be responsible for training teachers serving students with disabilities, and that the Secretariat of Health will provide orthopedic devices and prosthesis and medication for students with disability, favoring in particular students with limited resources (Article 12).

The National Development Plan (NDP, [PND, Plan Nacional de Desarrollo] 2013–2018) (Gobierno de la República [Federal Government], 2013) offers a diagnosis of the current situation, sets specific goals and provides the general guidelines for the education of people with disabilities. It acknowledges the existence of "five million seven hundred people with disabilities who, along with individuals from other vulnerable groups, live in inadequate, defenselessness and abandonment conditions which prevent them to demand their rights, satisfy their needs or face every day problems" (p. 45). It also mentions that despite the efforts made by the Federal Government to grant the fulfillment of the rights of people with disabilities and to contribute to their integral development and full inclusion, serious difficulties still remain for this population to have access to education under adequate conditions, as well as to have employment opportunities. In order to overcome these limitations, Strategy 2.2.4 of the NDP defines the two lines of action: "(1) to establish integral attention schemes for people with disabilities through actions that foster the detection of disability, the provision of early stimulation and rehabilitation; (2) to design and carry on strategies to increase the productive inclusion of people with disabilities by providing training for labor and connection with the productive sector" (Gobierno de la República, 2013, p. 117).

In turn, the Program for the Educational Sector 2013–2018 (DOF, 2013a) acknowledges that "despite the fact that the educational system has incorporated among its preoccupations the inclusion of all children and youth, there is still a long way to go in order to grant the conditions for access, permanence, participation and school achievement for all students with special educational needs" (DOF, 2013a). In response, Objective 3 of this program is "to ensure greater coverage, educational inclusion and equity among all groups of the population for the construction of a fairer society" (DOF, 2013a). One of the lines of action to fulfill this goal is to "Foster new educational forms and settings for the inclusion of people with disabilities, as well as gifted and talented, in all educational levels" (DOF, 2013a).

SPECIAL EDUCATION INTERVENTION MODELS

In Mexico, inclusive education serves students whose learning pace is different from that of the majority of their peers, this includes gifted and talented students, as well as students with and without disability, in other words, inclusive education supports students with SEN. Students with SEN can study in three different settings:

(1) Multiple Attention Centers (CAM);
(2) General schools with integration projects; which have the support of a General Education Support Units (USAER);
(3) General schools without USAER support.

As mentioned earlier, CAM are special education schools for students with disabilities or specific conditions that prevent them from being in the general classroom. CAM provide services for early childhood (45 days–5 years), preschool (3–8 years), elementary education (6–17 years) and for labor training (17 years and older). According to the Secretariat of Education (SEP, 2006), these centers offer education to students with multiple disabilities, pervasive developmental disorders and to students who due to their condition require generalized, permanent, or highly specialized adaptations. The guidelines offered by SEP indicate that these centers should offer the general curriculum with the necessary supports depending on students' needs. Advised group size in CAM is between six and eight students and students should be grouped in such a way that they share certain competencies and support needs and belong to a similar age group (SEP, 2006).

Research conducted on the functioning of CAM reveal that in many cases, the curriculum delivered in CAM tends to deviate significantly from the general curriculum and does not emphasize students' learning, limiting their possibilities to attend general schools and to achieve social inclusion. These studies also report that grouping strategies in CAM tend to differ from the recommended strategy, many centers group students by type of disability or by age and only a few, group students with similar characteristics, including age (Ezcurra, 2003; García et al., 2009; Ponce, Hernández, López, & Pérez, 2006).

CAM also offer extracurricular services to students enrolled in general education schools who need to learn specific forms of communication (Braille, sign language, alternative, and augmentative communication) or require additional teaching support, which cannot be provided by the general or special education teachers within the school they attend (SEP, 2006).

General schools with support of USAER offer education to students with SEN through collaborative work between general teachers, USAER staff and parents. The guidelines provided by the Secretariat of Education for this service indicate that the USAER staff should support general education teachers in planning and implementing pedagogical alternatives to meet students' educational needs. At the beginning and throughout the school year, general teachers and special education professionals work together in the identification of students with SEN. USAER conducts, with the support of general teachers and parents, psychoeducational assessment of identified students and along with general teachers design a plan for each class to accommodate students with SEN within the classroom. For some students, individual curricular adaptations are made and implemented with the participation of teachers and parents. Students with SEN receive support within the general classroom, and may also attend sessions in the resource room and receive support outside of the school, as needed (SEP, 2006).

Even though these guidelines emphasize collaborative and interdisciplinary work to meet students' educational needs it is common to see, in practice, that support teachers from USAER form groups of students to work with them in the resource room. Less frequently, USAER teachers work with general teachers to implement curricular adaptations in the classroom, and offer guidance to parents. General teachers tend to believe that the progress of students' with SEN is the responsibility of USAER (García-Cedillo & Romero-Contreras, 2012). Whenever a student requires specific personal supports such as eye-glasses, hearing aids, wheel chair, etc., the parents are the sole responsible to provide for these.

Research on the functioning of USAER show some good results, however the practice of pulling out students to offer them support in the resource room has been questioned as it does not seem to have a positive impact on their learning (García et al., 2003; Red Internacional de Investigadores y Participantes sobre Integración Educativa [International Network of Researchers and Participants on Educational Integration], 2004).

General schools without the support of USAER also receive students with SEN. In these cases, the possibility of having supports to meet their educational needs depends on the good will of their teachers who might seek information and guidance from USAER professionals serving near-by schools, CAM professionals or from the Resource and Information Centers for Educational Integration (CRIIE).

Special education currently serves 650 thousand students (143 thousand have a disability). A total of 28,000 schools (mostly preschools and elementary) have the support of USAER, which represents 10% of basic general schools (SEP, 2012). No data however is available on the number of students with SEN in regular classrooms. Due to the distribution of special education services, students with SEN have some access to preschool and elementary educational levels, but their access to middle school is limited, and even more so, to high school and college.

Special education services are rare in rural areas, even in those close to urban concentrations. A study conducted in the outskirts of the capital of the state of San Luis Potosí, showed that there is one USAER for a municipality with fifty schools. Because this USAER only has ten support teachers, it can only serve this amount of schools, so the rest are left without any support, even in communities (within the municipality) where 2.5% of the school population have SEN (Auces, 2013).

FAMILY PARTICIPATION

Family participation and involvement in education is promoted in Mexico through the School Boards for Social Participation (CEPS, Consejos Escolares de Participación Social) (DOF, 2010). In the case of students with SEN, family participation and involvement is promoted throughout the educational process; families, according to SEP guidelines, are part of the multidisciplinary team that conducts the psychoeducational assessment and elaborates and implements the curricular adaptation plan (SEP, 2006).

CEPS promote the involvement of the community, particularly parents, in the analysis and decision making of school planning, administration of resources, school infrastructure, educational evaluations, and extracurricular activities (DOF, 2010).

In practice, parental involvement and participation in children's education is rather limited. This is partly due to Mexican parents' cultural distance from school practices (Romero-Contreras, 2009) and to the lack of adequate training of teachers regarding how to work collaboratively with parents (Romero-Contreras, García-Cedillo, & Fletcher, 2013a).

In a study conducted to assess the current status of educational integration in the country (García-Cedillo & Romero-Contreras, 2012), general and special education professionals and parents of students with and without SEN from different states were interviewed. The interviews included several questions on the functioning of CEPS. Overall, general and special education professionals reported that the CEPS have been installed in most schools and that they are functioning well. The opinions of general education professionals tended to be more favorable regarding the functioning and usefulness of CEPS's and their positive impact for educational integration, than the opinions of special education professionals. Parent participation among interviewees was 20% ($N = 702$), however, very few declared that the CEPS has had an impact on the process of educational integration of their children.

Parent–teacher interactions tend to be informative as teachers take little advantage of parent' knowledge and experience to contribute to students' academic development. For example, in an interview-based study, parents declared that USAER staff offers them information (talks and workshops) on inclusive education and orientation on how to support their children with SEN at home (Romero-Contreras et al., 2013a).

TEACHER TRAINING

Special education teacher preparation in Mexico has evolved in a similar way as the models of service described in the first section of this chapter: from the medical model, to a more psychoeducational model and finally to an integrative/inclusive model. This evolution, however, has always lagged behind legislative changes and changes in the provision of services.

Prior to 1940, and for a long period of time, special education teachers were trained in clinics and hospitals under the medical model (Sánchez Escobedo, Acle Tomasini, De Agüero Servín, Jacobo Cupich, & Rivera Morales, 2003). Most teacher trainers were medical doctors with little or no experience in education, who offered courses and guidelines to work with people with disabilities. During this period, training emphasized diagnostic procedures and rehabilitation techniques. One exception to this, was the Normal School for Deaf and Mute, founded in 1867, where teachers learned sign language and how to teach students to read and write in Spanish, as well as the curricular subjects (SEP, 2004).

In 1940, the Normal School of Specialization was created to train general teachers, with at least two years of experience, in special pedagogies. In 1943, special education programs were offered to serve four types of disability: intellectual disability, blind, deaf, and mute and minor delinquents. In 1955, another program was created to serve motor disabled people, and in 1970, the specializations in language disorders and learning disabilities were created (Sánchez Escobedo et al., 2003). Between 1940 and 1960, several minor changes were made to the programs offered by the Normal School of Specialization. In the 1960s, the programs were reorganized sharing a core-curriculum with a medical-psychiatric focus (SEP, 2004). For almost 30 years, the Normal School of Specialization located in Mexico City was the only public institution in the country for special education teacher training. Teachers from other locations attended summer programs in this school. In 1969, the Normal School of Specialization of the State of Nuevo Leon was created. By 1980, 13 states were offering special education teacher-training programs (SEP, 2004).

In the 1970s, private and public universities also started offering special education undergraduate programs and later on master-level graduate programs in special education mainly in the areas of language, learning, and hearing (Sánchez Escobedo et al., 2003). However, the majority of special education teachers are trained in public teacher colleges called Normal schools (SEP, 2004).

All Normal schools in the country, public and private, have to follow the same curriculum for all undergraduate teaching degrees. The special education teacher-training curriculum has been modified several times; the two most important modifications took place in 1985 and 2004.

The 1985 curriculum had, for the first time, a psychoeducational focus, reducing the emphasis on the medical-clinic model and sharing core contents with the general education teacher-training program, but maintained the special education segregation model. This program had six areas of specialization or terminal options: hearing and language, visually impaired, intellectual disability, social maladaptation and delinquency, learning disability and neuromotor impairment. The specialization portion of the curriculum included subjects in the areas of normal and deviant development and treatment, as well as practicum with the target population (SEP, 2004).

The 2004 special education teacher-training curriculum adopted an integration/inclusive perspective. This is over ten years after the General Education Law mandated the integration of special education students in general education schools and classrooms. This curriculum is organized in three areas, general education, special education and one of four areas of specialization: hearing and language, intellectual, motor, and visual. The curriculum program is four-years long. During first three years, students take courses in the normal school premises and conduct observations and short practicum projects in varied school setting. In the last year, students conduct intensive supervised internship practice in a special education service setting, mainly USAER or CAM. The graduate of this curriculum should have didactic competencies to identify SEN associated or not with a disability, be able to conduct psychoeducational assessments and other relevant assessments, and to design intervention programs and curricular adaptations (SEP, 2004).

Once a teacher graduates he/she is licensed to teach in the National Educational System (NES) and, so far, requires no further certification. However, the recent educational reform foresees the implementation of teacher evaluation procedures to enter and remain in the NES; the guidelines and procedures to implement teacher assessment are being developed (DOF, 2013b).

In the school year 2004–2005, there were 2,700 undergraduate students enrolled in the 54 normal schools offering what would be equivalent to a B.A. degree in Special Education. Most normal schools were offering the program with the specialization in intellectual disability, followed by hearing and language, motor disability and visual impairment, in that order (Sánchez Escobedo et al., 2003).

Until 2010 there was no doctoral programs in special education offered in the country (Servicios Educativos Integrados al Estado de México [SEIEM, Educational Services of the State of Mexico], 2010). In 2012, the University of Baja California opened the first doctoral program on inclusive education (Universidad de Baja California [UBC, University of Baja California], n.d.).

MEXICO'S SPECIAL EDUCATION: PROGRESS ATTAINED

The education of students with special needs with and without disability in Mexico has evolved and gained momentum at a rather slow pace for multiple reasons. Statistics on the number of children and youth with SEN are scarce and not very reliable. Ignoring the magnitude and characteristics of the problem limits the possibilities for good planning and timely and adequate intervention. Also the lack of local scientific research on the relationship between intervention models and outcomes, limits the development of innovative and adequate educational programs. Teacher-training programs lag behind legislative advances to improve the quality of education of students with SEN, and in-service training is not well organized. Additionally, legislative changes are not timely implemented, as educational programs are not well articulated to secure the resources and the coordination among stakeholders to conduct the necessary actions. As indicated before, the supports for students with SEN are concentrated in the early grades, mainly kindergarten and elementary levels, in urban areas; and have not extended to serve the majority of this population. Many students with SEN do not attend school, and the few who have attained low educational levels.

Special education teacher preparation in Mexico has recently had some important improvements. For example, a study conducted to compare the two more recent curricular modifications (1985–2004), indicated that graduates from 2004 program, which has a new integration/inclusion perspective, are better prepared to educate students with disabilities in inclusive environments (Romero-Contreras et al., 2013a) than 1985-program graduates. In this study, Romero-Contreras et al. conducted follow-up in-depth case studies to examine the type and quality of services being provided by special education teachers in inclusive settings in Mexico. Interviews were conducted to elicit perceptions of special education services and inclusive education from a variety of perspectives. Interviewees included special education teachers, general education teachers, special education directors, regular school directors, parents of children with and without special needs and students with and without special needs. Results indicated that all stakeholders have a generally positive view of inclusive education; although everyone stated a need for additional training in how to accommodate students with special education needs in an inclusive environment. Interestingly, special education students from the 2004 program who are in their fourth year of preparation have significantly better attitudes toward students with disabilities, and higher self-efficacy perception than their peers studying in the earlier years (Romero-Contreras, García-Cedillo, Forlin, & Lomelí-Hernández, 2013b). This optimism and positive attitude was met head on with resistance from the established school routine, practices, and culture when the novice special education teacher enters the profession. Case study research carried out with novice special education teachers in the same study suggest that their efforts to reach out and collaborate with their general education peers was blunted. Novice special education teachers spoke of their retrenchment to their isolated resource settings and ultimately maintained a low profile in their school of practice (Romero-Contreras et al., 2013a). The school culture dictated the maintenance of a "business as usual" approach with little room for innovation or change. This lack of collaboration is frequently reinforced by the directors of schools, who have little knowledge or expertise regarding how to support and promote collaborative planning and delivery of instruction in their schools on behalf of children with disabilities.

Employment programs for people with disability are scarce. A recent survey conducted with people with disabilities found that the main problem they identify is the lack of employment (27.4%), followed by discrimination (20.4%) and the difficulty of being self-sufficient (15.6%) (INEGI, 2013). Since being self-sufficient is no doubt related to having employment, it can be concluded that for more than 40% of the people with a disability, employment and support programs to gain self-sufficiency and therefore a good quality of life, are ineffective.

CHALLENGES FACING INCLUSIVE EDUCATION IN MEXICO

One of the most important challenges that Mexico needs to address is transforming inclusive education into a more general and clearly defined public policy. Currently, inclusive education is part of an educational program under the responsibility of special education authorities and professionals. Until recently, the program in charge of inclusive education was the PFEEIE (National Program for the Strengthening of Special Education and Educational Integration [Programa Nacional para el Fortalecimiento de la Educación Especial y la Integración Educativa] SEP, 2002). Recently, a new program, which has not been implemented as of this writing, the Program for Educational Inclusion and Equity [PIEE, Programa para la Inclusión y la Equidad Educativa] was launched. The characteristics and objectives of this program have not been clearly described or defined, and the only document available includes a set of regulations by which to allocate resources and set specific priorities (DOF, 2013c). According to these regulations, the PIEE will provide support not only to basic education, but also to high school and higher education. While this is no doubt a step in the right direction, the vagueness of this new program raises concerns as to the possibility of making good use of resources when the objectives and procedures are still imprecisely defined. We have reason to believe that this program could result in a new paralysis in the advancement of inclusive education in Mexico given the lack of information on how this new and clearly top-down initiative emerged without the necessary consensus among all the parties involved.

In addition, the overall quality of education is a central concern for all children in Mexico. Both national and international assessments of learning outcomes for students show alarmingly poor results for school-aged students in Mexican public schools. Teachers' skill level is generally very poor as documented by the fact that 70% of teachers in Mexico flunked a new nationwide test to measure whether they had the basic skills to be educators (Oppenheimer, 2008). This has resulted in significant educational reform legislation being initiated and directed by the newly elected president, congress, and other constituents.

CONCLUSION

Mexico adopted the international educational policy of inclusive education and signed on to the Salamanca Declaration 20 years ago. Inclusive education is a strategy by which to strengthen the capacity of the current educational system to reach out and provide equitable learning opportunities for all learners. The need for shared responsibility between general and special education is critical for the education of all children in schools. The reality is that the policy and legislative actions underlying inclusive education implementation are in place, but the actual day to day, nuts and bolts operation of inclusive practices is a universal deficiency in educational systems around the world. Effective inclusive education programs require changes and modifications in content, approaches, structures, and strategies with a common vision that covers all children (UNESCO, 2003b). For the successful implementation of inclusive education to be achieved, increased collaboration and responsibility for all learners with SEN will need to be the primary educational strategy in ordinary schools carried out in collaboration with all stakeholders: teachers, administrators, parents, and the greater community. Most importantly legislation, policies, and practices must move from a position of rhetoric to one of conviction and commitment apparent in actions to provide an equitable and quality education with equal access for all children with and without disabilities.

REFERENCES

Auces, M. R. (2013). *Formación docente e inclusión educativa en el medio rural: Estudio de caso desde la narrativo de los sujetos* (Vol. 1). [*Teacher preparation and inclusive education in the rural area: Case study from the narrative of the participants.*] Colección Investigadores y Maestros. San Luis Potosí, México: BECENE-RIESLP.

Comisión de Política Gubernamental en Materia de Derechos Humanos [Commission on Government Policy on Human Rights]. (n.d.). *Glosario de términos sobre discapacidad.* [*Glossary of terms on disability.*] Retrieved from http://www.conadis.salud.gob.mx/descargas/pdf/glosario_terminos_sobre_discapacidad.pdf. Accessed on February 13, 2014.

Diario Oficial de la Federación [DOF, Official Gazette of the Federation]. (1973). *Ley Federal de Educación*. [*General educational law*.] México, DF: Cámara de Diputados. Retrieved from http://201.161.2.34/servicios/p_anuies/publicaciones/revsup/res008/txt5.htm

Diario Oficial de la Federación [DOF, Official Gazette of the Federation]. (1993). *Ley General de Educación*. [*General educational law*.] México, DF: Cámara de Diputados. Retrieved from http://www.diputados.gob.mx/LeyesBiblio/ref/lge/LGE_orig_13jul93_ima.pdf

Diario Oficial de la Federación [DOF, Official Gazette of the Federation]. (2010). *Lineamientos Generales para la Operación de los Consejos Escolares de Participación Social*. [*General guidelines for the functioning of the school boards for social participation*.] México, DF: Cámara de Diputados. Retrieved from http://dof.gob.mx/nota_detalle.php?codigo=5145508&fecha

Diario Oficial de la Federación [DOF, Official Gazette of the Federation]. (2011). *Ley General para la Inclusión de las Personas con Discapacidad*. [*General law for the inclusion of people with disability*.] México, DF: Cámara de Diputados. Retrieved from http://dof.gob.mx/nota_detalle.php?codigo=5191516&fecha

Diario Oficial de la Federación [DOF, Official Gazette of the Federation]. (2012). *Reglamento de la Ley General para la Inclusión de las Personas con Discapacidad*. [*Regulations for the general law for the inclusion of people with disability*.] México, DF: Cámara de Diputados. Retrieved from http://dof.gob.mx/nota_detalle.php?codigo=5281002&fecha

Diario Oficial de la Federación [DOF, Official Gazette of the Federation]. (2013a). *Programa Sectorial de Educación*. [*Program for the educational sector*.] México, DF: Cámara de Diputados. Retrieved from http://www.dof.gob.mx/nota_detalle.php?codigo=5326569&fecha

Diario Oficial de la Federación [DOF, Official Gazette of the Federation]. (2013b). *Ley General del Servicio Profesional Docente*. [*General law of professional teaching services*.] México, DF: Cámara de Diputados. Retrieved from http://www.dof.gob.mx/nota_detalle.php?codigo=5313843&fecha

Diario Oficial de la Federación [DOF, Official Gazette of the Federation]. (2013c). *Acuerdo 711. Reglas de operación del programa para la inclusión y la equidad educativa*. [*Agreement 711. Rules of operation of the program for educational inclusion and equity*.] México, DF: Cámara de Diputados. Retrieved from http://dof.gob.mx/nota_detalle.php?codigo=5328358&fecha

Diario Oficial de la Federación [DOF, Official Gazette of the Federation]. (2014). *Constitución Política de los Estados Unidos Mexicanos*. [*Political constitution of Mexico*]. México, DF: Cámara de Diputados. Retrieved from http://www.diputados.gob.mx/LeyesBiblio/pdf/1.pdf

Dirección de Educación Especial del Distrito Federal [DEE-DF, Direction of Special Education-Federal District]. (2010). *Memorias y actualidad en la educación especial en México. Una visión histórica de sus modelos de atención. Integración*. [*Past and present of special education in Mexico*.] México City, Mexico: Secretaría de Educación Pública. Retrieved from http://pdi.cnotinfor.pt/recursos/Integracion%20Educativa%2 0en% 20Mexico.doc

Ezcurra, M. (2003). *La calidad de la atención educativa de los niños y jóvenes con discapacidad en los Centros de Atención Múltiple. Resultados del Informe Final de la Investigación*. [*Quality of educational attention of children and youth with disability in the Multiple Attention Centers. Final research report*.] Unpublished manuscript.

García, I., Escalante, I., Escandón, M. C., Fernández, L. G., Mustri, A., & Toulet, I. (2003). *Proyecto de investigación: Integración educativa. Perspectiva internacional y nacional. Informe final de investigación (Ciclos escolares 1995–1996). En Integración educativa. 1996–2002 Informe final.* [*Research project: Educational Integration. International and national perspectives. Final research report (School years 1995–1996). In Educational Integration. 1996–2002. Final Report.*] Secretaría de Educación Pública, Subsecretaría de Educación Básica y Normal, Fondo Mixto de Cooperación Técnica y Científica y Cooperación Española [Compact Disc].

García, I., Romero-Contreras, S., Motilla, K., & Martínez, C. (2009). La reforma fallida de los Centros de Atención Múltiple [The failure of the reform of the multiple attention centers]. *Actualidades Investigativas en Educación, 9*(2), 1–22.

García-Cedillo, I., & Romero-Contreras, S. (2012). *Evaluación del proceso de integración educativa en México.* [*Evaluation of the process of educational integration in Mexico.*] Reseñas de Investigación en Educación Básica. Convocatoria 2006, Núm. 15. Secretaría de Educación Pública, México City, Mexico. Retrieved from http://basica.sep.gob.mx/dgdgie/cva/sitio/pdf/fomInv/rese/2006/r615.pdf

Gobierno de la República [Federal Government]. (2013). *Plan Nacional de Desarrollo 2013–2018.* [*National development plan, 2013–2018.*] México City, Mexico. Retrieved from http://pnd.gob.mx/wp-content/uploads/2013/05/PND.pdf. Accessed on November 1, 2014.

Instituto Nacional de Estadística y Geografía [INEGI, National Institute of Statistics and Geography]. (2000). *Tabuladores temáticos sobre la población con discapacidad. XII Censo General de Población y Vivienda.* [*Thematic figures on population with disability. XII general census of population and households.*] Mexico City, Mexico: INEGI. Retrieved from http://www3.inegi.org.mx/sistemas/productos/default.aspx?c=265&s=inegi&upc=702825000399&pf=Prod&ef=&f=2&cl=0&tg=0&pg=0&ct=102020800. Accessed on February 13, 2013.

Instituto Nacional de Estadística y Geografía. [INEGI, National Institute of Statistics and Geography]. (2001). *Presencia del tema de discapacidad en la información estadística.* [*Presence of the topic on disability in statistical information.*] Mexico: INEGI. Retrieved from http://www.inegi.org.mx/est/contenidos/espanol/metodologias/censos/marcoteorico3.pdf. Accessed on October 7, 2014.

Instituto Nacional de Estadística y Geografía [INEGI, National Institute of Statistics and Geography]. (2013). *Las personas con discapacidad en México, una visión al 2010.* [*People with disability in Mexico, a glance at 2010.*] México City, Mexico: INEGI.

Martínez, M. A. (2009). *Editorial. Educación especial.* [*Editorial. Special education.*] Educar, Revista de Educación. Secretaría de Educación. Gobierno del estado de Jalisco. Retrieved from http://portalsej.jalisco.gob.mx/comunicación-social/sites/portalsej.jalisco.gob.mx.comunicacion-social/files/pdf/edu47.pdf. Accessed on December 5, 2013.

Oppenheimer, A. (2008). My opinion Andrés Oppenheimer. Positive step for Mexican education. *Arizona Daily Star,* August 27. Retrieved from http://www.azbilingualed.org/NEWS_2008/2008b/positive_step_for_mexican_education.htm

OREALC-UNESCO. (2010). *Sistema Regional de Información Educativa de los estudiantes con Discapacidad (SIRIED). Propuesta metodológica.* [*Regional system of educational information of students with disabilities.*] Santiago, Chile: UNESCO.

Orizaba Noticias [Orizaba News]. (2003). Miguel Alemán Velazco entregó hoy la medalla "Adolfo Ruiz Cortines" a la profesora Odalmira Mayagoitia. [Miguel Alemán Velazco presented the medal "Adolfo Ruiz Cortines" to teacher Odalmira Mayagoitia]. *Orizaba Noticias*. Retrieved from http://www.orizabaenred.com.mx/cgi-bin/web?b=VERNO TICIA&%7Bnum%7D=16160. Accessed on December 5, 2013.

Padilla, A. (2010). La educación especial en México a finales del siglo XIX y principios del XX: Ideas, bosquejos y experiencias. [Special education in Mexico at the end of the XIXth century and the beginning of XXth]. *Revista Educación y Pedagogía, 22*(57), 15–29.

Ponce, V. M., Hernández, A. C., López, L. M., & Pérez, V. (2006). *La práctica y los significados educativos de los agentes de los Centros de Atención Múltiple en el Estado de Jalisco.* [*Practices and educational meanings of multiple attention centers' agents in the state of Jalisco.*] Guadalajara, México: Secretaria de Educación del Gobierno de Jalisco.

Red Internacional de Investigadores y Participantes sobre Integración Educativa [International Network of Researchers and Participants on Educational Integration]. (2004). *Evaluación externa del Programa Nacional de Fortalecimiento de la Educación Especial y de la Integración Educativa. Informe Final. Reporte Técnico.* [*External evaluation of the National program for the strengthening of special education and educational integration.*] Mexico City, Mexico: Subsecretaría de Educación Básica y Normal.

Romero-Contreras, S. (2009). Experiencia Temprana, Desarrollo y Aprendizaje Escolar: Interacciones, Influencias y Posibles Compensaciones. [*Early experience, school learning and development.*] In O. López (Ed.), *La investigación educativa: Lente, espejo y propuesta para la acción* (pp. 161–188). San Luis Potosí, Mexico: UASLP, El Polo Académico, SEGE, El Colegio de San Luis.

Romero-Contreras, S., García-Cedillo, I., & Fletcher, T. (2013a). The challenge of curriculum coherency and relevance in pre-service teacher training for inclusive education in Mexico. In P. Jones (Ed.), *Bringing insider perspectives into inclusive teacher learning: Potentials and challenges for educational professionals* (pp. 103–120). New York, NY: Routledge.

Romero-Contreras, S., García-Cedillo, I., Forlin, C. H., & Lomelí-Hernández, C. A. (2013b). Preparing teachers for inclusion in Mexico: How effective is this process? *Journal of Education for Teaching, 39*(5), 509–522. doi:10.1080/02607476.2013.836340

Sánchez Escobedo, P., Acle Tomasini, G., De Agüero Servín, M., Jacobo Cupich, Z., & Rivera Morales, A. (2003). Educación Especial en México, 1990–2001. [Special education in Mexico, 1990–2001.] In P. Sánchez Escobedo (Ed.), *Aprendizaje y desarrollo. La investigación educativa en México* (pp. 191–376). [*Learning and development. Educational research in Mexico.*] México, DF: COMIE.

Secretaría de Educación Pública [SEP, Secretariat of Public Education]. (2002). *Programa Nacional de Fortalecimiento a la Educación Especial e Integración Educativa. Tríptico de discapacidades.* [*PNFEEIE, National program for the strengthening of special education and school integration. Brochure on disabilities.*] México City, Mexico: SEP.

Secretaría de Educación Pública [SEP, Secretariat of Public Education]. (2004). *Plan de estudios 2004. Licenciatura en Educación Especial.* [*Curriculum 2004. Licentiate in special education.*] México, DF: SEP.

Secretaría de Educación Pública [SEP, Secretariat of Public Education]. (2006). *Orientaciones generales para el funcionamiento de los servicios de educación especial.* [*General guidelines for the functioning of special education services.*] México, DF: SEP.

Secretaría de Educación Pública [SEP, Secretariat of Public Education]. (2010). *Principales cifras del ciclo escolar 2009–2010.* [*Main figures from the school year 2009–2010.*]

Gobierno Federal [Federal Government]. Retrieved from http://www.snie.sep.gob.mx/princ_cifras/Principales_cifras_2009-2010.pdf

Secretaría de Educación Pública [SEP, Secretariat of Public Education]. (2012). *Datos del Programa Nacional de Fortalecimiento de la Educación Especial y la Integración Educativa (PNFEEIE)*. [*Figures from the National Program for the Strengthening of Special Education and Educational Integration – PNFEEIE.*] Retrieved from http://www.educacionespecial.sep.gob.mx/pdf/tabinicio/2012/Datos_pfeeie_2012.pdf

Servicios Educativos Integrados al Estado de México [SEIEM, Educational Services of the State of Mexico]. (2010). *Catálogo de instituciones de educación superior que ofertan posgrados en educación.* [*Catalogue of higher education institutions offering graduate studies in education.*] Gobierno del Estado de México. Retrieved from http://www.edomex.gob.mx/esuperior/doc/pdf/cat_ies.pdf

Sistema Nacional para el Desarrollo Integral de la Familia [SNDIF, National System for the Integral Development of Families]. (2012). *Informe de Rendición de Cuentas 2006–2012.* Retrieved from http://sn.dif.gob.mx/wp-content/uploads/2013/04/Informe Consolidado2006-2012.pdf

UNESCO. (1990). *World declaration on education for all and framework for action to meet basic learning needs.* Retrieved from http://www.unesco.org/education/pdf/JOMTIE_E.PDF

UNESCO. (1994). *The Salamanca statement and framework for action on special needs education.* Retrieved from http://www.unesco.org/education/pdf/SALAMA_E.PDF

UNESCO. (2003b). *Overcoming exclusion through inclusive approaches in education: A challenge and a vision.* Paris: UNESCO.

Universidad de Baja California [UBC, University of Baja California]. (n.d.). *Official web page of the University of Baja California.* Retrieved from http://ubc.edu.mx/oferta-educativa/doctorado-en-educacion-inclusiva/

SPECIAL EDUCATION TODAY IN GUATEMALA

Diane Rodriguez, Kenneth J. Luterbach and
Rocio Espinosa de Gaitan

ABSTRACT

*Special education in Guatemala started in the 1940s with the establish-
ment of schools for the blind. While there is a relatively large population
of persons with disabilities, the country has an insufficient number of
educational and rehabilitation programs because the country is very
impoverished. Guatemala has enacted a number of disability laws in the
1990s and early 2000s that enable persons with disabilities to participate
in educational services to develop their capabilities and to deter discrimination. The government has three categories of disability, namely, physical, sensory, and intellectual. Most of the special education schools and
rehabilitation workshops are in the capital city with few programs in
rural areas. Many children with special education needs do not attend
school. The government offers public service to families of children
with disabilities. In the 1980s, the government formed partnerships with
United States universities to help develop service plans for students with
disabilities as well as train school personnel in effective instructional
methods due to a shortage of licensed teachers. While special education
is improving it has a long way to go.*

Special Education International Perspectives: Practices Across the Globe
Advances in Special Education, Volume 28, 91–106
ISSN: 0270-4013/doi:10.1108/S0270-401320140000028010

INTRODUCTION

Guatemala has a population of approximately 15 million (World Bank, 2013) in a territory of 108,890 square kilometers. Guatemala is an autonomous legal entity with its own assets and coordinating nature (Article 22 of Decree 135-96). Guatemala City is the national capital. Twenty-four languages are spoken in Guatemala including Spanish, Mayan, Xinka, and Garifuna. The official language is Spanish. It is estimated that approximately 49% of the population are Indigenous people. Over 13 million people live in Guatemala and according to *Encuesta Nacional de la Discapacidad Insituto de Estadistica* [*National Disability Survey Statistics Institute*] [ENDIS] (2005); there were approximately 401,971 individuals with disabilities in Guatemala in 2005, which is approximately 3% of the population. In 2006 the Consejo Nacional para la Atencion de las Personas con Discapacidad [CONADI] (2006) [*National Council for People with Disabilities*] reported that one in every 135.48 homes in Guatemala has one or more persons with a disability. In Guatemala, CONADI serves advisory and advocacy functions pertaining to general policies on disability. Guatemala has 22 *departmentos* (which may be translated as departments, but in this case refer to political regions like the 50 states in the United States [US] states or Canadian Provinces). Guatemala is a picturesque country with diverse people who are working to enhance the country, in part by reducing the high rate of poverty and by improving services to people with disabilities. There is much work to do in pursuit of those goals.

Negotiations between the Guatemalan government and groups of citizens advocating for people in poverty and for individuals with a disability continue in order to tackle poverty and the exclusion of people with disabilities. Awareness of poverty and exclusion are critical to understanding the context of persons with disabilities in Guatemala. Extreme poverty is still high. Income per capita in Guatemala was $3,120 in US funds in 2012 (World Bank, 2013). The high level of existing poverty, evident in the low per capita income, is largely due to the high degree of inequality. In Guatemala and other countries, there is a positive correlation between education and income (CONADI, 2006). The United Nations Children Fund [UNICEF] (2009) noted: "for every quetzal obtained by a person who has completed only the primary level in school, one who has completed high school gets almost two quetzals" (p. 1). The income of a person who finished sixth grade is, on average, 79% higher than one who does not complete elementary education. Given that 50.3% of those with disabilities are illiterate and that 37.6% have attended only primary school, it is likely that their incomes are very low, which is to say that they probably live in extreme poverty. They face precarious employment, lack of basic services, and low-quality housing, which is accentuated in rural areas where the majority of Guatemalans, including persons with disabilities, reside. These circumstances are present throughout the nation; each political region in Guatemala needs to serve individuals with disabilities.

DEFINITION OF DISABILITY

To ensure a shared conception of disability in Guatemala, it is extremely important to know the legal definition of the term *disability*, which was used in the Diagnostic and Statistical Manual of Mental Disorders (American Psychiatric Association, 1983). In Guatemalan law, the term *discapacidad* (disability) is defined as "any physical, mental or sensory impairment, congenital or acquired impairment, which substantially limits one or more of the activities considered normal" (Decreto No. 135-96 de La Ley de Atención a las Personas con discapacidad [Decree No. 135-96 of The Law of Attention to Persons with Disability]). In such light, disability in Guatemala is regarded as any loss of normality of structure or loss of anatomical (physiological) or mental (psychological) function. The term disability is conceived in Guatemala as any restriction or diminished function resulting from an impairment of the ability to perform an activity within the range considered normal. In Guatemala the term disability is defined as a disadvantage for a given individual resulting from an impairment that limits or prevents the fulfillment of a role that is normal for the peer group, which depends on the individual's age and gender as well as social and cultural factors.

DISABILITY LAW

The Law of Attention to Persons with Disability (Decree 135-96) requires each political state in Guatemala to discuss how to enable people with disabilities to participate in educational services that support their conditions and development (UNESCO, 2010/2011). According to Decree 135-96, the Minister of Education is responsible for ensuring that people with disabilities in rural areas have access to education through appropriate programs in their geographical area. Further, an appropriate program includes provision of bilingual education in areas of predominantly indigenous people.

Also in the Ministerial Decree 34-2008 of January 11, 2008, the policy of inclusive education was approved for all Guatemalan people with special educational needs, which includes those with indigenous backgrounds. The inclusiveness policy provides a foundation for equal opportunities and conditions for students with special needs, which are commensurate with the rest of the population. In effect, this policy fosters the physical, intellectual, and emotional development of students with special needs in order to prepare them to participate fully in society. This policy also recommends expanding coverage and improving the quality of education, training, and retraining of teachers. Finally, this policy promotes community participation and management, advocacy, strategic partnerships, and evaluation. A brief summary of the history of special education in Guatemala follows.

HISTORY OF SPECIAL EDUCATION

In 1945, special education in Guatemala was first implemented at the School for St. Lucia Blind Children, on a private initiative through the Committee for Blind and Deaf of Guatemala. The School for Deaf Children Fray Pedro Ponce De Leon was created in 1965, along with the Open Rehabilitation Centre for Blind Adults. Since the early 1960s, special education theories and practices in Guatemala have been discussed and documented, as summarized in Table 1. Regarding the care of individuals

Table 1. Contributors to Special Education in Guatemala.

1961	Dr. Daniel Mac Alles IIME
1967	Dr. Daniel Mac Alles – Study Special Education in Central America
1969	Dr. Hernan Cortes – UNESCO
1970	Dra. BP de Braslavsky – UNESCO
1982	UNICEF – Education Especial en Centro America
1983	Miriam Ponce – Special Education and Actions in the Field in Guatemala
1989	UNICEF – Diagnosis of Special Education in Guatemala
1991	UNESCO – Profile of Special Education Services
1992	Diagnosis of Existing Services for People with Disabilities in Guatemala. Thesis of Búrbano G, Berducido Maritza
1994	UNICEF. Samayoa, Thomas y Valdez
1998	Database of the National Support Network for People with Disabilities Associación de Capacitación y Asistencia Técnica en Educación y Discapacidad (ASCATED)
2004	Diagnosis of the Situation of Special Education in Guatemala, DICADE, ASCATED

Source: Burbano and Berducido (1993). Diagnóstico de servicios para personas con discapacidad en Guatemala. Guatemala, Universidad Rafael Landivar.

with intellectual disability, the Neurological Institute of Guatemala has coalesced human resources in this area of disability in 1962 by forming and organizing a group of parents concerned about their children's education. In 1977 technical careers in special education, language therapy, and school counseling were implemented at various universities. According to Artiles (1995), special education programs modeling the services in the US were implemented in Guatemala in the 1980s.

CONCEPTIONS OF DISABILITY IN GUATEMALA

The term disability is used in Guatemala to describe three particular categories of disabilities, namely physical, intellectual, and sensory.

(1) A *physical disability* pertains to the body, limbs, and organs in general. Examples of physical disabilities include Muscular Dystrophy, Hemiplegia, and Cerebral Palsy.
(2) An *intellectual disability* (or mental impairment) is related to cognitive abilities, which affect learning, language, and chronological maturation.
(3) A *sensory impairment* (i.e., blindness and deafness) is related to the senses, especially hearing and vision, or the combination disability known as deaf/blindness.

The term disability in the International Classification of Impairments, Disabilities and Handicaps [ICIDH] (1980) refers only to activity limitations, but disability is now used as a generic term encompassing all human dimensions (physical, intellectual, and emotional).

The National Statistics Institute of Guatemala (Instituto Nacional de Estadistica [INE]) collects data and issues reports on a variety of issues pertinent to citizens in Guatemala, including data on individuals with disabilities. According to INE (2005) statistics, 27% of individuals with disabilities have congenital causes. Another 34% have disabilities caused by illnesses or accidents.

With respect to the provision of special education services, the INE (2005) reported that 78% of individuals with disabilities do not receive individualized services or attention. Individuals with disabilities in Guatemala may not receive services for a variety of reasons. In some cases, they do not know about the availability of services. In other cases, a suitable location for the services may not be available. Lack of money may also prevent an individual with a disability from being able to pay for transportation to the location of service. In other cases, services are not received due to lack of family support.

According to the National Survey on Disabilities from the National Statistical Institute *Encuesta Nacional de la Discapacidad Insituto de Estadistica* (ENDIS) (2005), people with disabilities have, in general, low educational levels. In particular, 50.3% of the total sector is illiterate. Further, according to ENDIS (2005), five of ten individuals with disabilities do not have any education or have completed only some primary education. Although both the Ministry of Education and the Ministry of Social Welfare of the Presidency of the Republic have established a small number of special education programs, the number of programs is small and they are generally concentrated in the capital city.

LEGISLATION ON DISABILITY AND ROLE OF GOVERNMENT

The national policy on disability in Guatemala has legal basis in national regulations, which were created in light of international guidelines. Within the legal framework, national policy on disability is based on the provisions of the Constitution of the Republic of Guatemala, The Law of Attention for People with Disabilities, Decree 135-96 (2005); the Authority Act Executive Decree 114-97 (2007), the Social Development Decree, Act 42-2001 (2001), the Urban Councils Act and Rural Development Decree 11-2002 (2002); the Ley de Organismo Ejecutivo Decreto 114–97 [Authority Executive Decree] (2007), and the General Act Decentralization Decree 14-2007 (2007). The rights of persons with disabilities are reflected in Article 53 of the Constitution of the Guatemalan Republic. In addition, laws specific to the Health Code, the Labor Code, and General Education law influence disability policy in Guatemala. Legislation and regulations support the principle of equality, which requires nondiscrimination.

The Law of Attention for People with Disabilities (Decree 135-96) upholds the principle of nondiscrimination in institutions of education and in workplaces. Under this law, people with a disability have the same rights as individuals without a disability. Decree 135-96 emphasizes training, which recognizes the need for individuals with a disability to develop intellectually, physically, socially, and emotionally in order to lead a fulfilling life. This decree also makes clear the government's duty to advise companies to create physical environments and conditions suitable for the performance of people with disabilities.

The Ministry of Education is responsible for policies and programs related to special education in Guatemala. The Directorate of Special Education is responsible for the existence and quality of special education programs. The Directorate is committed to implementing the special education policy to promote inclusive education and to facilitate access to schooling for youth with disabilities. Due to the policy of inclusion, special education students attend classes in the regular education system when possible. Such inclusive practices are beneficial to youth with disabilities because they learn that their disability is not too severe or limiting that the regular school system cannot accommodate them (Clark & Artiles, 2000).

The Social Welfare Department of the Presidency of the Republic is in charge of the of the country's largest Special Education Center, the Alida Arana Special Education Center. Personnel at that Center care for children and adolescents with special needs regarded as moderate to mild. In 2012, that Center provided services for a population of approximately 800 children and adolescents. There are multiple programs for Special Education in both the Ministry of Education and the Ministry of Social Welfare, just as there are multiple programs in the private sector, but the public and private programs combined are too few for the number of people with disabilities in Guatemala. Further, most of the programs are concentrated in Guatemala City.

OVERVIEW OF SPECIAL EDUCATION

In 2010, the Ministry of Education served approximately 15,609 children and youth with disabilities throughout the country. One may wonder why so few students with disabilities are served in a country with over 400,000 people with disabilities. First, most of those people are no longer of school age. Second, many children and youth with disabilities do not attend school. Third, the number of programs available to students is insufficient.

Guatemala has approximately 4,988 teachers. There are 930 teachers in inclusive settings, 460 special education teachers, and 3,598 teachers in traditional (non-inclusive) settings (Ministerio de Educación [MINEDUC], 2011). In 2005, a variety of special education programs exited in Guatemala, 47% for children with learning disabilities, 15% for children with speech and language impairments, 14% for children with intellectual disabilities, 12% for children with severe disabilities, and 12% for other disabilities (MINEDUC, 2005).

Before providing any special education service, testing occurs to determine whether an individual has a disability. Public schools use psycho-educational assessment for diagnosis and promotion. For purposes of admitting students to special education programs, as well as for formative evaluation of students in special education programs, schools use different assessment instruments, including: (a) adaptive behavior scales; (b) diagnostic academic tests; (c) basic ability tests; (c) psychological tests; (d) personality drawing tests; (e) intellectual knowledge tests; (f) development scale tests; (g) achievement tests; and (h) social/behavioral scales. Additionally student work samples are examined. After assessment, a student may receive special education services if there is significant discrepancy from peers their age.

Búrbano and Berducido (2005) identified the following special education services provided by the public sector: (a) integrated resource classrooms that are mandated by the Ministry of Education and located in national schools, which serve youth with learning, intellectual, and hearing, visual, and physical disabilities; (b) speech therapy; (c) counseling to parents; (d) special schools in rural sectors with educators hired by the Ministry of Education who teach students with different types of disability and work in coordination with parents to provide services; and (e) Institutions of the Ministry of Social Welfare in which employees serve people with intellectual disabilities (Búrbano & Berducido, 2005).

After schooling, people with disabilities have difficulty becoming employed in Guatemalan society because some employers lack knowledge and skills about disability or have negative attitudes and beliefs about persons with disabilities. Further, workplaces typically do not include adaptive technology that would enable a person with a disability to perform in a manner similar to other workers. Limited accessibility for people with disabilities to work and to engage in other economic, political, and social activities in Guatemala impedes progress and development. Such barriers to the world of education, culture and social life, in general, foster "social disability" (UNESCO, 1991).

WORKING WITH FAMILIES OF SPECIAL NEEDS STUDENTS

A Vignette

In October of 2003, Manuel Afredo Salazar Vásquez, son of Alfredo and Irene Salazar, was born in Guatemala. In June 2004, eight months later,

Manuel was diagnosed with Down Syndrome (DS). Like many other parents, the news shocked them, terrorized them, and produced other endless types of emotions in them.

After seeking assistance from laboratories, physicians, specialists, and therapists for more than a month, Alfredo and Irene realized that this reality was going to change the course of their lives. Two weeks later, they were informed that their son Manuel Alfredo had five congenital defects in his heart, which merited an open-heart surgery to correct them. They decided to travel to the US to seek help and then proceeded with the surgery and post-surgical care in the pediatric unit. The family returned to Guatemala and sought social services, which ultimately provided needed assistance. Throughout their experiences seeking care for their son, they realized that in their country there is a big scarcity of institutions that are able to provide guidance and therapy, which are so needed in the beginning months and years of the lives of children with Down Syndrome.

The great need for services and the scarcity of resources motivated Alfredo and Irene to create the Asociación Guatemalteca para el Síndrome de Down (AGSD, 2004) (Guatemalan Association for Down Syndrome).[1] Initially, the Salazars did not have the financial means or financial assistance to open the Association. To overcome that barrier, they decided to sell their house and when it sold, they opened the AGSD. In early September of 2005 the Salazars contracted qualified and experience personnel who began to provide early stimulation, physical therapy, and speech therapy for children with Down syndrome. AGSD has five classrooms with a capacity to support more than 55 children with Down Syndrome from birth through adolescence.

The AGSD provides multiple services for families. They group learners with Down Syndrome by age, as noted below.

– Program for early stimulation	0–2 years
– Classroom 1	3–6 years
– Classroom 2	7–10 years
– Classroom 3	11–14 years
– Classroom 4	15–older

Even with limited operational funds, which are acquired through donations, the impact of the AGSD has been tremendous, which is evident in the following comments from families who have benefitted from AGSD services.

1. *The family is really happy that Misael is receiving an education. His brother Jonathan said: I have noticed that he is the same as us, he has made a lot of progress. Before, he did not speak and now, even though he might be mad, he still talks. We have noticed his progress.*
2. *I knew that she had DS the instant that she was born. I heard the doctors say that there was something wrong with the child. I thought that everything was a dream. I was hoping that they would tell me that it was not true. I had a hard time accepting it. When the doctor confirmed my perspective, I had to accept it. I felt depressed and sad and at times I thought that she was going to die. When I was young, children with DS used to scare me because I didn't know how they were in reality. The process was really hard and I used to think how I was going to tell that to my husband, I thought that he was going to blame me for her condition. I used to think how it happened, probably something that I drank did me wrong. At the time of their first visit, my husband, my mother and my brother came and I had to explain everything to them. My husband was very serene and told me that she was our daughter and that we have to love her. Hilary was twice hospitalized for respiratory problems. She also had two small heart murmurs. Since the beginning she has been very close to our family and found our support. Hilary was one and a half months of age when she first visited AGSD. I felt good from the first time I arrived there. I have seen a lot of progress in her. I am happy because I communicate a lot with other families and relate to their experiences.*

Public Services for Families

Schools in Guatemala offer a variety of services to parents. At workshops for parents, school personnel address a multitude of issues, including the roles of father and mother to assist in the education of their daughter or son; awareness and critical involvement of the parent/family in their child's education; importance of favorable attitudes on the part of parents toward their child's development. Workshops for parents also address characteristics of disabilities, causes of disabilities, special education, behavioral problems, behavior modification, policies and rules for access to education for youth with special needs, inclusive education, self-esteem, child rights, family disintegration, learning disabilities, Adult Down Syndrome, intellectual disabilities, special education and sexual education, child maltreatment, and school performance.

PHILOSOPHICAL PRINCIPLES FOR INDIVIDUALS WITH SPECIAL NEEDS

In Guatemala, Special Education is based on a set of philosophical principles that guide regulatory policy in order to provide students with special needs access to appropriate educational materials and experiences. Explanations of the guiding principles appear below.

Standardization: This consists of making available to children and young people with disabilities special terms and conditions, for everyday life, that are as close as possible to those of all children and young people of the same age, living in a particular culture.

Integration: An educational system in which students with special educational needs are enrolled in regular classes in their neighborhood, next to peers without disability and where the students with special needs receive the support they need and are taught according to their own abilities and needs.

Equal Opportunities: Creating equal opportunity requires equitable provision of services, activities, and information, which includes service providers who present acceptable attitudes toward people with disabilities. Collectively, those conditions make educational spaces accessible for children and young people with disabilities.

Education: This is the idea that every human being, however limited the person may be, can benefit from an education. Any failure to take this principle into account is an attack on the concept of education and the mission of the educator.

Flexibility: Educational services are modified to accommodate the unique character and capability of every student.

Inclusion: For many children with a disability, inclusive education enables children with disabilities to attend regular schools in their community. Personnel at the schools make appropriate adjustments and provide the necessary support for each child to enjoy a high quality suitable education.

Investigators, who consider matters pertaining to special education in Guatemala, hold different perspectives on guiding principles. According to Jimenez and Garcia de la Cadena (2007), special education in Guatemala is regulated by the following four principles: normalization, school integration, the sectorization of services through interdisciplinary teams, and the individualization of the teaching process. Though conceptions of the guiding principles vary, on matters pertaining to students with special needs, the Ministry of Education in Guatemala has certainly been guided by principles favorable to this student population.

SCHOOL ENVIRONMENTS

In the early 1980s the Guatemalan Ministry of Education formed partnerships with US universities to help create plans to begin delivering special education services and to provide professional development workshops for teachers with a focus on services for students with learning disabilities (MINEDUC, 2001). Based on work completed through those partnerships, the Ministry of Education approved programs for students with learning disabilities in the elementary public schools.

The delivery of services to students with special needs varies by school (Association of Training and Technical Assistance in Education and Disability [ASCARED], 2004). There are public schools that have integrated children with special educational needs into regular classrooms and have a teacher serve this integrated population. With respect to programs taught in integrated classrooms and resource classrooms, a teacher working under the coordination of the Special Education Unit of the Ministry of Education attends to those programs. This is consistent with observations by Jimenez and Garcia de la Cadena (2007) who noted that in Guatemala students who require special resources, such as students with auditory or motor deficits or intellectual disabilities, received educational services in integrated classrooms that are organized to provide educational resources to children who have learning disabilities in reading, writing, or arithmetic.

Regarding the private sector, some institutions run special education programs, such as *FUNDABIEM, The Pro-Blind and Deaf Committee of Guatemala, Guatemala Neurological Institute, The Southern Education Foundation, School Kipling*, and the *Foundation Margarita Tejada* (Rodriguez, Espinosa de Gaitán, & Luterbach, 2008). Reports by the National Council for the Care of Persons with Disabilities (CONADI, 2006) also highlight the efforts of non-governmental bodies that drive special education in the interior of the country, such as work by ASCATED, FEDEGUAPA, EDECRI, and Schools Project Special Education "New Day," which began in 1982 in four departments of the Republic of Guatemala.

TEACHER TRAINING

With respect to teacher training, some universities in Guatemala provide teacher career programs at specialized Centers of Practice with attention focused on the implementation of special education programs. For example, the University of San Carlos of Guatemala, Universidad del Valle, and Universidad Rafael Landivar, among others, offer teacher training in special education (Rodriguez et al., 2008). La Universidad Del Valle de Guatemala offers two special education programs leading to licensure, one in the Education of Children with Special Needs and the second in Learning Disabilities. The objectives for the Education of Children with Special Needs program are to: (1) prepare specialized professionals in the care of people with specific problems of psychological, physical, or sensory type, favoring functionality and inclusion of individuals with disabilities; (2) train professionals to support social, academic, and professional inclusion of people with disabilities through school education; and (3) contribute to the educational development of the country by providing comprehensive quality care to people with special needs. The objectives for the Learning Disabilities program are to: (1) develop specialized professionals to teach students with Learning Disabilities; and (2) promote quality education attending to diversity in learning.

After initial training, in-service teachers receive psycho-pedagogical support through workshops. These training sessions, in different subjects and programs focused on the area of special education, allow teachers to update and improve their teaching (ASCATED, 2004).

Teachers in Guatemalan schools have attained different academic credentials. According to the Ministry of Education (2011), 40% of the teachers in Guatemala have attained the technical level; 24% of the teachers have a master of primary education degree; 23% of the teachers have an academic degree in psychology and education; and 13% of the teachers have attained the academic level of teachers in pre-primary education.

CONCLUSION

A social approach to disability aspires to continually improve conditions for people with a disability. In Guatemala, past efforts in public and private sectors have improved living conditions for people with a disability, but more work needs to be done. Every citizen in Guatemala, including those with a special need, deserves equal access and opportunity in the public sphere in Guatemala. Earnest citizens can ensure that attention is continually focused on the need to form a value system that upholds the dignity of individuals with a disability by providing equal access and opportunity in education and in all other public pursuits. It is important to note that Guatemala has a large number of individuals with disabilities, but only a small number of students receive educational services. The number of institutions serving children with disabilities in Guatemala is insufficient relative to the amount of people requiring special services. There is a shortage of licensed teachers trained in the area of special education and there is a need to open more programs and to increase the number of classrooms serving children and youth with disabilities. More programs would also enable schools to make inclusion programs available to learners earlier in their development.

The problem of limited inclusion of people with disabilities into mainstream society continues in Guatemala. People with disabilities have limited opportunities to integrate and participate in Guatemalan society. We hope that the Republic of Guatemala implements the principles and values identified in the national discourse on disabilities, which includes: (a) equity; (b) social solidarity; (c) equality; (d) respect; (e) freedom; (f) responsibility; (g) comprehensiveness; and (h) right to quality of life.

With regard to the status of special education in Guatemala, it is important to acknowledge the benefits of past efforts while calling for continual improvement through joint efforts by parents, politicians, administrators in government, teachers and other service providers, school administrators, and instructors in teacher training programs, as well as private sector groups and international and domestic partners in special education. Such a collective effort is necessary in the search for effective and efficient strategies to achieve equity and equal opportunities for diverse learners. Through such efforts, much needed educational opportunities and services for children with special educational needs in Guatemala can be expanded and strengthened. An improved system of special education in Guatemala would better prepare students with disabilities to absorb the humanistic, holistic, and dynamic spirit of life in Guatemalan society.

We hope that the quantity and quality of special education services increase by strengthening and creating more special education centers at the national level and by implementing more inclusive education programs. Special education programs in Guatemala may be strengthened through curriculum development and lesson development. Importantly, we hope that the Ministry of Education in Guatemala will strive to improve the educational experience for all children and youth in an inclusive society.

NOTE

1. For more information on the Guatemala Association for Down Syndrome, please contact Irene Salazar www.facebook.com/downguatemala

REFERENCES

American Psychiatric Association. (1983). *Diagnostic and statistical manual of mental disorders.* Washington, DC: American Psychiatric Association.

Artiles, A. (1995). The Guatemala challenge before the new millennium: Education for a multicultural society. *The Education, 39,* 213−227.

Asociación Guatemalteca para el Síndrome de Down (AGSD). (2004). *Family brochure.* Retrieved from www.downguatemala.org. Accessed on July 5, 2014.

Association of Training and Technical Assistance in Education and Disability. (ASCARED). (2004). *Facilitator in inclusive education approach to disability.* Guatemala City, Guatemala: Author.

Búrbano, G. C., & Berducido, M. E. (2005). *Situacion actual de la education especial en Guatemala.* [*Current status of special education in Guatemala.*] Asociacion de Capacitacion y Asistencia Técnica en Educación y Discapacidad (ASCATED). Retrieved from http://www.mineduc.gob.gt/portal/contenido/menu_lateral/programas/Educación_especial/documents/EducaciónEspecial.pdf. Accessed on December 29, 2013.

Búrbano, H. G., & Berducido, M. L. (1993). *Situational analysis of existing services for individuals with disabilities in Guatemala.* Guatemala City, Guatemala: University Rafael Landívar.

Clark, M. D., & Artiles, A. (2000). A cross-national study of teachers' attributional patterns. *The Journal of Special Education, 34*(2), 77−89.

Consejo Nacional para la Atencion de las Personas con Discapacidad (CONADI). (2006). *Politica nacional de la discapacidad.* Ciudad de Guatemala, Guatemala: Author.

Decreto Ministerial No. 34-2008. (2008). *Ministerio de Education Articulo 4.* [*Ministry of Education Decree 34-2008.*] Guatemala City, Guatemala: El Congreso de la Republica Guatemala.

Decreto No. 135-96. (2005). *The law of attention to persons with disabilities. Article 3.* Retrieved from http://www.ine.gob.gt/np/productos/index.htm#. Accessed on December 29, 2013.

Encuesta Nacional de la Discapacidad Insituto Nacional de Estadistica (ENDIS) [National Survey of the National Statistical Institute]. (2005). Retrieved from http://www.ine.gob.gt/np/productos/index.htm#. Accessed on December 29, 2013.

Instituto Nacional de Estatisticas en Guatemala (INE). (2005). Encuesta Nacional de la Discapacidad [National Survey of Guatemala]. Retrieved from http://www.ine.gob.gt/np/productos/index.htm#. Accessed on February 18, 2014.

International Classification of Functioning, Disability, and Health (ICIDH). (1980). *ICIDH-2 final draft.* Geneva, Switzerland: World Health Organization.

Jimenez, J. E., & Garcia de la Cadena, C. (2007). Learning disabilities in Guatemala and Spain: A cross-national study of the prevalence and cognitive processes associate with reading and spelling disabilities. *Learning Disabilities Research & Practice, 22*(3), 161−169.

Ley de Consejos Urbanos y el Decreto de Desarrollo Rural Decreto No 11-2002 Articulo 28 [Urban Councils Act and Rural Development Decree]. (2002). El Congreso de la República de Guatemala, Guatemala City, Guatemala.

Ley de Desarrollo Social Decreto 42-2001 [Social Development Decree]. (2001). El Congreso de la República de Guatemala, Guatemala City, Guatemala.

Ley de Organismo Ejecutivo Decreto 114-97 [Authority Executive Decree]. (2007). El Congreso de la República de Guatemala, Guatemala City, Guatemala.

Ley General de Descentralización 42-2007 [General Act Decentralization Decree]. (2007). El Congreso de la República de Guatemala, Guatemala City, Guatemala.

Ministerio de Educación (MINEDUC). (2001). *Política y normativa de acceso a la Educación para la poblacion con necesidades educativas especiales*. [*Policy and legislation on access to education for the population with special education needs.*] Guatemala City, Guatemala: Guatemala Government.

Ministerio de Educación (MINEDUC). (2005). *Documento base de educación especial*. [*Document-based on special education*.] Guatemala City, Guatemala: Guatemala Government.

Ministerio de Education (MINEDUC). (2011). *Educación especial para un mundo especial*. [*Special education for a special world*.] Guatemala City, Guatemala: Author. Retrieved from http://www.mineduc.gob.gt/portal/contenido/anuncios/EducaciónEspecial/documents/BoletinDIGEESP.pdf. Accessed on December 29, 2013.

Rodriguez, D., Espinosa de Gaitán, R., & Luterbach, K. (2008). Understanding the complexities of special education in Guatemala. *Journal of International Special Needs, 11*, 31–37.

UNESCO. (1991). *Perfil de servicios de educación especial en Guatemala. Seminario – taller planificación de servicios de educación especial en Guatemala*. [*Profile of special education services in Guatemala. Seminar-planning workshop for special education services in Guatemala*.] Guatemala City, Guatemala.

UNESCO. (2010/2011). *World data on education: Guatemala* (7th ed.) Author. Retrieved from http://www.ibe.unesco.org/fileadmin/user_upload/Publications/WDE/2010/pdf-versions/Guatemala.pdf. Accessed on December 15, 2013.

UNICEF. (2009). *At a glance Guatemala*. Retrieved from http://www.unicef.org/infobycountry/guatemala_48087.html. Accessed on December 31, 2013.

World Bank. (2013). *Data for Guatemala*. Retrieved from http://data.worldbank.org/country/guatemala. Accessed on December 30, 2013.

PART II
EUROPE

SPECIAL EDUCATION TODAY IN THE UNITED KINGDOM

Ron Smith, Lani Florian, Martyn Rouse and
John Anderson

ABSTRACT

This chapter aims to provide a critical analysis of special needs education within the United Kingdom today. Central to such an analysis is an understanding of the rapidly changing social and political milieu within which special needs education is embedded, including the rapidly changing demographics of schooling, and the devolution of political power into four separate but linked countries — England, Wales, Scotland and Northern Ireland. Following a discussion of such wider social, political and educational issues, the authors explore the convergences and divergences in policy and practice across the four devolved administrations. The authors describe a plethora of contemporary policy developments within each of the four administrations that speak to the need for special needs education to change in response to 21st century concerns about the problems of access to, and equity in, education for all children. Despite this, the authors remain extremely circumspect about the potential of many of these developments to lead to successful inclusive practices and developments on the ground — and explain why. The analysis in the

Special Education International Perspectives: Practices Across the Globe
Advances in Special Education, Volume 28, 109–145
ISSN: 0270-4013/doi:10.1108/S0270-401320140000028011

concluding section focuses on the issue of teacher education for inclusion and some very innovate UK research and development projects that have been reported to successfully engage teachers with new paradigm thinking and practice in the field of inclusive special needs education.

INTRODUCTION

Understanding that the United Kingdom (UK) is made up of four separate but linked countries – England, Northern Ireland, Scotland and Wales – is an essential starting point for considering special needs education in the United Kingdom today. However, while the strong similarities and links between the different countries and their own educational systems often justifies grouping them for general discussion purposes, this can obscure important differences. Differences in national contexts have resulted in variations in special education policy (e.g. in the language used), and practices (e.g. types of data collected), making some direct comparisons difficult – if not impossible. In this chapter, consequently, the shared concerns that are relevant across all of the countries of the United Kingdom are discussed broadly, while differences are identified to make the distinctive nature of each country context explicit. Where data is available, some examples are provided to enable the reader to make comparisons.

This chapter will consist of three major sections each with a number of relevant sub-sections. The common, but mistaken, use of the term England to refer to the United Kingdom or Britain reinforces the misunderstanding that the island of Britain is one country. This error further compounds confusion about the relationships between Britain and the other devolved countries of the United Kingdom. To clarify this situation, *Section 1* attempts to contextualize UK developments by, for example, describing changes in the broader UK social milieu within which education – and special needs education – are embedded. We will also discuss developments within the general school system and some of the recent educational agendas being forged within the devolved countries. *Section 2* focuses on UK developments with respect to special needs education more generally, as well as emerging trends within each of the devolved countries. With respect to special needs education, across the United Kingdom, three discursive influences can be seen to have impacted the consciousness and practice of UK educators, that is, 'exclusion', 'integration or assimilation' and, more recently, since the adoption and international use of the term inclusion (e.g. UNESCO, 1994, 2000), there has been much talk about 'inclusion' and 'inclusive education'. *Section 3* addresses selected current issues and challenges, and then discusses some of the implications of these for UK teacher education.

At this stage it should be said that, in order to maintain consistency throughout the book, we have endeavoured to address most of the topics suggested by the editor. However, of necessity, so as to take account of the specific UK context, the writing framework may take a slightly modified form. Nevertheless, the story told in this chapter makes use of the very substantial knowledge base and practical experience of four UK[1] practitioners, academics and researchers.

SECTION 1: THE UNITED KINGDOM: AN INTRODUCTION

Essentially, the interrelated but distinct nature of the national contexts of the countries of the United Kingdom is historical. The early 18th century political union of Great Britain brought England, Scotland and Wales under a single form of government in 1707. In 1800 a further Act of Union added Ireland until it was partitioned in 1921 to become the Irish Free State. However, during this time of political change, Northern Ireland opted to remain a part of the United Kingdom, hence today references to the United Kingdom are to Great Britain and Northern Ireland, also commonly (although incorrectly) referred to as Britain.

While education in each of the four countries has many features in common, Scotland and Northern Ireland have always had separate systems. Historically Scotland's education system has served as a distinctive marker of national identity and pride; an aspect indeed of resistance to assimilation with England (Anderson, 2003). In Northern Ireland, but for different historical and political reasons, in part due to the direct rule by the Westminster Parliament, educational reforms have generally followed developments in England and Wales, which until recently, operated a unified system. However, the devolution of political powers within the United Kingdom more broadly has led to the emergence of a distinct system of education in Wales since 2007 that is the responsibility of the Department for Children, Education, Lifelong Learning and Skills (DCELLS) (Welsh Assembly Government, 2010). Devolution has also led to further distinctions in Scotland and Northern Ireland.

The Social Fabric of the United Kingdom

Like other countries in Europe, the United Kingdom has been undergoing rapid economic changes brought about in part by the decline of many traditional industries and mining. Heavy engineering (e.g. iron and steel manufacturing, ship building, volume car making) has been replaced by hi-tech industries and the service sector (tourism and financial services). At the same time as these major economic changes, the United Kingdom is becoming increasingly urban and multicultural (de Blij, 2005). Government statistics estimate the population to be 67 million people (Office for National Statistics, 2012). Table 1 shows the 2011 census estimate for the main ethnic group categories. However, regional variations are substantial.

The United Kingdom has a long history of immigration and identifies itself as a multicultural society with a tradition of offering opportunity to others and refuge to those escaping persecution or hardship elsewhere (Home Office, 2007). After the Second World War, the government welcomed immigrants who were needed to help rebuild Britain. From the 1950s immigrants arrived from the former British colonies in the Caribbean and South Asia, and this is reflected in the relatively large ethnic minority groups from India and Pakistan. In recent years, the enlargement of the European Union (EU) has resulted in a new wave of immigrants from the accession states of Eastern and South Eastern Europe. Additionally, an

Table 1. The 2011 Census Estimate for the Main Ethnic Group Categories.

Ethnic Group	2011 (Population)	2011 (%)
White	55,010,359	87.1
White: Irish Traveller	63,193	0.1
Asian or Asian British: Indian	*1,451,862*	*2.3*
Asian or Asian British: Pakistani	*1,173,892*	*1.9*
Asian or Asian British: Bangladeshi	*451,529*	*0.7*
Asian or Asian British: Chinese	*433,150*	*0.7*
Asian or Asian British: Asian Other	*861,815*	*1.4*
Asian or Asian British: Total	4,373,339	7.0
Black or Black British	1,904,684	3.0
British Mixed	1,250,229	2.0
Other (Total)	580,374	0.9
Total	67,594,426	100

Source: Office for National Statistics (2012).

increasing number of refugees have sought asylum in the United Kingdom from conflicts elsewhere on the world.

In all countries of the United Kingdom, the majority of immigrants tend to be concentrated in urban areas, so, whilst overall numbers of some minority groups may be low, the concentration of groups within particular areas is often high. In addition, there has been an increase in East European migrants moving to rural areas to work in horticulture and farming. In recent years, many schools in these areas received non-English speaking children for the first time, while other schools in urban areas enroled a majority of students for whom English was not their first language. However, this is not the only language issue, as there are different dialects of English spoken throughout the United Kingdom. Many Welsh and Scottish people speak Welsh or Gaelic; Irish is also spoken in Northern Ireland, as is the dialect Ulster Scots (Home Office, 2007).

One of the many consequences of the Second World War was public demand for the post-war world to be better than the pre-war world. As part of the post-war reconstruction, the state took the view that full citizenship demanded the social rights of employment, health, housing and education (Carr & Hartnett, 1997). It was out of these expectations and aspirations that the United Kingdom moved to establish a welfare state, which included a new Education Act providing secondary education for all, and a National Health Service (NHS) that was free at the point of delivery (Board of Education, Education Act, 1944). More than sixty years after it was established, the NHS remains a crucial element of the social fabric of the United Kingdom and it continues to enjoy high levels of public approval. Nevertheless, since at least the mid-1980s, many of the socially progressive policies associated with the welfare state — particularly in England — have been replaced by a post-welfarist commitment to 'market democracy and competitive individualism' (Gewirtz, 2002, p. 2).

The General School System

The United Kingdom has a long history of universal provision of public education. Children between the ages of 5–16 years must attend school (in Northern Ireland the starting age is 4 years), and the majority remain in education beyond the age of 16 years.[2] Education is financed largely through national taxation with funds distributed through local authorities, although some schools are funded directly by government. Across the United Kingdom, primary schools generally educate both boys and girls, but a small number of secondary schools are single-sex schools.

It is important to point out that in all four countries of the United Kingdom, faith schools are part of the state funded education system. Since compulsory school attendance laws were introduced in the 1870s and 1880s, the state education system developed in partnership with the mainstream Christian churches. Today around a third of maintained schools in England have a religious character (Church of England, Catholic, with a small numbers of Jewish, Hindu, Buddhist and Muslim schools) (Teachernet, n.d.). In Scotland, the majority of schools are effectively secular and are known as 'non-denominational' schools.

Currently in England, Wales and Northern Ireland, after five years of secondary education, the majority of students take examinations in a range of subjects at the level of General Certificate of Secondary Education (GCSE). The GCSE is a single-subject examination set and marked by independent examination boards. Students usually take up to 10 (there is no upper or lower limit) GCSE examinations in different subjects, including Mathematics and English language. After taking GCSEs, students may leave secondary school or they may choose to stay on at school for two more years (years 12 and 13), or continue their education at a further education college where a range of courses are available. Students who are aiming for university normally take A-Level (short for Advanced Level) examinations. Results on GCSE and A-level examinations are not only important for individual young people; they are also used to compare schools.

Recent reports of poor performances in international tests of mathematics, reading and science made headline news across the United Kingdom. For example, the Programme for International Student Assessment Tests (PISA), which are administered every three years by the Organisation for Economic Cooperation and Development (OECD, 2007), indicated that the United Kingdom's recent performance had 'flat-lined' while competitors had improved. The United Kingdom remained stuck among the average, middle-ranking countries; in 26th place for mathematics and 23rd for reading, broadly similar to three years earlier. In science, the United Kingdom was reported to have slipped downwards, from 16th to 21st place, in a downward trend for results in the subject. In a breakdown of the UK results, England, Scotland and Northern Ireland were clustered around the average. Furthermore, the results were particularly poor for Wales which trailed behind the rest of the United Kingdom in all three subjects (British Broadcasting Corporation [BBC], 2013).

Within all four devolved administrations of the United Kingdom, recent curriculum reforms have resulted in what might be called the official curriculum (as opposed to the planned and informal or hidden curricula) becoming a much more demand-led system of skills acquisition with in-built flexibility and responsiveness. For example, from 2008 in England, schools have had a duty to consider the potential of the National Curriculum inclusion statement to improve teaching and learning – a duty to consider the flexibilities that exist to modify or personalize the curriculum and to make it relevant to student's strengths and interests.

Teaching—Learning Agendas within the Four Countries

There is a national curriculum in England, which consists of English, mathematics, science, design and technology, information and communication technology, history, geography, modern languages, music, art and design, physical education, and citizenship. In addition to these subjects, there are a number of other compulsory courses, such as religious education. Children also take national curriculum-based tests at age 7, 11 and 14 years. The school level results in England are public and are used to construct league tables of school performance (Qualifications and Curriculum Authority [QCA], 1999).

Since May 2010, with the formation of a new right-wing-leaning coalition Government between the Conservative and the Liberal Democratic parties, schooling in England has seen further significant changes. These have included: the introduction of Higher Education tuition fees; the eradication of the Education Maintenance Grant (EMA; financial support for 16 to 18 year-olds who want to continue their education after school leaving age); the introduction of Academies and 'Free Schools' and proposals to change the National Curriculum and assessment arrangements. Academies were almost exclusively opened by the former Labour Government in areas of multiple social deprivation to replace under-performing comprehensives. They are free of local authority control, gain funding directly from the government, and head teachers (Principals) are given almost complete freedom over such issues as, for example, budgets, the curriculum, hiring staff, term times and the length of school day. Now, however, all schools can apply for academy-style freedoms and Secondary schools ranked 'outstanding' by the statutory Inspection quango (Ofsted) are being fast-tracked into the programme while other schools will undergo a more rigorous screening process.

Education in Wales[3] is distinctly Welsh both in terms of the languages of education and the curriculum. Education is seen as playing a key role in the development of a bilingual country and Welsh Government policy is committed to upholding the right of all children to be educated through the medium of Welsh, if their parents so wish. There is also an expectation that the curriculum should be distinctly Welsh in terms of the opportunities learners get to develop and apply their knowledge across the curriculum. While the national curriculum initially applied to Wales, a National Curriculum Council has retained oversight of the curriculum and undertakes a 5-yearly review cycle. Recently there has been considerable investment in the development of the statutory curriculum for all 3–5 year-olds (the Foundation stage). The perception that Wales performs poorly in international comparisons of attainment with other countries of the United Kingdom has also had a major influence on recent education policy in Wales, with new literacy and numeracy frameworks and tests for 7–14-year-olds being introduced during 2012 (Welsh Assembly Government, 2012).

In 2000, the Scottish Executive of the newly created devolved Scottish Parliament set five national priorities for education. These were: achievement in attainment; a framework for learning that included supporting and developing the skills of teachers and the self-discipline of pupils; inclusion and equality to promote equity and help every pupil benefit from education; teaching values and citizenship and learning for life. Scotland is currently making the transition to a new 'Curriculum for Excellence' designed to give teachers and schools more flexibility and greater curricular coherence across the 3–18 age range. The purpose of the Curriculum for Excellence is encapsulated in what are called the four capacities – to enable each child or young person to be a successful learner, a confident individual, a responsible citizen and an effective contributor (Learning and Teaching Scotland, n.d.). The assessment and examination arrangements in Scotland are the responsibility of the Scottish Qualification Authority (SQA, 2006). The previous tiered system (called The Standard Grade) offered examination papers at three levels (foundation, general and credit). This system has been undergoing review and revision in light of the introduction of Curriculum for Excellence, mentioned above, in order to develop a new framework of national qualifications. As a result, new examination and assessment arrangements are expected to replace Standard Grades in 2014.

No matter the other similarities and differences between Northern Ireland and the rest of the United Kingdom, educational developments in the province need to be set against the backdrop of almost three decades of political violence which saw over 3700 people killed, and tens of thousands of people injured. The declaration of ceasefires by paramilitary groups in 1994 created an opportunity for political dialogue that led, in April 1998, to the Good Friday Peace Agreement (GFPA). The GFPA represented an attempt at a fundamental shift within society, a shift away from a 'culture of violence' through the establishment of new democratic structures. It enshrined commitments to pluralism, equality and human rights as essential parts of the settlement. It is now 15 years since the GFPA, and, whilst it represented social and political possibilities of immense significance, to imagine that Northern Ireland had crossed some invisible Rubicon where social conflict magically disappeared would be naïve. A realistic assessment of the present peace process suggests that reconciliation remains as yet an unfulfilled dream.

Segregation features in almost every aspect of life in Northern Ireland: people live, socialize, work and shop in areas where they feel safe (Leitch & Kilpatrick, 1999). Unsurprisingly, segregation also remains a distinctive characteristic of the school system. The vast majority of children and teachers attend schools that can be described as either Protestant (Controlled) or Catholic (Maintained) schools. There has been a trend towards Integrated schools that are attended in roughly equal numbers by Protestant and Catholic students, although, currently, only 7 per cent of the student population attend such institutions.

Northern Ireland retains a selective secondary education system as a result of transfer tests which are no longer regulated by the state because of contentious and unresolved policy changes relating to selective secondary education. This means that, at the age of 11 years, children in Northern Ireland are segregated at the post-primary stage by ability, and, in some cases, by gender.

Prior to 2008, Northern Ireland followed a curriculum framework similar to the English national curriculum. However, from that date, a revised 'Northern Ireland Curriculum' was implemented. This aimed to provide better access to the skills and competences perceived as more relevant to a 21st century economy, to provide a richer entitlement and greater choice, and to enable teaching to be adapted more readily to meet pupils' individual needs and aspirations. The curriculum also includes the study of the Irish language in all maintained schools and Irish is the language of instruction in a small number of Irish-medium schools (Council for the Curriculum, Examination and Assessment [CCEA], 2000).

In recent years, policy initiatives in Northern Ireland have prioritized issues of school improvement, raising standards, and addressing underachievement in literacy and numeracy (Department of Education Northern

Ireland, 2008, 2009, 2011). International commitments to establish the ability to read and write as a basic human right (UNESCO, 2000) have been mirrored in Northern Ireland by concerns to raise the literacy and numeracy standards of all children and young people – concerns brought to the fore by a number of influential enquiries and reports critical of the extant situation.[4]

At this point it should also be said that, there has been very little actual legislative reform affecting education in Northern Ireland in the last five years, due to the complexity of the political structures. Significant time lags between the planning and implementation stages of strategies, policies or action plans now appear to be a fact of life in the Province. For some, the peace process is now definitely just a protracted talking shop that, unfortunately, is heading into an abyss. The power-sharing arrangements resulting from the GFPA are viewed as only serving to perpetuate the sectarian divide, leaving no room for progressive and reforming voices to be heard. Furthermore, as suggested by O'Donnell (2013), it is the case that the Northern Ireland Executive was framed specifically to suit the post-conflict situation and that it was indeed a strange and limited democratic construct.

Others take a more positive and longer view, pointing to the inevitability of slow progress in the context of transitional societies, and, despite resolution, point to the significant amount of policy consultation and discussion that has occurred. Some academics also point to the work of conflict transformation theories and theorists, such as Lederach (1995, 1997), to help contextualize slow progress and lacunae in decision-making within societies emerging from violent conflict.

SECTION 2: SPECIAL EDUCATIONAL NEEDS

General Developments

As in many other countries, there is a long-standing tradition of special school provision in the United Kingdom and many such schools were established during the 20th century to educate children with disabilities. Although the numbers varied in different parts of the United Kingdom, about 2 per cent of children attended special schools. In addition, until the 1970s a very small number of children were in hospitals or attended 'junior training centres' run by health authorities. The 1970 Education Act in England and Wales, followed by similar legislation in Scotland in 1974,[5] and Northern Ireland in 1987,[6] ended the long-standing practice of classifying a small minority of children as uneducable, and put a stop to the arrangements for classifying children suffering from a disability of mind as children unsuitable for education at school. It also took away the power of health authorities and relocated responsibility to education authorities. For the first time in UK history, 100 per cent of school-age children were entitled to education (Vaughn, 2002).

In the 1970s the government established a Committee of Inquiry, chaired by the philosopher (now Baroness) Mary Warnock to undertake a review of special education policy and provision. The recommendations of the Committee report, commonly referred to as the Warnock Report (Department of Education and Science [DES], 1978), formed the basis for further legislative developments across all the four countries. That is, the Education Scotland Act (1980) (SOEID, 1980); the 1981 Education Act in England and Wales (Department of Education and Science [DES], 1981); and the Education Order (1984) in Northern Ireland, (DENI, 1984), which took place from January, 1986. These Acts were informed by Warnock recommendations that stressed the non-categorical nature of disability and an ecological or interactive view of special education need (SEN) which suggested that up to 20 per cent of students may have special educational needs at some point in their educational careers.

The idea that up to 20 per cent of all children might experience difficulty in learning at some time in their school careers required a definition of special educational need that was flexible and sensitive to the range and type of individual differences that make up the school-aged population. Subsequently, children with special educational needs were defined as having significantly greater difficulty in learning than other children of similar age, or having a disability preventing or hindering the child from making use of mainstream educational facilities, but the term has been problematic. For example, a student with a medical diagnosis or disability does not necessarily have a special educational need, unless special educational provision is needed to access the curriculum. Equally, a child with a special educational need does not necessarily have a disability.

The original intent of a flexible, non-categorical approach to SEN provision was to enable support to be provided to children experiencing difficulties in learning without the delay and expense of multi-disciplinary assessment or the stigma of a label. It shifted the focus of special education away from the comfortable certainty of categorical handicaps towards a consideration of learning needs. However, notwithstanding the efforts that had been made to replace individual categories of difficulty with one

overarching category, this has proved very difficult in practice for a variety
of reasons. Riddell, Weedon, and Harris (2012), for example, noted that
parents of children with particular types of difficulty, such as autistic
spectrum disorder, and voluntary organizations representing these groups
have campaigned for official recognition of specific categories. Government
have also found it useful to request local authorities to audit the incidence
of particular types of difficulty, partly as an accountability mechanism, but
also to inform funding decisions. In England, the practice of gathering data
by type of difficulty, which was abandoned following the Warnock Report,
was reinstated in the 1990s. More recently, in response to concerns about
the lack of specificity in SEN data, the English government has begun to
collect data from schools to include 11 categories of SEN: Specific Learning
Disability (SpLD), Moderate Learning Difficulty (MLD), Severe Learning
Difficulty (SLD), Profound and Multiple Learning Difficulty (PMLD),
Emotional and Behavioural Difficulty (EBD), Speech, Language and
Communication Needs (SLCN), Hearing Impairment (HI), Visual
Impairment (VI), Multi-Sensory Impairment (MSI), Physical Difficulty
(PD), Autism Spectrum Disorder (ASD) and other (OTH). However, such
data are not collected consistently across the United Kingdom. In Northern
Ireland and Wales, different categorical data are collected. In Scotland,
local authorities provide information to the government on the numbers of
children with particular types of difficulty (Riddell et al., 2012).

Despite the acknowledgement of the interactive nature of special educational needs, the administrative procedures which have been set out
to ensure that children are appropriately supported when they experience
difficulty are based on an individual needs approach to provision.
Commentators, such as Dyson (2005) have also argued that, in emphasizing
the requirement that children and young people should be educated within
the least restrictive environment (Frederickson & Cline, 2009), the view of
pluralism in practice actually underpinning the Warnock Report, and its
associated Education Acts, represented more of an 'integrationist' (assimila-
tionist) than inclusionist impulse. In other words, children and young
people were welcome in mainstream schooling as long as they could be
accommodated with additional resources and without having to make too
many changes to the regular curriculum. This integrationist discourse was,
as Slee (2011) remarked, little more than the calculus of equity, concerned
with measuring the extent of a student's disability with a view to calculating
the resource loading to accompany the student into school.

All of the UK countries use a variation of a staged assessment and intervention process that is specified in governmental guidance, called a *Code of*

Practice. In Table 2, the staged assessment procedure followed in Northern Ireland is outlined. England and Wales follow a similar approach but stages of action are simplified and refer to School Action (Stages 1 and 2), or School Action Plus (Stages 3 and 4), and Statement. In Scotland, a particular staged intervention model is not specified but local education authorities are encouraged to use a wide range of approaches that 'are built around discrete stages of intervention which seek to resolve difficulties as early as possible and with the least intrusive course of action' (Scottish Government, 2005).

As can be seen in Table 2, children with complex needs can be referred for what is known in the United Kingdom as 'statutory assessment' by a multi-professional team. Such an assessment might lead to a 'Statement of Special Educational Needs being issued (except in Scotland which issues a Co-ordinated Support Plan, or CSP). Requests for such assessment may be initiated by the school or by the parents and the Statement is reviewed at least annually. As in other countries, following an individual needs approach to SEN provision, there are guidelines to ensure parents' and children's views are included in this planning process. The Statement and CSP are statutory documents that specify the educational and other provision that is required to meet complex needs.

As in other countries, the relational definition of special needs education as that which is 'additional to' or 'different from' that provided to others of similar age characterizes the legal definitions of special or additional support needs in the United Kingdom. As a result, there are many forms of

Table 2. Code of Practice on the Identification and Assessment of Special Educational Needs: Northern Ireland.

Stage 1	Teachers identify and register a child's special educational needs and, consulting the school's SEN co-ordinator, take initial action.
Stage 2	The SEN co-ordinator takes lead responsibility for collecting and recording information and for coordinating the child's special educational provision, working with the child's teachers.
Stage 3	Teachers and the SEN co-ordinator are supported by specialists from outside the school.
Stage 4	The Board (similar to Local Education Authority in England and Wales) considers the need for a statutory assessment and, if appropriate, makes a multi-disciplinary assessment.
Stage 5	The Board considers the need for a statement of special educational needs; if appropriate, it makes a statement and arranges, monitors and reviews provision.

Source: DENI (1998).

provision in mainstream and special schools, some of which is categorical and some of which is not. Provision may be made in special schools, special units attached to mainstream schools or in mainstream classes. Many mainstream schools offer 'resourced provision' or special 'bases' for children with particular difficulties, but the majority of children with special or additional support needs are educated full-time in mainstream classes, bringing in specialist support as required. Schools in Northern Ireland, England and Wales have a designated SENCo (a special educational needs co-ordinator) responsible for managing provision for students with SEN. In Scotland, teachers who provide specialist support are referred to as Support for Learning Coordinators.

As suggested above, during the post-war period, and following the Warnock Report (DES, 1978) special needs education across the United Kingdom developed along broadly parallel lines. Following the prominence given to the concept of inclusion in education with, for example, the UNESCO Salamanca Statement (UNESCO, 1994), the language of inclusion started to become assimilated within UK legislation. Within England, Wales and Scotland for example, the Special Educational Needs and Disability Act 2001 (SENDA; Department for Education and Skills [DfES], 2001), amended Part 4 of the Disability Discrimination Act (DDA) enhancing the rights of disabled children and their parents by prohibiting discrimination against disabled pupils and prospective pupils. Discrimination was defined as failure to make reasonable adjustments or the provision of less favourable treatment for a reason relating to the pupil's disability. Similar legislation was introduced in Northern Ireland through the Special Educational Needs and Disability Order (NI) 2005 (DENI, 2005).

Early Years Provision

In the United Kingdom there is a long-standing tradition of early years education, and care for children under the age of 5 years is provided by a wide range of professionals. Childminders, private day care, voluntary sector playgroups, and local authority nursery classes and (in England) all are considered part of early years provision. For children under age 5 years, publicly funded nurseries and pre-schools are available for a limited number of hours each week. Providers of early years education vary enormously in terms of their qualifications and training. While trained teachers will be working in all classes based in school settings (reception and nursery classes), this is unlikely in private day nurseries or voluntary sector playgroups. In these settings staffs are likely to have qualifications relating to the care of young children, rather than a teaching qualification.

All of the countries of the United Kingdom make provision for children with disabilities and complex needs from birth. The Codes of Practice that accompany special education legislation outline a framework for the provision of services to children from birth through the school years. While the referral for services may be initiated by anyone, in many cases it is the early years practitioners who begin the process of identifying children with special or additional needs. It is common for practitioners to liaise (often through parents/carers) with other agencies – particularly medical – if children have been identified with an impairment of any kind. In these cases, families may be in receipt of disability living allowance, and additional funds will be available to settings and families to fund additional support in addition to access to specialist provision (e.g. speech therapy and physiotherapy). Children with statements of special educational need are given privileged access to settings offering specialist provision/provision that are considered particularly suitable. In some cases this may mean that a child attends a setting outside of the catchment schools their peers would be expected to attend. In such cases additional funding for transport is provided.

Contemporary Developments within the Four Countries

England

In England and Wales such inclusive policy developments have also existed alongside a broader set of educational reforms having very different policy intent. The 1988 Education Act introduced a national curriculum (which specified content), and a national assessment (which specified standards), along with a series of other changes designed to align the schooling system with the methods, cultures and ethical systems of private sector organizations. Ball (2003) described the processes and effects of this post-welfarist social policy realignment as the terrors of performativity. Privileged within performative cultures were outputs rather than beliefs, values or authentic relationships, and conformity to very narrowly defined attainment targets and performance criteria (Wrigley, 2005).

Initial optimism that the consumerism, marketization and manageralism pursued during the late 1980s across the English public sector would be moderated during the thirteen year period of the New Labour Government (1997–2010) was soon dampened. A plethora of educational policies were introduced during this period targeting special needs education, social, and educational inclusion (including SENDA; see above). Indeed, as Norwich (2013a) suggested, because social inclusion became a central pillar of social, economic and educational policy, the conditions for inclusive education were probably at their optimal during this time. Despite this, critical commentaries on the actual inclusive impact of what became known as New Labour's 'Third-Way', make uncomfortable reading. In terms of inclusive education, Dyson (2005) argued that wider post-welfarist social policy developments in England had contained inherent contradictions and ambiguities that changed very little in practice. Indeed, despite its laudable aims, he argued that the most disadvantaged children and young people – who traditionally make up the largest proportion of children identified as having special educational needs – continued to be at the greatest risk of impoverished educational experiences, low achievement and limited life chances. Children living in poverty, and/or those with special educational needs, had been made more vulnerable as schools serving areas of deprivation struggled to compete in the educational market (see also, Gillborn & Youdell, 2000; McLaughlin & Rouse, 2000).

In May 2010, a Coalition between the Conservative and Liberal Democratic parties came to power with a manifesto dedicated to opposing the previous Government's 'bias to inclusion',[7] as well as legislate for a more choice-based approach to provision for children with disabilities and difficulties in English schools (Norwich, 2013a). In March 2011, a Green Paper (DFE, 2011) laid out the government's vision for a new system to support children and young people identified as having special educational needs and disabilities. Following consultation, the government (DFE, 2012) set out its next stage towards new legislation in the form of a Children and Families Bill (DFE, 2013). This had its first reading in the House of Commons in February 2013 and covered six key areas of reform. The key measures with regard to special needs education included:

- A single assessment process (0–25) axing the current system of 'School Action' and 'School Action Plus' assessments, and replacing them with a single stage called 'SEN Support';
- An Education, Health and Care plan (EHC) to replace the Statement;
- An offer of a personal budget for families with an Education, Health and Care plan;
- A requirement for local authorities and health services to jointly plan and commission services;
- A requirement on local authorities to publish a local offer indicating the support available to those with special educational needs and disabilities and their families.

(Friswell & Petersen, 2013, pp. 14–15)

The general direction taken by this government has attracted criticism from many educators. Far from creating greater equality, some changes are anticipated to perpetuate inequalities both in schools and higher education (Bhopal & Maylor, 2014). With regard to special educational needs, inclusion is viewed narrowly in terms of school placement and is seen as a private as opposed to a public policy matter. Whether this 'SEN market' leads to better provision and services, or becomes a recipe for chaos, remains to be seen. However, what seems clear, as Norwich (2013b) suggested, is that the policy was not evidence-informed. Though the Government had initiated pilot developments across the country to test out its broad ideas, legislation was forging ahead before lessons had been learned from these pilots (Norwich, 2013b).

Data collated in 2012 by the European Agency for Development in Special Needs Education (European Agency for Development in Special Needs Education [EADSNE], 2012)[8] indicated that there were 7,504,300 children and young people in publicly funded schools in England. Approximately 18 per cent of these were categorized as having an SEN, whilst an additional 2.7 per cent – representing those with the greatest physical or mental health needs – held a statement of SEN. Overall the proportion of children in English special schools reduced from about 1.8 per cent of the school population in 1983 to about 1.3 per cent in the year 2000 (Norwich, 2002). Since then, depending on the formula used, the proportion in special schools has remained largely unchanged at about 1.1 per cent (Ofsted, 2010; cited in Norwich, 2013a). The most prevalent type of SEN are those children and young people identified as having moderate learning difficulties (MLD), and the second largest group consists of those identified as having behavioural, social and emotional difficulties (BSED).

Scotland

Scotland did not adopt the same market-based reforms as England and continues to have a largely comprehensive system of education. Until fairly recently, special needs education in Scotland was governed by a legal framework established within the Education (Scotland) Act 1980 as amended by the 1981 Act (Hodkinson & Vickerman, 2009). However, in the Education (Additional Support for Learning) Scotland Act 2004[9] (Scottish Executive Education Department [SEED], 2004a), the language of special education was dropped and replaced with the arguably more inclusive terminology of 'additional support needs' (ASN). The inclusiveness of the ASN term, and its differentiation from SEN, was explained in a summary handout provided by the Scottish Executive Education Department (SEED, 2004b). This indicated that ASN referred to any child or young person who would benefit from extra help in order to overcome barriers to their learning (SEED, 2004b). The Act stipulated that an ASN might arise from any factor which caused a barrier to learning, whether that factor related to social, emotional, cognitive, linguistic, disability, or family and care circumstances. For example, additional support needs might be required for a child or young person who: was being bullied; was identified as having behavioural difficulties; had a sensory of mobility impairment; was at risk or was bereaved (SEED, 2004b). The legislation put into place a raft of additional measures to increase parental rights and local authority accountability. It abolished the Record of Needs and established a new document called the Co-ordinated Support Plan (CSP) to record the needs of children with multiple, complex and enduring difficulties requiring significant multi-agency support (Riddell et al., 2012). Finally, as Riddell et al. (2012) noted, the ASL Act put in place a number of new dispute-resolution mechanisms, outlined in a new Code of Practice (Scottish Executive, 2005).

Data collected by EADSNE indicated that, in January 2012, there were 585,289 children and young people in publicly funded schools (369,093 in primary schools, 216,196 in secondary schools and 5,595 in special schools) in Scotland. The proportion of children in special schools was approximately 1 per cent. A larger number of categories of difficulty are used in Scotland (18 in total) for monitoring purposes. The largest category (learning disability) accounted for about a fifth of all pupils with ASN, while the second largest category (social emotional and behavioural difficulties), accounted for just over 15 per cent. Together, these two included just over one-third of the ASN population (Riddell et al., 2012).

Wales

The organization of special needs education in Wales (Welsh Assembly Government, 2009), and the definition of SEN, are exactly the same as those to be found in England (Hodkinson & Vickerman, 2009). As suggested above, Wales does have its own Code of Practice and the legal provision of special education is governed by the Education (SEN) (Wales) Regulations 2002.[10] However, at the present time, the Welsh Government is consulting on a new legislative framework having many elements in common with the English Children and Families Bill (DFE, 2013). For example, the new legislation proposes:

- As part of a policy to make the field more inclusive of other children who have additional needs — but not disabilities/impairments — to replace the SEN terminology and give a statutory footing to the concept of Additional Learning Needs (AN);

- To replace SEN statements with new integrated Individual Development Plans (IDP);
- For those with severe and/or complex needs, extend multi-agency arrangements from birth to twenty-five;
- Set out the duties to be imposed on relevant bodies such as local authorities and the National Health Service (NHS);
- Shift the emphasis away from dealing with disputes and complaints from parents/ carers, towards a strategy of prevention and early resolution of concerns and disagreements;
- Impose a duty on the Welsh Ministers to issue a code of practice in relation to the new statutory framework for AN;
- Impose a duty on relevant bodies to collaborate in respect of AN provision.

(Welsh Assembly Government, 2012, p. 4)

According to Ware (2013), the scale and diversity of the legislative changes currently underway in Wales, combined with the bilingual nature of Wales and a demographic that is quite distinct from England,[11] makes it difficult to predict their overall effects on special needs education. There are, none-the-less, some concerns over the impact of certain of these changes including the cost of the Welsh Language/Welsh Medium Education Strategy and the problem of distinguishing whether initial difficulties with the curriculum are as a consequence of being educated through a second language or of learning difficulties. Differences between Welsh Medium (W-M) and English Medium (E-M) schools have also been reported. For example, the former are reported to have: less diverse populations than E-M schools; a lower proportion of children with statements (2 per cent in W-M and 3 per cent in E-M) and significantly fewer children having free-school meals[12] (Ware, 2013).

Northern Ireland

As described in Section 1, as a result of direct rule, the philosophy underpinning educational special needs legislation and guidance in Northern Ireland has historically closely mirrored developments in England. Indeed, the present framework, as implemented by the Education Order (Northern Ireland) 1984, was effectively outlined by the Warnock Report (DES, 1978). However, shortly after devolved powers were restored to a Northern Ireland Assembly (October, 2009), the new Northern Ireland Minister of Education initiated a process of public consultation on the policy text entitled: *Every School a Good School: The Way Forward for Special Needs Education and Inclusion in Northern Ireland*[13] (DENI, 2009). Uniquely in the history of Northern Irish educational policy-making, this policy text was initially conceived under direct rule from the English Parliament at

Westminster (April, 2006), and consulted upon at a time when devolved powers had been restored to a Northern Ireland Assembly.

The consultation document presented an extremely comprehensive set of 26 policy proposals (see Table 3), with the stated intention of operationalizing ... 'a new, stronger, more comprehensive, more robust, inclusive framework for meeting a wide diversity of educational need, based on the broader inclusive concept of additional educational needs' (DENI, 2008, p. 3).

Whilst the reasons for the fundamental review were overwhelmingly framed in instrumental terms, not dissimilar to some of those related to English and Welsh proposed reforms (e.g. the bureaucracy of the current SEN framework, inconsistencies and delays in assessment and provision, the steeply rising cost of the provision for SEN, the year on year increase

Table 3. Outline of Main Proposals in the DENI Fundamental Review of SEN and Inclusion.

1. Inclusion – Additional Educational Needs (AEN) Model
2. Inclusion – role of special schools
3. Early identification and intervention framework
4. Early identification and intervention – personal learning plans
5. Pre-school settings – PEAGs settings within revised SEN framework
6. Pre-school settings – pupil support services in PEAGs settings
7. Pre-school settings – early identification officers
8. Training and development – initial teacher education
9. Training and development – INSET/capacity building
10. SENCo – name change to learning support co-ordinator
11. Learning support co-ordinator – career pathway
12. The learning support co-ordinator – diagnostic testing
13. Stages of the SEN framework
14. Co-ordinated support plans (CSPs)
15. Co-ordinated support plans – complex and multiple needs criteria
16. Co-ordinated support plans – annual reviews of CSPs
17. Transition points – Access to transitions support services
18. Developing effective partnerships – between education and health and social care
19. Multi-disciplinary groups (MGs)
20. Effective partnerships with parents and carers
21. Effective partnerships with children and young people
22. Resolution and appeals mechanism – dispute avoidance and resolution services (DARS)
23. Resolution and appeals mechanism – special educational needs and disability tribunal
24. Funding – local management of schools
25. Introduction of CSPs – transitional arrangements
26. Introduction of CSPs – transitional arrangements

in the number of children issued with statements and the need for clear accountability on resource utilization[14]), there were some value-driven proposals that provided much encouragement to Northern Irish practitioners and researchers who had long advocated for a genuine 're-visioning' of the SEN task. For example, on the occasion of the introduction of the Code of Practice in Northern Ireland, some 25 years earlier, just such a re-visioning had been recommended by Dyson and Millward (1998) as part of their DENI commissioned research to baseline the introduction of the SEN Code of Practice. At that time, Dyson and his team intimated that policy and practice in many N. Irish schools was based on a model which was not fully aligned with the model implied by the Code. Discerning practitioners read this comment as suggesting that extant practice was underpinned by a deficit model of SEN including: a narrow conception of SEN (relating principally to difficulties in literacy and numeracy); a tendency to respond to those difficulties outside the mainstream class (in withdrawal groups or 'bottom' sets) and undeveloped ideas of how children identified with a wide range of SEN could be supported throughout the school.

The Fundamental Review spoke to the aim of setting in place a dynamic programme of transformation of Special Needs Education in Northern Ireland. However, seven years further on, the final text has yet to see the light of day. On the other hand, during April 2012, the Minister of Education presented his recommendations, or 'directions for travel,' to the Northern Ireland Education Committee (DENI, 2012a). From this it appears that only 4 of the original 26 policy targets will form part of the new framework[15]; that is, Personal Learning Plans will replace individualized learning plans; SENCos will be called Learning Support Coordinators (LSCs); there will be a 3 phase SEN framework instead of 5, and some Statements will be set out in the form of a Co-ordinated Support Plan or CSP (DENI, 2012b).

For a number of years, one of the co-authors of this chapter has undertaken research designed to illuminate the way in which Special Needs Education policy is made and implemented in Northern Ireland (see, e.g. Barr & Smith, 2009; Smith & Barr, 2008). Drawing mostly upon critical policy analysis (see, e.g. Ball, 1994, 2003, 2008; Ozga, 2000), he has undertaken a probing case study of the text and trajectory of the Fundamental Review. While his analysis tells a fascinating story of Special Needs Education in Northern Ireland (Smith, 2013), his conclusions are extremely disappointing from the perspective of progressing an inclusive special needs education that supports and welcomes diversity amongst all learners.

He persuasively demonstrates that very little of a fundamental or transformatory nature has actually occurred as a consequence of this protracted policy cycle; apart from the strengthening and formalising of procedures chiefly as a means of regulating the contents around identification and resource allocation. The transformative nature of these proposals was initially breached below the waterline by some extremely confusing and contradictory messages related to the key concepts of 'additional educational needs', 'inclusion' and 'barriers to learning'. Then, during policy discussions, further erosion occurred as these incoherent messages were variously interpreted and misinterpreted by competing interests. For example, from the perspective of inclusive education understood in terms of access, equity and quality education for all, the 'barriers to learning' concept refers specifically to features of the school and classroom context that discriminate and exclude. However, this was clearly not what the concept meant within this policy text. With its frequent use of language that referred to 'children with barriers to learning' and 'children's difficulties', little if any progress appeared to have been made in moving away from conceptualizing educational difficulties in terms of individual pathologies. The maintenance of a highly individualized needs-orientated view of resourcing within these proposals was the logical outcome of the highly individualistic gaze adopted. The vision of inclusion has retained some very traditional approaches towards special needs education, and for this reason, reinforces some less enlightening views of children who experienced difficulties or disabilities (see also, Armstrong, Armstrong, & Spandagou, 2011).

Finally, Smith (2013) drew attention to some interesting discursive continuities with New Labour policy on inclusive education. Whilst these continuities tallied with English SEN discourse at the time of its inception, it was their implications for the trajectory of inclusive education in Northern Ireland that fuelled concern. Here, the author was particularly anxious not to leave unchallenged the way in which a human capital notion of economic development might destabilize the development of a more local and relevant model of inclusion. Embracing as it does the moral and ontological primacy of the person over claims of social collectivity, post-welfarist policy developments in England provide an inappropriate worldview for advancing the sorts of transformations in human relationships required for a society emerging from 30 years of violent ethnopolitical conflict. As Bottery (2000) starkly remarked, the first part of the Third-Way agenda involved accepting the reality of the market, whilst the second part meant devising policies that 'brought the losers' along' (Bottery, 2000, p. 33).

SECTION 3: SELECTED CONTEMPORARY ISSUES AND CHALLENGES FOR INCLUSIVE TEACHER EDUCATION

As contemporary societies become more heterogeneous, and, as inclusive education reforms gain currency across the world, educational systems are being challenged to address some very fundamental questions related to the accommodation of difference. In tandem with the demographic developments described in Section 1, there has been a growing recognition across the United Kingdom that the field of special needs education requires to change in response to 21st century concerns about the problems of access to, and equity in, education for all children. For example, in 2006, a House of Commons Report into Special Educational Needs in England suggested that the Warnock framework for supporting pupils identified as having special educational needs was based on an outdated model of society and was now 'not fit for purpose' (House of Commons Education and Skills Committee [HCESC], 2006, p. 12). It recommended a thoroughgoing examination of provision for special educational needs (Warnock, Norwich, & Terzi, 2010). In 2009, the Lamb Inquiry on Special Educational Needs and Parental Confidence in England reported that securing appropriate educational support could be a battle for some families. Furthermore, whilst almost all students (98—99 per cent) were now educated in mainstream schools, and many were indeed well supported and made good progress, too many others had a far less positive experience (Department for Children, Schools and Families [DCFS], 2009). As Kilpatrick and Hunter noted, albeit with reference to the situation in Northern Ireland, a great deal remained to be done before school systems could be said to be ... *inclusive* (cited in Donnelly, McKeown, & Osborne, 2006).

While subsequent legislative changes have indeed been considerable, our analysis in Section 2 leaves us rather circumspect about the potential of a number of these policy innovations to encourage successful inclusive practices and developments on the ground. The way in which inclusive values work out in practice is extremely complex, messy and problematic (Dyson, 2005). They need to be seen as embedded within wider national social, economic and political processes and the prevailing meaning structures, values and range of pedagogies and curricula within these wider political contexts (Clark, Dyson, Millward, & Skidmore, 1997). We intimated, for example, that messy, contradictory, confused and unclear policy discourses, as well as the effects of competing reforms (especially those geared towards school's performance and measurable outcomes), left the practice of inclusion open to interpretation and distortion (see also, Armstrong et al., 2011). Slee (2011) argued that policy discourses should always be interrogated in order to determine whether they connoted a signing on to an agenda for cultural work, or liberal assimilation. His warning to never underestimate the resilience of the traditional forms of thinking to appropriate new turf appeared to us to be compellingly prescient. As Thomas (2013) suggested: 'inclusion has to be conceived with many surfaces, disability certainly, and social justice no less, but now other facets of life at school: community, social capital, equality, and respect' (p. 474). The emphasis in relation to inclusion was now on looking to the classroom and school context for barriers to learning, and ensuring that provision for the majority of students is sufficiently flexible to accommodate students who cause concern.

Despite this, and despite the fact that special educational needs within the United Kingdom are not actually defined in law by child characteristics (see Section 2), limited concrete progress appears to have been made in moving away from deficit views and beliefs about children and young people whose school progress causes concern. Furthermore, limited movement has occurred away from a highly individualised needs orientated view of resourcing. The dominant model of SEN in policy texts seems to have remained firmly focused on viewing difference as an individual deviance, problem or pathology.

Throughout this period, a number of attitudes and practices derived from the difference as individual deviance viewpoint have remained central to the discursive consciousness of teachers, such that that they continue into the 21st century as taken-for-granted assumptions underpinning practice. For example, when learning differences are viewed as having arisen from pupil shortcomings, then this all too easily translates into an acceptance that such children require provision that is 'different from' or 'additional to' that which is ordinarily available in classrooms (Florian, 2009). Despite the scarce empirical evidence to substantiate a specific pedagogical distinction for pupils labelled as having SEN, the latter continue to be seen by mainstream teachers as requiring to be dealt with by experts; in other words, seen to be 'someone else's problem' (Avramidis, Bayliss, & Burden, 2002). This 'ideology of expertism' serves to relieve mainstream schools of the pressure to respond to diverse students and consequently perpetuates and even strengthens a divisive ideology that impinges upon efforts to create more inclusive schooling environments (Troyna & Vincent, 1996, p. 385). The research programme undertaken in primary and secondary settings by Avramidis et al. (2002), identified a culture where teachers, pressurized by the 'standards agenda', felt that they were only responsible for the learning outcomes of 80 per cent of the children in their classes, the remaining 20 per cent being the responsibility of the SEN teacher. Finally, there is evidence that dominant modes of assessment associated with deficit models of SEN are discriminatory to a diverse range of groups and neglectful of areas such as ethnicity, gender and class (e.g. Fernando, 2010). As Thomas (2013) noted, statistics reveal that it is minority populations of various kinds who were (and still are) identified as having learning or behaviour difficulties, and who were (and still are) disproportionately selected for special provision (e.g. Tomlinson, 1982).

Today, across the United Kingdom, there is a conflict between the protection offered by the individual needs approach to meeting special educational needs as operationalized by Statements or CSPs and the resources that accompany them, and contemporary views of good practice in educating all students. For example, research on teaching assistants (TAs) (Farrell, Balshaw, & Polat, 1999) urges a shift away from the one-to-one allocation of TAs to individual pupils with Statements in favour of model whereby TAs work alongside teachers in support of learning for all pupils. But problems occur when Statements specify resource allocations (such as a fixed number of hours of adult support) that are at odds with good practice. Ironically, the manner by which Statements specify resources for children may not support their learning. That there is a conflict between contemporary knowledge of good practice and Statements, a tool developed twenty years ago when a different view of provision prevailed is not surprising. Statements were designed to ensure that resources followed children. Today's challenge is to separate the protection offered by the Statement from the means by which that protection is offered.

Teacher Education for Inclusion

The effective preparation of teachers through Initial Teacher Education (ITE) and the further development of teachers through career long professional development (CLPL) are two crucial (and challenging) spaces through which education can try to meet the needs of diverse groups of learners (Beck, 2014). Calls for reform in teacher education (TE) are increasingly made in response to dissatisfaction with student performance and poor outcomes, particularly relating to the 'long-tail of underachievement' of specific groups such as students from ethnic majorities, those living in poverty, or those who may have additional needs associated with disability or language.

In 1988 separate training of special education teachers at pre-service level was ended, in part, because such separate training had created a group of teachers who were themselves segregated and were seen as a barrier to inclusion. Currently, most initial teacher education modules, courses or inputs on additional needs, multicultural education, and 'inclusion', are offered as optional extras, available to only some students. Even in cases where these options are required, courses tend to focus on the characteristics of particular kinds of learners, how they should be identified and specialist teaching strategies; that is, a Grey's Anatomy approach to special education where they are 'instructed in the pathology of human differences and defects' (Slee, 2011, p. 155). As Florian (2013) noted, the main problem here is that the content knowledge of such courses is often not well integrated into the broader curriculum and pedagogical practices of mainstream classroom settings. On courses where input on inclusion is 'infused' across all course elements, the coverage is limited, and tends to reinforce the view that the education of students identified as having difficulties in learning is the primary responsibility of specialists rather than class teachers with the support of specialists (Florian & Pantic, 2013). Smith (2010) found that a popular approach to infusion within subject disciplines was the intuitively appealing, but fundamentally deterministic and limiting approach, focused on matching teaching to the apparent deficit characteristics or attributes of categorized groups of learners. Not only this, despite the research evidence demonstrating that the judgements teachers make about students' learning ability limited what was possible for students to achieve (see, e.g. Ball, 1981; Boaler, William, & Brown, 2000; Hart, Dixon, Drummond, & McIntyre, 2004), he found that ability grouping and ability labelling held very high associations amongst student teachers in Northern Ireland at the end of their course as a strategy for meeting special educational needs.

However, over the past few years, the authors of this chapter have witnessed how innovative inclusive teacher education can help prepare teachers to respond to diversity without relying on different kind of programmes, and transform deficit thinking about ability and disability. Limitations of space here permit only a cursory mention of four very innovative UK Research and Development Projects.

Scotland's Inclusive Practice Project (IPP; 2006–2011)
The IPP was funded by the Scottish Government and aimed at preparing primary and secondary teachers to enter a profession in which they took

responsibility for the learning and achievement of all learners (Rouse & Florian, 2012). The IPP adopted an approach to initial teacher education based on the idea that a child's capacity to learn was not fixed, but could be enhanced based on what teachers did today. The project Directors (Professors Lani Florian and Martyn Rouse, then at the University of Aberdeen, School of Education) began with the view that there was a need to change current thinking about inclusive education as providing something 'additional to' or 'different from' that which was 'otherwise available' to others of similar age in mainstream schools (Rouse & Florian, 2012). A key aspect of this approach was to think of inclusive teaching as making a range of opportunities available to everyone in the classroom so that all children could participate in learning activities. In this way, individual needs could be catered for but individual pupils were not singled out as being 'less able' or different. This position was based on the view that the central task in preparing new teachers was not to defend the need to accommodate learner differences, but to challenge assumptions about the adequacy of what was 'otherwise available' to the majority of learners. The follow up study of programme graduates confirmed that the approach was helpful to newly qualified teachers. Programme graduates reported that the course provided a framework for supporting the development of inclusive practice in the classroom. Observations of their practice supported this claim (see also Florian, 2012; Florian, 2013; Florian & Black-Hawkins, 2011; Florian & Linklater, 2010; Rouse & Florian, 2012).

The National Framework for Inclusion (Scotland)
The Scottish Government (2009) recognized that inclusive education was of high priority and that teachers needed to be well prepared and appropriately supported throughout their careers if they were to succeed in developing and sustaining inclusive practices. With the support of the Scottish Government (2009), the Scottish Teacher Education Committee (STEC) set up a working group in order to develop a National Framework for Inclusion. This group consisted of course Directors and inclusion specialists representing all seven universities involved in initial teacher education. Their remit was to develop a framework which would identify what was to be expected of student teachers and of qualified teachers at whatever stage of their careers, that is values and beliefs; professional knowledge and understanding; and skills and abilities. The STEC Framework highlights the principles of inclusive practice, social justice, inclusion, and learning and teaching, in the context of current policy and legislation. It adopts a broad definition of inclusion covering additional support needs, poverty,

culture and language, and is informed by relevant aspects of UK Government's new Equality Bill (Government Equalities Office, 2010). It attempts to promote inclusion as being the responsibility of all teachers, in all schools, and builds upon existing innovative practice within the universities of Scotland, to provide a secure basis for planning courses in teacher education and professional learning.

The Contribution of Planned Activities in One-Year Postgraduate Teaching Programmes (PGCE) in England
During 2007–2008, evaluative research was carried out by the PGCE Tutor Team at Exeter University (Lawson & Nash, 2010) on the idea of requiring student teachers, during one of their Teaching Practices (TPs), to undertake a piece of assessment and teaching with one pupil whose name was on the school's SEN register, or had a Statement of SEN. As reported by Lawson and Nash (2010), this intensive and extensive evaluation led to further developments and improvements which, in turn, led to the type of task becoming promoted by the Training Development Agency for Schools (TDA) for use across all English PGCE Programmes (see, Training and Development Agency for Schools, 2009a, 2009b). The specific aims of the task were to help student teachers: develop their practical knowledge, skills and positive attitudes by teaching a pupil identified as having learning difficulties; extend their knowledge and understanding of this aspect of inclusive teaching and learning; and learn to cooperate and relate effectively with other staff in school having responsibilities related to SEN, for example the Special Educational Needs Co-ordinator or SENCo.

Recently, Lawson, Nash, and Norwich (2013) disseminated the results of their most recent research into the contribution of planned activities in PGCE programs and what student teachers learned about teaching pupils with special educational needs/disabilities in their school-based placements. Three kinds of school-based approaches were compared:

1. A personalized teaching task involving student teachers working with a pupil identified as having SEN over 6–8 hours, carried out in-class or through withdrawal;
2. An alternative non-teaching pupil-focused SEN task, for example, a classroom pupil observation around inclusion or a pupil pursuit study;
3. No specific pupil-focused SEN task other than class teaching practice.

Lawson et al. (2013) reported that, what student teachers learned about teaching pupils identified as having special educational needs was strongly interlinked with what they learned about teaching in general. A planned pupil-focused SEN task, when carried out in favourable conditions, could make a contribution to their pedagogic knowledge, especially in understanding personal learning needs. This was something that was less likely to be achieved from whole-class teaching experience. The value of the planned pupil-focused task was that it enabled student teachers to become aware of individual pupils' perspectives and learning needs that went beyond differentiation in terms of sub-groups. Paradoxically in many ways, in spending specific time focusing on a pupil, student teachers learned about the interactive nature of the teacher–learner relationship, and the importance of planning appropriate learning processes. This enabled them to understand greater pedagogic complexity beyond what could often be regarded as a 'mechanistic and piecemeal' curriculum coverage approach (Lawson et al., 2013).

The MAINSEN Project in Northern Ireland 2010–2013 (The Post-Primary PGCE in Main Subject with Special Needs Education and Inclusion)
In 2010, the Department of Education in Northern Ireland funded Queen's University Belfast (QUB) and the University of Ulster (UU) to research and develop new ways of ensuring that all student teachers approached the task of creating inclusive classroom contexts with confidence and skill (Smith, 2014). The Universities were required to collaborate in order to develop an approach to Initial Teacher Education that enabled student teachers to:

- Develop a range of practical teaching strategies with an emphasis on the development of literacy;
- Develop their assessment for learning skills, for example make an assessment of what learners do best, what they find difficult, and then plan a programme of learning and teaching to meet these needs within a whole-class situation;
- Develop their language of learning;
- Develop their understanding of the importance of pupil meta-learning; that is, pupil self-awareness and learning about learning.

The MAINSEN project was both underpinned and informed by a cluster of ideas that linked and overlapped, such as contemporary UK research on the question of whether some children required specialist teaching methods (see, e.g. Lewis & Norwich, 2005), and contemporary currents of thinking that conceptualize the individual in social terms and behaviour as socially embedded and socially meaningful. The coordinating lecturers were greatly influenced by the Scottish IPP. Indeed, the Directors of the latter very kindly acted as critical friends to the Northern Ireland Project. Consistent with the IPP approach, the MAINSEN Project set out to challenge the idea that classroom teachers did not have the necessary skills to teach pupils identified as having special educational needs. Salient educational differences were considered to be found in learners' responses to tasks and activities, rather than in the diagnostic criteria used to categorize them in order to determine eligibility for additional support – and thereby render them beyond the responsibility of the class teacher (Florian, 2010a, 2010b). The project also developed strong links with a small, international, collaborative network of teacher educators – the Inclusive International Teacher Education Research Forum (IITERF) – who are interested in addressing questions of access and equity in relation to diversity education.

The MAINSEN was both a development and also research project. Over the three-year project period, much evidence was gathered about the ability of the MAINSEN approach to engage teachers with new paradigm thinking and practice in the field of Special Needs Education (see, e.g. Bell et al., 2012; Education and Training Inspectorate [ETI], 2012; Smith, 2014).

CODA

Schools across the United Kingdom are becoming much more diverse. Throughout the four nations of the United Kingdom, the demographics of schooling are changing, for example, the growth in cultural and linguistic diversity, the growth in the number of children identified as living in disadvantaged circumstances (McKinney, Hall, Lowden, McClung, & Cameron, 2012), and the movement towards increased inclusion of children and young people with more diverse additional support needs (Florian, 2012). Across the United Kingdom, we presently live in a time of unprecedented change, and, as a result of devolution, the policy context of the United Kingdom is also changing rapidly. Of immediate relevance is the forthcoming 2014 Scottish Independence Referendum. This represents an extremely important political milestone in Scotland's history when the Scottish electorate will have the opportunity of voting 'yes' or 'no' to remaining part of the United Kingdom (The Scotsman on Sunday, 2014). As said previously, further policy developments will likely continue to mark the distinctive approach each country is adopting, and it remains to be seen whether, to what extent, and how, these policy options will affect outcomes for students identified as having special educational needs (England and Northern Ireland), additional support needs (Scotland), or additional learning needs

(Wales). However, as we move forward, it seems very clear that the fields of inclusive special needs education, and teacher education for diversity, will remain amongst the most challenging and important tasks facing education in the United Kingdom.

NOTES

1. We also draw upon an earlier chapter by Florian, Rouse, and Anderson (2011). Consequently, here, we record our deepest gratitude to Gallaudet University Press for written permission to make use of this earlier work.

2. The leaving age in England is being raised to 18 by 2015.

3. Thanks to Dr Jean Ware, University of Bangor, Wales, for this information on very recent educational developments in Wales.

4. All countries in the United Kingdom have school systems that produce very high academic attainments for some students, but, there is concern in all countries, not just Northern Ireland, about the long-tail of underachievement for the lowest performing 20 per cent (OECD, 2007) and the steep rise in the numbers of young people not in education, employment and training (NEET) (Leper, 2010).

5. The Education (Mentally Handicapped Children) (Scotland) Act (1974) (Scottish Office Education and Industry Department [SOEID], 1974).

6. The Education Order (Northern Ireland), 1987 (Department of Education for Northern Ireland [DENI], 1987).

7. However, as Norwich (2013a, p. 98) remarked 'what the Government really meant by bias towards inclusion was the previous Government's inclusive-oriented policy initiatives, rather than extensive inclusion practices and developments'.

8. The agency SNE data collection is a biennial exercise with data provided by the representatives of the agency. In all cases this data is from official Ministerial sources.

9. Amended in 2009.

10. In January 2012, there were 363,765 young people in publicly funded schools in Wales (EADSNE, 2012). This involved 193,374 in primary, 170,391 in secondary, and 3005 in special schools. The proportion of children in special schools was approximately 1 per cent.

11. Demographic differences between Wales and the rest of the United Kingdom include the following: it is a small country of 3,000,000 people representing less than 5 per cent of UK population; it has two official languages (Cymraeg/Welsh and English); it is very rural with 60 per cent of the country sparsely populated; one in three primary school children attend a school with fewer than ninety students; it has a lower average salary than any other UK region and one in five children live in poverty (Ware, 2013).

12. A commonly accepted indicator of social disadvantage.

13. Locally referred to as the 'Fundamental Review'.

14. Northern Ireland has a school population of 313,600 children and young people. There are 4600 students in 40 special schools and this comprises 1.4 per cent of the population. Special school enrolments have remained relatively static since

2003–2004. Twenty-one per cent of children and young people in mainstream schools are placed on the SEN register (3.3 per cent having statements, and 18 per cent at Code of Practice stages 1–4 (EADSNE, 2012).

15. On the other hand, as part of a new statutory Code of Practice, the Minister has recommended a number of minor amendments and revisions to the Education Committee.

REFERENCES

Anderson, R. (2003). The history of Scottish education, pre-1880. In T. G. K. Bryce & W. M. Humes (Eds.), *Scottish education* (2nd ed., pp. 215–224). Edinburg, UK: Edinburg University Press.

Armstrong, A., Armstrong, D., & Spandagou, I. (2011). *Inclusive education: International policy and practice*. London: Sage.

Avramidis, E., Bayliss, P., & Burden, R. (2002). Inclusion in action: An in-depth case study of an effective inclusive secondary school in the Southwest of England. *International Journal of Inclusive Education, 6*(2), 143–163.

Ball, S. (1981). *Beachside comprehensive. A case study of secondary schooling*. Cambridge: Cambridge University Press.

Ball, S. J. (1994). *Education reform: A critical and post-structural approach*. Buckingham, UK: Open University Press.

Ball, S. J. (2003). The teacher's soul and the terrors of performativity. *Journal of Education Policy, 18*(2), 215–228.

Ball, S. J. (2008). *The education debate*. Bristol, UK: Policy Press.

Barr, S., & Smith, R. A. L. (2009). Towards educational inclusion in a transforming society: Some lessons from community relations and special needs education in Northern Ireland. *International Journal of Inclusive Education, 13*(2), 211–230.

Beck, A. (2014, March 21). Teacher education for the changing demographics of schooling: Policy, practice and research, Towards education reform in Scotland: Implementing the Donaldson report. Presentation at the ESRC Seminar Series, University of Edinburgh, Edinburgh, UK.

Bell, D., Bradley, E., Dennison, J., Duke, S., Elliott, E., Johnston, N., … Smith, R. A. L. (2012). *Essays on inclusive pedagogy* (Vol. 1). Belfast, UK: The School of Education, Queen's University Belfast.

Bhopal, K., & Maylor, U. (2014). Educational inequalities in schools and higher education. In K. Bhopal & U. Maylor (Eds.), *Educational inequalities: Difference and diversity in schools and higher education* (pp. 48–72). London: Routledge.

Boaler, J., William, D., & Brown, M. (2000). Students' experiences of ability grouping – Disaffection, polarisation and the construction of failure. *British Educational Research Journal, 26*(5), 631–648.

Board of Education. (1944). *The 1944 Education Act*. London: HMSO.

Bottery, M. (2000). *Education, policy and ethics*. London: Continuum.

British Broadcasting Corporation. (2013, December 3). *Pisa tests: UK stagnates as Shanghai tops league table*. Retrieved from http://www.bbc.co.uk/news/education-25187997. Accessed on January 1, 2014.

Carr, W., & Hartnett, A. (1997). *Education and the struggle for democracy: The politics of educational ideas.* Buckingham, UK: Open University Press.

Clark, C., Dyson, A., Millward, A., & Skidmore, D. (1997). *New directions in special needs: Innovations in mainstream schools.* London: Cassell.

Council for the Curriculum, Examinations and Assessment. (2000). *Developing the Northern Ireland curriculum. Advice to the Northern Ireland minister of education on curriculum review.* Belfast, UK: CCEA.

de Blij, H. (2005). *Why geography matters.* New York, NY: Oxford University Press.

Department for Children, Schools and Families. (2009). *DCSF: Special educational needs in England.* Retrieved from http://www.education.gov.uk/rsgateway/DB/SFR/s000852/index.shtml. Accessed on November 27, 2010.

Department for Education and Skills. (2001). *Special Educational Needs and Disability Act.* London: Department for Education and Employment.

Department of Education and Science (DES). (1978). *Special educational needs: Report of the committee of enquiry into the education of handicapped children and young people (the Warnock report).* London: HMSO.

Department of Education and Science (DES). (1981). *Education Act.* London: HMSO.

Department of Education for Northern Ireland. (1984). *The education order (NI) 1984.* Belfast, UK: HMSO.

Department of Education for Northern Ireland. (1987). *The education order (NI) 1987.* Belfast, UK: HMSO.

Department of Education for Northern Ireland. (1998). *Code of practice on the identification and assessment of special education needs.* Bangor, UK: Department of Education NI. Retrieved from http://www.deni.gov.uk/index/7-special_educational_needs_pg/special_need-codes_of_practice_pg.htm. Accessed on November 25, 2010.

Department of Education for Northern Ireland. (2005). *The education order (NI) 2005.* Belfast, UK: HSMO.

Department of Education Northern Ireland. (2008). *Every school a good school: A policy for school improvement.* Bangor, UK: Department of Education NI.

Department of Education Northern Ireland. (2009). *Every school a good school: The way forward for special educational needs and inclusion.* Bangor, UK: Department of Education NI. Retrieved from http://www.deni.gov.uk/every_school_a_good_school__the_way_forward_for_special_educational_needs__sen__and_inclusion___8211__consultation_document__english__pdf_434kb.pdf. Accessed in November 2013.

Department of Education Northern Ireland. (2011). *Count read succeed.* Bangor, UK: Department of Education NI.

Department of Education Northern Ireland. (2012a). *Summary report of responses to the consultation on every school a good school: The way forward for special educational needs and inclusion and the associated equality impact assessment.* Bangor, UK: Department of Education NI. Retrieved from http://www.deni.gov.uk/every_school_a_good_school__the_way_forward_for_special_educational_needs__sen__and_inclusion___8211__consultation_document__english__pdf_434kb.pdf. Accessed in November 2013.

Department of Education Northern Ireland. (2012b). *Review of SEN and inclusion: Minister's presentation to the committee for education.* Retrieved from http://www.deni.gov.uk/every_school_a_good_school__the_way_forward_for_special_educational_needs__sen__and_inclusion___8211__consultation_document__english__pdf_434kb.pdf. Accessed in November 2013.

DFE. (2011). *Support and aspiration: A new approach to special educational needs and disability — Consultation.* Green Paper. London: HMSO.

DFE. (2012). *Support and aspiration: A new approach to special educational needs and disability — Progress and next steps.* London: HMSO.

DFE. (2013). *Children and families bill.* London: HMSO.

Donnelly, C., McKeown, P., & Osborne, B. (Eds.). (2006). *Devolution and pluralism in education in Northern Ireland.* Manchester, UK: Manchester University Press.

Dyson, A. (2005). Philosophy, politics, and economics? The story of inclusive education in England. In D. Mitchell (Ed.), *Contextualizing inclusive education: Evaluating old and new international perspectives* (pp. 63–88). London: Routledge.

Dyson, A., & Millward, A. (1998). *The research report series: Practice in mainstream schools for children with special educational needs.* Department of Education, University of Newcastle upon Tyne, Special Needs Research Centre, Newcastle, UK.

Education and Training Inspectorate. (2012). *An evaluation of the joint post-primary 'post graduate certificate in education: Main subject with special education and inclusion (PGCE with SEN and Inclusion)' by Queen's University Belfast and University of Ulster 2011–2012.* Bangor, UK: Education and Training Inspectorate.

European Agency for Development in Special Needs Education. (2012). *Special needs education country data.* Brussels, Belgium: European Agency for Development in Special Needs Education.

Farrell, P., Balshaw, M., & Polat, F. (1999). *The management, role and training of learning support assistants.* London: DfEE Publications. Research Brief No. 166.

Fernando, S. (2010). *Mental health, race and culture* (3rd ed.). Basingstoke, UK: Palgrave.

Florian, L. (2009). Preparing teachers to work in 'schools for all' [Editorial]. *Teaching and Teacher Education, 25*(4), 533–534.

Florian, L. (2010a). Special education in an era of inclusion: The end of special education or a new beginning? *Psychology of Education Review, 34*(2), 22–30.

Florian, L. (2010b). The concept of inclusive pedagogy. In F. Hallett & G. Hallett (Eds.), *Transforming the role of the SENCO* (pp. 61–72). Buckingham, UK: Open University Press.

Florian, L. (2012). Preparing teachers to work in diverse classrooms: Key lessons for the professional development of teacher educators from Scotland's Inclusive Practice Project. *Journal of Teacher Education, 63*(4), 275–285. doi:10.1177/0022487112447112

Florian, L. (2013). Preparing teachers to work with everybody: A curricular approach to the reform of teacher education. *FORUM: For promoting 31-19 comprehensive education, 55*(1), 95–102.

Florian, L., & Black-Hawkins, K. (2011). Exploring inclusive pedagogy. *British Educational Research Journal, 37*(5), 813–828. doi:10.1080/01411926.2010.501096

Florian, L., & Linklater, H. (2010). Preparing teachers for inclusive education: Using inclusive pedagogy to enhance teaching and learning for all. *Cambridge Journal of Education, 40*(4), 369–386. doi:10.1080/0305764X.2010.526588

Florian, L., & Pantic, N. (2013). *Learning to teach: Part 2: Exploring the distinctive contribution of higher education to teacher education.* York, UK: The Higher Education Academy.

Florian, L., Rouse, M., & Anderson, J. (2011). Education for all in the countries of the United Kingdom. In K. Mazurek & M. Winzer (Eds.), *Special education in an international perspective* (pp. 67–86). Washington, DC: Gallaudet University Press.

Frederickson, N., & Cline, T. (2009). *Special educational needs, inclusion and diversity* (2nd ed.). Maidenhead, UK: McGraw-Hill.

Friswell, J., & Petersen, L. (2013). *The NASEN guide to SEN.* Tamworth, UK: NASEN.

Gewirtz, S. (2002). *The managerial school: Post-welfarism and social justice in education.* London: Routledge.

Gillborn, D., & Youdell, D. (2000). *Rationing education: Policy, practice, reform, and equity.* Buckingham, UK: Open University Press.

Government Equalities Office. (2010). *Equality Act.* Retrieved from http://www.equalities.gov. uk/equality_bill.aspxe. Accessed on November 27, 2010.

Hart, S., Dixon, A., Drummond, M. J., & McIntyre, D. (2004). *Learning without limits.* Maidenhead, UK: Open University Press.

Hodkinson, A., & Vickerman, P. (2009). *Key issues in special educational needs and inclusion.* London: Sage.

Home Office. (2007). *Life in the United Kingdom: A journey to citizenship.* Norwich, UK: TSO.

House of Commons Education and Skills Committee. (2006). *Special educational needs: Third report of session 2005–2006.* London: Stationery Office.

Lawson, H., & Nash, T. (2010). SENCOs: A partnership role in initial teacher education? In F. Hallett & G. Hallett (Eds.), *Transforming the role of the SENCO: Achieving the national award for SEN coordination* (pp. 50–61). Maidenhead, UK: Open University Press, McGraw-Hill Education.

Lawson, H., Nash, T., & Norwich, B. (2013). Research dissemination: What trainees learn about teaching pupils with special educational needs/disabilities in their school based work: The contribution of planned activities in PGCE programmes. Exeter, UK: Graduate School of Education, University of Exeter.

Learning and Teaching Scotland. (n.d.). *What is curriculum for excellence?* Retrieved from http://www.ltscotland.org.uk/understandingthecurriculum/whatiscurriculumforexcellence/index.asp. Accessed on June 1, 2014.

Lederach, J. P. (1995). *Preparing for peace: Conflict transformation across cultures.* Syracuse, NY: Syracuse University Press.

Lederach, J. P. (1997). *Building peace: Sustainable reconciliation in divided societies.* Washington, DC: US Institute of Peace.

Leitch, R., & Kilpatrick, R. (1999). *Inside the gates: Schools and the troubles.* Belfast, UK: Save the Children.

Leper, J. (2010). *Rising numbers of NEET young people a key issue for coalition government.* Retrieved from http://www.cypnow.co.uk/news/ByDiscipline/Youth-Work/100 3023/Risingnumbers-Neet-young-people-key-issue-coalition-government. Accessed on December 1, 2010.

Lewis, A., & Norwich, B. (Eds.). (2005). *Special teaching for special children? Pedagogies for inclusion.* Maidenhead, UK: Open University Press.

McKinney, S., Hall, S., Lowden, K., McClung, M., & Cameron, L. (2012). The relationship between poverty and deprivation, educational attainment and positive school leaver destinations in Glasgow secondary schools. *Scottish Educational Review, 44*, 33–45.

McLaughlin, M., & Rouse, M. (2000). *Special education and school reform in Britain and the United States.* London: Routledge.

Norwich, B. (2002). *LEA inclusion trends in England 1997–2001: Statistics on special school placements and pupils with statements in special schools.* Bristol, UK: CSIE.

Norwich, B. (2013a). *Addressing tensions and dilemmas in inclusive education: Living with uncertainty.* London: Routledge.

Norwich, B. (2013b, November 15). Changing legislation and its radical effects on inclusive and special education in England. Presentation at the Inclusive Education Day conference, Faculty of Education, University of Cambridge.

O'Donnell, L. (2013, November 7). Parties should renew vows of the Belfast agreement. Belfast Telegraph Newspapers, Belfast, UK.

Office for National Statistics. (2012). *Population estimates.* Retrieved from http://www.ons. gov.uk/ons/taxonomy/index.html?nscl=Population+Estimates. Accessed on December 15, 2013.

Ofsted. (2010). *The special educational needs and disability review.* London: Ofsted.

Organization for Economic Cooperation and Development. (2007). *Quality and equity of schooling in Scotland.* Paris, France: OECD.

Ozga, J. (2000). *Policy research in educational settings: Contested terrain.* Buckingham, UK: Open University Press.

Qualifications and Curriculum Authority. (1999). *The national curriculum for England.* London: QCA.

Riddell, S., Weedon, E., & Harris, N. (2012). Special and additional support needs – Current dilemmas and solutions. In L. Peer & G. Reid (Eds.), *Special educational needs: A guide for inclusive practice* (pp. 99–115). London: Sage.

Rouse, M., & Florian, L. (2012). *Inclusive practice project: Final report.* Aberdeen, UK: University of Aberdeen School of Education.

Scottish Executive. (2005). *Supporting children's learning: Code of practice.* Edinburgh, UK: HMSO.

Scottish Executive Education Department. (2004a). *Education (Additional Support for Learning) (Scotland) Act 2004.* Edinburgh, UK: SEED.

Scottish Executive Education Department. (2004b). *Summary handout on the Additional Support for Learning Act.* Edinburgh, UK: Scottish Executive Education Department.

Scottish Government. (2005). *Supporting children's learning code of practice.* Retrieved from http://www.scotland.gov.uk/Publications/2005/08/15105817/58273

Scottish Government. (2009). *Statistical bulletin education series: Pupils in Scotland.* Retrieved from www.scotland.gov.uk/Publications/2009/11/05112711. Accessed on November 15, 2013.

Scottish Government. (2010). *Implementing getting it right for every child: Summary for practitioners.* Retrieved from www.scotland.gov.uk/Resources/Doc/1141/0100658. Accessed on November 15, 2013.

Scottish Office Education and Industry Department. (1974). *The Education (Mentally Handicapped Children) (Scotland) Act (1974).* Edinburgh, UK: SOEID.

Scottish Office Education and Industry Department. (1980). *The Education (Scotland) Act.* Edinburgh, UK: SOEID.

Scottish Qualifications Authority. (March 2006). *National qualifications: A quick guide.* Retrieved from http://www.sqa.org.uk/files_ccc/nq_quick_guide.pdf. Accessed on November 27, 2010.

Slee, R. (2011). *Their irregular school: Exclusion, schooling and inclusive education.* London: Routledge.

Smith, R. A. L. (2010). *Student teachers' understanding of special needs education after one year of initial teacher education.* Unpublished report. School of Education, Queen's University, Belfast, UK.

Smith, R. A. L. (2013, November 15). Critical reflections on policy-making for inclusive and special needs education in a transitional society. Presentation at the Inclusive Education Day conference, Faculty of Education, University of Cambridge, Cambridge, UK.

Smith, R. A. L. (2014). The post-primary PGCE in main subject with special needs education and inclusion (MAINSEN). Final report to the Department of Education Northern Ireland. Queen's University Belfast, Belfast, UK.

Smith, R. A. L., & Barr, S. (2008). Towards educational inclusion in a contested society: From critical reflection to cultural action. *International Journal of Inclusive Education, 12*(4), 401–422.

Teachernet. (n.d.). *Faith schools*. Retrieved from http://www.teachernet.gov.uk/wholeschool/ faithschools. Accessed on November 23, 2010.

The Scotsman on Sunday. (2014). New polls show shift to yes. The Scotsman on Sunday, The Scotsman Publications Ltd., Edinburgh, UK.

Thomas, G. (2013). A review of thinking and research about inclusive education policy, with suggestions for a new kind of inclusive thinking. *British Educational Research Journal, 39*(3), 473–490.

Tomlinson, S. (1982). *The sociology of special education.* London: Routledge and Kegan Paul.

Training and Development Agency for Schools. (2009a). *Special educational needs and disabilities training toolkit for 1 year ITT programmes.* London: TDA.

Training and Development Agency for Schools. (2009b). *Secondary undergraduate courses: A training resource for initial teacher training providers' user guide.* London: TDA.

Troyna, B., & Vincent, C. (1996). The 'ideology of expertism': The framing of special education and racial equality policies in the local state. In C. Christensen & F. Rizvi (Eds.), *Disability and dilemmas of education and justice* (pp. 79–92). Buckingham, UK: Open University Press.

UNESCO. (1994, June 7–10). The Salamanca Statement and framework for action. Presented at the World conference on Special Educational Needs Education: Access and quality, Salamanca, Spain.

UNESCO. (2000). The Dakar framework for action. Education for all: Meeting our collective commitments. Paris, France: UNESCO.

Vaughn, M. (2002). *Milestones on the road to inclusion 1970–2002.* Bristol, UK: University of West of England. Retrieved from http://inclusion.uwe.ac.uk/inclusionweek/articles/ milestones.htm. Accessed on November 22, 2013.

Ware, J. (2013, November 15). The context for special/inclusive education in Wales. Presentation at the Inclusive Education Day conference, Faculty of Education, University of Cambridge, Cambridge, UK.

Warnock, M., Norwich, B., & Terzi, L. (2010). *Special educational needs: A new look.* London: Continuum.

Welsh Assembly Government. (2009). *Pupils with statements of special educational needs government.* Retrieved from http://wales.gov.uk/docs/statistics/2009/090617sdr932009en. pdf. Accessed on November 25, 2013.

Welsh Assembly Government. (2010). *Education and skills.* Retrieved from http://wales.gov. uk/topics/educationandskills/?langen. Accessed on November 20, 2013.

Welsh Assembly Government. (2012). *Forward in partnership for children and young people with additional needs. Proposals for reform of the legislative framework for special educational needs.* Cardiff, UK: Author. Retrieved from http. //wales.gov.uk/topics. Accessed on December 25, 2013.

Wrigley, T. (2005). Misunderstanding school improvement. *Improving Schools, 3*(1), 23–32.

SPECIAL EDUCATION TODAY IN SPAIN

Shaila Rao, Cristina M. Cardona and Esther Chiner

ABSTRACT

The focus of special education around the globe may be to provide specialized instruction to meet unique needs of children to help them achieve their full potential. However, each country around the globe may also have its own unique issues, barriers, legal frames, policies, and practices, as well as a history of its origin and evolution of policies and practices that govern special education in that country. This chapter describes how special education in Spain originated and evolved to its current state. It includes the following chapter sections: origins of special education in Spain; legislative acts; prevalence and incidence of various recognized disability areas; an overview of Spain's education system including special needs education; current assessment and intervention practices; teacher education practices; family involvement considerations; and future challenges to special education.

INTRODUCTION

The Government of Spain was a leader in organizing a conference on inclusion in Salamanca, Spain in 1994. The conference in cooperation with

Special Education International Perspectives: Practices Across the Globe
Advances in Special Education, Volume 28, 147–180
ISSN: 0270-4013/doi:10.1108/S0270-401320140000028012

the United Nations Educational, Scientific, and Cultural Organization (UNESCO) was represented by 300 participants, representing 92 governments and 25 international organizations. During the conference, the Salamanca Statement or the Salamanca Statement on Principles, Policy, and Practice in Special Needs Education and Framework for Action (UNESCO, 1994) was adopted. The major tenet of the document is an equitable education for *all and a worldwide consensus on future directions for special needs education*. This conference was an impetus for Spain to continue its leadership in inclusive education. Spain's leadership was recognized by the International Peto Institute in their the statistics published after the 1995 conference of UNESCO in France which showed that Spain was one of the leading European countries in terms of integrated education (see Deak, 1999). The inclusive education movement in Spain had its roots during the decade 1975−1985 via the work of the National Institute of Special Education. This institute had as one of its major tenets the educational integration of students with special education needs and improvement of the rights for people with disabilities. In a national overview document about Spain's special education practices, the European Agency for Development in Special Education (EADSP) stated that the promotion of inclusive education practices was enhanced by the Spanish constitution which recognizes the right to education as one of the essential rights that public powers must guarantee to every citizen (EADSP, 2009a). This was quite a compliment because the EADSP is an independent and self-governing organization established by Ministries of Education of its 28 member countries (Spain is a member) to act as their platform for collaboration in the field of special needs education. The EADSP overview further states that the Spanish education system, set up in accordance with the values of the Constitution, is inspired by three main principles:

a) Quality education for all students, regardless of their condition and circumstances. b) Equity that guarantees equal opportunities, educational inclusion and non-discrimination and that acts as a compensating factor for the personal cultural, economic and social inequalities, with special emphasis on those derived from disabilities. c) The transmission and application of values that favor personal liberty, responsibility, democratic citizenship, solidarity, tolerance, equality, respect and justice and that also help to overcome any type of discrimination. (https://www.europea-agency.org/country-information/spain)

The above perspective provides an introduction to this chapter which is a description of special education in Spain today. This chapter will provide readers with detailed information related to the following topics: an insight into the origins of special education in Spain; a comprehensive perspective on the development of special education in Spain; data on the prevalence of students with special educational needs; impactful trends in educational legislation and litigation; parameters related to teacher education and special education training; prevailing educational interventions and policy, standards, and research related to educational interventions; insightful information about working with families who have children with special education needs; and a synopsis concerned with the future challenges that remain in the contemporary scene of special education in Spain.

ORIGIN OF SPECIAL EDUCATION IN SPAIN

The earliest origin of special education in Spain occurred during the middle ages because of the influence of Christianity in the western countries. During this period, Christianity affected all spheres of life and had an impactful influence on society that lead to an important change in the practices carried out with people with disabilities. Christianity rejected the infanticide of people with disabilities and adopted an attitude of understanding and care toward these people. This attitude prevented children with disabilities from being eliminated but, at the same time it resulted in an increase of people with disabilities being abandoned. To remedy the increase in the abandonment of people with disabilities, society across Europe built asylums and shelter to house these people. For instance, in Spain, Pedro IV of Aragón, created in Aragón, Valencia and later in Navarra, under the name of *Pare d'Orfans*, the first institution to shelter orphan children after taking over the guardianship and education of these children (Vicente & De Vicente, 2006). However, as time went by, the caring and humanistic attitudes of politicians and the general population changed into more radical positions in which people with intellectual or mental illness were persecuted as they were considered to be possessed and condemned to be burnt. This attitude and practice remained throughout the Inquisition period which was established in Spain during the 15th century.

Hope spring a new for people with disabilities with the start of the Renaissance period. The Renaissance led a new way of understanding of science and human development and behavior based on contributions and important changes in scientific and medical conceptions. For instance, human behavior was not explained based on under demonic premises. Instead, the explanation of human behavior was based on nature and the physical and biological processes of the body (Illán & Arnáiz, 1996). Positively, during this time, some ecclesiastical institutions still took care of poor people, orphans, indigents, and people with mental illness and intellectual impairment. Unfortunately, the religious wars that took place at that time undermined the power of the Church which consequently led to the abandoning of many of these institutions (Vicente & De Vicente, 2006). Interestingly, there were some private initiatives from prominent people of that period who dedicated their lives and fortune to create hospitals and shelters for socially disadvantaged people, such as Doña Teresa Enríquez, Santo Tomás de Villanueva, and Miguel de Giginta. Fray Gelabert Jofré deserves a special mention because he created a hospice for people with mental illness in Valencia, which is considered to be the first psychiatric hospital in Spain.

The Renaissance in Europe became a fertile environment for people with humanist's goals and perspectives. This was true in Spain also and the pioneering figure of Juan Luis Vives (1492–1540) is especially remarkable for his contributions to the special education. This humanist advocated for the education of children with disabilities in special schools because they were being separated from non-disabled children. His goal was to provide them with individualized special education so that they could be educated. To some extent, his educational ideas were a precursor to the 1970s' idea of an education for all handicapped children which occurred in the United States and the United Kingdom (Vicente & De Vicente, 2006). Also, during the 16th century Juan Huarte de San Juan considered that each person had different talents and aptitudes, and that they should be assessed individually. Because of these ideas he is considered to be the father of Differential Psychology and Vocational Counselling (Galino, 1968).

During the 16th and 17th centuries, one can find the first mention of special education, and more specifically, the education of people with sensory impairments. In fact, a highly important contribution for the education of the deaf was put forth by the Spanish Benedictine monk, Pedro Ponce de León (1509–1584). This monk demonstrated that it was possible to develop thinking/though processes and speech of deaf adults and children. He considered that there was a causal relationship been deafness and mutism and he developed the first oral method for the education of deaf people. The social dissemination of the oral method took some years due to the high cost at that time and there was difficulty using this oral method with big groups (Jiménez & Vilà, 1999). However, the method developed by Ponce de León crossed many territories and borders and eventually was enhanced in 1620 by another Spaniard named Juan Martín Pablo Bonet

(1579–1633) who wrote the first book about education of deaf children (*Reduction de las letras, y arte para enseñar à ablar los mudos*, 1930). Interestingly, this method was further enhanced during the 18th century in Abbot L'Epée in France where it was adapted to the French phonetics and alphabet.

Despite Spanish educators being outstanding pioneers in the education of the deaf during the 16th and 17th centuries, the further development of special education practices and innovations did not materialize until the second half of the 20th century. Thus for many years, Spain was far behind other European countries with respect to special education practices and policies. For people with hearing disabilities some education innovations and programs continued to be initiated such as the one by Joan Albert i Martí, who taught reading and writing to people with hearing impairments and founded the "Royal School of Deaf-and-Dumbs" in 1802 in Madrid. However, advances for other people with disabilities did not occur until the 20th century when a real interest the education of people with intellectual and other disabilities emerged. Another helpful impetus to special education occurred with the passage of The Public Instruction Act of 1857, which is also known as Moyano Law (*Ley Moyano*). This Act established compulsory education for children aged 6 to 9 years and initiated the creation of schools for deaf people. A number of decades after this Act In 1907, the siblings Francisco and Amador Pereira founded the "Pedagogical Psychiatric Institute" for mentally retarded people with intellectual impairments. A few years later, in 1911, local authorities established a "School for blind, deaf-and-dumb and abnormal people" in Barcelona, and in 1914 the "National Board of Abnormals" was created.

These and other such initiatives were not enough for the progressive development of special education in Spain and, despite the influence of the pedagogical reform movements taking place mainly in Catalonia, and the more innovative pedagogical principles from Europe, the new ideas "did not crystallize into an adequate system for meeting the needs of handicapped children" (García Pastor, 1998, p. 46). Because the implementation of the compulsory education elapsed slowly, special education was also delayed. Thus, at the beginning of the 20th century special education was poorly developed in Spain.

The development of special education was further delayed from 1936 to 1939 because of the Spanish Civil War which lead to the disappearance of the pedagogical reform movements. Positively, private initiatives continued to meet the needs of children with disabilities. For instance, in 1939 the National Organization for Blind People (Organización Nacional de Ciegos

Españoles, ONCE) was founded. Its contribution for the education and inclusion of blind people in Spain has been outstanding. Further ONCE continues today to strive for the promotion of inclusive practices and to attend to the educational, vocational, and recreational needs of people with visual disabilities. Lastly, since its foundation, the ONCE has created schools for the blind in several cities such as Pontevedra, Alicante, Sevilla, and Madrid.

Eventually with the passage of the Elementary Education Act *in 1945* (LEP, 1945) an opportunity for special education to grow materialized. This legislated Act created special schools for people with blindness, deafness, and intellectual impairment. About a decade after this Act in 1955 the National Board of Special Education (previously named National Board of Abnormals) proposed the development of a Plan for Special Education that did not crystallize until 1978 (García Pastor, 1998).

In summary, the progress of special education in Spain during the 20th century was slow and the events such as the Civil War and the subsequent dictatorship of General Francisco Franco during his 35-year reign in the century did not help its development. While there were a number of hopeful aspects and legislation, it was not until Public Law 14/70, General Law of Education and Financing of the Educational Reform (LGE, 1970) was enacted that the special education became part of the educational system.

OVERVIEW OF SPAIN'S EDUCATIONAL SYSTEM INCLUDING SPECIAL NEEDS EDUCATION

The legislative framework components governing and guiding the Spanish education system comprises the Spanish Constitution (1978), the Organic Act on the Right to Education (LODE, 1985) and the Organic Law of Education 2/2006, May 3 (Ley Orgánica de Educación LOE, 2006) which develops the principles and rights established in it (EADSP, 2009b). Table 1 provides an overview of the stages constituting Spain's education system.

Similar to other countries around the world, legislative actions in the 1990s became a primary influence behind the major educational reforms in Spain. For example, two governmental Acts, the General Educational System Organizational Act or LOGSE in 1990, and Participation, Evaluation, and Administration of Schools Organization Act, or LOPEG in 1995 "culminated 30 years of continuous education reform that began

Table 1. Stages Constituting the Spanish Education System.

Stages	Brief Description		
Preschool Education: 0–3 years	Provided on a voluntary basis for families with a focus on early childhood education		
Infant Education: 3–6 years	Cost-free, voluntary and is the first level of school education organized as a single three-year cycle.		
Compulsory Education: Free of charge 6–16 years	Compulsory Primary Education 6–12 years, three 2-year cycles and is cost-free	Secondary Education	
		Compulsory Secondary Education (ESO) leading to Compulsory Secondary Education certificate, cost-free 12–16 years	Bachillerato: Compliments ESO, with The Compulsory Secondary education certificate as a prerequisite, 2-years, and is non-compulsory	Specific Vocational Training: Education to prepare for work in specific professional field. Provides an all-round and practical education, and is non-compulsory

Source: Complete National Overview – Spain – European Agency for Development in Special Needs Education (2009b).

with LGE or the General Act of Education of 1970" (Arco-Tirado & Fernandez-Balboa, 2003 p. 586). These Acts brought about significant changes to the education system in Spain. Furthermore, the concept of "special educational needs" and "integration of students with special needs" in the mainstream classrooms that began in 1985 was strengthened by LOGSE (Moliner, Sales, Ferrández, & Traver, 2011). The LOGSE which regulates and governs special education within general plan education, asserts that the incorporation special education into the mainstream system and also introduced the concept of special educational needs. The passage of this act also initiated integration of students with special education need in *mainstream establishments* (schools) where the programs offered needed to be adapted to needs of the students with special educational needs. The law also established that although students with special educational needs could attend either mainstream or special education establishments (schools), this should only be an option if their needs could not be met in mainstream establishments. Special education schools are intended for pupils who are unable to be integrated into mainstream schools. If there are no special education schools available, students with special educational needs are then educated in special classes (special units) within the mainstream centers (Spain- European Agency for Development in Special Needs Education, 2009b).

Spain subscribed to the principles of inclusion early in the 1980s and then carried out several educational reforms in order to transform a selective educational system into a more comprehensive one. Although these reforms arrived a bit later than in other developed countries, in the last three decades, a big effort has been made by the Government of Spain to develop a legislative body in accordance with the international declarations as regards to people with disability or with special educational needs (Chiner & Cardona, 2013).

The first educational reform took place in the 1970s with Public Law 14/70, General Law of Education and Financing of the Educational Reform (LGE, 1970). This law introduced important changes into the Spanish educational system. The focus of these changes was incorporated into Article 49 which was an adoption of the Spanish Constitution in 1978. The changes of this Article lead led to a policy requiring schools to integrate and educate people with disabilities. The effect of these changes was enhanced after the death of General Francisco Franco.

In addition, the 1970 Education Act guided a significant reform in education as it extended compulsory elementary education to children aged 14 years. Also, this act regulated secondary education and vocational training, and led to the recognition of special education as part of the educational system. However, during the 1970s, students with special educational needs still attended school in segregated settings (self-contained classrooms inside regular schools or special schools) with a parallel curriculum. According to Illán and Arnáiz (1996), the 1970 Education Act should be considered as the starting point of the national special education system. Unfortunately, the provisions under this Act were too general and they were not fully implemented.

Twelve years after the Education Act was passed, the Government of Spain passed Public Law 13/1982, Social Integration of Disabled People Act (LISMI, 1982). This law provided the process for the integration of students with special educational needs into regular schools. The law is considered a major special education landmark in all life aspects (society, school, and work) for people with disabilities. The LISMI was inspired by the United Nations Declaration on the Rights of Mentally Retarded Persons (United Nations [UN], 1971) and the Declaration on the Rights of

Disabled Persons (UN, 1975). It is a very progressive law which recognized that the principles of normalization, social integration, community services, and individualization in education and integration in schools will only be possible if the society provides the resources and support services that is necessary to meet the needs of people with disabilities (Jiménez & Vilà, 1999).

In 1982, an additional legal disposition, namely, the Royal Decree 2639/ 1982 of Arrangement of the Special Education (Real Decreto 2639/1982, de 15 de Octubre, de Ordenación de la Educación Especial) established three different alternatives to integration: full integration, mixed integration, and partial integration. However, the Public Law 13/1982, LISMI, required more precision and in 1985, the Royal Decree 334/1985 of Arrangement of the Special Education (Real Decreto 334/1985, de 6 de marzo, de Ordenación de la Educación Especial), developed the LISMI established guidelines to begin the integration process in Spain. This legal disposition recognized that, among other aspects, (a) special education was part of the general educational system, (b) special schools should coordinate and work together with the regular schools, (c) schools should be provided with resources and supports to avoid the segregation and to promote the integration of students with disabilities, (d) there is a need of assessment and counseling, and (e) a need for the development of early intervention programs for children with disabilities was critical to the successful education of young students with special needs. The Royal Decree 334/1985 also marked the beginning of an eight-year experimental program for the integration of students with disabilities in general schools and classrooms.

The United Kingdom's concept of "special educational needs" (SEN) was gaining momentum in Spain at the same time. In fact the United Kingdom's Warnock Report (Department of Education and Science, 1978) had a great influence on the Spanish educational policies and which culminated in an ambitious educational reform carried out in 1990 with the LP 1/1990, Organic Law of General Arrangement of the Educational System (LOGSE, 1990). In general terms, the 1990 Education Act reaffirmed the mandate of the Royal Decree 334/1985 stating that special education is to be a part of the general education system with a common flexible curriculum for all students. Further, curricular adaptations and educational differentiation were to be made based on students' educational needs. This new concept of "special educational needs" resulted in a more comprehensive and open education. Adopting this model necessitated that all schools accept diversity while responding to the particular needs of each student. Most importantly, the principle of inclusion guided the process of the education of all students with special educational needs, and since 1990, all students, regardless of their educational needs, must be taught in regular classes together with their peers. Only when this is not possible will students learn in self-contained classrooms within the regular schools or special schools.

The new demands of the 1990 Education Act led to the revision of the previous Royal Decree 334/1985 that was finally replaced by the Royal Decree 696/1995 for education of students with special educational needs (Real Decreto 696/1995, de 28 de abril, de Ordenación de la educación de los alumnos con necesidades educativas especiales). This new document included some changes such as (a) the use of the concept of students with special educational needs instead of special education students, (b) the introduction of educational response to gifted students, (c) the gradual transformation of special schools into special education resource centers, (d) the replacement of the individual development programs (PDI) by the individual curricular adaptations (ACI) which made adapting the official curriculum at different levels possible, depending on the context and the students' needs, and (e) the diversification of the multidisciplinary teams in general, special and early intervention. Following the general guidelines of the LOGSE mandate, each Autonomous Community developed its own legislative body which has been, in some cases, interpreted and applied differently in each region (García Pastor, 1998).

The subsequent laws enacted after the LOGSE (Public Law 10/2002 and Public Law 2/2006) only introduced minor changes (mostly centered on terminology) regarding the education of students with special needs. The Public Law 10/2002, Organic Law of Quality of Education (LOCE, 2002) introduced the generic term "specific educational needs" to refer to several groups of students, such as foreigners, gifted students, and students with special educational needs. This last group of students with specific educational needs included students with physical and intellectual disabilities, sensory impairments or severe personality and behavior disorders. The current Education Act, the Public Law 2/2006, Organic Law of Education (LOE, 2006) refers to "students with specific educational support needs" and includes students with special educational needs derived from a disability, behavior disorders, or gifted students and students with a late entry to the Spanish educational system. The 2006 Education Act also included a section on policies to avoid educational inequalities based on ethnicity and social, economic, cultural, or geographical factors.

The above legislative acts and educational reforms allowed Spain to progress a long way in twenty years in its efforts to promote inclusive education. Although its implementation started late in the 1980s, today Spain is considered to have one of the most inclusive educational systems in Europe. However, the current Government which is run by the conservative party, Popular Party (Partido Popular), is preparing a draft of a new Education Act, the Organic Law of Improvement of the Quality of Education (Ley Orgánica de Mejora de la Calidad Educativa, LOMCE) which contains important changes in the organization of the educational system which may affect the education of students with special needs. This law has been questioned for its neoliberal principles. It has the risk of promoting inequality among students from different social backgrounds and with diverse abilities. Moreover, the current new millennium worldwide economic and financial crisis has affected the Spanish economy strongly and has prompted the Government to carry out significant cuts in education. These cuts include a reduction in teachers, a considerable increase in the student-teacher ratio, a diminishment in resources and supports that are provided to schools, and a reduction in the number of programs attending to diversity.

Table 2 provides the reader with a framework of various pieces of legislation within the last three decades of the 20th century and the first decade of the 21st century that have influenced development of inclusion in Spain.

The 1990 Education Act is probably the most important educational reform enacted in the Spanish educational context, especially in regards to the education of students with special educational needs and their inclusion in the general education system. Although the term inclusion was not included in the text, the LOGSE mandate shared the principles of inclusive education that later many countries subscribed to after the publication of the Salamanca Statement and Framework for Action on Special Needs Education (UNESCO, 1994). A May 2012 report by the Organization for Economic Cooperation and Development (OECD) on children with special education needs (SEN) in OECD countries contended that "despite international consensus on the right of children with SEN, and efforts to find an international definition agreed by all countries, data on children with SEN are still being collected according to national definition" (OECD, 2012, p. 1). The report highlighted two main issues in terms of reporting *prevalence* of students with SEN. The first issue is that some children's SEN are not recognized and the second being reported data covers only the national definitions. Understanding how special educational needs are decided and defined within the Spanish educational system will be a precursor to understanding issues and challenges that exist in attempting to state the number of students with special educational needs included in general

Table 2. Framework of Legislation Leading to Inclusion in Spain.

Year	Law	Influence
1970	General Law of Education and Financing of the Educational Reform (LGE)	• Introduces the special education as part of the educational system. • It establishes that the special education will be provided in general schools and special schools.
1978	Spanish Constitution	• Recognizes the right of all citizens to education. • It establishes the need of planning, rehabilitation, and integration of people with disabilities.
1982	Social Integration for the disabled people Act (LISMI)	• Attends to personal, medical, school, and work issues of people with disabilities. • Integrates special education in the general educational system. • It is based on the principles of normalization, integration, community services, and individualization.
1985	Royal Decree 334/1985 of Arrangement of the Special Education	• It develops the demands of the LISMI. • It represents the beginning in the practice of the school integration in Spain.
1990	Organic Law of Arrangement of the General Educational System (LOGSE)	• Introduces the concept of "special educational needs." • It is based on the principles of normalization and school integration. • Promotes the use of curricular adaptations and diversifications to attend to the SENs.
2002	Organic Law of Quality of Education (LOCE)	• Replaces the concept of SENs for "specific educational needs." • It is based on the principles of normalization, non-discrimination, and integration.
2003	Law on Equal Opportunities, Non-Discrimination and Universal Access for People with Disabilities	• Compliments the 1982 Act on Social Integration of Disabled People (LISMI). Marked an unambiguous shift in Spanish disability policy toward a human rights perspective based on the social model of disability. • One of the measures was setting of basic guidelines for the educational framework to ensure pupils with handicap achieved general objectives of education to the maximum extent.
2006	Organic Law of Education (LOE)	• It is based on the principles of equity in education, normalization, inclusive education, and non-discrimination. • Introduces the term of "students with specific educational support needs."

Note: Students with Special Educational Needs Included in General Education in Spain.

education system. The OECD (2012) reported the definition of SEN in Spain is "Students with SEN refer to those who require certain support and specific educational attention due to disability or serious behavioural disorder, either for a period or throughout the whole of their schooling. The schooling of these students in special education centers will take place only when their needs cannot be met by the special needs provisions available in mainstream schools" (p. 10).

The Organic Law of 2006 (LOE) differentiates support for *three* distinct groups of students: students with special educational needs, high ability (gifted) students, and students with a late entry into education system.

- Students with special educational needs (SEN) as per the definition above are further classified into the following categories according to Ministry of Education, Culture, and Sports: hearing disability, motor disability, intellectual disability, visual disorders, pervasive developmental disorders, and severe behavioral and personality disorders.
- Students with High Intellectual Abilities: Students receiving curricular adaptations for an extended, enriched curriculum, flexible schooling options, and/or participation in extracurricular enrichment.
- Students from other countries who may have joined the Spanish education system and are enrolled in courses offered to students who are at a lower age or grade level. Schools provide necessary support to students who may have language problems and difficulty integrating into the normal classes according to their age.

The 2006 Organic Law of Education stipulates procedures to be followed for identification of children with SEN and requires that only teams of qualified personnel should carry out identification and evaluation process and decide subsequently on a program, support needs, or a plan for students. The qualified teams may include speech therapists, audiologists, psychologists, guidance counselors, social workers, and teacher consultants, appointed by regional education authorities (Teese, Aasen, Field, & Pont, 2006). Such needs are to be established with necessary input from and consultation with parents, teachers, and administrators from the educational establishments. Students with special education needs identified by the team of experts have a choice of attending either special education establishments or mainstream establishments with appropriate adaptations made to the curriculum to meet the needs of these students. The following section reports some statistics on the enrollment of students with SEN in various educational establishments (schools), including students with SEN who are integrated/included.

The Ministry of Education, Culture and Sport (MECD), Government of Spain released a report in July 2013 about students with special education needs in the year 2011–2012. According to the reported statistics, during 2011–2012 year the total number of pupils who received care and support in the three categories defined by LOE (students with SEN, students with high intellectual disabilities/gifted and students with a late entry in schools) amounted to 399,083 students or 5.1% of the total student population. Of these 117,385 students or 1.48% were students with disabilities integrated into regular schools. This category includes those integrated into public regular schools and private regular schools. A total of 32,233 students were in special schools or special units within the regular schools, which again included both public special schools and private special schools and special units within public regular schools and special units within private regular schools. Table 3 provides longitudinal data for school years 1999–2000 to 2010–2011 of students with special educational needs in various schools.

The categories of special needs included hearing impairments, motor/physical impairments, mental/intellectual/cognitive impairment, visual impairments, and autism/other developmental disabilities, and other multiple disabilities including pervasive developmental and behavioral disorders. The number of students with special educational needs fully integrated in regular education schools and in regular education classes increased by 7,610 over the period between 1999–2000 and 2012–2013 with an increase of 4,896 in the reported number of students with special educational needs who were in special schools and in special education units within the general education schools in the same period. The inception of inception of Public Law 13/1982 (LISMI, 1982) had a positive effect on the number of students identified as having special educational needs who were in special education schools and/or in special education units within regular schools in the previous decade. An overview of longitudinal data (1990–1991 to 1999–2000) reported a remarkable decrease, from 42,329 students in 1990–1991 school years to 27,321 students in 1999–2000 school years (Cardona, 2009).

According to the July 2013 report by the Ministry of Education, Culture, and Sport – Government of Spain (MECD) for the school year 2011–2012, the total number of pupils who received care and support in the three categories defined by LOE (students with SEN, students with high intellectual disabilities/gifted and students with a late entry in schools) amounted to 399,083 students. Of these 149,618 were students with various disabilities. The prevalence of various disabilities reported within *this* student population was 70,594 students or 47.2%, the highest percentage occurred with cognitive/mental/ intellectual disabilities, followed by 43,644

Table 3. Students with Special Educational Needs in Schools in the 21st Century.

School Year	Overall Total of All Students in Education at Different Levels and in Different Public and Private Regular Schools	Total Number of Students with Special Educational Needs Integrated in Regular Schools in Regular Classes at Different Levels	% of total school population fully integrated	Total Number of Students with Special Educational Needs in Special Schools and in Special Education Units within the Regular Schools (Includes Public Schools and Private Schools)
2011–2012	7,923,293	117,385	1.48	32,233
2010–2011	7,782,182	110,383	1.41	31,043
2009–2010	7,608,292	111,034	1.46	30,643
2008–2009	7,443,625	107,998	1.45	30,819
2007–2008	7,241,299	106,320	1.47	29,427
2006–2007	7,088,662	104,793	1.48	28,871
2005–2006	6,983,538	107,410	1.54	28,665
2004–2005	6,933,472	109,823	1.58	28,145
2003–2004	6,903,063	117,582	1.70	27,799
2002–2003	6,843,646	123,960	1.81	27,057
2001–2002	6,830,185	116,456	1.71	27,090
2000–2001	6,882,363	114,844	1.67	27,334
1999–2000	6,972,500	109,775	1.57	27,337

Source: Ministry of Education, Culture and Sports-Government of Spain (2013a).

students or 29.2% with pervasive developmental disorders. Other disabilities reported included 12,878 students with physical disabilities/motor impairments, 7,288 students with hearing impairments, 3,000 students with visual impairments, and 10,222 students with multiple disabilities.

ASSESSMENT OF STUDENTS FOR SPECIAL EDUCATIONAL NEEDS

The Public Law 2/2006, Organic Law of Education (LOE, 2006) stipulates that the identification and evaluation of students with special educational needs will be carried out by multi-professional (multidisciplinary) teams. These teams assess students' needs, as well as all the relevant elements regarding the teaching-learning process. The evaluation of the student and the context is to be done to help professionals make decisions about the type of schooling, the special education provisions, and the curricular adaptations that are necessary for the personal, intellectual, social, and emotional development of the students.

In order to fulfill the requirements of the Public Law 2/2006, the Ministry of Education published in *Order EDU/849/2010 of arrangement* in 2010 regulations governing the education of students with specific educational support needs. According to this Order the student's assessment is to be conducted by the school counselor with the cooperation of teachers, parents, and other professionals.

The school counselor gathers information about (a) the student (e.g., individual traits, personal and social development, curricular competence, learning styles), (b) the school context (e.g., school and classroom organization, student's relationship with the professionals and peers), and (c) the social and family context (e.g., family and environment information, parents' expectations, and relationship with school, and community resources). For this purpose, the professionals use informal instruments, measurements, and procedures that they consider necessary to collect information about the students and their context, especially, systematic observation, questionnaires, interviews, samples of school works, and class tests.

Once the assessment has been carried out, the school counselor writes a report which reflects the current developmental and educational profile of the student. This a confidential document that includes all the information about the student and his or her context, the instruments used for assessment, the main results and conclusions of the assessment, the specific educational support needs, the expected organizational and curricular measures to be adopted, and the personal and material resources that will be necessary. It also provides recommendations for the education of the student with special educational needs that includes specific adaptations to the curriculum.

An assessment report indicating such needs for curricular adaptations and the type of schooling that may be a better match for the educational needs of the student is a requirement for any adaptations to be provided. In conclusion, a student being transferred to any special education school is required to have a complete schooling report to help find a good match for the student's ability and needs. This schooling report includes (1) a final assessment report prepared by multidisciplinary team specifying student's present level of performance, student's abilities, needs, and needed modifications, (2) recommendations for educational approaches that will better respond to the student's needs, and (3) recommendations for specific other equipment and resources. The comprehensive report concludes with a recommendation for the best fit (special school, special unit with a general education school, or a general education classroom) to meet the child's needs determined by the multidisciplinary team, including the type of resources needed, thus justifying the placement recommended.

To avoid referrals that may lead to unnecessary and stigmatizing formal and comprehensive assessments, teachers are expected to adapt their instruction to the particular needs of each student in collaboration with the school counselor and other professionals (e.g., the special education teacher). Teachers may adapt their teaching strategies and the curriculum as long as the elements of the core curriculum (objectives and curricular contents of each level) are not significantly modified. And only when all these general accommodations are not sufficient to respond to students' educational needs, a formal assessment will be conducted by the school counselor (Giné & Ruiz, 1991; Ruiz i Bel, 1988). Teachers need to have documentation of previous assessment results and measures adopted in the classroom to respond to student's needs and documentation to justify the need of a formal assessment.

PROVISION, SUPPORTS, AND EDUCATIONAL INTERVENTIONS

Considering the trend in the last decade where inclusion has become a preferred model for the education of all students, the key question is how the

Spanish educational system organized to meet the needs of learners identified as having disabilities or severe special educational needs (SEN).
According to the European Agency for Development in Special Needs
Education (2009a), the Spanish educational system supports a multi-track
structure in the sense that students with disabilities and/or severe educational needs can be enrolled: (1) in mainstream schools with almost full
inclusion into all school activities and following the school core curriculum;
(2) in self-contained special education classrooms for students in need of
ongoing educational support in some periods of their timetable combined
with mainstream classes; and (3) in special schools, both public and/or private schools.

In the first approach (inclusion), students with disabilities or special
educational needs spend all, or at least more than half, of the school day
with students who do not have special educational needs. Because inclusion
can require substantial modification of the general curriculum most schools
use this approach only for selected students with mild to moderate
special needs for which is accepted as a best practice (Echeita et al., 2009;
Verdugo & Rodríguez-Aguilella, 2012). Specialized services may be provided inside or outside the regular classroom, depending on the type of service. Students may occasionally leave the regular classroom to attend
smaller, more intensive instructional sessions in a resource room or to
receive other related services that might require specialized equipment or
might be disruptive to the rest of the class, such as speech and language
therapy, occupational therapy, physical therapy, rehabilitation, or
counseling.

Self-contained special education classrooms or mainstreaming refers to
the practice of educating students with disabilities in classes with non-
disabled students during specific time periods based on their skills. These
classes are exclusively for students with special needs such as deafness,
severe intellectual disabilities or personality disorders. The students in this
setting usually do not get to spend any time with their non-disabled peers.
Although these students attend the same school where regular classes are
provided, they spend almost all instructional time exclusively in a separate
classroom for students with specific needs. If their special class is located in
an ordinary school, they may be provided opportunities for social integration outside the classroom.

Recently, the overall number of special schools in Spain has tended to
decrease (Ministry of Education, Culture, and Sport, Government of
Spain, 2012). While some special institutions have been transformed into

resources centers, others have been dismantled as a result of inclusive policies but still exist. The public administration gives students the necessary support from the beginning of their schooling or as soon as they are identified as having special needs. The schools develop the curriculum through Individual Educational Plans (IEP), which have to take into account the student's needs and characteristics.

Since the introduction of the Organic Law 2/2006 of Education (LOE, 2006), inclusion has been a key principle within the Spanish educational structures at different levels, recognizing the need to fit provisions to a wide range of needs and students' abilities, motivation, mother tongue, etc. The Organic Law 2/2006 of Education establishes the concept of "pupils with *specific* need of educational support" which includes students with special educational needs, gifted students, and immigrant students/pupils who were incorporated late into the Spanish education system. The law is based on the following basic principles: (1) quality education for all students; (2) equity for equal opportunities, inclusion and non-discrimination; and (3) flexibility to adapt education to special needs, interests, aptitudes, and expectations.

A key component of the definition of "special educational needs" (SEN) in the Spanish legislation is that children have special educational needs if they require additional provision or different supports that are not normally available in schools. With the introduction of the term "special need of educational support," increasingly, the population of children with disabilities is no longer defined in terms of categories of need, but inextricably linked to resourcing (European Agency for Development of Special Needs Education [EADSNE], 2013). This has opened the way to greater inclusion while placing the emphasis on funding rather than on educational issues.

In Spain as in most countries across Europe, learners seen to have "special or additional" needs that are assessed to ascertain the level and nature of support required. Agencies usually use national systems of classification or categorization to identify problems and assess students' educational or supports needs. Recommendations emerging from the Spanish Minister of Education, Culture, and Sport, Government of Spain (2012a) advocate a move away from any form of classification system that leads to labeling and/or placement based on categories toward of an understanding of what benefits the students. In this sense, the Ministry recommendation is to use *ordinary measures* for attending to diversity, such as successive levels of curricular adaptation, or organization and delivery of support activities in regular settings before using more specific measures of support. Once ordinary measures have been applied and have proved to be insufficient to respond to the educational needs of a student, the education system considers a series of *extraordinary measures*: for example, significant curricular adaptations, curriculum diversification, repeating a cycle or school year, and ultimately social guarantee programs. Other specific support measures are: alterations of school building facilities, additional support provided by specialist teachers, specific teaching methods or materials for students having sensorial (visual, auditory) disabilities or other specific needs, reduced class sizes, support specialist teachers, or special arrangements for assessment and evaluation. There is also the possibility of prolonging schooling up to the age of 18 years.

To meet the needs of the students with disabilities in inclusive classrooms, teachers usually emphasize instruction in functional academics and daily living, social, and vocational skills. To teach these skills, teachers use a variety of teacher-directed, student-directed, and peer-mediated approaches. Teachers-directed models include: (a) task analysis to determine prerequisite skills and component skills (what skills are needed to complete the task); (b) modeling, a method in which the teacher demonstrates the behavior to be learned, and facilitates mastery by providing much practice, reinforcement, and feedback; or (c) scaffolding, an approach that can be defined as an adjustable and temporary support. In addition, educators are increasingly facilitating students' use of self-regulation procedures, such as self-monitoring, self-administering consequences, and self-instruction to promote student independence. Further, given the context of large heterogeneous classes, reflective teachers are increasingly using peer-mediated procedures to provide additional practice and individual help to students with and without disabilities. One such arrangement is peer tutoring, a technique that under certain conditions has been shown to benefit both tutor and tutee academically, behaviorally, and socially. Specific examples of peer tutoring in the areas of reading and math with Spanish students are reported by Cardona, Reig, and Domene (2000) and Cardona (2002) respectively. These researchers used class wide peer tutoring (CWPT) to accommodate the diversity of reading and math abilities of Spanish students in a bilingual programs that included students with moderate intellectual disabilities.

Additionally, the inclusion of students with disabilities in general education classrooms has resulted in increased interest among educators in procedures that promote academic improvement and skills and enhance the social acceptance of these students. Recent reviews of methods suggest that teachers in Spain are increasingly using mastery learning (Martín, Torres, Santaolalla, & Hernández, 2013; Torres, 2013), computer-assisted instruction (Cascales, Martínez, & Laguna, 2013; Navarro & Camús, 2013), cooperative learning (Hernández & Olmos, 2011; Pujolàs, 1997), and co-teaching (Devesa, 2004). However, little information exists regarding teachers' perceptions of within-class instructional adaptations. With this as a focus, Cardona (2003) examined how teachers (kindergarten, elementary, and secondary) perceive such adaptations in terms of feasibility, effectiveness, and desirability of implementation. This researcher found that instructional adaptations have a moderate teachers' acceptance and that although a majority of the teachers believe that are feasible and effective only a minority perceive them as desirable. In another study, Cardona and Chiner (2006) found that teachers reported a *limited* use of instructional adaptations which significantly differed among kindergarten, elementary, and secondary school teachers. Cardona and Chiner indicated that a possible interpretation for this finding is that teachers were not involved in systematic consultation or collaboration with support personnel and viewed most of these adaptations as incompatible with the prevailing structure of the general education classroom. Other explanations could be that teachers had specific concerns involving availability of supports and time for planning and implementation.

In summary, educational goals for students with disabilities emphasize readiness skills at younger ages and functional academics and vocational training at older ages. After finishing the compulsory secondary education, all students, including special education students, receive a certificate with the number of years of study and the grades they have received in the different subjects with non-prescriptive and confidential guidance regarding their academic and professional future. In addition, provision has been made (LOCE, 2002; LOE, 2006) for students with disabilities who finish basic education without having reached the objectives of compulsory secondary education to continue their schooling under three different vocational training-related options: (1) social guarantee programs adapted to their personal circumstances as well as to their level of skills and development, (2) special social guarantee programs specially designed for students with disabilities wishing to continue schooling beyond compulsory education (ESO), and (3) transition to adult life programs (initial vocational training) for those students with disabilities associated with more severe and permanent disabilities. The special social guarantee programs have the same structure as the social guarantee programs designed for students without disabilities but are organized around the following areas: basic training, training and career guidance, vocational training, complementary activities, and educational guidance. On the other hand, transition to adult life programs are programs designed for students with more severe disabilities who are unable to take advantage of the two other training alternatives. These programs, which are generally provided in specific special education schools, last two years but they may be extended to three years.

As a result of the above process of schooling, the Spanish Government aims to increase the opportunities and participation of young with disabilities in employment and full participation in their communities. Therefore, a variety of vocational training and employment approaches have been available since the passage of Public Law 13/1982, Ley de Integración de los Minusválidos (LISMI, 1982). These approaches include the following: (1) protected employment in occupational canters; (2) sheltered workshops, structures environment where a person receives training a works with other workers with disabilities on jobs requiring relatively low skills; and (3) supported competitive employment. Despite this specific legislation that promotes access to regular employment, a low percentage of people with disabilities (36.6%) work in inclusive environments (Colectivo IOÉ, 2003; Instituto Nacional de Estadística [INE], 2012; Jordán & Verdugo, 2011; Pallisera, Vilà, & Valls, 2003). In reality, several studies (Caleidoscopia, 1996; Fernández, Arias, & Gallego, 1999; Fundación Equipara, 2008) that have examined employment rates of people with disabilities has shown that: (a) there are low social expectations for about employability, and (b) that family members and professionals negative expectations about employability of people with disabilities may be real barrier to attaining and keeping jobs. With this in mind, Gómez (2013) studied the employability beliefs and perceptions of 118 families, 54 educators and 60 people with intellectual disability belonging to a non-governmental association from the Valencian Community and found that families, educators and people with a disability believe that only some people with intellectual disability can work and that family fears can affect real possibilities of their employability. Although current employment figures and perspectives may look bleak (Colectivo IOÉ, 2003; INE, 2012), evidence also shows (Carabaña, López de la Nieta, & Andreu, 2006) that employers are taking a more favorable attitude toward hiring workers with disabilities. Thanks to these employers' efforts, many people with disabilities are achieving levels of independence in employment that were never thought possible.

In conclusion, as has been largely recognized, inclusive education and its implementation may differ depending on the context in which it is developed and implemented but the literature (Alexander, 2012; European Agency for Development in Special Needs Education [EADSNE], 2011, 2013) has shown that there are common elements across different contexts as to "what works" in helping all learners to succeed. In the context of the Spanish educational system, these elements include:

- Changes in the whole educational system, rather than simply where learners with disabilities are educated.
- The need to increase the capability of regular schools and develop their competence to benefit all learners.
- The importance of listening to learners and their families in the organization of any additional support.
- The development of inclusive attitudes and beliefs in teachers and the will to take responsibility for all learners.
- The importance of distributed leadership to ensure a positive culture and ethos in all schools.
- The importance of networking and collaboration in providing support at all levels (community, school, and individual).
- The development of equitable funding approaches which aim to improve the school system for all learners through collaboration, rather than providing an incentive to identify and label learners (p. 63).

Ultimately, inclusion involves changing the culture and the organization of regular schools and the communities they serve in order to ensure the full participation of all learners (Mittler, 2000).

TEACHER EDUCATION FOR SPECIAL AND INCLUSIVE EDUCATION

Preparing new teachers to be "inclusive" educators requires so much more than the addition of a special education course or a specific intervention module. To be successful in this effort, teacher educators must develop expertise to deal with contentious issues and address their own personal deeper values and attitudes. Special and inclusive education is different terms. Both terms have roots in the worldwide campaign to achieve education for all but its meaning differ. According to Florian (2009), special education has focused on those things that are *additional to* and *different from* that which is otherwise available, while inclusive education has focused on *extending the scope of the ordinary school* to accommodate a greater diversity of learners ensuring their meaningful participation in the culture, curriculum, and community of mainstream schools. In any case, prospective teachers require a bachelor's degree with an emphasis in Special Education to qualify as a special education teacher at a public school.

Spain has a decentralized system of teacher education and certification. Each Autonomous Community and University is responsible for initial certification and credentialing of its teachers. In a decentralized system, the central government, in this case, the Ministry of Education, governs almost all aspects of the teacher education and verification process. The Ministry sets minimum guideline entry and exit requirements, as well as curriculum content for teacher education programs. While the Autonomous Communities and their respective institutions of higher education monitors compliance with these guidelines there has to be an adaption of the state core program to their particular needs and demands. Therefore, in Spain, the Ministry of Education and the Department of Education of the diverse Autonomous Communities share responsibility for teacher education and certification, but higher education institutions (universities) develop from these guidelines their own programs.

Types of Institutions that Prepare Teachers

Prospective teachers in Spain have to complete a *four-year* undergraduate program for initial certification. Teacher education programs are offered by public universities and private universities and almost all of them provide initial teacher certification in two majors (*kindergarten education* and *primary education*). Teacher certification in secondary and high school requires all prospective teachers to complete a master's program for initial certification.

Entry Requirements

The majority of teacher education programs require a minimum GPA in high school (grades C or above) and a pass on an entrance examination (Selectividad). Performance on both is combined into a university entrance score which is determinant to be accepted or not in one of the two major teacher education programs (kindergarten or primary education). Also, Spain has entry requirements based on students' performance in secondary school. Each student has a university entrance score that is calculated based on marks obtained on assessments and examinations in high school and results from university entry examination. Each university sets its own cut-off scores, acceptance being more competitive for kindergarten than primary education.

Teacher Education Curriculum

The curriculum content of the four-year undergraduate programs is determined by individual teacher training institutions (universities) within the context of state and community accreditation policies. Institutions typically require 60 ECTS credits per year to complete 240 credits during the four years.

A typical undergraduate teacher education program (e.g., *Maestro*: Primary Education) consists of 240 credits (1 credit = 25 hours of student work at the university): 60 ECTS credits of general studies (core courses), 100 ECTS credits of professional studies and certification teaching (core courses), 30 ECTS credits of electives courses and mentions (specialization), 44 ECTS credits of practicum (student teaching and other field-based experiences), and 6 ECTS credits Final Degree Project. To obtain a mention in Special Education, prospective teachers are required to take 18 ECTS common courses for the itinerary (three 6 ECTS compulsory courses and two 6 ECTS elective) (see Table 3 for the mention of Special Education).

A teacher education program in *special education* (e.g., *Maestro*, Emphasis in Special Education) consists of 240 ECTS credits. On average, 60 credits of general studies (core courses), 100 ECTS credits of major credits (courses in certification teaching subject area and professional studies), 12 ECTS credits of electives courses and 18 ECTS credits for the mention (special education), 44 ECTS credits of practicum (student teaching and other field-based experiences), and 6 ECTS credits Final Degree Project (FDP).

Teacher training programs in kindergarten or primary education majors have similar structures. All are composed of at least 240 credits distributed between common core courses, courses in certification teaching subject

Table 4. Common Courses for Teacher Certification (Maestro: Primary
Education, Emphasis in Special Education).

Plan 2012 (University of Salamanca, Spain): Itinerary of Special Education	
Course	# ECTS Credits
Minor common courses	
Disability studies	6
Response to diversity: students with disabilities	6
Psychological disorders	6
Minor electives courses	
Behavioral interventions programs	6
Communication and speech intervention programs	6
Teaching maths to students with special educational needs	6

area, student teaching and other field-based experiences, elective courses,
and FPD (Table 4).

Exit Requirements

In Spain, exit standards for the undergraduate training programs of
Maestro include completion of required courses, passage of classroom
examinations with adequate PGA (above C), and a *Practicum* composed of
field activities (observation in classes, assisting teachers, and collaboration
in extracurricular activities) and student teaching. The length of time
required for the Practicum is a semester approximately. This Practicum is
supervised and evaluated by selected teachers of the schools and staff from
the higher education institutions.

Degree Earned

Upon completion of the teacher education program undergraduates are
awarded a bachelor degree (*Diploma of Maestro*). Depending on the major,
students can obtain the following degrees:

- *Maestro:* Kindergarten Education.
- *Maestro:* Primary Education.

With emphasis in: Music Education, Physical Education, Foreign
Language Education, Special Education, and Speech Therapy depending
on the institutions.

FAMILY AND PARENT INVOLVEMENT

Parents have a crucial role to play in the education of their children with disabilities in Spain. This role is guaranteed by law (LISMI, 1982; LOE, 2006) which requires the school system to ensure that parents have the opportunity to participate in the educational decisions affecting their children with special needs education. Special education legislation, namely, Public Law 13/1982 (LISMI, 1982), stipulates that parents of students with disabilities are entitled to the following rights to: (1) a free and appropriate public education for their children; (2) an independent psycho-educational evaluation when placement and program decisions have to be made; (3) a notice before the multidisciplinary team initiates or changes the identification, evaluation, or placement of the child; (4) give or withhold consent before an evaluation is conducted and before initial placement in made in special education; (5) revoke consent at any time; (6) request an impartial due process hearing to question identification, evaluation, or placement of the child; (7) have a full and individual evaluation of the child's educational needs in all areas related to the suspected disability conducted by a multi-disciplinary team; and (8) have their child educated in regular schools and classrooms to the maximum extent possible with a continuum of alternate placements and supplementary services such as a resource room or itinerant instruction. In addition, this law stipulates that when a student is identified as having a disability, parents or guardians must be involved in developing individualized education program (IEP) and that the school should make every effort to provide their child with the necessary services and supports needed so that their child can be taught with children who do not have disabilities.

Parent and family responsibilities are less clearly defined in the law than are parental rights but strong recommendations exists for how schools can develop partnerships with families such as: engaging in quality communication; inviting parents to participate in schools activities; soliciting parents' input on decisions about their child's education; or empowering parents to take action that addresses their own needs. Some of these partnerships can be developed thorough the Association of Mothers and Fathers (AMPA) at their child's school, however, these partnerships will only be successful with strong commitment and collaboration.

Despite these requirements of collaboration between schools and families as stipulated by law, many parents have little or no involvement in their children special and/or inclusive education process. They often attend their child's Individualized Education Program meeting but have little or no involvement in developing objectives or interventions (Antequera et al., 2008). Quite frequently, families have also reported that they were not given choices to participate or reporting that their children are not receiving the kind of services they need (Gómez, 2013). However, there are several other schools where professionals, specialist personnel, regular and special education teachers, and families work together. Inclusion Europe (2006) described one such example of good practices followed by Padre Jerónimo Elementary School. This school has been practicing and striving to enhance their integration program for students with special needs since the year 1987–1988. The school encourages active participation by all stakeholders in education of students with special education needs specifically, parents and families. Some specific ways this school involves families are by: informing them how the school works with their children; by inviting them to participate in the follow-up and evaluation of the educational process of their children; and by providing them with proper information at the end of every school year and, most crucially, at the end of the school attendance (Inclusion Europe, 2006, pp. 9–10).

To promote family involvement in the lifelong learning of their children with disabilities parents in recent decades have engaged in united efforts, and sought awareness regarding their child's education, care, and guidance by creating national, regional, and local associations. Calvo, Regueiro, and Ramirez (2011) published a resource guide that provides information about various organizations and associations which band together to share problems and promote awareness regarding needs and education of children, youth, and adults with disabilities. It is an excellent resource for individuals with various disabilities and their families. Each page in the document lists details of organizations/associations including contact information, types of services individuals with disabilities and families can expect, and their outreach activities. https://www.uclm.es/to/fcsociales/pdf/GuiaPersonasDis capacidad.pdf.

The Spain's State Board of Education in their *Proposals for Improvement 2012 Report on the State of the Spanish Education System* called for greater involvement of families in education states that "social participation in general, and students' parents, mothers in particular are one of the fundamental pillars of education" (Ministry of Education, 2012, p. 21). In recognizing the direct positive correlation between family involvement and student success, the report also called for setting avenues for school–family/parent communication. Another recommendation from the report stresses the need to provide a wider choice of centers of education for children with disabilities and greater autonomy and freedom for *parents* to choose the centers they deem best for their children.

FUTURE TRENDS AND CHALLENGES

Now that Inclusion is a reality in the Spanish educational system, more attention should be paid to the quality of the process of inclusive education. Administrators, professionals, and the school community should be aware that inclusion is not just having students with special educational needs in the ordinary schools and classrooms, but also the full participation of these students in all the activities that are taking place in their school and social context (Inclusion International, 1996). To achieve real inclusion of all students, administrators, professionals, and the school community must guarantee equal opportunities to these students and be able to respond adequately to their special educational needs in order to fully develop their personal, social, educational and vocational development. For this purpose, professionals, and especially regular education teachers, must believe in inclusion and understand it as a right. Positively, research has shown that teachers in Spain hold positive attitudes toward inclusion (Chiner & Cardona, 2013). Teachers have been found to generally agree with the concept of inclusion, but they also think that it is not easy to implement due to the lack of: time, resources, supports, and training (Chiner & Cardona, 2013). This latter aspect may hinder the right conditions to promote inclusion and can lead teachers to a discouragement that will negatively affect the students' learning and development. Another study conducted by Chiner and Cardona (2012) also showed that, despite the positive attitudes toward inclusion, teachers do not adapt their instruction sufficiently to meet students' special needs. Further Chiner and Cardona pointed out that teachers usually implement general adaptations oriented to the whole group rather than more specific inclusive practices. In other words, they usually provide accommodations that are easy to implement.

In light of the above, the schools educational administration should provide teachers with enough resources and supports, as well as necessary pre-service and in-service training through professional development courses on inclusion and specific instructional adaptations to attend students' special educational needs in inclusive classrooms. Special attention should be paid to secondary education teachers. These teachers are well trained in specific subjects, such mathematics, history, and science, but they have very little knowledge about teaching, and more specifically, teaching students with special educational needs. Currently, prior to becoming secondary education teachers, they must complete a sixty-credit program, teaching strategies (especially in their specific subject area) and, in some cases diversity strategies. However, this training is clearly not enough for secondary education teachers to feel prepared to address students' special education needs. Given this situation, higher education programs should include more credits related to teaching students with special educational needs in order to prepare teachers to be more sensitive toward diversity and be confident to adapt their instruction to the specific needs of each student.

CONCLUSION

In spite of the significant progress made to date in Spain's inclusive education practices, it still has a system based on a *continuum* of services that go from total inclusion in regular classrooms to the segregation in special education schools. The decision of placing the student is often based on categories of disabilities, forgetting the principles of the special educational needs concept. The LOE (2006) mandates that students must be placed in regular classes and schools, and only when that is not possible, they will be taught in special education units or schools. However, the latter policy makes the mandate ambiguous and subject to different interpretations. Therefore, it is critical that administrators work on developing what was initially stated by the LOGSE (1990): promoting special schools as resource centers, more than direct teaching schools, and including most of the students in ordinary schools.

REFERENCES

Alexander, R. (2012, May). International evidence, national policy and classroom practice: Questions of judgment vision and trust. *Closing session keynote given at the third Van Leer international conference on education "from regulation to trust"*, Jerusalem, Israel.

Antequera, M., Bachiller, B., Calderón, M. T., Cruz, A., Cruz, P. L., García, F. J., ... Ortega, R. (2008). *Handbook for the education of students with specific need of educational support due to intellectual disability.* Sevilla, Spain: Junta de Andalucía.

Arco-Tirado, J. J., & Fernandez-Balboa, J. (2003). Contextual barriers to school reform in Spain. *International Review of Education, 49*(6), 585–600.

Bonet, J. P. (1930). *Reduction of words and the art of teaching mute people how to speak.* Madrid, Spain: Beltrán.

Caleidoscopia. (1996). *Personal and social factors of the employment of people with disabilities.* Madrid, Spain: Real Patronato de Prevención y Atención a Personas con Minusvalía.

Calvo, S. M., Regueiro, E. M., & Ramirez, A. P. (2011). *Guide of associations for people with disabilities.* Universidad de Castilla la Mancha. Retrieved from https://www.uclm.es/to/fcsociales/pdf/GuiaPersonasDiscapacidad.pdf

Carabaña, J., López de la Nieta, M., & Andreu, S. (2006). Analysis of interactions and impact of the Spanish educational system on the labour market: The case of pupils with special educational needs with particular reference to students with intellectual disabilities. In J. M. Ibáñez (Ed.), *Libro verde sobre los itinerarios hacia el empleo de los jóvenes con discapacidad intelectual* (pp. 73–352). Badajoz, Spain: Aprosuba.

Cardona, C. M. (2009). Current trends in special education in Spain: Do they really reflect legislative mandates of Inclusion? *The Journal of International Association of Special Education, 10*(1), 4–10.

Cardona, M. C. (2002). Adapting instruction to address individual and group educational needs in math. *Journal of Research in Special Educational Needs, 2*(1), 1–16.

Cardona, M. C. (2003). Classroom change and inclusion through/via instructional adaptations. *Revista De Investigación Educativa, 21*(2), 465–487.

Cardona, M. C., & Chiner, E. (2006). Use and effectiveness of instructional adaptations in inclusive classrooms: A study of perceptions and training needs of teachers. *Bordón, 58*(3), 5–24.

Cardona, M. C., Reig, A., & Domene, D. (2000). *Theory and practice of instructional adaptations.* Alicante, Spain: Universidad de Alicante Press.

Cascales, A., Martínez, M. J., & Laguna, M. I. (2013). Methodology to work with tablets with students with specific needs of educational support in regular classrooms. In M. C. Cardona, E. Chiner, & A. Giner (Eds.), *Investigación e innovación educativa al servicio de instituciones y comunidades globales, plurales y diversas* (pp. 718–724). Alicante, Spain: AIDIPE (Asociación Interuniversitaria de Investigación Pedagógica).

Chiner, E., & Cardona, M. C. (2012). Teachers' use of inclusive practices in Spain. *The International Journal of Learning Diversity and Identities, 19*(1), 29–45.

Chiner, E., & Cardona, M. C. (2013). Inclusive education in Spain: How do skills, resources, and supports affect regular education teachers' perceptions of inclusion? *International Journal of Inclusive Education, 17*(5), 526–541. doi:10.1080/13603116.2012.689864

Colectivo IOÉ. (2003). *The employability of people with disabilities.* Barcelona, Spain: Fundación La Caixa.

Deak, A. (1999). *Children with special educational needs: The position in Spain.* International Peto Institute. Retrieved from epa.oszk.hu/01400/01428/00004/pdf/0402-Deak-Spain.pdf

Department of Education and Science. (1978). Special educational needs. *Report of the committee of inquiry into the education of handicapped children and young people (The Warnock report).* London, UK: HMSO.

Devesa, M. C. (2004). Effects of co-teaching in learning to read and write in 5-year-old students. Trabajo del período de investigación (suficiencia investigadora) del programa de doctorado "Atención a la Diversidad en Ámbitos Educativos". Universidad de Alicante, Alicante, Spain.

Echeita, G., Verdugo, M. A., Sandoval, M., Simón, C., López, M., González-Gil, F., & Calvo, I. (2009). FEAPS opinion about the process of educational inclusion. *Siglo Cero, 39*(4), 26–50.

European Agency for Development in Special Needs Education (EADSP). (2009a). Special needs education within the education systems: *Spain*. Odense, Denmark: Author.

European Agency for Development in Special Needs Education (EADSP). (2009b). *Teacher education for inclusion: International literature review*. Odense, Denmark: Author.

European Agency for Development in Special Needs Education (EADSP). (2011). *Teacher education for inclusion across Europe: Challenges and opportunities*. Odense, Denmark: Author.

European Agency for Development in Special Needs Education (EADSP). (2013). *Organization of provision to support inclusive education: Literature review*. Odense, Denmark: Author.

Fernández, D., Arias, E., & Gallego, L. (1999). *Enterprise culture: Employers' motivation for the inclusion of people with disabilities*. La Coruña, Spain: Fundación Paideia.

Florian, L. (2009, July). Special and inclusive education in Europe. *Session keynote given at 11th IASE biennial international conference on special education, broadening the horizon: Recognizing, accepting, and embracing differences to make a better world for individuals with special needs*, Alicante, Spain.

Fundación Equipara. (2008). *2008 Equipara report: Observatory for improving the labour equity of people with disabilities*. Barcelona, Spain: Author.

Galino, M. A. (1968). *History of education: Ancient and middle ages*. Madrid, Spain: Gredos.

García Pastor, C. (1998). Integration in Spain: A critical review. *European Journal of Special Needs Education, 13*(1), 43–56.

Giné, C., & Ruiz, R. (1991). Curricular adaptations and school educational project. In A. Marchesi, C. Coll, & J. Palacios (Eds.), *Desarrollo psicológico y educación, III. Necesidades educativas especiales y aprendizaje escolar* (pp. 337–349). Madrid, Spain: Alianza Editorial.

Gómez, J. M. (2013). *Beliefs and perceptions of employability of people with intellectual disability*. Unpublished doctoral dissertation, University of Alicante, Alicante, Spain.

Hernández, A., & Olmos, S. (2011). *Collaborative learning methodologies through technologies*. Salamanca, Spain: Ediciones Universidad de Salamanca.

Illán, N., & Arnáiz, P. (1996). Historical evolution of special education: Background and current situation. In N. Illán (Coord.), *Didáctica y organización en educación especial* (pp. 13–43). Málaga, Spain: Aljibe.

Inclusion Europe. (2006). *Towards inclusive education: Examples of good practices of inclusive education*. Brussels, Belgium: Inclusion Europe and European Commission.

Inclusion International. (1996). *Inclusion: News from inclusion international*. Brussels, Belgium: Author.

Instituto Nacional de Estadística. (2012). *Employability of people with disabilities. Series 2008–2011*. Retrieved from http://www.ine.es/jaxi/menu.do?type=pcaxis&path=/t22/p320/serie&file=pcaxis

Jiménez, P., & Vilà, M. (1999). *Special education and diversity education*. Málaga, Spain: Aljibe.

Jordán, de U. B., & Verdugo, M. A. (2011). *Evolution of supported employment in Spain (1995–2010) and adjustment to the quality standards of EUSE.* Retrieved from http// sid.usal.es/idocs/F8/FDO25798/Informe_INICO_ECA_1995-2010.pdf

LEP. (1945, July 18). *Act of elementary education.* Boletín Oficial del Estado.

LGE. (1970, August 6). *Act on education and financing of the educational reform.* Boletín Oficiadel Estado.

LISMI. (1982, April 20). *Act on social integration of people with disabilities.* Boletín Oficial del Estado.

LOCE. (2002, December 24). *Organic act on educational quality.* Boletín Oficial del Estado.

LODE. (1985, July 4). *Organic act on the right to education.* Boletín Oficial del Estado.

LOE. (2006, May 4). *Organic act on education.* Boletín Oficial del Estado.

LOGSE. (1990, October 4). *Act on general arrangement of the education system.* Boletín Oficial del Estado.

LOPEG. (1995, November 21). Organic act on the participation, evaluation, and administration of schools. Boletín Oficial del Estado.

Martín, J. F., Torres, J., Santaolalla, E., & Hernández, V. (2013). The competence of learning to learn: Teacher perceptions of its development in elementary and secondary school in the community of Madrid. In M. C. Cardona, E. Chiner, & A. Giner (Eds.), *Investigación e innovación educativa al servicio de instituciones y comunidades globales, plurales y diversas* (pp. 776–786). Alicante, Spain: AIDIPE.

Ministry of Education. (2012). *The figures of education in Spain.* Madrid, Spain: Author.

Minister of Education, Culture, and Sport-Government of Spain. (2012). *Proposals for improvement 2012 report on the state of the Spanish education system.* Retrieved from http://www.mecd.gob.es/dctm/cee/informe2012/pm2012cee.pdf? documentId = 0901e72b 8145b4f3

Ministry of Education, Culture, and Sport-Government of Spain. (2013a). *Report on non-university education: Students with special educational needs, 2011–2012.* Retrieved from http://www.mecd.gob.es/servicios-al-ciudadano-mecd/estadisticas/educacion/no-univer-sitaria/alumnado/matriculado.html

Ministry of Education, Culture and Sport-Government of Spain. (2013b). *Report on non-university education: Students enrolled 2000–2011.* Retrieved from http://www.mecd. gob.es/servicios-al-ciudadano-mecd/estadisticas/educacion/no-universitaria/alumnado/ matriculado.html

Mittler, P. (2000). *Working towards inclusive education: Social contexts.* London: David Fulton.

Moliner, O., Sales, A., Ferrández, R., & Traver, J. (2011). Inclusive cultures, policies and practices in Spanish compulsory secondary education schools: Teachers' perceptions in ordinary and specific teaching contexts. *International Journal of Inclusive Education,* *15*(5), 557–572.

Navarro, A., & Camús, M. (2013). The interactive whiteboard in the educational process of students with specific learning disorders. In M. C. Cardona, E. Chiner, & A. Giner (Eds.), *Investigación e innovación educativa al servicio de instituciones y comunidades globales, plurales y diversas* (pp. 1080–1087). Alicante, Spain: AIDIPE.

OECD. (2012). *Child well-being module, CX3.1, special education needs.* Organization for Economic Cooperation and Development. Retrieved from www.oecd.org/social/family/ 50325299.pdf

Order EDU/849/2010. (2010, March 18). *Order on the educational arrangement of students with specific needs of educational support and the regulations of school counselling services.* Ministerio de Educación, en las ciudades de Ceuta y Melilla. Boletín Oficial del Estado.

Pallisera, M., Vilà, M., & Valls, M. J. (2003). The current situation of supported employment in Spain: Analysis and perspectives based on the perception of professionals. *Disability and Society, 6*(18), 797–810.

Pujolàs, P. (1997). A methodological and organizational classroom proposal for diversity. *Aula de Innovación Educativa, 59*, 23–27.

Royal Decree on Arrangement of the Education of Students with Special Education needs. (1995, June 2). Boletín Oficial del Estado.

Royal Decree on Arrangement of the Special Education. (1982, October 22). Boletín Oficial del Estado.

Royal Decree on Arrangement of the Special Education. (1985, March 16). Boletín Oficial del Estado.

Ruiz i Bel, R. (1988). *Individualized teaching techniques.* Madrid, Spain: Cincel.

Teese, R., Aasen, P., Field, S., & Pont, B. (2006). Equity in education thematic review: Spain country note. *Proceedings of Organization for Economic Co-Operation and Development (OECD).* Retrieved from http://www.oecd.org/spain/36361409.pdf

Torres, B. (2013). Alternative assessment strategies for children with disabilities in inclusive classrooms. In M. C. Cardona, E. Chiner, & A. Giner (Eds.), *Investigación e innovación educativa al servicio de instituciones y comunidades globales, plurales y diversas* (pp. 1152–1158). Alicante, Spain: AIDIPE.

United Nations. (1971, December 20). *Declaration on the rights of mentally retarded persons.* General Assembly resolution 2856(XXVI).

United Nations. (1975, December 9). *Declaration on the rights of disabled persons.* General Assembly resolution 3447(XXX).

United Nations Educational, Scientific, and Cultural Organization. (1994). *The Salamanca statement and framework for action on special needs education.* Paris, France: Author.

Verdugo, M. A., & Rodríguez-Aguilella, A. (2012). Inclusion in Spain from the perspective of students with intellectual disability, families, and professionals. *Revista de Educación, 358*, 45–56. doi:10.4438/998-592X-RE-2010-358-086

Vicente, A., & De Vicente, M. P. (2006). *An approach to the history of special education.* Murcia, Spain: Diego Marín.

SPECIAL EDUCATION TODAY IN NORWAY

Rune Sarrormaa Hausstatter and Harald Thuen

ABSTRACT

The rise of special education in Norway dates back to the early 1880s. Originally, special education was strongly influenced by the Age of Enlightenment and religious and philanthropic commitment to disadvantaged children. This chapter describes the development of special education by examining five critical eras, namely, The Era of Philanthropy, the Era of Segregation — Protection for Society, The Era of Segregation-Best Interest of the Child, The Age of Integration — Social Critique and Normalization, and The Age of Inclusion. Also, included are sections on the origins of public education, teacher preparation aspects, approaches to special education, working with families, and important legislative acts that support the right to education for students with disabilities. The chapter also explores the tension that exists today between regular and special education due to Norwegian legislation that emphasizes that students that do not benefit from regular education have a right to special education. The chapter concludes with a discussion about the future challenge to special education, namely, the efficacy of special education.

Special Education International Perspectives: Practices Across the Globe
Advances in Special Education, Volume 28, 181–207
Copyright © 2014 by Emerald Group Publishing Limited
All rights of reproduction in any form reserved
ISSN: 0270-4013/doi:10.1108/S0270-401320140000028013

INTRODUCTION

A central study in the development of special education is offered by Werner-Putnam (1979). This pioneering work presents a model where the development of special education follows certain, almost law like histori-cal development, starting with support for children with sensory impair-ment and ending with children struggling with severe learning disabilities. This stage like development seems to be in keeping with the experiences of most Western countries. However, the reason for why we experience this development can be debated. Warner-Putnam's explanation is that the development of special education follows the economic development of each country. Special education is expensive and might therefore be seen as a luxury activity – something that a state will spend resources on after other national challenges are solved. In Warner-Putnam's view the development of special education is a hierarchical and linear development based on the nation's wealth. Richardson and Powell (2011) present an alternative model to Putnam. In their view, the development of special education must be looked at as the sum of both international, global trends, and national challenges. The debate about human rights (e.g. United Nations, 1975, 2006) and the quality of education are exam-ples of global processes that both constrain and force nations to develop their support for people with disabilities. As pointed out by Richardson and Powell, special education is not always about the wish to help people with problems; special education strategies can also be used as national strategies to secure the international position of the nation. Several aspects of the development of special education in Norway support the claim made by Richardson and Powell. The aim of this chapter is there-fore to describe the development of special education in Norway as responses to international trends and link this historical development to future challenges of this support system in Norway.

A FEW HISTORICAL FACTS ABOUT NORWAY

Before we go into the description of the development of the special educa-tional system in Norway, it is necessary to emphasize a few general facts. Norway is a very small country with a population of about five million peo-ple and is one of the richest countries in the world – with a wealth that is reasonably shared by all citizens. The financial situation changed dramatically when Norway became an oil-producing nation in the early 1970s. Before the oil, Norwegian society was mainly dependent on the fishing industry, shipping, agriculture and after the Second World War an energy demanding metal industry supported by hydro power.

Norway, which is situated on the outskirts of mainland Europe, has held no vital historical position since the last Viking rides. Norway was part of a union with Demark for 436 years. Supporting Napoleon, the Danish King found himself on the losing side, and as part of the Treaty of Kiel, Norway was ceded to Sweden in 1814. Norway used the opportunity to declare its own independence and build its own constitution – resulting in the Norwegian-Swedish War, and a new union where Norway was under the Swedish king but with a Norwegian Parliament. A Norwegian Parliament meant partly Norwegian independence and the growth of the nation.

In a peaceful separation with Sweden in 1905, Norway established itself as an independent kingdom. Although, Norway was neutral in the First World War the neutrality strategy did not work in the Second World War, and Norway was occupied by Germany in 1940. Norway become part of the Western block after their political and financial support in World War II. This situation led eventually to Norway joining the North Atlantic Treaty Organization in 1949.

These brief facts about Norway might seem to be of no importance in a chapter dealing with the trends in Norwegian special education. However, they are important in order to understand the role of special education in Norway. First of all, the marginal position of Norway in today's world history means that the country has never imposed any major changes on the field of special education in a global perspective. On the contrary, Norway's strive towards national independence and the growth of a new nation has resulted in strategies where the goal has been to adapt to the international trends of education. The development of Norwegian special education must therefore be understood as one of several areas where Norway should prove its ability to be an independent nation (Froestad, 1999). The second point is the fact that the financial situation has changed a lot in Norway over the last 40 years. One result of this is that Norway can afford to use a lot of resources on its school system, and subsequently Norway might be a nation that tries to adapt to international trends more actively than many other nations.

ORIGINS OF EDUCATION

The Public School

The first traces of organized education in Norway date back to 1152 when the first cathedral schools were established and later changed into Latin-schools. The public school system in Norway was established in 1739, and the public school has since had a dominant position in Norwegian education. While this school legislation stated that the school should be for everybody, in practice many children did not get any education and illiteracy was the norm. The first round of modernization, finished in 1827, of the public school came as a reaction to Norwegian independence from Denmark and stated that all places with more than 30 habitants should have a permanent school. This school should offer education to children from 7 years old until about 15 years of age, for a minimum of two months per year. In 1845, a new legislation for schools in cities was declared, which ensured 18 to 24 hours teaching a week for 45 weeks a year. In 1889, the public school was reorganized into the national elementary school, which offered education for children from 7 to 14 years old. The school system was then modernized in 1936 and in 1959. In 1969 the elementary school was changed to 9 years of school (age 7–16 years) and in 1997 this was changed to 10 years of school (from age 6 years). Today there are about 600,000 students in compulsorily school from grades 1–10 (6–16 years of age). Norway has a school system that is divided into primary school (grades 1–7) and secondary school/middle school (grades 8–10). In addition, all students have the right to a 3-year high-school education. Today, 97 per cent of children in grades 1–10, and 94 per cent of youth at high-school (grades 11–13) attend public school, and the rest join private schools (Ministry of Education and Research [MER], 2012).

Teacher Education

The development of the school system was also dependent on the development of the teaching profession. The first state owned teacher training seminary was opened in 1826, and several others were established later in the 1800s. As pointed out by Karlsen (2005), the first phase of the period of teacher education was very liberal in the sense that there was no state defined curriculum and no general tests. This, however, changed in the late 1800s when the state took more control over the content of the teacher training seminaries to ensure the quality of the education, and this education is still today controlled by a national framework. Teacher training education was offered as a semi-academic degree in Norway until 1973. After that teacher education was established as 3-year education study at the college level until in 1993 it was changed to 4 years of study.

THE RISE OF SPECIAL EDUCATION IN NORWAY

The history of Special Needs Education in Norway dates back to the early 1800s, when it was strongly influenced by the ideas of the Age of Enlightenment and an increasingly religious, philanthropic commitment to disadvantaged children. The origins of the first special needs educational institutions are to be found in a coming together of the rational and the humane, a meeting between the Enlightenment's fascination with and exploration of man's possibilities and limitations on the one hand and a Christian charity on the other. For Norway and the Western World in general, new perspectives in knowledge, institutional models and methods for deaf, blind, intellectually impaired and socially maladjusted children and young people emerged in the Western World in the years between 1770 and 1830.

Two different approaches can be identified in the early history of institutions in Norway. The first approach originated in Paris and derived from a scientific, medical interest in children and young people with physical or intellectual disabilities. It came to Norway with the establishment of our first institution for special education, the institute for the deaf in Trondheim which opened in 1825, and was later followed by an institute for the blind (1861) and an institute for the educationally subnormal or those whom we now refer to as having intellectual disabilities (1874). In 1881, the above three groups were brought within the remit of a common law – the Act on 'Teaching of Abnormal Children', or *Abnormal School Act (Government of Norway, 1881)*, as it was called. This was a sign that special needs education was now a public concern, an undertaking that required 'Society's Contribution', although it also continued to rely on private support.

The other approach is associated with children and young people who are socially maladjusted either because of their background or behaviour.

They were not classified as 'abnormal', but described by words such as 'neglected' or 'morally corrupted children'. This approach was not intended to develop specific teaching methods and technology to deal with the students' problems, but to establish a completely new environment for upbringing and care as a substitute for the child's family. The first establishment of this type to arrive in Norway was established in Oslo in 1841 under the name Toftes Gave, originally referred to as a 'rescuing institution' and after a few decades as an 'educational care establishment'. In 1896, the Norwegian educational care establishments were brought within the scope of the 'Law on the Treatment of Neglected Children', known as the Child Welfare Council Act (Government of Norway, 1896) and were now called 'reform schools', and the model institution Bastøy was opened at the same time.

On the basis of this the first era in the history of special needs education during the 1800s can be described as the era of philanthropy. The next era begins with two separate laws at the end of the 1800s, the Abnormal Schools Act and Child Welfare Council Act, indicating that the state now steps in and takes responsibility for the upbringing, education and care of disabled children. They become 'children of the state' with the development of a system of institutions based on strict segregation through the first half of the 1900s. The third era was ushered in by the Special Schools Act of 1951 (Government of Norway, 1951). This act gave Norway a general special schools system which embraced institutions that previously fell under the Abnormal Schools Act (1881) and Child Welfare Council Act (1896), bringing the blind, deaf and dumb, intellectually impaired and children with maladjusted social behaviour, behavioural difficulties, as they were called, under one and the same law. The two historical approaches were thus combined under one and the same law – and Norway ended up with one system. This system would still be based on an ideology of segregation, but at the same time people began to have doubts about the effect of the institutions and the treatment of children. The change came in 1975 with the 'integration reform'. The Special Schools Act was now integrated with the Primary and Lower Secondary Schools Act (Government of Norway, 1975). Special needs teaching in principle are incorporated within 'normal schools', that is to say primary and lower secondary schools, the integration of the acts being based on an ideology of normality. The era of integration lasted until 1997, when it gave way to a new era, as we can describe the Reform Document which introduced the fifth and current epoch, the Norwegian Curriculum Plan of 1997 (Government of Norway, 1997). The plan is based on 'adapted learning' rooted in the principle of inclusive education, which had some years beforehand had been adopted as the guiding principle at the UNESCO World Conference on Special Needs Education in Salamanca (UNESCO, 1994).

Having outlined the five eras, we shall now go on to demonstrate more specifically how the changing ideologies and reforms shaped the development of special needs education in Norway.

The Era of Philanthropy (1825–1880)

The philanthropists, who took the initiative to establish institutions in the 1800s, wanted to perform their good works without any help from the Government or public funds. They were only answerable to God. The concept of philanthropy was far from new. It derived from the Greek expression *fil antropos* – 'friend of humanity', and was best understood in everyday parlance as an expression for benevolence, kindness or generosity – a Christian charity. The spirit of philanthropy was able to flourish in Norway in the 1800s on the basis of the principle of liberalism, which required the state and the government to exercise restraint in favour of private initiatives. This created the political basis for a flourishing, Christian, private benevolence, primarily directed towards children and young people, who in their innocence were considered to be 'the deserving poor' that prevailed over other groups who were themselves considered to be 'to blame' for their situation.

The guiding principle for the philanthropists was charity – love for a stranger. 'Love thy neighbour as thyself'. In the Christian concept of love, your neighbour is someone who needs help, but from whom you cannot expect anything in return (Nygren, 1965, 1966). Love for a 'neighbour' is not like love for a relative or friend; it is directed at strangers – even your enemies. This distinguishes Christian charity from other forms of love, such as erotic love, parental love or affection between friends. The philanthropists wanted to get back to Augustine's caritas synthesis (compassionate love) – which arose from the connection between *eros* and *agape*, eros stood for man's longing and striving upwards to God, a yearning to be loved and gain salvation, whereas *agape* expressed a universal love for man in God's image which seeks to help and save mankind. In terms of the caritas synthesis, charity is not a love that sacrifices all, because it considers love to be a need in man. Considered in this way charity is not just a means of giving, but also a way of receiving.

The blind, deaf, disturbed and morally maladjusted children were all given prominence in the name of charity. But they also attracted a rational, scientific interest, particularly based on medical knowledge. The mythical delusions on witchcraft and other devious causes of disability common in the Middle Ages had been cast aside, it was understood and accepted that the disabled were not to blame for their own fate. This also applied to socially and morally maladjusted children, it was accepted that they could not be held responsible for the situation in which they found themselves, which had been caused either by poverty or parental neglect. All the above groups represented a deviation from what was considered normal. Questions were asked about the limits that could be set. What could be achieved from teaching, development and improvement within the different groups? How the message of charity would be reflected in the establishments' teaching work and particularly in the pastors' meeting with the child.

International pioneers included the theologian and lawyer, Charles-Michel de l'Épée, in the education of the deaf, the linguist, Valentin Haüy, in the teaching of the blind and the psychiatrist, Jean Marc Gaspard Itard, and his student, the physician Édouard Onesimus Séguin, in the teaching of the educationally subnormal (Thuen, 2008, p. 88). These individuals established the first institutions for children with medical disabilities on a universal basis – or institutes as they preferred to call them, to give their work a more professional image. l'Épée opened his institute for the deaf in 1770, in 1784 it was the turn of Haüy's institute for the blind, and in 1837 Séguin commenced education for pupils who had been diagnosed as 'idiots'. All three pioneers were located in Paris, where they also gained recognition and honours in the French Academy of Sciences. Common to all of them, apart from the medical-diagnostic approach, was a desire to stimulate the development of children's moral, intellectual and mental capacity through education. Particular importance was attached to identifying the wishes of the child. Diagnostics, teaching technology and education together formed a new blueprint for the institutions, adapted to suit the different groups. In Norway the first institute for the deaf and dumb was established in 1825 (Trondheim), the first institute for the blind in 1861 (Oslo) and the first institute for the educationally subnormal in 1874 (Oslo), all significantly influenced by the above Paris institutes.

The moral educational care institutions for their part sought inspiration from the writings of Johann Heinrich Pestalozzi and the establishments he and his successor, Philipp Emanuel von Fellenberg, set up in Switzerland. Then Johann Hinrich Wichern's established *Das rauhe Haus*, a model for many outside Hamburg. A number of observers from the Norwegian establishments visited Wichern's establishment and returned home bursting with enthusiasm. The educational care establishments took over full responsibility for the care and education of children from their parents. Their institutional educational theory either aimed at family model along the lines of Pestalozzi's or Wichern's establishments, or they could organize their activities on the model of a military 'barracks', which some preferred. The educational care establishment was a total institution along the lines of a prison, but based on the principle of educational care and not punishment of children, whereby children were not imprisoned after a judgement passing a sentence for a specific number of years. The educational care establishment could on the contrary detain the child as long as it was considered necessary; it was up to the establishment's directors to assess when the child was sufficiently 'improved' to be discharged. In individual cases the Norwegian establishment could have custody of children from the age of six years until they were 19–20 years old. In other words, this approach involved the development of an all-embracing institutional system of education.

Elsewhere in Europe and in North America the educational care establishments were prolific from the 1820s onwards and were referred to as 'Houses of Refuge' (North America), 'Reformatory Schools' (England), 'Rettungsanstalten' (Germany) and 'La Colonie Agricole' or 'Le Péntencier Agricole' (France). In Norway, the first educational care establishment was founded in Oslo in 1841. One particularly distinctive feature of the Norwegian establishments was their location on islands. This was partly because the island establishments were more difficult to escape from than establishments on the mainland and partly because educational work on an island could be accomplished away from and undisturbed by their surroundings.

The Era of Segregation: Protection of Society (1880–1950)

International research literature tends to make a distinction between private, philanthropic child care and public care by using the terms 'child rescue' and 'child saving' (Thuen, 2002). The difference in concepts is based on the idea that 'rescue' (child rescue) derives from a private commitment rooted in civil society. It is the charity of the individual, the act of rescuing a fellow human in need that is the driving force in this form of child care. The shift to 'child saving' takes place when the Government intervenes in the care by means of laws, making it part of a public commitment. This coincided with the transition from a constitutional to a social basis for the government's action, which is evident in significant parts of the Western world between 1870 and 1920. Care was now increasingly to be motivated as a 'safeguard' in a spirit of solidarity with society. There was a desire to protect the individuals who were least capable of protecting themselves and a desire to protect society from the individuals who might harm it.

The emergence of the welfare state in the early 1900s gave rise to questions: What responsibility should the Government take for the education of the disabled? Should legislation also provide for their compulsory education? If so what would be the best way to provide for education outside 'normal school'? The answer was given by the act concerning 'Treatment of Abnormal Children', or the Abnormal Schools Act of 1881, as it was known. With this law, Norway became the first country in Europe to introduce a common law for disabled children. The term 'abnormal' had been used for some years as a generic term for the blind, deaf and dumb and the educationally subnormal. Similar questions were asked with reference to the concept of child protection: What responsibility should the Government have for the care, upbringing and education of the children who displayed deviant social behaviour at school and in the home environment or whose parents were unable to take care of them? The answer was provided by the act on 'Treatment of neglected Children', or the Child Welfare Council Act of 1896 as it was known. The Abnormal School Act and the Child Welfare Council Act heralded a decline in importance of philanthropy and special needs education and child protection now became a public concern. Special needs education was still reserved for children with medically diagnosed disabilities, whereas children with social behavioural difficulties were allocated to child protection.

The two acts must be seen in the context of the introduction of the Norwegian Elementary School Acts in 1889. These laws, one for the towns and one for the country, were intended to modernize and bring democracy to primary and lower secondary school education. The fundamental aim was to create a standard common school for all children between the ages of 7 and 14 years, and thus do away with the old school system divided by class. But the concept of a common school did not apply to everyone. Disabled children were left out. Both the Abnormal Schools Act and the Child Welfare Council Act sought to separate disabled and difficult children from the elementary schools, based on a desire to create a 'good' elementary school for 'normal pupils', avoiding the disruptive effect that disabled and maladjusted children might have on the teaching. There was no issue with the right of the disabled to education in general and their obligation to participate, but with their rights within the context of the elementary school, or normal school. It was decided that children who had 'intellectual or physical Deficiencies', who had contagious diseases, or who influenced other school children with their bad behaviour, could be excluded. At the same time, the Elementary School Acts gave the local authorities the right to establish extra tuition or special tuition, but without obligation. Rather paradoxically, the idea of making schools more democratic, enshrined in the acts of 1889, led to a separation of pupils who were considered not to belong there. If the idea of a school for all, even for children from the upper social strata of the community, was to become a reality, the children who it was feared would tarnish the quality of teaching, had to be left out.

The Abnormal Schools Act and the separation paragraphs in the Elementary Schools Act actually laid the foundations for an extensive, differentiated special school system in Norway. The reason was twofold. The Abnormal Schools Act was conceived out of a professional interest in the disabled who were 'educationally competent'. Thus, the law was itself a segregating law that separated the disabled into two groups, the educationally competent and the non-educationally competent. The law represented a continuation of the concepts of the Enlightenment and the belief that teaching and education of disabled children was of value and beneficial. The aim was to impart to children 'as far as possible' a knowledge that corresponded to the common schools' aim of a Christian and civic education, but the abnormal schools were also supposed to prepare the students for working life. The law was effectively a law of enforcement based on the practice that all abnormal children had to be registered and assessed for a place in a school which was almost always a long way from home, thus representing a drastic infringement of parental rights. The decision to separate made in the Elementary School Acts was not justified out of any consideration for the disabled but as a way of protecting the elementary schools as a normal school. In other words, it was an institutionalized protection of normality. Although the basic motivation was different the Abnormal Schools Act and the Elementary Schools Act became coordinating aspects of a system of segregation that gradually produced a system of institutions ranging from extra tuition and special tuition to boarding schools and work and foster homes.

How did this system fit into the era? In Norway the educational concepts were taken from Europe. The German periodical *Der Heilpädagog*, was particularly well known. It discussed educational and teaching issues associated with a broad spectrum of children with disabilities. There may have been several reasons why Norway nevertheless became the only European country to introduce a common law in the 1800s. In the preparatory and processing stages of the act practical considerations, such as the additional work involved in the development of three laws and the fear of favouring one group over the others, were raised (Aas, 1954; Simonsen, 1998). Froestad (1995) thinks that the fundamental explanation is more likely to lie in the understanding of handicap as a social construct. The various 'deviant groups' were lumped into the common category 'abnormal' as a separate group in relation to the 'normal'. This enabled the normal classes to be freed from deviant children who were to be transferred to 'auxiliary schools'.

By the beginning of the 20th century, Norway had by virtue of the Elementary Schools Acts and the Abnormal Schools Act established a system of segregation that classified students into three groups: normal school pupils, special school pupils and the non-educationally competent pupils. An institutional system that would embrace all would gradually be developed. But at the same time this system was beset by inconsistencies in regulation and organization, which could make a big difference in how children were treated. Gradually as the institutions were established, a general need emerged for testing and measuring children's mental condition and level of ability, so that they could be classified and be allocated into the right place in the system. For example, measurement of a student's intelligent quotient (IQ) was developed by Binet and Simon (1905), who worked from the French Ministry of Education, just after the turn of the century. The objective was to identify children with intellectual impairment and their level of intellectual deficiency. On the basis of their IQ and level, they could be placed in special classes with tuition adapted to suit their needs. The tests rapidly won recognition as the best tool in the task of separating the individual student groups from one another. It was thought that children's intelligence could be measured purely in terms of ability, but that their mind, which indicated their moral level, could also be assessed.

It was not many years before the institutions under the two laws came in for sharp criticism from the public, in both literature and professional contexts. Initially, there were criticisms of abuse and mistreatment, lack of staff and resources and degrading living arrangements, primarily issues of human and material shortcomings. But soon people were not just asking about the material and resources aspects of the operation but also about the professional justification for the institutional placements. Several big cases were brought before the courts (Thuen, 2002). The revelations in these cases triggered a broad public debate about the work of the various institutions. For instance, they were accused of a lack of love and affection and a tough regime, and at worst of being concentration camps for children. Prominent politicians and members of the Government also voiced strong criticism. In practice, however, the criticism did not have much effect, investigations and official reports show that abuse and mistreatment of children continued on a significant scale right up to the 1970s (NOU, 2004, p. 23).

In the 1930s another form of criticism was expressed based on empirical and professional research (Arctander & Dahlstrøm, 1932). Arctander and Dahlstrøm reported that the research showed a high level of recidivism among children placed in institutions for children with behavioural difficulties or criminality. Furthermore, half of the boys in these institutions had committed criminal offences in the years immediately after being discharged and the rate of recidivism increased with the passing of time after they left. Also, compared with children in foster homes, the rate of recidivism of children from institutions was up to three times as high. In addition, psychiatric studies of institutionalized children conducted at the same time showed that: large groups suffered from various forms of mental disorders; and many of these children were also IQ tested and labelled as 'backward'. In short the institutions had failed in everything from the admissions procedure to the educational content and outcome.

The Era of Segregation: In the Best Interests of the Child (1950–1975)

The period after the Second World War was dominated by a strong focus on the development of the welfare state. The Nordic welfare state model became the Norwegian strategy. The Nordic welfare state model, dominated by a social democracy, focused on universalism by giving equal benefits and services to all citizens regardless of the status of the family or market. The development of a good school system was in this framework important, and all children had the right to education.

In 1951, Norway introduced the Special Schools Act, replacing the old abnormal schools and expanding the field of practice for special needs education. This law now applied to five groups of persons with disabilities, where previously there had been three. The individual groups were also extended. Where the old law included blind children, the new one would apply to the blind and the visually impaired. Likewise for the deaf; the new law included the deaf and hard of hearing. As well as these two groups, the law would apply to children with mental impairments with speaking, reading and writing difficulties and children with social behavioural difficulties, which previously fell under the Child Welfare Council Act and child protection. Terms like 'educationally subnormal' and 'retarded' were replaced by the collective term 'mentally impaired', which indicated that they should be the focus for the professional educational experts, while the other mentally impaired were brought back into the fold of the medical profession (Korsvold, 2006). At the same time, Norway got into a two-pronged system for special needs education; alongside separate special schools, special needs education could also be given as extra tuition in normal schools. The system expanded sharply in the decades to come. For example, in 1950, 1,500 students were received extra tuition in primary and lower secondary schools while in 1975 the number had jumped to 46,000 (SSB, 1975), or around 8 per cent of all students. Then special schools tripled during the period. The peak year was in 1978, when Norway had 100 special schools in the country with a total of 3,700 pupils (SSB, 1994).

Under the two-pronged system, special needs education was distinctly segregated during the years 1950—1975. It was an intentional policy, thus expressed in a Ministerial Recommendation in 1849: 'A system must be devised so that pupils who belong in special tuition classes can be separated as soon as it is advisable' (Samordningsnemda for skoleverket). The old system would be modernized, but without letting go of the diagnostic philosophy of segregation. The terms 'special schools' and 'special needs teacher' were introduced and brought into use a few years before the Special Schools Act was introduced (Ravneberg, 1999). The teachers in the various special schools were about to move closer and the use of the generic term 'special needs teacher' can be interpreted as a desire to define a common professional status. It was to be the introduction to an epoch defined by professional action and an increasingly professional approach.

One significant aspect of the new segregation policy was that the various groups of disabled children were not mixed together within the institutions which had particularly been the case in the previous era. The diagnosis of children using different tests, primarily IQ tests, was central to this work (see Table 1). The problem with this type of testing was that it set IQ boundaries between the various groups. Scales for division of intelligence according to IQ were developed based on international research, but the borderline cases were and still are problematic. Because of these borderline cases, teachers in normal schools, auxiliary schools, and special schools needed to discuss where borderline students were to be placed (Ravneberg, 1999). Finally, there were also pupils with 'character defects' which made

Table 1. Proposed Division of Students in the Norwegian School System in 1948.

	IQ	Percentage of Student Population
Normal school	Above 90	93.75
Support/help school	66–90	4.9
Schools for mentally retarded	41–65	1.1
Nursing home	0–40	0.25

Source: Developed from Ravneberg (1999).

them unsuitable for admission to special schools. These pupils had to be separated from the special school system and sent to separate homes for the educationally subnormal but it was not clear what 'character defects' entailed. In hindsight due to these aspects, many children were wrongly placed in this heartless system of segregation.

It may be debated whether special needs education in the years directly after the war was anything more than a pure organizational convenience. Were the activities based on educational theories and principles? A common point of reference appears to have been the Swiss psychologist, teacher of the deaf and later a professor of mental health education, Heinrich Hanselmann (Thuen, 2008). A central theme to his theory was to bring the treatment of the deaf, educationally subnormal, those with speech impediments or nervous conditions, socially difficult and unprincipled children under one heading. The common feature was that they all suffered from defects in personal development that advocated a special therapeutic educational approach, an overall view of their human spiritual life. The old term 'abnormal' was replaced by 'developmentally impaired', an expression that is found in the Norwegian reform philosophy at the end of the 1940s. Therapeutic educational theory focussed on the upbringing of children, not their health, which fell within the medical profession and this is where it would be necessary if it would separate the children. The general impression is however that up to the 1960s special educational needs teaching both in primary and lower secondary schools and in the special schools largely muddled along on the basis of trial and error, without any foundation in a tradition of scientific knowledge (Haug, 1999). The knowledge was primarily based on an exchange of practical experience. The content of special needs education would therefore be mainly driven by practical experience.

To increase the level of professionalism of the special education support system, the national college of special teacher training was established in

1961. Training of special teachers developed slowly from short courses in the 19th century, into a 2-year study course offered by the special teacher training college from 1961. The first year offered an introduction to five areas of special education: intellectually impaired, blind, deaf, language and speech problems, and behavioural problems. The education of teachers focused on practical challenges faced by teachers in the special schools. The second year offered a specialization within one of the five areas of specialization. The establishment of a special teacher training school led to an increased awareness of the need to also develop special education as a research area as part of the training and development of special teachers. This focus on research led to the first MA course in special education in 1976, and the PhD in special education was established in 1986. The special teacher college became part of the University of Oslo in 1990.

In the 1970s, several other colleges were given the opportunity to offer the first and second year of training to special teachers. This development came, as discussed later, at the same time as the normalization ideology (Wolfensberger, 1972) became a political factor in education. As a result of this, the new colleges for training special education teachers divided themselves into more or less two directions: one group following the system in the already established national special teacher training school and a second group with a clearer support of the normalization ideology and later integration.

The Era of Integration: Social Critique and Normalization

Not until the mid-1960s can we detect the signs of a political shift in the direction of a policy of integration. It was now recognized 'that the objectives of the special schools are in principle the same as for normal general education schools' (St.meld 42, 1965–1966). The separated children had a 'need for the same broad general educational, cultural and social development objectives as other children and young people'. These were fundamentally new perspectives in special school policy, derived from 'experience and new developments in psychology, psychiatry and sociology', as it was said. Special needs education had to look after 'the person behind the handicap' (St.meld 42, 1965–1966). The separated children must not 'get used to thinking of themselves and their peers as patients, cases or clients'. It is true the term 'deviants' was still used in referring to children with disabilities, but the causal pattern behind their 'deviant condition' was assumed to be more complicated and complex than had been believed from previous knowledge. Reference was made to England, where special educators' attention focussed on 'children at risk', and the need for supervision and observation of children assumed to be in the danger zone for 'dysfunctional development'. An effort was made to get away from the 'old' segregating methods and the way was opened for new, extended forms of understanding. In the first instance, the shift was expressed in a cautious scepticism in regards to institutions. For example, there was an argument in favour of using more day schools as opposed to boarding schools in regards to the further development of the special schools system. But in a broader perspective they were looking for a new type of expertise, an expertise based on three aspects, as envisaged by the Spesialskolerådet (Norwegian Council for Special Schools): educational diagnosis, educational treatment, and educational research (St.meld 42, 1965–1966). The aspects looked promising. It was essential for the research to be based on practical experience. Special needs educational research and special needs educational practice should be mutually stimulated by long-term cooperation.

The concept of integration entered the debate about the further development of special needs education at the end of the 1960s when the so-called Blom Committee was appointed in 1970. In spite of the ideological shift promoted by the Government in the mid-1960's criticism of the system had not abated. There are several explanations for the negative reactions. They are partly due to the lack of political vigour on the part of the Government, and partly the treatment the children in the institutions could be exposed to. A new era was approaching. It started in 1975, when the Special Schools Act was integrated in the Primary and Lower Secondary Schools Acts. The long tradition in special needs education would now finally be replaced by 'integration'. Science had brought a new sensitivity to the child's inner life and psyche that indicated that the security of the child was a vulnerable and delicate quantity. With their alienation and formalism the institutions represented a danger for children. The question was no longer whether the institutions were beneficial and effective for society, but also whether they were in the 'best interests of the child'. The Blom Committee proposed one common school law for all children. This was effectuated in 1975 (St.meld 98, 2009). This common school law emphasized that all children should have the right to education based on their abilities. The right to special education should not be connected to a medical situation or age, but to the pedagogical needs of each child. The principle of education to all children gave also the last group, severe mentally disabled children, the right to education. The main focus on integration and the goal of integration was accordingly:

(a) all should be part of a social community,
(b) all should have a share in the goods of the community,
(c) all should have the responsibility for tasks and obligations in the community.

The goal of integration was according to this committee to reduce barriers on human, social, and organizational levels. People with disabilities should have the same rights as everybody else to an education to foster personal, academic, and social development. How this equality should be reached was still much to be debated. The committee proposed a mix of both local support in ordinary schools and a national special school system (Kiil, 1981). This mixed support system continued to be offered in Norway for over 20 years, but the process of integration had begun.

The academic discussion in the same period was divided into two areas. As already presented, it had a strong focus on the scientific basis for the special education profession. This development was mainly within the already established categories of special needs that dominated the second year of the national teacher training college. The second area was established as part of the critique of the segregated strategy – the perspectives of normalization. The concept of normalization related to people with disabilities did partly exist as an organizational concept in the Nordic countries just after the Second World War, however, its development as a democratic and political concept took place in the 1960s by those at the forefront; Bengt Nirje from Sweden and Niels Erik Bank-Mikkelsen from Denmark. Bank-Mikkelsen first discussed the concept in 1959 (Biklen, 1985) but the word itself was first authored by Nirje (1969, 1985). Their perspectives on normalization had an international impact in the late 1960s, and these thoughts also brought new aspects into the special education debate in Norway by particularly emphasizing that the area of education must be related to the general social principles of the community. This focus on normalization as part of the general social development gave strong support to the goal of integration. Compared to several other Western countries the development of integrating children and adults with disabilities had taken place relatively slowly. However, in the late 1980s this changed, and already in 1993 most of the nursing homes and national special schools were closed down (Tøssebro, 2010). All children were then to have their education in the normal school and adults were to have the possibility to live a normal life as participants of the local community. Vislie (1995), one of the main Norwegian contributors to the academic discussion on integration, points to two strategies of integration that were developed during the 1970s and 1980s. The first strategy was related to the development of the special educational area to meet the new demands of integration. The second strategy was to reformulate the regular school system to meet an increased diversity of students.

The changes made in the Norwegian school system in the 1970s and 1980s reflect the first strategy described by Vislie (1995). The special school system was slowly reduced and almost all special schools were closed in 1993. Only a few schools for pupils with hearing and visual problems remained. The next strategy − the reformulation of the regular school system − became the next challenge for the special education system in Norway. It must be added that these radical changes in the late 1970s came at the same time as Norway became an oil-producing nation. Norway's wealth grew extensively from the mid-1970s, and with this wealth came both the international wave of new ideas of how to meet diversity and the financial possibility to carry through and pay for new reforms.

The Era of Inclusion: The Last Phase of Norwegian Special Education?

The goal of integrating students physically into the ordinary school system was more or less fulfilled in 1993 − one year before Norway ratified the Salamanca Statement. The closing of special schools and the strong drive towards integrating students with special needs in the 1980s and the early 1990s meant that the ratification of the Salamanca Statement (UNESCO, 1994) did not lead to any new national strategy when meeting children with special needs. The process of integration had already fulfilled most of the organizational strategies of the Salamanca Statement. However, for the concept of inclusion to mean more than just integration, the academic field of education presented definitions of this concept that emphasized the change that inclusion meant. In the Norwegian framework the definition presented by Peder Haug covers the Norwegian understanding of inclusion. An inclusive educational environment shall according to Haug (2003) focus on increasing *fellowship* among students, giving all students the possibility of *participation* as part of a process of *democratization*, and on top of this giving all students the necessary support so that they *benefit* from the education offered. The Norwegian understanding of inclusive education is as seen, not about integrating students in ordinary education, but about the transformation of teaching so that it supports all learners. In other words, it was the second aim of integration presented by Vislie (1995) that became the dominant focus for the Norwegian inclusion debate. A central reason for this focus was the high emphasis on normalization that led to the changes in the early 1990s. Theoretical perspectives of inclusion seem to follow the same line of argument and advocate for normalization would then also support the new concept of inclusive education. The political area had a strong drive towards fulfilling the normalization reform, and in this context special education was understood as not compatible with the goal of inclusion. In other words, the choice of this strategy meant that the approach of special education was reduced, and Norwegian educational policy from the mid-1990s was highly influenced by the criticism raised by advocates for inclusive education and the goal was to reduce the amount of special education to a minimum.

WORKING WITH FAMILIES

An examination of the early historical working relationship between families with special needs children and the special education profession in Norway reveals the absence of an established cooperative relationship. As you may recall, Norway's original special education support system cared for children with special needs that did not have parents. However, there was no formal policy in the early system that addressed the parents of students receiving educational services. Briefly, The Special Education Act of 1950 addressed the involvement of the family by noting that the family of child with special needs should be respected by allowing them the opportunity to visit their child once a month. Positively, after World War II, many parent interest groups were formed. Also, authors began to write about the rights of the handicapped. One noted book *The Rights of the Handicapped* was composed by Arne Skouen in 1966. In this book, Shouen compared the special schools to concentration camps (Haug, 1999). This author's engagement via national lectures was one of the reasons why the Blom Committee was established and why changes in special schools occurred in the 1970s.

Parent involvement changed significantly from the 1970s onwards due to Norway's legislations. For instance, today, parents have the right to ask for an evaluation of their child if they suspect he/she has special needs and they have to approve the offering of special educations services to their child. Fundamentally, changes related to working with families has been more juridical and only limited attention has been given to the practice collaboration of special education professionals and parents

(Befring & Tangen, 2008; Wilson, Hausstatter, & Lie, 2010). Certainly, this is an area that needs to be developed within Norwegian special education.

SPECIAL EDUCATION IN NORWAY TODAY

A central reason for the tension between ordinary and special education is due to the §5 in the Norwegian education law. The Norwegian legislation emphasizes that students that do not benefit from ordinary education have the right to special education (§5-1). An increase in special education is then a sign of a failing general educational system. Special education is thus used as a measurement of how well the ordinary education is able to educate all students and is hence also a measurement of inclusion in the Norwegian context.

The increased focus on inclusive education led to a reduction of special education in ordinary schools in Norway during the 1990s. The amount of special education was reduced to about 5 per cent in the late 1990s and early 2000s. However, this changed around 2005. Two central factors contributed to this change: first, the focus on international test results (mainly the Programme for International Student Assessment [PISA test]), and secondly, a new school reform in 2006 – the Knowledge Promotion Reform (Ministry of Education, 2006), that incorporates national tests into the Norwegian school. Even though the Knowledge Promotion Reform claimed that the goal of Norwegian schools should be to reduce the amount of special education to a minimum, the amount increased dramatically (see Fig. 1). One central reason for this might be the reform itself. The Knowledge Promotion Reform was mainly developed due to the poor Norwegian results in the first round of the PISA test (Norway performed about average – and still does). The reform clearly focused on increasing the academic standard of the Norwegian student; one central strategy here was the introduction of national school tests and competition between schools. The reason for the increase of special educational needs in Norway is debated (Hausstätter, 2013), and this increase is presented as one of the most clear challenges for the Norwegian school system today. In addition to a political goal of reducing the need for special education to a minimum the special education support system is very expensive – hence, this increase is therefore extremely politically challenging. The increase is also challenging the goal of creating an inclusive school in Norway because of the idea that inclusion and special education are strategies that are not

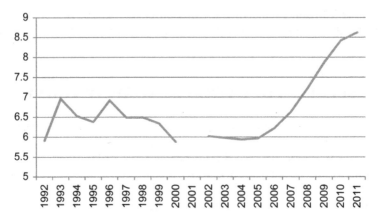

Fig. 1. Amount of Special Education in Norway Grades 1–10. *Source*: GSI
Norway (2013).

compatible (Gallagher, Heshusius, Iano, & Skrtic, 2004; Mostert, Kavale, &
Kauffman, 2007).

Adapted Education

The political alternative to the special education strategy is 'adapted education'. This strategy is logically linked to the school legislation and especially
to §5-1 presented above. An increase in special education is thus a sign that
the ordinary education system is not good enough. So in order to try to
reduce the amount of special education in Norway a lot of national
resources have been put into the development of a better normal educational system linked to the idea of 'adapted education'. The theoretical framework for this approach is presented by Bachman and Haug (2006).
According to them, two solutions are outlined to meet the goal of adapted
teaching: a student-centred approach (narrow approach) and a classroom
approach (wide approach) as can be seen in Table 2.

The student-centred approach is the dominant way of meeting the goal
of giving adapted teaching to all students among Norwegian teachers.
This approach focuses on the abilities and possibilities of each student.
The academic level of each student is evaluated and necessary teaching is
then planed accordingly. The problem with this approach according to
Bachman and Haug (2006) is that it supports an individualistic learning
environment and not necessarily an inclusive learning environment. It

Table 2. Adapted Teaching.

Student-Centred Approach	Classroom Approach
Individualization of teaching through individual plans, work schedules, and learning styles	Focus on collective approaches in teaching as well as individual approaches
Focus on intrinsic motivation	
Portfolio assessment of individual work	Focus on both internal and external motivation
Emphasis on the individual instead of the community	Development of a collaborative school culture
The focus is on the individual student when students have problems in school	Emphasis on structure and clarity in teaching
	The students' problems in school are put into a contextual relationship where the focus is on
Differentiation and possible segregation of students	the learning environment and teaching
	Emphasis on social participation for all students

also reduces the teacher's responsibility for the students' learning progress (Biesta, 2004), and the ability for the teacher to create an environment for learning where students learn to relate to each other to become good citizens. The alternative to this student-centred approach is the classroom approach. The entity of teaching within this framework is the whole group of students. The idea is that the teacher should give students the possibility to work together and to share their different knowledge. As part of this teaching the student also has to relate to others and through this develop their social skills. The point of this approach is to emphasize that learning is something that goes on in a social environment and in this case it is the classroom that is the environment for teaching. The teacher is in this approach is a facilitator of the communication between students in relation to the goal of the teaching. Classroom management is therefore emphasized as a crucial competence for the teacher in relation to adapted teaching.

However, it is important to emphasize that the distinction between the student-centred approach and the classroom approach has mainly been through an academic way of dealing with the concept of adapted teaching. In general, the practical field of education has practiced adapted teaching within the framework of the student-centred understanding. This focus on the student-centred approach can also be the third reason for why there has been an extreme rise in the amount of special education in Norway. The student-centred approach to teaching is very similar to the way special education knowledge is developed. It is the child's specific needs and situation that defines the pedagogical strategy necessary. So, in other words, the student-centred approach and special education is based on the same fundamental understanding where teaching should be planned and carried through, and hence special education is a good way to carry through a student-centred education.

FUTURE CHALLENGES: THE EFFICACY OF SPECIAL EDUCATION

One hundred and ninety years after the first special school was established in Norway, the role of special education is highly debated. For the last 40 years, the main debate regarding special education has been whether this type of support system stigmatizes and marginalizes students. The challenge of stigmatization was the main aspect in this debate for a long time; however, this has slightly changed during the last 10 years. The main question today is not whether special education stigmatizes students but whether it is effective or not and the main question today is: Can we continue supporting a special education support system if we cannot prove its efficiency?

The question of efficacy in special education is crucial for the whole existence of special education. This teaching profession is based on the first examples of successful teaching of 'idiots' as part of a scientific and philanthropic strive towards giving help and support to children that was excluded or found to be a problem for society for more than 200 years. To raise the question of whether special education is effective or not is therefore to challenge the essence and existence of this professional field in general. This question of efficacy is raised towards a profession that in a Norwegian context has based its professional knowledge on practical experience adapted from central Europe to begin with and later from the special schools in Norway itself. The research-based knowledge for this profession is quite young, with a slow development at the beginning of the 1960s through to the establishment of the first teacher training college in special education. The need for research-based knowledge within this field was further challenged by views on normalization, integration, inclusion, and adapted teaching supported by a political goal of reducing the need for special education in Norwegian schools. In other words, the research area of special education is still relatively young and has not yet been able to overall establish high quality research approaches. In addition, there has not been a political and ideological milieu in Norway for supporting the development of special educational research. To make things even more complicated, the area of professional practice has changed extensively over the last 40 years. The special education profession was developed to meet the need for professional knowledge in special schools and care institutions. These institutions were closed down early in the 1990s and the special education profession had then to adapt to the new practical environment in ordinary schools and as pointed out by Vislie (1995), needed to become part of the reformulation of the regular school system to meet the increased diversity of students. This new situation demanded a new set of knowledge both practical and scientific; however, the development of such new special educational knowledge has not yet been developed. The reason for this is that due to the established criticism of special education within the political context, there has not been any political support for developing an effective special education support system within schools, and due to the lack of academic experience within the special education area itself there has not been developed extensive research proving the effectiveness of special education support. Hence, the challenge faced by the question of efficiency in special education that we face today is, therefore, quite troublesome.

However, things seem to be changing. The increase in volume of children receiving special education support has made authorities aware of the challenges facing the special education support system. The lack of a clear understanding in this field led to a new green paper in 2009 (St.meld 98, 2009) that focuses on the right of every child to have the right to a good learning situation in schools. One recommendation in this paper was to establish an expert group that should evaluate the situation for special educational knowledge in Norway. This expert group was established and their report is expected to be presented to the ministry of education in February 2014. A second sign of change is seen at the national research council in Norway. The national research grant for education for the next 3–5 years has a total budget of 163 million Norwegian kroner (about 26.7 million United States dollars) and has explicitly devoted 28 million Norwegian kroner (about 460, 000 United States dollars) towards special educational research. For the first time in over 20 years, there is a national grant supporting special education research and this can be understood as a sign of a changing attitude towards the need for a further development of special educational knowledge in Norway.

REFERENCES

Aas, O. E. (1954). *Public care for mentally retarded in Norway from 1870–1920.* Oslo, Norway: Hovedfagsoppgave, Universitetet i Oslo.

Arctander, S., & Dahlstrøm, S. (1932). *The status on children in public care from 1990–1928.* Oslo, Norway: Olaf Norlis forlag.

Bachman, K., & Haug, P. (2006). *Research on adapted education.* Volda, Norway: Høgskulen i Volda.

Befring, E., & Tangen, R. (2008). *Special education.* Oslo, Norway: Cappelen.

Biesta, G. (2004). Against learning: Reclaiming a language for education in an age of learning. *Nordisk Pedagogikk, 24*(1), 70–82.

Biklen, D. (1985). *Achieving the complete school: Strategies for effective mainstreaming.* New York, NY: Teachers College Press.

Binet, A., & Simon, T. (1905). Methodes nouvelles pour le diagnostic du niveau intellectuel des anormaux. *L'Annee Psychologique, 11,* 191–244.

Froestad, J. (1995). *Professional discourses and public policy in the care for the handicapped in Scandinavian in the 1980s.* Dr. Avhandling, Rapport No. 34. Bergen, Norway: Institutt for administrasjon og organisasjonsvitenskap, Universitetet i Bergen.

Froestad, J. (1999). Normality and discipline. In S. Meyer, & T. Sirnes (Eds.), *Normality and identity formation in Norway* (pp. 76–98). Oslo, Norway: Gyldendal.

Gallagher, D. J., Heshusius, L., Iano, R. P., & Skrtic, T. M. (2004). *Challenging orthodoxy in special education: Dissenting voices.* Denver, CO: Love Publishing.

Government of Norway. (1881). *Abnormal Schools Act of 1981.* Oslo, Norway: Parliament of Norway.

Government of Norway. (1896). *Children Welfare Council Act of 1896.* Oslo, Norway: Parliament of Norway.

Government of Norway. (1951). *Special Schools Act of 1951.* Oslo, Norway: Parliament of Norway.

Government of Norway. (1975). *Primary and Lower Secondary Schools Act.* Oslo, Norway: Parliament of Norway.

Government of Norway. (1997). *Norwegian curriculum plan of 1997.* Oslo, Norway: Parliament of Norway.

GSI Norway. (2013). *The schools information system.* Retrieved from https://gsi.udir.no/. Accessed on December 31, 2013.

Haug, P. (1999). *Special education in primary school: Fundamentals, development and content.* Olso, Norway: Abstrakt forlag.

Haug, P. (2003). Qualifying teachers for the school for all. In K. Nes, M. Strømstad, & T. Booth (Eds.), *Developing inclusive teacher education* (pp. 34–51). New York, NY: Routledge.

Hausstätter, R. (2013). *The twenty percentage rule.* Spesialpedagogikk nr 6.

Karlsen, G. E. (2005). Norwegian teacher education, a historical perspective. *Norsk pedagogisk tidsskrift nr, 6,* 403–416.

Kiil, P. E. (1981). *Legislation for special education after 1945.* Oslo, Norway: Pedagogisk forskningsinstitutt.

Korsvold, T. (2006). *The value of the child: A childhood as mentally retarded in the 1950s.* Olso, Norway: Abstrkt forlag.

Ministry of Education. (2006). *The knowledge promotion reform.* Retrieved from http: //www. udir.no/Stottemeny/English/Curriculum-in-English/_english/knowledge-promotion—Kunnskapsloftet/. Accessed on December 31, 2013.

Ministry of Education and Research (MER). (2012). Retrieved from http://www.regjeringen.
no/en/dep/kd/news-and-latest-publications/News/2012/regjeringen-har-begrenset-
privatskolene.html?id=686534
Mostert, M. P., Kavale, K. A., & Kauffman, J. M. (2007). *Challenging the refusal of reasoning
in special education.* Denver, CO: Love Publishing.
Nirje, B. (1969). The normalization principle and its human management implications. In
R. B. Kugel, & W. Wolfensberger (Eds.), *Changing patterns in residential services for the
mentally retarded* (pp. 179–195). Washington, DC: President's Committee on Mental
Retardation.
Nirje, B. (1985). The basis and logic for the normalization principle. *Australia and New
Zealand Journal of Developmental Disabilities, 13,* 65–68.
NOU. (2004). Care institutions for children: National evaluation of the institutions from
1945–1980. Olso, Norway: Ministry of Education.
Nygren, A. (1966). *Eros och Agape.* Stockholm, Sweden: Aldus/Bonmers.
Ravneberg, B. (1999). *Discourses of normality and professional processes.* Rapport No. 69.
Bergen, Norway: Institutt for administrasjon og organisasjonsvitenskap.
Richardson, J. G., & Powell, J. J. W. (2011). *Comparing special education: Origins to contem-
porary paradoxes.* Stanford, CA: Stanford University Press.
Samordningsnemda for skoleverket, VII. (1949). Olso, Norway: Kirke-og undervisnings
depatementet.
Simonsen, E. (1998). *Science and professional battles: Teaching of deaf and mentally retarded in
Norway from 1881–1963.* Dr. Avhandling. Oslo, Norway: Det utdanningsvitenskape
lige fakultet, Universitetet i Olso.
SSB. (1975). *Educational statistics.* Oslo, Norway: Ministry of Education.
SSB. (1994). *Statistics Norway.* Oslo, Norway: Ministry of Education.
St.meld 42. (1965–1966). *On the development of special education schools.* Oslo, Norway:
Ministry of Education.
St.meld 98. (2009). *Special education.* Oslo Norway: Ministry of Education.
Thuen, H. (2002). In the place of parents, child and institutions from 1820–1900. Oslo,
Norway: Pax.
Thuen, H. (2008). *About the child, upbringing and care through history.* Oslo, Norway:
Abstrakt forlag.
Tøssebro, J. (2010). *What is disability.* Oslo, Norway: Universitetsforlaget.
UNESCO. (1994). *Salamanca statement and framework for action on special education needs.*
Paris, France: United Nations.
United Nations. (1975, December). Declaration on the rights of disabled persons. General
assembly resolution 3447(xxx). New York, NY: United Nations.
United Nations. (2006). *United Nations treaty collection 15. Convention on the rights of persons
with disabilities.* New York, NY: United Nations.
Vislie, L. (1995). Integration policies, school reforms and the organization of schooling for
handicapped pupils in Western societies. In C. Clark, A. Dyson, & A. Milward (Eds.),
Towards inclusive schools? (pp. 42–53). London: David Fulton.
Werner-Putnam, R. (1979). Special education – Some cross-national comparisons. *Comparative
Education, 15*(1), 83–98.
Wilson, D., Hausstatter, R. S., & Lie, B. (2010). *Special education in primary school.* Bergen,
Norway: Fagbokforlaget.
Wolfensberger, W. (1972). *The principal of normalization in human services.* Toronto, Canada:
National Institute on Mental Health.

SPECIAL EDUCATION TODAY IN SWEDEN ☆

Girma Berhanu

ABSTRACT

This chapter provides a comprehensive presentation and discussion of special education in Sweden. The presentation and discussion are tied deeply to the country's general education system which incorporates social and political aspects as well as beliefs in equity for all.

The municipalities in Sweden have a large degree of independence as such special education can be organized in different ways. Yet, within each municipality's educational structure is the common theme that students are different therefore teaching cannot be the same for everyone. The following chapter sections provide the reader with a better understanding of Sweden's general special education system today: legislative acts that ensure equal access to education; the special education context; the history of special education and service in Sweden; the expansion of special education starting in the 1960s and early 1970s; current prevalence data; a clarification of differentiation, inclusion and categorization;

☆Some sections (paragraphs) of this chapter have been adapted from the author's own texts (Berhanu, 2008, 2009, 2011).

Special Education International Perspectives: Practices Across the Globe
Advances in Special Education, Volume 28, 209–241
Copyright © 2014 by Emerald Group Publishing Limited
All rights of reproduction in any form reserved
ISSN: 0270-4013/doi:10.1108/S0270-401320140000028014

teacher preparation advances; problems in schools and student's difficulties; a description of inclusive education; and current challenges to inclusive education.

INTRODUCTION

A presentation of special education in Sweden is deeply tied to a discussion of the general educational system, structure, history, and political culture of Sweden and of the Nordic welfare model. Swedish social welfare/ educational policy has traditionally been underpinned by a strong philosophy of universalism, equal entitlements of citizenship, comprehensiveness, and solidarity as an instrument to promote social inclusion and equality of resources, which helped facilitate both the quality of special educational services as well as inclusive education. While Swedish education policies have a solid history and culture of solidarity, community, and social responsibility, Sweden also has deep cultural values and historical heritage that support self-realization, individual productivity, competition, and social competence. Democratic values and participation in school and society are essential elements in the Swedish social fabric. Democracy is a cornerstone and founding value of the Swedish curricula and educational legislation. Fostering democracy and raising democratic citizens are principal functions of schools. Equity is also an essential element. Since the early nineteenth century, when elementary school was regarded as a basic school for all, equity has been and is still a central element in the Swedish educational policies, ordinances, and directives. "Equity is a general term indicating 'fairness;' for example, that principles of justice have been used in the assessment of a phenomenon" (Wildt-Persson & Rosengren, 2001, p. 307). Equity in the school is guaranteed by the Swedish Education Act (Skollag, 1985, 2010). This act stipulates that consideration must also be afforded to pupils with special needs. Each school has a special responsibility for those pupils who, for different reasons, experience difficulties in attaining the established educational goals (Skollag, 1985, 2010).

Within the past decades, however, Sweden has undergone a dramatic transformation. The changes are framed within neo-liberal philosophies such as devolution (devolvement of responsibilities to local authorities), market solutions, competition, "effectivity," and standardization, coupled with a proliferation of individual/parent choices for independent schools, all of which potentially work *against* the valuing of diversity, equity, and inclusion. Marginalization and segregation of socially disadvantaged and ethnic minority groups have increased. Result and resource differences have widened among schools and municipalities and among pupils. Swedish efforts in the past to promote equity through a variety of educational policies have been fascinating. Those early educational policies, including the macropolitical agenda focused on the social welfare model, have helped to diminish the effects of differential social, cultural, and economic background on outcomes, and on the development of special educational services as well as inclusive learning settings. This has come under threat. There is still some hope, however, of mitigating the situation through varied social and educational measures combined with an effective monitoring system and a stronger partnership and transparent working relationship between the central and local government systems. Research and follow-up are crucial in this process. At the time of writing this chapter, Sweden has gone through a range of policy reforms. The changes were triggered partly by Swedish children's disappointing performance or lower levels of knowledge in International studies such as PISA (Programme for International Student Assessment) and TIMSS (Trends in International Mathematics and Science Study). To help combat this trend, the country has introduced several changes to its school system, such as a new education act, new curricula, introduction of teacher certification, and new grading system. These policy changes and reforms have yet to be thoroughly evaluated.

Some studies (Berhanu & Dyson, 2012; Wernersson & Gerrbo, 2013, and references therein) indicate that the number of special needs education pupils has increased mainly in large cities and that different forms of segregated education have expanded. Dubious assessment methods and unreflective application of individual evaluation and educational plans have led to many students being viewed as derailed from the "norm" (Isaksson, Lindqvist, & Bergström, 2010; Skolverket [The Swedish National Agency for Education], 2005, and references therein). In addition, the share of Swedish pupils who fail in core subjects when leaving compulsory education and face problems finalizing their upper secondary education has increased steadily.

As more and more reports indicated that pupils were entering special educational placements within the regular school framework and in special schools, the government began financing a number of projects that will map out the processes that lead to exclusionary measures in an attempt to mitigate the situation and therefore enhance full participation of pupils with special needs in all aspects of school life (e.g., Berhanu, 2006).

The Swedish constitution recognizes equal human worth and respect for the freedom and dignity of the individuals. The principles laid down there are sources for the curriculum's goals and objectives. In that respect, an important principle in achieving equity has been and still is the compensatory principle, that is, that the state should not remain neutral in issues relating to equal opportunity. Differences among geographical regions, social or economic groups must not be attributable to any form of discrimination that would indicate that the principle of equality has been neglected (Wildt-Persson & Rosengren, 2001).

Equity carries a particular significance for children with special educational needs. The majority of these children are integrated into regular child-care activities, compulsory schools, and upper secondary schools. There are, however, eight special schools for pupils with hearing/vision and physical disabilities, as well as some schools for those who are mentally handicapped. A total of 1% of all pupils in the compulsory and upper secondary school levels are in such segregated settings (Skolverket [The Swedish National Agency for Education], 2005; Vislie, 2003; Wildt-Persson & Rosengren, 2001). This is minimal by international comparison according to the Organization for Economic Cooperation and Development (OECD) (1999a, 1999b, 2000a, 2000b). Nonetheless, since the early 1990s the situation has *a different and complex picture*. The number of pupils placed in educational programs for learning disabled students has increased dramatically. In general, the number of children defined as "special needs" has shown a steady increase. In addition, there has been a dramatic increase in the number of Independent/Free schools. Variances between schools and municipalities and student achievement including segregation and persistent socioeconomic differences among the school populations have been the post-decentralization policy phenomena. All the indicators of the National Agency for Education compiled through evaluations, case studies, and supervision, testify to this fact.

THE SWEDISH EDUCATIONAL SYSTEM: THE GENERAL CONTEXT

Sweden has signed the United Nations (UN) Convention on the Rights of the Child (United Nations [UN], 1989), the UN Standard Rules on the Equalization of Opportunities for Persons with Disabilities (United Nations [UN], 1993), and UNESCO's Salamanca Statement and

Framework for Action (UNESCO, 1994). These are all powerful standards and statements to prevent exclusionary activities in the school sector and make a strong case for inclusion. These documents have shaped a number of important government reports, directives, and policies and have worked to place inclusive education firmly on the agenda. Political expression, however, has not matched practice. As Emanuelsson, Haug, and Persson (2005) noted, "the school act, the School ordinances and the National Curricula all emphasize the importance of solidarity, the right to education of equal value and the right for pupils who experience difficulties for various reasons to receive the help and support they need. Local schools, however, often find this unrealistic, which indicates that the gap between political intentions and practical realities is considerable" (p. 122).

The Swedish Education Act (Skollag, 1985, 2010) states that all children shall have equal access to education, and that all children shall enjoy this right, regardless of gender, residence, or social or economic factors. Special support shall also be given to students who have difficulty with the schoolwork. Most students with a need for special support are taught in regular classes in compulsory and upper secondary schools. There are also a certain number of special remedial classes for students with functional disabilities, and for students with social and emotional problems. Effective July 1, 1994, programs for pupils with learning disabilities use the same curriculum as do regular compulsory and upper secondary schools. This is a way of *delineating* that all pupils, regardless of learning development, fall under the same fundamental values. The special programs do, however, use their own syllabi adapted to this form of education and to the different needs they must meet for each one of their pupils. On paper and in accordance with Swedish law, parents have a right to choose between the two school forms. Whether it is an opportunity in reality was questioned in an evaluation by the National Board of Education (Skolverket [The Swedish National Agency for Education], 2002, cited in Göransson, 2006).

Government concern to provide appropriate services to special needs children within the regular school framework has been outlined in the first Swedish National Curriculum (LGR 62, 1962) where "the contents and organization of special education were carefully specified and the accompanying proposal was for a system of coordinated special education as alternative to remedial and special classes" (p. 120). However, it was not until the 1969 National Curriculum (LGR 69, 1969) came into force that increased emphasis was given to integrating children with various forms of disability into regular education. The discourses in this new curriculum have many similarities with the current inclusive agenda, although the term used then was *integration*. One significant perspective shift in the curriculum and official reports of the time and the 1970s was the statement that the school's environment represents a possible cause of children's difficulties in school (Skolverket [The Swedish National Agency for Education], 2005). Consequently, the discourses of the *categorical* versus the *relational perspective* evolved (Emanuelsson, Persson, & Rosenqvist, 2001; Emanuelsson et al., 2005). Since then a number of school reforms have taken place that aim at a school system combining quality and equality. Education can be described as one of the cornerstones of the modern welfare state. This has been manifested heavily in Sweden, which was dominated by a social democratic model. Strong Labor parties were able to secure broad support for their policies during the interwar period and after the Second World War, with *solidarity*, *community*, and *equality* as the key words. There were high hopes that uniform, free-of-charge education for children from all social strata would contribute to equality and justice, and promote social cohesion. Although the belief in the potential of education in this respect may have faded, education is still regarded as one of the major methods of preventing unemployment, social exclusion, and ill health (Arnesen & Lundahl, 2006). "Hence, contemporary policy for equity is very much a latter day echo of the social democrats' age-old concept of the '*peoples' home*'" (OECD, 2005, p. 14).

Sweden's reputation for successfully combining effective economy and social welfare measures is still unscathed in many ways. By OECD's (2005) measure, Sweden is an affluent, healthy and well-educated society. Its population is about 9 million, of which approximately 20% come from an immigrant background. Its strongly unique combination of social equality and equity measures, underpinned by high levels of taxation and public spending based on redistributive policies, together with a regulated capitalist economic system, has brought about this success. Its Gross Domestic Product (GDP) per capita is $28,100, compared to $26,000 GDP per capita total OECD. Overall educational attainment is quite high, with at least 80% of the population having attained upper secondary education and an average life expectancy at birth of 82.8 years for women and 77.7 for men. Furthermore, it has one of the highest OECD employment-to-population ratios, with 74% of the population at work. This is third only to Switzerland and Denmark. Sweden also has one of the highest OECD employment rates for mothers, second only to Portugal. Around 78% of all mothers of children under age 7 years were working in 2003 (OECD). Compared with OECD nations, Sweden is one of the leading countries by many standards, be it educational achievement or literacy levels. It is among the highest in social expenditure as a proportion of GDP; it has one of the lowest poverty rates and the lowest levels of income inequality in OECD countries.

Most of the modern history of Sweden is characterized by collective action spearheaded by a social democratic welfare state and is a prominent example of social democratic welfare states favoring full employment and a focus on minimizing differences, social alienation, and exclusion, as opposed to individual responsibility and market solutions (Arnesen & Lundahl, 2006; OECD, 1999a, 1999b, 2000a, 2000b, 2005; Wildt-Persson & Rosengren, 2001). This political and cultural background has been instrumental in creating an early and fertile platform from which to criticize the traditional special educational and exclusionary approach and to formulate concepts such as normalization, integration, and mainstreaming (Nirje, 1992; Wolfensberger, 1972). This background has fostered awareness and cultural messages of the significance of social inclusiveness and has resulted in organization changes such as closing large institutions for intellectually disabled persons and building community-based residential, learning, and working environments. This was a remarkable achievement by any standard. The social motives of education that are citizenship, social integration, social equality, and democracy had as much importance as economic motivations not only in Sweden but also in Scandinavia as a whole.

The slogan "A school for all" (En skola för alla) embellished most of the policy documents and government-commissioned reports and propositions in the 1960s, 1970s, and through the late 1980s as a component of the inclusive and caring welfare state. In the 1962 Curriculum for the Compulsory School System (LGR 62, 1962), a 9-year unified compulsory school program for all children ages 7 to 16 years was introduced. This compulsory curriculum emphasized that pupils come at the center of the learning process and that they should be helped to achieve multisided development within the framework of a school for all or a common frame of reference.

Current Swedish educational policy documents recognize that students are *different*. That has important implications in how schooling is organized and therefore the learning process and the avenues to reach goals. The curriculum states clearly that consideration should be taken of the different abilities and needs of the students. There are different ways to reach the goal. "Hence teaching cannot be designed in the same way for everyone" (LPO, 1994; LGR 11, 2010; Skolverket [The Swedish National Agency for Education], 2011).

THE SPECIAL EDUCATIONAL STRUCTURE

The Swedish public education system is composed of compulsory and non-compulsory schooling. Compulsory education includes regular compulsory school, Sami school, special school, and programs for pupils with learning disabilities (Sami is an ethnic group with ill-defined genetic origins, living in the northern areas of the Scandinavian Peninsula and Russia). Noncompulsory education includes the "preschool class," upper secondary school, upper secondary school for pupils with learning disabilities, municipal adult education, and adult education for adults with learning disabilities. The 9-year compulsory school program is for all children between ages 7 years and 16 years. All education throughout the public school system is free. There is usually no charge to students or their parents for teaching materials, school meals, health services, or transport. The education system has focused on providing equality of opportunities and equivalence of outcomes (http://www.skolverket.se, OECD, 2005). However, the system has undergone a number of important reforms in the past 18 years that have a strong bearing on equity.

Due to the large degree of independence of the municipalities, Special Needs Education can be organized in different ways. Support could include variations of the following options:

- all pupils in need of special support have written action plans of provision set up in cooperation with the pupils themselves, parents and professionals involved;
- the teachers of the pupil are consulted by a specialist teacher;
- a specialist teacher or assistant helps the teacher or works with the pupil concerned for longer or shorter periods within the frames of the activities of the larger group;
- the pupil receives teaching materials adapted for his or her needs;
- the pupil leaves the larger group for limited periods to work with a specialist teacher;
- a classroom assistant works with the pupil in need of special support or in the class of the pupil concerned;
- the pupil in need of special support works in a group for pupils with similar needs for longer or shorter periods within the same organization;
- teachers are supported by a resource center at the local level;
- resource centers at the local level may be supported by an advisor at the National Agency for Special Needs Education and Schools.

The majority of pupils in need of special educational support are educated in general basic compulsory classes. If this is not possible, then the school must indicate very clearly why other educational options for pupils should be considered. This is an important philosophical standpoint for child-care organization and operation. Earlier debates focused upon prerequisites for mainstreaming. Now the focus has shifted to the need for justification for segregated options to be considered for pupils (The European Agency for Special Needs and Inclusive Education, 2014).

The schools have a pupil-welfare team made up of a representative of the local school board, and the pupil-welfare staff (i.e., a school doctor, nurse, psychologist, counselor and Special Educational Needs (SEN) teachers). Pupils' progress toward educational goals should be supported (Skollag, 2010).

Action plans of provision are set up for each pupil in need of special support in cooperation with teachers, parents, and the pupil concerned. Those plans indicate the responsibility of each partner in the development of the pupil's abilities and knowledge. Municipal child care, pre-primary activities, compulsory schooling, after-school centers, and youth centers are often part of the same organization with a common school board. Several of these activities are often integrated, with the staff organizing joint work together. This facilitates a complete view of each pupil. It is common practice to provide for the pupils' needs in close cooperation with their parents. The National Curricula states the importance of the parents' participation in the planning of pupils' education. Diversity is considered as a general standard in this social development and all children should as far as possible, irrespective of their needs, and be a part of such a group. All children in need of special support have written action plans of provision set up in cooperation with the pupils themselves, parents, and professionals involved (Skollag, 2010).

For pupils in need of special support, technical aid is available from the regional counties, and adaptations of teaching materials are provided from the state. Schools and teachers are consulted by local resource centers which, in turn, are consulted by the National Agency for Special Needs Education and Schools. The Agency is the national authority which coordinates government support in respect to special needs education for children, young people, and adults with disabilities. The Agency is a resource for people working with children, adolescents, and adults with disabilities. Its primary task is to provide support under central supervision to those responsible for special needs education in government-operated schools and independent schools. It does this by distributing information and providing knowledge about special needs education, and by initiating and participating in developmental work in this field (http://www.spsm.se/sv/Om-webbplatsen/English).

THE HISTORY OF SPECIAL EDUCATION AND SPECIAL EDUCATION SERVICES

Early Beginnings

In 1842, a policy termed *allmän folkskola* (folk school) came into force. Before that, education was reserved only for middle-class and upper-class society. The policy was primarily meant to provide schooling for all citizens, although in practice two parallel school systems evolved: one for the poor and disadvantaged, and the other for stronger elements of society. Even so, the policy's intention was noble, and we can still trace Sweden's long tradition of comprehensive, compulsory, and equivalent education from this time. It is also from this time that special needs education established its roots as a two-track system (i.e., special education and regular education settings crystallized). In the special education track the so-called *problem-child* was categorized using different nomenclature such as *idiot, poor, feeble-minded, imbecile,* and *dullard.* As we entered into the mid-twentieth century, these categories changed into *intellectually disabled, learning disabled,* and *mentally retarded.* During the last two decades, the general category became *pupils with special needs* but with a new culture of diagnosis based on neuropsychiatric methods, such as Attention Deficit Hyperactivity Disorder (ADHD), Deficits in Attention, Motor Control and Perception (DAMP), autism, or Asperger's syndrome. The above reflects how classification and categorization has been an activity "as old as schools themselves" (Mehan, 1993, p. 243; see also Hjörne, 2004; Skolverket [The Swedish National Agency for Education], 2005).

Special education in its modern, rational, and scientific form has a brief history in Sweden. As Rosenqvist (1993) outlined already in the early 1990s, three main periods can be discerned in the history of special education in Sweden: (a) the stage of non-differentiation, (b) the stage of differentiation, and (c) the stage of integration.

In the early years after *Allmän folkskola* students who did not meet the requirements were considered to be *different* from the "norm." At first it was all about the blind and deaf children, and it resulted in the creation of three parallel tracks. The first track symbolized the school where students who fulfilled their duty and were not considered *different* from the "norm" were served or fully included. The second track represented the students who at some time during their school years did not meet the objectives and requirements set and were placed in so-called "Help classes," "special classes," and "private instruction." The third track, *built* in 1807, represented a school for various disabilities whose purpose was to serve disabled children to get some form of education, or rather, skills (Nilhom & Björck-Åkesson, 2007; Skolverket [The Swedish National Agency for Education], 2005).

Special education in Sweden arose as in most countries as a response to the assumption that the usual teaching did not suit all children. In this regard, one wonders about the driving forces behind the establishment and early expansion of special education in Sweden. According to Ahlström (2011), it presumably did not come into existence merely to provide disabled children with remedial training and an education adapted to their needs but to fulfill many other functions. Is it not likely, for instance, that teachers as well as "normal" and "well-adjusted" pupils were expected to profit from having "misfits" dismissed from ordinary classrooms? Or, could special education not be regarded as a method to deal with too heterogeneous classes? Certainly — but there are also reasons to believe that various professional groups had private interests in the expansion of special education, like teachers to whom a new career path was opened, and physicians who realized that their professional knowledge might be demanded in that context. Special education may, of course, also have had more covert tasks to fulfill than these, which must be considered when looking for an answer to the introductory question.

Because elementary school became compulsory in 1842, schools expanded and reached a larger segment of the population, the diversity of the student population became obvious, and the ability to meet these variations within the student population was a challenge to the school authorities. There were a range of proposed solutions.

One solution seemed to present itself in the form of intelligence tests as instruments of selection. In Sweden they were first used for this purpose in Stockholm in 1920 (Nordström, 1968), but until the early 1940s there were few good instruments and trained testers. Some physicians could perform testing, but the schools wanted their own school psychologists. Regular programmes of study for school psychologists did not appear until the late 1950s, although annual courses in intelligence testing for teachers were arranged from 1944 .... Before the appearance of intelligence tests, 2 percent of the population was estimated as being slow learners (Ramer, 1946). Now it became the norm to follow international trends that advocated an "SL class interval", first between IQs of 80 and 70 and later between 85 and 70 (Skolöverstyrelsen, 1947, p. 347). The proportion of slow learners, defined in this way, was substantially higher than had originally been envisaged, which prompted numerous appeals for greater numbers of SL classes. (Ahlström, 2011, p. 185)

Expansion of Special Education Starting

During the latter part of the 1960s to the early 1970s, special education expanded and one could see that about 20% of students did not perform well (Nilhom & Björck-Åkesson, 2007). It turned out also that the special education became *too costly* for the state. The situation forced the government to set up an inquiry committee.

After a detailed investigation into the school's inner workings by the inquiry committee Swedish Government Official Report (SOU, 1974) the concept of mainstreaming was introduced. Class teachers were now faced with the requirement to deal with diversity of students in their class and thus adapt teaching to pupils' differing abilities and needs. Teachers would take care of several students who previously had special education support. When the Curriculum for the Compulsory School (LGR, 1980), came into being, it was stressed with even greater force that the services of the school should be adapted to the individual student's abilities and that the school would work proactively to prevent the onset of school difficulties. Special education as an organizational form was not mentioned in the curriculum. This curriculum's hallmark was a "school for all."

As a consequence of a growing number of young people leaving school without a full education, subsequent policy measures came up, with a whole new approach to special education as a field of knowledge and profession. A motive was that the adaptation of mainstream education in schools should work better so that fewer students would need special education. Consequently, the dominant individual-based and medically oriented approach to school problems was replaced largely by the system-based approach (or school-based or context-based approach with regard to school difficulties). In practice, the policy change led to the introduction of the profession, Special Pedagogues (Special Educators), whose functions were more than just teaching pupils with special needs but also working at the organizational level in helping teachers to include pupils with special needs and to help meet their needs within a regular school/class settings so that fewer students would need special education in a segregated setting (Ahlberg, 2007b; Nilhom & Björck-Åkesson, 2007). These special Pedagogues [as opposed to Special Teachers] are entrusted with the responsibilities to serve mainly as mentors and advisors for colleagues who have special needs pupils/students in their classes. They also conduct school improvement tasks as well as teach students with the greatest problems in school.

Current School Prevalence Data

In academic year 2008–2009, the number of students in special schools amounted to approximately 22,600. Of these some 13,300 students study at one of 714 special compulsory schools and 9,300 students study in one of the 271 special upper secondary schools. Of all pupils in the compulsory school system, the share of pupils in the special compulsory school has nearly doubled from 0.8 percentage points at the start of the 1990s to 1.4 percentage points in academic year 2007–2008. Every seventh pupil in the special compulsory school was integrated (i.e., attended compulsory school in the academic year 2008–2009). An ever larger share of the special school pupils have been integrated into compulsory school since the end of the 1990s. The teacher–pupil ratio is 27 teachers per 100 pupils (Statistics Sweden, 2009).

Differentiation, Inclusion and Categorization

As mentioned earlier, the post-war Swedish educational policy measures are characterized by comprehensiveness, equity, and *inclusion* as coined in the slogan "A school for all." That did not stop differentiation, classification, and categorization of children or segregated educational placements. In fact, paradoxically, the amount of special education, as Emanuelsson et al. (2005) noted, has increased steadily. Vast differences have been observed in how pupils with special needs are actually defined and registered in different municipalities. This is partly the consequence of a decentralized education system that manifests itself in divergent local practices (Göransson, Nilholm, & Karlsson, 2011).

There are different interpretations of the importance of levels, categories, and differentiation, particularly in relation to receiving support or eligibility for special schools or special programs. Göransson et al. (2011), who conducted a series of studies in this problematic area, concluded:

> Regarding the importance of categories in obtaining support, policy documents do not clearly state that a medical diagnosis is necessary for receiving extra support in regular compulsory schools. Instead, these documents mention educational categories. But medically based categorizations are needed for: (1) determining the eligibility for special schools and special programs, and (2) receiving support from the National Agency of Special Needs Education and Schools. So, one conclusion of the present analysis is that *national policies and practices leave a lot of room for interpretation at municipal and school levels, which generates vast differences*. Regarding support in municipalities, we can first conclude that there is a need for additional overarching data. But clearly, there are vast differences between the municipalities. This applies to: (1) issues related to values and goals; (2) the organization and placement of pupils; and (3) the importance of categorization. For example, more than 60% of the municipalities indicated that medical diagnosis was of little or no relevance for receiving special support, whereas other municipalities indicated that such a diagnosis was relevant. (p. 550)

The *categorical* model described in several Swedish reports is the one referred to in the international research (see Mitchell, 2005) as the *within-child model*, the *medical model*, the *psych-medical model*, the *discourse of deviance*, the *defect model*, and the *pathological model*. In this paradigm, school failure is ascribed to some defect, pathology, or inadequacy located within the student. The *relational* model is variously referred to as the *social model*, the *socio-political model*, the *socio-political paradigm*, and the *deficient system model*. In line with this, the term *students with difficulties* was challenged and began to be replaced by *students in difficulties* (Emanuelsson et al., 2001). Fierce criticism against the traditional and categorical special pedagogical perspective has brought about a paradigmatic shift and a policy deeply ingrained with a relational perspective (which is more environment oriented) as a guiding principle. However, the categorical perspective, which is associated with traditional, segregative, and exclusionary approaches, has not given way to the relational perspective. In fact, the categorical perspective made an upsurge in the 1990s and has since then dominated both special education research and praxis in Sweden. The recent growth in categorization, identification, and classification within the framework of "redesigning regular education support" in the ordinary school system in an effort to facilitate inclusion has been criticized by one prominent Swedish professor of special education:

> Once children are identified as "different" ... they become problematic to mainstream schools and teachers. From within the categorical perspective the process of labelling children as "having difficulties" has the effect of investing the source of any difficulty or

problem within the child. Once this process is complete, then it becomes easier to transfer the responsibility to "specialists" trained to deal with the "problems" exhibited by the child. (Emanuelsson, 2001, p. 135)

Many of the social and educational changes made in the early 1990s were dramatic. Observers might ask why there occurred such a huge shift from the traditional inclusive, collective frame of reference and social justice toward individual rights, parental choice, and market-oriented policies. In particular, the impact of the decentralized educational policy on equity is pervasive. Two studies confirm that

... educational expenditure per student (measured in terms of money or teacher density) has fallen rather dramatically during the 1990s − followed by a slight increase after the turn of the millennium. According to Björklund et al. (2004), the teacher/student ratio has decreased by 18.7% during the 1990s. Whether this can be directly attributed to the decentralization or to the impact of the economic downturn of the 1990s remains an open question. (Ahlin & Mörk, 2005; Björklund, Edin, Frederiksson, & Krueger, 2004 as cited in OECD, 2005, p. 17)

Paradoxically, in the footsteps of the introduction of inclusive education, the number of pupils labeled as having special needs increased dramatically. Teachers found themselves incapable of dealing with pupil diversity in the classroom and meeting individual student needs. This has often been regarded as schools' failure to meet the diverse needs of pupils, manifesting itself in resignation and distress among teachers and pupils not achieving set targets.

One in five compulsory school pupils in Sweden is judged to be in need of special needs education (Asp-Onsjö, 2006). This means that approximately 200,000 pupils in Sweden receive some kind of special educational support during the school year. At the same time, the number of pupils enrolled in special schools for the intellectually disabled (*särskolan*) has increased from 0.9% to 1.4% during the last 5 to 6 years (Skolverket [The Swedish National Agency for Education], 2002). "From 1992 to 2001 the number of students registered in schools and classrooms for students with severe learning disabilities ... has increased by 67%" (Rosenqvist, 2007, p. 67).

The "School for all" movement was transformed to a structure of capitalism in the 1990s and the rhetoric of inclusion became a metaphor for the dominance of human capital, manifested in personal choice, over social justice. Citizenship was replaced by stress on individualization of rights and promotion of dominant social interests (Persson & Berhanu, 2005). On the positive side, there are still commendable activities and policies in Sweden that promote social inclusion. For instance, the system offers a possibility for youngsters who fail at some stage to move on into further education via individual or tailored programs. A generous school system guarantees free education (including free books, meals, and transportation to the nearest school) for all in compulsory education. Free access is also guaranteed in state-run higher education and in municipal adult education.

Teacher Preparation

In the beginning of the 1990s, a Special Educator Program was launched that would have significant impact on the praxis of special/inclusive education in Sweden. The program was in line with a relational or system-based perspective on educational difficulties. In addition to carrying out teaching tasks, Special Educators are expected to supervise, consult, and counsel regular teachers on how to meet the needs of all pupils. In line with this, all teacher trainees study special needs education within the so-called General Field of Education and may also study this field of knowledge within an eligible field of study or in specialization courses. The program was well under way until 5 years ago. Then, a new conservative government came into power and "discredited" it. In 2008, the government reinstituted a special teacher program in which trainees will be expected upon completion to work directly with individual pupils (The programs are: Postgraduate Diploma in Special Needs Training with specialization in Intellectual Disabilities; Postgraduate Diploma in Special Needs Training with specialization in the Development of Language, Writing, and Reading; Postgraduate Diploma in Special Needs Training with specialization in Mathematical Development). The teacher preparation focus is the student, not the system, a dramatic shift from the previous perspective. Currently both programs exist side-by-side, are offered at an advanced level, comprise 90 credits, 1–1/2 years of full-time study, and qualify graduates for specialist tasks in schools. The new Special Education Teachers should be able to analyze school difficulties at the individual level in different learning environments and be able to *personalize* the school activities regulated by the Swedish Code of Statutes (SFS, 2008). The vision from the government's side is now that equivalence is strengthened through early identification/detection and interventions for students in need of special education and individualized support measures. From school authorities, the importance of special education expertise of all categories of teachers is strongly emphasized. The tricky question is whether this trend enhances or hinders the inclusive school agenda that the government itself set as a goal. All these changes have implications on the process of differentiation, individualization, segregation, and categorization.

School Problems and Students' Difficulties

In a recent large-scale study conducted by Giota and Emanuelsson (2011) on head teachers' judgments of school difficulty, the traditional conception of school difficulties emerged that is "social background and context as well as schoolwork content and teaching habits are judged as key factors behind the students' difficulties and need for special education support. In general, however, school problems and students' difficulties seem still to mainly be seen as caused by student characteristics and disabilities rather than as shortcomings of school and teaching" (see also, Persson, 2008).

A similar study conducted by Isaksson et al. (2010) indicated that there were three different patterns or models for identifying and supporting pupils with special educational needs: a *pedagogical*, a *social*, or a *medical* model. Various professionals were involved in different ways in each model. Another finding was that school personnel did not find it easy to sort out and assess "special educational needs" and that the identification of such needs was conditioned upon resources available for the schools.

> Until the early 1990s, resources to the schools, including resources for special education, were strictly regulated and distributed based on the total number of pupils in the school. Currently, the municipalities distribute economic resources to the schools in terms of unspecified block grants. This system encourages schools to identify as many pupils with special educational needs as possible, since they may then generate additional economic resources for the school (Jóhanneson, Lindblad, and Simola, 2002). To the extent that individual shortcomings take center stage at the expense of social and environmental aspects of teaching, a built-in conflict regarding the demand for individual adjustment on the one hand and inclusion within the social group on the other becomes apparent. (Egelund, Haug, & Persson, 2006; Telhaug, Mediås, & Aasen, 2004). (Isaksson et al., 2010, p. 134)

Inclusive Education

Integration and inclusion have been used interchangeably in Swedish educational discourses. Most people are familiar with the term *integration*. The term *inclusion* has been difficult to translate into Swedish. That has left many with considerable ambiguities about the use of the term. As in many other countries, there is confusion and controversy over the semantics of inclusion. This demonstrates the problematic nature of terms when they cross over into use in other cultures. Many have questioned whether the new terminology means only a linguistic shift or a new agenda. In the first translations into Swedish of UNESCO's Salamanca Statement and Framework for Action (1994), *inclusion* was translated as *integration*.

Although there is still a conceptual problem of clarity, the difference between integration and inclusion has been sorted out and technically defined by the experts (see, e.g., Nilholm, 2006a, 2006b). The message of inclusive education as outlined in the Salamanca statement has now begun to permeate the Swedish language, at least in official documents. The social model of disability and the relational nature of disablement have been officially accepted, which implies that schooling as such "is more or less disabling or enabling" (Corbett & Slee, 2000, p. 143). This in turn requires schools to restructure and adjust their learning environments, pedagogical methods, and organizational arrangements. Despite or, rather, because of the inflated discourses of inclusion and revamping of inclusion policies, the practice is often short of advocacies. For instance, "the number of pupils in 'special units' (*grundsärskolan*) increased by as much as 62% during 1993–1999, despite promises and statutes" (Westling Allodi, 2002). Unless a whole range of activities, including branding activities and attitudes, are brought under control, legislation alone will not bring about the desired results.

Unfortunately, there are too few comprehensive studies that map out the level of participation and the extent of inclusiveness of disabled children in the ordinary school system in Sweden, in particular in terms of comparing pupils' development in special and regular education. However, the indication (in terms of children's social and cognitive development) is in line with the international studies that show that special-needs students educated in regular classes do better academically and socially than students in non-inclusive settings (Baker, Wang, & Walberg, 1995; Peetsma, Vergeer, & Karsten, 2001). Some Swedish studies have shown that inclusion has a positive effect on pupils' self-concept (e.g., Persson & Persson, 2012; Westling Allodi, 2000, 2002). This is in line with international research (Baker et al., 1995; Lipsky & Gartner, 1996).

One exemplary action in Sweden in relation to monitoring participation and inclusive/segregative processes is the recent establishment of a Forum for Inclusive Education by Örebro University and the Swedish Institute for Special Needs Education. The main goal of the forum is to enhance knowledge on inclusive and segregative processes in school and identify good examples that promote participation in the common education. As many authors have pointed out (Kivirauma, Klemelä, & Rinne, 2006; Thomas & Loxley, 2001; Westling Allodi, 2002), this is no longer a question of compulsory education or the children's special needs, but rather, the right to participate in a common education.

Challenges to Inclusive Education

A couple of factors that challenge inclusive education and/or the concept of inclusive education in Sweden appear to be, according to Göransson et al. (2011):

> (1) Parents and children increasingly select the schools. (2) Work within the schools is of an increasingly individualized character; it emphasizes individuality at the expense of other values such as fellowship, solidarity and equal opportunity. However, the authors concluded that comparing inclusiveness with standards of what inclusive education should be is one thing. Comparing inclusiveness of various education systems is something else. So, we are content that *in an international comparison, Swedish classrooms are largely democratic; most pupils enjoy participating in school activities and influencing them.* (p. 551)

Similarly, Tideman (2007) wrote "although the overall picture in some respects is complicated and problematic, Sweden might still be considered in the vanguard of special education development in inclusive education, thus making the further development of policy and practice intriguing and worthy of attention" (p. 1947).

Ethnic Minority and Socially Disadvantaged Pupils

Sweden explicitly adopts multiculturalism and cultural diversity in an atmosphere of mutual tolerance in Sweden's Curriculum for the Compulsory School System, the Preschool Class and the Leisure-Time Centre (LPO, 1994); however, terms such as ethnicity, color, and race remain obscure in official taxonomies, educational policies, and school practices. The complex relationships that exist between ethnicity, socioeconomic factors, special needs education, gender, and so forth have recently become a subject of research interest (Berhanu, 2008; Fridlund, 2011; Rosenqvist, 2007).

A recent report by Gustafsson (2006) concludes that from 1992 to 2000 a consistent and linear increase occurred in school segregation in relation to immigration background, educational background, and grades. A national tracking system enables observation of variable achievement among groups of students. Students with foreign backgrounds receive lower average grades than do their peers, have a higher dropout rate from upper secondary education while fewer qualify for higher education. Some recent Swedish studies on disproportionality indicate an over-representation of immigrant students and socially disadvantaged students in special schools and classes (Bel Habib, 2001; Hahne Lundström, 2001; Skolverket [The Swedish National Agency for Education], 2000; SOU, 2003). These students were categorized in diffused, vague, symptom-based, and pedagogical-related terms such as *concentration and behavioral problems*, *speech and language difficulties, unspecified "poor talent,"* or *developmental retardation*. However, extensive and longitudinal studies have yet to be carried out in this specific problem area (see Rosenqvist, 2007) and there is a need for a coherent cumulative body of disproportionality research.

A recent literature review (Berhanu, 2008; Berhanu & Dyson, 2012), demonstrates that the above problem is related to, among other reasons, unreliable assessment procedures and criteria for referral and placement; lack of culturally sensitive diagnostic tools; the static nature of tests, including embedded cultural bias; sociocultural problems, family factors, and language problems; lack of parental participation in decision-making; power differentials between parents and school authorities; institutional intransigence and prejudices; and large resource inequalities that run along lines of ethnicity and class.

Disproportionality is a significant phenomenon in all of the education systems for which good evidence is available. This is the case regardless of the demographics of the school population or the structures and procedures of the special education system. Disproportionality is not confined to countries (such as the German-speaking ones) that have historically had high levels of segregation. On the contrary, education systems (such as those in Scandinavian countries) that are relatively inclusive place a high value on equitable provision and outcomes, and are located in relatively equal societies also display disproportionality. So too do special education systems (such as those of the United Kingdom) that offer additional provision to children on the basis of educational "need" without requiring a diagnosis of disability (Berhanu & Dyson, 2012).

Disproportionality is most marked in those categories of special education that lack precise diagnostic criteria. In practice, this means those that relate to general learning or social difficulties rather than to physical, sensory, or intellectual impairment. One interpretation of this is that the prejudices of teachers and administrators operate unchecked by objective criteria during the identification and assessment process; this then results in negative interpretations of over-represented groups' characteristics and behaviors. However, it is notable that these groups also tend to do poorly in regular education systems and experience the greatest socioeconomic disadvantages. It is equally plausible; therefore, that over-representation reflects accurately the actual difficulties these groups experience in education systems. These difficulties may in turn be attributable to the marginalized social status of these groups, which education systems fail to address, but for which they are by no means entirely to blame. Overall, there is no one group that is particularly at risk of over-representation in special education (or exclusion from access to its resources), and there is no single explanation for disproportionality. However, although multiple explanations are needed in order to cover the multiple forms of disproportionality in the United States, Europe in general, and in Sweden in particular, a common theme is that those groups that are most at risk of wider social and educational marginalization tend also to be most at risk of disproportional representation (usually, over-representation) in special education. Disproportionality can therefore be regarded as a product of social marginality rather than as a product of the structures and procedures of special education systems.

Although Swedish legislation guarantees bilingual education or mother-tongue instruction at preschool and compulsory school, there is a huge gap between practice and legal commitments. This glaring gap has lessened the active participation of immigrant students in school. In particular, the lack of mother-tongue assistance at preschool, combined with a fee requirement, creates an unfavorable start for many immigrant children. In fact, considering Sweden's generosity in all aspects of schooling when it comes to fees, it is surprising that preschool education is not *gratis* (see, e.g., OECD, 2005). In addition, the National Agency for Education "points to the paradox that mother-tongue instruction is nearly non-existent in special education or assimilated programs, where immigrant children are strongly over-represented. Materials are hard to find — and mostly imported from the countries of origin" (OECD, 2005, p. 46).

SPECIAL EDUCATION RESEARCH AND KNOWLEDGE CONSTRUCTION

The last two decades of research show not only the lack of well-founded and sound theories in special education (see, e.g., Clark, Dyson, & Millward, 1998; Emanuelsson, 1997, 2003; OECD, 1995; Persson, 1998; Skrtic, 1991) but also the crisis in special education knowledge. This phenomenon is not only confined to Sweden but also to other countries with similar levels of development of special educational services. Special educational research is a subject of debate, and various criticisms have surfaced. Some of the criticisms are that the research is more focused on deviations, abnormalities, and exceptionalities (Ahlberg, 2013; Dyson & Millward, 1997; Haug, 1998; Persson, 1998). In recent years, however, the criticism has a different character, which is that the research is ideological, rhetorical, and lacks theoretical basis and is remote from the daily teaching, practice, and school life (Giota, Lundborg, & Emanuelsson, 2009).

Special pedagogy/education as a knowledge and research field has thus been strongly criticized, from researchers in the field, but also from other sources. In this regard, Emanuelsson (1997) who reviewed special education research in Sweden from 1956 to 1996, has correctly captured the issue:

> Special-education research in Sweden has until rather recently as elsewhere, been restricted to questions and problems dictated within existing school teaching practices. The focus of interest in the majority of studies is on different kinds of remedial-education organization environments, and it is more or less tied up to what happens or is supposed to happen in such situations .... The need to broaden this narrow perspective was pointed out rather early (for example, Emanuelsson, 1974). However, the fact that special education was at risk of being locked in as an "artefact of regular education" (Skrtic, 1991) by not theoretically taking into account conditions dictated within regular teaching regulations and practices has influenced the research that has taken place only to a small extent.... This means that the vast majority of studies have concentrated on special needs being understood as consequences of certain individual disability characteristics and the measures taken against them. As a rule, these measures were formulated in terms of responses to diagnose related needs of individual help and support in order to decrease or "cure" such difficulties. The fact that special education was also organized as a response to the needs in regular teaching settings of getting rid of disturbances in terms of deviant diagnosed students .... has only recently been taken into full consideration, at least to such an extent that it can be said to be characterizing special education research in the country. (p. 462)

Generally, special education research in Sweden is multifaceted. Foci, theoretical underpinnings, and methods vary. Some variations in this regard can be seen from one University (or research setting) to another. The research usually targets the participation, communication, and learning of children, youth, and adults in various contexts and situations. In the author's research department, a more specific description of the research environment is to use inclusion as a foundation for studying different aspects of the three processes of *participation, communication, and learning*. These processes are regarded as an integrative area and can be studied at the level of the individual, group, organization, and society. The object of study may vary, which means that studies have varying foci in terms of content. Participation, however, constitutes the unifying base. The three processes are considered to be predicated on each other. Even though they are intertwined, it is possible to distinguish them on an analytical level, which is a necessary condition for them to be elucidated and researched. On this common platform, research issues vary, which means that the focus of studies pursued will shift. Some studies focus on all three processes. However, other studies may have a clear focus on one or two of the processes, which means that the other one(s) form a background against which the research is carried out. Studies focusing on participation target processes of exclusion and inclusion in preschools, schools, and society. People's participation is studied in various contexts. Causes and consequences of categorization and classification are analyzed (Ahlberg, 2007a, 2009, 2013).

Research interests comprise studies both of processes that lead to marginalization, stigmatization, and exclusion and of processes that lead to participation and community. Studies focusing on communication target language and interaction. The linguistic and behavioral forms of expression involved in communication are studied, as is how these are created and built up through social and cultural experience. Research may be directed toward identifying and analyzing dilemmas and various discourses that take place in schools and other institutions. Research issues also may deal with language development or the creation of identity, or they may target various types of collaboration and cooperation at different levels in society. Studies that target learning focus on the formation of knowledge and cognitive, as well as emotional, physical, and social development. This includes studies of people's learning at individual and collective levels and studies of what people learn and how various forms of knowledge, values, abilities, and skills are developed in different situations and contexts. Learning is understood as something that is created in the interaction between human beings and the contexts in which they are involved (Ahlberg, 2007a, 2009, 2013).

Multifaceted "problem complexes" require a multiplicity of theoretical and methodological approaches, and researchers in most research teams in Sweden use as points of departure systems theory, sociocultural perspectives, the communicative relational perspective, social constructionism, and the phenomenological life-world perspective (e.g., Berndtsson & Sunesson, 2012). Approaches such as ethnography, ethnomethodology, action research, and discourse theories are also used. Large-scale studies with quantitative methods are conducted in collaboration with other research environments or research institutes (Giota & Emanuelsson, 2011; Giota et al., 2009). Most of the research comprises critical analyses of concepts, phenomena, processes, and structures such as the following: Processes of inclusion and exclusion (e.g., Berhanu, 2008; Berhanu & Dyson, 2012; Fridlund, 2011; Harling, 2014); identity formation; cooperation; school documentation culture (e.g., Andreasson & Carlsson, 2013); function of special education; supervision; content and organization of education for students in need of special support; management and leadership of education at various levels; specific areas of *disability* or specific problem areas, such as reading and writing (e.g., Lundberg & Reichenberg, 2013; Reichenberg, 2012) and groups of students receiving special education, such as students with intellectual disabilities, with socioemotional and behavioral problems (see also PRIS [Platform for Research in Inclusive education and School development] (2013) http://www.ips.gu.se/forskning/ forskningsmiljoer/pris/ for a range of research project in one single University).

Generally, a distinctive feature of special education research is that it is a multidisciplinary field of knowledge with *natural* links not only with education but also with medicine, psychology, and sociology. It is then inevitable that the influence of different theories and perspectives will be very important for research in the field. The diversity offers rich opportunities to expand the research field, but it can also contribute to the image that special education research is suffering from "identity crises," and the theories are diffuse (Ahlberg, 2009; Emanuelsson et al., 2001). More special education perspectives need to be developed; what Emanuelsson (1997) stated a long time ago rings true now that:

> Further theory development in special education will necessitate collaboration with other research disciplines, but at the same time there will be a need for clearer relations between special-education research, handicap research and other fields of research on exclusional processes in society. In this respect it might be fair to say that special-education research in Sweden today is in an exciting and demanding phase of its history. (p. 472)

CONCLUSION

As elsewhere, special education in Sweden in general describes an educational alternative that focuses on teaching students with academic, behavioral, health, or physical needs beyond those met by traditional educational programs or techniques. In Sweden, special education or special needs education is the education of students with special needs in a way that addresses the students' individual differences and needs. Ideally, this process involves the individually planned and systematically monitored arrangement of teaching procedures, adapted equipment and materials, accessible settings, and other interventions designed to help learners with special needs achieve a higher level of personal self-sufficiency and success in school and community than would be available if the student were given access only to a typical classroom education (Mitchell, 2010).

As a research domain, special education in Sweden, as in many other countries, has been criticized for being weak in theory and perspectives. The school practice in that regard has also been a subject of debate. "It is often said to be too narrowly bound to established traditional ways of teaching, in regular as well as in special education. In a way therefore, it can, be [sic] said to be too loyal to the existing educational system and too uncritical of established educational politics ..." (Emanuelsson, 1997, p. 471).

However, in a range of parameters that are believed to favor inclusive education, special education research, and services, Sweden is in the forefront. Sweden is a wealthy, highly educated and healthy society with one of the highest standard of living in the world. In comparison to even many well-developed countries, Sweden is one of the leading countries at successfully combining equity and social inclusion with high economic efficiency. The tradition of universalism and comprehensiveness with minimization of streaming and tracking has been the hallmark of the Swedish education system. Redistribution policies underpinned by high levels of taxation and public spending still appear to have strong social consensus. Sweden has, at the same time, undergone a dramatic transformation within the past two decades. The changes are framed within neo-liberal philosophies that place greater emphasis on devolution, marketization (driven by principles of cost containment and efficiency), competition, standardization, individual choices and rights, development of new profiles within particular school units, and other factors that potentially work *against* the values of diversity, equity and inclusion. This all has obvious implications related to special education.

While there are signs that inclusive education as envisaged in the Salamanca declaration is being exercised at different levels, gaps in research and follow-ups are most noticeable in this area. Finally, an over-representation of minority pupils in special educational placements (Berhanu, 2008; Berhanu & Dyson, 2012) and significant gender differences in specific disability categories (Skolverket [The Swedish National Agency for Education], 2005) as well as in general learning outcomes and methods of testing and assessment are areas of grave concern requiring further studies.

National evaluations and OECD (1999b, 2000b, 2005) reports indicate that differences in a number of aspects (e.g., socioeconomic, educational achievements, and resources) have increased between schools and municipalities, as well as among pupils. Differences in achievement can be linked to the new goals and an achievement-referenced operating system. The number of children who are placed in special educational settings and in particular in Särskolan (education for learning disabled pupils) has increased. The proportions of students who fail in core subjects when leaving compulsory schools and students who drop out from upper secondary schools have increased. Increased segregation by place of residence, variation in classification and placement decisions of pupils with special needs (diverging local practices), a proliferation of independent schools, class differences, individual choices, marginalization, exclusion, and other factors have been documented and have become a subject of heated debate during the last few years. In particular, "growing ethnic inequalities are probably the Achilles heel of the present-day Swedish education system" (OECD, 2005, p. 47; see also Beach & Dovemark, 2007; Beach & Sernhede, 2011).

The paradox is that all these trends that work against inequity are happening while at the same time the rhetoric advocating a school for all and inclusive education have become policy catch-words while having very little effect on the ground. As Skidmore (2004) observed, based on his experiences in the United Kingdom, inclusion has become a buzzword in educational discourse. Although inclusion has been adopted as a policy goal, to date much of the Swedish debate has amounted to little more than the trading of abstract ideological positions, which has little connection with the daily realities in schools. In practice, the trend may be described as *excluding the included*.

Responses and challenges to inclusive education in general and the quality and extent of special education services are varied and complex. Sweden's cultural and political heritage could have been ideal to fully implement inclusive education as envisaged in The Salamanca Statement and Framework for Action (UNESCO, 1994). However, the new political movements and policies that dominate the Swedish educational system have created contradictory and conflicting realities that work not only against fundamental equity issues but also against the long Swedish tradition of universalism, comprehensiveness, and egalitarianism (e.g., Beach & Dovemark, 2007; Korp, 2006).

Apart from the obvious policy shifts that brought about contradictions in the education system, the very nature of our humanity and social activities also are filled with some dilemmas and contradictions. However, policies and practices can either strengthen or weaken the complexities emanating from this. The dilemmas revolve around individually and collectively based ideas of democracy and categorization (social stigmatization/segmentation) versus individuality, utility and culture, the public and personal domains, economy and welfare, individual agency versus collective action, autonomy, and communitarianism. This has definitely shaped the policy and services for special needs pupils and the general structure of special education.

A number of government funded studies have been conducted recently to investigate the participation and inclusion of disabled pupils at different levels of the education system, particularly at individual, classroom, and school levels, and conferences are being held linked to these studies. There is therefore some hope that the studies will reveal micro-level and meso-level activities that hinder or enhance full participation of students with special needs and *problematize* further real-world dilemmas, including the growing culture of diagnosis. Significant factors that may facilitate physical, social, and curricular inclusion have been identified: competent personnel, differentiation in the curriculum, favorable assessment methods, collaboration between the teaching staff, class size, involvement by school leadership, continuous and intensive in-service staff training, partnership with parents, and economic factors. Moreover, the concept of participation has to be further *problematized*. It is one of the least empirically defined core concepts and is broadly misconceived. It is complex, multidimensional, subjective, and context-bound.

On the positive side, there are still commendable activities and policies in Sweden that promote special education and social inclusion. Acclaiming Sweden's past achievements with regard to special education, inclusion, and equity as well as social justice, an OECD (2005) report has stated that "the tools to achieve equity in Sweden have not been added as corrections to the education system — they are at the heart of the Swedish model." That model includes:

- a strong, popular, and successful preschool combining care, nurture, and education;
- a well-designed, broad and attractive comprehensive curriculum;
- an encouraging and non-threatening learning culture for all;
- opportunities for bridges and second chance provision at all levels;
- absence of dead ends;
- equivalence of qualifications; and
- a long-standing tradition of democratic adult education (pp. 48—49).

According to my observation the statement still rings true. There is, however, a cause for concern for how long Sweden's positive reputation, particularly in the areas of integration. "A school for all," equity, and social welfare will persist given the drastic changes that have taken place within a short span. Caution is needed if the traditional model that favored the development of special education and inclusive education in Sweden is to survive.

REFERENCES

Ahlberg, A. (2007a). Specialpedagogik — ett kunskapsområde i utveckling [Special Education — A knowledge domain in the process of development]. In E. Björck-Åkesson & C. Nilholm (Eds.), *Reflektioner kring specialpedagogik — sex profes-sorer om forskningsområdet och forskningsfronten*. Stockholm, Sweden: Vetenskaps-rådet.
Ahlberg, A. (2007b). Specialpedagogik av igår, idag och imorgon [Special education of yester-day, today and tomorrow]. *Pedagogisk forskning i Sverige, 12*, 257—268.
Ahlberg, A. (Ed.). (2009). *Specialpedagogisk forskning. En mångfacetterad utmaning.* [*Special Education. A multifaceted challenge.*] Lund, Sweden: Studentlitteratur.
Ahlberg, A. (2013). *Specialpedagogik i ideologi, teori och praktik — Att bygga broar.* [*Special education as ideology, theory and practice — Building bridge.*] Stockholm, Sweden: Liber.
Ahlström, K.-G. (2011). The origin of special education in Sweden. *Education Inquiry, 2*(2), 179—192.
Andreasson, I., & Carlsson, M. A. (2013). Individual educational plans in Swedish schools: Forming identity and governing function in pupils' documentation. *International Journal of Special Education, 28*(3), 58—67.
Arnesen, A., & Lundahl, L. (2006). Still social and democratic? Inclusive education policies in the Nordic welfare states. *Scandinavian Journal of Educational Research, 50*(3), 285—300.
Asp-Onsjö, L. (2006). *Åtgärdsprogram — dokument eller verktyg: En fallstudie i en kommun.* [*Individual educational plan — Document or Tools: A case study in one municipality.*] Göteborg, Sweden: Acta Universitatis Gothoburgiensis.
Baker, E. T., Wang, M. C., & Walberg, H. J. (1995). The effects of inclusion on learning. *Educational Leadership, 52*(4), 33—35.

Beach, D., & Dovemark, M. (2007). *Education and the commodity problem: Ethnographic investigations of creativity and performativity in Swedish schools.* London: The Tufnell Press.

Beach, D., & Sernhede, O. (2011). From learning to labor to learning for marginality: School segregation and marginalization in Swedish suburbs. *British Journal of Sociology of Education, 32,* 257–274.

Bel Habib, I. (2001). *Elever med invandrarbakgrund i särskolan: Specialpedagogik eller disciplinär makt.* [*Pupils with immigrant background in education for intellectually disabled.*] Kristianstad, Sweden: Högskolan i Kristianstad. Enheten för kompetensutveckling.

Berhanu, G. (2006). *Framgångsfaktorer för delaktighet och jämlikhet.* [*Favorable factors to enhance participation and equality.*] Goteborg, Sweden: Specialpedagogiska institutet.

Berhanu, G. (2008). Ethnic minority pupils in Swedish schools: Some trends in overrepresentation of minority pupils in special educational programs. *International Journal of Special Education, 23*(3), 17–29.

Berhanu, G. (2009, February 1–5). Challenges and responses to inclusive education in Sweden: Mapping issues of equity, participation and democratic values. Presented at a Research Forum: A comparative analysis of equity in inclusive education. Center for Advanced Study in the Behavioral Sciences (CASBS), Stanford University, Palo Alto, CA.

Berhanu, G. (2011). Challenges and responses to inclusive education in Sweden: Mapping issues of equity, participation and democratic values. In J. A. Artiles, E. B. Kozleski, & F. R. Waitoller (Eds.), *Inclusive education: Examining equity on five continents.* Cambridge, MA: Harvard Education Press.

Berhanu, G., & Dyson, A. (2012). Special education in Europe, overrepresentation of minority students. In J. Banks (Ed.), *Encyclopedia of diversity in education* (pp. 2070–2073). Thousand Oaks, CA: SAGE Publications.

Berndtsson, I., & Sunesson, L. (2012). Introducing echolocation into O & M University courses for professionals. *International Journal of Orientation & Mobility, 5*(1), 34–39.

Clark, C., Dyson, A., & Millward, A. (Eds.). (1998). *Theorizing special education.* London: Routledge.

Corbett, J., & Slee, R. (2000). An international conversation on inclusive education. In F. Armstrong, D. Armstrong, & L. Barton (Eds.), *Inclusive education: Policy, contexts and comparative perspectives* (pp. 133–146). London: David Fulton.

Dyson, A., & Millward, A. (1997, May). Theory and practice in special needs education. Paper presented at the International seminar "Theoretical perspectives on special education", Ålesund, Norway.

Emanuelsson, I. (1997). Special education research in Sweden 1956–1996. *Scandinavian Journal of Educational Research, 41*(3&4), 461–474.

Emanuelsson, I. (2001). Reactive versus proactive support coordinator roles: An international comparison. *European Journal of Special Needs Education, 16*(2), 133–142.

Emanuelsson, I. (2003). Differentiation, special education, and equality: A longitudinal study of self-concepts and school careers of students in difficulties and with or without special education support experiences. *European Educational Research Journal, 2*(2), 245–261.

Emanuelsson, I., Haug, P., & Persson, B. (2005). Inclusive education in some Western European countries: Different policy rhetorics and school realities. In D. Mitchell (Ed.), *Contextualizing inclusive education: Evaluating old and new international perspectives* (pp. 114–138). London: Routledge/Falmer.

Emanuelsson, I., Persson, B., & Rosenqvist, J. (2001). *Specialpedagogis forskning: en kunskapsöversikt.* [*Special education research – A literature review.*] Stockholm, Sweden: Skolverket.

Fridlund, L. (2011). *Interkulturell undervisning – ett pedagogiskt dilemma. Talet om undervisning i svenska som andraspråk och i förberedelseklasser.* [*Intercultural education – A Pedagogical dilemma. Professional talk about the teaching of Swedish as a second language and in preparatory classes.*] Doctoral thesis. Gothenburg Studies in Educational Sciences 310, Acta Universitatis Gothoburgensis, Göteborg, Sweden.

Giota, J., & Emanuelsson, I. (2011). Policies in special education support issues in Swedish compulsory school: A national representative study of head teachers' judgements. *London Review of Education, 9*(1), 95–108.

Giota, J., Lundborg, O., & Emanuelsson, I. (2009). Special education in comprehensive schools: Extent, forms and effects. *Scandinavian Journal of Educational Research, 53*(6), 557–578.

Göransson, K. (2006). Pedagogical traditions and conditions for inclusive education. *Scandinavian Journal of Disability Research, 8*(1), 67–74.

Göransson, K., Nilholm, C., & Karlsson, K. (2011). Inclusive education in Sweden? A critical analysis. *International Journal of Inclusive Education, 15*(5), 541–555.

Gustafsson, J. E. (2006). *Barns utbildningssituation: Bidrag till ett kommunalt barnindex.* [*Children's educational situation: Contribution to a local child index in Swedish.*] Stockholm, Sweden: Rädda Barnen.

Hahne Lundström, K. (2001). *Intagningskriterier till gymnasiesärskolan i Göteborg.* [*Admission criteria to upper high school for educationally disabled in Gothenburg*]. Projektarbete vid Arbetslivsinstitutets Företagsläkarutbildning 2000/2001.

Harling, M. (2014). *A fair (af) fair? On subjectivitism and differentiation in educational capitalism.* Licentiate dissertation, Department of Education and Special Education, University of Gothenburg, Gothenburg, Sweden.

Haug, P. (1998). *Pedagogisk dilemma: Specialundervisning.* [*An education dilemma: Special needs instruction.*] Stockholm, Sweden: Swedish National Agency for Education.

Hjörne, E. (2004). *Excluding for inclusion? Negotiating school careers and identities in pupil welfare settings in the Swedish school.* Göteborg, Sweden: Acta Universitatis Gothoburgensis.

Isaksson, J., Lindqvist, R., & Bergström, E. (2010). Pupils with special educational needs: A study of the assessments and categorizing processes regarding pupils' school difficulties in Sweden. *International Journal of Inclusive Education, 14*(2), 133–151.

Kivirauma, J., Klemelä, K., & Rinne, R. (2006). Segregation, integration, inclusion: The ideology and reality in Finland. *European Journal of Special Needs Education, 21*(2), 117–133.

Korp, H. (2006). Lika chanser i gymnasiet? En studie om betyg, nationella prov och social reproduktion [Equivalence in upper high school? A study of grades, national tests and social reproduction]. *Malmö Studies in Educational Sciences, 24,* 34–38.

LGR. (1980). *Läroplan för grundskolan – allmän del.1980 (Lgr 80).* [*Curriculum for the compulsory school system.*] Stockholm: Skolöverstyrelsen och Liber.

LGR 11. (2010). *Läroplan för grundskolan, förskoleklassen och fritidshemmet.* [*Curriculum for the compulsory school system, the preschool class and the leisure-time centre.*] Stockholm, Sweden: Fritzes.

LGR 62. (1962). *Läroplan för grundskolan.* [*Curriculum for the compulsory school system.*] Kungl. Skolöverstyrelsens skriftserie. Stockholm: SÖ-förlaget.

LGR 69. (1969). *Läroplan för grundskolan.* [*Curriculum for the compulsory school system.*] Allmän del. Svenska utbildningsförlaget: Liber.

Lipsky, D. K., & Gartner, A. (1996). Inclusion, school restructuring and the remaking of American society. *Harvard Educational Review, 66*(44), 762–796.

LPO. (1994). *Läroplan för det obligatoriska skolväsendet, förskoleklassen och fritidshemmet.* [*Curriculum for the compulsory school system, the preschool class and the leisure-time centre.*] Stockholm, Sweden: Skolverket och Fritzes AB.

Lundberg, I., & Reichenberg, M. (2013). Developing reading comprehension among students with mild intellectual disabilities: An intervention study. *Scandinavian Journal of Educational Research, 87*, 89–100.

Mehan, H. (1993). Beneath the skin and between the ears: A case study in the politics of representation. In S. Chaiklin & J. Lave (Eds.), *Understanding practice: Perspectives on activity and context* (pp. 241–268). Cambridge: Cambridge University Press.

Mitchell, D. (2005). Introduction: Sixteen propositions on the contexts of inclusive education. In D. Mitchell (Ed.), *Contextualizing inclusive education: Evaluating old and new international perspectives* (pp. 1–21). London: Routledge/Falmer.

Mitchell, D. (2010). *Education that fits: Review of international trends in the education of students with special educational needs.* Wellington: New Zealand Ministry of Education.

Nilholm, C. (2006a). *Including av elever 'I behov av särskilt stöd' – vad betyder det och vad vet vi.* [*Including children with special needs – What does it mean? What do we know?*] Myndigheten för Skolutveckling: Forskning i fokus nr 28.

Nilholm, C. (2006b). Special education, inclusion and democracy. *European Journal of Special Needs Education, 21*(4), 431–445.

Nilhom, C., & Björck-Åkesson, E. (2007). *Reflektioner kring specialpedagogik – sex professorer om forskningsområdet och forskningsfronterna.* [*Reflections on special education: Six professors' comments on the research domain and the research front.*] *Vetenkapsrådets Rapportserie, 5*, 7–16.

Nirje, B. (1992). *The normalization principle papers.* Uppsala, Sweden: University of Sweden, Centre for Handicap Research.

OECD. (1995). *Integrating students with special needs into mainstream schools.* Paris: OECD.

OECD. (1999a). Early childhood education and care policy in Sweden, *Country Note.* Paris, France: Organization for Economic Cooperation and Development.

OECD. (1999b). *Inclusive education at work, students with disabilities in mainstream schools.* Paris, France: Organization for Economic Cooperation and Development.

OECD. (2000a). *Education at a glance.* Paris, France: Organization for Economic Cooperation and Development.

OECD. (2000b). *Special needs education: Statistics and indicators.* Paris, France: OECD Organization for Economic Cooperation and Development.

OECD. (2005). *Equity in education: Thematic review. Sweden, Country Note.* Paris, France: Organization for Economic Cooperation and Development.

Peetsma, T., Vergeer, M., & Karsten, S. (2001). Inclusion in education: Comparing pupils' development in special and regular education. *Educational Review, 53*(2), 125–135.

Persson, B. (1998). *Den motsägelsefulla specialpedagogiken – motiveringar, genom-förande, konsekvenser Specialpedagogiska rapporter nr 10 Göteborg.* Göteborg, Sweden: Göteborgs universitet, Institutionen för specialpedagogik.

Persson, B. (2008). On other people's terms: Schools encounters with disabled students. *European Journal of Special Needs Education, 23*(4), 337–347.

Persson, B., & Berhanu, G. (2005). *Politics of difference: The emergence of special needs in a school for all.* Göteborg, Sweden: (Research Programme) Project Document, Göteborg University.

Persson, B., & Persson, E. (2012). *Inkludering och måluppfyllelse –att nå framgång med alla elever.* [*Inclusion and goal attainment to achieve success too all pupils.*] Stockholm, Sweden: Liber.

PRIS [Platform for Research in Inclusive education and School development]. (2013). Retrieved from http://www.ips.gu.se/forskning/forskningsmiljoer/pris/. Accessed on February 17, 2013.

Reichenberg, M. (2012). "I liked the text about the little bird" Five intellectually disabled persons talk about texts. *Scandinavian Journal of Disability Research Peer Review, 15*(2), 108–124. Retrieved from http://www.tandfonline.com/loi/sjdr20

Rosenqvist, J. (1993). Special education in Sweden. *European Journal of Special Needs Education, 8*(1), 59–74.

Rosenqvist, J. (2007). *Specialpedagogik i mångfaldens Sverige: Om elever med annan etnisk bakgrund än svensk i särskolan.* [*Special education in multicultural Sweden: Ethnic minority pupils in education for intellectually disabled.*] Ett samarbetsprojekt mellan Special pedagogiska institutet och Högskolan Kristianstad (HKr), Specialpedagogiska institutet. Specialpedagogiska skolmyndighetens webbplats.

SFS. (2008). *Förordning om ändring i högskoleförordningen.* [*Ordinance amending the higher education.*] Stockholm, Sweden: Utbildningsdepartementet.

Skidmore, D. (2004). *Inclusion: The dynamic of school development.* Buckingham, UK: Open University Press.

Skollag. (1985). *The Education Act.* Stockholm, Sweden: Utbildningsdepartementet.

Skollag. (2010). *The Education Act.* Stockholm, Sweden: Utbildningsdepartementet.

Skolverket [The Swedish National Agency for Education]. (2000). *Hur särskild får man vara? En analys av elevökningen i särskolan.* [*How different one has to be? A study of the increase of pupils in education for intellectually disabled.*] Uppföljning/Utvärdering Dnr 2000:2037 2000-09-29. Stockholm, Sweden: Skolverket.

Skolverket [The Swedish National Agency for Education]. (2002). *Barnomsorg, skola och vuxenutbildning i siffror 2002 del 2.* [*Childcare, school and adult education in numbers 2002 part 2.*] Rapport 214. Stockholm, Sweden: Skolverket.

Skolverket [The Swedish National Agency for Education]. (2005). *Handikapp i skolan. Det offentliga skolväsendets möte med funktionshinder från folkskolan till nutid.* [*Disability in schools. The public education's handling of handicap from Folk school to the present time.*] Rapport 270. Stockholm, Sweden: Fritzes. Retrieved from www.skolverket.se

Skolverket [The Swedish National Agency for Education]. (2011). *Läroplan för grundskolan, förskoleklassen och fritidshemmet.* Stockholm, Sweden: Fritzes kundservice.

Skrtic, T. M. (1991). The special education paradox: Equity as the way to excellence. *Harvard Educational Review, 61*, 148–206.

SOU. (1974). *Utredningen om skolans inre arbete.* [*Commission (inquiry) on school's internal workings.*] Stockholm, Sweden: Utbildnings-departementet.

SOU. (2003). *För den jag är. Om utbildning och utvecklingstörning.* [*For who I am: On education and developmental disability.*] Stockholm, Sweden: Skolverket. *The Education Act* Skollagen (1985:1000) i Svea Rikes Lag.

Statistics Sweden. (2009). *Education in Sweden 2009.* Örebro, Sweden: Statistics Sweden.

The European Agency for Special Needs and Inclusive Education. (2014). Retrieved from http://www.european-agency.org/country-information/sweden/national-overview/special-needs-education-within-the-education-system. Accessed on January 12, 2014.

Thomas, G., & Loxley, A. (2001). *Deconstructing special education and constructing inclusion.* Buckingham, Sweden: Open University Press.

Tideman, E. (2007). Special education in Sweden. In *Encyclopedia of special education: A reference for the education of children, adolescents, and adults with disabilities and other exceptional individuals* (pp. 1944–1947). New York, NY: Wiley.

UNESCO. (1994, June 7–10). The Salamanca statement and framework for action on special needs education. *Adopted by the World Conference on Special Needs Education: Access and Quality*, Salamanca, Spain.

United Nations. (1989). *Convention on the rights of the child.* New York, NY: UN General Assembly Document A/RES/44/25.

United Nations. (1993, December 20). The standard rules on the equalization of opportunities for persons with disabilities. *Adopted by the United Nations General Assembly, forty-eighth session, resolution 48/96, annex.* Retrieved from http://www.un.org/esa/socdev/enable/dissre00.htm

Vislie, L. (2003). From integration to inclusion: Focusing global trends and changes in the Western European societies. *European Journal of Special Needs Education, 18*(1), 17–35.

Wernersson, I., & Gerrbo, I. (2013). *Differentieringens janusansikte. [The double face of differentiation.] En antologi från Institutionen för pedagogik och specialpedagogik vid Göteborgs universitet. [Anthology from the Department of Education and Special Education.]* Göteborg, Sweden: University of Gothenburg.

Westling Allodi, M. (2000). Self-concept in children receiving special support at school. *European Journal of Special Needs Education, 15*, 69–78.

Westling Allodi, M. (2002). *Support and a resistance: Ambivalence in special education.* Stockholm, Sweden: HLS Förlag.

Wildt-Persson, A., & Rosengren, P. G. (2001). Equity and equivalence in the Swedish school system. In W. Hutmacher (Ed.), *In pursuit of equity in education: Using international indicators to compare equity policies* (pp. 288–321). Hingham, MA: Kluwer Academic Publishers.

Wolfensberger, W. (1972). *The principle of normalization in human services.* Toronto, Canada: NIMR.

SPECIAL EDUCATION TODAY IN SWITZERLAND

Judith Hollenweger

ABSTRACT

This chapter delineates the development of special education in Switzerland from its early first special needs classes in the 19th century to today's integrated and inclusive educational system which is promoted via many ventures. Along this developmental path, research revealed not only that self-contained special needs classes were less effective than integrated classes and that the classes contained an overrepresentation of children with migrant backgrounds. However, the movement to an inclusive education system has not always been easy. Included in this path to inclusion are sections on the following: legislative enactments to insure the rights of persons with disabilities, definitions of who is disabled, prevalence data, the influence of a strong private sector on special education practices, the scientific study of special education by researchers and academics, teacher and professional training endeavors, and challenges that remain today.

Special Education International Perspectives: Practices Across the Globe
Advances in Special Education, Volume 28, 243–269
ISSN: 0270-4013/doi:10.1108/S0270-401320140000028015

INTRODUCTION

Through the years, special education in Switzerland has developed into a diverse field with many different theoretical and practical approaches. Diverse institutional traditions have created a multi-voiced community contributing to policy making, research, and practice as well as to teacher education. To understand special education in Switzerland, it is important to understand its people; their outlooks on the state and their fellow citizens which influences their understanding of good practice and expertise as well as their attitudes toward life in general and people with disabilities in particular. Switzerland, also referred to as the Swiss Confederation, is a small landlocked country with a population of approximately 8 million people in 2013 and four national languages (Swiss German, French, Italian, Romansh). The Swiss are not united by a common ethnic or linguistic identity, but rather by a shared sense of identity, independence and civic spirit. These are reflected in Switzerland's direct democracy, federalism and armed neutrality and help explain why the country is not part of the European Union and joined the United Nations only in 2002.

Switzerland can be considered a consensus democracy (Lijphart, 1999). The principle of power-sharing is articulated in the composition of the government and complex systems of decision-making at national, cantonal, and municipal levels. Government power is always shared between the major parties at national, cantonal, and communal levels thus securing a broad range of opinions. Citizens enjoy extensive rights in decision-making due to Switzerland's direct democracy. They not only elect their communal, cantonal, and federal representatives but are called upon to vote on an average of four times a year on new laws, popular initiatives, or referendums (Swiss Confederation, 2013). Decisions taken by the federal or cantonal parliaments have to be voted on by the people if 50,000 citizens so demand (referendum). Through popular initiatives, votes on amendments to the federal or cantonal legislation can be requested if 100,000 signatures are collected within 18 months (Swiss Confederation). If desired, the citizens always have the last word in all important matters. Another mechanism by which the power of the central government is limited and local decision-making strengthened is the subsidiarity principle. The 26 cantons hold all powers which are not plainly assigned to the federation and similarly, the communes are autonomous in all matters not regulated by the cantons. Each canton retains its own constitution and all enjoy equal rights. For example, health care, education, and culture are largely under the jurisdiction of the cantons.

Direct democracy, the subsidiarity principle as well as the cultural and linguistic diversity have shaped education in Switzerland. Public education is under the authority of the individual cantons which grant varying autonomy to their communes in organizing the provision of education. Only a few essential principles are set out at the federal level. For example, the revised federal constitution of 1874 secured the right of education for all children to be managed by the cantons without interference of the church. In 2006, the Swiss voted in favor of an amendment to the federal constitution which demanded that the cantons "harmonize" their education systems to facilitate transfers of children between different cantonal education systems and to guarantee quality of provision. This will partly be achieved through national education goals and a common curricular framework for the German and French speaking cantons respectively. With no direct federal influence on educational matters, the responsibility to comply with this constitutional amendment lies with the cantons. The needed coordination effort at national level is the responsibility of the Swiss Conference of the Cantonal Ministers of Education (EDK). Harmonization is achieved through Inter-Cantonal Agreements or Concordats. Once such a Concordat has been approved at the inter-cantonal level, each canton will chart its own procedure to decide whether it will join the Concordat or not. Consequently, it is only legally binding for the cantons which join the Concordat. As with all changes to the legislation, concordats have to be either voted on directly by the population or in cantons where the parliament decides, a vote may be requested indirectly by a referendum. Educational reforms therefore are only successful if they consider the needs and interests of all constituencies. More often than not, this results in protracted change processes, but generally it leads to workable solutions. As a consequence of the citizen self-management rule which is firmly entrenched in the Swiss public services (Helmig et al., 2011); schools are governed by a local school board consisting of elected lay persons. This limits the influence of the Ministry of Education and gets citizens involved in public services.

The considerable influence and power of civil society is also reflected in the principle that the state should only be responsible for activities or problems that cannot be carried out or solved by other social actors such as associations, foundations, or private companies. Due to its liberal tradition and sense of independence, individual responsibility and self-help, the Swiss civil society sector is quite powerful (Helmig et al., 2011). Counting employed workers and volunteers, it comprises 6.9% of the country's economically active population thus surpassing the workforce in the construction, the financial or the agricultural sectors (Helmig et al.). Many of these private organizations or associations are supported financially by public funds either through direct contributions, provision of capital, or through service agreements. Service agreements are contracts that define the services which the respective private organization or association provide, for example, services for children with disabilities. This is still mirrored today in a high proportion of special schools and services for persons with disabilities governed by private organizations or foundations rather than by the state. Only recent developments in legislation have led to some changes which may have a further impact in the future.

To understand special education in Switzerland, it is important to recognize how public and private sectors as well as civil society cooperate; how they influence and are driven by research, policies and practices. Developments in special education since its beginnings as a field of study can be viewed as covering three separate periods. The *era of discovery and exploration* was initiated with the introduction of compulsory education as the responsibility of civil society rather than the church following the French revolution wars, the birth of the modern Swiss state in 1848 and the revision of the Swiss federal constitution in 1874 (see above). This era is marked by the creation of special education as a scientific field, leading to the first European chair for special education to be established in 1931 at the University of Zurich. A *second era of expansion and consolidation* is closely linked to developments in the social state culminating in the introduction of the national invalidity insurance in 1960 and the educational expansion after the Second World War. In this era, foundations, organizations and associations providing services for children with disabilities and their families or providing training for professionals underwent a process of institutionalization thus becoming part of a publicly funded network of service providers and partners in policy development. The *third era of special education in Switzerland lasts until today* and is marked by its dispersion and crisis. As a result of its expansion, the boundaries and contour of special education became increasingly blurred in the 1980s, raising questions about its purpose, effectiveness and legitimacy. A move toward integration and inclusion challenged the institutional self-image of the private sector service providers. More recently, changes in legislation have created financial and organizational challenges for the private sector because new laws promote special education as a matter of individual rights rather than social security and welfare.

Legislation and policy development have played an important role in institutionalizing special education during the second era and in challenging established structures in the third era. The next section therefore will be dedicated to developments in legislation. The impact of legislation is reflected in mechanisms of identification and definition of disability which will be explored in the third section. Prevalence data in Switzerland is scarce and only recently Switzerland has started to collect information on disability independent of service provision. Because the private sector has been instrumental in establishing special education in Switzerland, a section will be dedicated to it. It was also due to private initiatives that special education was established as a science and a field for professional training. Subsequent sections will be dedicated to describe developments in these areas and the current situation. Finally, in summing up, the last section will focus on how these developments have influenced current practices in special education and which challenges lay ahead.

DEVELOPMENTS IN LEGISLATION: FROM BENEFITS TO RIGHTS

In 1925, a new article in the federal constitution laid the foundation for the Swiss social state with a focus primarily on creating an old age and survivor pension. When the first corresponding law was rejected by the Swiss voters, the implementation of this pension took priority over disability issues. Finally, in 1948, the Federal Office of Social Insurance [Bundesamt für Sozialversicherungen] was charged with the provision of benefits in case of old age and survivors. Only much later in 1960, did the Federal Invalidity Insurance Law [Bundesgesetz über die Invalidenversicherung, IVG] come into effect. Undoubtedly, this was the most far-reaching legislation for Swiss people with disabilities in the 20th century, including for children with disabilities. The law defined "invalidity" as the "inability to earn an income," or – for the insured who were not gainfully employed – the "inability to continue to carry out day-to-day tasks (e.g., housework) because of a physical, psychological or mental disability." It required the disability to be long-term (minimum of one year). Whether a disability is "congenital or the result of an illness or accident is irrelevant" (Federal Social Insurance Office, 2010). The basic premise of the Invalidity Insurance system was and still is to promote the professional (re)integration of persons with disabilities as well as improve or restore their earning capacity. The guiding principle is "rehabilitation before pension" (Federal Social Insurance Office). Children with disabilities, including their education, were supported by the Invalidity Insurance to ensure their future integration into the workforce.

The implementation of the Federal Invalidity Insurance marks the beginning of an era of expansion and consolidation in special education. The Invalidity Insurance helped ensure adequate provision for children with disabilities through direct payments for services (e.g., language therapy), aids (e.g., wheelchair), and financial support for families and children. In addition, it co-financed organizations and associations, providing educational, social, and other services or training staff and professionals working in the respective institutions. According to article 74 of the Federal Invalidity Insurance Law, private national or regional organizations and associations providing services for people with disabilities or offering training courses for staff and professionals were entitled to receive funding. This encouraged the establishment and expansion of private organizations and associations as well as training institutions. As knowledge related to description, diagnosis and treatment grew, "new disabilities" were identified which − once approved by the Federal Disability Insurance − led to an increase in identified children and services provided. Over the years, this led to an inconsistent and ad hoc system of establishing eligibility that was mainly driven by parents, special schools and professionals. The significances for special education will be explored in further details in the following sections.

The year 2008 generated an important momentum for special education in a time of dispersion and crisis. As part of a major reform called the "new financial perequation and the repartition of tasks" [Neugestaltung des Finanzausgleichs und der Aufgaben zwischen Bund und Kantonen] between the federation and the 26 cantons, the federation withdrew from all obligations related to special education. In other words, the Federal Invalidity Insurance ceased to finance services or training institutions and no longer paid for special education measures. This had and still has far-reaching consequences for service providers and training institutions as will be illustrated in the next sections. The Cantons now assumed full financial responsibility for the education of all children, but also gained more control over identification, organization of services and training. Article 62, paragraph 3 was included in the Federal Constitution requesting the Cantons to "ensure that adequate special needs education is provided to all children and young people with disabilities up to the age of 20" (Swiss Federation, 2013). In preparation for assuming full legal, financial, and professional responsibility for the provision of children and youth with disabilities from birth to 20 years, the Cantons charged the Swiss

Conference of Cantonal Ministers of Education [Schweizerische Konferenz der Kantonalen Erziehungsdirektoren] to prepare an Inter-Cantonal Concordat for Special Education or short Special Education Concordat [Sonderpädagogik-Konkordat] (EDK [Swiss Conference of Cantonal Ministers of Education], 2007) which came into force on January 1, 2011 after a three-year transition period. It sets out some basic standards for all cantons joining the Concordat to adhere to, namely a shared terminology, quality specification for service providers as well as a standardized eligibility procedure.

There are some policy developments in disability legislation which are worth commenting on at this juncture because of their over-arching relevance or indirect impact on education. Due to the manifold articulated voices of the Swiss disability constituents supported by public funds and with so many diverse players each generally protective of their own subsidies, service contracts and interest groups, the motivation to promote legislation to strengthen the rights of individuals with disabilities has been less fervent than in other countries. Other reasons for the late efforts to promote social, economic, and cultural rights of persons with disabilities can be found its strong tradition of civic and political rights, the absence of war veterans as well as in its decentralized and consensus-oriented direct democracy. In 1996, the Swiss Center of Independent Living was established in Zurich and has since helped develop a new perspective on disability inspired by self-advocacy, political awareness, and activism. A new awareness is also reflected in Article 8 of the revised Federal Constitution which came into effect in 2000. For the first time, it explicitly states the principle of equalization of all persons, including persons with disabilities. A popular initiative was launched in 1999 to ensure "Equal rights for persons with disabilities" [Gleiche Rechte für Behinderte]. The requests of the initiative were considered too radical and the Federal Council subsequently drafted a counter-proposal, the "Federal Act on the Elimination of Discrimination against People with Disabilities" [Bundesgesetz über die Beseitigung von Benachteiligungen von Menschen mit Behinderungen]. After the popular initiative was rejected by the Swiss voters in May 2003, this new federal act came into force in 2004. Article 20 explicitly demands that the Cantons provide education which is adapted to the requirements and needs of children with disabilities and to promote a "general orientation towards inclusive education."

Switzerland does not have a tradition of litigation about matters of education, but this may change over the coming years. With the entry into force of this new federal legislation, a specialist center (Egalité Handicap) was founded in 2004 to provide legal services, monitor and document jurisdiction and to collaborate with public and private partners. Typical for Switzerland, this center is affiliated with the umbrella organization of private disability organizations and collaborates with the Federal Bureau for Equality of People with Disabilities. The current legislation does not guarantee children with disabilities the right to be included in regular schools; it only promotes inclusion and states it as the preferred model. It also ensures that children with disabilities are not discriminated against and that compensation is provided if children with disabilities are at a disadvantage. Notably in higher education, several cases were publicized where students did not receive adequate support or adaptations were not made to ensure their participation. In 2012, the Federal Supreme Court rejected a complaint of a family that requested that their 14-year-old son with a "perceptional disorder" be schooled in a special school rather than receiving special educational support in regular school.[1]

Despite much progress toward understanding people with disabilities as citizens and agents, children with disabilities are still today frequently treated as passive targets. Self-representation of children with disabilities is only an emerging issue. Identification depends on others and their expectations; the needs of the child are still defined by others. Changes are slow, despite efforts to give the child an independent voice in decisions that affect their lives. A new federal legislation on the protection of children and adults [Kindes- und Erwachsenenschutzrecht] which came into effect in January 2013 strengthens the influence of children and persons with disabilities in relation to legal guardianship and for the purpose of self-representation. A philosophy of improved self-representation is also embedded in the new Standardized Eligibility Procedure to secure the rights of children and youth with disabilities in the context of education (EDK, 2011). The procedure requires discussions with parents and teachers to develop recommendations. It encourages the participation of the child in this process but cannot legally ensure that the voice of the child is altogether taken into account. Last but not least it should be mentioned that Switzerland is one of the last countries in Europe to ratify the United Nations Convention on the Rights of Persons with Disabilities (2006). Only in 2013, the two chambers of the Federal Assembly approved the ratification and it is expected that the Federal Council will proceed with it in 2014. It remains to be seen whether the ratification will be followed by a national action plan and whether this will have a positive impact on education for children with disabilities over the coming years.

WHO HAS A DISABILITY OR SPECIAL EDUCATIONAL NEEDS?

While impairments create realities that people have to learn to live with, "disability" is a social construct and relative to expectations, attitudes and beliefs as well as physical and social characteristics of the environment. Whether a child is identified as having a disability depends on legislation and policies, the availability of services, financing mechanisms as well as specific diagnostic or eligibility criteria. Disability, therefore, is always defined in the specific social context in which it is used. Definitions of disability in education systems have been influenced mainly by medicine (e.g., to explain disorders) and psychology (e.g., to explain deviance), but also by expectations expressed in the curriculum (Hollenweger, 2013). In some countries, specific clinical categories (e.g., autism) are also used for administrative purposes, but not in other countries (OECD, 2005, 2007). Schools themselves create "disabilities" and consequently certain social groups tend to be overrepresented or underrepresented amongst children identified as having a disability. All these factors make it difficult to collect reliable data on childhood disability independent of service provision. Switzerland's decentralized structure adds to the difficulty of collecting comparable data unless the Federal government is given a mandate to do so. This is not the case with special education, although efforts have been made to improve data (see below). But since 2004, the federal government has a mandate to monitor the implementation of the national disability equalization law and thus has intensified its efforts to collect relevant data.

PREVALENCE DATA

According to the 2007 Swiss Health Survey carried out by the World Health Organization (World Health Organization [WHO], 2007) the self-reported disability prevalence in Switzerland is 14%. The Federal Office of Statistics[2] estimates that in 2011, around 1.4 million people in Switzerland aged 16 years and older have a "disability," of whom 541,000 experience severe restrictions and almost 40,000 live in an institution for the disabled (Bundesamt für Statistik, 2010a). It is estimated that 144,000 children with disabilities between the ages of 0 to 14 live in 122,100 households, amounting to 8.4% of all households (Bundesamt für Statistik [Federal Office of Statistics], 2010b). As judged by their parents or caregivers, 34,400 children experience substantial participation restrictions in their daily life due to their disability (Bundesamt für Statistik). Apart from data drawn from the Swiss Health Survey, available data on childhood disability is linked to service provision. For many years, the cantonal ministries of education merely provided information on the number of children in different types of special schools and the Federal Invalidity Insurance generated data along their different types of services. Thus, neither the education nor social sector is able to provide prevalence data. Over the last few years, the Federal Office of Statistics has modernized the Swiss education statistics to allow tracking of individual children throughout their school career and thus providing information on the outcomes of special educational support. A pilot data collection exercise for children with disabilities was carried out in 2012, but data for all cantons will only be available for the school year of 2014–2015.

These changes coincide with the cantons assuming full responsibility for special education as the Invalidity Insurance withdraws from financing education of children with disabilities. Both developments created the opportunity to move away from an insurance-based thinking that defined disability as impairment, thus strongly based in a medical model of disability. Until 2008, the definition of "childhood disability" has been profoundly influenced by the Federal Invalidity Insurance. Children were identified as being "disabled" if they received "special education measures" [sonderpädagogische Massnahmen] on the basis of the Invalidity Insurance Legislation. In 2009, the Invalidity Insurance no longer co-financed education, but still provided medical services to 71,139 children between the ages of 0 and 14 years, auxiliary aids (e.g., wheelchairs) to 4,978 children and paid a "helplessness allowance" to 5,892 children unable to carry out activities of daily living (Bundesamt für Statistik [Federal Office of Statistics], 2010b). Statistics of socio-medical institutions provide information on children with disabilities living in institutions; in 2008 this included 4,757 children of which many only spent some months there (Bundesamt für Statistik [Federal Office of Statistics], 2010b). As for early childhood intervention, data provided by the "curative education services" [Heilpädagogische Dienste], shows that in 2010 they served 6,756 children who were in 29 services that provided early childhood intervention covering 17 of the 26 Cantons (Kronenberg, 2012). Clearly, this information does not cover all the services as there are over 100 early intervention centers in Switzerland and many more professionals working in a private capacity.

In the school year 2008–2009, out of around 780,000 children in primary and secondary education, 25,000 were taught in special classes and 16,000 in special schools (European Agency, 2010). Although the situation will improve in the future as mentioned above, the data on disability in education is still linked to type of special school rather than characteristics of the child (OECD, 2007). As a consequence, children are only identified as being "disabled" if they attend a special school or receive additional resources for their education. Identification or segregation rates vary substantially between the different cantons and regions as a result of differences in policies, traditions and geography. In the Canton Basel-Town, for example, 10% of all school children either visit a special school or a special class, compared to 6.8% in the Canton of Zurich, 4.1% in the Canton of Geneva or 2% in the Canton of Ticino (Sieber, 2006). There has been an increase of segregated schooling between 1980 and 2000, a trend which was analyzed for six Cantons in 2004 (Häfeli & Walther-Müller, 2005). Some of the contributing factors identified were availability of services, identification and decision-making processes as well as financial mechanisms. Increased social pressure on regular schools is linked to overrepresentation of children from disadvantaged and migrant backgrounds in special education (Carigiet Reinhard, 2012; Sieber, 2006). The social bias in labeling children as being "disabled" or having "special needs" is not only a Swiss phenomenon, but in an education system which segregates a rather high percentage of children into special settings and streams children according to their achievement after 6th grade, the consequences may be more severe than in comprehensive systems where all children go to the same schools for compulsory education.

A challenge that remains is the need to implement data collecting mechanisms and generate survey data which does not only reflect service provision but is also able to inform policy makers about the effects of these services and the level of participation children with disabilities enjoy in education. With the Inter-Cantonal Concordat for Special Education, the participating cantonal education ministries are adopting the International Classification of Functioning, Disability and Health (ICF) Version for Children and Youth (WHO, 2001, 2007) as a common language, as the basis to establish eligibility (Hollenweger, 2011; Hollenweger & Moretti, 2012) and to facilitate collaboration in multidisciplinary teams. Disability is understood as the result of the complex interaction between characteristics of a person and the environment rather than as a fixed characteristic of an individual. In education, participation is the most central concept of the ICF as all children have a right to participate to the fullest possible level in all educational activities. Environmental factors contribute to functioning and disability and are the lever for improving participation. The ICF can be used to describe different dimensions and levels of functioning that may be present even in children with the same disorder. Thus, different sectors and professionals are able to highlight specific aspects related to their expertise and work without losing sight of other aspects. It is hoped that in the future, such a coherent conceptual basis will provide more meaningful and compatible data.

THE INFLUENCE OF A STRONG PRIVATE SERVICE SECTOR ON SPECIAL EDUCATION

Direct democracy, subsidiarity principle, decentralization, and a strong civic society sector have left their mark on special education in Switzerland. Policy developments related to the education of children with disabilities have been unhurried in Switzerland, partially due to the consensus-based decision-making processes typical for this country, but also due to a strong private sector. Private organizations and associations have been and some still remain today major players with considerable influence in policy, practice as well as in training and research. Their organization, governing principles and financing mechanisms are rooted in the diverse local scenes but through a network of umbrella organizations and other superstructures, the private sector is an important player at national level as well. In the era of discovery and exploration, private foundations, associations, and organizations were established as a reflection of the deep-seated Swiss civic sense, but they were able to expand and consolidate their position as a result of the Federal Invalidity Insurance legislation which not only paid for direct services but also operating subsidies for private associations and organizations delivering services for persons with disabilities. This includes many private schools and institutions for children with disabilities which were founded at various points in time both by parents and professionals. Notwithstanding, today more than half of Switzerland's special schools are run by such private bodies. A glance at their creation and expansion is central to an understanding of today's circumstances of special education in Switzerland.

Many umbrella organizations and associations go back 150 or more years. For example, in 1810, the Swiss Charitable Association [Schweizerische Gemeinnützige Gesellschaft] was founded and soon cantonal and regional structures followed all over Switzerland. These charitable associations not only established institutions for the disabled or trained "teachers for the poor" [Armenlehrerausbildung] since 1835 but also exerted their influence in shaping the nature of the emerging public education system (Schumacher, 2010). The Swiss Teacher Association was founded in 1849, mainly to promote education independent of state efforts. In 1844, the Swiss Association of Education for the Poor [Schweizer Armenerzieherverein] was founded to represent the growing number of institutions for the poor with an emphasis on their "moral development"; it survives until today as "Curaviva" and still defends the interests of homes and social institutions for persons with disabilities, old age and children with special needs. In 1882 the first special classes [Hilfsklassen] were installed in La Chaux-de-Fonds to support children unable to follow instruction in regular classes (Bless, 1995). To extend this practice was the declared goal of the "Swiss Conference for the Concerns of Idiots" [Schweizerische Konferenz für das Idiotenwesen], founded in 1889 and renamed as "Swiss Association for Curative Education" [Schweizerische Heilpädagogische Gesellschaft] in 1976 (Geisen & Riegel, 2009, p. 295). These associations also contributed substantially to the discovery and exploration of special education.

Pro Infirmis, founded in 1920, is a private umbrella organization with over 25 membership organizations and a network of offices in all parts of Switzerland. It has a special mandate by the federal and cantonal states to provide services to people with disabilities and their families. Sixty percent of the Pro Infirmis' expenditures are covered by the federal government. Counseling services for families are also offered by Pro Infirmis and other associations and private bodies. There are many parents' organizations providing services for parents and organized in national umbrella organizations, for example INSIEME (children with intellectual disabilities) founded in 1957, Visoparents (Children with visual impairments) founded in 1963 and AutismusSchweiz (children with autism spectrum disorders) founded in 1975 to name just a few. Parents' organizations work at the local or cantonal level, but are represented at the national and international levels for advocacy work and representation of their interests. Parents' organizations have recently created a "Union of Parents of Disabled Children" [Konferenz der Vereinigungen von Eltern behinderter Kinder] to represent their interests vis-à-vis society and the government. But the wide range of services available can be perplexing for families. A recent study (Wagner Lenzin, 2007) with a small sample of parents suggests that the social network and social capital of families with a disabled child are very important and facilitate access to helpful support. Counseling services offered by these private organizations can be overbearing and disempowering. It is also suggested that some of them are not providing highly professional services.

The emergence of the social welfare system and a shift away from a charity paradigm did not result in a decrease of these private activities. Rather on the contrary, it marked the beginning of an era of expansion and consolidation of the private sector. Switzerland's welfare state fits the residual social policy model as it relies on a high degree of personal responsibility and the involvement of non-government organizations (Desai, 2014). If the support and pensions of the Invalidity Insurance were insufficient, persons with disabilities could rely on a network of services provided by private organizations, for example, Pro Infirmis. With the introduction of the Federal Invalidity Insurance, these services for people with disabilities were institutionalized within the social welfare system. Despite remaining private, they functioned now with a public mandate and with public funding. Between 1960 and 2008, this also applied for private organizations providing special education. Coinciding with an over-all expansion of education and a growing knowledge in special education, more and more children were identified as having a disability and being in need of support by the Federal Invalidity Insurance. New knowledge created new labels which created new sources of income, new professions, and new institutions (Bühler-Niederberger, 1991). Eventually, the expansion led to dispersion and to a loss of a clear identity of the professionals working in the area. These developments were interrupted when the Federal Invalidity Insurance ceased to finance special education and the Inter-Cantonal Conference of Ministers of Education assumed responsibility for all teaching professions. But with regard to providing special education, the trend has not yet been turned around because many of the cantons are not in full control and private services still play an important role. In 2003, only less than half of the special schools in Switzerland were public (46%), compared to 92% in the United Kingdom or 97% in Finland (OECD, 2007). It will be interesting to see whether this will change as a result of a rights-based perspective requiring the state to assume full responsibility for the education of all children — rather than delegating the education of children with disabilities to private service providers.

THE SCIENTIFIC STUDY OF SPECIAL EDUCATION

Medicalization of the care of persons with disabilities in the 19th century and the gradual adoption of social policies mark the beginnings of special education in Switzerland (Kaba, 2007). In was during this period that the social construct of "backwardness" and the "pathologies of education" were created (Ruchat, 2003). In the German-speaking part of Switzerland, special education was established as a science between 1880 and 1930 by professionals working with children with disabilities. This development was strongly driven by the will to gain authority and responsibility for the "disabled" rather than leaving their treatment to medicine (Wolfisberg, 2002). In 1924, the first college for "curative care workers" [Heilerzieher] was founded in Zurich (later named "Heilpädagogisches Seminar Zürich," today "Interkantonale Hochschule für Heilpädagogik") with Heinrich Hanselmann as its first director. Heinrich Hanselmann also was appointed professor for "curative education" [Heilpädagogik] at the University of Zurich, which in 1931 created the pioneer university chair for special education in Europe (Wolfisberg). Both, Hanselmann and his successor, Paul Moor, emphasized that "curative education" was nothing other than education in order to ensure its scientific autonomy from medicine. This strong dissociation from medicine may be one reason why special education as a science – unlike in Germany – did not develop along the lines of impairment categories (e.g., special education of the blind or the physically disabled), but pursued more holistic approaches. Terminology like "developmental restraint" [Entwicklungshemmung] or "weakness of hold" [Haltschwäche] were used to establish the distance from medical terms like anomaly, degeneration, or defect (Gröschke, 2008). Since Paul Moor's retirement, the positions as director of a training institution and university professor were no longer held by the same person and subsequently the science of special education and the training of professionals developed separately until this day.

Developments in the French-speaking part of Switzerland were somewhat different and it is helpful to describe the diverse origins of scientific inquiry related to children with disabilities in order to understand today's regional differences in approaches, nomenclatures, and philosophies in the sphere of special education. In Geneva, the impetus for studying children with disabilities came from within the Department of Public Instruction which established a permanent medical-educational commission in 1908. This commission was later developed into the Geneva medical-educational services [Service médico-pédagogique de Genève] (Ruchat, 2008), which still exists today. The commission was chaired by Édouard Claparède who in 1912 established the "Institut Jean-Jacques Rousseau" to promote the "science of education" and to train teachers, including those in special education. The institute also provided "medico-educational" consultations

[consultations medico-pédagogiques] and developed various diagnostic and therapeutic methods (Droux & Ruchat, 2007; Ruchat, 2008). Jean Piaget worked in the "Institut Jean-Jacques Rousseau" since 1921 and became its director in 1932. It is therefore not surprising, that the concept of "intelligence" played an important role in the construction of the "backward child" (Ruchat, 2003). In 1975, the Institute – which since 1929 was associated with the University of Geneva – became part of its Faculty of Psychology and Educational Sciences [Faculté de Psychologie et des Sciences de l'Education, FPSE]. As a consequence, in Geneva the scientific study and teacher education in special education are in much closer dialogue than in the German-speaking part of Switzerland.

Not only political but also religious and philosophical differences added to the diversity of scientific study. A catholic "curative education" was established in Fribourg and Lucerne in 1935 but remained less influential over the coming years (Gröschke, 2008). This was partially due to the circumstances that Josef Spieler, professor of "Curative Education" at the University of Fribourg, was German by origin and a member of the NSDAP; he was extradited after the Second World War for his closeness to Nazi philosophy. Special education in the Protestant universities (e.g., Geneva, Zurich) generally relied more on education and psychology, while Catholic universities (e.g., Fribourg, Lucerne) emphasized the importance of philosophy and ethics. Eugenics was discussed in Switzerland with the entire scope between uncritical adoption, strategic use of some elements, critical debate, and total rejection (Wolfisberg, 2002). In 1942 in Pro Infirmis' first edition of its journal, Heinrich Hanselmann as its editor strongly rejected the notion of exterminating "worthless life." The era of discovery and exploration was dominated by developments in Zurich and Geneva which were also of international importance. In 1925, the "International Bureau of Education" (IBE) was founded in Geneva as a private non-governmental organization to promote scientific research in the educational field and to serve as a documentation and coordination center for institutions and associations concerned with education.[3] From 1929 to 1967, Jean Piaget was director of the IBE and professor of psychology at the University of Geneva. Heinrich Hanselmann was elected first president of the "International Association for Curative Education" [Internationale Gesellschaft für Heilpädagogik], founded in 1937 (Hänsel, 2008). This served the over-all efforts to establish special education as a discipline to promote the institutionalization of special education teacher training and to endorse "special education" rather than "curative education" as a scientific discipline. The Swiss school of special education remained constitutive for the study of special education until well into the post war period (Gröschke, 2008).

In the era of expansion and consolidation, the private organizations offering services for children with disabilities underwent a process of institutionalization and similar developments can be observed in the Swiss universities where institutes were founded. In the 1970s, the Institute of Special Education was established at the University of Zurich. The Institute for Special Education and Psychology [Institut für spezielle Pädagogik und Psychologie] in Basel was founded in 1971 and remained an independent institute associated to the University of Basel until its integration into the newly founded University of Teacher Education of Northwestern Switzerland [Pädagogische Hochschule Nordwestschweiz] in 2001. Its first director, Emil E. Kobi as well as Urs Haeberlin, professor at the University of Fribourg, were both instrumental in continuing the humanistic tradition of Switzerland's special education as a normative and value-based science. The importance of child development and systemic perspectives remained important as did a strong focus on what makes disability a disability beyond the underlying medical realities. More recently, sociological approaches have assumed more attention to improve understanding of issues encompassing institutions, the social realities of disability and the foundation of special education itself (Weisser, 2005). The "empirical turn" in policy development and research agendas influenced education in Switzerland only recently, mainly initiated by OECD's Programme for International Student Assessment (PISA) and a move toward outcome-based educational policies (Buchhaas-Birkholz, 2009). The influence of academic special education on practice has been limited not only because of the strong civic sector as described earlier but also because teacher education and professional training has developed rather independently. Until today, the separation between academic and professional studies of special education remains a reality in most Cantons.

TRAINING OF TEACHERS AND PROFESSIONALS IN SPECIAL EDUCATION

The training of all professionals contributing to the education of children with disabilities has its roots mainly in the private sector as described earlier. The era of discovery and exploration thus coincided with the motivation to become established as a profession with one's own area of work and authority independent of medicine. Similar to the institutionalization of services and academic studies, the expansion and consolidation of teacher training institutions was encouraged by the Federal Invalidity Insurance. Like other private service associations, teacher training institutions in special education benefited from subsidies by the Federal Invalidity Insurance independent of their legal status (e.g., part of a university, a private organization or public teacher training college). In 1959, the "Association of Training Institutions for Curative Education" [Verband heilpädagogischer Ausbildungsinstitute, VHpA] was created to act as the main coordinating body for the professions in the area of special education. The association founded the "Swiss Central Office for Curative Education" in 1972 as a documentation and research center. Today this "Swiss Center for Curative and Special Education" [Schweizer Zentrum für Heil- und Sonderpädagogik] still plays a central role, but is now an independent foundation charged with coordinating special education at national and international levels in close cooperation with the Swiss Conference of Cantonal Ministers of Education.

The term "curative education" [Heilpädagogik] is still used today for the teaching profession in the German-speaking part of Switzerland, while "special education" generally refers to academic studies. The gap between theory and practice is aggravated by the fact that private institutions and associations play an important role in policy development and were the main drivers of the expansion of services. Until recently, private organizations also played an important role in initiating new training courses. This came to an end when the Swiss Conference of the Cantonal Ministers of Education (EDK) assumed responsibility for teacher training in special education in 1998 and the training of language and psychomotor therapists in 2000 as part of the bologna process and the transformation of teacher training colleges into Universities of Teacher Education [Pädagogische Hochschulen] in the early 2000. Since then, all training courses have to comply with the accreditation regulations of the Swiss Conference of the Cantonal Ministers of Education. In most Cantons, this transition was used to integrate separate teacher training institutions for special educators into the newly founded Universities of Teacher Education, with the exception of the "Inter-Cantonal University for Curative Education" [Interkantonale Hochschule für Heilpädagogik], the successor organization of the "Heilpädagogische Seminar Zürich." This integration process was accelerated by the fact that as of 2008, the Federal Invalidity Insurance no longer subsidized these institutions.

Today, the Universities of Geneva, Fribourg and Zurich offer academic studies in special education which do not qualify for practical work with children. As for Speech and Language Therapy, the Universities of Geneva and Neuchâtel offer master degrees, while the University of Fribourg, the University of Teacher Education of Northwestern Switzerland in Basel, the Inter-Cantonal University of Curative Education in Zurich and the Swiss University for Language Therapy in Rorschach offer Bachelor degrees – as required by the accreditation regulations. Bachelor degrees in psychomotor therapy can be attained at the Geneva University of Applied Sciences or at the Inter-Cantonal University of Curative Education in Zurich. Master degree studies for special education teachers are available at the University of Teacher Education of Northwestern Switzerland in Basel, the University of Teacher Education in Bern, the French speaking University of Teacher Education of Berne, the Jura and Neuchâtel, at the University of Fribourg, at the University of Geneva, the University of Teacher Education in Lausanne, the University of Teacher Education in Lucerne and at the Inter-Cantonal University of Curative Education in Zurich. In addition, Geneva, Basel, and Zurich also offer master degrees for early childhood intervention. These training courses correspond with the services made available for children with disabilities. Early childhood intervention [Heilpädagogische Früherziehung] is provided for children from 0 to 6 years, subsequently special education [Schulische Heilpädagogik]. Pedagogical-therapeutical measures include language therapy [Logopädie] and psychomotor therapy [psychomotorische Therapie]. Psychomotor therapy reflects the holistic and systemic tradition of Swiss special education and works on the premise that physical and motor disturbances have an effect on well-being, self-esteem, cognition, and social interaction (Kobi, 1993).

Over the years, there have been several initiatives to improve the competence of regular teachers in the area of special education. In 1994, a first report "Special Education in Teacher Education" [Sonderpädagogik in der Lehrerbildung] (EDK, 1994) was published by the Swiss Conference of Cantonal Ministers of Education and initiated a nation-wide discussion on what regular teachers need to know about special education. This was taken up by regular teacher education when their curricula changed substantially to meet the new accreditation criteria as part of the change process from colleges to universities around 2000. But subsequently, better trained regular teachers suddenly shared more and more competencies and responsibilities with special education teachers working in special classes called "curative education teachers" [Schulische Heilpädagogen].

The decline of the over-all number of students between the 1990s and the early 2000 coincided with increased efforts to integrate children with disabilities in regular classes. Due to changes in legislation strengthening integration and inclusion, many special classes were abolished and special education teachers had to work alongside regular teachers in their classes. This led to a dispersion of their tasks and responsibilities in order to meet the specific needs of the local schools and teachers. Some special teachers developed into advisors, supervisors, coaches, or project managers; it was no longer clear what "curative school education" [Schulische Heilpädagogik] really was. In these times of crisis, several initiatives sought to re-invent special education as well as to strengthen the knowledge and skills of regular teachers to teach diverse groups of children (Cohep, 2008; VHpA, 2003). Today, all Universities of Teacher Education have taken up the call to prepare their students for a School for All, but clearly there are limits to what can be learned during bachelor studies leading to kindergarten and elementary school teacher certification. The "curative teacher training institutions" once proud to trained "generalists" for children with special needs rather than "specialists" for impairment groups, are now debating what this means in a time when regular education teachers have assumed many of their former responsibilities. The debate continues and Switzerland may see a move toward training "specialist special teachers" in the future.

SPECIAL EDUCATION TODAY AND FUTURE CHALLENGES

Once, the establishment of the first special classes in the late 19th century marked the birth of a new profession and field of work. It was the beginning of the long history of the "Schweizerische Heilpädagogische Gesellschaft" which shaped special education throughout the era of discovery and exploration and the era of expansion and consolidation (Schindler, 1990). The growth of special classes in the 1970s and 1980s lead to an over-all segregation rate of an average 6% in the late 1990s (Sieber, 2006). Since the 1980s, integration and inclusion of children with disabilities or special needs is promoted through many different ventures. Research into the effectiveness of these special classes not only identified them as less effective than integrated settings (Bless, 1995) but also uncovered an overrepresentation of children with migrant background (Kronig, 2007). Today, special classes for children with learning disabilities and behavioral problems are viewed with suspicion and have been abolished in some Cantons. The "Schweizerische Heilpädagogische Gesellschaft" is no longer a relevant player; it did not survive the era of dispersion and crisis. But the re-integration of children in special classes into regular classes was not always successful. It led to an increase in the rate of children educated in special schools for children with intellectual disabilities[4] and to the uncertainty for professionals described in the previous section.

The legacy of the Federal Invalidity Insurance is still discernible in the service provision today. Financing special classes and other support measures for "mild" or high incidence disabilities was never part of the Federal Invalidity Insurance's responsibility and the private sector was not involved in providing education for this group. The Cantonal Ministries of Education therefore had a free hand to reform special classes and special educational support in regular classes. Special schools on the other hand serve children with low incidence disabilities and benefited from subsidies provided by the Federal Invalidity Insurance. Due to changes in federal and cantonal legislations, there is a trend toward inclusion, but regular and special schools adapt only slowly to the new circumstances. The Cantons encourage special schools to develop into resources centers, but generally they still retain some children in segregated settings while increasingly providing services to children in regular schools. Akin to Germany, special education was institutionalized by separate organizations and associations thus retaining its segregate tradition (Pfahl & Powell, 2010). As mentioned earlier, more than half of all special schools continue to function as private institutions to this day. Although the cantonal ministries of education co-finance, inspect, and supervise these special schools, they are not entirely part of the education system. Private foundations and organizations not only retain responsibility for these schools, but through their national networks and local players influence policy and practice.

Identification rates differ across cantons as described earlier. This has raised questions about equal opportunities and the quality of provision both in integrated and segregated settings. A new standardized eligibility procedure was introduced in 2011 with the withdrawal of the Federal Invalidity Insurance from financing special education. The standardized eligibility procedure (EDK, 2011) is used by the school psychological services (e.g., in Zurich) and the medical-pedagogical services (e.g., in Geneva). Generally, there is no specific need for a medical or clinical diagnosis; the procedure takes a dimensional rather than a categorical approach and is based on the ICF (WHO, 2001) and combines information on functioning, environmental factors and educational goals to herald required changes to the environment or special support. It is hoped that through the use of this standardized procedure, threshold criteria and other factors explaining differences in identification can be better understood. The identification of high incidence disabilities is not regulated by the Standardized Eligibility Procedure and therefore differs across cantons. In the Canton of Zurich for example, no formal clinical assessment is needed, if there is consensus amongst parents and teachers and if the necessary resources are available at school level. Resources are allocated by the school team to groups or individuals, for example, based on a school-based cooperative assessment procedure [Verfahren Schulische Standortgespräche] where all parties, including the child, come together to discuss the problems and find a solution (Bildungsdirektion Kanton Zürich, 2007). These informal assessment practices may be challenged in the future as a result of a more rights-based approach to education. Schools may be confronted more and more with litigation cases as parents increasingly demand specific support, disability compensation or adaptations based on the new federal legislation and encouraged by the UN Convention on the Rights of Persons with Disabilities (United Nations, 2006).

As support for high incidence disabilities was never regulated by the Federal Invalidity Insurance, the cantons have developed diverse practices. Regular schools generally offer pedagogical-therapeutical interventions (e.g., psychomotor and speech therapy) and special education support not only for children with learning or behavior difficulties but also for children with migrant background. Switzerland has a greater rate of immigrant children (23.5%), compared to other European Countries such as France (13.2%) or Finland (2.5%) (OECD, 2010). In 2010, 42% of all regular classes in Switzerland consisted of a third or more "foreign students" (Bundesamt für Statistik, 2012). In some city districts, up to a 100% of children may be first or second generation migrants, with diverse cultural and linguistic backgrounds. Special support in regular or special "welcoming classes" is provided to learn the language of instruction and in some cantons (e.g., Basel and Zurich) programs were developed to support schools with high percentages of immigrant students. Not all regular teachers are appropriately prepared for this cultural and linguistic diversity. Over 50% of regular teachers declare that their work in the classroom is made more difficult due to the cultural backgrounds of their students (Reusser, Stebler, Mandel, & Eckstein, 2013). The management of diversity in schools remains a challenge to this day.

Another challenge for the future of special education today is the development of effective and efficient early childhood intervention for children aged 0−6 years. In the German-speaking region of Switzerland, "curative education services" [Heilpädagogische Dienste] were established by private associations in the 1960s and 1970s (Grob, 2010). Their strong roots in "curative education" and the private sector are typical for the special education scene in German-speaking Switzerland. However, today barriers against developing comprehensive, community-based services exist. In the French-speaking part of Switzerland, corresponding services are generally more interdisciplinary with a stronger emphasis on psychology and therapeutic approaches (Grob, 2010). These services, such as the "Mobile Educational Services" Service Educatif Itinérant] of Geneva (established in 1969), gradually assumed more and more responsibilities for children at risk or vulnerable (Bauloz, Cevey, & Métral, 2009). Similar services in the German-speaking region of Switzerland are presently developing (Lanfranchi & Neuhauser, 2011), but questions remain about the prevention of developmental delay and child abuse as well as how a better head start in life can help children from disadvantaged backgrounds. So far, early childhood intervention is the only area of special education where professionals work within the family (Grob, 2010). Traditionally, special education in Switzerland provides services for children when their problems seem related to their education, but it does not "interfere" with parents. Now that the cantons are fully responsible for the development and education of all children with disabilities, it is hoped that they will seize this opportunity to foster partnerships with parents and the private sector to ensure that all children grow up in the best possible circumstances and receive the support needed to develop into healthy adults and contributing members of the Swiss society − independent of the nature and extent of their disabilities or special needs.

NOTES

1. Documentation of case available at http://www.egalite-handicap.ch
2. Statistic available online at http://www.bfs.admin.ch/bfs/portal/de/index/themen/20/06/blank/key/01.html
3. Available at http://www.ibe.unesco.org/en/about-the-ibe/who-we-are/history.html
4. Table and graph available online at http://www.bista.zh.ch/sop/Sonder.aspx

REFERENCES

Bauloz, F., Cevey, A., & Métral, E. (2009). Le Service Educatif Itinérant de Genève: 40 ans de Soutien, d'Ecoute et d'Itinérance [Mobile educational services of Geneva: 40 years of support, listening and traveling]. *Schweizerische Zeitschrift für Heilpädagogik, 15*(5), 19−25.

Bildungsdirektion Kanton Zürich. (2007). *Schulische Standortgespräche: Ein Verfahren zur Förderplanung und Zuweisung von sonderpädagogischen Massnahmen.* [*School-based review meetings: A procedure for planning and allocating special educational provision.*] Zürich, Switzerland: Bildungsdirektion Kanton Zürich.

Bless, G. (1995). *Zur Wirksamkeit der Integration:* Forschungsüberblick, praktische Umsetzung einer integrativen Schulungsform, Untersuchungen zum Lernfortschritt. [*About the effectiveness of integration: Review of research, practical implementation of integrative schooling, analysis of learning progress.*] Bern, Switzerland: Haupt.

Buchhaas-Birkholz, D. (2009). Die "empirische Wende" in der Bildungspolitik und in der Bildungsforschung: Zum Paradigmenwechsel des BMBF im Bereich der Forschungsförderung [The "empirical turn" in educational policy and research: About the paradigm shift of the Federal Ministry of Education and Research in the area of research funding]. *Erziehungswissenschaft, 20*(39), 27−33.

Bühler-Niederberger, D. (1991). *Legasthenie: Geschiche und Folgen einer Pathologisierung.* [Dyslexia: *History and consequences of a pathologization.*] Opladen, Germany: Leske + Budrich.

Bundesamt für Statistik. (2010a). *Gesundheit und Gesundheitsverhalten in der Schweiz 2007: Schweizer Gesundheitsbefragung.* [Health and health behavior in Switzerland 2007: The Swiss health survey.] Neuchâtel, Switzerland: Bundesamt für Statistik.

Bundesamt für Statistik. (2012). *Bildungssystem Schweiz − Indikatoren. Unterrichts- und Lernbedingungen − Kulturelle Heterogenität der Schulabteilungen* [*Education system in Switzerland − Indicators. Conditions of instruction and learning − Cultural heterogeneity in schools*]. Retrieved from http://www.bfs.admin.ch/bfs/portal/de/index/themen/15/17/blank/01.approach.4002.html. Accessed on December 15, 2013.

Bundesamt für Statistik [Federal Office of Statistics]. (2010b). *Demos: Informationen aus der Demografie* [*Demos: Information from demography*]. Newsletter Nr. 4, Bundesamt für Statistik, Neuchâtel, pp. 4−8.

Carigiet Reinhard, T. (2012). Schulleistungen und Heterogenität: Eine mehrebenanalytische Untersuchung der Bedingungsfaktoren der Schulleistungen am Ende der dritten Primarschulklasse. [Achievement and heterogeneity: A multilevel analysis of causal factors of achievement at the end of grade three.] Bern, Switzerland: Haupt.

Cohep. (2008). *Analyse und Empfehlungen: Heilpädagogik in der allgemeinen Lehrerinnen- und Lehrerbildung.* [Analysis and recommendations: Curative education in general teacher education.] Bern, Switzerland: Schweizerische Konferenz der Rektorinnen und Rektoren der Pädagogischen Hochschulen cohep.

Desai, M. (2014). *The paradigm of international social development: Ideologies, development systems and policy approaches.* New York, NY: Routledge.

Droux, J., & Ruchat, M. (2007). L'«enfant-problème» ou l'émergence de figures problématiques dans la protection de l'enfance [The "problem child" or the emergence of problem figures in the protection of childhood]. *Carnet de Bord, 14*, 14−27.

EDK [Swiss Conference of Cantonal Ministers of Education]. (1994). *Sonderpädagogik in der Lehrerbildung.* [Special education in teacher education.] Dossier 27. Bern, Switzerland: EDK.

EDK [Swiss Conference of Cantonal Ministers of Education]. (2007). *Interkantonale Vereinbarung über die Zusammenarbeit im Bereich der Sonderpädagogik.* [*Inter-Cantonal Agreement on the coordination in the area of special education.*] Bern, Switzerland: EDK. Retrieved from http://www.edudoc.ch/static/web/arbeiten/sonderpaed/konkordat_d. pdf. Accessed on December 15, 2013.

EDK [Swiss Conference of Cantonal Ministers of Education]. (2011). Standardisiertes Abklärungsverfahren (SAV)*:* Instrument des Sonderpädagogik- Konkordats als Entscheidungsgrundlage für die Anordnung verstärkter individueller Massnahmen. [Standardized eligibility procedure: Instrument of the special education concordat as the decision basis to allocate reinforced individual provision.] Bern, Switzerland: EDK.

European Agency. (2010). *Country data 2010.* Brussels, Belgium: European Agency for the Development of Special Needs Education.

Federal Social Insurance Office. (2010). *Social security in Switzerland.* Bern, Switzerland: Federal Social Insurance Office.

Geisen, T., & Riegel, C. (2009). Jugend, Partizipation und Migration*:* Orientierungen im Kontext von Integration und Ausgrenzung. [Youth, participation and migration: Orientations in the context of integration and marginalization.] Wiesbaden, Germany: Verlag für Sozialwissenschaften.

Grob, F. (2010). *Heilpädagogische Früherziehung – Integrative Pädagogik – Frühe Bildung.* [*Early childhood intervention – Integrative pedagogy – Early education*]. Working Paper Nr. 1. Basel, Switzerland: Institut Spezielle Pädagogik und Psychologie Pädagogische Hochschule FHNW.

Gröschke, D. (2008). Heilpädagogisches Handeln*:* Eine Pragmatik der Heilpädagogik. [Curative educational practice: Pragmatics of curative education.] Bad Heilbrunn, Germany: Klinkhardt.

Häfeli, K., & Walther-Müller, P. (2005). Das Wachstum des sonderpädagogischen Angebots im interkantonalen Vergleich*:* Steuerungsmöglichkeiten für eine integrative Ausgestaltung. [Growth of special education provision – A cross-cantonal comparison: Regulation options for an integrative design.] Luzern, Switzerland: SZH Edition.

Hänsel, D. (2008). *Karl Tornow als Wegbereiter der sonderpädagogischen Profession: die Grundlegung des Bestehenden in der NS-Zeit.* [Karl Tornow as a pioneer of the special education profession: Establishment of the existing in the era of the Nazis.] Bad Heilbrunn, Germany: Klinkhardt.

Helmig, B., Gmür, M., Bärlocher, C., von Schnurbein, G., Degen, B., Nollert, M. … Salamon, L. M. (2011). The Swiss civil society sector in a comparative perspective*:* VMI research series (Vol. 6). Baltimore, MD: Johns Hopkins University and University of Fribourg.

Hollenweger, J. (2011). Development of an ICF-based eligibility procedure for education in Switzerland. *BMC Public Health, 11*(S4), 7.

Hollenweger, J. (2013). Developing applications of the ICF in education systems: Addressing issues of knowledge creation, management and transfer. *Disability and Rehabilitation, 35*(13), 1087–1091.

Hollenweger, J., & Moretti, M. (2012). Using the international classification of functioning, disability and health children and youth version in education systems: A new approach to eligibility. *American Journal of Physical Medicine and Rehabilitation, 91*(13 Suppl. 1), 97−102.

Kaba, M. (2007). Social health care access for the physically disabled in 19th century French speaking Switzerland. *Hygiea Internationalis, 6,* 67−77.

Kobi, E. E. (1993). *Grundfragen der Heilpädagogik: Eine Einführung in heilpädagogisches Denken (5. Auflage).* [Basic questions of curative education: An introduction to curative educational thinking.] Bern, Switzerland: Haupt.

Kronenberg, B. (2012). HFE-Statistik 2010: Im Anschluss an die Heilpädagogische Früherziehung besuchen mehr Kinder die Regelschule als die Sonderschule [HFE Statistics 2010: More children go to a regular rather than a special school after early childhood intervention]. *Schweizerische Zeitschrift für Heilpädagogik, 18*(4), 5−12.

Kronig, W. (2007). *Die systematische Zufälligkeit des Bildungserfolgs.* [The systematic randomness of educational success.] Bern, Switzerland: Haupt.

Lanfranchi, A., & Neuhauser, A. (2011). ZEPPELIN 0-3 − Förderung ab Geburt mit "PAT − Mit Eltern lernen" [ZEPPELIN 0-3 − Support from birth on with "PAT − Learning with parents"]. *Sonderpädagogische Förderung heute, 6,* 437−442.

Lijphart, A. (1999). *Patterns of democracy: Government forms and performance in 36 Countries.* New Haven, CT: Yale University.

OECD. (2005). *Students with disabilities, learning difficulties and disadvantages: Statistics and indicators.* Paris, France: OECD.

OECD. (2007). *Students with disabilities, learning difficulties and disadvantages: Policies, statistics and indicators.* Paris, France: OECD.

OECD. (2010). *PISA 2009 results: Overcoming social background − Equity in learning opportunities and outcomes* (Vol. 2). Paris, France: OECD.

Pfahl, L., & Powell, J. J. W. (2010). *The special education profession and the discourse of learning disability in Germany.* Discussion Papers No. *SP I* 2010-504. Wissenschaftszentrum Berlin für Sozialforschung (WZB), Forschungsschwerpunkt Bildung, Arbeit und Lebenschancen, Abteilung Ausbildung und Arbeitsmarkt, Berlin, Germany.

Reusser, K., Stebler, R., Mandel, D., & Eckstein, B. (2013). *Erfolgreicher Unterricht in heterogenen Lerngruppen auf der Volksschulstufe des Kantons Zürich* [*Successful instruction in heterogeneous learning groups in compulsory education in the canton of Zurich*]. Retrieved from http://www.zh.ch/dam/Portal/internet/news/mm/2013/166/Vielfalt_Volksschule_Bericht.pdf.spooler.download.1372834739198.pdf/Vielfalt_Volksschule_Bericht.pdf. Accessed on December 15, 2013.

Ruchat, M. (2003). Inventer les arriérés pour créer l'intelligence: L'arriéré scolaire et la classe spéciale: histoire d'un concept et d'une innovation psychopédagogique, 1874−1914. [Inventing backwardness to create intelligence: Educational backwardness and the special class: History of a concept and a psycho-educational innovation.] Bern, Switzerland: Haupt.

Ruchat, M. (2008). *Le Service médico-pédagogique de Genève: un centre pour dépister l'enfant-problème (1908−1958): 100ième anniversaire du Service médico-pédagogique 1908−2008.* [*The medical-educational service of Geneva: A center to detect the problem child.*] Genève, Switzerland: Département de l'instruction publique, Service médico-pédagogique.

Schindler, A. (1990). *Die Entwicklung der Schweizerischen Heilpädagogischen Gesellschaft seit 1889: Antworten auf Zeitfragen aus der Sicht einer Institution.* [The development of the Swiss Association for Curative Education since 1889: Answers to questions of the time from the perspective of an institution]. In D. Raemy (Ed.), *Heilpädagogik im Wandel der Zeit.* Luzern, Switzerland: Edition SZH/SPC.

Schumacher, B. (2010). Freiwillig verpflichtet: Gemeinnütziges Denken und Handeln in der Schweiz seit 1800. [Voluntarily obliged: Non-profit thinking and acting in Switzerland.] Zürich, Switzerland: Verlag Neue Zürcher Zeitung.

Sieber, P. (2006). *Steuerung und Eigendynamik der Aussonderung: Vom Umgang des Bildungswesens mit Heterogenität.* [Regulation and momenta of segregation: Managing heterogeneity by the education system.] Reihe, ISP-Universität Zürich, Bd. 13. Luzern, Switzerland: Edition SZH/CSPS.

Swiss Federation. (2013). *Federal Constitution of the Swiss Confederation.* Retrieved from http://www.admin.ch/ch/e/rs/1/101.en.pdf. Accessed on December 15, 2013.

United Nations. (2006). *UN Convention on the rights of persons with disabilities.* New York, NY: United Nations.

VHpA. (2003). *Positionspapier des VHpA: Vermittlung heilpädagogische relevanter Kompetenzen in der Lehrerinnen- und Lehrerbildung.* [Position paper of the VHpA: Conveying competences relevant for curative education in teacher education.] Luzern, Switzerland: Verband Heilpädagogischer Ausbildungsinstitute der Schweiz (VHpA).

Wagner Lenzin, M. (2007). Elternberatung: Die Bedeutung der Beratung in Bewältigung sprozessen bei Eltern mit ihrem Kind mit Behinderung. [Parent counseling: The relevance of counseling for coping processes of parents with a disabled child.] Bern, Switzerland: Haupt Verlag.

Weisser, J. (2005). Behinderung, Ungleichheit und Bildung: Eine Theorie der Behinderung. [Disability, inequality and education: A theory of disability.] Bielefeld, Germany: Transcript.

Wolfisberg, C. (2002). *Heilpädagogik und Eugenik: Zur Geschichte der Heilpädagogik in der deutschsprachigen Schweiz (1800–1950).* [Curative education and eugenics: The history of curative education in German-speaking Switzerland.] Zürich, Switzerland: Chronos Verlag.

World Health Organization. (2001). *International classification of functioning, disability and health (ICF).* Geneva, Switzerland: World Health Organization.

World Health Organization. (2007). *International classification of functioning, disability and health: Children and youth version (ICF-CY).* Geneva, Switzerland: World Health Organization.

SPECIAL EDUCATION TODAY IN ICELAND

Gretar L. Marinósson and Dóra S. Bjarnason

ABSTRACT

The purpose of the chapter is to give an overview of special education in Iceland, historically and with reference to modern use of terms, research, policy, legal trends and funding. Recent data is provided on demographic developments amongst children in Iceland and detailed account is given of practices in schools, including collaboration with parents and teacher education. Finally some issues and challenges are discussed that still remain to be solved with respect to meeting the special needs of students in school. One of the findings is that only 1.3% of students attend special schools and special classes and that the term special education has out-lived its usefulness except perhaps in the context of the three segregated special schools that still remain in the country. Official papers have replaced it with the term special support. Despite a diversity of views and practices the main implication is that a new model of education is required, in line with that proposed by Slee where the needs of individuals are served in all schools and the binary thinking related to regular versus special education is no longer necessary.

Special Education International Perspectives: Practices Across the Globe
Advances in Special Education, Volume 28, 271–309
ISSN: 0270-4013/doi:10.1108/S0270-401320140000028016

INTRODUCTION

Iceland: Country and Nation

Given its geographical size of 100,000 square kilometres and a population of just one third of a million inhabitants, Iceland is one of the most sparsely populated country and smallest independent nation states in the world. The island's location in the middle of the north Atlantic makes it relatively isolated but also well situated for the interception of cultural currents from both sides of the Atlantic. Icelanders have a distinct language and culture, which historically is closely linked to other Nordic nations. Reykjavik, the capital city, is by far the largest municipality with a population of about 120,000.

At the time of the establishment of the first public schools around 1850, Iceland was a Danish dependency and one of the poorest countries in Europe, its economy being largely based on farming and fishing. The population, numbering approximately 70,000, over 80% of whom lived in rural areas, was homogenous but literate (Guttormsson, 1983). The country gained independence step by step in the late 19th and early 20th century and became a republic with parliamentary democracy in 1944. Executive power lies with the cabinet formed usually by coalition of two or more political parties.

Iceland took a leap forward in the 20th century to become an urban, highly modern, capitalistic market society; from the 1960s it has ranked as one of the 10–15 most affluent nations within the OECD (Jónsson, 2009). Communication with other nations has always been dynamic, particularly with the Nordic states but also elsewhere. Economic prosperity after the Second World War was thus largely based upon transactions with Eastern Europe, Northern America, the European Union and, lately, Japan and China. More recently the bank crisis, the fall of the krona and the currency embargo since 2008 has seriously affected both public and private spending and set the nation's economy back several years.

EDUCATION IN ICELAND

For centuries children were educated in their homes by their parents and later by peripatetic teachers. This system continued well into the 20th century in rural areas. The history of public schools in Iceland is relatively short, compared to that of neighbouring countries, spanning merely 160 years (Guttormsson, 2008). The first Education Law on public schooling was passed in 1907 followed by subsequent Education Acts in 1926, 1936 and 1946. However, it was not until the 1974 Education Act that all children, including those with special needs and disabilities, were required to attend school. Legislation and curricula in the 20th century reflect continuing efforts towards increased equality between children in different parts of the country, of different gender and of varying learning ability. Recent PISA results show that this endeavour has borne fruit in relative homogeneity of school performance, at least at the compulsory school level (Halldórsson, Ólafsson, & Björnsson, 2013).

The educational system is structured at four levels of schooling:

- The preschool ('playschool' as it is called in Iceland), ages 2−5 years. Operated by local authorities.
- The compulsory school ('basic school'), ages 6−16 years. Operated by local authorities.
- The upper secondary school ('continuing school'), ages 16−20 years. Operated by the state.
- Universities and adult education provision. Independent but financed largely by the state.

This chapter deals with special education at the three first school levels, the preschool, the compulsory school and the upper secondary school. The university level is mostly left out, although students with a variety of disabilities are admitted for university study. Readers interested in more detailed information about the extent to which Iceland's seven universities cater to students with special needs are referred to Stefánsdóttir's (2013) comprehensive description.

The majority of Iceland's public schools operate under municipalities (preschools and compulsory schools) or the state (upper secondary schools and universities). Only a few schools are privately run with 70% contributions from the municipalities or the state. Students at compulsory schools are the only ones obliged to attend school but 95% of children attend preschools and up to 95% of children attend upper secondary schools although around 35% discontinue their studies before completion (Statistics Iceland, 2013). Today the annual public expenditure on education per student is slightly above the average for 21 Europe Union (EU) nations at preschool, primary school and upper secondary school levels but considerably lower at the tertiary/university level. The same applies when compared to the Organisation for Economic Co-operation and

Development (Organisation for Economic Co-operation and Development [OECD], 2000) average.

SPECIAL EDUCATION IN ICELAND

A review of the literature reveals little consensus on the meaning of the term 'special education', what it should contain, where it should ideally be practiced and how (Bjarnason, 2010b). Does the term refer to location, pedagogic methods and contents, the professionals who carry it out or to the additional resources needed to implement the special needs education? Indeed the term 'special support' is now used in official documents in Iceland in place of the term 'special education' that is seen to have outlived its usefulness except in the context of segregated special schools.

Although special education may strictly be understood as referring to what happens within the education system, the other side of the coin is what happens within the child. The term impairment is used here in the 'individual' or 'medical' theoretical perspective about what happens within the child (WHO, 1980). The term 'disability' is similarly debated but is used here as an over-arching term for all major barriers that prevent an individual from participating in society (and school), including personal impairments, social structures, physical structures and social prejudices. The term 'special educational needs' is used here to refer to all educational needs that the school does not manage to adjust to and meet in its daily work. This term overlaps with disability at the same time as it also extends beyond it to 'cover those who are failing for a wide variety of other reasons that are known to be likely to impede a child's optimal progress' (OECD, 2000).

The same perplexity applies to 'special educational needs' as to special education and disability. Does the term refer to all kinds of special needs or only some; should, for example, difficulties related to behaviour (e.g. Attention Deficit Hyperactivity Disorder [ADHD]), social interaction (e.g. bullying), giftedness and multiculturalism be categorised as special educational needs? Does the term only refer to difficulties experienced or observed in connection with education? Do these needs exist irrespective of whether they have been identified as such, diagnosed or met (OECD, 2000)? Discussing students with special educational needs implies that such a category can be identified. Many would argue that this is not so, and that such construction contributes to the maintenance of the status quo as regards meeting students' individual needs at school (see, e.g. Goodey, 1999).

However, the terms special education and special educator are mentioned neither in Icelandic law, ordinances nor the National Curriculum Guides for the pre-primary, primary or secondary sectors of the school system. Nor are they mentioned in a recent policy document on educational provision by the largest municipality, the City of Reykjavík (Reykjavíkurborg, 2012). Instead the term 'special support' is used. It is considered contradictory to maintain a system of education that should be inclusive of all children and still have special education. This makes for a rather peculiar point of departure for a chapter on special education. Notably, however, two Ordinances on students with special educational needs exists, one for the-Compulsory School (Regluerð um nemenur með sérþarfir í grunnskóla nr. 585, 2010) and another for the Upper Secondary School (Reglugerð um nemendur með sérþarfir í framhaldsskólum nr. 230, 2012), three special schools exist at the Compulsory School level and special classes within mainstream schools exist at these two levels. Special educators still function in mainstream schools at three school levels, although their professional status is no longer recognised by law or regulation. The situation regarding this branch of the education system is, therefore, complicated today as it always has been.

The policy of inclusive education has gained support in Iceland, as in most other countries in the world in recent years, following a runaway increase in the number of students placed in segregated special educational provision. The policy shift in Iceland was based on developments in Sweden, Denmark, Italy and the United States in the 1970s and later public missions, first on 'Education for All' in Jomtien, Thailand (UNESCO, 1990), Salamanca Statement and Framework for Action for students with special needs (UNESCO, 1994), the Convention on the rights of the child (United Nations, 1989), the Dakar Framework for Action on education for all (UNESCO, 2000) and the Convention on the Rights of Persons with Disabilities (United Nations, 2006). In a world where millions of children are deprived of education altogether, not the least girls with disabilities, the inclusion mission by UNESCO sounds utopic. Nevertheless, most governments in the world have chosen inclusion as their central education policy. To what extent or how they manage to make it a reality is another matter. There is indeed a large measure of integration of students with disabilities and special needs into mainstream schools in Iceland, as only 1.3% of the school age population attends special schools (0.5%) and special classes (0.8%). However, there are at present an increasing number of so-called 'participation classes' being established in Reykjavík mainstream schools, as branches from special schools, primarily for children who find it difficult to keep up with the speed of learning or exhibit difficult behaviour in mainstream classes. This is an example of local interpretation of the policy of inclusive education (Fræðslumiðstöð Reykjavíkur, 2002).

RESEARCH ON SPECIAL EDUCATION IN ICELAND

Although special needs education is probably among the fields of education in Iceland where there has been the greatest research activity over the past 50 years, the total number of research projects is less than 100 (Marinósson, 2005). The studies divide easily into two groups. On the one hand there are projects carried out by pedagogues studying school responses to student diversity in some form, from a social-relational theoretical perspective. On the other hand there are investigations of children's impairments by clinicians guided by an individual-medical perspective. Half of the projects carried out by the pedagogues are quantitative in their methodological approach and half qualitative. In addition there are a few action research projects. All the projects carried out by the clinicians are basically quantitative although they may include some interview or open observation data. Half of the projects by the pedagogues are (masters or doctoral) theses submitted as part of their research training. The overwhelming majority of research projects are initiated by individuals or groups, only a few are initiated by official institutions such as the Ministry of Education. It is difficult to talk about trends in research in this field where the number of research projects is as limited as this and significantly dependent on individual researchers. However, one can broadly portray the available research as belonging to either holistic or inclusive educational research or more categorical, clinical research.

The educational research is institutionalised at university education departments, the latter to a large extent at state assessment units and a university psychology department. The institutional basis for all educational research (indeed all social science research) in Iceland is weak on account of lack of resources: under funding, lack of trained researchers and the embryonic state of research institutions. It would therefore be considered essential for those few who engage in research within similar fields to collaborate. This is, however, rarely the case. The researchers at the different institutions hardly ever meet to discuss their research, probably precisely because of the weak structure that they operate within. As regards to research in special education this reflects the present uneasy relationship between the individual and the social theoretical perspectives in disability research (op. cit.; Barnes, Mercer, & Shakespeare, 1999). In the last few years, greater stress has been laid on research and publication within the universities, partly for reasons of international race for a place amongst the top 100, 300 or 500 universities in the world, partly because the value of research for society is better understood. At the same time, there has been a change in policy in allocation of competitive funds so that larger sums go to fewer applicants whilst there has been no increase in total sums, partly because of the bank crisis and the collapse of the Icelandic currency in 2008. The surge of research within special education that was felt before the bank crisis has therefore now slowed down.

Special education should not be studied separately from mainstream education but as an inherent part of it. One implication of such context-oriented approach is that the methodology should not solely be based on logical positivistic assumptions of truth and objectivity but also assumptions of the contextual nature of social phenomena. In an era where emphasis is on the strengths of individuals and the failings of the system to meet their needs, increasing collaboration between researchers within social, health, and educational institutions is called for. There is a need for larger and longer term projects that can gain an overview of the situation in education from policy to grass roots level over an extensive time period. This necessitates comparison with similar research projects in other countries.

ORIGINS AND HISTORY OF SPECIAL EDUCATION IN ICELAND

The development of Iceland's response to disability mirrors closely that of neighbouring countries, albeit at a slower pace and on a smaller scale. Thus small institutions for people with intellectual disability were established by the middle of the 20th century and abandoned before the end of the century. The exclusion of children from school on the grounds of 'amorality' and 'illness' as stipulated in the Education Act 1936 was annulled by the passing of the Education Act 1974 when the right of education was extended to all children and the concept of integration was introduced. Then for the first time the school was obliged to take account of its students' educational needs whereas before its major task was to teach prescribed subjects. To follow up on this policy legal responsibility for compulsory education was moved first from the state to eight education authorities (Lög um grunnskóla nr. 64, 1974) and then to the municipalities (Lög um grunnskóla nr. 66, 1995). The first ordinance on special education 1977 (Reglugerð um sérkennslu nr. 270, 1977) was revised in 1990 and the categorical system of provision replaced by a system geared to meeting special educational needs of all students in their home schools (Reglugerð um sérkennslu nr. 389, 1990). It was considered possible to evaluate more accurately each student's special needs in their daily context than by diagnostic labels alone, made on the basis of snapshots taken in a clinic in Reykjavík. This context bound assessment of special needs only survived a few years until funding was made conditional on diagnosis by 'recognised authorities'.

Since 1996, Compulsory Schools have been under the jurisdiction of the municipalities where Preschools were since 1994 (Lög um leikskóla nr. 78, 1944) while Upper Secondary Schools were under the state (Lög um framhaldsskóla nr. 92, 2008). Universities have gained authority over their own affairs (Lög um opinbera háskóla nr. 85, 2008) and the education of all pedagogic personnel has been moved to university level and extended from three years (Bachelor) to five (Master) (Lög um menntun og ráðningu kennara og skólastjórnenda nr. 87, 2008). Discussion of the Compulsory School's response to the diversity of students has developed in character from exclusion to inclusion to rights and thereby also through change in ideas and accompanying terminology from special education through integration to inclusion. This, however, is not a linear development in time as older theoretical perspectives, nomenclature and special educational provisions live alongside the more recent ones. Moreover the discourse on inclusion as a response to student diversity in Icelandic schools must be linked to similar policies in neighbouring countries.

Looking back in time at the institutionalisation of special education, schools for deaf and blind students started around 1870 and these students have moved increasingly into mainstream schools since. Special education for physically disabled students started in the mid-20th century and was provided in special schools and units after World War II but since 1970 it has increasingly taken the form of personal support within mainstream school surroundings (Sigurðsson, 1993). Children with intellectual disabilities who were considered uneducable were first offered a place in an institution in Sólheimar, a residential care home established in 1931 by a private individual. In the 1950s and 1960s, the population of children with intellectual disability in institutions expanded considerably with the establishment of other homes under the Ministry of Social Affairs and a medical institution, Kópavogshæli. Höfðaskóli, the first special school for children with IQs of 50–70 was opened in Reykjavík in 1961 and, after the education authorities had taken over the education and training of children who had been considered uneducable, special classes were established in mainstream schools. Special education for students with emotional and behavioural difficulties started in residential facilities in the countryside in the late 1940s. These two major categories of special educational needs have since gradually become an assignment for the preschool and compulsory school to solve largely inside the mainstream but the special classes and the special schools have also survived. In addition, a surprising number of students with new and previously unknown diagnostic labels have demanded the attention of teachers and school managers (e.g. autistic spectrum disorder and ADHD).

Special education in Iceland has generally developed from categorisation and segregation towards individualisation and inclusion. However, the development is more complicated as categorisation does not always have a corollary in segregation and individualisation is not always the result of inclusion. In fact, the processes can work totally independently of each other and run parallel in time. Furthermore, the process from categorisation to individualisation has turned back on itself so that the trend now is towards greater categorisation in the school system under the influence of funding control and medical diagnosis that support each other (Marinósson, 1999).

The development of disability studies as a sociological alternative to the medico- psychological paradigm of handicap was influential in moving the development of special education in the direction of looking more closely at the context of school problems and not merely at the students themselves (Bjarnason, 2010a). This social focus overshadowed special education and marginalised it, at least academically and politically.

The introduction of 'individualisation of instruction,' promoted by the Director of Education for Reykjavik, further diverted attention from special education to the work of the class teacher. The idea behind 'individualised instruction' was indeed that by realising the aim of providing for individual educational needs the requisite for special education was done away with and with it the considerable cost to the education directorate (Fræðslumiðstöð Reykjavíkur, 2000).

A fundamental principle of the Icelandic educational system is that everyone should have equal opportunities to acquire an education, irrespective of sex, economic status, residential location, religion, possible impairment, and cultural or social background. Only recently, however, was education seen as a medium for democratic aims in society: That by educating each and every individual to his or her full potential (s)he could be given an opportunity to take full part in society, this being considered the foundation of a fully democratic society (European Agency, 2011).

Earlier research in Iceland and elsewhere indicate, however, a number of factors that stand in the way of equal access to education for disabled people, such as badly co-ordinated official policy, lack of collaboration between service systems, lack of information, devaluation of students with disability, attitudes that regard diversity in the student group as a problem, lack of financial support, narrow definition of curriculum for disabled students, inflexible teaching methods and segregation of support from other types of school work (Bjarnason, 2004; Gunnþórsdóttir & Bjarnason, in press; Marinósson, 2011; Marinósson & Bjarnason, 2007). These are some of the challenges that still face Iceland and impact on the quality of education for special needs.

LEGAL TRENDS, LITIGATION AND THE FINANCING OF SPECIAL EDUCATION

Legal Trends

Although the needs of poor and disabled people for subsistence had been provided for since the middle ages, the first legislation that specifically concerned disabled people was the Law on institutions for imbeciles 1936 (Flóvenz, 2004). This legislation was a shift of emphasis 'from passive support, in the form of subsistence payments for disabled people, towards active welfare policies' (Ólafsson, 2005). Since the Second World War, the Icelandic legislative assembly has passed various acts of education designed to work towards equality of educational opportunity and against social inequality. Thus, a general Law on the affairs of the disabled was passed in the early 1990s (Lög um málefni fatlaðra, 1992). However, there is no separate legislation for special education at any of the four levels of education.

The legal context for what was to follow as regarded education for children with disabilities was the passing of three vital social legislations in 1936; the Law on social security (Lög um alþýðutryggingar), the Law on state subsistence for the sick and disabled (Lög um ríkisframfærslu sjúkra manna og örkumla) and the Law on institutions for imbeciles (Lög um fávitahæli) (Margeirsdóttir, 2001). The Education Act of 1936 explicitly excluded those from school who were unfit for reasons of 'moral deficiency or singular disobedience'. Those whom the doctor deemed lacking in mental or physical abilities, and were seen unable to learn with other children were excused from school (Lög um fræðslu barna, 1936). Perhaps the law's main purpose, to make school attendance mandatory for 7–14-year olds (previously 10–14 years), should be understood in the context of the social legislation passed at that time, as some of these children were provided with instruction and support elsewhere than in school. The Education Act of 1946 was the first piece of legislation in Iceland to mention the school's role in adjusting to the needs of the students:

> Schools shall endeavour to organise their work *in accordance with the nature and needs of their students*, to help them adopt healthy attitudes and habits, observe their physical health and instruct them in subjects stipulated by law, each according to his or her developmental capacity. (Lög um fræðslu barna, 1946, authors' translation and emphasis)

At that time, it indicated a shift from a systems orientation to a more child-centred view. This was consistent with the child-centred view that had its provenance in the 'age of enlightenment'. Under its banner, it was considered necessary to 'take account of the child's nature and adjust one's expectations of children to their development and ability' (Guttormsson, 1983).

Whilst the 1946 Education Act shifted the main focus from school subjects to the students' needs, it was the 1974 Education Act that recognised in law for the first time that all children of a given age had an equal right to education in the state school system and that the school had a role in meeting the full diversity of student needs (Lög um grunnskóla nr. 64, 1974). The view that this should be done in the child's neighbourhood school rather than as a segregated provision has been stated since then in an increasingly unequivocal fashion by those who formulate official education policy (Mennta- og menningarmálaráðuneytið, 2012b). Following this legislation in 1974, the field of intellectual disability was transferred from under the jurisdiction of health authorities to education. This coincided when special schools replaced instruction within the subnormality institutions with the first Ordinance on special education 1977 (Reglugerð um sérkennslu nr. 270, 1977).

The Law on the Affairs of People with Disabilities, which was passed in 1992 (Lög um málefni fatlaðra nr. 59, 1992), stipulates that all individuals with disabilities (defined as intellectual disability, psychiatric illness, physical disability, blindness and/or deafness as well as disabilities resulting from chronic illness and accidents) are to be enabled to live and function in the community. For this purpose, where a disabled person's needs are not covered by general services within the fields of education, health and social services, special services, detailed in the law, shall be provided. The law has been criticised for interpreting the concept of disability too narrowly since it does not cover groups that undoubtedly need this service, such as children with ADHD, epilepsy and dyslexia. These and some other groups with special needs are not defined as disabled, which perhaps throws a light on the influence of the funding system on medical criteria. The aim is now to bring this policy of social inclusion into practice by covering the rights of people with disabilities by common law and thus make special legislation unnecessary. Thus, service would be provided on the basis of what an individual needs within his or her social context instead of on the basis of a diagnosis of disability (Margeirsdóttir, 2001).

Next, the legislative assembly, passed an Education Act-Preschools in 1994 providing for special needs of preschool children in their local preschools (Lög um leikskóla nr. 78, 1994). The Education Act-Compulsory Schools in 1995 stipulated 10 years of compulsory schooling for children aged 6–16 years. However, there is no mention of special education in that law (Lög um grunnskóla, 1995). The idea is that the 'basic school' shall be inclusive, catering for all educational needs of all its students. Around the same time, an Ordinance from 1986 stipulating the sole right of those having a particular university degree to practise special education was annulled by the Ministry of education and culture. Thereafter, a school principal could hire any qualified teacher to provide support for those students who needed it. Another landmark made in the 1995 Education Act was the transfer of compulsory schools from the state to the municipalities. According to law on Upper Secondary School (Lög um framhaldsskóla nr. 80, 1996) everyone is entitled to education at that school level and students with special needs are to be provided with support and instruction according to their needs. Although students are expected to follow the ordinary curriculum as far as possible there is the possibility of establishing special units for students with disabilities (Mennta- og menningarmálaráðuneytið, 2011b; Eurypedia, 2014).

New Education Acts of Law were agreed in 2008 for all educational levels, that is the Preschool, Compulsory School, Upper Secondary School and Higher Education Act. In addition a number of implementing Ordinances have been issued providing for various policy details (Mennta- og menningarmálaráðuneytið, 2012a; Mennta- og menningarmálaráðuneytið, 2012b;

Mennta- og menningarmálaráðuneytið, 2012c). The Icelandic government ratified: the UN Convention on the Rights of Persons with Disabilities (United Nations, 2006) in 2012; the United Nations Convention on the Rights of Child (United Nations, 1989) in 2013; and adopted the Salamanca Declaration (UNESCO, 1994) in 1995.

The Education Acts for Preschools, Compulsory Schools and Upper Secondary Schools all stipulate that students shall have education according to their needs (Lög um framhaldsskóla, 2008; Lög um grunnskóla, 2008; Lög um leikskóla, 2008). If this stipulation was followed to the extreme and individualisation of instruction was complete there would be no need for special education as there would be no special educational needs at school. However, there is an escape clause saying that for those, whose needs the school does not meet there shall be a service that assesses these needs and advises the school on how to meet them. This also applies to children with Icelandic as a second language. Guidelines for services for students with special educational needs in Preschool and Compulsory Schools are given in Ordinance on students with special needs and Ordinance on municipalities' expert services in schools. Here students with special educational needs are defined as 'students who find learning hard for reasons of specific learning difficulties, social or emotional difficulties or disabilities according to paragraph 2 of the Act on the Affairs of the Disabled nr. 59/1992, students with dyslexia, students with chronic illness, developmental impairment, mental disorders and other students with health related special needs' (Reglugerð um nemendur með sérþarfir í grunnskóla nr. 585, 2010; Reglugerð um sérfræðiþjónustu sveitarfélaga nr. 584, 2010). Responsibility for providing this service is divided between the schools, the local authority's services and services provided by the four state diagnostic and advisory centres for disability, hearing, sight and psychiatric problems. Three of these state institutions fall under the Ministry for Social Affairs and one under the Ministry of Health but none under Education.

According to the Preschool Act, Compulsory School Act and Upper Secondary School Act, the staff of each school are obliged to write a working guide, a kind of school policy, which is to be based on the National Curriculum Guidelines (see Mennta- og menningarmálráðuneytið, 2012a, 2012b, 2012c). However, each school has an opportunity to take into account its circumstances and special characteristics. The school working guide is also an administrative plan for each school. It is to account for the school year and to include an annual calendar, the organisation of teaching, the aims and content of the education offered, student assessment procedures, assessment of the work that goes on in the school, extra-curricular activities and other aspects of the operation of the school including how it is going to meet students with special needs. Compulsory schools display their policy on special needs education on their website and introduce it to teachers and parents (European Agency, 2011; Reykjavíkurborg, 2012).

Inclusive education is mentioned in the Education Act 2008 for the first time as the basic education policy in Iceland from early years to the period of transition to university or the labour market. The general aims of the legislation on each school level apply to all students including those with disabilities and special needs. This means addressing and responding to the learning needs of all students. In short Education for All means that:

- There is equal opportunity for all to attend school and acquire education in accordance with their ability and needs.
- Schools must attend to the ability and needs of all students.
- Students and/or their parents decide on which school they attend.
- Students in need of special support have the right to special provision.

(European Agency, 2011)

The education policy places emphasis on the Icelandic National Curriculum Guides for Preschool (2012a), Compulsory School (2012b) and Upper Secondary School (2012c).[1] The curriculum guidelines assure conformity of goals for all three levels of schooling. The National Curriculum Guide based on the Compulsory School Act of 2008 stipulates that

Compulsory schools must educate all children in an effective manner. According to law, all children are entitled to appropriate education in compulsory school, academic, vocational and artistic, and local authorities are required to offer appropriate study opportunities regardless of their children's physical or mental capabilities, emotional or social situations or linguistic development. This applies to all children; children with or without disabilities, with long-term illnesses, exceptionally intelligent children and children with mental disabilities, children from remote communities and children from ethic, linguistic or cultural minorities. (Mennta- og menningarmálaráðuneytið, 2012b)

Similar stipulations of inclusive education appear in the curriculum guides for the Preschool and the Upper Secondary School. The central principle as laid down in the Act and the National Curriculum Guides is to make it possible for all children to study in their local inclusive schools.

A National Curriculum Guide for special units in Upper Secondary Schools, called 'practical departments', was published in 2005. The programme offered by the units has three levels depending on the needs of students and lasts four years (Mennta- og menningarmálaráðuneytið, 2011b).

Litigation

Litigation regarding educational issues is not common in Iceland. There is, however, no dearth of disputes dealing with everything from the violation of privacy to hospital mistakes at the birth of a child. The most common cases concern compensation for a loss of some kind. There is a trend to solve educational disputes at a lower level of administration before taking them to court. Thus the Education Acts refer disputes to the Ministry of Education that publishes its arbitration on its website. The following is an example of such a case.

Ruling on a charge brought by parents stating that a ruling by the City of Reykjavík to refuse entry into a special school to a student with mild intellectual disability was wrong.

The parents stated that the ruling by the City of Reykjavík to refuse their daughter entry into Klettaskóli special school was based on rules set by the Education committee that all children with an IQ of 50–70 were expected to attend a mainstream school. The charge was that this rule contravened the Education Act for compulsory school, no. 91/2008; Ordinance on students with special educational needs, no. 585/2010; Law on the affairs of disabled people, no. 59/1992; the Constitution for Iceland, no. 33/1944 and the UN Convention on the Rights of Children. The City Advocate claimed that the Education Act for the Compulsory School clearly states that the school should be inclusive and adjust its services to suit the needs of the child. This intention is then detailed in the Ordinance for students with special educational needs and the National Curriculum Guide. He further claimed that the rules of acceptance of students to the school were set on the basis of all these laws, ordinances and curriculum guides and stated quite unequivocally that the school is for students of 1st – 10th class in the compulsory school who have been assessed with medium, severe or deep intellectual disability or with mild intellectual disability with additional impairments such as Autistic Spectrum Disorders, Cerebral Palsy and blindness. Furthermore, the school should be able to offer the applicant education suitable for him or her and that demonstrably the local school is unable to offer the same. The Ministry ruled that the Reykjavík Education Authority was within its rights to refuse the child entry into the special school (Mennta- og menningarmálaráðuneytið, 2011a; authors's translation).

If a child is unequivocally disabled the parents can seek the assistance of the Guardian of the Rights of People with Disabilities who helps with redressing whatever wrong has been alleged. The next stage may be the Ombudsman of the Althingi who has an advisory role towards official instances on behalf of members of the public who appeal to his office. Nevertheless, several cases related to special education or disabilities appear before the courts annually. Mostly, they are demands for financial compensation because services have not been provided, but in rare cases the right of entry into a mainstream school or a special school are sought. The following is an example of such a case.

Supreme Court Case no.169/2007. H.Ó. vs. S-town.

> A local authority was charged by parents of maltreating their 12 year old daughter by excluding her from a primary school. The parents demanded a considerable sum of money as compensation. The daughter had been diagnosed with autistic spectrum disorder combined with intellectual disability. For reasons of behaviour the school found it impossible to integrate her into mainstream classes and suggested to the parents that they move the child to a special school. The parents claimed that, according to Compulsory School Act where inclusion was the main policy, their daughter had an undeniable right to attend a mainstream school. The verdict which fell in the municipality's favour was supported by the argument that since the Compulsory School Act had the provision that a special school was an option if the parents and professionals considered the child's needs were not met in his or her home school then this child did not have an unequivocal right of attendance at a mainstream school. (Iceland Supreme Court, 2007; authors' translation)

Both these cases are instructive as the Education Act is not crystal clear on the point as to whether parents can choose a school for their child or not. It is left to 'parents, teachers, school managers, or other experts' to decide whether the mainstream school does or does not meet the needs of the child; then parents can apply to transfer him or her to a special school. Apparently the authority that runs the school can then wield its power to refuse the application although the law does not say so.

Financing

Without additional resources, it is questionable whether instruction or support for students with special needs that is provided as part of the daily work of the mainstream classroom teacher would be labelled special education, even though it may be carried out in accordance with an individual education plan and although the general education teacher may have a further degree in special education. One of the central characteristics of special education is that it involves financial contributions over and above the ones required for group instruction. Resources required may be ten times greater per child than that in the mainstream. Thus, it matters a great deal how this funding is allocated and used.

Preschool is financed by the municipalities but they may determine a fee collected from the parents for their child's attendance. There are no separate funds for special education at the preschool level. Compulsory schooling is free of charge but in order to meet the needs of students with disabilities funds are provided by central government to the municipalities via the Municipalities Equalisation Fund. The students funded must be residents of the municipality, their disabilities must have been diagnosed and it must be clear that they need considerable and extended additional support at school (Jöfnunarsjóður sveitarfélaga, 2014).

Payments to the municipalities for students with impairments depend on the levels of disability. The same amount is expected to be paid per student with the same degree of disability to each municipality irrespective of whether the special education provided varies from one municipality to another. This amount is determined on the basis of medical diagnoses and is in accordance with the amount the individual and his/her family gets from the national security system because of a given disability as described in the Act on the Affairs of the Handicapped (Lög um málefni fatlaðra nr. 59, 1992). The State Diagnostic and Advisory Centre, which has created the rules for the Advisory Committee of the Equalisation Fund, has the final say in whether the amount suggested by other specialists is in accordance with the given degree of disability. The amount allocated for each student is meant to provide an educational opportunity for that student. This can be in the form of a special class or a special school run by the local authority itself, shared with other authorities or stationed in a different authority (European Agency, 2011). The Equalisation Fund is now in the process of adapting the Supports Intensity Scale (SIS) for the evaluation of needed funds for support for children as well as adults (Jöfnunarsjóður sveitarfélaga, 2012).

In addition to the funding provided for individual students with diagnosed impairments by the Equalisation Fund, the municipalities allocate funds for students with disabilities in collaboration with the schools and their expert services (special educators, schools advisory services, school health service, etc.). This is usually done on the basis of an annual survey in the schools updated twice a year, that is according to need rather than a disability category. However, some local authorities take account of whether the children have been assessed to receive family support from State Social Security and at what level (Elín S. Jónsdóttir, personal communication, 2014, Akureyri). For this, the State Social Security Institute assesses the child's level of disability (five levels), the need for care, support or treatment and finally the cost involved (Tryggingarstofnun ríkisins, 2012). Many municipalities follow the example from the City of Reykjavík that has a two-tier system of allocation of funds for special education: One allocation for students with disabilities and another general allocation for the whole student body, including students with special needs such as learning disabilities, ADHD or language and speech impairment. The allocation for students with disabilities is made following an application by the school, only for students diagnosed by authorised state agencies and on the basis of a plan of intervention submitted by the school. The general allocation is a sum proportional to 0.14–0.25 of a weekly lesson multiplied by the number of students in the school. Some municipalities allocate this latter sum on identified students, others in a lump sum to be used by the schools as they see fit. Reykjavík adds a third tier in its allocation for schools that apply for it on the basis of a disproportional number of students with special needs compared to other schools. A separate allocation is made for students who need support for reasons that they have a mother tongue other than Icelandic. All allocations are made on the condition that the school organise its work in accordance with the policy of inclusive education (Reykjavíkurborg, 2012). The state pays upper secondary school operating costs. Funds for educating students in need of special support are applied for to the Ministry of Education on an individual and/or group basis.

As detailed above, the funding of special education is to some extent linked to diagnostic labelling of impairments. One of the consequences is that schools try to identify students with disabilities who might fetch extra funds for the school. A system based on diagnostic labels thus has perverse incentives for over identification of disabilities and special needs. Some municipalities are therefore transferring more of their special education resource distribution from the 'bounty' system to a 'base' funding system where schools get a general sum estimated on the basis of the totality of educational needs of its students as observed in the school context at that time ('difficulty model') as opposed to being based on formal diagnosis only ('disability model'). This later approach to funding has been adopted by Finland (Jahnukainen, 2011).

THE CHILDREN: PREVALENCE AND INCIDENCE OF IMPAIRMENT

Official information on the prevalence and incidence of disability in Iceland is hard to come by. The State Diagnostic and Counselling Centre, which has as one of its roles to keep an overview of children's disability in the country does not have this statistic, neither does the Ministry of Welfare that has disability as one of its tasks, nor any other state institution. One wonders how it is possible to plan to meet the needs of these individuals with disabilities without having some idea of the size and composition of the task. The larger municipalities do, however, keep data on the children with disabilities and special needs that they serve in their schools. In addition, Statistics Iceland (2013) keeps data on education and finally there are a few carefully done studies on the epidemiology of some disability groups that we can rely on (see Tables 1 and 2).

The proportion of students who receive special support in compulsory schools has risen gradually over the last two decades after remaining relatively stable for two decades before that. Thus, in 1974 around 15% of students received special education. In 1984 and 1994 the figure remained unchanged but, as Table 3 shows, in 2005 it had risen to 23.7% and in 2013 to 27%. One of the reasons may be the tendency to provide short-term help for a variety of reasons (e.g. help at break-time and lunch-time)

Table 1. Prevalence of Impairment amongst Children.

Disability	%	NB	n^{a}	Age
Autism spectrum disorder	1.20[b]	Boys 1.72%; girls 0.64%	22.229	14−18
Intellectual disability (severe)	0.51[c]	Medium ID: No data Mild ID: No data	Not provided	5−18
Cerebral palsy	0.22[d]		139	5−6
Visual impairment	0.1[e]		73,459	0−17
Hearing impairment	0.05[f]		4,000	0−18
Psychiatric disorders	10.1[g]		317	4−6

[a]$n = $ *size of population from which % is calculated.*
[b]Sæmundsen, Magnússon, Georgsdóttir, Egilsson, and Rafnsson (2014).
[c]Bakel et al. (2013).
[d]Sigurðardóttir, Þórkelsson, Halldórsdóttir, Thorarensen, and Vik (2009).
[e]Rosenberg, Hansen, Rudanko, Viggósson, and Tornquist (1996).
[f]Ingibjörg Hinriksdóttir, chief physician, personal communication, National Hearing and Speech Institute (2014).
[g]Guðmundsson et al. (2012).

Table 2. Number of Compulsory School Students with Formal Diagnosis.

Year	No. of Diagnosed Students	Total No. of Students	%
2010−2011	6,527	42,320	15.42
2012−2013	6,955	42,320	16.43

Source: Statistics Iceland (2013).

Table 3.   Proportion of Preschool and Compulsory School Boys and Girls who Receive Special Support or Special Education.

Years	Preschool			Compulsory School		
	Boys (%)	Girls (%)	Total (%)	Boys (%)	Girls (%)	Total (%)
2004–2005	7.7	4.0	5.9	28.7	18.5	23.7
2008–2009	6.6	3.5	5.1	30.0	18.7	24.5
2012–2013	7.6	3.7	5.7	33.0	20.9	27.0

Source: Statistics Iceland (2013).

to a greater number of students than before for the purpose of preventing learning or social problems from becoming entrenched. This development is an indication of greater flexibility in the provision of learning support within mainstream schools (Svavarsdóttir, Ólafsdóttir, & Logadóttir, 2011). Considering that only 5.25% of compulsory school students in Reykjavík are diagnosed with impairments and 1.3% of these are in special schools and special classes (Hrund Logadóttir, personal communication, 2014, Reykjavíkurborg) these figures warrant observations on how the system of special education has a tendency to blow up despite the fact that the number of students per teacher (1:10) and group (1:19) is low compared to many other countries (OECD, 2013).

EDUCATIONAL PROVISION AND TEACHER EDUCATION FOR SPECIAL NEEDS

Identification and Intervention

Most children with severe disabilities are identified at preschool age (0–5 years of age) by medical personnel, health visitors or preschool teachers. They are then generally referred to the State Diagnostic and Counselling Centre (Greiningar- og ráðgjafarstöð ríkisins, 2014) for a medical examination, psychological assessment and evaluation by social workers as well as physical and occupational therapists. The National Institute for the Blind, Visually Impaired and Deaf Blind is a public institute governed by the Ministry of Welfare. It provides services mainly in the rehabilitation and education area and does not provide initial medical diagnosis or medical treatment. This institute is responsible for a national database regarding visually impaired and blind individuals. A corresponding facility, The National Hearing and Speech Institute of Iceland is the centre of knowledge in the field of hearing and speech impairments. This centre offers the diagnosis and treatment, sales and services of hearing aids and assistive equipment. Children and adolescents with serious emotional and psychiatric problems are referred to the Child and Adolescent Psychiatric Unit of the National Hospital for diagnosis and treatment. Children with suspected disabilities at preschool can be referred by preschool teachers for diagnosis and intervention to the expert services operated by social and educational departments of the municipalities (European Agency, 2011). The same applies to students at compulsory schools where parents and teachers play a major part in identifying and evaluating students' need for support. For this purpose a variety of methods are used for screening in the fields of language, literacy, maths and social interaction (Svavarsdóttir et al., 2011). The next step is often a conference in the Child Welfare Committee of the school where the student's teachers, special educators, a representative of the school health service, the school psychologist, the principal and others share their evaluation of the situation. The conclusion may be a referral to a school psychologist for formal assessment who may then recommend special educational support in or outside the classroom (Björnsson, 1991).

The law concerning compulsory education underlines the right of every child to receive appropriate education in a school nearest to his or her home. However, parents have the right to apply for a special school for their child should the mainstream school fail to provide education suited to his or her needs. This is, however, limited to students with considerable learning or behaviour problems so that those with milder level of difficulty cannot expect to gain access to a special school. This has led to conflicts between parents and the local authority (Ólafsdóttir, 2013; Mennta- og menningarmálaráðuneytið, 2011a). Decisions as to who is eligible for education at a segregated facility are, in the case of students at the compulsory level, reached in consultation between head teachers and their special educators, parents and the school advisory services or other experts. At the compulsory, level special educators and guidance counsellors located in schools provide counselling and support to their fellow teachers and parents. Students can also be referred by teachers and parents to the municipality's school expert services for diagnosis and intervention (European Agency, 2011).

Provision of Special Support

According to the law on preschools children who, because of disability, emotional or social difficulties, need special support or training are provided with such support in their own preschool under the guidance of experts. Similarly, the compulsory 'basic schools' have inclusive catering for special needs as well as other educational needs of its students. The main policy is that such instruction should take place in their local home school. Special needs education in the mainstream school is organised on a short-term or long-term basis depending on the needs of the student, possibly lasting all of his or her school years. The municipalities are also obliged to offer education for children who are in hospitals or are sick for a long period (Lög um grunnskóla, 2008). Recent immigrants receive special instruction in Icelandic, both at the compulsory and upper secondary levels, in addition to some provision for instruction in their native language (European Agency, 2011).

Everyone is entitled to education at Upper Secondary School level. Students with disabilities (as defined in the Law on the Affairs of the Disabled) are to be provided with instruction and special support in their studies. Expert advice and suitable conditions are to be ensured. In their studies, disabled students are to follow the mainstream curriculum with other students as far as possible. The law provides for the possibility of establishing special units within upper secondary schools for students with disabilities. The law also stipulates that deaf students have the right to special instruction in the Icelandic sign language (Lög um framhaldsskóla nr. 92, 2008). In addition, there is increasing emphasis on educational and vocational counselling.

The Ordinance on students with special needs in compulsory schools (Reglugerð um nemendur með sérþarfir í grunnskóla nr. 585, 2010) and its counterpart for the upper secondary school (Reglugerð um nemendur með sérþarfir í framhaldsskólum nr. 230, 2012) state that support for individual students and student groups involves a flexible and multifarious learning context and teaching methods and that the support shall take place within a local school. According to this special support, which is not seen as separate from other teaching, involves changes of educational aims, curricular content and teaching context and/or methods as compared with what other students of the same age are offered. It involves the writing of an education plan for an individual or a group of individuals, implementation of the plan and finally written reports and evaluation of the education plan and its implementation.

Special educational support in the Compulsory School is provided by a variety of arrangements:

1. Special needs education in mainstream classes (within class or pull-out).
2. General special education classes in regular schools (for students seen to have learning and behavioural problems).
3. Specialised special classes or units for students seen to share the same problem or label such as autism spectrum disorders.
4. Special schools (Reykjavíkurborg, 2012, p. 16).

Outside of Reykjavík, the first arrangement mentioned above would be seen widely but the second, third and fourth arrangements would only apply in rare instances. Students in the special units within regular schools have a home class and spend a part of the day taking part in that programme.

According to those in charge of providing for special needs of children in Akureyri, a town on the north coast of Iceland, each mainstream school makes an education plan for an individual with special needs, a group or a special class. The plan includes teaching, materials and assistants and is reviewed two to four times a year. The teaching plan is carried out by a class teacher and in some instances a support person in the class. In many schools, teachers work in teams so that the teaching load of students with disabilities is spread within the team. A team is created around each child with disabilities, including a representative from the school, who supervise the use of funding provided for the student's education (Elín S. Jónsdóttir, personal communication, 2014, Akureyri).

There are three segregated special schools in the country that serve students with disabilities at the compulsory school age: A school for students with intellectual and multiple disabilities and two schools for children with socio-emotional and behavioural difficulties. In addition to the above-mentioned special schools, there are special classes in 49 Compulsory Schools (30%) with 1–40 students each. This includes temporary classes (for students with learning and behaviour issues) as well as more long-term special classes (e.g. for students diagnosed on the autistic spectrum disorder). All these special classes are located in mainstream schools and the students participate in regular class part of the time. Students with hearing impairment attend a 'twin school' together with students with unimpaired hearing. In that school, sign language is on equal footing with the Icelandic language. Two 'participation' classes have just been established in Reykjavík mainstream compulsory schools, one for students with 'mild' intellectual disability and another for students with behaviour problems operated by the special school for those students. The idea is that the students will have easier access back into the mainstream school from these 'participation' classes than from the special schools. In addition to short-term home support teaching for sick children, there are facilities available for children who are hospitalised for longer periods in two national paediatric wards. Surveys by the City of Reykjavík also reveal that in all year school groups, special support is more often provided in 'pull-out groups' than inside the classroom, despite the policy of inclusive education, according to which as much instruction as possible should be provided within the classroom and despite the fact that all schools employ support personnel in mainstream classrooms (Fræðslumiðstöð Reykjavíkur, 2002; Reykjavíkurborg, 2012). No statistics exist on the learning outcomes and grades of students with special educational needs or diagnostic labels in comparison with other students.

At upper secondary level, students with disabilities and students with emotional or social difficulties are to be provided with instruction and special study support. Extra teaching hours are provided to schools wishing to give special support to individuals or groups of students so that they can either follow the mainstream curriculum or a special programme. Many Upper Secondary Schools now provide extra support to students who have difficulties with reading and writing. There are special programmes (called 'practical departments') operated in all (19) upper secondary schools for students who find learning difficult in the mainstream classes because of disabilities or special educational needs. The ratio of teachers and students in the units is 1:1 to 1:4 and the students are offered instruction for four years, the same length of time as students in mainstream classes. Many of the students receive part of their instruction in mainstream classes and mingle with other students in the cafeteria. In mainstream courses, students with disabilities are assisted with their studies by, for example, sign language interpreters, co-students acting as scribes or other assistants, but in other respects they are subject to the same rules as other students. The upper secondary schools have, in collaboration with the Ministry of Education, done a great deal in recent years to meet the needs of all their students at that level; this is in accordance with the law and regulations as well as official policy, which emphasises offering courses to match everyone's abilities. The new programs are especially intended for students with poor preparation for enrolment in the more difficult programs. The results of an evaluation of these programs indicate that direct interaction between the students in these programs and their non-disabled peers is minimal. The students themselves and their parents and teachers, however, all consider their enrolment in the mainstream schools beneficial (Leiknisdóttir, Jónsdóttir, & Jónsdóttir, 2012). No special schools for students with disabilities exist at the Upper Secondary School level.

At the University of Iceland, where an official policy exists on how to meet the needs of students with dyslexia, physical disabilities, blindness and psychological problems, students can apply to the Counselling Service for special study arrangements and special examination procedures. The School of Education offers a two-year diploma programme for students with intellectual disability where they can prepare for work on the open market (Stefánsdóttir, 2013).

Most preschools and compulsory schools put someone in charge of special support arrangements who maintain contact with the municipality's expert services. For the Compulsory School this service offers general curricular advice, specialist advice on the teaching of the main school subjects, guidance for students and psychological counselling. The focus shall be not only on support for teachers and head teachers in day-to-day school work, including how to meet special educational needs, but also on teachers' projects aimed at school improvement. The purpose is to strengthen the professional capacity of the school to solve its own problems. Specialists of the service, such as teachers, psychologists and other specialists, are also expected to assess students with psychological or social problems, should these difficulties impede their education. Some advice to parents is also expected (Lög um grunnskóla nr. 91, 2008). The service has been criticised for being too clinically oriented and not providing enough support for leadership and development work in schools that may help with building inclusive education (Sigþórsson, 2013, 212). No such expert service is operated for the Upper Secondary Schools on an area basis, but guidance counsellors employed by the schools deal with learning and personal problems presented by individual students. For more complicated problems, they direct students to specialised evaluation and services outside the school (European Agency, 2011).

Special needs education cannot be considered without reference to its social and institutional context. For special needs education to work in practice a network both inside and outside the schools must exist between all those who serve the needs of the children in question. Ordinance no. 585 (Reglugerð um nemendur með sérþarfir í grunnskóla nr. 585, 2010) for expert services in municipalities, paragraph 5 stipulates that head teachers of preschools and primary schools shall take the initiative in entering into collaboration with the local authority's school expert service, social service, child protection service and health service in connection with chronic illnesses or other health needs of individual student. In the City of Reykjavik, for example, there are several institutions run by the City involved in meeting the needs of individuals. At the Compulsory School level there are additionally two special schools with limited advisory role to mainstream schools and parents. Finally, there are third-level institutions serving children with disabilities and a hospital for children, all run by the state. Inside the schools, there are student counsellors whom special educators need to collaborate with. In most schools, this collaboration is managed by a special educational needs co-ordinator. Parents are usually in good collaboration with the schools on how to plan and organise special education for their child. Without collaboration there is a danger of cross-over advice to teachers and parents.

TEACHER EDUCATION

Teacher education is at the university level. Teacher education for the Compulsory School level started in 1971 whereas teacher training for the Preschool level started in 1994. A three year bachelor degree in education was required for teacher certification at the preschool and compulsory school level until 2011. Teachers in upper secondary school were required to add 60 ECTS in pedagogy to their bachelor degree to fulfil requirements for teaching their school subjects. A recent study showed that preparation for student teachers at university undergraduate level for work in an inclusive school is far too limited (Guðjónsdóttir & Karlsdóttir, 2012). In 2011 a new law on teacher education took effect requiring a master's degree (5 year of study) for teacher certification at all school levels. Teachers wishing to specialise in special needs education complete a 120 ECTS (European Credit Transfer System) programme leading to a masters in special and inclusive education at the University of Iceland, School of Education in Reykjavík (Marinósson & Bjarnason, 2011).

WORKING WITH FAMILIES

The role of parents as advocates for their children's education has been strong in Iceland as in many other western countries, but the advocacy has taken the form of lobbying the Ministry of Education, local educational authorities and individual schools and preschools, through the media, personal contacts and parent associations (Bjarnason, 2010a). Thus, in Iceland the development has been impacted by parents but driven by professionals and politicians.

Hardly any services or formal support beyond the family doctor was available to disabled children living at home and their families until after the middle 20th century. Parents of blind and deaf children formed support societies for those categories of children in the late 1930s and 1940s.

In the 1950s, when the post-war welfare system was taking shape two benefit societies were established to aid people with disabilities. The Benefit Society for Children with Disabilities (Styrktarfélag lamaðra og fatlaðra) was established by medical doctors and other health professionals in 1952 to support and care for children and young people diagnosed with polio. The society has broadened its clientele and now supports children with a variety of physical and intellectual impairments. Its mission today is 'to support people with disabilities, particularly children, in every possible manner that contributes to their participation, competence and quality of life'. The Benefit Society manages a community based rehabilitation centre and a camp for disabled children and youth in Reykjadalur, just out of Reykjavík. In 1958, some parents of children with intellectual impairments joined together to solve their private problems. They initiated the opening up of a non-governmental organisation (NGO) service for children and adults with intellectual and multiple impairments. The association was called 'Styrktarfélag vangefinna' which translates as The Benefit Society for the Mentally Retarded. The name was changed in 2008 to Ás Benefit Society (Ás Styrktarfélag). From the beginning, this organisation attempted, as did many similar organisations on both sides of the Atlantic, to fill gaps in services by building up, administering and operating segregated services for people with intellectual disabilities, from group homes, day-services to supported workshops, respite homes, summer camps and more. The organisation financed these services by selling lottery tickets and from public collections and benefits. In 2002, a contract was made with the Ministry of Social Services and Municipal Service Centres (svæðisstjórnir) for financial support towards the running of the services (Gunnarsdóttir, 2009). By the late 1960s and early 1970s a more radical group of parents and a few professionals joined forces, disappointed with the focus of The Benefit Society for the Mentally Retarded, and in 1976 they formed the advocacy movement Þroskahjálp (literally 'Help with development'), an umbrella association of parents and professionals pressing not only for services but also for normalisation, integration, inclusion and human rights. This group grew in strength and importance and developed into a powerful pressure group, being involved in shaping national disability policy and leg-islation. Þroskahjálp was instrumental in shifting the focus of government and public opinion from that of disability in the family as a private pro-blem to it being recognised as a public issue based on citizenship and human rights. The focus on disability in the family being recognised as a public issue grew in strength and influence such that young parents in the late 1990s and the new millennium expected better and more generic and/or special services for their disabled children as a right. Þroskahjálp lost some of its attraction for some parents who established a number of associations for the support of children with particular labels, such as Downs Syndrome, harelip, Tourette, ADHD, autism spectrum disorder and so forth. These parental societies have gained in voice and, from the parents' perspective, have been more accessible than Þroskahjálp. It may be argued that parents pulled the wagon for change in policy and practice shifting the focus gradually away from disability in the family as a private problem towards framing it as a public issue (Bjarnason, 2010a).

ISSUES AND CHALLENGES

Special Education versus Special Support

The theoretical position of special education vis-à-vis other disciplines is now more uncertain than before. It used to be considered an expert area within education drawing on a legacy from psychology, medicine, law, phi-losophy, and even religion but always operating within education. Now it is seen by some as an impostor in the inclusive school, an unwelcome propo-nent of the medical model in the context of a social model. The reason for this is based on a categorical perspective, where diagnostic tests are used for the classification of students into diagnostic categories. This is despite the fact that special education has been offered as a master's degree study at the Iceland University of Education and later at the School of Education at the University of Iceland and not at the Faculty of Psychology; and the focus of the study has, for the last 25 years been an inclusive one.

By eliminating the term 'special education' from the Education Act, the legislative assembly (or those who prepared the bill) were not only trying to be consistent with the policy of inclusive education, but also attempting to transfer power from the professionals to the parents and to widen parental choice. Eliminating the professional title of special educator was, for instance, designed to reduce the possibility of a student's education being limited to instruction by such a teacher (Marinósson, 2011). Thus, depro-fessionalisation of the school was being achieved as part of a bill promoting inclusion. Other issues have also impacted the development of special education in recent years both directly and indirectly.

Neoliberalism versus Child-Centred Views

In the last few decades, the major change in Icelandic education policy has been away from state control of education towards local responsibility; away from curriculum guided by content towards one assuming that teaching is guided by objectives; from bureaucratic control of schools towards their self-evaluation and accountability; from a social pedagogy towards an individual, competitive one; from annual budgets to contractual management of schools; from a social to a technical conception of change and development; and from a central administration towards the devolution of responsibility for administration and finances monitored through performance indicators (Mýrdal, Jóhannesson, Geirsdóttir, & Finnbogason, 1999). This development conceals a number of complexities and contradictions. There appears, for example, to be a paradox inherent in the principles of social inclusion on one hand and the policy of competition and accountability on the other. How does the decentralisation of decisions coincide with national testing and the monitoring of standards? How may standardised common goals coexist with 'providing effective and efficient education for all students'? Are strong individuals and democratic communities not best maintained through collaborative education? Is new knowledge not better produced through diverse perspectives rather than 'more teaching'? The central question is how a small nation state, like Iceland, can sustain its success in the global market place and simultaneously maintain a just democracy where different voices are listened to?

The Categorical versus the Contextual Model of Special Education

There is no legal basis for the categorisation of disabilities or special needs amongst students, but nevertheless there are several systems of categorisation in use for administrative purposes: One is used by the State Diagnostic and Counselling Centre, another by the Equalisation Fund for

Municipalities, a third by local authorities for use in their schools and a fourth is used by the State Social Security Institute.

It can reasonably be maintained that special education based on diagnostic categories builds on the categorical perspective, while inclusive education builds on the relational perspective. Persson (2003) is of the opinion that, although both models incorporate knowledge useful for students with special needs (see Table 4), they are both imperfect and that their proponents need to collaborate to produce a better one that takes us a step forward in search for a model that takes pedagogic practice better into account.

The categorical model represents an attractive choice for professionals as it is based on traditional principles of scientific research methodology and focuses on delimited areas of study, be that individuals or designated categories or sub-categories of impairments. In comparison, the social or contextual model represents a complex research field involving, for example, different participants' perspectives (e.g. that of students, parents, teachers or assistants), a variety of processes and routines (e.g. processes of social construction and institutional routines), outcomes (e.g. of instruction) and cultures (e.g. of schools). Within this model, special needs and special

Table 4. Implications for Special Education Support Depending on Theoretical Perspective.

	Categorical Perspective	Relational Perspective
Ontology of special needs	Special needs refer to actual characteristics of individuals	Special needs are social constructs
Approach to difference	Differentiating and categorising	Unifying
Major contribution	Mapping and systematising the field	Problematising and deconstructing the field
Disciplinary basis	Establishing special education as a 'scientific' discipline	Establishing special education as a *social* scientific discipline
Implication for provision	Special provision	Integrated/inclusive provision
Understanding of special educational competence	Superior support directly related to diagnosed difficulties among students	Superior support for incorporating differentiation into instruction and content
Reasons for special educational needs	Students *with* difficulties. Difficulties are either innate or otherwise bound to the individual	Students *in* difficulties. Difficulties arise from different phenomena in educational settings and processes

Source: Persson (2003).

education are looked at in the context of mainstream education and larger service systems thus overlapping with and facilitating links with other disciplines (Persson, 2003). This chapter is written with the latter model in mind.

The Perennial Tension between Full Inclusion and a Variety of Provision

There is still disagreement as to whether to expect the mainstream school to cater for all educational needs of its students or to provide a diversity of educational offers and leave it to parents and guardians to decide what kind of schooling is most suitable for their children. Iceland's Education Acts and the National Curriculum Guides reflect this dichotomy where the demands for a School for All is unequivocal but there still is an escape clause that provides for a special school or special class in individual cases. Some parents fight for the alleged right of their child to attend a special school although the school may not be authorised to accept him or her because the child is not disabled enough. Thus, the policy of inclusive education is enforced although parental choice (in collaboration with experts) is given a central place in the Compulsory School Act.

Inclusive Education: Ideology versus Practice

It would be incorrect to assume that a change in government policy towards inclusive education has been accompanied by a general change in pedagogic practice. The shift from a general child-centred perspective of the post-war years towards a whole school approach, characterised by collaboration and democratisation combined with individualisation of instruction seems not yet to be reflected in the classroom. Teachers are still fundamentally preoccupied with getting the content of the curriculum across to their student group (Óskarsdóttir, in press). According to a survey conducted by the City of Reykjavík in 2011 around a third of compulsory school teachers found it hard to follow the policy of inclusive education. They felt that funds, knowledge and time were lacking, but another third of the group thought it easy. The remaining third were neutral on this point (Svavarsdóttir et al., 2011).

The City of Reykjavík has a policy of inclusive education that it carries out partly by making funding of 'special support' for students conditional on the schools demonstrating that they follow the policy. This, however, is not yet fully functional in Reykjavík or in other local authorities. Thus, the 'bounty system' in combination with the 'base system' as the two are used together in many municipalities for funding special support has a perverse incentive on the schools to identify a greater number of students with special educational needs and disabilities than otherwise would be the case. Furthermore, it entails escalating costs of expert diagnosis and assessment that could otherwise be used for supporting the school in its efforts towards inclusion. Icelandic authorities should seriously consider changing over to a needs-based system where educational needs are assessed according to the learning context.

How to Integrate Special Education in an Inclusive School?

It seems that the term special education is disappearing in official documents concerning education in Iceland. It has perhaps outlived its usefulness and is being replaced by the term 'special support' which covers educational support that entails additional resources provided within the inclusive school to all those who need it irrespective of the reason. Thus, it works towards greater equality.

Iceland needs a new model instead of the special education model that also replaces the 'pure' inclusion model. The country needs an approach that is helpful, transparent and easily understood instead of standing in the way of development. This should describe an inclusive school where individual needs are catered as part of daily school work (cf. the 'irregular' school proposed by Slee, 2011). There is no regular and exceptional in this school but variegated tasks to meet a diversity of interests, types of talent, culture, character and needs. For this to work all available knowledge is utilised: pedagogic, medical, sociological, psychological and managerial. Thus, expert knowledge is part of school work but geared towards the aims of education. Not surprisingly this is precisely what the 1974 Education Act stipulated among the aims of education. Perhaps Iceland will reach the unreachable before too long?

CONCLUSION

With its roots in the age of enlightenment, special education had its heyday as part of the construction of a welfare state after World War II as a measure to remediate children's problems, particularly children who were ill equipped for formal school work or from poor families. Over the years special education has been overtaken by developments in related fields, such as disability theory and ideas of inclusive education, equality, equity and democracy in the day-to-day work of the school. At the same time, the proportion of children who benefit from special support within their schools has risen constantly. In Iceland it has reached 27% and is still growing. This raises burning questions of the system's adequacy in meeting every child's learning needs. The usual culprits are all under scrutiny: families and their circumstances, the children and their problems, the teachers and their teaching and the schools and their system. It may reasonably be argued that the main reason for the increase in this proportion is how all these players understand and use the service on offer in flexible way. This is a sign of an increasingly inclusive system. Schools have started to see parents as collaborators rather than customers or even adversaries and this is reciprocal; the children's school problems also need to be seen in the context of their school work rather than independent of it; all teachers need to embrace the principle of inclusive education and prepare their teaching in light of a diverse group of learners. The school system has to see students' educational needs as a general concept rather than tied solely to individuals and to provide resources for these to be met in the mainstream.

At the classroom level, there has been a lessening of identification and labelling of impairments or categories of impairments; however, at the administrative level there has been an increase in this trend. Under the influence of neoliberal policies, diagnostics and categorisation for the purpose of controlling the expenses of special education has been imported from the health system into the education system. This has, as far as identifiable disabilities are concerned, become a routine for deciding educational resources. It has replaced the principle of needs-based provision that is still, however, used for special needs that lie outside the disability quota. So the dilemma of equality of access to services in the face of limited resources is still very much present producing solutions such as the selection of individuals into predetermined quotas.

In order to find a way out of the dilemma, Iceland needs to rethink its conception of special education's role in the school system. Iceland needs to rethink the schools and their use of special education to solve their system-wide issues instead of focusing on the children. Special education needs to be integrated to an even greater degree into the mainstream work of the school by becoming part of the teachers' teamwork. It should also function as an expert support service for individuals and groups to participate actively in school work. This should be done in collaboration with the schools expert service operated by the municipalities. School work in general needs to be reoriented to a greater extent towards students' potentials instead of their shortcomings. Special education will then lose its identity as a separate service and become a support service for all students.

This chapter has traced the history of special education in Iceland from its inception to the present day. Special education research in Iceland, policy and legislation trends has been addressed. Information on the children with disabilities with respect to prevalence and types of disabilities has been presented, along with information on the practices of educating children with special needs. Teacher education has been addressed noting that Icelandic teacher education programs have followed the trend from segregated special education, through integration to inclusive education. The perspective of families of children with disabilities has been discussed. The chapter concludes with some of the ongoing challenges for special education in Iceland including the dichotomy of categorical and contextual responses to the diversity of student needs; the tension between inclusion and a cascade of provision and between the ideology and the practice of inclusive education. The role of special education in the inclusive school is still uncertain as it is vis-à-vis multicultural education but it seems that before long it will become part of the support system that serves all students.

NOTE

1. The Icelandic versions of the National Curriculum Guides were published in 2011.

ACKNOWLEDGEMENTS

We are grateful for the help we have received from a number of people in varying positions of administration and education around Iceland to provide the picture of special education presented here.

REFERENCES

Bakel, M. V., Einarsson, I., Arnaud, C., Craig, S., Michelsen, S., Pildava, S., … Cans, C. (2013). Monitoring the prevalence of severe intellectual disability in children across Europe: Feasibility of a common database. *Developmental Medicine & Child Neurology*, 6, 2013.

Barnes, C., Mercer, G., & Shakespeare, T. (1999). *Exploring disability. A sociological introduction.* Cambridge: Polity press.

Bjarnason, D. S. (2004). *New voices from Iceland: Disability and young adulthood.* New York, NY: Nova Science.

Bjarnason, D. S. (2010a). *Social policy and social capital. Parents and exceptionality 1974–2007.* New York, NY: Nova Science Publishers.

Bjarnason, D. S. (2010b). Gjenom labyrinten: Hva er (special) pedagogikk I et includerende miljö? [Through the maze: What is (special) education in inclusive settings?]. In S. Reindahl & R. S. Hausstatter (Eds.), *Spesialpedagogikk og etikk: Kollective ansvar og individuelle rettigheder. [Special education and ethics: Collective responsibility and individual rights.]* Lillehammer, Norway: Höjskoleforlaget.

Björnsson, K. (1991). *Sálfræðiþjónusta skóla: þáttur hagnýtrar sálfræði.* Reykjavík, Iceland: Háskólaúgáfan. Fræðsluskrifstofa Reykjavíkurumdæmis.

European Agency for special needs and inclusive education. (2011). *Complete country overview − Iceland.* Retrieved from http://www.european-agency.org/country-information/iceland/national-overview/complete-national-overview. Accessed on January 20, 2014.

Eurypedia. (2014). Compulsory school education: Statistics. In *European encyclopedia on national education systems.* Iceland. Retrieved from https://webgate.ec.europa.eu/fpfis/mwikis/eurydice/index.php/Iceland:Educational_Support_and_Guidance. Accessed on February 22, 2014.

Flóvenz, B. G. (2004). *Réttarstaða fatlaðra [The legal status of people with disabilities].* Reykjavík, Iceland: Háskólaútgáfan.

Fræðslumiðstöð Reykjavíkur. (2000). *Stefna í málefnum barna með íslensku sem annað tungumál í grunnskólum Reykjavíkur [Reykjavík school board's policy on children with Icelandic as a second language in Reykjavík schools].* Retrieved from http://www.grunn skolar.is/fraedslumidstodin. Accessed on January 15.

Fræðslumiðstöð Reykjavíkur. (2002). *Stefna fræðsluráðs Reykjavíkur um sérkennslu, 2002. [Reykjavík school board manifesto on special education.]* Reykjavík, Iceland: Fræðslumiðstöð Reykjavíkur.

Goodey, C. (1999). Learning disabilities: The researcher's voyage to planet Earth. In S. Hood, B. Mayhall, & S. Oliver (Eds.), *Critical issues in social research. Power and prejudice.* Buckingham, UK: Open University Press.

Greiningar- og ráðgjafarstöð ríkisins. (2014). *The state diagnostic and counselling centre, homepage.* Retrieved from http://www.greining.is. Accessed on February 22.

Guðjónsdóttir, H., & Karlsdóttir, J. (2012). Skóli án aðgreiningar og kennaramenntun. *Tímarit um menntarannsóknir, 9*(1), 132−152.

Guðmundsson, O. O., Magnússon, Sæmundsen, E., Lauth, B., Baldursson, G., Skarphéðinsson, G., & Fombonne, E. (2013). Psychiatric disorders in an urban sample of preschool children. *Child and Adolescent Mental Health, 18*(4), 210−217. doi:10.1111/j.1475-3588.2012.00675.x

Gunnarsdóttir, H. (2009). *Viljinn í verki: Saga Styrktarfélags vangefinna 1958−2008.* Reykjavík, Iceland: Ás styrktarfélag.

Gunnþórsdóttir, H., & Bjarnason, D. S. (in press). Conflicts between professional development and inclusive education among Icelandic compulsory school teachers.

Guttormsson, L. (1983). *Bernska, ungdómur og uppeldi á einveldisöld: Tilraun til lýðfræðilegrar greiningar. [Childhood, youth and upbringing: An attempt at a demographic analysis.]* Reykjavík, Iceland: Sagnfræðistofnun. Háskóla Íslands.

Guttormsson, L. (Ed.) (2008). *Almenningsfræðsla á Íslandi 1880–2007, fyrra bindi* (Vol. 1). [*Public education in Iceland 1880–2007.*] Reykjavík, Iceland: Háskólaútgáfan.

Halldórsson, A. M., Ólafsson, R. F., & Björnsson, J. B. (2013). *Helstu niðurstöður PISA 2012. Læsi nemenda á stærðfræði og náttúrufræði og lesskilningur.* [*Findings from PISA 2012. Mathematics and science literacy and reading comprehension.*] Reykjavík, Iceland: Námsmatsstofnun.

Iceland Supreme Court. (2007). *Court case collection.* Retrieved from http://www.haestirettur. is/control/index?pid=330. Accessed on February 22, 2014.

Jahnukainen, M. (2011). The history and trends of inclusive and special education in Alberta (Canada) and in Finland. *Scandinavian Journal of Educational Research, 55*(5), 489–502.

Jöfnunarsjóður sveitarfélaga. [Municipalities' Equalisation Fund]. (2012). Málefni fatlaðra, SIS matið. [*The Supports Intensity Scale for people with disabilities*]. Retrieved from http://www.jofnunarsjodur.is/malefni-fatladra/sis-matid/. Accessed on February 22, 2014.

Jöfnunarsjóðu sveitarfélaga [Municipalities' Equalisation Fund]. (2014). *Framlög til sveitarfélaga vegna fatlaðra nemenda í almennum grunnskólum* [*Contributions to municipalities because of students with disabilities in compulsory schools*]. Retrieved from http://www. jofnunarsjodur.is/framlog/grunnskolar/. Accessed on February 22.

Jónsson, G. (2009). Efnahagskreppur á Íslandi 1870–2000 [Economic crises in Iceland 1870–2000]. *Saga, 47*(2), 45–74.

Leiknisdóttir, A. M., Jónsdóttir, H. H., & Jónsdóttir, G. A. (2012). *Mat á starfsbrautum framhaldsskóla* [*Evaluation of the 'practical programmes' in upper secondary schools*]. A report written for the Ministry of Education, Culture and Sport 2011–2012. Reykjavík, Iceland: Mennta- og menningarmálaráðuneytið.

Lög um fræðslu barna nr. 34. (1946). Law on the instruction of children.

Lög um fræðslu barna nr. 94. (1936). Law on the instruction of children.

Lög um framhaldsskóla nr. 80. (1996). *Education act: Upper secondary schools.* Reykjavík, Iceland: Menntamálaráðuneytið.

Lög um framhaldsskóla, nr. 92. (2008). *Education act: Upper secondary schools.* Reykjavík, Iceland: Menntamálaráðuneytið.

Lög um grunnskóla nr. 64. (1974). *Education act: Compulsory schools.* Reykjavík, Iceland: Menntamálaráðuneytið.

Lög um grunnskóla nr. 66. (1995). *Education act: Compulsory schools.* Reykjavík, Iceland: Menntamálaráðuneytið.

Lög um grunnskóla nr. 91. (2008). *Education act: Compulsory schools.* Reykjavík, Iceland: Menntamálaráðuneytið.

Lög um leikskóla nr. 78. (1994). *Education act: Preschools.* Reykjavík, Iceland: Mennta málaráðuneytið.

Lög um leikskóla nr. 90. (2008). *Education act: Preschools.* Reykjavík, Iceland: Menntamála ráðuneytið.

Lög um málefni fatlaðra nr. 59. (1992). *Law on the affairs of people with disabilities.* Reykjavik, Iceland: Félagsmálaráðuneytið.

Lög um menntun og ráðningu kennara og skólastjórnenda við leikskóla, grunnskóla og framhaldsskóla nr. 87. (2008). *Act on the education and employment of teachers and principals at preschools, compulsory schools and upper secondary schools.* Reykjavík, Iceland: Menntamálaráðuneytið.

Lög um opinbera háskóla nr. 85. (2008). Law on state universities. Reykjavík, Iceland: Menntamálaráðuneytið.

Margeirsdóttir, M. (2001). *Fötlun og samfélag. Um þróun í málefnum fatlaðra.* [*Disability and society on the development of affairs of people with disabilities.*] Reykjavík, Iceland: Háskólaútgáfan.

Marinósson, G. L. (1999). Specialundiervisningens elever: Fra kategorisering til individualisering – og tilbage [*The students of special education: From categorization to* individualisation – and back again]. In *En skole for alle I Norden: 100 års samarbejde omkring undervisning av elever med særlige behov.* [*A school for all in the Nordic countries: One hundred years' collaboration on the education of students with special needs.*] Copenhagen, Denmark: Nordisk kontaktgruppe om specialunervisning.

Marinósson, G. L. (2005). Special education research in Iceland 1970–2002. *Netla- veftímarit um uppeldi og menntun.* Retrieved from http://netla.hi.is/articles-in-english. Accessed on February 22, 2014.

Marinósson, G. L. (2011). *Responding to diversity at school. An ethnographic study.* Saarbrücken, Denmark: LAP Lambert Academic Publishing.

Marinósson, G. L., & Bjarnason, D. S. (2007). Making sense of the educational contexts of students with intellectual disability in Icelandic mainstream schools. Paper presented at the European conference on Educational Research, Ghent, Belgium.

Marinósson, G. L., & Bjarnason, D. S. (2011). Þróun náms í sérkennslufræðum við H.Í. [The development of post-graduate programme in special needs education at the university of Iceland]. *Glæður, 21*(1), 34–40.

Mennta- og menningarmálaráðuneytið. (2011a). *Úrskurðir og álit.* [*Ministry of culture and education. Rulings and reports*]. Retrieved from http://www.urskurdir.is/Menntamala/urskurdir/. Accessed on February 22, 2014.

Mennta- og menningarmálaráðuneytið. (2011b). *Námskrá fyrir sérdeildir framhaldsskóla, Starfsbrautir.* [*National curriculum guide for special units in upper secondary schools.*] Reykjavík, Iceland: Author.

Mennta- og menningarmálaráðuneytið. (2012a). *Aðalnámskrá leikskóla – Almennur hluti á ensku.* [*Icelandic national curriculum guide for pre-schools – General section.*] Reykjavík, Iceland: Author. Retrieved form http://eng.menntamalaraduneyti.is/publications/curriculum/. Accessed on February 19, 2014.

Mennta- og menningarmálaráðuneytið. (2012b). *Aðalnámskrá grunnskóla – Almennur hluti á ensku.* [*Icelandic national curriculum guide for compulsory schools – General section.*] Reykjavík, Iceland: Author. Retrieved from http://eng.menntamalaraduneyti.is/publications/curriculum/. Accessed on February 19, 2014.

Mennta- og menningarmálaráðuneytið. (2012c). *Aðalnámskrá framhaldsskóla – Almennur hluti á ensku.* [Icelandic national curriculum guide for upper secondary schools – General section.] Reykjavík, Iceland: Author. Retrieved from http://eng.menntamalaraduneyti.is/publications/curriculum/. Accessed on February 19, 2014.

Mýrdal, S., Jóhannesson, I. A., Geirsdóttir, G., & Finnbogason, G. (1999). Governance and inclusion in Icelandic secondary education: Emerging issues and stories. Paper presented at the Annual Convention of the American Educational Research Association, Montreal, Canada.

Ólafsdóttir, A. K. (2013). Brotið á fötluðum börnum [The rights of children with disabilities violated]. *Vísir.is, 03*, 19.

Ólafsson, S. (2005). *Disability and welfare in Iceland from an international comparative perspective*. Reykjavík, Iceland: University of Iceland Social Science Institute.

Óskarsdóttir, G. G. (Ed.). (in press). Starfshættir í grunnskólum við upphaf 21. aldar [*Teaching and Learning in Icelandic Compulsory Schools at the Beginning of the 21st Century*]. Reykjavík: Háskólaútgáfan.

Organisation for Economic Co-operation and Development [OECD]. (2000). *Special needs education: Statistics and indicators*. Paris, France: OECD Publishing.

Organisation for Economic Co-operation and Development [OECD]. (2013). *Education at a glance, 2013: OECD indicators*. Paris, France: OECD Publishing. doi:10.1787/eag-2013-en. Retrieved from http://www.oecd.org/edu/eag2013%20(eng)–FINAL%2020%20June% 202013.pdf. Accessed on February 22, 2014.

Persson, B. (2003). Specialpedagogisk forskning i Sverige. Problemställningar, erfarenheter och perspektiv [Special educational research in Sweden. Questions, experiences and perspectives]. *Psykologisk Pædagogisk Rådgivning, 40*(2).

Reglugerð um nemendur með sérþarfir í framhaldsskólum No. 230. (2012). *Ordinance on students with special needs in upper secondary schools*. Reykjavík, Iceland: Mennta- og menningarmálaráðuneytið.

Reglugerð um nemendur með sérþarfir í grunnskóla No. 585. (2010). *Ordinance on students with special needs in compulsory schools*. Reykjavík, Iceland: Mennta- og menningar málaráðuneytið.

Reglugerð um sérfræðiþjónustu sveitarfélaga við leik- og grunnskóla og nemendaverndarráð í grunnskólum. No. 584. (2010). Reykjavík, Iceland: Mennta- og menningarmálar áðuneytið.

Reglugerð um sérkennslu No. 270. (1977). *Ordinance on special education*. Reykjavík, Iceland: Mennta- og menningarmálaráðuneytið.

Reglugerð um sérkennslu No. 389. (1990). *Ordinance on special education*. Reykjavík, Iceland: Mennta- og menningarmálaráðuneytið.

Reykjavíkurborg. (2012). Skóli án aðgreiningar og sérstakur stuðningur við nemendur í grunnskólum. *Stefna skóla og frístundaráðs Reykjavíkurborgar*. [School and Leisure Board: Inclusive education and special support for students.] Reykjavík, Iceland: Skóla og frístundasvið.

Rosenberg, F., Hansen, D., Rudanko, J., Viggósson, G., & Tornquist, K. (1996). Incidence of registered visual impairment in the Nordic child population. *British Journal of Ophthalmology, 80*, 49–53.

Sæmundsen, E., Magnússon, P., Georgsdóttir, I., Egilsson, E., & Rafnsson, V. (2014). Prevalence of autism spectrum disorders in an Icelandic birth cohort. *BMJ Open, 2013*(3), e002748. doi:10.1136/bmjopen-2013-002748

Sigþórsson, R. (2013). Sérfræðiþjónusta við leik- og grunnskóla [Expert services for compulsory schools and preschools]. In R. Sigþórsson, R. Eggertsdóttir & G. H. Frímannsson (Eds.), *Fagmennska í skólastarfi*. [Professionalism in school work.] Reykjavík, Iceland: Háskólaútgáfan og Háskólinn á Akureyri.

Sigurðardóttir, S., Þórkelsson, P., Halldórsdóttir, M., Thorarensen, O., & Vik, T. (2009). Trends in prevalence and characteristics of cerebral palsy among Icelandic children born 1990 to 2003. *Developmental Medicine & Child Neurology, 23*, 2009.

Sigurðsson, P. (1993). *Þættir úr sögu sérkennslunnar*. [Strands from the history of special education.] Reykjavík, Iceland: Þórsútgáfan.

Slee, R. (2011). *The irregular school: Exclusion, schooling and inclusive education*. London: Routledge.

Statistics Iceland [Hagstofan]. (2013). *Grunnskólinn: Nemendur sem njóta sérkennslu eða stuðnings [Compulsory schools: Students receiving special education or support]*. Retrieved from http://www.hagstofa.is/?PageID=2604&src=https://rannsokn.hagstofa.is/pxis/Dialog/varval.asp?ma=SKO02107%26ti=Nemendur+sem+nj%F3ta+s%E9rkennslu+e%F0a+stu%F0nings+2004%2D2013+++%26path=../Database/skolamal/gsNemendur/%26lang=3%26units=Fj%F6ldi/hlutfall. Accessed on February 22, 2014.

Stefánsdóttir, G. V. (2013). Atvinnuþátttaka fólks með þroskahömlun sem lokið hefur starfstengdu diplómunámi frá Háskóla Íslands [The employment of young people who have completed the semi-professional diploma program at the University of Iceland]. *Tímarit um menntarannsóknir, 10*, 85–103.

Svavarsdóttir, H. B., Ólafsdóttir, S. B., & Logadóttir, H. (2011). *Framkvæmd sérkennslu í almennum grunnskólum*. [Special education in mainstream schools.] Reykjavík, Iceland: Menntasvið Reykjavíkur.

Tryggingarstofnun ríkisins [State Social Security Institute]. (2012). *Greiðslur til foreldra fatlaðra barna [Payments to families of children with disabilities]*. Retrieved from http://www.tr.is/spurt-og-svarad/umonnunarmat/. Accessed on February 22, 2014.

UNESCO. (1990). *World declaration on education for all and framework for action to meet basic learning needs*. Adopted by the World Conference on Education for All, Meeting Basic Learning Needs, Jomtien, Thailand, 5–9 March. Paris, France: UNESCO.

UNESCO. (1994). *Final report. World conference on special needs education: Access and quality*. Salamanca, Spain, 7–10 June. UNESCO and the Ministry of Education and Science, Spain.

UNESCO. (2000). *The dakar Framework for Action. Education for all: Meeting our collective commitments*. Adopted by the World Education Forum, Dakar, Senegal, 26–28 April. Paris, France: UNESCO.

United Nations. (1989). Convention on the Rights of the Child. New York, NY: Author.

United Nations. (2006). *Convention on the rights of persons with disabilities*. Retrieved from http://www.un.org/disabilities/default.asp?navid=12&pid=150. Accessed on February 22, 2014.

WHO. (1980). *International classification of impairments, disabilities and handicaps*. Geneva, Switzerland: World Health Organisation.

SPECIAL EDUCATION TODAY IN UKRAINE

Alla Kolupayeva, Oksana Taranchenko and
Elyana Danilavichute

ABSTRACT

Special education today in the Ukraine is dramatically different than its early origins which stressed communal guardianship for persons with disabilities to its current movement to inclusive education. The journey to inclusive education was inconsistent due to a variety of elements such as the collapse of the Russian Monarchy, a series of different governments and social-political structures, World War II and membership in the USSR which stressed a unification of the education system. However, special education professionals who worked at the Special Education Pedagogy Institute of the National Academy of Pedagogical Sciences continued to research and develop a philosophical instructional framework to educate students with disabilities that includes theoretical and practical aspects of inclusive education. This chapter provides a detailed description of this framework as well as prevalence and school placements aspects, classification and assessment parameters, and the impact of legislation for free public education. The chapter concludes with challenges to inclusive education such as attitude modification, infusing

Special Education International Perspectives: Practices Across the Globe
Advances in Special Education, Volume 28, 311–351
Copyright © 2014 by Emerald Group Publishing Limited
ISSN: 0270-4013/doi:10.1108/S0270-401320140000028017

necessary teacher instructional strategies, and the incorporation of best practices from special education to regular education settings.

INTRODUCTION

Ukraine is country in Central Eastern Europe that is located in the south-eastern part of East European Plain. It has a population a little over 45 million. Until 1991, it was a part of the Soviet Union as one of the 15 Republics. In Ukraine, special education teaching had been in existence for a long time. During the early periods individual ideas and concepts emerged and then disappeared to reappear again in new forms. Eventually, these ideas and concepts grew into an independent field of special educational practice and academic research. As this independent field grew, learning institutions, special schools and a formal special education system for persons with disabilities evolved in Ukraine. It should be noted that the evolvement of this special education system was a controversial process that followed diverse societal trends.

As in other countries, the education of persons with disabilities in Ukraine has developed as a result of an evolutionary process – from unconnected attempts at individual instruction, to group instruction, and later to separate learning institutions. For centuries the specific nature of the development of the education system for persons with disabilities in Ukraine was defined by the complicated history of the Ukrainian people and its struggle against enslavement, oppression, purges, imperialistic invasions by neighboring countries, and overcoming internal disunity (both social and territorial) through its territory being divided up between other states (Poland, Lithuania, Austria-Hungary, Moldovia, Russia, USSR).

Several distinct stages may be distinguished in the formation of a special education system for the education of persons with disabilities in Ukraine:

- Stage I (10th–first half of the 19th century) – establishment of church charity structures that operated as institutions under churches and monasteries.
- Stage II (first half of the 19th–early 20th century) – philanthropy and the first private institutions for different categories of children with disabilities.
- Stage III (till 1930s) – the regulatory framework was developed and structures established to create an education system for people with disabilities; assessment approaches were formalized as well as the relevant

screening practices to identify children and place them in different types of school.

- Stage IV (1930s–1950s) – the unification of the education systems in the USSR; institutionalization of a separate special education system for persons with disabilities and special needs; theoretical rationalization of segregated schooling for children with different types of disabilities and special needs; practical implementation of this approach in different types of school.
- Stage V (1950s–1990s): improvement and growth of the special school network; research-based refining of approaches to reflect advancements in science and technology.
- Stage VI (1990s – present): the development of the national education system; reconsideration of conceptual approaches to the education of persons with disabilities and special needs taking into account international legislation and social changes in the country; implementation of inclusive practices.

EARLY ORIGINS OF SPECIAL EDUCATION

Communal Guardianship for Persons with Disabilities

In pre-Christian times pagan Slavs showed tolerance toward persons with disorders or injuries. At the end of the 10th century, a system of church-based charities began to emerge in the Kievan Rus',[1] then an influential European power. The state laws defined the groups of persons in need of help and those obligated to care for them. The adoption of Christianity in AD 988 with the extensive building of temples, churches, and monasteries started the age of charity work for persons with disabilities, which was institutionalized and regulated by the national legislation of the time. The monasteries maintained special institutions that provided care to such persons and, additionally, taught them basic literacy and handicrafts. Thus, as evidenced by historic and archive records, in the Kievan Rus' children with disabilities were surrounded by the atmosphere of care and sympathy.

To a large extent the evolution of teaching ideas and education in Ukraine was influenced by the Renaissance, the Reformation, and the humanist ideas of the Enlightenment. This closely intertwined with the formation of cultural and ethnic solidarity, raising to a new level the self-awareness of the Ukrainian people as a distinct nation and reaffirming the uniqueness of its model for the education of the younger generation. In the 16th century literacy became more or less universal in the Ukrainian lands. Schools had orphanages attached to them for orphans and children with various disabilities under the patronage of the community (Taranchenko, 2013).

During the 17th and 18th centuries, with the strengthening of secular authorities, another form of care became widespread, which was provided by the state, alongside church-based care and private charities. The Agency for Poorhouse Construction, founded in 1670, oversaw these institutions that became homes for old people with physical disabilities and children. Some of them had special divisions that served orphaned children, blind children, deaf-mute children, and others together, where they were observed and studied, taught basic work skills, and skills for independent living in the community (Taranchenko, 2013).

At the end of the 18th century to the beginning of the 19th century institutions and departments appeared that were directly responsible for charity work, as a new phenomenon in the evolution of social guardianship in the Russian Empire. The first and the most influential was the Office for Empress Maria's Institutions which oversaw virtually all social care institutions in the country: hospitals, schools, shelters, asylums, poorhouses, etc. (in the late 1890s there were almost 300 charitable societies and institutions). Ninety-eight percent of school-age children did not receive any education in the Russian Empire (Siropolko, 2001; Taranchenko, 2013). For this reason (lack of a compulsory education system) and the existing social, political, and economic situation, the country had no educational network for persons with hearing, visual, mental, and other disabilities.

First Private Institutions for Different Categories of Children with Disabilities

From the start of the 19th century, riding on a tide of enthusiasm for education in Ukraine, physicians, teachers, and public leaders increasingly paid more attention to the education of persons with disabilities. Segregated private schools were founded for deaf-and-blind children, and those with intellectual disabilities (10 schools for persons with hearing disabilities, 6 for children with visual disabilities) which followed a rather progressive instructional approach, matching western European practices. For example, some schools had pre-school units, offered well-organized vocational training programs, and applied the latest teaching methods. The instructional process was founded on the principles of nature-aligned education, continuity of teaching and learning (beginning from pre-school age), and drew on the individual characteristics of children to guide the selection of relevant teaching strategies. For instance, schools for children with hearing disabilities, in spite of the predominant speech-based instruction, used other modes of communication (sign language, finger-spelling) at the initial stages and when necessary to facilitate learning and create a supportive and natural environment for children (Kulbida, 2010; Taranchenko, 2007). Ukrainian schools were organized according to a family pattern: life and learning at school were structured in such a way as to help students acquire a broad range of skills for independent living in a wider community. Ukrainian teachers believed that the main purpose of schooling was to prepare people with disabilities for independent life in the community, and therefore, in addition to academic targets, they paid a lot of attention to their vocational training. This added a unique flavor to Ukrainian special education. The growing number of schools for persons with disabilities and the broader range of disabilities they served created the need to differentiate the student body. In the 19th century medical and educational professionals made considerable efforts to organize a system of education for persons with disabilities and carried out theoretical research and field studies to explore specific teaching approaches for different categories of children. The cohort of academics and practitioners engaged in the discussion of various issues related to assessment, teaching and learning, character building and socialization of children with developmental disorders included names that are now famous in Ukrainian education circles as well as, in some cases, internationally: Tarasevych (1922), Vladimirskyi (1922a, 1922b), Kashchenko (1910, 1912), Sikorskyi (1904), Maltsev (1902, 1910), Vetukhov (1901), Grabarov (1928), Leiko (1906), Sokolyanskyi (1925), Shcherbyna (1916), and others.

Regulatory Formalization of Education for Persons with Disabilities

After the collapse of the Russian monarchy in 1917, Ukraine had a number of different government and social-political structures (Central Council (*Tsentralna Rada*), Hetmanat, Western Ukrainian People's Republic (*ZUNR*), Directorate, Communist Party of Ukraine, Soviet government). In 1919 the Workers' and Peasants' Government of the Ukrainian Soviet Socialist Republic adopted a number of national policies (decrees) on organizing public education in the Republic. According to these decrees, schools for children with disabilities became a part of the general state system of public education. Obviously, the turbulent politics and social hardships had an adverse effect on the existing schools for persons with disabilities. Moreover, some of these schools had to close down due to the lack of funding, staff, etc. The difficult social, economic, and political situation continued to persist (lack of social stability for people to return to normal life, warfare, destruction of infrastructure, hunger, and repressions). During this period, the number of homeless children and orphans went up to 1.5 million (Likarchuk, 2002; Taranchenko, 2007).

At the same time, it should be noted that during that brief period of national independence from 1917 and in the 1920s, the national system of education acquired its theoretical and teaching framework, which was based on democratic principles, and domestic and international best practice. This became possible because of the administrative autonomy that Ukraine enjoyed for some time in education matters (Ukrainian and Russian education policies were not associated with each other).

The structures and working protocols of the education system for persons with disabilities were formalized in the regulatory act "Declaration of the Social Education Subdivision" of 1920 (People's Commissariat of Education of USSR, 1922). The directives in this act were research-based, humanistic, underpinned by the concept of children's rights and in tune with the most provisions of modern education laws and regulations, which indicates the advanced professional knowledge and progressive views of the Ukrainian developers of this policy. The Declaration stipulated that best practice from the assessment services (monitoring and placement offices) were to be disseminated across the republic and incorporated into the education system for persons with disabilities. They were an early prototype of the Psychology, Medical, and Pedagogical Consultations (*PMPC*) and support services that continue to the present day and are described in greater detail below. Ukrainian academics and practicing teachers gave the highest priority to the organization of education for children and youth with disabilities such as: the need to ensure compulsory universal pre-school education; differentiation of children and setting up separate schools for each category; creating specialized assessment institutes; forming special education departments at universities and founding institutes for teacher training; ensuring the continuity of education and adequate medical services; providing vocational training to youth with disabilities and creating vocational training schools for them.

Table 1. Schools for Children with Various Impairments and Student Numbers in 1924.

No.	Category	Number of Schools	Number of Children in Those Schools
1.	Juvenile offenders (or "morally defective" according to the accepted terminology of the time)	17	534
2.	Children with intellectual disabilities	11	440
3.	Deaf-mute children	9	525
4.	Blind children	6	224
Total		43	1,723

Table 1 gives a brief statistical overview of the school network established for children with disabilities (i.e., "defective children" or "defective childhood" according to the terminology of the day) in 1924.

Development of Differential Diagnosis and Educational Intervention

The key question during those years was how to identify "defective" children and study the nature and pattern of their development, how to explore ways of providing social, medical, pedagogical, and psychological support. In addition, research in medicine, psychology, and pedagogy boosted the advancement of the new academic field of pedology (child development) that encompassed a multitude of teaching, psychological, medical, and social issues and combined different areas of study. In the 1920s, pedology became the dominant experimental science about the child. It drew on the theories of Decroly, Dewey, Montessori, Lay, Meumann, Key and laid the foundations for further pedagogical research by Ukrainian scholars and teachers (Vladymyrskyi, Zaluzhnyi, Makarenko, Protopopov, Rusova, Sokolyanskyi, Tarasevich, Chepiga, and others), who were inspired by the concept of progressive education. These ideas were the most conducive ones to create supportive settings to facilitate learning and the all-round development of children with disabilities.

Of particular interest are studies that explored approaches to the classification of children with disabilities. The first publications on this issue had a significant impact, and the titles and content of the articles reflect the thinking of the time: "Classification of defective children" (Tarasevych, 1922), "Defective individual in the context of social education" (Vladimirskyi, 1922a), "Person in the general change of events" (Vladimirskyi, 1922b).

A new approach to the classification of children with disabilities was proposed by Tarasevych (1922), reflecting his long-term studies. He assumed that children with deficiencies in psychological and/or physical development make up the group of "defective children." In his view, the group also includes children without any disabilities, but with specific traits in their psychological-physical organization or health conditions which impede a person's development. Tarasevych emphasized in particular that different types of disability were not equivalent socially and pedagogically. Based on this, Tarasevych identified three groups of "defective" children: children with physical disabilities, children with sensory disabilities; and children with neuropsychic disabilities. Even before the theoretical reasoning by Vygotsky (1924), he deliberated on secondary manifestations of disabilities and the range of factors that complicate the disability pattern. In Tarasevych's view, the diversity of the types of neuropsychological disorder depends on a number of complicating factors (adverse environment, upbringing, various health conditions, etc.). Recognizing the dependency of different types of primary neuropsychological disorder on the localization, nature, and degree of organic disorders in neuropsychological domain, he distinguished, specifically regarding intellect, four degrees of disability of increasing severity. He argued persuasively that a delay or disorder in mental development had different causes and discriminated between children with mental disabilities, educationally neglected children and children with developmental delays caused by various unstable conditions which manifested themselves at an early age and influenced the child's development (Tarasevych).

According to Tarasevych (1922), the purpose of educational and psychological assessment is to identify the causes of the disability that is the primary disorder responsible for the disability. Thus assessment might involve a medical and psychological examination of the child as well as a review of his/her prior experiences and family background. This assessment data would subsequently be used to select appropriate educational approaches and instructional strategies for such children. He also believed that in selecting learning content and instructional strategies it was essential to differentiate secondary symptoms, which are due to adverse effects of the surrounding environment and poor education, and the primary disorder caused by congenital or acquired organic disorders. This idea formulated by Tarasevych became fundamental for implementing differential assessment, designing research into different types of disabilities, and in selecting educational intervention strategies.

Tarasevych (1922) also stressed the significant diversity within each category of children with disabilities. He postulated that an individual's psychological constitution, the structure of disorder within the intellectual, psychic, and education development will be different in each individual case and, consequently, different educational interventions may be required to compensate for the disability of a particular child; likewise, the prognosis for further development may vary from one child to another.

These insights into the role of different factors in the structure of the disorder and how they influence child's development, enabled Tarasevych (1923) to suggest specific approaches to teaching and learning, and formulate the goal, objectives, and methods of special education. The above concepts are also present in later research conducted by other academics. For example, they are reflected in Boskis' (1959) thinking, specifically in her psychological-pedagogical classification of children with hearing disabilities that is described in more detail below.

Another noteworthy piece of research during the same period is that of Vladimirskyi (1922a, 1927), who also emphasized the need for a comprehensive study of disabilities. In particular, he pointed out that "defectiveness" in a person is conditioned by quantitative and/or qualitative deficits in their experience, which becomes incomplete or distorted in nature. Hence, it is necessary to study a child thoroughly and in every aspect, compare his/her performance with the data about inherited and acquired experiences, determine what was missing in their past experience in order to gradually fill this gap in the course of education. So, academics and practitioners focused on studying the child with a disability and their social environment in order to influence the child's experience and transform that environment to support his/her development (Sokolyanskyi, 1928a, 1928b; Tarasevych, 1927, 1929; Vladimirskyi, 1927).

The main functions of the medical and pedagogical offices included a review of child's medical history data, clinical assessments, examination of the central nervous system, physical development, etc. During that time the first attempts were made to determine biological, constitutional, psychological and social factors at the heart of a child's disability and to design therapies and teaching strategies to influence these factors.

The works by Ukrainian researchers published during that time period underlined the need to start medical and pedagogical preventive measures and special education interventions from an early age. They presented findings from experimental research involving clinical studies of children with intellectual and psychological disabilities; considered the issues of etiology and anatomic-morphological disorders that cause mental retardation. Based on these findings the authors generally concluded that mental retardation is a typical, but not the only, feature of impaired psychological development of a child with the respective disability. They went on to state that a central nervous system disorder, being the cause of mental retardation, quite often affects the sensory-motor mechanisms of mental activity, as well as the emotional and volitional sphere.

In research, priority was given to somatic-neurological, psychological, and pedagogical aspects to identify the patterns of a child's psychological development; explore and record the specific features of the disability and compensatory abilities of a child with mental retardation. They indicated the need to study children with intellectual disabilities in the dynamics of their development as part of teaching and learning, which is vital for understanding individual differences. These ideas were fundamental for constructing a research-based framework for the new education system and for designing the curriculum and a new set of teaching approaches for students in special schools for children with intellectual disabilities.

In 1921 two instructors from the Kharkiv School for the Blind – Przhyborovska and Slyeptsov – created a Ukrainian version of Braille's point ABC that made it possible for children to learn in their mother tongue. The leading Ukrainian experts in the education of blind children (Leiko, 1901, 1906, 1908; Shcherbyna, 1927; Sokolyanskyi, 1928a, 1928b; and others) developed teaching strategies for different groups of students with visual disabilities (including deaf-and-blind children).

In their efforts to ensure that children with mental and physical disabilities received specific training to prepare them for independent life in the community and provide them with the necessary social skills, Ukrainian academics initiated a wide-ranging program of theoretical and methodological studies to look into the general patterns and peculiarities of a child's development. These studies were conducted by the employees of medical and pedagogical offices. To this end they were gathering and analyzing data on the mental and physical development of children, exploring various educational intervention strategies that helped master the school curriculum and acquire practical skills. Every potential candidate for placement in a special school underwent the assessment process. For this purpose, medical and pedagogical offices designed tools for medical, psychological, and pedagogical assessment.

In the 1920s, a distinctive assessment network was established in Ukraine, consisting of medical and pedagogical units, observation and placement offices, special collector institutions, medical and pedagogical offices, and research and pedological centers. The network operated all over the republic and became an integral element in the structure of the national education system for persons with disabilities. It may be described as the prototype of the contemporary support services provided to students with disabilities in schools. At that time, the network performed all the relevant functions: statistical recording; assessment (both short-term and long-term in specially organized classrooms and schools); research; consultation and advice (for parents, regular and special school teachers); professional training and awareness-raising (arranging training courses, practical internships, conferences and seminars); design of research-based guidelines and curriculum materials, diagnostic tests and techniques (e.g., related to occupational guidance); development of integrated initiatives, psychological and didactic principles of comprehensive education for urban and rural schools (separately); study of children's groups, etc. In addition, Ukrainian scholars and practitioners experimented with placing children with disabilities in the same classrooms with their typically developing peers in regular schools (although society was not yet ready for it). Methodological guidelines were developed for regular school teachers to equip them with specific strategies and techniques that are effective with students with disabilities. The achievements of this network later made it possible to differentiate within and further expand the regular education system and the system of education for persons with disabilities as a separate part of it. This is evidence of a quite original and progressive approach to establishing a national system for the education of persons with disabilities at that time and demonstrates the novel way of thinking within the cohort of Ukrainian scholars (Vladymyrskyi, Grabarov, Sokolyanskyi, Tarasevych, Sikorskyi, Kaschenko, Leiko, and many others).

At the center of the Ukrainian education system was the idea of social education for children from 4 to 15 years of age. This approach was based on the increasing influence of the community on the child's life. It included healthcare provision, and education and character development in the course of academic learning that was combined with extra-curricular activities. This model was underpinned by national traditions and relied on the use of best national and international educational practice in schools. A children's community was envisioned as the main type of learning setting for children (this format of "social education" was chosen specifically to address the pressing issue of homeless and orphaned children). Such a community would combine different types of learning and extra-curricular facilities under one roof (pre-school, school, and extra-curricular center). The plan was to provide social education not just to orphans, but to cover all children, including those with disabilities. The existing institutions for children with disabilities were in fact implementing this model in practice, so they were to be smoothly integrated into this new system. This period was crucial for establishing the regulatory framework for education. Following the Resolution "On introducing compulsory universal primary education in Ukraine" adopted by the Central Committee of the Communist Party in 1930, universal compulsory education became a legal norm. In 1931 the People's Commissariat for Education of the Ukrainian Soviet Socialist Republic passed the Resolution "On introducing compulsory universal education for children and adolescents with physical defects, mental retardation and speech defects" (1931).

At the start of the 1930–1931 school year, Ukraine had 25 special schools for children with mental disabilities including: 6 special non-residential schools, 17 special boarding schools; 2 children's communities (4,470 children) and 1 pre-school for children with speech disabilities (the school only opened in 1937, since before that speech disabilities were addressed through a clinical approach and fell under the responsibility of professionals with medical qualifications, while the psychological and pedagogical dimensions of speech support were just emerging). In total, 7,628 children aged between 6 and 13 were identified as having hearing disabilities, while only 1,100 of them were receiving education (Likarchuk, 2002; Siropolko, 2001; Taranchenko, 2013). In 1932, that number increased to 8,400, and 24 schools served 1,445 students (including segregated classrooms in regular schools). Children with visual disabilities were placed at special boarding schools for the blind or separate classrooms in regular schools (see Table 2).

During that time, the unification of the education system was underway in the USSR which marked the transition to the administrative command methods in education management, led to its final centralization and set a new course — toward a Soviet education system where all teaching and learning was indoctrinated with Soviet ideology. In those years and later the majority of Ukrainian scholars were declared "enemies of the people" (on various charges) and their works were destroyed as "anti-Soviet." As a consequence, their ideas and know-how regarding differential assessment, specific teaching and learning strategies for different age groups of persons with disabilities were practically rejected; the prototype of the service

Table 2. Schools for Children with Visual Disabilities, 1932–1937.

	1932	1933	1934	1935	1936	1937
Special boarding schools	5	12	14	16	18	21
Segregated classrooms	39	95	114	133	141	175

network (medical offices, collector institutions, etc.) that existed only in Ukraine and offered support to children with disabilities in the course of their education was undermined; academic and experimental research centers that designed and piloted new tools and models, provided training and professional development to teachers were closed down. The policy paper "The second five-year plan: targets for defective childhood" (Direktyvy VKP(b) (Directives of the All-Union Communist Party), 1932) was adopted as a supplement to the Resolution "On introducing compulsory universal education for children and adolescents with physical defects, mental retardation and speech defects" passed by the People's Commissariat for Education in 1931. It laid down the directions for special education teaching and the education system for children with disabilities in the Ukrainian USSR. This policy identified the Moscow Defectology Institute as the single authority in the field with the responsibility to design the theoretical framework for the education of this group of children. Since all policies of that level were construed as absolute commands, and given rather serious difficulties at the Ukrainian Institute of Physical Defectiveness in 1930s (that was later shut down), it was the academics from the Moscow Research Institute of Defectology who initiated studies into the development and education of children with disabilities (Direktyvy VKP (b) (Directives of the All-Union Communist Party), 1932).

The period between 1930 and 1941 saw the introduction of compulsory primary education and universal seven-year basic education. Universal compulsory education for children with hearing and visual disabilities was to be provided through the expanding network of special schools with increasing student numbers, the creation of separate schools for children and adolescents who were deaf, blind, had other hearing and visual disabilities (letter of instruction from the People's Commissariat for Education of the Ukrainian SSR dated April 1934 "On expanding the network of schools for persons with physical defects, mental retardation and speech disorders in 1934 in the view of universal compulsory education for defective children").

The years of the third five-year plan (1938–1942) were about preparing for and surviving the Second World War. The greater part of the national budget was channeled to the needs of the army, whereas education was funded residually and mostly from local budgets. Still, the school network continued to grow:

- During 1937–1938 Ukraine had 49 schools for children with hearing disabilities (5,281 students); 82 literacy schools were run for illiterate youth

with hearing disabilities; 1 school for children with speech disabilities
(100 students);
- In 1940 there were 65 schools for deaf children, 1 school for children
  with hearing disabilities (who became deaf from an older age) serving the
  total student body of 8,145; 4 schools for deaf-mute children had classrooms for students who lost their hearing at an older age;
- In 1941 the number of schools grew further to 83 schools for deaf children (9,419 students), 1 school for children with hearing disabilities (182
  students), 3 pre-school children's communities (200 children), 93 schools
  for adults (3,000 persons), 17 schools for blind children (957 students), 1
  school for children with visual disabilities (182 students), 3 schools for
  children with speech disabilities (251 students), 4 schools for children
  with behavior problems (578 students).

During this period, Boskis (1959, 1969, 1972) and her team conducted
research into psychological and physical development of children with
hearing disabilities to design a new didactic model for their special education. Between 1920 and 1930, Boskis worked at the Jewish school for deaf-
mute children (from 1931 – at the Institute for Experimental Research
in Defectology under the People's Commissariat for Education of the
RSFSR; from 1944 – at the Defectology Research Institute of the
Academy of Pedagogical Sciences of the RSFSR). She had extensive experience of observing and teaching diverse groups of students with hearing disabilities at that stage of her academic career in the Ukrainian Soviet
Socialist Republic. This enabled her to learn about the latest methods
designed by the leading assessment and audiology experts, take part in the
meetings of Ukrainian hearing specialists (Tarasevych, Sokolyanskyi,
Vladymyrskyi, and others). This professional background prompted her
interest in creating a pedagogical classification of children with hearing disabilities who were at the heart of her research. Considering that the majority of works authored by Ukrainian researchers were not published for
ideological reasons, it was the Boskis (1972) classification that eventually
became accepted and further promoted (Marochko & Hillig, 2003).

The pedagogical typology of children with hearing disabilities suggested
by Boskis (1972) was based on certain general assumptions that describe
peculiarities in the development of a child with impaired sensory receptors.
She argued that in the case of a partial defect, in order to determine the
nature and structure of development it is first of all necessary to: discriminate the norm from pathology; differentiate between total and partial
defects; identify the unique secondary anomalies with impaired receptor

partially functioning; study the conditions that determine peculiarities in the abnormal development of functions impaired at the secondary level; identify the techniques to help compensate for and adjust to the defect that may be applied to different forms of partial hearing disability; design tools to assess secondary defects as opposed to similar primary defects; etc. (Boskis, 1959, 1969, 1972). These principles made it possible to describe a category of children with partial loss of hearing (or hard-of-hearing).

With speech being the closest function dependent on the auditory analyzer, all studies on the development of the hard-of-hearing led by Boskis (1959) took into account the interaction between hearing and speech. She noted that impairments in speech development in a child caused by a hearing disability can be observed even with a hearing loss of 15–20 dB. Hence, it was suggested to use this measure as a conventional boundary between a hearing disability and normal hearing in a child. Using it to assess a hearing disability (the capacity for speech development with the respective degree of hearing) helped to find a solution to another problem – how to draw a line between deafness and significant loss of hearing in order to provide differentiated instruction for children. As the same time, Boskis (1969) observed that speech development depends not just on the degree of the primary disorder, but on a number of other factors as well: the age when hearing became impaired, the pedagogical environment created for the child after the impairment occurred, and his/her individual peculiarities. Taking all these other factors into account, a clear differentiation was made within deaf and hard-of-hearing groups to ensure an appropriate pedagogical environment and specially organized instruction. Deaf children were divided into two categories:

1. deaf children with no speech (who lost their hearing at early age) who lost their hearing at an early age and did not acquire any speech skills;
2. deaf children with speech preserved (who lost their hearing at a later age).

Two categories for children with partial hearing disabilities were proposed:

1. hard-of-hearing children with well-developed speech and minor speech shortcomings;
2. hard-of-hearing children with serious impairments in speech development.

Boskis (1972) suggested a conceptually new definition of the term "hard-of-hearing children."

This psychological and pedagogical research revealed the dialectic inter-action between biological and social factors in the development of child's psyche. At the most fundamental level, it confirmed the importance of spe-cial speech instruction as a key factor for providing relevant developmental interventions in this category of children, helping them master the basics of sciences and live full lives in their communities. This research laid a theore-tical foundation for further exploration of issues related to special educa-tion of children with partial hearing disabilities in the decades to come.

However, this period was also marked by a clash of theoretical views on the differentiation of children with hearing and speech disabilities. Over a period of 15 years, and simultaneously with Boskis' (1959, 1969, 1972) research, Shklovskyi (1938, 1939) was establishing his theory of cortical deafness with the central assumption that many children with hearing dis-abilities have a cortical brain dysfunction. He argued that in all cases when hearing loss is combined with a profound speech disorder it was not just a loss of hearing, but a separate kind of disorder, whereby the hearing dis-ability is the result of a cerebral lesion that disturbs the normal functioning of the cerebral cortex in auditory-and-speech areas. Shklovskyi (1939) named this disorder "combined auditory-and-speech lesions." He con-tended that a previously unknown category of children had been discovered and "brought through from their practically deaf-mute condition." Based on this theory, he created a distinct classification of persons with hearing disabilities that was actively promoted within the educational practice of educating children with hearing impairments and in the system of schools for children with disabilities.

Even a new type of school was created for children "brought through from their practically deaf-mute condition" (which existed for several years). Thus, deaf-mute children, children with late deafness, partial hear-ing loss, and other disabilities were placed in the same classrooms. This practice impeded the differentiation of schools and led to confusion among teachers and education authorities. However, the efforts to restore the dif-ferentiated system of schools for persons with hearing disabilities persisted. Eventually, the truth of Boskis' (1959) views was officially recognized and Shklovskyi's (1939) theory refuted as invalid. Thus, the system of special schools for children with hearing disabilities relied on the psychological and pedagogical typology of persons with hearing disabilities designed by Boskis. Policies adopted at this stage enabled a clearer definition of cate-gories and groups of children with hearing and speech disabilities. In addi-tion to the categories of children with hearing disabilities in Boskis' typology, children with combined hearing and speech disabilities (combination of hearing disabilities with aphasia) were isolated in a separate group. Based on this classification, schools for children with speech disabilities served children with aphasia, stutter (when they could not attend regular schools) and other severe speech disabilities.

The final stages of introducing universal education and the further development of differentiated schooling for persons with disabilities were halted by the Second World War. This war became an immense disaster for the Ukrainian people (in 1945 the population of the Ukrainian SSR was estimated at 27.4 million people compared to 41.7 million in 1941) and inflicted grave economic damage (Petrovskyi, Radchenko, & Semenenko, 2007). Still, once Ukrainian territory was taken back, the network of special schools began its gradual renewal.

In those years, the Ministry of Education of the Ukrainian Soviet Socialist Republic obliged local departments of people's education to complete the implementation of universal compulsory education for children with disabilities. The resolution of the Council of Ministers of the Ukrainian SSR "On measures to provide universal education for children with hearing, speech, vision and mental disorders" (1950) and other policies specified the types of schools for children with disabilities. Also, they set out a streamlined system of schools that was supposed to provide education separately to groups of students differentiated according to the nature of their disabilities and ensure the continuity of such education (these levels of schooling, i.e., primary, lower, and upper secondary, exist to this day).

After Stalin died in 1953, Ukrainian society experienced certain trends toward liberalization touching upon all aspects of Soviet society. In addition, the scientific and technical revolution that was getting underway required a transformation in the economy, hence the need for skilled workers and better qualified mid-level staff, which called for reforms in education. Yet, contrary to the liberalization process, Moscow maintained its control over practically all spheres including scientific research (in 1955 the Ukrainian Defectology Research Institute was closed down, which affected the progress of Ukrainian special pedagogy).

However, even under these circumstances steps were made (a series of orders and resolutions issued at the government and departmental levels) to improve the education system for persons with disabilities. In the 1950s, the network of schools for different categories of persons with disabilities expanded considerably; there was further differentiation; special classrooms were organized in factory apprenticeship schools; special pre-schools opened and segregated classrooms for different categories of children with disabilities were established at regular pre-schools. This growth is illustrated in Table 3 using the schools for children with visual disabilities as an example.

Similarly, positive dynamics were observed in the network of schools and pre-schools for children with hearing disabilities:

- school year 1952–1953 – 50 schools (6,231 students);
- school year 1953–1954 – 55 schools (7,328 students);
- school year 1954–1955 – 63 schools for deaf children, 2 for hard-of-hearing children (with a total of 7,155 students);
- school year 1966–1967 – 56 pre-school classrooms at 19 boarding schools (674 children), 10 schools for hard-of-hearing children (1,500 students), 35 schools for deaf children (5,600 students) (Taranchenko, 2013).

In the late 1950s, special classrooms appeared at vocational schools and special schools to train students with disabilities who, on the completion of such training, went into jobs at enterprises run by the deaf society or the blind society. Steps were taken to further enlarge the vocational training system. Special vocational schools for persons with disabilities were established under the Ministry of Social Welfare and special classrooms were organized at regular vocational schools. So, it may be said that in the early 1960s the right of persons with disabilities to vocational education, special secondary education and higher education was enshrined at the legislative level and implemented in practice. The first such classroom for persons with hearing disabilities opened at the Kyiv Training School for Light Industry in 1958. A year after a similar classroom was created at the Kharkiv School of Engineering and at the School for Mechanical Wood Processing in Zhytomyr in 1960.

Table 3. The Network of Schools for Children with Visual Disabilities, 1955–1961.

School Year	Total
Schools for blind children	
1955–1956	14 (1,075 students)
1959–1960	8 (894 students)
1960–1961	8 (904 students)
Schools for partially sighted children	
1955–1956	4 (355 students)
1959–1960	6 (559 students)
1960–1961	6 (721 students)

Advancements in Special Education Teaching and Legislative Directives (1960–1990)

The period between the 1960s and 1990s was marked by significant challenges in the development of Ukrainian special education teaching even though there were restrictions in the selection of research themes and quotas placed on degree candidates and doctoral theses. Nevertheless, this period saw advancements in special education. Ukrainian researchers and practitioners drafted a policy framework for special schools (the "Provision on special schools for children with different developmental disorders," curricula, syllabi, etc.) to ensure sustained teaching and learning process in these settings. Basic sets of teaching and learning materials were designed (textbooks, teacher's guides, other teaching and learning aids). During these years the majority of persons with disabilities of all age groups were covered by special school and pre-school services (Taranchenko, 2013).

The decades of 1970s–1980s witnessed continued encroachment on the national interests of Ukraine from the central authorities and increasing government centralization. The Ukrainian SSR became a large field for uncontrolled initiatives by central institutions against the background of a growing economic and social crisis. During this period, the first steps were made to draft new education legislation. In 1973 the new law "On approving the fundamental principles for the legislation if the USSR and the Union Republics regarding people's education" (1973) laid down the basic principles and objectives for the public education system. For example, this law stipulated that special schools and boarding schools were to provide their students with appropriate education, therapy and training for socially useful work. In 1974 the Supreme Council of the Ukrainian SSR passed the corresponding Law of the Ukrainian SSR "On People's Education." It envisaged creating special pre-schools for children with disabilities and specified the respective staffing and class-size policies. It also contained provisions on establishing special evening schools and correspondence schools for persons with disabilities who were employed in the national economy and special classrooms at regular schools (for working young people). In addition, in the 1970s higher education institutions resumed the practice of providing separate group instruction for persons with disabilities.

One of the most pressing problems in the 1970s–1980s (and, in fact, during the following decade) was the quality of education actually provided to most students with hearing disabilities during their 10–12 years of special school. When they graduated, at the age of 19 years as a minimum, their knowledge and skills were just at the lower secondary level. This hampered their transition to active working life. Consequently, some of them dropped out after the end of primary education. Often special school graduates had inadequate levels of general and speech development and lacked the skills to proceed to vocational training and continue their education at evening classes organized at special or regular schools or vocational schools which, in addition to vocation training, also taught the upper secondary curriculum. This created a challenge for researchers to find ways to significantly improve the attainment levels of special school students. To respond to these challenges, a number of measures were suggested that included improving school practices and creating opportunities to provide complete secondary education in the following couple of years. The proposed strategy for special schools was to continue to operate as a unique learning setting, taking into account the peculiarities of students with disabilities rather than copying the respective stages of regular school education. The transition to compulsory universal secondary education required substantial improvements in the educational content offered to students with visual disabilities, hearing disabilities, mobility problems, and speech and language disabilities (Taranchenko, 2013).

In the early 1980s, the Ukrainian SSR entered a new stage of social, political and economic development, initiated by the spread of democratic ideas in society. These trends were directly relevant to pedagogical science and the education system that, too, embarked on a new phase of development. These years were characterized by the school reform that started in practically all developed countries (which moved into post-industrial societies). The USSR also had to launch a period of reform, since the disparities in the education levels of the population and scientific advances between the Western world and the "country of full-fledged socialism" were quite obvious.

On the whole, the evolution of the special education system to serve persons with disabilities during the Soviet period may be described as complicated and quite controversial, since it was happening in a closed and authoritarian society. The growth of the special school network and the differentiation of educational services for persons with disabilities were very slow; and in fact during this period it became a closed system with some partial integration observed in vocational and tertiary education. The government policy and the economic system of the USSR based on administrative command and central planning held back the progress of Ukrainian special education, which could have worked as a catalyst and driving force for the evolution of the education system for persons with disabilities during that period.

From Totalitarianism to Inclusion: Toward Irreversible Progressive Changes in Education

The disintegration of the Soviet empire, of which Ukraine was a part up to 1991, and the fall of the totalitarian communist regime have led to a gradual value shift within the Ukrainian state. It began to reconsider its view of human rights, children's rights, and the rights of persons with disabilities. This reconsideration laid the foundation for a new social philosophy were the Ukraine citizens accept holistic approaches to social relationships, acknowledge the rights of minorities, including the rights of persons with disabilities.

After gaining independence, Ukraine declared that it recognized the key international legal instruments regarding persons with disabilities. However, national policy is still largely compensatory in nature and mainly focuses on providing some small financial assistance and services. Until recently, making actual changes to various aspects of life to meet the needs of persons with disabilities and enable their successful integration into the community wasn't formulated as an objective.

Both the general public and the authorities describe the state of the Ukrainian special education system that has been serving the majority of children with special needs and the prospects for its development as being in crisis. "Criticism was and is expressed regarding the social labeling of children with special needs as 'defective' or 'abnormal'; the failure of the special education system to cover the total student body that require its 'services' (e.g., it does not reach children with profound disabilities or provide specialized psychological and educational support for children with milder disabilities); its rigidity and one-option approach to the provision of special education services; and the supremacy of the academic curriculum over the personal development of the child" (Kolupayeva, 2009). Ukrainian legislation regarding persons with disabilities formerly contained a range of legal norms. These norms: were formalized in different policy documents enacted at different times; were related to different categories of persons with disabilities; and are conflicting and inconsistent. All this created challenges for practical implementation.

Until a few years ago, in Ukraine children with various special needs were educated within the special education system. This system consists of a network of differentiated schools and other settings that operate in innovative formats (e.g., rehabilitation centers, recreation centers, social and pedagogical centers, social, medical and pedagogical centers). In Ukraine, the responsibility for special schools for children with disabilities and special needs falls under the auspices of different government ministries. Therefore, such schools are funded separately from different sources. Also, this situation created a certain degree of isolation, because these facilities operate as treatment centers where children stay for a month or as educational settings where children are placed for the entire period of their schooling. It also affects material and technical resources in these learning institutions, the provision of teaching and learning aids, and staffing. The Ministry of Education and Science is responsible for special schools and pre-schools, psychological, medical and pedagogical support centers, education and rehabilitation centers. Recreation centers, early intervention centers, and children's homes fall within the remit of the Ministry of Health. The Ministry of Social Policy maintains children's orphanages, social and pedagogical rehabilitation centers, and special children's homes. The lack of integrated responsibility for settings for children with special needs poses a range of problems, because these departmental barriers hinder efforts to create a complete register of children with special needs and to establish an integrated system of social and pedagogical assistance and support.

The Ukrainian special education system is characterized by vertical and horizontal structures. The vertical structure is based on age groups and the levels of schooling accepted in regular education. The horizontal structure takes into account the psychological and physical development of a child, his/her learning needs and the nature of the disability. The vertical structure is determined by age group:

- early childhood (from 0 to 3 years);
- pre-school (from 3 to 6—7 years);
- school and vocational training (from 6—7 to 16—21 years).

During the early childhood period (0—3 years) children stay with their families, at pre-schools and orphaned children are placed in children's homes. Children with various disabilities can access specialized services at early intervention centers, rehabilitation centers, psychological, medical and pedagogical support centers and at special pre-schools. For pre-school children with special needs there are special pre-schools, pre-schools that provide compensatory intervention services, special classrooms at regular pre-schools, pre-school classrooms at special schools, and rehabilitation centers.

The horizontal structure of the special education system in Ukraine consists of eight types of special learning settings: for children with severe hearing disabilities (including deaf children); for children with hearing disabilities; for children with severe visual disabilities (including blind children); for children with visual disabilities; for children with severe speech disabilities; for children with musculoskeletal disabilities; for children with intellectual disabilities, and for children with psychological disabilities.

The experience of Ukrainian special schools demonstrates a number of achievements within such learning settings, such as a good pool of material resources; well-established processes for providing rehabilitation interventions; vocational training, arrangements for academic learning and recreation. But alongside these undeniable positive aspects, it is important to highlight the weaknesses of the modern special education system, as described below.

- Due to its unified nature the special education system fails to meet the learning needs of all students with disabilities. It impedes the use of syllabi that could offer multiple options for teaching and learning and makes it more difficult to change or add to the existing curricula, as required.
- Being the main type of special learning settings today, special schools create an isolated environment for children with disabilities, which have multiple social implications of a negative nature, for example, alienation of families from the education and upbringing of their children; social immaturity of students; limited opportunities to acquire life skills.
- The teaching and learning process at special schools lacks social and practical aspects. As a result, students graduate with low social and economic skills; have difficulties in understanding social norms and rules; lack independent living skills, etc.
- Because of limited individualization and the lack of a student-centered approach in teaching and learning, students experience emotional and personal challenges, have an inadequate view of their own characteristics, strengths and capabilities.
- As a result of ineffective therapy and interventions students fail to develop communication skills and experience feelings of social withdrawal and isolation.
- The lack of licensed instruments for psychological and educational assessment creates difficulties in making the right decisions regarding placement and appropriate organization of teaching and learning.
- In addition, there is a gap in theoretical and methodological guidelines, teaching and learning materials that can be used with children who have severe and atypical disabilities and require additional educational, intervention and rehabilitation services.

PREVALENCE AND SCHOOL PLACEMENTS

According to the Ministry of Education and Science of Ukraine, there are currently 396 special schools serving 60,000 children and young people. Also, this Ministry maintains 40 education and rehabilitation centers for children with different disabilities, 142 special pre-schools and 1,200 special classrooms at regular pre-schools with a total of 45,000 children.

The Ministry of Labour and Social Policy operates 298 rehabilitation centers: 208 of them provide early rehabilitation services to children with disabilities, while the remaining 90 are concerned with medical, social and vocational rehabilitation. Additionally, children and young people with disabilities can access rehabilitation services at 46 social and psychological rehabilitation centers which, also, come under the Ministry of Labour.

In Ukraine there are no complete state statistics about children with special needs because of interdepartmental barriers, the lack of a single categorical classification, and a variety of approaches to keeping a record of such children. According to the statistics of the Ministry of Education and Science of Ukraine, in 2010 there were over 160,000 children with special needs. However, the data of Psychological, Medical and Pedagogical Consultations (PMPCs), which are based on medical assessment as well as psychological and educational evaluation, show that the total number of children with physical and/or mental disabilities who require developmental interventions in the country is 1,194,031 (or 15% of all children in Ukraine).

In Ukraine, a significant number of children with special educational needs don't receive any special services and can't access support to meet their needs. Apparently, this may be attributed, *inter alia*, to the fact that in the not so recent Soviet past the two education systems − regular and special − divided up their areas of responsibility. In this situation, children with minor disabilities, who were not identified in time and did not have access to special educational support, were placed in regular schools that could not offer appropriate psychological and educational services. This "spontaneous integration" is fully typical for Ukrainian schools of today (Kolupayeva, 2009).

On the other hand, the larger numbers of children currently being identified as having special needs may be explained, first of all, by improved assessment practices. These improvements were a direct result of democratic trends and reforms in education. These progressive developments also affected the PMPC system, the selection functions of which, set out back in Soviet times, were changed to advice and consultation. PMPCs take an objective and unbiased approach to collecting statistical data thanks to a certain degree of autonomy and independence that the majority of these structures enjoy at the regional level, being separate legal entities rather than divisions of the respective oblast education authorities. This situation is observed in many regions of Ukraine, for example, in Crimea, Volyn, Dnipropetrovsk, Zhytomyr, Kirovograd, Lugansk, Lviv, Poltava, Ternopil, Kharkiv, Cherkassy, Chernivtsi oblasts, and in the City of Sevastopol.

THE IMPACT OF LEGISLATION FOR FREE PUBLIC EDUCATION

After Ukraine became independent, the grassroots integration processes were boosted by the adoption of the Law "On Education" (1991) that stipulates the right of Ukrainian citizens to free education in public schools and pre-schools irrespective of any specific characteristics, including health conditions (Article 3); the Law "On Comprehensive Secondary Education" (1991) that states that "Parents or persons acting in their place are entitled to: choose educational settings and formats of education services for their underage children ..." (Article 29); the Law "On the Protection of Childhood" (2001) that prohibits the discrimination of children with disabilities and children with special mental or physical needs; as well as other legal instruments that enshrine the right of the parent to choose an educational setting for their child. A considerable number of parents have exercised this right, clearly, not wanting their children to be in a boarding school that is often located far from their community, sometimes in another oblast, or because an appropriate boarding school does not exist. The economic crisis of the 1990s also did not assist the process of placing children in special schools, since some of them were restructured for a different function or closed down, while the remaining ones faced funding shortages. As a consequence, increasing numbers of children with special needs went to regular schools and pre-schools − the arrangement termed as "spontaneous integration." It should be noted, that for the country as a whole there are generally no official statistics on the numbers of children with disabilities in regular schools. So, in Ukraine large numbers of children with special needs attend regular schools (and pre-schools) as part of the process of so-called "spontaneous" integration. This situation brought to the surface issues regarding their teaching and learning as well as the necessary special supports, which required immediate solutions.

MOVEMENT INTO INCLUSIVE EDUCATION

Vygotsky (2003) stressed the importance of integration processes in education. He pointed to the need to create an education system that would seamlessly combine special education and regular education for children without disabilities. He further emphasized, that, "With all its advantages, our special school system has one key fault of enclosing its students ... in a narrow circle of the school, creating a cut-off and self-contained world where everything is adjusted and adapted to the child's defect, focuses his/her attention on their bodily deficiency and does not prepare him/her for real life. Rather than help the child out of this isolated world, our special schools generally foster skills that lead to more isolation and enhance his/her segregation. Due to these shortcomings it is not just the general education of the child that is paralyzed, but special training, too, almost comes to nothing" (Vygotsky, p. 96).

In Ukraine the implementation of an inclusive approach to the education of children with special needs started over 10 years ago. The main driving force for putting the ideas of inclusive education into practice were the parents of children with disabilities and nongovernmental organizations (NGOs) which advocated inclusion and lobbied the authorities to proceed in this direction. The Ukrainian Step-by-Step Foundation and the National Assembly of Persons with Disabilities were and are particularly active in this field. The Institute of Special Pedagogy, a unit within the National Academy of Pedagogical Sciences of Ukraine (NAPSU), initiated government reforms in the Ukrainian system of education for persons with special needs. The researchers from this Institute developed theoretical and methodological principles to support inclusive education in Ukraine. These principles are based on the new methodology of education development and include: education for persons with disabilities as a priority; democratic transformation of education through the transition to shared public and private management of education; continuity of education to create opportunities for life-long learning for persons with disabilities; variable forms of education services to offer a choice of educational options; individualization based on a system of assessment measures; and collaboration between all social institutions – families, schools and communities. The vision behind these reforms was developed in the course of long-term cooperation with Canadian experts launched by the Ukrainian Resource and Development Centre, an institute within MacEwan University led by Dr. Roman Petryshyn. This cooperation helped to study international best practice in inclusive education, to analyze them and identify the key priorities in introducing an inclusive model in Ukraine, as the next evolutionary stage in the development of the national education system. The Canadian experience of educational transformations proved highly valuable for Ukraine where education reforms are currently underway. It can offer new insights into ensuring equal access to quality education and inclusion. The Canadian education system has moved from the complete exclusion of persons with special needs from the education system to full recognition and acceptance of their differences, acknowledgment of the necessity to meet their educational needs and provide the relevant supports (Andrews & Lupart, 2000; Loreman, Deppeler, & Harvey, 2010).

The analysis of theoretical research, experimental evidence and best practice in including children with special needs within regular schools in Canada has been of great importance. In spite of the diverse types and levels of educational settings, *inter alia* for students with special needs, education systems are one of the essential elements in the existing global model of social order. This model is attractive to countries that overthrew their totalitarian regimes. It is also relevant for Ukraine today, when considering the challenges and opportunities that arise in attempts to find solutions to urgent educational and social problems.

A detailed study of foreign experience in implementing inclusion in schools helps to streamline the modernization of the national education system in order to upgrade and align it with the United Nations Convention on the Rights of Persons with Disabilities (United Nations, 2006). There is a growing understanding of the deep conceptual underpinnings that are reflected in the theories of social justice, human rights, the role of social systems in human development, social constructivism, structuralism; the ideas of information society and social criticism (Loreman et al., 2010). Based on these theories and ideas, education is increasingly viewed as a common good that involves providing equal access to this social asset. The path to overcoming social inequality lies in education that creates opportunities for individuals to take a meaningful place in society, and the understanding of this fact becomes crucial. It is broadly acknowledged that people with special needs should be able to achieve appropriate levels of academic training, acquire social experiences and relevant competencies, and develop social adaptation skills that constitute functional literacy, according to UNESCO. Society recognizes the importance of these objectives, which proves its readiness to move forward in this direction. This conclusion is also supported by the first positive outcomes of the individualized teaching and learning model that is being introduced in regular neighborhood schools to help children with special educational needs deal with their social and academic challenges.

Today, inclusion is gradually gaining an equal formalized place in the education system supported by the conceptual rationale mentioned above; by new inclusive policies developed at the national level; by systemic measures to manage and promote the national strategies of educational inclusion; and through awareness campaigns to disseminate the idea of inclusion. For example, in 2001 the Ukrainian Ministry of Education launched a nation-wide experimental program to facilitate social adaptation and the integration of children into their local communities through inclusive education. The program was initiated by the Ukrainian Step-by-Step Foundation, and the Special Pedagogy Institute of the National Academy of Pedagogical Sciences of Ukraine provided academic supervision and advice. The Canada-Ukraine Project "Inclusive Education for Children with Disabilities in Ukraine" began in 2008 (its education component was managed by Yuri Konkin, MacEwan University). The purpose of this five-year initiative (2008–2013) was to bring about changes in the attitudes of government officials, schools and NGOs toward people with special educational needs. The effects of these changes were demonstrated in two pilot regions: Lviv oblast and the Autonomous Republic of Crimea (Simferopol City). The analysis of the project outcomes and the resulting suggestions on the specific nature of inclusive education processes in Ukraine had a considerable impact on the design of key national policies. The project participants directly contributed to the drafting of these policies in collaboration with the relevant government agencies. A series of changes introduced in 2010 to the Law of Ukraine "On Comprehensive Secondary Education" opened the way for regular schools to set up special and inclusive classrooms to educate children with special needs, which signified the new formal status of inclusion in national policy. Further achievements included the "Concept of the development of inclusive education" adopted by the Ministry of Education, Science, Youth and Sports of Ukraine, and later, in August 2011, the "Procedure of organizing inclusive education in regular schools." Both documents were developed by leading professionals from the Special Pedagogy Institute.

It is noteworthy that at the beginning of the 21st century Ukraine experienced a wave of spontaneous basic inclusion, or rather integration, when parents started to exercise their constitutional rights by placing their children with disabilities into neighborhood schools. However, at the time Ukraine did not have adequate learning materials or teachers or teacher aids, who were prepared to provide adequate support in inclusive settings.

Approximately 130,000 children with disabilities were placed into mainstream schools as a result of such spontaneous integration.

It is only recently that the country started to introduce full inclusive education enhanced by necessary resources and supports. A total of 22 schools in Ukraine take part in the inclusion pilot project, which was launched by the Ministry of Education several years ago. The Canadian-Ukrainian project "Inclusive Education for Children with Disabilities in Ukraine" (2008—2013) proved to be a powerful catalyst for dissemination of inclusive education across the country, particularly in two pilot regions, Crimea and Lviv oblast. For example, over 50 schools in Crimea started to provide education in inclusive settings in 2012—2013.

CHALLENGES TO INCLUSIVE EDUCATION

Attitude Modification

Putting inclusive principles into practice "may involve not only a change in the way our schools are structured and work, but also in the attitudes of many special and regular education teachers who view their job as to educate a certain 'type' of student" (Loreman et al., 2010). Therefore, a national policy on inclusive education will need to address both social and organizational barriers. To overcome them it is necessary to improve professional teacher training, raise the awareness of parents and the community about special education, adapt school facilities to suit the special needs of children and develop research-based methodological guidelines and other support materials for teaching and learning. All these elements "come together" in the classroom where such a child is placed. Here success will depend on the style or method used to present new information, which becomes the basis for selecting the appropriate teaching and learning strategies. In this context it is essential to acknowledge that every child in the classroom has his/her own interests and abilities, preferences in processing new information, which follow from his/her individual learning style. Therefore, Ukrainian education is currently moving away from the traditional "authoritarian" instructional approach (that was dominant until the 1990s), that viewed the teacher as the "subject" and a student as the "object" in the teaching and learning process and led to "subject-object" relationships in the school. This structure of relationships resulted in a set of standard curricula that was the same for all students; the teacher communicated with all students in the classroom as a homogeneous group; there were uniform expectations to knowledge and behavior; there were generally rather strict discipline codes and rather few cases of understanding the essence of the student-centered approach. It is important to emphasize that the position of the student as an "object" of pedagogical influence envisages a specific type of teacher-student interaction. In this type of relationship, the stakeholders assume specific roles: the teacher as manager and student as a subordinate. It also assigns a certain degree of power that results in strategies based on authority (obligation) and manipulation (suppression of individual's will). In such circumstances the teacher, thanks to his/her position, achieves obedience relatively easily; and his/her will is perceived by students as such that requires immediate and unquestioning submission. This atmosphere is not conducive to creativity in the classroom, and later, in lower and upper secondary grades, the authority of power works less and less because teenagers start to look at the teacher through the lens of his/her professional and personal qualities.

In the light of modern views on teaching and learning, a student-centered, or humanistic, pedagogical interaction takes a central place and shapes the core of a fundamental innovation in the education field. A student becomes a "subject" and the "subject-object" relationship is replaced by the "subject-subject" one that is based on collaboration between the adult and the child. Instead of "brining the values of the society to the child" an alternative approach is growing in popularity — "travelling with the child towards the values of society." In this respect, priority is given to the development, rather than the shaping of inherent qualities. Guided by the capabilities and needs of students, the modern teacher organizes truly collective learning, delegates some of his/her functions to them, encourages self-direction, and in this way stops being the central figure in the pedagogical process. This facilitates personal development and helps avoid situations in which the teacher manipulates a child, because effective pedagogical interaction is based on the four principles identified by Orlov (2002). The first principle involves *the dialogical nature of such interaction*, which means that the teacher gives up his/her "superior position" and accepts the rules of collaboration — this creates a foundation for mutual understanding. The second principle — *the issue-based nature of pedagogical interaction* — changes the functions of both the teacher and the student. According to it, the task the teacher has is no longer to instruct and purposefully shape the desired qualities in a child, but rather to nurture motivation to explore new things, support personal growth by creating opportunities for him/her to actualize their knowledge, perform moral actions, and formulate issues independently. The third principle – *persona- lized nature of pedagogical interaction* – means that the teacher should cre- ate a supportive environment for students to adequately express their feelings and talk about their experiences, perform actions that do not fit in the standard roles of "manager" and "subordinate," which helps to get rid of the "masks" imposed by these roles. The fourth principle – *individualiza- tion of pedagogical interaction* – involves studying each student's capabil- ities, designing the learning content and selecting teaching and learning strategies that are age-appropriate and take into account students' indivi- dual differences.

So, without any doubt, the inherent features of humanistic pedagogical interaction – its dialogic nature, individual orientation, and therefore crea- tivity – make it unique. It relies on the humanistic paradigm that is based on the ideal of the unlimited creative potential of the individual and his/her freedom. This paradigm helps one to grasp'the purpose of one's existence and fosters an intrinsic feeling that makes them match their actions with the duty to mankind and leads people toward altruism. More and more Ukrainian educators recognize that pedagogical interaction between the teacher and the students founded on the best humanistic ideas is the ideal basis for successful inclusion in a particular classroom.

Developing a Philosophical Instructional Framework

To support inclusion in regular education settings, a supporting philosophi- cal framework was designed, drawing on the theoretical and methodologi- cal guidelines suggested by Professor Alla Kolupayeva (see Kolupayeva, Danilavichute, & Lytovchenko, 2012; Kolupayeva & Savchuk, 2011; Kolupayeva & Taranchenko, 2010). Additionally, a set of teaching and psychological tools was compiled and the relevant knowledge and skills were shared with the staff of pilot schools #3 in Simferopol and #95 in Lviv during a series training activities specially organized by the Canada- Ukraine "Inclusive Education for Children with Disabilities in Ukraine" project. Although a vital piece of progress in technical terms, it was only the first step toward innovative transformation of school structures. The second step was to find effective teaching and learning strategies for an inclusive setting. It helped to answer the question, "How to meet the learn- ing needs of every child and promote maximum academic achievements in a diverse classroom where all students have their individual abilities, inter- ests and needs?"

Therefore it was important to acknowledge and master the practical aspects of another key principle in humanistic pedagogical interaction, the leading role of which was recognized at the level of international inclusive practice long ago. This principle is differentiation (Loreman et al., 2010) that essentially means taking into account individual strengths and needs in one way or another when dividing students into groups to work separately during a lesson. Following on from this principle, in the two pilot schools mentioned above teachers organized differentiated learning activities to help bring the instruction as close as possible to the learning needs of students and their individual differences (Taranchenko, Naida, & Kolupayeva, 2012). Teachers in differentiated classrooms learned to vary the instructional strategies to enable every student to maximize their abilities when working in a group of peers who are selected based on the common individual typological characteristics in their development (i.e., their abilities, interests, the level and the speed of intellectual processes, preferred ways of receiving, processing and reproducing information).

Thanks to the positive experience of the pilot inclusive education programs, differentiation came to be viewed as a tool to implement a student-centered approach that presupposes the design of an individual educational trajectory, taking into consideration the subjective experiences of the child, his/her values and preferences, and enables the actualization of the personal function in the process of solving learning problems. Today the inclusive education teacher should know, and be able to use, a variety of strategies to differentiate learning within the classroom. Planning and implementing differentiated lessons happens in several stages: identifying the criteria to group students for differentiated activities; using these criteria for prior assessment; dividing students into groups based on the assessment results; selecting differentiation tools; designing multi-level learning activities for the groups; differentiating certain stages of the lesson; monitoring student progress within the groups and using this evidence to change the group composition and/or the nature of differentiated activities. Moreover, in a differentiated classroom the elements of the didactic system (aims and objectives, content, methods, activity formats and expected learning outcomes) may vary for different groups in the course of instruction. Today, self-determination and self-actualization of the individual come to the fore in the teaching and learning process. Moreover, it should be noted that in the light of the educational trends described earlier, individual instruction may be seen as a variant of differentiation (when the teacher or teacher assistant may interact with only one student for some time or a student may interact with a learning aid, for example, a computer, textbook, any other didactic source, etc.). The main advantage of individual instruction is that it helps to fully adapt the content, methods and pace of instruction to suit the child's strengths and needs, monitor his/her gradual progress from "not knowing" to "knowing" and adjust the teaching strategies, as required.

Necessary Teacher Instructional Strategies
All the above gives an idea of the range of knowledge and skills that the teacher is expected to have and to formulate the question that naturally arises before every beginning teacher, "What instructional strategies are the most effective in inclusive classroom settings?" The attempts to answer this question have led to the conclusion that, on the whole, the first and foremost objective of the teacher is to identify learning situations that are relevant for the child. Such situations should create opportunities for him/her to act within his/her capabilities, while relying on the teacher's assistance (that the latter provides in a sensitive way, i.e., mostly without appearing to do so, or, when necessary, in a clearly friendly manner), and to achieve meaningful positive outcomes. This line of reasoning demonstrates that any strategy must be based on a pedagogical framework that ensures a balance between the resources that the child needs to complete a learning assignment and the resources that can be offered by the teacher taking into account rather limited opportunities of the classroom environment (Danilavichute, Lytovchenko, & Kolupayeva, 2012).

According to Vygotsky (1991), instruction should "lead" the development and stimulate it. This becomes possible only when we consider factors such as: patterns of mental development, age, individual differences and needs of students, as discussed earlier. This approach forms the basis of the most effective instruction models known in Ukraine and internationally, that is, planned incremental development of mental actions and concepts (Galperin, 2002); development of theoretical thinking (Davydov, 2008; Elkonin, 1989); highest effectiveness of instruction to facilitate multi-faceted student development (Zankov, 1981); problem-based learning (Lerner, 1974); programmed instruction (Skinner, 1989; Talyzina, 1998); student-oriented instruction and personal development through education (Rogers, 1969); pedagogy as a factor in the child's psychosomatic health (Steiner, 1975); sensory development (Montessori, 1977), and social interaction in learning contexts (Rubtsov, 1996). Each of these theories offers its own answer to the aforementioned question about the most effective instructional strategies in inclusive classroom settings.

CONCLUSION

In this chapter, particular attention was given to an analysis of the subsystems evident in special education in Ukraine. These subsystems dominated Ukrainian special education and were concerned with specific categories of children with special need, that is, children with hearing disabilities, children with visual disabilities, children with intellectual disabilities, children with speech and language disabilities, children with musculoskeletal disabilities, children with delayed psychological development, children with infantile autism, children with complex disabilities, children with reactive states and internal conflict experiences, and children with psychopathological behaviors. The starting point in the design of these special education subsystems is the teaching about the structure of the disability: the primary and secondary disorder, the possibility to use the child's compensatory capacities and draw on them to plan teaching and learning activities. It is important to underline the fact that all these subsystems are based on the deep understanding of the patterns in a child's development according to the ontogenetic sequence in the development of the components of mental and physical domains. Secondly, they reflect the special needs of the individual determined by a certain type of developmental disability. Special education teaching contains elements of all the above subsystems and its best practice often becomes the core of innovations that find their place in regular education. Experimental evidence in special education teaching shows that some instructional methods, which are only now being criticized by regular schools, received similar negative feedback from special schools long ago. Teaching that relies solely on explanations and examples (when the teacher imparts information to the student, while the latter remains a passive recipient of it) was pronounced ineffective due to the specific nature of teaching and learning of children with special needs (Danilavichute et al., 2012).

Based on the in-depth analysis of good practices of supporting children with a variety of special needs within the special education system, the academics from the Special Pedagogy Institute of the NAPSU found that the experience accumulated over many years by special education professionals should be used as a resource to establish a national model for designing and implementing the teaching and learning process in inclusive settings. The validity of this conclusion was substantiated by the results of training conducted for regular education teachers from pilot schools to equip them with the necessary knowledge and skills in the area of special pedagogy. This training was organized as an experimental initiative within the

Canada-Ukraine project. Later the participants applied this knowledge and these skills in their daily practice and integrated them smoothly with the advanced pedagogical approaches mentioned above. This established a precedent which provided the impetus for the design of the relevant theoretical and methodological tools to support the education of children with special needs and to seek practical formats to enable the transfer of best practice from special schools to regular education settings. This strategy helped to maximize the available in-country capacity taking into account existing educational traditions and to implement the necessary innovations in a consistent (evolutionary) way.

On the whole, the content of the theoretical and practical resources of inclusive education reflects educational trends and approaches that gained international popularity over recent decades and attained their leading positions due to their universality. A profound understanding of the philosophy of inclusion and the distinct nature of its development in our country, the efforts to define its place and grasp its role within a unified education system provide the key to start thinking about how to design the teaching and learning process, taking into account the needs of children who follow a typical development process and children who develop at their own individual pace within a common educational environment. The search for ways of organizing effective pedagogical interaction between the teacher and the students in the inclusive classroom has created a range of options that based on different pedagogical models and their constituent parts. They have been tried and tested through practice in many countries and may be applied in various combinations. The best examples of protocols for using these pedagogical models and their constituent parts based on international experience and the first steps in the design and implementation of inclusive education made by the pilot schools within the Canada-Ukraine Project have confirmed that the strategies presented in the latest research and methodology publications produce significant positive results. At the same time, it should be pointed out that the innovative movement that is gradually gaining traction in Ukrainian education includes a number of specific features, and, therefore, further research is required to analyze and summarize existing good practice. Moreover, particular attention needs to be paid to the practical aspects of implementing professional collaboration between regular education and special education professionals. The experience accumulated by special education teaching over many decades can offer rational solutions to ensure that related services for children with special needs are provided in inclusive settings; to help design efficient protocols for using qualified special education staff as a resource to assist with assessment and interventions.

For example, resource centers are now being established at schools for children with special needs. This gives an opportunity to restructure special schools while preserving their core function, which is to educate children with similar disabilities/special needs, and offering parents of children with special needs a choice in deciding where to send their children. Such an evolutionary approach to educational modernization is valuable and the optimum one for the country, because it respects traditions with a long history and a large number of followers, and time is an important factor in changing those beliefs and attitudes. Increasingly popular are the Inclusive Resource Centres that have databases of available special services, their location and providers; they also keep case records with comprehensive information about children with special needs who would like to be included in their neighborhood schools. In our view, the emerging Ukrainian model of inclusive education, as a result of the daily practice and research conducted by the Special Pedagogy Institute of the NAPSU, will provide a sound foundation to improve the existing instructional strategies and create new ones for inclusive settings. Such is the long-term goal for the development of this sphere of social life in Ukraine.

NOTE

1. Kievan Rus' is the name of the early feudal state with the center in Kyiv that rose between the 7th and 9th centuries and existed till the mid-13th century. It was one of the influential powers of its time and had a significant impact on the development of the European civilization. However, starting from the mid-12th century its political unity was gradually undermined and, eventually, disintegrated into 15 principalities and lands. The name "Ukraine" (edge, border area) means the territory that was formally the central part of Kievan Rus' of the 11th−12th centuries.

ACKNOWLEDGMENT

Special acknowledgment to Tetiana Klekota who translated this chapter.

REFERENCES

Andrews, J., & Lupart, J. (2000). *The inclusive classroom: Educating exceptional children.* Calgary, Canada: Thomson Learning.

Boskis, R. M. (1959). Osnovnye tipy uchashchikhsia s nedostatkami slukhovogo analizatora i osnovania ikh rasdelnogo obuchenia v spetsialnykh shkolakh [Main groups of students with impaired auditory analyzer and rationale for their separate education in special schools]. *Obuchenie i vospitanie glukhikh.* [*Education of the Deaf.*] Moscow, Russia: Prosveshcheniye.

Boskis, R. M. (1969). Printsypy diagnostiki anomalnogo razvitia rebenka pri chastichnom defekte slukha [Principles of assessing anomalous development of a child with partial hearing defect]. *Defektologia.* [*Special Education.*], *1*, 18–26.

Boskis, R. M. (1972). Pedagogicheskaya klassifikatsia shkolnikov s nedostatkami slukha [Pedagogical classification of school students with hearing impairments]. *Defektologia.* [*Special Education.*], *1*, 10–19.

Danilavichute, E. A., Lytovchenko, S. V., & Kolupayeva, A. A. (Eds.). (2012). *Strategiyi vykladannia v inkliuzyvnomu navchalnomu zakladi: Navchalno-metodychnyi posibnyk. Seria Seria "Inkliuzyvna osvita." [Instruction strategies in inclusive classroom. Training and methodological guide. Inclusive education series.]* Kyiv, Ukraine: ASK.

Davydov, V. V. (2008). *Vidy obobshchenia v obuchenii.* [*Types of generalization in education.*] Kyiv, Ukraine: Direkt-Media.

Direktivy VKP (b). (1932). *i postanovlenia sovetskogo pravitelstva o narodnom obrazovanii: Sb. Dokumentov za 1917–1947 gg./Sost. N. I. Boldyrev [Directives of the All-Union Communist Party of Bolsheviks and the resolutions passed by the Soviet government in the area of people's education: Collection of documents adopted between 1917 and 1947. Compiled by N. I. Boldyrev].* Moscow, Russia: Academy of Pedagogical Sciences of the Russian Soviet Socialist Republic.

Elkonin, D. B. (1989). Svyaz obuchenia i psikhicheskogo razvitia detei [Links between teaching and psychological development in children]. In D. B. Elkonin (Ed.), *Izbrannye psikhologicheskie trudy* (pp. 78–94). [*Selected works on psychology.*] Moscow, Russia: Academia.

Galperin, P. Y. (2002). *Lektsii po psikhologii.* [*Lectures on psychology.*] Moscow, Russia: Academia.

Grabarov, A. N. (1928). Osnovnye dostizhenia v oblasti izuchenia detskoi defectologii i borba s nei za 10 let [Major achievements in the study of childhood defectology and efforts to overcome it over 10 years]. *Voprosy pedagogiki.* [*Issues in the field of pedagogy.*], *3–4*, 89–104.

Kashchenko, V. P. (1910). *Defektivnye dyeti shkolnogo vozrasta i vseobshchee obuchenie.* [*Defective school-age children and universal education.*] Moscow, Russia: Tip, Typography of Amoldo-Tretiakovskogo School for the Deaf and Mute.

Kashchenko, V. P. (1912). Istoricheskyi obsor i sovremennoye sostoyanie vospitania i obuchenia defektivnyhk detei v Rossii [Historical background and modern state of education and upbringing of defective children in Russia]. In V. P. Kashchenko (Ed.), *Defektivnye deti i shkola* (pp. 255–277) [*Collection of articles "Defective children and school."*] Moscow, Russia: Publishing House of K.I. Tikhomirou.

Kolupayeva, A. A. (2009). *Inkluzyvna osvita: Realii ta perspektyvy. Monographia.* [*Inclusive education: Realities and prospects. A monograph.*] Kyiv, Ukraine: Sammit-Knyga.

Kolupayeva, A. A., Danilavichute, E. A., & Lytovchenko, S. V. (2012). *Profesiyne spivrobitnytstvo v inkluzyvnomu navchalnomu zakladi: Navchalno-metodychnyi posibnyk. Seria "Inkluzyvna osvita." [Professional collaboration in inclusive schools. Training and methodological guide. Inclusive education series.]* Kyiv, Ukraine: ASK.

Kolupayeva, A. A., & Savchuk, L. O. (2011). *Dity z osoblyvymy osvitnimy potrebamy ta organizatsia ikh navchannia. Vydannia dopovnene ta pereroblene: Nauk.-metod. posib. Seria "Inkluzyvna osvita"* (Rev. ed.). [*Children with special educational needs and how to organize their education. A methodological guide. Inclusive education series.*] Kyiv, Ukraine: ATOPOL.

Kolupayeva, A. A., & Taranchenko, O. M. (2010). *Dity z osoblyvymy potrebamy v zagalnoosvitnyomu prostori: Pochatkova lanka. Putivnyk dlia pedagogiv: Navchalno-metodychnyi posibnyk. Seria "Inkluzyvna osvita."* [*Children with special needs in regular education settings: Primary education. Handbook for teachers: Training and methodological guide. Inclusive education series.*] Kyiv, Ukraine: ATOPOL.

Kulbida, S. V. (2010). *Teoretiko-metodologichni zasady vykorystannia zhestovoi movy u navchanni nechuyuchykh: Monographia.* [*Theoretical and methodological foundations of using sign language in the education of deaf people. A monograph.*] Kyiv, Ukraine: Poliprom.

Leiko, K. (1901). O razvitii vneshnikh chuvstv u slepykh [On the development of external senses in blind people]. *Slepets.* [*The Blind.*], *8*, 85−87.

Leiko, K. (1906). O pravovom polozhenii slepykh v Rossii [On the legal status of the blind in Russia]. *Slepets.* [*The Blind.*], *7*, 121−135.

Leiko, K. (1908). K psikhologii slepykh [On the psychology of blind people]. *Slepets.* [*The Blind.*], *4*, 61−65.

Lerner, I. Y. (1974). *Problemnoe obuchenie.* [*Issue-based learning*]. Moscow, Russia: Znanie.

Likarchuk, I. L. (2002). *Ministry osvity Ukrainy: V 2-kh t. − T. 1 (1017−1943 rr.). Monographia.* [*Ministers of Education in Ukraine. In two volumes. Vol. 1 (1017−1943). A monograph.*] Kyiv, Ukraine: Eshke O.M.

Loreman, T., Deppeler, J., & Harvey, D. H. P. (2010). *Inclusive education: Supporting diversity in the classroom.* Abingdon, UK: Routledge.

Maltsev, A. A. (1902). *Istoria i nastoyashchee sostoyanie prizrenia dushevnobolnykh v Poltavskoi gubernii.* Dis. d-ra meditsyny [*Historical perspective and the current state of care for mental patients in Poltava province.* Doctoral dissertation in medicine], V.P. Meshchersky Typography, Saint Petersburg, Russia.

Maltsev, A. A. (1910). *Uchilishche-khutor glukhonemykh v Aleksandrovske, Ekaterinoslavskoi gubernii (1903−1910).* [*Training school-farm for deaf-mute people in Aleksandrovsk settlement of Ekaterinoslav province, 1903−1910.*] Aleksandrovsk, Russia: Typography of the Training School-Farm.

Marochko, V., & Hillig, G. (2003). *Represovani pedagogy Ukrainy: Zhertvy politychnogo teroru (1929−1941).* [*Ukrainian pedagogues persecuted for political reasons: Victims of political terror (1929−1941).*] Kyiv, Ukraine: Naurovyi svit.

Montessori, M. (1977). *Education for human development.* New York, NY: Schocken Books.

Orlov, A. B. (2002). *Psikhologia lichnosti i sushchnosti cheloveka: Paradigmy, proektsii, praktiki: Ucheb. posobiye dlia stud. psikhol. fak. vuzov.* [*Psychology of personality and essence of individual. Paradigms, perspectives and practices, Study guide for psychology students.*] Moscow, Russia: Akademia.

People's Commissariat of Education of the Ukrainian SSR. (1931). Postanova Kolegii NKO URSR "Pro zagalne oboviazkove navchannia defektyvnykh ditei ta pidlitkiv" (10.07.1931 r.) // Buleten Narodnogo Komisariatu osvity URSR [Resolution of the Collegium of the People's Commissariat of Education of the Ukrainian Soviet Socialist Republic "On compulsory universal education of defective children and adolescents" of

July 10, 1931]. *Bulletin of the People's Commissariat of Education of the Ukrainian Soviet Socialist Republic*, p. 49.

People's Commissariat of Education of USSR (1922). *Zbirnyk dekretiv, postanov, nakaziv, rozporiadzhen' po Narodnomu Komisariatu osvity USSR*. [*Directives, Resolutions, Orders, and Instructions adopted by the People's Commissariat of Education of the Ukrainian Soviet Socialist Republic.*] Kharkiv, Ukraine: Soviet Socialistic Republic.

Petrovskyi, V. V., Radchenko, L. O., & Semenenko, V. I. (2007). *Istoria Ukrainy: Neuperedzhenyi pogliad: Fakty, Mify, Komentari.* [*History of Ukraine: An unbiased view: Facts, myths, comments.*] Kharkiv, Ukraine: Shkola.

Rogers, C. (1969). *Freedom to learn: A view of what education might become.* Columbus, OH: C. E. Merrill Pub. Co.

Rubtsov, V. V. (1996). *Osnovy sotsialno-geneticheskoy psikhologii.* [*Fundamentals of social and genetic psychology.*] Moscow, Russia: Institute of Practical Psychology and Voronezh, NPO MODEK.

Shcherbyna, A. M. (1916, March 16). Neudovletvorennaya potrebnost slepykh v prosveshchenii [The unmet need for the blind for education]. *Russkie vedomosti. [Russian Bulletin.]*, *62*, A2–A3.

Shcherbyna, A. M. (1927). Rol' vrachei v dele vospitania slepykh [The role of medical professionals in the education of the blind]. *Trudy 1-go Vsesouzh. s'yezda glaznykh vrachei. Proceedings of the 1st all-union congress of ophthalmologists.* Moscow, Russia (pp. 72–75).

Shklovskyi, M. L. (1938). *Printsypy komplektovania shkol dlia detei s rasstoistvami slukha i rechi [Guidelines for placing children to special schools concerned with hearing and speech disorders].* Abstract of the report made at the pan-Russian meeting on the issues related to education and upbringing of deaf-and-mute children. Moscow, Russia.

Shklovskyi, M. L. (1939). Klassifikatsia i differentsialnaya diagnostika rasstroistva slukha i rechi v detskom vozraste [Classification and differential assessment of hearing and speech disorders in children]. In M. L. Shklovskyi (Ed.), *Klassifikatsia i differentsialnaya diagnostika glukhonemoty, glukhoty i tugoukhosti.* [Classification and differential assessment of deaf-muteness, deafness and partial hearing loss *(Part 1)*.] Leningrad, Russia: Kargosizdat.

Sikorskyi, I. A. (1904). *O lechenii i vospitanii nedorazvitykh, umstvenno otskalykh i slaboumnykh detei.* [*On treatment and education of underdeveloped, mentally retarded and weak-minded children.*] Kyiv, Ukraine: I.N. Kurshev & Co.

Siropolko, S. (2001). *Istoria osvity v Ukraini.* [*History of education in Ukraine.*] Kyiv, Ukraine: Naukova dumka.

Skinner, B. F. (1989). The school of the future. In B. F. Skinner (Ed.), *Recent issues in the analysis of behavior* (pp. 85–96). Columbus, OH: Merrill.

Sokolyanskyi, I. (1925). Pro metodyku pratsi v komdytgrupakh i ustanovakh sotsvykhu [On the methods of organizing work in children's community groups and social education institutions]. *Radianska osvita. [Soviet Education.]*, *12*, 23–35.

Sokolyanskyi, I. P. (1928a). Ustanova dlia slipoglukhonimykh na Ukraini [The institution for blind deaf-mutes in Ukraine]. *Vsesvit*, *21*, 14–15.

Sokolyanskyi, I. P. (1928b). Deshcho z osnovnykh pytan' radianskoi pedagogiky [Selected main issues of Soviet pedagogy]. *Radianska osvita. [Soviet Education.]*, *12*, 6–12.

Steiner, R. (1975). *The education of the child in the light of anthroposophy.* London: Rudolf Steiner Press.

Talyzina, N. F. (1998). *Pedagogicheskaya psikhologia*. [*Pedagogical psychology*.] Moscow, Russia: Akademia.

Taranchenko, O. M. (2007). *Systema spetsialnogo navchannia ditei zi znyzhenym slukhom v Ukraini (istorychnyi aspect): Monographia*. [*System of special education for children with hearing impairments in Ukraine: A historical perspective. A monograph*.] Kyiv, Ukraine: LITO.

Taranchenko, O. M. (2013). *Rozvytok systemy osvity osib z porushenniamy slukhu v konteksti postupu vitchyznianoi nauky ta praktyky: Monographia*. [*Development of the education system for people with hearing impairments: A retrospective view on the evolution of theory and practice in Ukraine. A monograph*.] Kyiv, Ukraine: O.T. Rostunov.

Taranchenko, O. M., Naida, Y. M., & Kolupayeva, A. A. (Eds.). (2012). *Dyferentsiovane vykladannia v inkliuzyvnomu klasi: Navchalno-metodychnyi posibnyk, Seria "Inkliuzyvna osvita."* [*Differentiated instruction in inclusive classroom: Training and methodological guide, Inclusive Education Series*.] Kyiv, Ukraine: ASK.

Tarasevych, M. M. (1922). *Klassifikatsia defektivnykh detei*. [*Classification of defective children*.] Kharkov, Ukraine: Glavsotsvos NKP.

Tarasevych, M. M. (1927). Odeskyi krayevyi collector dlia defektivnykh ditei [Odesa regional collector institution for defective children]. *Shlyakh osvity*. [*The Path of Education*.], *10*, 147–152.

Tarasevych, N. (1929). Odeskiy likarsko-pedagogichnyi cabinet [Medical and pedagogical office in Odesa]. *Shlyakh osvity*. [*The Path of Education*.], *8–9*, 142–146.

Tarasevych, N. N. (1923). Pedagogicheskie instituty, kak samostoyatelnye nauchnye tsentry [Pedagogical schools as independent research centres]. *Put' prosveshchenia*. [*The Path of Education*.], *4*, 126–149.

United Nations. (2006). *United Nations treaty collection 15: Convention on the rights of persons with disabilities*. New York, NY: United Nations.

Vetukhov, V. (1901). *Uchilishche glukhonemykh v Kharkove*. [*School for deaf-mute people in Kharkiv*.] Kharkov, Russia: Prosveshcheniye

Vladimirskyi, A. V. (1922a). Defektivnaya lichnost v idee sotsialnogo vospitania [Defective individual in the context of social education]. *Prosveshchenie i iskusstvo*. [*Education and arts*.], *2–3*, 54–66.

Vladimirskyi, A. V. (1922b). Lichnost v obshchei tsepi yavlenii [Person in the general change of events]. *Put' prosveshchenia*. [*The Path of Education*.], *3*, 10.

Vladimirskyi, A. V. (1927). Kabinet indyvidualnoi pedagogiky v Kyevi [Centre of individualized pedagogy in Kyiv]. *Shlyakh osvity*. [*The Path of Education*.], *10*, 144–147.

Vygotsky, L. S. (1924). K psikhologii i pedagogike detskoi defektivnosti [On psychological and pedagogical approaches with defective children]. In L. S. Vygotsky (Ed.), *Voprosy vospitania slepykh, glukhonemykh i umstvenno otstalykh detei* (pp. 5–30). [*Issues of educating blind, deaf and mute and mentally retarded children*.] Moscow, Russia: SGON NKP.

Vygotsky, L. S. (1991). Problema obuchenia i umstvennogo razvitia v shkolnom vozraste [The issue of education and mental development in school age]. In L. S. Vygotsky (Ed.), *Pedagogicheskaya psikhologia* (pp. 374–391). [*Educational psychology*.] Moscow, Russia.

Vygotsky, L. S. (2003). Printsypy vospitania fizicheski defektivnykh detei [Principles of educating physically defective children]. In L. S. Vygotsky (Ed.), *Osnovy defektologii* (pp. 56–72). [*Fundamentals of special education*.] St. Petersburg, Russia: Lan'.

Zakon Soyuzu Radianskykh Sotsialistychnykh Respublik "Pro zatverdzhennia osnov zakono-davstva SRSR I soyuznykh respublik pro narodnu osvitu" [The Law of the Union of Soviet Socialist Republics "On approving the fundamental principles for the legislation of the USSR and the Union Republics regarding people's education"]. (1973). Radianska Shkola (Vol. 9, p. 3) [Soviet School].

Zakon Ukrainy "Pro okhoronu dytynstva" [The Law of Ukraine "On the Protection of Childhood"]. (2001). Vidomosti Verkhovnoi Rady (Vol. 30, p. 9) [Gazette of the Ukrainian Parliament].

Zakon Ukrainy "Pro osvitu" [The Law of Ukraine "On Education"] (1991). Vidomosti Verkhovnoi Rady (Vol. 34, p. 7). [Gazette of the Ukrainian Parliament].

Zakon Ukrainy "Pro zagalnu seredniu osvitu" [The Law of Ukraine "On Comprehensive Secondary Education"] (1991). Vidomosti Verkhovnoi Rady (Vol. 28, p. 3). [Gazette of the Ukrainian Parliament].

Zankov, L. V. (1981). Obuchenie i razvitie [Education and development]. In L. V. Zankov (Ed.), *Khrestomatia po vozrastnoi i pedagogicheskoi psikhologii* (pp. 21–26). [*Reader on developmental and pedagogical psychology.*] Moscow, Russia: Moscow State University.

SPECIAL EDUCATION TODAY IN RUSSIA

Iuliia Korolkova

ABSTRACT

Recently, the interaction of mass education and the education of people with disabilities has been widely discussed in Russia. This is positive aspect because for a long time these systems were isolated from the other. There are a lot of reasons for such isolation including the political processes in Russia, the peculiarities of the educational system, and the education and training of general and special education staff.

Lately, some positive tendencies in the development of special education have developed; however, it still needs to be accelerated. For example, recently, a series of legal documents defining the fundamental rights of people with disabilities have occurred as well as the adoption of a state regulatory policy in relation to them. The new law on education, which clearly defines the concepts that had not been fixed in any normative act earlier, has come into force and has improved the opportunities for people with disabilities not only to provide secondary education but also to expand the opportunities for vocational education for them. However, there is still a lot of work to be done.

Special Education International Perspectives: Practices Across the Globe
Advances in Special Education, Volume 28, 353–373
Copyright © 2014 by Emerald Group Publishing Limited
All rights of reproduction in any form reserved
ISSN: 0270-4013/doi:10.1108/S0270-401320140000028018

This chapter will present the system of special education in Russia as it has been shaped throughout the years and will describe the prospects for continued development and existing problems. It should be noted that the Russia's disability system involves persons with physical and mental impairments for which it has been difficult or impossible to provide education in general education classes.

HISTORY OF THE ESTABLISHMENT OF SPECIAL EDUCATION IN RUSSIA

In Russia, as in other countries, the historical development of a national system of special education was closely associated with (a) the socio-economic conditions in the country, (b) the level of cultural development of society, and (c) the legislation related to education. It is also important to note that the basis for the development of a national special education system in Russia and in the world is a reflection of the attitude of the state and the society of people with disabilities. On the basis of the above, the author describes five periods of special education evolution that cover a time span of two and a half millennia.

First Period: Intolerance to Understanding

The first period of evolution moved from aggression and intolerance to understanding of the necessity to care for persons with disabilities. A close examination of the history and culture of Kievan Rus' indicates that the pagan Slavs did not show aggression and hostility toward people with disabilities which occurred in Western European societies, but rather treated them with compassion and tolerance. Furthermore, the Kievan princes treated orphans and the poor with mercy and persons with disabilities were cared for by the church and they were given some income. This treatment was connected to the Byzantine system of monastic charity that had been prepared by the national cultural traditions. Therefore, the hallmark of this period is that in Russia, unlike in Western Europe, the period of aggression and intolerance toward people with disabilities was replaced with understanding, charity, and care.

This environment of charity was greatly enhanced by Peter I. He was responsible for creating a secular system of charity (Malofeev, 2010a,

2010b). His reign occurred during a period of forced and radical Europeanization of Russia. During this period, however, Russia lacked a broad network of church shelters and there was a lack of city governments. The lack of city governments stalled the European introduction of rest homes for the disabled. During this period there were no civil rights institutions or specialists to administer and supervise rest homes and secular and religious authorities stayed inactive. Positively, the above flaws were offset by a compassionate attitude of all social groups toward people with impairments.

Domestic zakonoulozhenie was the prevailing legal status. However, unlike Roman law and the subsequent European legislation, it did not address the status of people with severe disabilities until almost the 16th century. In fact, the first regulation of life for disabled people was introduced by "Stoglavy Sudebnik" (1551). It prescribed legislation aimed at protecting the "unblemished majority" from the "defective minority" by placing the deaf (believed to be bound by demons) in monasteries.

Second Period: Care of the Disabled

The second period of evolution covered the Russian society's awareness for the need to care for the disabled as well the understanding to provide opportunities to teach deaf and blind children. This period saw the movement of persons with disabilities from living in community shelters to having individual learning experiences in special schools. The first educational schools (Deaf −1806, Blind − 1807) were established in Petersburg when Alexander I invited the French visual specialist Valentine Hauy to Russia. While this movement began later in Russia than in Europe, it quickly ended in the national precedent for opening of the first special schools across Russia. Because there was a serfdom system in Russia at that time, it was almost impossible to discuss the social status of people with disabilities (Ermakov & Yakunin, 1990).

Peter I did not find much support in matters of charity for the disabled and budding innovations in the matters of state social policy withered during the reign of Anna Ivanovna. Unfortunately, everything conceived by the reformer remained on paper and the government forgot about it. After Peter, charity was not popular, and the charity traditions weakened, and the new ideas about care and creating learning opportunities could not take root.

With the arrival of Catherine the Great, the Russia government acquired all types of charitable institutions similar to those in Protestant countries. However, a genuine development of secular charity was difficult due to the vast territory of the Russian Empire and the absence of preconditions in the country.

Third Period: Development of Teaching and Special Schools

The focuses of the third period of evolution involved an awareness of teaching opportunities for children with sensory impairments, the recognition of the right to education for children with abnormalities and the development of a special education system. These focuses started at the beginning of the 19th century. During this period, positive attitudes of the public toward people with disabilities occurred and the first specialized institutions for the blind and deaf children were opened (Ermakov & Yakunin, 1990; Golovchits, 2001). Funding for these institutions was through charity and was beyond the scope of the domain of the government. Positively, Alexander's I liberal reforms led to a surge in charity. However, during the reign of Nicholas', the network of charitable institutions slowed considerably due to restrictions of freedom and persecution for dissenters. The situation improved considerably with the reign of Alexander's II and his reforms which included the abolition of serfdom, the establishment of municipal government, and the judicial reform. His reign created the development of philanthropy. Unfortunately, the development of special education was not under state control as such there was no regulatory framework.

At the turn of the 19th century, Russia experienced a growth in the number of hearing and visual impairment specialists'. Because of the success by these specialists in working with hearing and visually impaired students, physicians, teachers, and community leaders decided to teach people with cognitive impairments (Zhigoreva, 2006). This state of affairs was considered to be the beginning of a special education system in Russia. Once this occurred, legislation on universal compulsory primary education was passed. Furthermore, this universal conscription led to the inevitable reflection by the government and society of the presence of children and adults with cognitive impairments. The organization of a network of educational institutions for children with cognitive impairments began shortly after the above legislation (Baryaeva & Zarin, 2001). Prior to this organization of institutions, no attempts by teachers were made to educate individuals with cognitive impairments in Russia and any teaching that was carried out was by physicians. Positively, from this movement, the Russian Society of Psychiatrists organized a network of institutions for children with mental illness in 1908 (Aksenov, Arkhipov, & Whites, 2004).

Special education in Russia changed dramatically after the revolution of 1917. The revolution led to a change in the political system and Russia was in a crisis due to the civil war. The institutions which were established for children with mental illness were taken over by governmental agencies. All charity and philanthropy was strictly prohibited by the government. The new government saw the purpose of education of children with disabilities as an important political goal to develop them as socially useful citizens. Thus, the formation of Russian special education developed into a monarchical socialist state with totally different values, goals and ethical standards.

Fourth Period: Understanding the Need for Special Education

The fourth period of special education evolution was concerned with its movement away from the awareness of the necessity of special education for certain categories of children with impairments to the understanding of the need of special education for all who needed it. This period, as well as the previous ones, is full of contradictions in the development and establishment of special education. The main contradiction is that the Soviet Union announced the care for defective children a priority, but did not constrain the expansion of the network of special institutions.

This period is characterized by the widespread development and differentiation of the system of special education, the introduction of new types of educational institutions for children with disabilities, and the extension of the age range of special education up to preschool and after school. Unfortunately, the development of special education was interrupted twice by world wars. During this period, a national law on special education was not adopted in the USSR. Further, special education specialists were not evenly distributed across the country. For example, in some large regions, there are no special education institutions or speech pathologists. Also, there was a political tendency to keep a close secret on the state of special education system from the media.

However, the development of the special education field continued to grow against the backdrop of social and economic growth. For instance, research on the methods to diagnosis and remediate impairments was undertaken, the need for education of children with all disabilities was recognized, and special educational institutions for children with disorders of the musculoskeletal system, emotional, and behavioral disorders were added across the USSR.

Classification System
During this period, a classification evolved from the historically shaped system of educational institutions for children with disabilities. Classification focuses on a system of special education categories related to the specific characteristics exhibited. The classification includes the following disabilities categories: deaf; hard of hearing; late hard of hearing; blind; visually impaired; impaired function of the musculoskeletal system; emotional-volitional impairments; intellectual disabilities; cognitive impairments (learning difficulties); severe speech disorders; and complex developmental disabilities. Also, there is a more generalized classification, which is based on the grouping of the above categories of defects in accordance with the localization of them in a particular system of the body: physical (somatic) disorders (musculoskeletal system, chronic diseases); sensory impairments (hearing, vision); disorders of the brain (mental retardation, movement disorders, mental and speech disorders) (Aksenov et al., 2004).

Medical and social assessments determine the level of disability in accordance with which the individual rehabilitation program is built upon. Persons assigned to group one are considered disabled with persistent and significantly expressed body defects. They have deficits in the ability for self-care, movement, orientation in the surrounding environment, and the ability to control their actions may be impaired. Persons assigned to group two are disabled due to expressed and persistent health problems that lead to learning, employment, and self-care disabilities. Persons assigned to group three are disabled due to persistent but not significant or moderately expressed body impairments.

Types of Schools
Beginning in the 1950s, the special education schools in Russia have been differentiated within five types, namely, deaf, hard-of-hearing, blind, visually impaired, and cognitively impaired. Since 1954, the number of special schools has doubled because of new types of education and training methods. Beginning in the late 1970s and early 1980s, special elementary classrooms for children with cognitive impairments began to appear in regular schools. At the end of the 1980s, the first experimental classroom for children with severe cognitive impairments appeared in regular schools. By

1990, the total number of special schools was 2,789 (approximately 575 thousand students) and the network of preschools developed rapidly and there are more than 300,000 children with developmental disabilities in these programs (Russian Ministry of Labor, 2013).

Fifth Period: Equal Opportunities and Integration

The fifth stage of special education evolution involved moving from equal rights to equal opportunities and from the "institutionalization" of students with disabilities to the integration of students with disabilities. The main focus during this period focused on the integration of the people with disabilities into social life. The onset of the fifth period was not a logical continuation of the development of Russia society, but the result of one more reorganization of the government and a rethinking of the countries values. The government wanted to develop a special education model specially designed for Russia. This was due in part because in the previous period the system of special educational institutions and enrollment of children into special classes in regular schools, which was to a large extent modeled after the European model, was not achieved. From that endeavor, it became clear that Russia needed to develop its own model, which would promote integration but not result in a haphazard reduction of special educational institutions.

In developing its domestic education pedagogy model, the scientific activities of Vygotsky (1896–1934) were considered. Vygotsky had laid the foundations of modern special education His fundamental theoretical principles included: (a) the concept of the structure of a defect (the basic defect and related disorders); (b) biological and social unity (at the prevailing social role) in the concept of "defect"; (c) the defect and the possibility of its compensation; (d) the idea of the unity of the laws of development of normal and abnormal children; (e) the conception of qualitative uniqueness in the development of an abnormal child; (f) the postulation of the unevenness and selectivity in intelligence impairments (in mental retardation); and (g) the unity of intelligence impairments and affect (in mental retardation) (Malofeev, 2010a, 2010b). These important theoretical conceptions were utilized by Russian researchers to establish: (a) the important principles of special education and diagnosis of abnormal development, (b) the principle of using detours in teaching and development, (c) collective education, (d) structural and dynamic study of mental activity, and (e) the all-around, comprehensive study of the abnormal child's psychic state. Currently, these principles are applied in Russia's era of change and reform. This applies to the education of nondisabled children and those with disabilities.

PREVALENCE OF STUDENTS WITH DISABILITIES

The variety of classifications to some extent hinders the statistical treatment of data of people with disabilities. Problematic is the fact that the term "children with disabilities" is applied to a sufficiently large number of students with various physical and psychological disabilities. Previously, reported data on persons with disabilities was carried out by describing a category of children with terms such as "mentally retarded children," "emotionally disturbed children," and "behaviorally abnormal children." Nowadays, for ethical reasons these terms are not used because they undermine the dignity of these children.

The prevalence of people with disabilities is important and interesting. Here are some statistics provided by the Ministry of Labor Decree for the last 5 years: the number of people with disabilities of Type I and III groups has been steadily increasing; and the number of people with disabilities in Group II has been reducing. From the data, one can assume that the reduction in Group II is a positive tendency, however, one may need to consider the fact that in recent years the criteria of disability assessment has changed, and this could have led to a redistribution of people over Groups I and III (Russian Ministry of Labor, 2013).

The Ministry's data relating to children less than 18 years of age arouses ones attention. The data shows that in 2012 the number of children with congenital disorders is the most. While among children with behavior disorders it remains unchanged possibly due to the government's greater emphasis of attention on early diagnosis and prevention of defects.

In 2012, 1.6 million Russian children (4.5% of the total number of children), belonged to the category of people with disabilities and need special education appropriate to their special educational needs. Of these, 352,900 children attend Groups (I, II, and III) and preschool educational institutions of compensating types. Moreover, 63.6% of these students with disabilities regularly communicate and interact with nonhandicapped children who are in preschool institutions. In total, 277,700 school age children with special educational needs go to special educational establishments for children with hearing, vision, musculoskeletal, speech impairments, and cognitive impairments. A total of 203,000 students go to special schools,

2,500 students are taught in comprehensive schools, 2,500 students needing long-term care are taught in 145 health educational sanatoriums, and 34,000 students are taught at home and in schools with individual instruction. Only 38% of children with developmental disabilities are integrated into the regular education environment. Data provided by the Ministry of Education and Science of the Russian Federation indicates that there is a growth of children attending regular educational institutions over time (Russian Ministry of Labor, 2013).

CURRENT SYSTEM OF SPECIAL EDUCATION IN RUSSIA

Today in Russia, the problem of educating children with disabilities is becoming increasingly more relevant because legislation acts mandate that a child with a disability has the right to be educated in special and comprehensive schools or at home by their parents. A comprehensive school can offer a student with disability opportunities that include education in: (a) a regular class, (b) a class for remedial developmental training, (c) a class for children in need of special education, and (d) their home. There is considerable education debate among Russian special education professionals regarding the best practice to educate students with special needs. Some experts say that there is a need for education in special environments while some would argue the opposite, defending the idea of educating them in conjunction with normally developing peers. Currently across the globe, the idea of integrating children with special needs into mainstream schools is widely implemented. Positively, various forms of integration (combined, partial, temporary, and full) have been developed in Russia as well. The positive evidence for integration as an approach to teach children with developmental delays, social deficits, and psychological and pedagogical conditions comes from a number of studies (Aksenov, Arkhipov, & Belyakova, 2001).

Currently in Russia, the most important philosophy in general and special education in particular, is humanization. This philosophy can be valuable in overcoming the anonymity of special education. The philosophy stresses that schools make the student with a disability the center of attention and incorporate educational strategies to meet needs and interests. Based on the requirements of modern life in Russia and the challenges of integrated education, the interests and needs of the students with special needs and their parents becomes paramount to their future success in the community. Accepting this philosophy and emphasis, necessitates that teachers in Russia significantly upgrade the instructional intervention and adopt curriculum geared toward the students' needs and interests. Knowing the current state of special education in Russia today, it is obvious that Russia needs to development of a new teaching ideology in the field of special education as well as redesigning the standard curriculum for children with disabilities.

The fact that the government's attitude toward people with disabilities has changed is of special significance. Across the globe, the rights of children with disabilities are governed by domestic legislation, international conventions and United Nations agreements. The legislation of the Russian Federation in the field of education is in accordance with international standards that guarantees equal rights to education for people with disabilities and disabled people. As evidence of Russia's compliance with these standards, Table 1 describes three approaches to teaching children with special educational needs.

Table 1.   Approaches to Teaching Children with Disabilities in Russia.

1. Differentiated instruction for children with speech, hearing, vision, musculoskeletal, intellect impairments, and with cognitive disabilities in special institutions.

There are eight types of special schools for different categories of children with developmental disabilities:

• Special educational institution Type I (boarding school) for deaf children.
• Special educational institution Type II (boarding school) for hard-of-hearing children.
• Special educational institution Type III (boarding school) for blind children.
• Special educational establishments Type IV (boarding school) for visually impaired children.
• Special educational institution Type V (boarding school) for children with severe speech disorders.
• Special educational institution Type VI (boarding school) for children with disorders of the musculoskeletal system.
• Special educational establishments Type VII (boarding school) for children with cognitive impairments.
• Special (remedial) educational establishments Type VIII (boarding school) for children and adolescents that are cognitively impaired.

Children with moderate cognitive impairments are organized in Type VIII schools while children with lower intelligence are organized in schools Types I–IV.

2. Integrated education of children with disabilities in comprehensive schools.

3. Conjoined education when children with special educational needs are taught in the classroom with normal children (Kaliagin, Matasov, & Ovchinnikova, 2005).

Today, the Russian system of education for children with special educational needs is on the verge of inevitable change. The educational integration of students with special needs, for more than a decade, has been mainly put into practice in Russia through experimental transfer and adaption to domestic conditions and modification of some well-established and proven forms of educational integration from other countries. However, now the organization of special education for children with disabilities in regular preschool institutions, comprehensive and other educational institutions, together with other children is considered to be a priority.

INCLUSION AND STUDENTS WITH DISABILITIES IN RUSSIA

Today, Russia has more than 2 million children with disabilities (8% of all children). About 90,000 children have physical impairments, which makes their travel and access to social and educational resources difficult (Russian Ministry of Labor, 2013). To expand the access to education for children with disabilities who need to be taught at home, distance education of children with disabilities is being intensively developed in Russia. The systematic implementation of inclusive (conjoined) education is being introduced in Russia very slowly and irregularly. In some regions (Moscow, Samara, and Arkhangelsk), these processes have been well advanced while in other regions they are only beginning to emerge.

The Ministry of Education and Science of the Russian Federation reported that from 2008 through 2010, inclusive education models were implemented on a trial basis in the educational institutions of various types in several Russian regions, including Moscow, Arkhangelsk, Samara region, the capital of the Republic of Buryatia, Ukhta (Komi Republic), the Republic of Karelia (Petrozavodsk, Sortavala), Tomsk, Voronezh, St. Petersburg, Khabarovsk, and the North Caucasus republics (Russian Ministry of Labor, 2013). The development of inclusive education in Russia is mostly carried out in partnerships between government agencies and non-governmental organizations. The initiators of including children with disabilities in the learning process in regular educational institutions were associations of parents of children with disabilities, organizations advocating for the rights and interests of people with disabilities, and professional societies and educational institutions.

Reforming of any social system, including special education, involves the development of the necessary legal framework for this process.

Nowadays, the inclusive education in Russia is regulated by (1) the Constitution of the Russian Federation, (2) the Federal Law "On Education," (3) the Federal Law "On Social Protection of Disabled People in the Russian Federation," and (4) the Convention on the Rights of the Child and the Protocol No. 1 of the European Convention on Human Rights and Fundamental Freedoms. In 2008, Russia signed the United Nations Convention "On the Rights of People with Disabilities." In addition, the Russian Health Ministry has developed a draft concept of the federal target program "Accessible Environment" for years 2011–2015. The concept of "accessible environment" includes not only the adaptation of the physical environment, but a number of other issues including teachers training, the change in the system of additional support, and support to the individual.

An examination of the state of higher education for people with disabilities in the Russian Federation reveals profound changes in its organization and content. These changes were caused by some sustained trends in social policy and the emergence of a new holistic and semantic vocational education endeavors. In Russia, only a small number of universities focus on teaching individuals with disabilities. The focus is mainly for students with sensory impairments or movement disorders. More than 24,000 people with disabilities are enrolled in state universities and more than 34,000 thousand are taught in special secondary schools (Russian Ministry of Labor, 2013). The question of university involvement in the professional self-determination of people with intellectual disabilities is being asked.

CURRENT ISSUES AND INDIVIDUALS WITH DISABILITIES

There is still a big problem with the employment of people with disabilities. According to governmental statistics, the Russian Federation is home to about 10 million people with disabilities yet only 13–15% of them have permanent jobs. Moreover, the number of persons with disabilities, who have completed program of higher professional integrated education, that have employment does not exceed 60%.

There still remains the problematic issue of dilution of the concepts of "integration" and "inclusion." Some experts state that these concepts are identical, but more and more practitioners are inclined to the position that they are different concepts, especially in the areas of focus. The classification of defects is one of the challenging issues in special education and psychology in Russia. Mental impairments or lack of mental development may occur at any point in a person's life, and can develop and grow over time. The defect can be eliminated or decreased (in whole or in part) with the help of medicine or educational intervention. Further related to this issue is the lack of statistical treatment data with children with disabilities. No absolutely clear and comprehensive statistics in Russia's public records has yet been presented.

Social rehabilitation of people with disabilities is one of the most important and difficult tasks for the modern special education assistance system developed in Russia. Unfortunately, even with the positive trends in the development of special education, the public awareness of the problems people with disabilities have is limited. One of the critical problems is working with the family of persons with disabilities. This problem is complicated due to the lack of special education specialists and the poor communication with the family by educational and health services providers. Therefore, parents, being in the situation of having a child born with special needs are often left to solve problems all by themselves. New service trends and models of care that are occurring in global societies are increasingly requiring us to deal with these issues. Unfortunately, the existing system shows that teachers very often become involved with a child with special needs only when he/she is enrolled or is enrolling in the special educational institution. This practice often results in wasted educational time. Another important issue is when individuals with disabilities turn 18 years old. Under the current legislation anything done prior to the age of 18 years to help the student cannot be implemented after the child turns 18.

Today, there are a lot of citizens who were born and raised in the era of 1990s in Russia. We know it was not the easiest time for nonhandicapped citizens due to changes in the social system, values, lifestyles, mentalities, and education. For persons with disabilities it was even more difficult as they experienced a lack of concern by others, a lack of opportunities to enroll in educational institutions, or engage family members and others about work opportunities.

WORKING WITH THE FAMILY

Children with intellectual disabilities especially those with severe cognitive impairments are the most vulnerable in matters of socialization. Today, these children are at a disadvantage because some comprehensive schools are not fully staffed with specialist such as psychologists and the majority of them dismissed social workers years ago. Therefore, a problem arises in how to organize the systematical work that needs to be carried out with the family when they are placed into a seemingly dire situation of caring for a child with a disability. Russia's rehabilitation system does provide a significant set of services not only for children but also their parents, the family as a whole, and the wider environment. All the services are coordinated in such a way as to assist the individual and the family development and protect the rights of all family members. Help is provided at every opportunity in the natural environment, namely, in the home with the family. However, this does not extend to families with children in institutions.

The rehabilitation system provides a comprehensive plan aimed at the development of the child and the whole family. The plan is developed together with parents, a team of experts, physicians, social workers, teachers, psychologists, and speech pathologists, when possible. For the successful implementation of the plan, a system of activities is worked out for each individual child and family. The activities consider both the health and development of the particular child and the family needs and opportunities. The plan is typically developed six months or for shorter periods, depending on the age and the conditions of the development of the child.

At the end of the plan period, the specialist, who coordinates services for the child and family, meets with parents to discuss the achievements, successes, and what was not achieved. After this meeting, the parents together with the specialist or specialists, design a plan for the next six-month period. Sometimes, parents do not express any desire to cooperate and do not ask for help or advice. Some parents consider rehabilitation services primarily as an opportunity to get a break for themselves as it relieves them from the responsibility of caring for their child and gives this responsibility to the school or rehabilitation institutions.

Psychological-Medical-Pedagogical Committees

In the context of working with families, as well as child support, the question of the child's psychological and medical well-being occurs. Such special care matters are evaluated by the psychological-medical-pedagogical committees (PMPC). Special care as a new educational technology in Russia was developed by Kazakova (2009). She identified several sources for domestic special care system, namely, (1) the experience of comprehensive care and support for children in need of special education, (2) the experience of the special services providing psychological and educational various medical and social support to children (e.g., advisory services, remedial centers, diagnostic centers, service "Trust," and crisis services), (3) the long-term work of psychological, medical, and educational guidance and commissions for children with developmental problems, (4) the experience of coordinating, scientific and methodological expert boards to ensure appropriate development of the child in educational institutions, (5) the communication of studies of various major research universities and research centers, (6) the implementation of international programs to create a system of tracking students' progress in the country, and (7) need for experimental and innovative work of groups of educators, psychologists, and special teachers (Kazakova, 2009).

The establishments of psychological-medical-pedagogical commissions (PMPC) are priority goals and objectives in Russia's modernization of education. The accomplishment of effective PMPC requires the construction of an adequate system of comprehensive psycho-pedagogical, medical, social and legal support for children with problems in development and learning. Under the system of PMPC it is understood there is a three-level organizational structure, which consists of: (1) at the regional level – State Regional psychological-medical-pedagogical consultation within the State educational institution for children in need of psychological, educational, medical and social assistance, which is central with respect to municipal PMPC; (2) at the municipal (district) level – municipal psycho-medical-pedagogical commissions, which are the principal in relation to the psychological, pedagogical consultation of educational institutions; and (3) at the primary level (the level of educational institution) – psychological and pedagogical boards (Kazakova, 2009).

To qualify for the right to define the educational route for children with disabilities, the PMPC passes mandatory examination procedures that are established by the Department of Education. According to the results of the examination, PMPC receives a permit. The activities of the PMPC and its individual units are financed by the budget of the education system of the certain region, municipal (district) educational formations, as well as through the targeted payments on establishment and operation of PMPC. PMPC works in close contact with agencies and organizations of education, health, guardianship authorities, social security, internal affairs agencies and prosecutors, community organizations, and educational institutions providing assistance in the education and development of students and pupils. The main purpose of PMPC is to provide help to children with developmental disabilities on the basis of a comprehensive diagnostic examination and evaluation of the special provisions for their education and adequate health care. Table 2 describes the activities and related tasks of PMPC.

The examination of children by PMPC is done at the municipal level by the recommendation of PMPC of educational institutions. However, it should be noted, in all cases, the consent of parents or legal guardians of the child, who are present during the examination of the child, is necessary. The examination is performed by specialists, individually or collectively. According to the results, a compiled collegial conclusion of PMPC together with the recommendations is issued, taking into account the opinions of each expert. The collegial conclusion consists of conclusions and recommendations. The conclusion is a document confirming the right of children and pupils with developmental disabilities to ensure optimal conditions for their education. PMPC commission's conclusion is the basis for the enrollment of the child (only with the consent of the parents or legal representatives) in a special educational institution.

Table 2.   Tasks Focused on by Activities of PMPC.

1. Timely detection, prevention, and dynamic monitoring of children with developmental disabilities from 0 to 18 years of age.
2. Counseling the children and adolescents attending a PMPC; parents (legal representatives), educational, health and social workers, directly representing the interests of the child in the family and the educational institution on matters within the competence of PMPC.
3. Methodological support at the municipal level – PMP Consilium of educational institutions at the regional level – municipal PMPC.
4. The coordination of interaction of PMPC specialists with special care services of educational institutions, parents (legal representatives) to achieve continuity of rehabilitation.
5. Overseeing the implementation of the PMPC recommendations and monitoring the dynamics of children's development who have been screened under the PMPC.
6. The analysis of its own activities and the activities of PMPC and PMPC of educational institutions at the municipal level and municipal PMPC activities at the regional level (by order/request of the Office/district Department of Education/region).
7. To collect the data about the children and adolescents with developmental disorders.
8. To establish an information database of the institutions, to which parents (legal representatives) may appeal for help when difficulties arise in diagnostic or the aid is inefficient.
9. Participation in educational activities aimed at improving the psycho-pedagogical and medico-social and legal culture (Kazakova, 2009).

Source: http://www.gks.ru/ (Federal Service of Governmental Statistics).

The Educational System

The major components of the process of medical, social and pedagogical patronage are early diagnosis and early comprehensive care. Early diagnosis and early educational assistance are pressing problems for Russia at the moment. Despite the attention of researchers to these problems, the development of the science of special education in general is in its infancy.

Russia also has a number of domestic scientists (e.g., Matyukova, Strebeleva, Pechora, Pantyukhina, and Frucht) who have made a number of methodological recommendations for the development of the science of special education. Their recommendations have focused on programs of early diagnosis and psychological educational assistance to children with developmental disabilities. These scientists have stressed the practical application in psychological, medical and social centers, psychological, medical, and pedagogical consultations (PMPC) (Levchenko & Prihodko, 2001; Strebeleva, Wenger, & Ekzhanova, 2002).

Unfortunately, there are very few institutions providing programs for early diagnosis and early intervention for children with developmental disabilities operating in Russia today. Positively, there is a wide enough differentiated network of preschools for special purposes that include the following: nursery-gardens, kindergartens, preschool children's homes, preschool groups in nursery-gardens, kindergartens and orphanages, as well as in special schools and boarding schools. During the formation and development of special preschools, scholars, and practitioners adopted traditional special education preschool structures, polices, and curriculum. The organizational principles of the special education preschool education are discussed in the next section.

Children are recruited for the special education preschools based on their primary impairment. The special education preschools employ specialists such as special teachers (e.g., blind, deaf, and cognitive impairment), pedagogues for children with oligophrenia, speech therapists, and other health professionals (Mozgovoy, Yakovleva, & Eremina, 2006). The educational process in the special education preschools is carried out in accordance with the special integrated training and education programs designed for each category of preschool children with developmental disabilities and approved by the Ministry of Education of the Russian Federation. Best practice special education standards are implemented in all special educational establishments (Boryakova, 2000; Golovchits, 2001; Smirnov, 2003).

The educational institution designs and implements the curriculum and educational programs which are based on the characteristics of individual developmental needs and abilities of children, taking into consideration the special educational standards. In recent years, special educational institutions for other categories of children with disabilities (e.g., Autistic spectrum disorder traits, and Down's syndrome) have been introduced. The graduates of special educational institutions (except school Type VIII) can receive a state sample of completion which confirms their level of education or a state certificate indicating they have meet the standards of the special educational institutions which they attended (Boryakova & Kasitsyna, 2004; Mamaychuk & Ilina, 2004; Nicholskaya et al., 2003).

By analyzing remedial developmental work with all categories of children, it should be noted that all educational institutions are trying to help all participants' progress in their educational, social, and self-determinate goals. Also, the educational institutions work endlessly in solving the problems of the child and family with the help of various experts. However, the amount of progress that can be made and the number of problems solved is highly correlated with how well the staff has been trained (Shevchenko, 1999; Ulenkova & Lebedeva, 2002; Vodovatov & Bumagina, 2000). Russia is making a serious effort to improve the higher education training of special and general education teachers and specialists. In fact, the entire Russian higher education system is being reformed and rebuilt. This process started after Russia joined the Bologna process. Prior to joining the Bolonga process, there existed a specialist degree in higher education. When a candidate completed this degree, the graduate received a diploma of a specialist. The graduate had the option of continuing their education at the postgraduate level where the graduate could enroll in doctoral studies. Doctoral studies require the candidate to complete a thesis that is submitted to the Scientific Council which recognizes the right of the candidate to have a degree or a doctorate. Now, Russia has a multi-level system of higher education where a candidate can earn an undergraduate, graduate, and postgraduate degree. The doctoral level of education has disappeared and its status is not fixed in Russia's higher education regulations. With this change, the postgraduate school is now regarded as a stage of higher education. Also, students can earn either an academic bachelor degree or an applied bachelor degree. The applied degree is considered to be more practically oriented. It should be noted that this transition to the new system of higher education has led to a reduction of hours for a number of academic subjects, including compulsory ones, while other subjects simply disappeared from the curriculum.

The system of staff specialist (remedial) training in special education evolved over a long period of time and has had difficult developmental periods. Specialists training exist in several forms and as such there are several ways of getting qualifications as a special education specialist, namely, full-time (or day), evening and part-time training, or earning a qualification through upgrading courses and retraining.

It should be noted, that despite the fact that Russia has quite a number of ways of earning special education certifications, staff recruiting on the periphery is considered to be rather topical. For example, universities and institutes that are far from the center of the country don't train all the necessary specialists. Therefore, experts working in the regions are retrained for special education. Positively, in Russia, all special education professionals need to improve their qualifications at least once every 5 years.

CONCLUSION

In general, special education in Russia has progressed a long way the past few decades, but it is still in its infancy. Some of the problems of special education in Russia are already being solved, but many still remain. For example, while education is becoming more accessible to people with disabilities there are many tasks that are not completed due to the introduction of inclusive education. Also, full educational coverage for students with disabilities in rural regions remains problematic. Lastly, a shortage of special education specialists continues to exist and retraining of professionals to be specialists remains difficult.

It is also clear that Russia does not have enough progressive-minded, academically proficient, culturally developed teachers and professors. Part of this is due to inadequate funding of education. Another aspect is the absence of a moral and spiritual stimulus. Being a special education professional requires enormous commitment from those who have taken up these careers and not many people are able to perform such noble deeds every day. There is a need for the Russian government leadership to take ownership of these aspects and help move special education forward.

There is also a need for: (1) a broad public support of special education policy, (2) the restoration of governmental responsibility and a more active role of the government in this area, (3) the state to financially support programs that are comprehensive, and (4) a more efficient use and coordination of available resources. In addition, all Russian citizens need to develop ethical and moral responsibility for education in general as well as promote laws aimed at improving education. Positively, the recent documents defining the development strategy of general education in Russia ("New School" national project "Education") arouse a certain hope, as the intended objectives correspond to the needs of our society. Hopefully, the Russian modernization of education, in our case, special education, will not be in vain and soon everyone who works in this field or are its consumers will feel these improvements.

REFERENCES

Aksenov, L. I., Arkhipov, B. A., & Belyakova, L. I. (2001). Integration as an approach to teach students with disabilities. In N. M. Nazarova (Ed.), *Special pedagogy: Textbook for teacher training university students* (2nd ed.). Moscow, Russia: Publishing Center "Academiya".

Aksenov, L. I., Arkhipov, B. A., & Whites, L. I. (2004). Educating individuals with cognitive impairments. In N. M. Nazarova (Ed.), *Special pedagogy: Textbook for teacher training university students* (3rd ed.). Moscow, Russia: Publishing Center "Academiya".

Baryaeva, L. B., & Zarin, A. (2001). *Teaching children with intellectual impairments subject-role-play: Guidance notes.* St. Petersburg, Russia: Herzen State Pedagogical University of Russia.

Boryakova, N. Y. (2000). *A step in development. Children's early diagnosis and correction of mental retardation: Guidance notes.* St. Petersburg, Russia: Gnom-Press.

Boryakova, N. Y., & Kasitsyna, M. A. (2004). *Correctional and pedagogical work in the kindergarten for children with mental retardation (Organizational aspect).* Moscow, Russia: Tvorcheskiy Tsentr Sfera.

Ermakov, V. P., & Yakunin, G. A. (1990). *Development, training and education of children with visual impairments: Reference handbook for teachers.* Moscow, Russia: Prosvescheniye.

Golovchits, L. A. (2001). *Preschool surdopedagogy: Education and training of preschool children with hearing impairment: Guidance notes for university students* (pp. 252–261). Moscow, Russia: Humanity Publishing Center VLADOS.

Kaliagin, V. A., Matasov, U. T., & Ovchinnikova, T. S. (2005). *How to organize psychological support in educational institutions.* St. Petersburg, Russia: LOIRO.

Kazakova, E. I. (2009). *Basic techniques and technology in the work of the tutor.* Samara, Russia: The Academy.

Levchenko, I. Y., & Prihodko, O. G. (2001). *Technology training and education of children with disorders of the musculoskeletal system: Textbook for secondary teacher training institutions.* Moscow, Russia: Publishing Center "Academiya".

Malofeev, N. N. (2010a). *Special education in a changing world* (Vol. 1). *Textbook for teacher training university students.* Moscow, Russia: Prosvescheniye.

Malofeev, N. N. (2010b). *Special education in a changing world* (Vol. 2). *Textbook for teacher training university students.* Moscow, Russia: Prosvescheniye.

Mamaychuk, I. I., & Ilina, M. N. (2004). *Psychologist's help to a child with mental retardation. Scientific and practical guidance.* St. Petersburg, Russia: Rech.

Mozgovoy, V. M., Yakovleva, I. M., & Eremina, A. A. (2006). *Basics of oligophrenopedagogics.* Moscow, Russia: Publishing Center "Academiya".

Nicholskaya, O. S., Baenskaya, E. R., Liebling, M. M., Costin, I. A., Vedenina, M. Y., Arshatsky, A. V., … Arshatkaya, O. S. (2003). *Autism: Age, characteristics and psychological assistance.* Moscow, Russia: Terevinf.

Russian Ministry of Labor. (2013). *Russian military of labor data.* Moscow, Russia: Russian Ministry of Labor.

Shevchenko, S. G. (1999). *Correction and development: Organizational and pedagogical aspects: Guidance notes for teachers working in remedial developmental teaching.* Moscow, Russia: Humanity Publishing Center VLADOS.

Smirnov, I. A. (2003). *Special education preschool children with cerebral palsy. Textbook– Guidance notes.* St. Petersburg, Russia: Detstvo-Press.

Strebeleva, E. A., Wenger, A. L., & Ekzhanova, E. A. (2002). *Special preschool pedagogy: Textbook.* Moscow, Russia: Publishing Center "Academiya".

Ulenkova, U. V., & Lebedeva, O. V. (2002). *Organization of special psychological care for children with developmental problems: Textbook for teacher training university students.* Moscow, Russia: Publishing Center "Academiya".

Vodovatov, F. F., & Bumagina, L. V. (2000). *Organization of activities of remedial educational institutions: Textbook for secondary and university teacher training institutions.* St. Petersburg, Russia: Publishing Center "Academiya".

Zhigoreva, M. V. (2006). *Children with complex developmental disorders: Pedagogical assistance: Textbook for university students.* Moscow, Russia: Publishing Center "Academiya".

PART III
AFRICA

SPECIAL EDUCATION TODAY IN NIGERIA

Festus E. Obiakor and C. Jonah Eleweke

ABSTRACT

*Special education and related services began in Nigeria, the most popu-
lous nation of Black people in the world, only a couple of decades ago
courtesy of the efforts of missionaries from Europe and America.
Although the government took over the responsibility of providing special
education and related services to individuals in the late 1970s, evidence
indicates that the provision of these services is beset by numerous formid-
able obstacles such as the absence of supporting laws, inadequacies in
funding of services, inclusion programs, early identification and intervention services, personnel training programs, facilities, and educational
materials. This chapter discusses these issues and focuses on current
ways to improve the provision of meaningful special education and
related services for people with disabilities in Nigeria.*

Historically, the formal provision of special education and related services
developed in Nigeria only a couple of decades back. Nigeria is a country
located in the west coast of Africa. With an estimated population of over 155

Special Education International Perspectives: Practices Across the Globe
Advances in Special Education, Volume 28, 377–395
Copyright © 2014 by Emerald Group Publishing Limited
All rights of reproduction in any form reserved
ISSN: 0270-4013/doi:10.1108/S0270-401320140000028019

million people, it is the most populous nation of Black people in the world (Index Mundi, 2011). Nigeria's population is greater than that of the other 15 countries in West Africa combined. The country covers an area of 932,768 square kilometers and it is bordered on the north by Niger Republic, on the east by the Republic of Cameroon, on the west by the Benin Republic and on the south by the Atlantic Ocean (Eleweke, 1999a). Like in other developing countries, individuals with disabilities constitute a significant portion of the population due to inadequacies in nutrition, health care, and social services (Lang & Upah, 2008). Evidence is consistent that 80% of people with disabilities in the world live in Nigeria and other developing countries where inadequate nutrition, diseases, accidents, and poverty are common causes of disabilities (Lang, Groce, Kett, Trani, & Bailey, 2009; United Nations, 2011). Clearly, reliable data on the population of people with disabilities in Nigeria are lacking; and no valid census has been conducted in the country since after independence from Britain in 1960 (Obiakor, 1992; Obiakor & Maltby, 1989). However, going by World Health Organization and the World Bank (2011) estimates that disabilities occur in at least 15% of the world's population (i.e., one billion people), it can be assumed that there are at least 22 million people with disabilities in Nigeria.

As it appears, the provision of special education and related services is of immense benefits to the teeming population of people with disabilities in Nigeria. Effective special education and related services ensures that these individuals are able to receive education and services that would help in the development of their talents and contribution to national and global developments. The provision of such services could be achieved by ensuring that educational programs for them adequately address important issues such as early intervention, parent education and participation, personnel training, facilities, effective inclusion programs, funding arrangement, and enabling policies and legislations (Obiakor, Eskay, & Afolayan, 2012). Thus, this chapter looks at the current conditions of special education services in Nigeria. In addition, it discusses future directions of special education in Nigeria.

DEVELOPMENT OF SPECIAL EDUCATION IN NIGERIA

As indicated, the provision of special education and related services as a professional field is only a couple of decades old in Nigeria. This provision was instituted due to efforts by foreign missionaries in early and middle parts of the twentieth century (Obiakor & Bragg, 1998; Obiakor & Offor, 2012; Taiwo, 2007). Prior to the coming of missionaries and their efforts to initiate special education services, individuals with disabilities in Nigeria were neglected and in some instances rejected (Abang, 2005). Among the early Christian Missionaries were the Sudan United Mission (SUM), Roman Catholic Mission (RCM), Church Missionary Society (CMS), the American Southern Baptist Convention, the Seventh Day Adventist Mission, and the Sudan Interior Mission (see, Abang, 2005). Each of these religious organizations established special schools and other "regular" educational institutions. For instance, in 1953, the SUM established the first special school for the blind in Gindiri, Plateau State in Northern Nigeria. The Training Center for the Blind, Ogbomosho (Osun State, Western Nigeria) was established by the Baptist Mission in 1960. Between 1957 and 1962 efforts of the Methodist Mission resulted in the establishment of Schools for the Deaf in Ibadan and Lagos (Abang, 2005; Obiakor & Offor, 2012; Okeke, 2001; Shonibare, 1997). Other pioneer special education institutions established by missionaries included (a) Special Education Center, Orji River (Enugu State, Eastern Nigeria), which was established by the CMS in 1958 to cater for the deaf, blind, physically and mentally challenged; (b) Pacelli School for the Blind, Lagos which the RCM established in 1962 to provide a wide range of academic programs for learners with visual disabilities; and (c) Atunde-Olu School for the Physically Handicapped (sic) Children, Lagos which was established by the Anglican Diocese of Lagos in 1965 to provide educational opportunities for the physically challenged. Based on these details, one can conclude that special education programs in Nigeria were started by the efforts of religious organizations. The major concern of the missionaries was to provide training in crafts, arts, music, and other manual training with few academic subjects in reading, numeracy, and writing to enable individuals with disabilities to acquire the skills to become independent and contributing members of the society (Obiakor, 1992; Obiakor & Maltby, 1989; Okonkwo, 2007).

After the Nigerian civil war in 1970, awash with millions of dollars from crude oil exports, the Federal Government of Nigeria embarked upon massive rehabilitation and re-building programs that included setting up special education programs for the benefit of war veterans and other citizens with disabilities (Obiakor, 2004; Obiakor et al., 2012; Obiakor & Offor, 2012). In 1976, the Federal Government took over all the regular and special schools that were established by foreign missionaries and introduced the Universal Primary Education (UPE) program. The goal was to ensure free primary education for every Nigerian child regardless of disabilities (Obiakor et al., 2012; Obiakor & Offor, 2012; Taiwo, 2007). To demonstrate its seriousness of ensuring the success of the UPE for learners with disabilities in the country, the government established the Federal College of Special Education (FCOE, Oyo) in 1977. In addition, Departments of Special Education were established at federal universities located in Ibadan, Jos, Calabar, Nsukka, and at the Federal Polytechnic, Kaduna (Abang, 2005; Taiwo, 2007). These initiatives began to ensure that special education teachers of all kinds were trained and available to meet the demands of implementing the UPE (Obiakor & Bragg, 1998).

PREVALENCE AND INCIDENCE OF DISABILITIES IN NIGERIA

Reliable and valid data on the incidence and prevalence of disabilities in Nigeria are scanty given that the country has held no valid census since after independence from Britain in 1960. Nonetheless, a recent national baseline survey of persons with disabilities (PWDs) in Nigeria in 2011 by the Federal Ministry of Women Affairs and Social Development (FMWASD) provided some interesting insights. The FMWASD is the ministry responsible for issues affecting PWDs in Nigeria. The survey was necessary because the government recognized that the absence or inadequacy of data on disabilities prevents appropriate policy formulation, planning, and implementation of effective rehabilitation programs. Accordingly, the survey was designed to generate comprehensive data on the size and characteristics of PWDs in Nigeria, to provide appropriate support mechanisms to facilitate the delivery of relevant, effective, and timely services to persons with disabilities. The nation-wide baseline survey, covered 10,648 households in the 36 States of the country and the Federal Capital Territory, Abuja. The data indicated that 95.9% of the Questionnaires/Modules used for the survey were completed and found useable. This meant a great enthusiasm to participate in the survey by PWDs. Further, the report indicated that the response rate was more than 60% in all survey locations.

The data on geographical distribution, spread, and spatial magnitude of PWDs revealed that disabilities are very common in all parts of Nigeria. The report indicated a national average of 3.2% prevalence of PWDs vis-à-vis the national population, thus suggesting that about 15 million

Nigerians are living with one form of disability or the other. The rates of disabilities in the total population were found to vary in the geo-political zones in the country, namely: North-West (5.0%), South-East (4.5%), South-South (3.3%), North-Central (2.6), North-East (2.4%), and the South-West (2.1%). Data from the survey indicated that variations in the gender distribution of PWDs among the geo-political zones with more men than women living with disabilities. Such observation was significantly elevated in the North-West (5.6% vs. 3.5%), South-East (5.3% vs. 3.8%), South-South (3.7% vs. 2.8%) and North-Central (3.4% vs. 2.2%) than North-East (2.8% vs. 2.0%) and the South-West (2.3% vs. 1.6%). Data from the survey indicated that, taking the country as a whole, the majority of the PWDs were living in urban areas (58.6%) as compared to rural areas (41.4%). As per the geo-political zones, the data for the percentages living in urban centers versus rural areas were the South-West (77.1% vs. 22.9%), North-Central (68.2% vs. 31.8%), South-South (61.2% vs. 38.8%), North-West (51.7% vs. 48.3%), and North-East (51.3% vs. 48.7%). The result of urban–rural distribution of PWDs in the South-East was different. There were more PWDs in rural areas (63.8%) than urban areas (36.2%). It remains an issue of concern that majority of PWDs in Nigeria are living in urban areas and depend on begging for alms as the means of survival.

Based on the aforementioned survey, the data indicated that causes of disabilities in Nigeria were mainly traced to *illnesses, accidents, congenital abnormalities,* and *unknown factors*. In the North-Central zone, *illnesses* (60.4%) followed by *congenital abnormalities* (12.7%), *accidents* (12.1%) and *unknown factors* (0.7%) were major causes of disabilities. Similarly, *illnesses* accounted for most of the PWDs in in the North-East (70.1%), North-West (73.2%), South-East (60.2%), South-South (51.0%), and the South-West (64.3%). The data indicated that the causes of disabilities among PWDs in general were: *illnesses* (59.6%); *accidents* (20.1%); *congenital abnormalities* (16.0%); and the *unknown factors* (0.4%). The disabilities of 70% PWDs in the North-East were results of *illnesses* as against 66.8% in the North-West, 56.9% in the South-East, 52.7% in the South-South, and 48.4% in the South-West. Accident-induced disabilities were reported by more in the South-East (22.8%), South-South (22.0%) and South-West (21.6%), than in the North-Central (19.4%), North-East (14.3%), and North-West (12.6%). In addition to investigating the causes of disability, the survey also examined the prevalence of various types of disabilities in Nigeria. The types were *physical disabilities* (27.09%), *deafness/hearing loss* (23.76%), *mental illness* (13.44%), *visual/blindness* (12.22%) and *intellectual disability* (7.26%), *speech defect* (6.41%), *cerebral palsy* (3.68%), the unspecified category of disabilities referred to as *others* (3.11%), and *autism* (3.02%). These rates, however, could be questionable given that they are well below WHO and World Bank (2011) estimates of 15% of the population in developing countries to be PWDs. Apparently; it is only from a valid national census that reliable data on disability issues can be gleaned. Nonetheless, the effort to conduct this aforementioned survey is commendable.

NIGERIA'S NATIONAL POLICY ON EDUCATION

The National Policy on Education (NPE) which was first formulated in 1977 has a section devoted to educational services of individuals with special needs. This policy that was revised in 1981 contains numerous promises concerning the provision of appropriate educational and relevant services to citizens with special needs in Nigeria (Federal Republic of Nigeria, 1981). According to article 55 of the document, the purpose and objectives of special needs provision specifically include:

(a) to give concrete meaning to the idea of equalizing educational opportunities for all children, their physical, mental and emotional disabilities notwithstanding;
(b) to provide adequate education for all handicapped (sic) children and adults in order that they may fully play their roles in the development of the nation; and
(c) to provide opportunities for exceptionally gifted children to develop at their own pace in the interest of the nation's economic and technological development.

To achieve the above goals, the next article in the document highlighted actions that the government would embark upon (see Federal Republic of Nigeria, 1981). These proposed actions noted that:

1. The Federal Ministry of Education will set up a committee to co-ordinate special needs provision in collaboration with the ministries of Health, Social Welfare and Labour.
2. A census of individuals with disabilities in the country will be conducted in order to adequately plan services to meet their needs.
3. Government will accept the responsibility for the training/provision of qualified personnel in all aspects of special needs provision.
4. Government will provide the necessary facilities to ensure effective integration of most learners with special needs and those who are academically gifted in regular educational institutions.
5. The education of individuals with disabilities will be free up to university level.

6. Vocational institutions will be established and suitable employment opportunities will be created for individuals with disabilities.
7. Children's clinics will be attached to most hospitals in order to encourage prevention, early detection, and timely initiation of curative/rehabilitative measurês.
8. A committee on special education and a national council for rehabilitation of individuals with disabilities will be established to ensure full implementation of these programs.

Clearly, the promises in the policy document for individuals with disabilities in Nigeria are lofty. However, with the exception of the training of special education teachers, virtually all other promises of the policy document have remained at the theoretical level (Eleweke, 1999a, 1999b; Eleweke, 2002a, 2002b; Mukuria & Obiakor, 2004; Obiakor, 1992, 2000, 2004; Obiakor et al., 2012; Obiakor & Offor, 2012). Consequently, services for individuals with disabilities in Nigeria remain inadequate and unsatisfactory. For instance, the majority of public buildings such as schools, places of employment, libraries, health and recreation facilities are not accessible to wheelchair users in the country (Hamzat & Dada, 2005). Discussed below are a few important factors accounting for this situation and the unsatisfactory implementation of special education and related services in Nigeria.

Absence of Legislative Support

The provisions of effective special education and related services cannot be achieved without relevant legislations outlining implementation steps. Evidence indicates that Nigeria has no serious civil rights legislation that supports the implementation of special education services or protects the rights of citizens with disabilities to receive specific services (Eleweke, 1999a, 1999b; Hamzat & Dada, 2005; Lang & Upah, 2008). The issues contained in the NPE ought to be important elements of any special education legislation for the country. In the absence of such a law the provisions in the NPE document cannot be implemented for the benefit of Nigerians with disabilities. Interestingly, Nigeria had signed and ratified numerous United Nations Declarations on *Rights of the Disabled* and the *UN Convention on the Rights of People with Disabilities* (United Nations, 2006). The 50 Articles in the *UN Convention* are similar to those in the NPE, although with more details. Their goals are basically the same. A major over-riding goal is that governments should ensure the provision of conditions that should enable people with disabilities to develop to their fullest potential and become productive and contributing members of the society. Clearly, the UN Convention is significant because it is the first internationally legally binding instrument that will hold nations that sign it accountable for appropriate robust policies and effective implementation procedures geared toward upholding the rights and dignities of persons with disabilities (Lang & Upah, 2008; Mukuria & Obiakor, 2004).The question then is, Why will the Nigerian government rectify these international documents that outline actions for enhancing the lives of people with disabilities and not have the political will to enact supporting laws for these individuals? This critical question remains an enigma.

The importance of enabling legislation that ensures the implementation of special education and related objectives such as those contained in the *UN Convention* and NPE cannot be underestimated (Mee & Michael, 2011). Evidence is consistent that mandatory policies and laws are essential to ensure that required services will be provided to individuals with disabilities. Mandatory policies and laws are important in the implementation of policy objectives and provision of services because they are powerful orders that must be obeyed. Clearly, these policies and laws are necessary in Nigeria because they provide: (a) protective safeguards which guarantee the rights of Nigerians with disabilities to receive services specified in the NPE, (b) time of onset and phase plans, (c) consequential effect (i.e., punishment) for non-compliance, (d) room for litigation, (e) accountability, evaluation and monitoring procedures, and (f) financial backing and structure (Eleweke, 1999a, 1999b; Mukuria & Obiakor, 2004; Obiakor, 1992, 2000, 2004; Obiakor & Offor, 2012).

The enactment and implementation of mandatory laws and regulations will greatly facilitate the implementation of goals of the NPE for people with disabilities in Nigeria. To a large measure they provide guidance for the delivery of appropriate special education and related services to individuals with disabilities and guaranteeing their rights to receive these services. Clearly, the key elements of appropriate legislation that would facilitate the implementation of provisions in the NPE document are: (a) clear policy guidelines on provisions, (b) coherent framework for provisions, (c) conduit of resources and guarantee of client satisfaction, and (d) enforcement of provisions. Thus, a framework for implementing and monitoring legislative enactments needs to be developed if they are to have the intended effects. Obviously, without a legislation to support implementation as it is currently the case in Nigeria, provisions in the NPE document may not be mandatory or even obligatory (Lang & Upah, 2008; Obiakor, 2000; Obiakor et al., 2012; Obiakor & Offor, 2012).

Absence of Funding Structure

It is not surprising that since Nigeria has not enacted a law to support the provision of special education and related services, the financial supports necessary for implementation will be lacking. In other words, financial backing and structure for program implementation should be an important component of a law supporting the provision of special education and related services in Nigeria. Evidence indicates that Nigeria has so far made no commitment to give robust financial support to the implementation of the goals of NPE or other services and programs that would enhance the lives of citizens with disabilities (Lang & Upah, 2008). No doubt, a well-structured funding arrangement is desirable for meeting the cost of providing adequate services for these individuals.

Data available on the structure of funding of services for individuals with disabilities in Nigeria are at best scanty. In general, these services are not adequately funded (Barnes & Sheldon, 2010; Lang et al., 2009). Evidence suggests that in Nigeria expenditure on disability programs remains a low priority area (Eleweke, 1999a, 1999b; Garuba, 2003; OnlineNigeria, 2011). Sadly, it has been argued that governments in Nigeria and other developing countries perceive financial investment in the provision of services for individuals with disabilities as a waste (Mba, 1995). These governments consider providing adequate funding for meaningful and qualitative services for individuals with disabilities as a kind of contribution of surplus fund to charity (Mukuria & Obiakor, 2004; Obiakor, 1992, 2000, 2004). Consequently the rights of these individuals to receive services such as those articulated in the NPE document remain a deferred dream.

Lack of Effective Inclusion Programs

Although evidence indicates that most educational institutions for students with special needs in Nigeria are segregated, the need for these learners to be integrated and educated in regular schools is acknowledged. Thanks to numerous United Nations Declarations on the "Rights of the Disabled," inclusive education has been accepted, at least in principle, in Nigeria and many other developing countries (Cherema, 2010; UNESCO, 2009). The question is whether the necessary resources and supports to ensure the success of inclusive programs are available in the country. Clearly, the provision of effective special education and related services for individuals with disabilities requires more inclusive environments to enhance equality and access to programs and services.

The NPE document in Nigeria highlighted the need for people with disabilities to access services and programs in inclusive settings. While there seems to be some awareness that inclusion is necessary to fight discrimination and negative attitude toward people with disabilities, practices seem to continue to foster exclusion. Hence, Part 8 of the NPE document, for instance, considers inclusion as "the most realistic form of special education" for learners with disabilities in the country. Nonetheless, evidence is consistent that inclusion programs, in educational milieu, are not being satisfactorily implemented in Nigeria (Ajuwon, 2008; Garuba, 2003; Obiakor & Bragg, 1998; Obiakor & Offor, 2012). Factors such as the absence of support services, relevant materials and support personnel are major problems that hinder the implementation of effective inclusion of learners with disabilities in Nigerian schools. It is evident that due to architectural barriers, most places of education, employment, and recreation remain inaccessible to wheelchair users (Hamzat & Dada, 2005). Alade (2004) reported that some school administrators in the country would not accept students with physical disabilities even if such students crawl to get around because of architectural barriers. Consequently, many of such learners stay at home and the opportunity to learn is denied to them. In other words, they are denied the chance of developing their skills and contributing their quota to national development.

Lack of Early Identification and Intervention Policies and Programs

The importance of early identification and intervention for effective special needs provision is well documented in the literature (Guralnick & Albertini, 2006; Steele, 2004). Evidence is consistent that early identification and intervention for any form of disability is critical to their early childhood development (Goode, Diefendorf, & Colgan, 2011). It is during this period that the child's social, emotional, physical, and intellectual developments take place. Early identification and intervention are important to facilitate the implementation of programs in the early formative years. Such programs assist children with special needs to realize their maximum potential. Timely identification leads to the initiation of individualized programs, counseling of parents, appropriate school placement, and public awareness campaigns (Derrington, Shapiro, & Smith, 2003). These identification and intervention programs should be planned as ongoing aspects of effective special education programs, which respond to different needs of developing persons at different stages of their development (Mukuria & Obiakor, 2004; Obiakor et al., 2012).

While the importance of early identification and intervention is acknowledged in the NPE document, evidence indicates clearly that in Nigeria early identification and intervention programs are lacking because educational and health services remain grossly inadequate (Muga, 2003; Ogbonna, 1990). Indeed, research suggests that there exists no policy or guidelines on early infant hearing screening in the country (Eleweke, 1997). As a result, children with deafness, for example, are not identified early and provided with the necessary services to facilitate their development. The late detection and resultant delay in the initiation of rehabilitative programs pose adverse consequences for children's language, communication, educational, and socio-emotional developments. Clearly, early identification and intervention programs remain a myth in Nigeria as a result of (a) absence of an enabling policy, (b) financial constraints, (c) limited human resources, and (d) lack of political will.

Inadequate Personnel Training Programs

The provision of effective special education and related services for students with special needs necessitates the involvement of different professionals to assist in the identification, referral, diagnosis, and providing services to these students (Obiakor, 2000, 2004). Such professionals include (a) special needs teachers of different kinds, (b) psychologists, (c) guidance counselors, (d) peripatetic teachers, (e) educational technologists, (f) speech and language therapists, (g) audiologists, and (h) communication support workers such as interpreters and note takers. Research indicates that adequately trained teachers and support personnel of different kinds are necessary to provide meaningful educational services to all students. Almost two decades ago, Prater, Savage-Davis, Fuhler, Marks, and Minner (1997) observed that properly trained, bright, and hard-working staff can improve the chances of any new program to be successful. Through creative staff development, initiatives, and innovative ideas many barriers such as lack of funding and poor physical facilities could be tackled. Well-trained personnel are needed to lead classrooms and promote high academic achievements for learners with special needs. Evidently, effective training programs are required to produce competent professionals needed to work in various aspects of special education and related services.

One of the goals of the NPE that has been put into practice is that of training special education teachers in universities at Ibadan, Jos, Nsukka, Calabar, the Oyo Federal College of Special Education, and the Kaduna Polytechnic to mention a few. However, training programs for specialist personnel such as educational audiologists, psychologists, guidance counselors, educational technologists, speech and language pathologists and communication support workers such as interpreters are not available in many of these institutions (Eleweke, 1999b; Obiakor, 1992, 2000, 2004; Okeke, 1998). Further, concerns remain about the adequacies of the special education teacher training programs in Nigeria in view of the lack of relevant special materials and facilities in the institutions (Eleweke, 1999b). Many years ago, Adima (1988) explained that many of Nigeria's teachers might be incompetent because "special education is a dumping ground for students who have been rejected by other disciplines ....They come into special education as students who have nothing else to do. One of the implications of this is that poor students are offered admission leading to the production of mediocre special education teachers" (pp. 54—55). Data compiled by Adima indicated that between 1974 to 1985 the three main institutions in Nigeria offering training programs for specialist teachers had produced a total of 1,366 teachers of students with special needs (of different categories and levels: certificate, diploma, National Certificate of Education, bachelor degree in education and post graduate), yet only 10% of these teachers were working in institutions for students with special needs. Adima inferred from the data that 90% of the special teachers trained had no interest in working with students with disabilities and that they used their qualifications in special education as "stepping stones" to the realization of other career goals.

Lack of Facilities

The provision of quality special education and related services for students with special needs requires the availability of sufficient varieties of materials and facilities (Obiakor et al., 2012; Obiakor & Offor, 2012). Pertinent questions are: What materials are to be used? Where will they be found? Who will provide them and when? Indicators of sufficiency or availability of facilities and materials for education of students include adequately stocked libraries, science laboratories with the necessary equipment and chemicals, vocational and technical workshops with equipment and devices, adequate dormitories, and recreational facilities.

Available evidence indicates that the necessary equipment and materials for effective instruction to these students are inadequate or non-existent in many educational institutions in Nigeria (Eleweke, 2002a, 2002b). For instance, a survey of educational programs for deaf students in the country indicated that most of the schools lacked libraries, science laboratories, and workshops for vocational training (Eleweke, 2002a). The lack of materials, facilities, and support services in educational institutions affects adversely the success of students with disabilities at all levels (Mukuria & Obiakor, 2004; Obiakor & Offor, 2012). Clearly, this situation suggests that students with special needs in Nigeria are not receiving the right type of education they deserve. The inadequacies in the provision of facilities deprive Nigerian students their right to proper education and makes a mockery of the ideals of equalizing educational opportunities for all children as stated in the NPE document.

FUTURE PERSPECTIVES

It is evident from the foregoing discussions that the provision of special education or related services in Nigeria leaves much to be desired. For the present condition to improve, actions are required in several areas. Despite the prevailing developmental difficulties, economic and political upheaval in the country, improvements in the provision of special education and related services is possible if the government could strive to take appropriate actions and utilize the available resources as efficiently as possible. Most importantly, strong determination by the government characterized by concrete actions rather than mere rhetoric is imperative for marked improvements to occur. Actions are required in the areas that follow in order to achieve this goal (Obiakor, 2000, 2004; Obiakor & Offor, 2012).

It is obvious that the improvements in the provision of special education and related services cannot be achieved without strong legal framework. It is therefore a big challenge to the government in Nigeria to take affirmative actions that would lead to enacting and implementing relevant laws. There has been disability legislation in the works since Nigeria return to civilian rule in 1999. The bill was passed and harmonized by both chambers of the

National Assembly in 2010 but has been awaiting presidential assent (Businessday, 2011). There is an urgent need to enact that law to give legal support to the provision of special education and related services in Nigeria. Enacting this law will give impetus to improving services for Nigerians with disabilities so that they could develop their potential and contribute to national development (Obiakor & Maltby, 1989; Obiakor et al., 2012; Obiakor & Offor, 2012).

If improvements are to manifest in the implementation of meaningful and effective special education programs in Nigeria, it is essential that all educational institutions in the country be adequately equipped and staffed to welcome all learners regardless of abilities or disabilities. It remains a challenge to the Nigerian government and educational authorities to ensure that schools are provided with facilities necessary for the implementation of meaningful special education and related services. The government should encourage selected firms in the country, for instance, by providing necessary incentives such as tax breaks and inexpensive lands for expansion, to boost the production of educational equipment and materials. The goal must be to ensure that all schools are adequately equipped for the implementation of meaningful special education programs in the country.

Given the ever-increasing population of the country, there is a need to establish more teacher training programs to ensure that all schools are adequately staffed for the effective implementation of special education programs for all learners with special needs. If improvement is to be achieved in the country, it is imperative that these training institutions develop programs for the training of support staff such as interpreters for deaf people, educational audiologists, educational psychologists, speech and language therapists, and guidance counselors. More institutions of higher learning in the country must be equipped and upgraded to offer programs for training these professionals. These training institutions should consider the use of the UNESCO Teacher Resource Pack (Ainscow, 1994) in their training programs. The pack has been specifically designed to facilitate the training of teachers for implementing inclusive education by restructuring schools and classrooms along inclusive lines so that the needs of all learners could be identified and addressed. Mittler (2000) reported that the pack is now in use in over 50 countries in both pre-service and in-service training programs and it has been translated into 15 languages. The pack clearly has been found to be extremely useful and thus could assist greatly in teacher training programs to improve special education services in Nigerian schools.

It is recommended that the Nigerian government give adequate attention to the issue of making services *accessible* and *inclusive* for people with disabilities in the context of the new community-based rehabilitation (CBR) guidelines launched in Nigeria's capital city of Abuja in 2010 (World Health Organization, 2010). These guidelines were designed to empower persons with disabilities by supporting their inclusion in health, education, employment, recreation, skills training, and other community services (Christian Blind Mission, 2010). This is essential because the vast majority of people with disabilities in Nigeria live in rural areas and need to access service to develop their potential. An effective CBR program is one positive means of improving special education and related services. It focuses on enhancing the quality of life for people with disabilities and their families, meeting basic needs and ensuring inclusion and participation. Initiated in the mid-1980s, it has evolved to become a multi-sectorial strategy that empowers persons with disabilities to access and benefit from education, employment, health and social services. It has been implemented through the combined efforts of people with disabilities, their families, organizations and communities, relevant government and non-government, health, education, vocational, social, and other services. Clearly, it is a community-based approach that helps to ensure that development reaches the poor and marginalized, and facilitates more inclusive, realistic, and sustainable initiatives (World Health Organization, 2010).

Alade (2004) reported that the community-based vocational rehabilitation program the International Labour Organisation and the United Nations Development Program (ILO/UNDP), initiated in Western Nigeria that could be one means to enable more people with disabilities in the country to acquire skills that could lead to self-employment. However, reliable data on the progress of the program in the country are scarce. It seems to be the case that too much bureaucracy and inadequate funding adversely affect this program.

A ministry responsible for disability and rehabilitation should be created at federal, state, and local government levels. Presently, the Ministry of Women Affairs and Social Development is charged with disability issues in Nigeria. Sadly, these issues, such as developing and implementing CBR programs, are put at the back burner (Lang & Upah, 2008). Nonetheless, if adequately planned and implemented, CBR will facilitate addressing many of the challenges of disability services articulated in the NPE document in Nigeria.

Advocacy organizations for people with disabilities in Nigeria should strive to become more active to exert sufficient pressure on the government (at both state and federal levels) to take the needs of people with disabilities into consideration in policy formulation and implementation. The history of special education and related services provision in many countries of the world acknowledge the important roles of pressure groups for people with disabilities in bringing about the needed changes and improvements in services (Obiakor, 2000, 2004). Evidence indicates that in many countries, these pressure groups have continued to assume greater responsibility by exerting pressure on governments to provide needed services and to enact and enforce legislations guaranteeing the rights of people with disabilities. Indeed, Lang and Upah (2008) argued that the main reason for the existence of organizations for people with disabilities is to advocate for the advancement and enforcement of the rights of people with disabilities because at its foundation, disability is a human rights issue. Hurst (1995) argued this point nearly two decades ago when he concluded that powerful disability movements are required to influence governments to enact laws on disability services in many western countries. People with disabilities must take a leading role in their own empowerment process to agitate for the enactment of laws and provision of appropriate services. In addition, various associations of people with disabilities in Nigeria under their national umbrella – Joint National Association of Persons with Disabilities (JANOPWD) must play significant roles in persuading the government to recognize the needs of citizens with disabilities by enacting a law that will facilitate improvements in the provision of services.

CONCLUSION

This chapter has focused on the current nature of special education in Nigeria. In addition, it has dealt with prospects and future directions of services for persons with disabilities. No doubt, the provision of special education services in Nigeria remains unsatisfactory. In other words, the majority of individuals with disabilities in Nigeria are not receiving services. Although the government included a section on special education provision in the *National Policy on Education*, it remains the case that apart from establishing institutions of higher education that train teachers for learners with special needs, virtually all other promises in the policy document remain at the theoretical level. There is no legislation to support the implementation of the provisions in the policy document. In the absence of an enabling law, it is not surprising that obstacles to implementation such as lack of funding structure, facilities, materials, and personnel remain. Nonetheless, we believe progress in implementing the provisions of the policy document can occur, if the government enacts the disability legislation that has been in the works since 1999. A presidential commission should be set up to ensure full implementation of the disability legislation. Reporting directly to the President of the Republic, the Commission will achieve much. Clearly, the current arrangement whereby disability issues are handled by the Ministry of Women Affairs and Social Development is making no impact. It seems to be the case that disability issues are not considered important. Consequently, very little funding is provided to improve services. We recommend that in addition to the Commission, Ministries of Disability and Rehabilitation should be created at the federal, state, and local government levels. Given that disabilities affect a significant portion of the population, it is proper to establish ministries that will be in charge of special education and rehabilitation services. Such ministries will plan their own budget and programs to ensure people with disabilities in Nigeria receive all the needed services to develop to their fullest potential and contribute to national and global developments.

REFERENCES

Abang, T. B. (2005). *The exceptional child: Handbook of special education.* Jos, Nigeria: Fab Anieh.

Adima, E. (1988). Handicapping the handicapped in Nigeria: Will the paradox end? *Ibadan Journal of Special Education, 4*, 51–60.

Ainscow, M. (1994). *Special needs in the classroom: A teacher education guide.* London: Jessica Kingsley and UNESCO.

Ajuwon, P. M. (2008). Inclusive education for students with disabilities in Nigeria: Benefits, challenges and policy implications. *International Journal of Special Education, 23*(3), 11–16.

Alade, E. B. (2004). Community-based vocational rehabilitation (CBVR) for people with disabilities: Experiences from a pilot program in Nigeria. *British Journal of Special Education, 31*(3), 143–149.

Barnes, C., & Sheldon, A. (2010). Disability, politics and poverty in a majority world context. *Disability & Society, 25*(7), 771–782.

Businessday. (2011). Group appeals to Jonathan on Nigeria disability bill. *Businessday*, Lagos, Nigeria. Retrieved from http://www.businessd ayonline.com/NG/index.php/typography/the-news/21509-group-appeals-to-jonathan-on-nigeria-disability-bill

Cherema, J. (2010). Inclusive education in developing countries in Sub-Sahara Africa: From theory to practice. *International Journal of Special Education, 25*(1), 87–93.

Christian Blind Mission. (2010). *New CBR guidelines launched in Abuja.* Retrieved from http://www.cbm.org/New-CBR-guidelines-launched-at-Abuja-Conference-272070.php

Derrington, T., Shapiro, B., & Smith, B. (2003). *The effectiveness of early intervention services.* Hawai'i, HI: University of Hawai'i Center on Disability Studies. Retrieved from http://www.seek.hawaii.edu/Products/4-Info-Binder/LR-Effectiveness.pdf

Eleweke, C. J. (1997). *Analysis of service provision for deaf people in Nigeria: Implications for future developments.* Unpublished Ph.D. thesis, University of Manchester, UK.

Eleweke, C. J. (1999a). The need for mandatory legislations to enhance services to enhance services with people with disabilities in Nigeria. *Disability & Society, 14*(3), 227–237.

Eleweke, C. J. (1999b). Improving special needs professional preparation and development programs in Nigeria. *African Journal of Special Needs Education, 4*(2), 41–49.

Eleweke, C. J. (2002a). A review of issues in deaf education under Nigeria's 6-3-3-4 education system. *Journal of Deaf Studies and Deaf Education, 7*(1), 74–82.

Eleweke, C. J. (2002b). Issues and problems in the education of deaf children in Nigeria. In A. Ali & B. Okeke (Eds.), *Philosophy and education: A book of readings: Honour of Msgr. Prof. F. C. Okafor* (pp. 191–224). Onitsha, Nigeria: Africana-FEP.

Federal Ministry of Women Affairs and Social Development. (2011). *Report of the national baseline survey of persons with disabilities (PWDs) in Nigeria.* Abuja, Nigeria: Author.

Federal Republic of Nigeria. (1981). *The national policy of education.* Lagos, Nigeria: Author.

Garuba, A. (2003). Inclusive education in the 21st century: Challenges and opportunities for Nigeria. *Asia Pacific Disability Rehabilitation Journal, 14*(2), 191–200.

Goode, S., Diefendorf, M., & Colgan, S. (2011). *The importance of early intervention for infants and toddlers with disabilities and their families.* Retrieved from http://www.nectac.org/~pdfs/pubs/importanceofearlyintervention.pdf

Guralnick, M. J., & Albertini, G. (2006). Early intervention in an international perspective. *Journal of Policy and Practice in Intellectual Disabilities, 3*(1), 1–2.

Hamzat, T. K., & Dada, O. O. (2005). Wheelchair accessibility of public buildings in Ibadan, Nigeria. *Asia Pacific Rehabilitation Research Journal, 16*(2), 115–124.

Hurst, R. (1995). Choice and empowerment: Lessons from Europe. *Disability & Society, 10*(4), 529–534.

Index Mundi. (2011). *Nigeria population.* Retrieved from http://www.indexmundi.com/nigeria/population.html

Lang, R., Groce, N., Kett, M., Trani, J.-F., & Bailey, N. (2009). *The potential impact of the global economic downturn on people with disabilities in developing countries.* Retrieved from https://www.ucl.ac.uk/lccr/centrepublications/workingpapers/WP08_Impact_of_the_Global_Economic_Downturn.pdf

Lang, R., & Upah, L. (2008). *Scoping study: Disability issues in Nigeria.* Retrieved from http://www.ucl.ac.uk/lc-ccr/downloads/scopingstudies/dfid_nigeriareport

Mba, P. O. (1995). *Special education and vocational rehabilitation.* Ibadan, Nigeria: Codat.

Mee, K. K., & Michael, F. (2011). A comparative examination of disability anti-discrimination legislation in the United States and Korea. *Disability & Society, 26*(3), 269–283.

Mittler, P. (2000). *Working towards inclusive education: Social contexts.* London: David Fulton.

Muga, E. (2003). Screening for disabilities in a community: The "10 Questions" screening for children in Bondo, Kenya. *African Health Sciences, 3*(1), 33–39.

Mukuria, G., & Obiakor, F. E. (2004). Special education issues and African diaspora. *Journal of International Special Needs Education, 7,* 12–17.

Obiakor, F. E. (1992). Education in Nigeria: A critical analysis. *International Education, 21,* 55–66.

Obiakor, F. E. (2000). Special education in Nigeria. In C. R. Reynolds & E. Fletcher-Janzen (Eds.), *Encyclopedia of special education: A reference for the education of the handicapped and other exceptional children and adults* (2nd ed., pp. 1263–1266). New York, NY: Wiley.

Obiakor, F. E. (2004). Building patriotic African leadership through African-centered education. *Journal of Black Studies*, *34*, 402–420.

Obiakor, F. E., & Bragg, W. A. (1998). Exceptional learners in Nigeria and the USA: The placement issue. *The Journal of International Special Needs Education*, *1*, 31–36.

Obiakor, F. E., Eskay, M., & Afolayan, M. U. (2012). Special education in Nigeria: Shifting paradigms. In K. Mutua & C. S. Sunai (Eds.), *Advances in research and praxis in special education in Africa, Caribbean, and the Middle East* (pp. 23–36). Charlotte, NC: Information Age Publishing Inc.

Obiakor, F. E., & Maltby, G. P. (1989). *Pragmatism and education in Africa: Handbook for educators and development planners*. Dubuque, IA: Kendall Hunt.

Obiakor, F. E., & Offor, M. T. (2012). Special education contexts, problems and prospects in Nigeria. In M. A. Winzer & K. Mazurek (Eds.), *International practices in special education: Debates and challenges* (pp. 138–148). Washington, DC: Gallaudet University Press.

Ogbonna, P. (1990). *Early intervention services for children with disabilities in Nigeria*. Boston, MA: Boston University.

Okeke, B. A. (1998). The status of disability rehabilitation centers in Enugu State – Nigeria: An appraisal. *African Journal of Special Needs Education*, *3*(2), 67–74.

Okeke, B. A. (2001). *Essentials of special education*. Nsukka, Nigeria: Afro-Orbis.

Okonkwo, H. C. (2007). Special needs education for the future. In E. D. Ozoji & J. M. Akuoyibo (Eds.), *The practice and future of special needs education in Nigeria* (pp. 130–146). Jos, Nigeria: Department of Special Education and Rehabilitation Sciences, University of Jos.

OnlineNigeria. (2011). *Other educational developments*. Retrieved from http://www.online nigeria.com/education/?blurb=535

Prater, G., Savage-Davis, E. M., Fuhler, C., Marks, L., & Minner, S. (1997). The preparation of special educators in school-based settings: Program descriptions, lessons learned and recommendations. *The Journal of the International Association of Special Education*, *1*(1), 31–44.

Shonibare, D. O. (1997). Emerging curriculum in special education. In U. M. D. Iyowi (Ed.), *Curriculum development in Nigeria*. Ibadan, Nigeria: Sam Bookman.

Steele, M. C. (2004). Making the case for early identification and intervention for young children at risk for learning disabilities. *Early Childhood Education Journal*, *32*(2), 75–79.

Taiwo, S. A. (2007). Special education in Nigeria: Past, present, and future. *The Journal of Advocacy and Rehabilitation in Special Education*, *5*(1), 60–65.

UNESCO. (2009). *Toward inclusive education for children with disabilities: A guideline*. Bangkok, Thailand: UNESCO Bangkok.

United Nations. (2006). *United nations treaty collection 15: Convention on the rights of persons with disabilities*. New York, NY: United Nations. Retrieved from http://treaties.un.org/pages/ViewDetails.aspx?src=TREATY&mtdsg_no=IV- 15&chapter=4&lang=en

United Nations. (2011). *World program of action concerning people with disabilities*. Retrieved from http://www.un.org/disabilities/default.asp?id=23

World Health Organisation. (2010). *CBR guidelines: Towards community-based inclusive development*. Retrieved from http://whqlibdoc.who.int/publications/2010/9789241548052_introductory_eng.pdf

World Health Organisation, & World Bank. (2011). *World report on disability*. Retrieved from http://whqlibdoc.who.int/publications/2011/9789240685215_eng.pdf

SPECIAL EDUCATION TODAY IN SOUTH AFRICA

Sigamoney Naicker

ABSTRACT

The chapter on special education in South Africa initiates with a very comprehensive historical account of the origins of special education making reference to the inequalities linked to its colonial and racist past to a democratic society. This intriguing section ends with the most recent development in the new democracy form special needs education to inclusive education. Next, the chapter provides prevalence and incidence data followed by trends in legislation and litigation. Following these sections, detailed educational interventions are discussed in terms of policies, standards and research as well as working with families. Then information is provided on regular and special education teacher roles, expectations and training. Lastly, the chapter comprehensively discusses South Africa's special education progress and challenges related to budgetary support, staff turnover, and a lack of prioritizing over the number of pressing education goals in the country's provinces.

Special Education International Perspectives: Practices Across the Globe
Advances in Special Education, Volume 28, 397–429
Copyright © 2014 by Emerald Group Publishing Limited
All rights of reproduction in any form reserved
ISSN: 0270-4013/doi:10.1108/S0270-401320140000028020

INTRODUCTION

The policy of inclusive education in South Africa, adopted in 2001 at a country level, is a radical departure from its previous special education policy. The radical changes that have taken place in South Africa after the transition from an apartheid state to a new democratic country in 1994 did not leave special education untouched. The policy process underpinned by the human rights culture impacted significantly on shifting thinking from special education towards an inclusive approach to education. Like general education, special education was one of the most unequal areas of education with resources skewed leaving the majority of the black population neglected in terms of access to schooling, teacher training and almost all aspects of schooling.

The post-apartheid dispensation, in view of a lack of a human rights culture, advanced human rights as a key component of transformation towards a non-racial society. Special Education was targeted as a very important area that required a human rights culture. The South African education system in developing White Paper Six on Special Needs Education: Building an Inclusive Education and Training System which was launched in 2001, prepared the foundation for the transformation of special education. The major plan was to rupture theories, assumptions, models, tools and practices of Special Education thus creating the conditions for Inclusive Education strongly underpinned by a human rights culture.

Similar to the other policy processes, South Africans had to contend with a number of policy interventions that were competing in a tough fiscal environment. Besides the financial constraints, there were several backlogs as a result of 350 years of colonial rule that favoured the minority population whilst the majority of black people occupied the status of either the working class or underclass. The policy intention and how it played itself out in different contexts will be some of the issues that are given consideration in this chapter.

ORIGINS OF SPECIAL EDUCATION IN SOUTH AFRICA FROM ITS COLONIAL AND RACIST PAST TO A DEMOCRATIC SOCIETY

The history of South African special education provision and education support services, like all other aspects of South African life during the

Table 1. Different Phases and Stages in the Development of Special
Education in South Africa.

Phase	Stage	Characterization
1		Lack of provision
2	1	Provision by church and private organizations
	2	Development of standardized tests
	3	Development of medical model
3	1	Beginning of institutional apartheid and the provision of disparate services
	2	Racially segregated education and the development of special education services
	3	Special education in homelands and Bantustans and the promotion and politicize of ethnic differences by the apartheid government
4		Developments in the new democracy

colonial and apartheid era was largely influenced by fiscal inequalities in terms of race (Naicker, 2005). In the light of the different and complex developments in special education and education support services in South Africa, the history of special education and education support services has been divided into historical phases(see Table 1) (Naicker, 1999, 2005).

There are difficulties in clearly demarcating the above phases and in portraying the complexities which existed within the fragmented African section of the South African population. These complexities include: (1) the introduction of the Homelands with their own separate policies (or rather, lack therefore) which was manifested in very limited provision in, for example the Transkei, Ciskei, and Bophutswana; (2) different policies of the South Africa Department of Education and Training which is responsible for the nation's education; (3) policies shaped by South Africa's Bantu Education Act of 1953; (4) the fragmented nature of South Africa's society based on racial distinction; and (5) the varying state policies with different intervention times for whites, Africans, who were divide into Homelands and locally, coloureds, and Indians. With these complexities in mind, the following section delineates the four phrases.

PHASE ONE: ABSENCE OF PROVISION (1700S–1800S)

Here, as everywhere else in the world, the South African society in the 1700s and early 1800s saw little provision for any type of special education need. Mostly, persons with disabilities were viewed by society as a sign of 'divine displeasure', a superstitious attitude which led to the chaining, imprisonment and killing of people later recognized as persons with intellectually impairments, physical disabilities, visual impairments, hearing impairments, and emotionally disturbance. The 'divine displeasure' attitude influenced to a large extent the negative treatment of people who were constructed as disabled within the South African context since it was a colonized territory.

PHASE TWO: WHITE-DOMINATED PROVISION, AND THE IMPORTANT ROLE OF THE CHURCH (FROM LATE 1800S–1963)

Stage One: Provisioning by Church, Private Organizations and Society, and the Racist Nature of the State

The title of this phase is self-explanatory and intentionally used to reflect the oppressive nature of special education policy on the part of the South Africa state during the period 1863–1963. Whilst the effect of racial practices is still being felt today, long after 1963, this particular phase began to set the pattern for later years and was most striking in terms of racial disparities. These disparities become evident when one looks at the chronology of special education provisions. For example, no special education provision was made by the South Africa state for African children. In fact, it took a century for the state to provide subsidies for African persons with hearing impairments, visual impairments, and physical disabilities. These subsidies occurred in 1963.

The church played an important role during this phase. It initiated the first provision of special education for children with disabilities for both white and 'non-white' children, through the Dominican Grimley School for the Deaf in 1863. In 1863, Dr Grimley, Vicar Apostolic of the Cape of Good Hope, who had been actively associated with the education of the deaf in Dublin, invited the Irish Dominican sisters to work in South Africa. The superior of the pioneer group of sisters, Mother Dympna, began to teach some deaf children on her arrival at the Cape and shortly afterwards the Grimley Institute (now known as Dominican Grimley School) was founded under the patronage of the Vicar Apostolic.

More importantly, the church continued to provide a service to 'non-white' children in the absence of state provision for these children for the next century. The church's special education provision was an important factor in South Africa's recognition of the existence of white church-run schools in 1900 which lead to the state's promulgation of the White Education Act 29 in 1928. This Act, allowed the State Education Department to establish vocational schools and special schools for 'white' children with disabilities.

The White Education Act 29 of 1928 provides the first signal of the model of special education in South Africa. Although it mainly concerned white learners, it provided the foundation for South Africa's Special Education Act of 1948. This Act made provision for separate special schools for several categories of disability which include the: deaf, hard of hearing, blind, partially sighted, epileptic, cerebral palsy and physically disabled. Act 29 worked on the assumption that learners were deficient and that their deficiencies were pathological, a perspective that was strongly influenced by the medical thinking of professionals at that time. Unfortunately, this pathological perspective associated disability with impairment and loss and it did not take systemic deficiencies into consideration.

The state increasingly favoured white students with special needs and in 1937 passed the Special Schools Amendment Act which created the first provision for hostels in special schools for whites. The provision of hostels meant that provision was made for learners to live in the schools they attended. Positively, the church and other private associations and societies continued to provide support for 'non-white' children. For example, they were responsible for establishing (1) the Athlone School for the Blind for coloured children, (2) a school for blind Indian children and (3) the Worcester School for coloured children with epilepsy. South Africa has a fairly long history with regards to the education of learners with disabilities. It started 1863 when the Roman Catholic Church established the first school for deaf children in Cape Town.

From the initiatives taken by the Catholic and other churches, the service gradually grew to the current 20 schools for blind, 47 for deaf, 54 for physically disabled and cerebral palsied, 2 for autistic and quite a number for intellectually disabled learners. The establishment of schools for disabled learners was mainly due to private initiative (churches, other private organizations and individuals) and for specific disability groups.

Stage Two: Development of Tests as a Precursor to Institutional Special Education and Education Support Services

The 1920s saw the first development of intelligence tests in South Africa. Professor Eybers, of the then University College of Orange Free State, published an individual intelligence scale called the Grey Revision of the Stanford-Binet Scale (Behr, 1980, 1984). The development of tests to evaluate students with special education needs continued in white education and their usage in schools increased. For instance, in 1924, a committee, appointed by the Research Grants Board of the Union Department of Mines and Industries and under the chairmanship of Professor R. W. Wilcocks, designed a test, which came to be known as the South African Group Test of Intelligence. This marked the first connection between education and the labour market in South Africa and was the precursor to aptitude tests. Later, in 1926, Professor J. Coetzee of Potchefstroom University published the first standardized arithmetic test in South Africa for whites. In 1929, both the Wilcocks and Coetzee tests were used in the Carnegie Poor White Survey and later in the Bilingualism Survey (Behr, 1980). The Poor White Survey was commissioned to establish ways in which the poor whites could be uplifted. There was a fear that that poor whites and poor blacks will socialize which could lead to a multi-racial society.

In 1939, Dr. Fick developed the individual Scale of General Intelligence for South African Schools. This scale was used in schools to assess the cognitive capacity of students with disabilities until the mid-60s. The scale was the precursor of categorization and labelling of students with intellectual and learning disabilities. Unfortunately, since IQ tests were later used not only for whites, but also for all children to assess intelligence in children and place them in special education programmes, it perpetuated the 'exclusive' education philosophy in the 1960s, 1970s and 1980s. In addition, these tests became a highly valued component to psychological services in schools (currently associated with education support services), a basis for adaptation classes (in Coloured Education), adjustment classes (in Indian Education) and remedial education.

Stage Three: The Genesis of the Medical Model

The 1948 Special Schools Act in white education introduced into special education a model that incorporated a medical and mental diagnosis and treatment. This model focused on the individual deficit theory and viewed the person as a helpless being. The model was firmly entrenched in the charity and lay discourses (Fulcher, 1989). The medical discourse shaped and largely influenced 'exclusive' special education practices in the field which continued for decades after its introduction in South Africa's education system due to its highly convincing theme which, according to Fulcher (1989):

> Suggests, through its correspondence theory of meaning, that disability is an observable or intrinsic, objective attribute or characteristic of a person, rather than a social construct. Through the notion that impairment means loss, and the assumption that impairment or loss underlies disability, medical discourse on disability has deficit individualistic connotations. Further, through its presumed scientific status and neutrality, it depoliticizes disability; disability is seen as a technical issue, (and) thus beyond the exercise of power. Medical discourse individualizes disability, in the sense that it suggests individuals have diseases or problems or incapacities as attributes. (p. 28)

Thus, disability was associated with an impairment or loss. The entire focus was on the individual who was viewed as helpless and dependent. The individual deficit theory viewed the person as in need of treatment and assistance outside regular education. No attempt was made to establish the deficiencies of the system; for example, a person with physical disability using a wheelchair required a ramp to gain access to a mainstream school, which was not provided for by the system. Access to education was prevented as a result of barriers, which reflect a deficient system and not a deficient person.

This medical discourse model was also the beginning of the professionalization, and consequently the mystification, of special education in South Africa for regular education teachers. Fulcher (1989) is appropriate here in her comments about the medical discourse:

> it professionalizes disability: the notion of medical expertise allows the claims that this (technical) and personal trouble is a matter for professional judgment. (p. 28)

Following this prevailing belief, regular education teachers were led to believe that it was beyond their level of expertise to teach learners who were classed as disabled and these students must be educated by specialists. Unfortunately, such beliefs perpetuated the idea that students with disabilities must be excluded from regular education thus making inclusive education not possible. This idea, according to Fulcher's (1989), led to the proliferation of educational psychology and related disciplines practice, namely, a

medical discourse, through its language of body, patient, help, need, cure, rehabilitation, and its politics that the doctor knows best, excludes a consumer discourse or language of rights, wants and integration in mainstream social practices. (p. 28)

Therefore, the depoliticizing, individualizing and professionalizing of
disabilities led to the notion that learners who were viewed as disabled
had to be taught in special schools and/or classes, while their rights
were ignored. Parents of learners were intimidated by the knowledge of
professionals and therefore did not challenge the decisions concerning
placement.

PHASE THREE: 'SEPARATE DEVELOPMENT' AND ITS IMPACT ON SPECIAL EDUCATION AND EDUCATION SUPPORT SERVICES (1963–1994)

*Stage One: Institutional Apartheid and Disparate Service Provision
for the Four Race Groups*

The year 1948 ushered in the introduction of institutional apartheid into
every facet of South African life. The National Party's policy of separate
development ensured apartheid by dividing students into four groups,
namely, 'Africans', 'coloureds', 'Indians' and 'whites'. This had significant
implications for special education and education support services. Whilst
the concept of education support services (known traditionally as psychological services, or auxiliary services) evolved only at a much later stage
(1992) in South African education, it must be noted that the initial precursor was the introduction of the psychological services that were initiated after the above introduction of separate development. The School
Psychological and Guidance Services of South Africa's Department of
Education in the Transvaal, after the promulgation of Act No. 39 of 1967
for 'whites', saw, the clinics established and staffed by clinical psychologists, vocational guidance psychologists, orthodidacticians, speech therapists, sociopedagogic psychologists and occupational therapists (Behr,
1980). These clinics which were staffed by multi-disciplinary professionals
proved to be a workable model and paved the way for special education
support services several decades later (National Education Policy
Investigation, 1992).

Stage Two: Segregated Education Departments Take
Control of Special Education and Education Support
Services Provision

Education, as one of the pillars of separate development, was used as an instrument to ensure that all four groups accepted the idea of that policy. The passing of the Coloured Persons Education, Bantu Education and Indian Education Acts, in 1963, 1964 and 1965 respectively, saw special education and education support services being taken over by the various departments. Unfortunately, the disparities in special education and education support provision were clearly racial and became very visible with the unfolding of separate development. Table 2 illustrates these disparities (Behr, 1980).

Behr (1980) reported that 'Whites' made up 17.5%, 'Africans' 70.2%, 'Coloureds' 9.4% and 'Indians' 2.9% of the population. Table 2 shows clearly that special education provision favoured 'whites'. The provision problem with regard to bias towards 'whites' was actually worse than it appeared since churches and private associations and societies had initiated the development of 'non-white' special schools while special education for whites had been provided mainly by the State.

In psychological services (a precursor of today's special education support services) there were major discrepancies on racial lines. For example, in the Transvaal, under the wing of the School Psychological and Guidance Services, an elaborate system of child guidance clinics was

Table 2. Provision and Schools for the Different Types of Disability.

Disability	White	African	Coloured	Indian
Aural	5 schools	7	2	1
Visual	2 schools	4	1	1
Cerebral palsy	4 schools	3	1	1
Physically disabled	4 schools	None		
Epilepsy	3 schools	None	1	None
Autism	2 schools	None	None	None
Mental retardation	41 centres	None	None	3
Industry/reform	3	None	5	1
Remedial	Provision exists	None	None	Provision exists
Educable mental retardation	Provision exists	None	Provision exists	Provision exists

Source: Behr (1980).

established for each of the 24 inspection circuits. In this system, a clinic served a group of schools. A multi-disciplinary team carried out intellectual, scholastic, and emotional assessments of pupils, and provided help in the form of psychotherapy, pelotherapy and speech therapy. In addition, clinics were concerned with identifying and guiding children with learning deficits, cultural deprivation and behavioural problems. Other provinces had similar services, but not as elaborate as the Transvaal's (Behr, 1980).

While the Department of Bantu Education did establish a section with psychological services, it was restricted to assessing all pupils in Form I and Form III (Form 1 is grade 6 and Form III is Grade 10) to help teachers and lecturers assess their teaching. Also, psychological services for coloureds were instituted and at least one teacher in each school was concerned with guidance. In addition, training was provided for secondary teachers who had taken psychology as part of degree course responsible for guidance. School Psychological Services in Indian Education focused mainly on assessing and placing pupils needing special education (Behr, 1980).

Except for Indian Education, which had several psychologists, an inspector of psychological services and a school guidance office, there was little comparison between the resources of white education and other race groups. This disparity resulted in poor supervision of adaptation classes, remedial education and facilities at special schools where they existed.

Stage Three: The Homeland or Bantustan Phase

In 1968, the South Africa state conferred Territorial Authorities to six 'Homeland' government departments, with each having a separate education department. However, this did not result in any significant changes for African children with special education needs. Furthermore, there was little information on the actual development of special education and education support services in these territories (National Education Policy Investigation, 1992). However, it followed the pattern and trends of the 'separate development' phase relating to the number of pupils in special schools as a ratio of total enrolment for the various races: Indians 1:42; whites 1:62; coloureds 1:128; and Africans 1:830 (National Education Policy Investigation, 1992).

PHASE FOUR: DEVELOPMENTS IN THE NEW DEMOCRACY; FROM SPECIAL NEEDS EDUCATION TO INCLUSIVE EDUCATION

As mentioned earlier, the advent of the democratic government in 1994 saw wide-scale transformation taking hold throughout the country in many aspects including education. This included the unification of 19 education departments into a single Ministry of Education. The unification was tantamount to a revolution. The disparities and lack of provision for mainly black South Africans clearly reflected the need to conduct intensive research with a view to providing educational service that could benefit all South Africans. It was against this background that the democratic government appointed the National Commission on Special Education Needs and Training (NCSNET), as well as the National Committee on Education Support Services (NCESS), in 1996. While the NCSNET and NCESS were established as separate entities by the Ministry of Education, the two agencies decided to work jointly as a single group in the light of overlapping functions. This was clearly spelt out in the Department of Education (1997) single report of the NCSNET and NCESS:

> In the early stages of the work of the NCSNET and NCESS, it became evident that the links between these areas were so close that they required a joint investigation. The first meeting of both bodies was held in mid-November 1996. The NCSNET and NCESS initially commenced their investigations within separate task groups. By the third meeting in January 1997, it was evident that the investigations overlapped in so many ways that it was necessary to amalgamate and conduct both consultative and research work through joint structures and processes. (p. 10)

The work of NCSNET and NCESS lasted for a year (1996–1997), during which these bodies consulted widely with key stakeholders in education. Workshops and public hearings were held in all provinces, since consultation with all interested parties formed part of the terms of reference of the NCSNET and NCESS and was regarded as crucial.

The terms of reference adopted by NCSNET and NCESS had to heed the major proclamations and other policy documents during the period of transformation. For example, the new Constitution of the Republic of South Africa had this to say: 'Every person shall have the right to basic education and equal access to educational institutions' (p. 16). The

Department of Education's (1996) White Paper on Education and Training
was also clear on the question of rights:

> It is essential to increase awareness of the importance of ESS (Education Support
> Services) in an education and training system which is committed to equal access, non-
> discrimination, and redress, and which needs to target those sections of the learning
> population which have been most neglected or are most vulnerable. (p. 16)

Further, the White Paper on an Integrated National Disability Strategy,
produced by the Disability Desk of the Office of the Deputy State
President (1997), offered very clear direction to the NCSNET and NCESS:

> An understanding of disability as a human rights and development issue leads to a
> recognition and acknowledgement that people with disabilities are equal citizens and
> should therefore enjoy equal rights and responsibilities. A human rights and develop-
> ment approach to disability focuses on the removal of barriers to equal participation
> and the elimination of discrimination based on disability. (p. 10)

In November 1997, in the Department of Education report titled,
'Quality education for all: Overcoming barriers to learning', the NCSNET
and NCESS recognized the need for all learners to gain access to a single
education system and thus be able to participate in everyday mainstream
economic and social life. The recommendations of the NCSNET and
NCESS were largely phrased in the language of human rights, which differed radically from that of the medical discourse perspective as it moved
away from individualizing, professionalizing and depoliticizing disability
by stating that:

> ... Barriers can be located within the learner, within the centre of learning, within the
> education system and within the broader social, economic and political context. These
> barriers manifest themselves in different ways and only become obvious when learning
> breakdown occurs, when learners 'drop out' of the system or when the excluded become
> visible. Sometimes it is possible to identify permanent barriers in the learner or system,
> which can be addressed through enabling mechanisms and processes.
>
> However, barriers may also arise during the learning process and are seen as transitory
> in nature. These may require different interventions or strategies to prevent them from
> causing learning breakdown or excluding learners from the system. The key to prevent-
> ing barriers from occurring is the effective monitoring and meeting of the different
> needs among the learner population and within the system as a whole. (Department of
> Education, 1997, p. 14)

By identifying the education system and individuals with disabilities as
reflecting or experiencing potential barriers to learning, the NCSNET and
NCESS had moved away from viewing disability as only an individual loss

or impairment. Furthermore, NCSNET and NCESS suggested that these barriers could be addressed in a regular school and that regular education teachers needed to be trained to identify and deal with barriers to learning and development. These barriers could include the following: socio-economic factors, attitudes, inflexible curriculum, language and curriculum, inaccessible and unsafe built environments, inadequate support services, lack of enabling and protective legislation and policy, lack of parental recognition and involvement, disability (learning needs not met) and lack of human resource development strategies. In their recommendations, and as part of the principles on which their work was based, the NCSNET and NCESS called for 'equal access to a single, inclusive education system' in which:

> Appropriate and effective education must be organised in such a way that all learners have access to a single education system that is responsive to diversity. No learners should be prevented from participating in this system, regardless of their physical, intellectual, social, emotional, language, or other differences. (Department of Education, 1997, p. 66)

An educational development that preceded the work of the NCSNET and NCESS was the introduction of a general curriculum, namely, the Outcomes-Based Education (OBE). The NCSNET and NCESS recommended that a single education curriculum and urged that diverse special education needs be firmly incorporated within the OBE that had already been under way in South Africa. This NCSNET and NCESS argued that OBE had the capacity to deal with diversity as a result of its flexibility and its premise that 'all students can learn and succeed, but not on the same day in the same way' (Spady, 1994, p. 9).

EDUCATIONAL INTERVENTIONS (POLICY, STANDARDS, RESEARCH)

Education White Paper Six on Special Needs Education: Building an Inclusive Education and Training System (Department of Education, 2001) suggests a 20-year plan to transform the system from a dual to a single system of education. The 20 years include short-term, medium-term and long-steps. It must be noted that the previous dispensation also neglected rural education. White Paper Six has both an urban and rural focus. With White Paper 6, the government's short-term intent was to:

- Implement a national advocacy and education programme on inclusive education.
- Plan and implement a targeted outreach programme, beginning in Government's rural and urban nodes, to mobilise out-of-school children and youth with disabilities.
- Complete the audit of special schools and implement a programme to improve efficiency and quality.
- Designate, plan and implement the conversion of 30 special schools into resource centres in 30 districts.
- Designate, plan and implement the conversion of thirty primary schools to full-service schools in the same 30 districts above.
- Within all other public education institutions, on a progressive basis, the general orientation and introduction of the inclusion model to management, governing bodies and professional staff.
- Within primary schooling, on a progressive basis, the establishment of systems and procedures for the early identification and addressing of barriers to learning in the Foundation Phase (Grades R-3). (Department of Education, 2001, p. 42)

Therefore, White Paper Six introduced a three tier inclusive education system which includes Full-Service Schools, District-Based Support Teams and Special Schools as Resource Centres. These three systems are described below.

Full-service/inclusive Schools, further and higher education institutions are first and foremost mainstream education institutions that provide quality education to all learners by supplying the full range of learning needs in an equitable manner (Department of Education, 2010). A full-service school would be equipped and supported to provide for a greater range of learning needs. As learning needs and barriers to learning arise within a specific context and vary from time to time, it is obvious that full-service schools should be supported to develop their capacity and potential for addressing and reducing barriers to learning, as well as seeing their educational provision in a flexible manner. Following this thinking, a full-service school may, but not necessarily need to have all possible imaginable support to learners in place but it would have the potential and capacity to act in such a way that a support needed for a learner could be provided.

The guidelines for *District-based Support Teams* refer to integrated professional support services at the district level. Support providers employed by the Department of Education will draw on the expertise from local education institutions and various community resources. Their key function is to assist education institutions (including early childhood centres, schools, further education colleges and adult learning centres) to identify and address barriers to learning and promote effective teaching and learning. This includes both classroom and organizational support, providing specialized learner and educator support, as well as curricular and institutional development (including management and governance), and administrative support (Department of Education, 2005).

It is believed that the key to reducing barriers to learning within all education and training lies in a strengthened education support service. This strengthened education support service will have, at its centre, new district-based support teams that will comprise staff from provincial, district, regional and head offices and from special schools. The primary function of these district-based support teams will be to evaluate programmes, diagnose their effectiveness and suggest modifications. Through supporting teaching, learning and management, they will build the capacity of schools, early childhood and adult basic education and training centres, colleges and higher education institutions to recognize and address severe learning difficulties and to accommodate a range of learning needs.

Special Schools as Resource Centres imply the qualitative improvement of special schools for the learners that they serve and their phased conversion to special school resource centres that provide professional support to neighbouring schools and are integrated into district-based support teams (Department of Education, 2007). According to the White Paper Six, in an inclusive education and training system a wider spread of educational services will be provided according to the learners' needs. The priorities and goals of special schools will include orientation to new roles within the district support teams which include support to neighbouring schools and full-service schools. The new approach should focus on problem solving skills and the development of learners' strengths and competencies rather than focusing on their shortcomings and disabilities only. The special school as resource centre should be integrated into the district support team to provide support to full-service schools and ordinary schools in that district. The District Support Team should be the overseer of support required by learners within the district.

The intention here is to ensure that there is sufficient human resource development so that teachers are well equipped to deal with diversity. Further, through physical resource/material resource development, schools will be made accessible. District Support Teams, which comprise curriculum specialists, psychologists, early childhood education specialists and related personnel, will also undergo training in the area of inclusive education. The purpose of identifying a relatively small number of schools is to ensure that there is rigorous development and research that is able to establish the strengths and weaknesses of the plan. Ultimately, Full-Service schools (ordinary primary school) will be converted into a school, which caters for difference. Special Schools within this plan should have more of an outreach role to assist and support, together with the District Support Team, the Full-Service School and the Ordinary School. Advocacy focusing on inclusive education will be conducted within the 30 districts, as well as system-wide, to ensure that there are sufficient common understandings about government's plans. It is envisaged that this process will lead to the following outcomes:

- Costing of an ideal district support team.
- Cost of conversion of special schools to special schools/resource centres.
- Costing of an ideal full-service school.
- Costing of a 'full service' technical college.
- Determining the minimum levels of provision for learners with special needs for all higher education institutions.
- Devising a personnel plan.
- Costing non-personnel expenditure requirements. (Department of Education, 2001, p. 44)

According to White Paper Six, the completion of the short-term steps should take three years. Once the research has been completed and the findings known, the medium steps should involve more schools, further education and training and higher education institutions, depending on available resources.

The notion of inclusive education, as mentioned earlier in this chapter, is shaped directly by the recommendations of the NCSNET and NCESS. Therefore, the focus is not merely on disability but rather on all vulnerable children, including over-age learners, children in prison, learners who experience language barriers, or barriers such as the attitudes of others, lack of parental recognition and poverty. The transformational goals mentioned at the beginning of this chapter becomes very relevant to inclusive education where the emphasis is on creating access and skewing funding so that it is pro poor.

What emerges clearly from the government's inclusive education intention is that the system is being geared towards creating possibilities for the first time in the history of South Africa, pedagogy of possibility, not only in terms of race but ability, interest, intelligence and styles. Whilst the intentions are very clear, several challenges face policy implementers within the South African context.

Learners will follow programmes and receive support based on the level of support they require. The Screening, Identification, Assessment and Support strategy specifically aims to identify (1) the barriers to learning experienced, (2) the support needs that arise from barriers experienced and

(3) the support programme that needs to be in place to address the impact of the barrier on the learning process.

The nature of support programmes that will be addressed within the SIAS strategy covers the following areas:

- Vision;
- Hearing;
- Mobility;
- Communication;
- Learning/Cognition;
- Health (including Mental Health);
- Behaviour and social skills;
- Multiple and Complex Learning Support.

The provisioning drivers for the support programmes are:

(1) curriculum and assessment adjustments;
(2) training requirements;
(3) availability of specialized staff;
(4) specialized LTSM /assistive devices and other resources to ensure access to education.

The strategy rates the level of the identified support that is required as a low, moderate or high level of provision. The organizers that guide this rating process include the *frequency, scope, availability and cost of the additional support service, programme or specialized learning and teaching support material.* The support provisions that are rated low cover all the support provisions in all departmental programme policies, line budgets and norms and standards for public schools. Support provisions that are rated moderate cover support provisions that are over and above provisions covered by programme policies, line budgets and norms and standards for public schools. Such provisions are provided once-off or for a short-term period or on a loan system. Implementation of such provisions can generally be accommodated within the school or regular classroom. Support provisions that are rated high are over and above provisions covered by programme policies, line budgets and norms and standards for public schools support. These provisions are specialized, requiring specialist classroom/school organization, facilities and personnel. A resource package and guidelines concerning the use of technology is currently being developed by the Department of Basic Education.

PREVALENCE AND INCIDENT ASPECTS

The issue of prevalence and incidence has always been a controversial issue in South Africa. For example, the 2010 national household survey estimates that 6.3% of people older than five years in South Africa have some form of disability. This might be an underestimation as the World Health Organization's 2011 World Report on Disability placed the global disability population at about 15%. Therefore, there is little consensus on issues of prevalence and incidence. However, when the Department of Education's White Paper Six was developed, disability in the schooling system utilized the World Health Organization data. It was estimated between 2.2% and 2.6% of learners in any school system could be identified as disabled or impaired. This meant that about 400,000 of South African children had disabilities or impairments. When White Paper Six was written only 64,200 children were accommodated by the schooling system. Since then, considerable progress with regards to building of special schools has been achieved.

The data collected in Census 2001 indicates that there were 2,255,982 people with various forms of disability. This number constituted 5% of the total population enumerated in this census. Of this number, 1,854,376 were African, 168,678 were coloured, 41,235 were Indian/Asian, and 191,693 were white. The number of females affected was 1,173,939, compared to 1,082,043 males.

The provincial prevalence levels show that the most affected province was Free State with a prevalence of 6.8% and the least affected province was Gauteng (3.8%). The prevalence increased by age from 2% in the age group 0–9 years to 27% in the age group 80 years and above. Those who had post-secondary education had the lowest prevalence (3%) compared to those who had no schooling (10.5%). Lastly those with primary level and secondary level of education had prevalence of 5.2% and 3.9%, respectively.

The prevalence of sight disability was the highest (32%) followed by physical disability (30%), hearing (20%), emotional disability (16%), intellectual disability (12%) and communication disability (7%). A comparison of the demographic and socio-economic characteristics of disabled and non-disabled persons shows that disabled persons were on average older. About 30% of disabled people had no education while only 13% of the non-disabled population fell in this category. However, the most affected population group in this regard were African (Census, Government of South Africa, 2001, p. 2).

TRENDS IN LEGISLATION AND LITIGATION

At this time, national legislation concerning entry and exit to special schools do not exist. The countries nine provinces accept children at the age of 3 years and the exit age is 21 years. Provinces will have to indicate what provision is made once children leave at the age of 21 years.

In revising policies, legislation and frameworks, the Ministry of Education promised in White Paper Six to give particular, but not exclusive, attention to those that relate to the school and college systems. Policies, legislation and frameworks for the school and college systems were required to provide the basis for overcoming the causes and effects of barriers to learning. Specifically, White Paper Six promised admission policies will be revised so that learners who can be accommodated outside of special schools and specialized settings can be schooled within designated full-service or other schools and settings (Department of Education, 2001).

At this time, there are no national laws concerning placement of learners with regard to age and related matters. The government indicates that provincial authorities should create placement options based on broad guidelines. Regarding admission, the South African Schools Act (Act 79 of 1996) through section 5 makes provision for all schools to be full-service schools by stating that: public schools must admit learners and serve their educational requirements without unfairly discriminating in any way; governing bodies of a public school may not administer any test related to the admission of a learner to a public school; and in determining the placement of a learner with special education needs, the Head of Department and principal must take into account the rights and wishes of the parents and of such learner while taking into account what will be in the best interest of the learner in any decision-making process (Department of Education, 2010).

The government specifies that The Screening, Identification, Assessment and Support (SIAS) Strategy (SIAS) should be used to maximize learners' participation in schools and classrooms. The aim of introducing the SIAS strategy in the education system is to overhaul the process of identifying, assessing and providing programmes for all learners requiring additional support so as to enhance participation and inclusion. One of the key objectives of the strategy is to provide clear guidelines on enroling learners in special schools and settings which also acknowledge the central role played by parents and educators. In essence these guidelines provide a strategic policy framework for screening, identifying, assessing and supporting all

learners who experience barriers to learning and development within the
education system, including those who are currently enroled in special
schools.

Reasonable accommodation of individuals' requirements should be
made. This can in turn be realized by making provision for individualized
support measures that could include facilitating the learning of Braille,
using alternative script, communicating through augmentative and alternative modes, means and formats of communication, the introduction of
orientation and mobility skills, and facilitating peer support and mentoring,
facilitating the learning of sign language and the promotion of the linguistic
identity of the Deaf community (Department of Education, 2010).

Until now only two major cases were disputing the service provision
regarding learners who are disabled. The first one involved a claim against
the state regarding South African Sign Language (SASL). A learner
claimed that by not offering SASL as a school subject, the Department of
Education is acting in contradiction to the constitution of the country.
A matric Grade 12 student, Kyle Springate, took the Department of
Education to court in his quest to have sign language recognized as an
exam subject. Springate discovered in 2009 that, despite having taken sign
language as a subject throughout high school, sign language would not
form part of his matric exam. He appealed for sign language to be recognized as an additional language, believing that it formed part of the school
curriculum. Springate discovered that sign language was not a recognized
subject, which meant that he faced losing points in his university application. This student ended up taking dramatic art as an extra subject and had
to study three years of work for his final school year at Westville Boys'
High School in Durban. Kyle's mother, Paige McLennan-Smith, said that
this turn of events had placed her son at a disadvantage. Kyle's mother
argued that her son was exhausted after a normal day at school 'as a result
of lip-reading', which required him to concentrate all the time during the
school day. With the burden of taking dramatic arts as a subject, he was
even more exhausted after a day at school. Paige argued that 'If Kyle fails
dramatic arts and his application to the university is assessed on the basis
of only six subjects, he stands little chance of being accepted'. Springate
hoped to study fine art at Rhodes University.

In the court papers filed at the KwaZulu-Natal High Court in
Pietermaritzburg, the Department of Basic Education said that there had
not yet been any consensus among organizations representing the deaf
about the exact definition or components of sign language, and that this
had resulted in a delay in the process of formally recognizing sign language

as a subject. The court requested that the Department of Education offer sign language as a subject in view of the challenges posed to learners. Since this court case, the Department of Education has taken steps to introduce SASL as a subject (Legal Resources Centre, 2009).

The second court case (High Court of South Africa, 2010, Case No: 18678/2007-Western Cape Forum for Intellectual Disability vs. Government of the Republic of South Africa) involved a right to education of children with severe intellectual disability. In November 2010, the Western Cape Forum for intellectual disability challenged the state in the high court with concerns for the rights of the children with profound and severe cognitive deficits. They argued that the: (i) the state establishes and funds schools which include schools known as 'special schools' which cater for the needs of children who are classified as having moderate to mild intellectual disabilities (IQ levels of 30−70); (ii) children with an IQ of under 35 are considered to be severely (IQ levels of 20−35) or profoundly (IQ levels of less than 20) intellectually disabled and as such children are not admitted to special schools or to any other state schools; and (iii) the state makes no provision for the education of children with severe or profound intellectual disabilities (the affected children) nor does It also does it provide schools in the Western Cape for such children.

The High Court decided that the State has failed to take reasonable measures to make provision for the educational needs of children with severe and profound intellectually disabilities children in the Western Cape, thus being in breach of the rights of those children to basic education, protection from neglect or degradation, equality and, human dignity. The State was instructed to take reasonable steps and interim measures in order to address the above challenges experienced by the children.

WORKING WITH FAMILIES

South African parents, teachers and learners are important partners in attempting to improve performance of learners. However, the social portrait even in the second richest province, namely, Western Cape, suggests that many parents do not have the requisite levels of education. Quite clearly there is a relationship between parent's education and their commitment to socializing children into education. This of course is a universal experience. Departments of Education have played a role in advocacy regarding the involvement of parents by maintaining close links with a number of parent organizations. Parent organizations as well as school governing body organizations have also been involved in the development of policy regarding White Paper Six. Regular meetings have been held between the Department of Education and school governing bodies and parent organizations at both the national and provincial level. These organization include, Disabled Children's Action Group (DICAG) South Africa, Downs Syndrome Association of South Africa, South African National Organization for the Deaf, Special Education Parent Teacher Organization, Disabled People South Africa (DPSA) and, South African National School Governing Body Association.

Of all the above-mentioned groups, DICAG was one of the most powerful and influential. Their representatives sat on almost all major transformation committees when White Paper Six was developed. DICAG was established in 1993 by the parents of children with disabilities. Their main aim is to empower themselves to educate children in an inclusive environment to ensure equal opportunities for children with disabilities.

DICAG was initially affiliated to Disabled People South Africa (DPSA), the national disabled people's umbrella organization before it became an independent organization. It has 311 support centres, 15,000 parent members and 10,000 children actively involved. DICAG has served as a campaigning organization to help raise the level of awareness of disability as well as challenge stereotypes and perceptions of people with disabilities in South Africa.

The issue of cultural capital and education is an issue that favours middle-class families that are in the minority in South Africa. Working class families do not have the cultural capital and therefore are unable to empower their children. Many working class parents do not attach value to education since education has not helped them. They do not see the value in education based on their experiences.

In South Africa, there are many non-governmental organizations that worked with families during the apartheid era. Many of these organizations that survived financially are helping parents and families. In the disability sector, there are many parent empowerment groupings that rely on one another for support. Typically, these groups consist of parents who have children who have a particular category of disability, for example, the Downs Syndrome Organization, which comprises parents of Downs Syndrome Children. Other disability categories of children have similar organizations. These organizations are composed of mainly middle-class parents who fell into the white race group. With the transitions towards inclusive education, many black parents have joined these groupings. This is the most dominant grouping of family support but the existence of these grouping in working class areas is minimal. Positively, more and more parents are joining these organizations from different classes and races across the country with the movement towards inclusive education in South Africa. Many of these organizations continue to play a very important role in schools and various communities through outreach programmes, conferences and other forums. They are an indispensable part of the South African special education scenario with many parents playing particularly active roles. A good example is the role of the Western Cape Inclusive Education Forum. They established a resource centre and other forms of support. Many of these parents have worked in townships and have been extremely helpful to disadvantaged black children. One of the pioneers in this movement was Michelle Belknapp.

An example of a more formal organization is the South African National Council for the Blind. Traditionally, this organization has served mainly white learners but with the transition to a democracy, they serve all children. This movement towards serving all children has been adopted by most other categorical disability organizations.

In more privileged areas, there is a close relationship between the school governing body which includes parents and representatives of the school. Children who attend middle-class schools have a formal network in terms of the school governing body that establishes goals for students with their parents input at individual schools. Whilst this does not happen at a systemic level, more progress is being in underprivileged areas. Schools increasingly are required to take children from all backgrounds and parents receive support from schools where the goals of their children are discussed. For example, at the De La Bat School in the Western Cape, parents of 3-year-old children are being involved in the school's Sign Language programmes. Parents at De La Bat School are made aware of the possibilities for their child' learning and teaching. School personnel report that the parents play a constructive role in the lives of their children and get exposed to Sign Language once their children are admitted in school. Hopefully over the next decade, South African special school administrators will make a major systemic effort to replicate the successful parental involvement example from De La Bat School.

There are no formal transitional living and vocational training programmes that are provided in South Africa schools. However, many parents of children with disabilities get involved in this area. For example, national organizations such as the Downs Syndrome Association create awareness and opportunities for children to obtain employment. While such organizations can be helpful in this area, much work has to be done in the public schools.

TEACHERS AND SPECIAL EDUCATION (ROLES, EXPECTATIONS, TRAINING)

Teacher training requirements in South Africa require teachers to hold a 4-year teaching degree or a 3-year degree and a higher education teaching diploma. Special Education/Inclusive Education is part of the teacher training packages. Specialist training in areas of disability is lacking in South Africa with very few specialized training programmes on offer. Universities are currently working with the Department of Basic Education working on these programmes.

Teaching practice at schools is mandatory at universities and each student has to complete teaching practice for a specific period of time. This is normally a six-week period. At this time there, is a huge teaching shortage in South Africa regarding various categories of disabilities. However, this shortage in particular areas was acknowledged by White Paper Six. This also includes South African Sign Language (SASL) teachers and teachers of the visually impaired. Steps have been taken to ameliorate the challenge but it will take a significant period of time to address the backlogs. In view of White Paper Six and related White Papers, the government is playing a major role in creating the conditions for quality teacher education. Bursaries are provided for all teachers provided they commit themselves to teaching for a period of time. The bursaries are generous and cover the four-year study programme.

When White Paper Six was developed, it was envisaged that teacher education should be a priority. White Paper Six articulated the vision that classroom educators will be the primary resource for achieving the goal of an inclusive education and training system. The main thrust of the plan was to ensure that educators will need to improve their skills and knowledge, and develop new ones. Staff development at the school and district level was regarded as critical to putting in place successful integrated educational practices. White Paper Six had the following foci:

- In mainstream education, priorities will include multi-level classroom instruction so that educators can prepare main lessons with variations that are responsive to individual learner needs; co-operative learning;

curriculum enrichment; and dealing with learners with behavioural problems.
- In special schools/resource centres, priorities will include orientation to new roles within district support services of support to neighbourhood schools, and new approaches that focus on problem solving and the development of learners' strengths and competencies rather than focusing on their shortcomings only.

Along with the above foci, the Ministry of Education has been training teachers within the framework of the OBE curriculum. Also, there has been an emphasis on diversity by the Department of Education. For example, in his forward to the teacher's curriculum guide, South Africa's Director-General of Education, Mr. Thami Mseleku, has clearly expressed a focus on diversity. In the curriculum guide, he states 'These guidelines are geared to assist teachers in accommodating Learning Outcomes and Assessment Standards that are prescribed, yet create space and possibilities for the use of judgments and insights based on particular contexts and a diverse learning population' (Department of Education, 2003). This curriculum document further states:

> The guidelines are intended to be implemented in conjunction with other policies, for example, the White Paper Six: Special Needs Education: Building an Inclusive Education and Training System needs to be read to provide background information on issues related to barriers to learning, as these have crucial impact of what happens in the classroom. (Department of Education, 2003, p. 1)

Positively, inclusive education has been on the teacher education agenda in most of the teacher training forums across the country for the last 10 years. A dedicated section on inclusion has been a key feature in all training and orientation session relating to the South African school curriculum.

Government provides support for teachers and at this time in view of the Year of Inclusion links are being fostered with South Africa's major universities to train prospective teachers in specific disabilities. For example, an agreement has been concluded with South Africa's largest university, University of South Africa, for teachers to be trained to teach the visually impaired. South African Sign Language and other areas are being looked at. During the apartheid era, many teachers who taught in black schools did not have specialist qualifications in specific disabilities. Of course universities were segregated and provision was made for white teachers.

Student teaching, practicums and internships are being made available to teachers at various universities and inclusive education is receiving a lot of attention. Teachers are certified with four-year degree programmes which include practicums and teacher training at school sites. Bursaries will be offered to teachers as part of the National Bursary Scheme if current negotiations come to fruition.

Teacher Development Priorities in Inclusive Education include the following:

Focus 1: Training all teachers on Screening, Identification, Assessment and Support (SIAS) and Curriculum Differentiation – CAPS training and one per school (2012–2014).

Focus 2: Improving specialized skills – visual impairment, deaf and hard of hearing, autism, intellectual disability, communication disorders, cerebral palsy – short courses and bursaries for Higher Education Institutions accredited courses (2012–2014).

Focus 3: District support teams – effective management of special schools, full-service schools and supporting implementation of inclusion at all levels (guidelines training) (2012).

PERSPECTIVE ON THE PROGRESS OF SPECIAL EDUCATION

In assessing the progress of the Department of Education's White Paper Six, a number of factors have to be considered. South Africa became a democracy about 18 years ago and merged 19 separate ethic and provincial departments into one unitary system of education. New appointments were made in the various state departments and there was a total transformation in terms of demographics, leadership and policy.

Whilst inclusive education was embraced as an ideology and practice by a large majority of South Africans, there remain several challenges. Many people who embraced inclusive education were the marginalized, black people, progressive white people and those that saw merit in the concept based on educational thinking. However, the inclusive system had to be implemented in an education system that did not have a sound and developed practices in the majority of schools that previously were characterized as disadvantaged. Another challenge related to the fact that the expertise in the field were in the hands of people who promoted special education. The majority of the structures and organizations in the field of special education were led by people who promoted special education. The transformation of knowledge and organizations was a huge stumbling block in terms of advancing inclusive education. Paradigmatic change is a difficult concept. However, to advance paradigmatic change in an environment where people's views were so entrenched in the opposing discourse is a gargantuan task.

Within this context seven white papers were developed and implemented. Table 3 provides the foci of the different White Papers.

In South Africa's relatively new democracy, there has been a major commitment in principle to special education or inclusive education. Many South Africans who came into power in the new democracy developed a demonstrated passion and commitment to inclusive education as a major part component to change the system. This passion emerges from the fact that substantial numbers of South Africans operated in the margins and cracks of Apartheid society.

The context into which White Paper Six was implemented differed but presented a range of challenges. A closer look at the education profile within the province of the Western Cape, the second richest province, provides some sense of the challenges facing policy implementation. According to the Human Capital Strategy developed by the provincial education department, only 23.4% of the population complete grade 12 (final school year), 36.5% drop out during the secondary school phase, only 7.9% complete primary education, 15.2% drop out during the primary phase and 5.7% of the population have no schooling. Looking at this across racial divides, it is evident that enrolment and completion of school to the age of 17 years is highest amongst the whites (at 100%), with the enrolment and completion is significantly lower amongst the African population, and still lower amongst Coloured adolescents. For those who are at school

Table 3. Foci of South Africa's Department of Education White Papers.

White Paper	Foci
White Paper 1	First White Paper of the Democratic Era that lays the framework for education and training in South Africa
White Paper 2	Organization, Funding and Governance of Schools
White Paper 3	Transformation of Higher Education
White Paper 4	Further Education and Training Colleges
White Paper 5	Early Childhood Education
White Paper 6	Inclusive Education
White Paper 7	e-Learning

currently, only 37% of learners at grade 3 level are achieving grade-appropriate literacy and numeracy levels while at grade 6 level, numeracy performance drops to 15%, and literacy performance to 35%. These statistics are very problematic especially considering that the Western Cape's education department receives 38.1% of the provincial budget (Western Cape Education Department, 2007). It is evident that these children are not receiving a high quality education in spite of the ample funding that occurs.

It is quite logical given South Africa's history to conclude that the poorest children are black. It is also logical conclude that black poor children are the ones that experience the least success in the education system. After 15 years of funding education on a pro-poor basis with the emphasis on equity, it seems there is much more work to do if inclusion has to become a reality. The challenge is to break the cycle of failure and poverty using education as a point of departure. The high dropout rate and the low pass rates in literacy and numeracy suggests a relationship between parents level of education referred to above and school results.

In the light of the above discussion, it becomes obvious that one of the main interventions of White Paper Six was to introduce the notion of barriers to learning and the introduction of systemic issues instead of focussing mainly on individual deficits as the only challenge of special needs education. Many learners experience barriers to learning or drop out primarily because of the inability of the system to recognize and accommodate the diverse range of learning needs typically through inaccessible physical plants, curricula that is geared for general education students, ineffective assessment, insufficient learning materials and ineffective instructional methodologies. The approach advocated in White Paper Six is fundamentally different from traditional ones that assume that barriers to learning reside primarily within the learner and accordingly, learner support should take the form of a specialist, typically medical interventions (Department of Education, 2001, p. 60). The notion that performance could be affected not only by individual weaknesses but systemic weaknesses was introduced by White Paper Six. This shift in thinking could be characterized as follows. Different learning needs may also arise because of:

- Negative attitudes to and stereotyping of difference.
- An inflexible curriculum.
- Inappropriate languages or language of learning and teaching.
- Inappropriate communication.
- Inaccessible and unsafe built environments.
- Inappropriate and inadequate support services.
- Inadequate policies and legislation.

- The non-recognition and non-involvement of parents.
- Inadequately and inappropriately trained education managers and educators. (Department of Education, 2001, p. 60)

In the long term, understanding the above weaknesses to effective learning and systemic challenges may assist educators in addressing challenges facing the South Africa's education system. Positively, after a decade, the educational policy process and understandings are taking hold. Further, current performance suggests that South Africa has to consolidate and entrench the insights generated by White Paper Six.

South Africa has many challenges and there is a considerable amount of work that is yet to be done. However, a 2012 Department of Basic Education (previously Department of Education) report indicated that the following has been achieved with regarding to implementing White Paper Six:

- Piloted the implementation of White Paper Six through a Field Test in 30 districts, 30 special schools and 30 designated full-service schools;
- Developed the screening, identification, assessment and support (SIAS) strategy for early identification of learning difficulties and support;
- Developed Inclusive Learning Programmes to guide the system on how to deal with disabilities in the classroom;
- Developed Funding Principles to guide provinces on how to fund the implementation of White Paper Six as an interim measure;
- Submitted two funding bids to Treasury for the Expansion of Inclusive Education Programme from which R1.5bn was allocated for 2008 and R300m for 2009 on Equitable Share basis;
- Converted 10 ordinary schools to full-service schools;
- Incorporated inclusivity principles in all curriculum training;
- Trained 200 district officials related to educational aspects for students with visual impairment and hearing impairment;
- Developed Guidelines for Responding to Learner Diversity in the Classroom through the National Curriculum Statement and orientated: 2,474 district officials and grade 10 subject advisors in 2011; 110 stakeholders in 2011; 3,035 district officials and subject advisors for grade 11 in 2012; 163 stakeholders and special schools lead teachers in 2012; and 968 district officials and subject advisors for grades 4–6 in 2012;
- Is developing the South African Sign Language curriculum as subject for grades R-12;
- Has developed a framework for qualifications pathways at NQF level 1 for learners with moderate and severe intellectual disability;

- Is developing an Action Plan to provide access to education for out-of-school children and youth including those with severe and profound intellectual impairments;
- 98 Special Schools have been converted to Special Schools as Resource Centres;
- 25 New Special Schools have been built;
- 225 Full-Service Schools have been created;
- District-Based Support Teams have been created across the country.

After a little more than a decade of implementation, it is clear that progress has been achieved; however, the achievement of learners and learning outcomes is not at a desirable level.

CHALLENGES THAT REMAIN

It must be noted that the above pilot study was initially envisaged as a three-year pilot but was concluded within a ten-year period. Whilst government committed itself to completing the pilot in three years, a number of factors contributed to delaying the implementation. These included provinces not dedicating budgets to advance the pilot, staff turnover in the Department of Basic Education, lack of human resource capacity in the provinces and in general a lack of prioritizing given the number of pressing priorities in the provinces.

The Department of Basic Education (DBE) in South Africa committed 2013 to the entrenchment of Inclusive Education thus calling 2013 the year of inclusion. This was a very bold approach by the education authorities. As mentioned earlier, there is much more to do for inclusive education to be successful in South Africa. Whilst progress in the area of inclusive education is at a theoretical stage, the planning and the beginning steps of White Paper Six has been achieved. It is obvious that more work has to be done in the area of teacher education, human resource development, building and developing full-service schools, support and creating special schools as resource centres and empowering district-based support teams. The following presentation to the education standing committee (Department of Basic Education, 2012) reveals the limitations of the implementation:

- Analysis found glaring disparities in the provision of access to specialist services to schools across provinces and within each in terms of types of the professionals;

- There is a huge lack of specialist professionals and in three of South Africa's provinces the availability of specialists is below 0.5%. These provinces are yet to budget for inclusive education. There is a lack of therapists, psychologists, social workers and professional nurses;
- The ratio for teachers without knowledge of South African Sign Language (21.8%) is higher than that for teachers without knowledge of visual impairment (10.9%). Areas of deafness and visual impairment appear to experience major challenges. Although South African Sign Language development has begun, this is one of the most neglected sectors.

The lack of quality and trained staff is a major problem that hinders the further development of Inclusive Education/Special Education in South Africa. Specialists are central to the assessment and identification process. Availability of therapists is also critical for assessment of learners for provision of assistive devices and technology particularly for students with physical disabilities. If the three provinces that have not budgeted for the expansion of Inclusive Education do not occur, White Paper Six will ultimately fail in these provinces. According to the report made by the Department of Basic Education (2012) to the standing committee, visual impairment and deafness are isolated because they are the highly specialized compared to other disabilities that largely depend on Curriculum Differentiation. The report also cautioned about appropriate and relevant conversion of ordinary schools to full-service schools. Specifically, the report stressed that a conversion is more than making schools environmentally accessible for learners with physical disabilities as there is an accompanying need for an inclusive education ethos. Ultimately, the report calls for provinces to get more involved in the inclusive education process through adequate budgeting, increased advocacy and effective training.

At a general level, it seems that the envisaged White paper Six educational shift in paradigm has been largely underestimated. Paradigm shifts are complex and ambitious projects and poor results in the South African education system suggest that deeper training of teachers should take place to address the challenge of poverty and education. If poor learners and poor achievers are to be advanced in the system, teachers need effective; special education knowledge based instructional tools that will create a different consciousness within the school cultural so that inclusive education can flourish.

CONCLUSION

For a developing country and a relatively young democracy, South Africa has made some bold attempts at moving towards an inclusive education system. The country's progress in this endeavour is noted but not currently sufficient given the documented learning outcomes of South Africa's learners in their formative years.

While the 2013 year dedicated to inclusive education has led to advancement in achieving White Paper Six goals, it also pointed out the needs to focus on the employment of specialists and support personnel. Psychologists, therapists and related personnel are indispensable to successful inclusive education particularly for full-service schools, special schools as resource centres and district-based support teams. The results of academic achievement and advancement in the early grades of schooling suggest that not much progress has been made with regard to the paradigm shifts anticipated in White Paper Six concerning barriers to learning. Teacher training should focus on content knowledge but also provide teachers with effective instructional and intellectual tools to deal with poverty. The alienation of South African children who experience barriers to learning due to hearing and visual impairments is problematic. This cannot continue as any human rights culture should ensure that learners who are hearing or visually impaired should be at the centre of the inclusive education process.

REFERENCES

Behr, A. L. (1980, 1984). *New perspectives in South African education*. Durban, South Africa: Butterworths.

Department of Basic Education. (2012). *Presentation to standing committee*. Pretoria, South Africa: Department of Basic Education.

Department of Education. (1996). *White paper on education and training*. Pretoria, South Africa: South Africa Department of Education.

Department of Education. (1997). *Quality education for all. Report of the national commission for special education needs and training and national committee for education support services*. Pretoria, South Africa: South Africa Department of Education.

Department of Education. (2001). *Education white paper 6 on special needs education: Building an inclusive education and training system*. Cape Town, South Africa: South Africa Department of Education.

Department of Education. (2003). *Outcomes-based education in South Africa: Background information for educators*. Pretoria, South Africa: South Africa Department of Education.

Department of Education. (2005). *Conceptual and operational guidelines for district based support teams.* Pretoria, South Africa: South Africa Department of Education.

Department of Education. (2007). *Guidelines to ensure quality education and support in special schools and special school resource centres.* Pretoria, South Africa: South Africa Department of Education.

Department of Education. (2010). *Guidelines for full service schools/inclusive schools.* Pretoria, South Africa: South Africa Department of Education.

Disability Desk: Office of the Deputy State President. (1997). *Integrated national disability strategy document.* Pretoria, South Africa: Office of the Deputy State President.

Fick, M. L. (1939). *An individual scale of general intelligence for South Africa.* Pretoria, South Africa: SA Council for Educational and Social Research.

Fulcher, G. (1989). *Disabling policies? A comparative approach to education policy and disability.* London, UK: Farmer Press.

Government of South Africa. (2001). *Census.* Pretoria, South Africa: Government Printer.

High Court of South Africa. (2010). *Western Cape forum for intellectual disability vs. Government of South Africa.* Case 18678. Cape Town, South Africa.

Legal Resources Centre. (2009). *Update in the matter of Kyle Springate.* Bulletin. Retrieved from www.lrc.org.za/

Naicker, S. M. (1999). *Curriculum 2005: A space for all, An introduction to inclusive education.* Cape Town, South Africa: Tafelburg.

Naicker, S. M. (2005). An emerging pedagogy of possibility. In D. Mitchell (Ed.), *Contextualizing inclusive education* (pp. 230–251). London, UK: Routledge.

National Education Policy Investigation. (1992). *National education policy investigation: Education support services.* Cape Town, South Africa: Oxford University Press.

Spady, W. (1994). *Outcomes-based education: Critical issues and answers.* Alexandria, VA: American Association of School Administrators.

Western Cape Education Department. (2007). *Human capital development strategy.* Cape Town, South Africa: Edumedia.

SPECIAL EDUCATION TODAY IN GHANA

Ahmed Bawa Kuyini

ABSTRACT

The Ghana chapter on special education begins with the history of service provisions for persons with disabilities. It includes information on educational and rehabilitation services, special schools and integrated education. Detailed data is related concerning prevalence and incidence rates and special needs among the Ghana population. This is followed by a comprehensive section on regular and special education teacher roles, expectations, and training. An important aspect of Ghana's special education is its movement towards inclusive education. The support for this movement comes from the Ministry of Education's policy, namely, The Education Strategic Plan (ESP), which adopts inclusive education and promotes it as the future special education direction for the country. The chapter provides detailed information on the issues related to the implementation of the ESP plan, four models that have been developed for inclusive education, the progress and effort that Ghana has made towards inclusive education as well as significant challenges that are present.

Special Education International Perspectives: Practices Across the Globe
Advances in Special Education, Volume 28, 431–469
ISSN: 0270-4013/doi:10.1108/S0270-401320140000028021

INTRODUCTION

Ghana is a country with a population of 25 million people. It is located in West Africa and has borders Cote D'Ivoire, Burkina, and Togo. Ghana has many natural resources that include major sea ports on the Atlantic Ocean, fertile land, and reserves of oil, gold, and bauxite. Also, it has a young population and its people are among the best educated in the world. The population of Ghana is very diverse and includes more than 50 different ethnic groups. The country was given its independence from in 1957. Special educational in Ghana is mainly a public sector endeavour with the Government establishing and running the majority of schools. However, the private sector, including religious and non-religious organizations has been an integral part of the historical development and current provision of special education. From a humble and unknown component of the education system at independence in 1957, special educational provision has now expanded and has a presence in all aspects of educational considerations in Ghana.

ORIGINS OF SPECIAL EDUCATION IN GHANA

History of Service Provision for Persons with Disabilities

Historically, services for people with disabilities began with the Christian missionaries such as the Wesley and Basel missionaries who made special provisions in schools for children and adults with hearing and visual Impairment in the early part of the 20th century. Some missionaries set up limited forms of rehabilitation services. However, broad service provision involving the government of Ghana began after the Second World War.

Rehabilitation Services
Formal recognition for the need to develop services for persons with disabilities in the newly independent Ghana began with Dr. Kwame Nkrumah's motion in parliament on the plight of persons with disabilities. This motion culminated in the setting up of the John Wilson committee in 1959, which was to examine the needs of the disabled and to make recommendations to the Government (Walker, Marfo, & Charles, 1986). The committee among others recommended the establishment of eight rural rehabilitation units across the country (Korsah, 1983). Following the committee's report, the Government provided these rehabilitation

institutions through the Department of Social Welfare starting in the middle of 1961. By 1970, there was at least one rehabilitation centre in each region of Ghana (Walker et al., 1986), providing services mainly to the blind, deaf and physically disabled. Thus, Ghana like many developing countries employed the Institution-based rehabilitation approach; in which the bulk of the cost is borne by Government.

Educational Services
The Government's participation in educational provision for persons with disabilities was minimal before Ghana's independence in 1957. Under the British Colonial Government, all attempts at providing educational services to children with disabilities were undertaken by Christian missionaries. The missionaries established and ran schools specifically for blind children, and only in 1945 did the colonial government take on some of the responsibility for providing these services (Avoke, 2001). After independence and following the recommendations of the parliamentary committee on the plight of the persons with disabilities, some provisions were made in the Education Act of 1961 (Government of Ghana, 1961) to provide for the needs of persons with disabilities. The Education Act of 1961 stated among other things that every child who had attained the going school age as determined by the Minister of Education was to attend a course of instruction as specified by the MoE in a school recognized for that purpose (Government of Ghana, 1961). In essence, the provisions of the Education Act of 1961 laid the foundation for a free compulsory education for all children in Ghana. The Act thus gave recognition to the right to education for all children with disabilities in Ghana and resulted in the establishment of schools for children with disabilities. Successive Governments from the 1960s continued with the pre-independence approach to educational provision, such that residential special schools remained the main form of schooling for children with disabilities in Ghana, even into the 1990s.

Special Schools
The MoE set up a number of special schools for different categories of disabilities from the 1960s. Two schools for the blind were established at Akropong and Wa and followed by the opening of schools for persons with hearing impairment across the regions of Ghana in 1962. The Society of Friends of the Mentally Impaired started a school for children with intellectual disability, namely, the Accra Psychiatric Hospital in 1968 (Avoke, 2001; Ofori-Addo, Worgbeyi, & Tay, 1999). Between 1970 and 1980 many more segregated 'special schools' were established for the 'visually impaired',

the 'hearing impaired', and the 'intellectually disabled'. Increasing national recognition of the need for additional education services led to the formation of the Special Education Division (SED) within the Ghana Education Service (GES) in 1985.

At the threshold of the inclusion initiative in 1992, there were two basic schools for students with visual impairments in Akropong and Wa. Additionally, resource centres were established in three primary schools (Avoke, 2001; MoE, 1996). There were four public and two private schools for students with intellectual disabilities. For students with hearing impairment, there were eleven schools for primary education and one for secondary education (a demonstration secondary school) was located at Mampong–Akwapim. Students with learning disabilities were educated in five primary schools. There were also four primary schools connected to hospitals. Two of such schools were connected to teaching hospitals, and the other two were connected to local hospitals for children receiving orthopaedic services. Most students with moving difficulties attended regular schools in their local communities, and this arrangement represented some kind of informal integration (Avoke, 2001; MoE, 1996).

Integrated Education
In the late 1970s, formal attempts were made to integrate children with visual impairments into the regular education system. In 1975, resource centres were established in two secondary schools, and units for hearing impaired education opened in two regular schools at Kibi and Koforidua. In addition, a teachers' training college was established to train teachers with the capacity to support students in integrated settings. In spite of the good underlying intentions, the experimental integrated education programmes were not sustainable because of the lack of clear policy, and resources, both human and material. As a consequence, the unit for the hearing impaired eventually operated like other special schools, with qualified teachers of the hearing impaired providing classroom instruction. Furthermore complicating this situation at education integration was the fact that higher educational opportunities were limited for students with visual impairments such that only a few students were offered places in teacher training colleges such as The University of Ghana and The University of Cape Coast (MoE, 1996; Ofori-Addo et al., 1999).

Limitations of the Rehabilitation Service and Special School Systems in Ghana
By the 1980s, the general rise in the cost of managing both institutional rehabilitation centres and special schools had become a strong issue of

concern. This situation arose because, not only was the cost of running the institutions high, but also services were meeting the needs of only about 2% of the disabled population (Ofori-Addo, 1994; O'Toole, Hofslett, Bupuru, Ofori-Addo, & Kotoku, 1996). This situation reflected the general trend in many developing countries, including: Zimbabwe, Indonesia, Nigeria, Zambia, Pakistan, Philippines and Jamaica. The inadequacies of the institution-based rehabilitation as echoed in these developing countries exposed a huge discrepancy between the number of people needing services and the availability of appropriate services. Though many of these countries had recognized the inadequacies of these approaches, not much was done to augment the volume and quality of services. Such inaction was not necessarily the result of insensitivity on the part of governments, but rather the result of resource constraints and the implementation of inappropriate methods to service delivery (O'Toole, 1990).

The use of inappropriate methods of service delivery (including institutionalized rehabilitation centres, and special schools) was seen as undesirable and in many countries culminated in the call for reforms in rehabilitation and educational provision for persons with disabilities. In the United States (USA) in particular, the 1970s saw the coming into force of legislation such as the Education of All Handicapped Children Act (EAHCA) (1975, Public Law 94-142), which called for the provision of free public school education for all students with disabilities. Not long after the passage of EAHCA, several bodies including UNESCO (1990, 1994) and World Health Organization [WHO] (2006) also proposed some reforms in both rehabilitation and educational service provision for persons with disabilities. These developments marked the knick-point for new thinking and arrangements in area of special needs education at the international level and ultimately in Ghana.

PREVALENCE AND INCIDENCE OF DISABILITY AND SPECIAL NEEDS

Defining Exceptionality, People, and Ideas

Traditional views about disability are quite diverse, and divergence from the norm has been influenced by superstitious beliefs. Generally, in Ghana, people with disabilities were believed to be possessed by evil spirits and can be a source of bad omen for the family or community. For example among the Dagomba people of northern Ghana, some children with disabilities such as Down's Syndrome – who usually have low muscle tone – are believed to be snake-spirits in disguise, who are capable of turning into big snakes at night to devour their enemies. Historically, these beliefs culminated in cruelty, infanticide or negative attitudes towards such children and hampered efforts at providing rehabilitation in the family and community. These negative views about the causes and potential of disability to do harm have meant that people only see the negative attributes and fail to see the needs of people with disability. Such negative attitudes within society seem to influence teachers' attitudes towards students with disabilities in the classroom (Agbenyega, 2007; Kuyini & Desai, 2007, 2008). It evident therefore that work needs to be done to change attitudes in the Ghanaian society.

In the formal sector, the definition of disability in Ghana appears to be confined to the more obvious sensory and physical disabilities. In other words people with disability have been defined as those with physical, hearing, vision, intellectual and multiple impairments. According to the SED of the GES, the main types of special needs students provided for in schools include *intellectual disability, hearing, and visual impairment.* Although in recent times other disabilities such as *autism spectrum disorder* and *psychiatric disabilities* have been given attention, however, it is clear that this definition does not include other forms of disability or special needs such as *attention deficit hyperactivity disorder* and conduct disorder.

Prevalence

As in any other society, there is range of disabilities in Ghana. However, given no accurate data on disabilities in Ghana, The Ministry of Employment and Social Welfare (MESW) suggested calculating the number of persons with disabilities using a 10% formula. Thus, for an estimated population of 25 million people, the percentage of people with disabilities would be about 2.5 million. At the turn of the century, The National Disability Policy Document (Government of Ghana, 2000) reported a much higher percentage (about 14.3%) based on reports from the regions (see Table 1). On the other hand, the a study by the National Community-Based Rehabilitation Programme (NCBRP) undertaken in the Upper East Region of Ghana in 1998 revealed a lower disability prevalence rate of 5.5% of the total population for that region (SUNEPED, Report, Ministry of Employment and Social Welfare [MESW], 1998), which conflicts with the estimates contained in the National Disability Policy

Table 1. Disability Prevalence by Gender and Region.

Region	Male %	Female %	Total %
Western	19.6	21.6	20.7
Central	19.0	23.9	21.6
Greater Accra	21.2	22.7	22.0
Volta	16.8	19.4	18.1
Eastern	10.2	11.5	10.9
Ashanti	11.4	14.1	12.8
Brong Ahafo	12.0	13.5	12.8
Northern	7.8	4.7	6.3
Upper East	3.5	1.0	2.3
Upper West	6.2	7.2	6.7
Total	13.4	15.2	14.3

Source: National Disability Policy Document, Government of Ghana (2000).

Document. On the basis the National Disability Policy Document (Government of Ghana, 2000), it would appear therefore that the national average is well above 10% of the population.

The lack of accurate statistics on disability in the general population also applies to children of school going age. The GES in 2006 estimated that there were about 676,000–804,000 children with disabilities using the United Nations estimation of 10–12% of any given population. The Ghana Education Service [GES] (2006) indicated that children who are officially registered included only those with physical/severe learning disabilities, visual impairment and hearing impairment. In their 2008 study Kuyini and Desai reported that there was an average of 4–5 children with mild-moderate disabilities in inclusive classroom settings of 45–50 students. This represents about 2–2.5% of the classroom populations. Since many children with severe disabilities do not attend schools at all or often attend special schools, there is every indication that the population of children with special needs who should in educational settings is well above 5%.

The above high estimates of disability underscore the need for conscious effort in pursuing effective measures to provide rehabilitation, educational and other services to persons with disabilities. More importantly, the composition of the disability population shows that a substantial percentage is within the school going age. These young persons with disabilities have a right to, and require access to education as all other citizens. No doubt, if the educational needs of such a substantial percentage of the population were to be met by only special schools, it would require enormous amounts of resources to provide the appropriate variety of specialists, equipment and space in special education classrooms. It is this recognition that underpins the recent Ghana Government's drive to ensure that all children (with and without disabilities) attend their local schools. However, there appears to be a variety of barriers to realizing this objective of providing access to education for all children.

As in several other countries, many children with disabilities in Ghana are required to and often attend special schools. However, the bulk of children with disabilities have difficulty accessing education (both special and general), resulting in low levels of educational participation compared to the rest of the population. The National Disability Policy Document (MESW, 2000) in confirming the difficulty of children with disabilities in accessing basic education also estimated that about 53% of females with disabilities were without education, in contrast with 37.3% of males. In the last 10 years, the benefits of the Free Compulsory Universal Basic Education (FCUBE) programme have resulted in increased school participation nationally. For example, the low enrolment rate of 75–78% in 1992 and 1996 of children attending school has increased to 84% in 2011 (World Bank, 2012). However, educational participation by children with disabilities is still lower than those without disabilities. Such low levels of educational participation by children with disabilities has been blamed on a general limited educational provision in the communities, social rejection due to negative attitudes towards disability and the attendant social stigma which induces parental restrictions to participation in society (World Bank, 2012).

TRENDS IN LEGISLATION AND POLICY

Since independence in 1957, major legislation relating to educational and service provision and wellbeing of people with a disability include the Education Act of 1961, The 1992 Constitution, Children's Act of 1998, Persons with Disability Act (Act 715) of 2006, and the New Policy on Inclusive Education (SED, 2013). However, the provisions of the Education Act of 1961 which provided all children access to education irrespective of ability or disability set the stage and provided the momentum towards Ghana's eventual movement to an inclusive education system (Anson-Yevu, 1988; Avoke, 2001). The section below describes in detail Ghana's development towards inclusive education.

Developments Towards Inclusive Education in Ghana: 1987–2004

Ghana's participation in the international developments in regard to providing special needs education had some positive impact on the situation at home, and culminated in the 1980s witnessing significant steps to reform the entire educational system, and to improve on services for persons with disabilities. By 1986, reports indicated that service provision for persons with disabilities including educational provision in Ghana, were inadequate (Kuyini, 1998; Ofori-Addo, 1994; O'Toole et al., 1996). The reports specifically noted that:

- The existing rehabilitation institutions were unevenly distributed across the country.
- Many of the institutions were urban-based, whereas the majority of the disabled lived in the rural areas.
- More importantly, special education in schools only benefited a small number of disabled children and rarely equipped the individual for employment in adult life.
- Vocational education provided through government rehabilitation institutions was of poor quality and lacked viability as to employment prospects (Ofori-Addo, 1994; O'Toole et al., 1996).

As a consequence, The Government of Ghana outlined and implemented a new educational reform programme in 1987. The reform called The New Educational Reform Programme of 1987 was aimed at improving access to and quality of education for all children. It had the following key objectives:

- Reverse the steady decline in the quality of education and address the negative outcomes.
- Tailor the organizational structure and content of the educational system to match the professional needs of the country.
- Create an effective and well-integrated management system of the educational sector at the national level for all manner and levels of education.

The purpose of this last goal was to develop policy-based activities in line with national development objectives; provide a quality educational system in terms of content and services offered; and integrate special education into the regular educational system (Ofori-Addo et al., 1999). Such a goal required liaising with international bodies for advice and support and led to the invitation of the UNESCO team to Ghana.

The UNESCO Consultation on Special Education
The Ghana Government participated in, and committed itself to the processes and activities associated with the international decade of the disabled, including The United Nation's *World Program of Action for the Disabled* (United Nations, 2006). In line with this commitment, The Government of Ghana reached out to UN bodies including UNESCO to initiate ways of tailoring policy and educational provisions towards meeting the needs of persons with disabilities. Consequently, the UNESCO *Consultation on Special Education* at the invitation of the Ghana Government visited Ghana in 1988. The consultation team's objective was to ascertain the nature and level of need for educational provision for persons with disabilities in Ghana. The team's finding reflected an imbalance between a huge need for educational services for persons with disabilities and limited resources for meeting the need (O'Toole et al., 1996). Against the background of the team's belief in the potential of integrated education to be effective in providing desired outcomes, as happened in countries with similar conditions, the team recommended the concurrent initiation of a community-based rehabilitation and inclusive education programme in Ghana. Having carefully studied the recommendations, another UNESCO team was invited Ghana in 1991. The team assessed the possibility of establishing a Community-Based Rehabilitation (CBR) programme (Ofori-Addo, 1994), and provided valuable recommendations to the Government of Ghana on how best to implement such a programme. The team's recommendations, taking into account Ghana's unique socio-economic and cultural context resulted in a convenient approach, where the general reform in the entire system of rehabilitation service delivery was tied to the development of an inclusive education programme (Ofori-Addo et al., 1999; O'Toole et al., 1996).

The CBR Programme and Inclusive Education Initiative
The reform in the rehabilitation service delivery saw the initiation of the CBR programme (Ofori-Addo, 1994). The programme was implemented on a pilot basis in ten districts in 1992. In 1994, it was extended to 10 other districts following the initial successes in the first implementation areas. The aims of the CBR programme were to:

- Create awareness and mobilize resources at the community level to better enable parents to help their disabled children attend school, to learn skills and participate productively in family and community life.

- Establish links with service providers in health, education community development and social welfare at the district level. In this way the needs of the disabled can be more effectively met.
- Strengthen the association of persons with disabilities to play a role in the mobilization of the community for the implementation and management of the CBR programme.
- Promote human rights of persons with disabilities (Ofori-Addo, 1994).

Outcome of CBR Programme

Literature on CBR programmes in some developing countries had revealed that implementation was saddled with problems, and doubts had been expressed about the appropriateness and potential of the approach to ensure any effective or successful rehabilitation (Jaffer & Jaffer, 1990; O'Toole, 1987). However, Ghana's programme showed promising results. In fact, evaluation reports of Ghana's CBR programme Kuyini (1998), Ofori-Addo (1994) and O'Toole et al. (1996) indicated positive results in the direction of the programme objectives. In particular an outsider evaluation of the CBR programme in Northern Ghana by Kuyini (1998) indicated the following:

- The CBR programme, as conceived by the programme management, had been well implemented with respect to the administrative and structural arrangements.
- There was a substantial positive impact in line with some programme objectives such as; assistance to persons with disabilities, recruiting and engaging volunteer-local supervisors, getting parents to become trainers of the persons with disabilities, and the formation of disabled peoples' organizations.
- The programme, however, faced clear problems with respect to the mobilization of local community resources and sustaining the concept of volunteer-local supervisors.

Educational Outcome of the CBR Programme

One important outcome of the CBR programme was that it provided an avenue for establishing inclusive school environments. The Principle of Normalization (Wolfensberger, 1972) and the principle of belonging as grounded in Maslow's Hierarchy of Needs (Kunc, 1992) were cardinal considerations underpinning the Government's desire to implement the Community-Based Rehabilitation and Inclusive Education programmes. Since the implementation of the two programmes were all aimed at providing services to many persons with disabilities who were without services in the community, it also entailed the acceptance of the principles underlying the Primary Health Care Project, promoted by the World Health Organization (WHO). The development of the Primary Health Care Project entailed the acceptance of two important principles. The first was that it was more important to bring about small improvements for many than to provide the highest standard of care for a privileged few. And the second was that non-professionals with limited training could provide crucial services (O'Toole, 1989).

In the development of the CBR concept, it was envisioned that the most effective way of bringing about a change in the status of majority of the disabled (who were without services) was for the communities themselves to take on the task of rehabilitation. It was thought (in line with the above principles underscoring the usefulness of the Primary Health Care concept), that it was not possible to meet all needs of the disabled at the community level. However, up to 70% of needs could be dealt with at the community level. This would be a tremendous improvement on the 2–3% of needs that were being met in developing countries. The remaining needs could be addressed through referrals at the district and national levels (Helander, Mendis, & Nelson, 1989). Furthermore in line with these principles, the CBR and inclusive education programmes in Ghana could provide crucial services, and lead to tremendous improvements in the percentage of needs being met among the population persons with disabilities. With respect to education, the evolving inclusive local schools could provide the needed services to students with disabilities who were not able to enrol in the few special schools. The initiation of the inclusive education programme was therefore the outcome of the implementation of the CBR programme, with the posting of trained peripatetic teachers to support students with disabilities attending their local schools (Ofori-Addo, 1994; O'Toole et al., 1996).

Policy Initiatives for Special/Inclusive Education: 2000–2012

Since the CBR and inclusive education initiative in the 1990s, many educational provisions have been made that support inclusive education. Firstly, provisions in the 1992 constitution (Articles 36–39) allowed for the FCUBE agenda. Flowing from this provision, the government launched the free FCUBE programme in 1996, which increased educational access to many children with special needs in local schools. Then in 2000, the government released the National Disability Policy Document (MESW, 2000), which sought to respond to the need to provide opportunities for people with disability in education and increase social participation. The document became the basis for the Persons with Disability Act of 2006.

The Ministry of Education Strategic Plan (2003–2015, MoE, 2003) and its extension 2010–2020 has been designed by the MoE in collaboration with UNESCO, non-governmental organizations (NGOs), and other stakeholders in education. The aim of the Strategic Plan is to develop a model for Inclusive Education within the overarching framework of Education for All (EFA). The Plan (2003–2015) envisions the achievement of an inclusive education system by 2015 through a Special Educational Needs Policy Framework that would address the issues of educational segregation and inequality to the education of students with disabilities (Ghana Education Service [GES], 2005). As a result, the SED of GES developed a policy in 2004 that aimed to contribute to the vision of progressive expansion of inclusive education (GES, 2006). The policy framework required the Special Education Division of the GES to explore and implement measures for progressing social and educational inclusion of students with disabilities. The SED is expected to work towards equal educational opportunities (access, participation and quality) for students with special needs. One of the methods for achieving equal opportunity is to expand inclusive education across Ghana (GES, 2006).

In 2006, the Parliament of Ghana passed The Persons with Disability Act (Act 715). The Act makes several provisions for people with disability in terms of rehabilitation and education. Among others, the Act obligates the Government to enhance social participation, provide educational opportunities for people with disabilities and progressively establish rehabilitation centres in regions and districts for people with disabilities. In addition, the Act states that a CBR approach shall be used such that as far as practicable persons with disability shall be rehabilitated in their communities to foster their integration. Finally, The Mental Health Bill, 846 is being considered by parliament and the provisions of this bill will serve the needs of people with psychiatric disabilities and other conditions that have impacts on psychosocial functioning of children and young people in educational settings. Table 2 provides a summary of Ghana's special education policy initiatives.

Table 2.   Policy Initiatives.

Date	Name of Policy	Policy Provision
	The 1992 Constitution of Ghana	The 1992 Constitution of Ghana makes provisions for people with disabilities and special needs in relation to: Protection from discrimination and abusive (Article 29) Access to education for people with disabilities/special needs (Article 37 and 38). These articles formed the basis for the FCUBE programme of 1996.
June 2000	National Disability Policy Document	This document was jointly developed by the Ministry of Employment & Social Welfare, Federation of the Disabled in Ghana, and the Ministry of Education. It is the first comprehensive document focusing on situational analysis of people with disability, rights to education and participation and service provision. It outlined rights with regard to education, transportation, community acceptance, housing and employment (MESW, 2000). Informed by Ghana's experience with implementing the CBR programme, the UN Convention on the Rights of the Child (1989) and the UN Standard Rules on the Equalization of Opportunities for People with Disabilities (1993). It provided the foundation for the Persons With Disability Act, 2006.
2003–2015	Government of Ghana's Education Strategic Plan (ESP) 2003–2015 and 2010–2020	The strategic plan advances five key issues: Achieving the Goals of Education For All and the Millennium Development Goals Progressing social and educational inclusion of students with disabilities Equalizing Educational Opportunity-Increasing educational access for students with disabilities/special needs through special schools and expanding inclusive schools environments (MoE, 2003) The Basis for the Special Educational Needs Policy Framework.
2005	Special Educational Needs Policy Framework	The framework outlines/addresses the challenges of marginalization, segregation and inequality that have previously constituted barriers to the education of students with disabilities (GES, 2005).
June 2006	Persons with Disability Act	The main legislation for rights and service provision for people with disabilities in Ghana. Informed by the National Disability Policy Document (2000) The 1992 Constitution of Ghana, the UN Convention On The Rights Of Persons With Disabilities (2006) and the UN Convention on the Rights of the Child (1989).
2011–2012	Special Needs & Inclusive Education (SNIE) Policy	National consultation around the development of a new Special Needs and Inclusive Education (SNIE) Policy was started in 2011 and is yet to be finalized.

EDUCATIONAL INTERVENTIONS: POLICY AND STANDARDS

The MoE and the GES are responsible for policy and administration of educational services in Ghana. The GES is the main implementing and supervisory agent of primary and secondary education services. The GES provides basic education services to all children regardless of ability or disability. The criteria and standards employed for the education of students with disabilities are no different from those without disabilities. Both regular and special schools run pre-school programmes and also provide full basic level education for all children consisting of six years primary and three years junior secondary schooling. In special schools additional support to students with extra learning needs was and is provided by trained special education (GES, 2006).

The Special Education Division of Ghana Education Service

The GES is the implementation organ of the MoE for basic education services. The GES has 12 divisions, one of which is SED. The SED, established as a unit in 1976, became a full division in 1985. The mission and responsibility of the division is the provision of education services for children and young people with disabilities and/or special learning needs in primary and secondary schools. It also has specific oversight responsibility for the inclusive education programme. The GES outlines the vision of the special education division as endeavouring to establish 'An inclusive education system, where children with disabilities and those with Special Education Needs (SEN) benefit from quality education to make them independent and employable in order to contribute their quota to the development of the nation' (Ghana Education Service [GES], 2010). This vision is expected to be achieved through observing three key principles:

- The Right to Education.
- The Right to Equality of Education Opportunity.
- The Right to fully participate in the Affairs of the Society (GES, SED, 2010).

Current Activities

In collaboration with other Ghana government Ministries and non-government organizations the Division of Special Education oversees

educational provision to all children and youth with identified disability
and/or special needs through the following activities:

1. Establish and supervise special schools, special education units and support inclusive schools.
2. Assess the educational needs of children through three National
   Assessment centres.
3. Support the planning, implementing individualized Educational
   Programmes for students with special needs.
4. Assess curriculum in schools and contribute to the training of special
   educators through curriculum development and instruction in colleges
   of Education and Universities.
5. Resource Special schools, assessment centres and Braille and sign
   Language facilities.

Today, the Division has supervisory oversight of 1,468 special schools, unit
schools, and inclusive schools across the country. Details of educational
provision at these schools is discussed later under the heading 'Perspective
on the progress of special education'.

Interventions and Standards

In general, policy intentions such as those contained in the National
Constitution and Acts of Government are more or less broad intentions for
service delivery. Thus, the crux of policy making and implementation
relates to the identifying what is intended to be done backed by a narrow
formulation of what can be done at a point in time bearing in mind the
actors and resources allocation to the cause. The government has made
attempts at improving access to schools for students with special needs
building school infrastructure and school level implementation initiatives.

There is no comprehensive policy on school level intervention standards
across the country. Intervention standards applied to mainstream schools
also apply to special schools. However, in terms of access, parental responsibility, assessment of learning needs and use of Individual education Plans
(IEPs) there are provisions in different policies that lead to a definition of
standards for interventions in schools. The different policies summarized in
the previous pages, advocate and prescribe some interventions, which are
more or less a guide to the expectations pertaining to institutions and
actors. For example, under the Education Strategic Plan (2003–2015) the
Government initiated pilot inclusive education programmes in 30 schools

in Central, Eastern and Greater Accra regions. This effort was supported by some international NGOs, such as Volunteer Services Overseas (VSO), Sight Savers International (SSI) and the United States Agency for International Development (USAID). In the inclusive schools, emphasis is placed on ensuring that students showing signs of learning difficulties/ special needs are assessed and learning support plans put in place to support their learning. The lessons from these schools were intended to inform practice for future broad national implementation and in the last few years the research and experiences from the initial 30 schools have been used to guide further expansion in all regions of Ghana.

The Persons with Disability Act (Act 715) of 2006 makes provision in regard to educational participation. First, it obligates parents, guardians or custodians of a child with disability who is of school going age, to enrol the child in school. Further, The MoE shall by legislative instrument designate schools or institutions in each region, which shall provide the necessary facilities and equipment that will enable persons with disability to fully benefit from the school or institution. More importantly, the Government shall provide free education for a person with disability, and establish special schools for persons with disability who by reason of their disability cannot be enroled in formal schools. The Government shall also provide appropriate training for basic school graduates who are unable to pursue further formal education and this includes the designation, in each region, of a public technical, vocational and teacher training institutions which shall include in their curricula special education, such as sign language, and Braille writing and reading. Finally, the acts make it an offense for any educational institution to refuse admission on account of disability.

Teaching: Principles and Methodology

The standard of teaching to be provided for children with disabilities includes the following:

(1) Children with visual impairment learn through the Braille and are capable of accessing basic education up to the university education.
(2) Education for the hearing impaired is for children from basic education to tertiary-university education.
(3) Education for intellectual disability is limited to only basic education level. However efforts are being made to have a transition programme

in the technical and vocational models that can make them have skills
for daily living.
(4) Inclusive teaching methodologies, deriving from the UNESCO
Resource Pack and others sources will be used.

The inclusive interventions include: methodology, reinforcing, prompting,
accommodation modification and adaptation, chaining, and task analysis.
Whereas strategies include: collaborative problem solving, peer tutoring,
staff development, classroom and student management, cooperative
learning, multi-level instruction, peer—peer coaching, peer-led teaching,
and twinning. These strategies are integral to any training programme
for teachers and there is an expectation that they will be used in classrooms. However, recent studies show that many teachers report having
limited knowledge of these skills (Agbenyega & Deku, 2011). The challenges of implementing instructional provision are discussed later in this
chapter.

WORKING WITH FAMILIES

Working with families of children with a disability is a highly recommended strategy for providing the best education and support to students
with special needs. In pre-colonial Ghana traditional systems prevailed,
where parents educated their children with disabilities in the home (Anson-
Yevu, 1988). With the institution of schools for students with disabilities,
school authorities had to establish a liaison with parents. Anson-Yevu
(1988) reports that the first evidence of families taking an advocacy role in
Ghana occurred on in 1964, when parents of children with intellectual disabilities formed an association called the 'Society of Friends of the
Mentally Retarded'. The work of this group of parents led to the establishment of the first 'home for the mentally handicapped' in 1966, which later
became a special school (GES, 2005). This was the beginning of parental
involvement in children's education in a proactive and meaningful way
and many parents began to be involved in some way in their children's
education.

Although nothing substantive has been written about this in the
Ghanaian literature, it is evident in written school reports that all special
schools have parent associations, which are committed to the welfare of
their children.

It is important to note that collaborating with parents needs to happen in all schools (mainstream and special schools). And while special schools and rehabilitation institutions had embraced parental collaboration with schools, this was more erratic in mainstream schools. However, the 1990s witnessed a big paradigm shift in formalizing parental roles both in rehabilitation institutions and schools. First, the inception of CBR brought a new dimension to the parental participation in that parents received training in rehabilitation techniques and also on how to support their children through the inclusive education settings that were integral to the programme. The establishment of the CBR saw one of the best attempts to work comprehensively with parents of children with a disability. The CBR programme required parents of disabled children to assume training roles that would allow them to assist their children educationally. It also required that the parents would assume the training role for other family members. Evaluation studies (Kuyini, 1998; Ofori-Addo, 1994; O'Toole et al., 1996) showed that parents did assume training roles for their children. In fulfilling these roles they developed liaisons with CBR programme officers, local supervisors, disabled people's organizations and Community Rehabilitation Committees. This initiative culminated in many parents joining disability organizations in their local communities/ districts; a development that has enhanced parental collaboration with schools.

Another major change occurred with the implementation of the FCUBE programme. FCUBE envisioned increased access to achieve Education for All Goals. As part of the FCUBE policy, schools were required to set up School Management Committees (SMCs) and Parent-Teacher Associations (PTAs) as a way to enhance communities' sense of ownership and participation in school governance. Today, most schools have PTAs, which have a good understanding of how the schools are run, their achievement, challenges and needs of learners in the school.

In special schools teachers and peripatetic teachers work with parents to facilitate assessments and support learning in other ways. Many parents honour school visits and help in the school administration and school improvement. Parents participate in setting policy such as rules and regulations governing bully, name-calling, stigmatization and marginalization of children with special needs. They also can be brought in to provide inservice education training sessions around attitude towards children with disabilities and special needs. Finally, they support schools to raise funds to meet the schools' needs.

TEACHERS AND SPECIAL EDUCATION: ROLES, EXPECTATIONS AND TRAINING

Role of Special Schools Teachers

In special schools the roles of teachers are quite specific. They are required to do the following:

- Liaise with District Special Education to ensure pupils are regularly screened and assessed.
- Ensure Individualized Education Plans developed and administered for children with disabilities and special needs are reviewed regularly.
- Ensure that Children with disabilities and Special Educational Needs have access to the relevant educational materials, specialized equipment and assistive devices.
- Ensure the curriculum is adapted.
- Submit term reports on Children with disabilities and Special Educational Needs to the head teacher (school principal).

Roles of Peripatetic and Resource Teachers

Peripatetic teachers are itinerant teachers working in clusters of schools. The peripatetic teachers operate within the special education unit of the District office of The Ghana Education Service. The responsibilities of the peripatetic teachers include coordinating the inclusion programme in the district, providing in-service training on inclusion to teachers in the district, assessing students' special needs, recommending appropriate remedial measures to teachers, and supervising/evaluating the inclusion programme in the district. The role of peripatetic teachers is crucial in that they not only identify children with special needs in the schools under their jurisdiction, but also have to ensure that such students receive the best possible education, given the circumstances and the means available. At present peripatetic teachers and/or resource teachers are attached to pilot inclusive schools to offer support to students and teachers. They are expected to work in schools where students with identified special needs are and provide guidance and instruction where needed.

Regular Classroom Teachers

The above-mentioned roles of special educators and peripatetic teachers differ from regular classroom teachers. With the advent of inclusive education the role of regular classroom teachers have also changed. As the government progressively rolls out inclusive schools many regular classroom teachers are expected to play a much broader role that reflects the philosophy and principles of inclusive education. According to Mamlin (1999) regular classroom teachers must play a critical role in making schools more inclusive. This researcher stressed that the classroom teacher is the single most important indispensable factor to the successful implementation of inclusion as it is the responsibility of the classroom teacher to determine whether or not the innovations and accommodations will be implemented and have any chance of succeeding (Mamlin, 1999).

Under inclusive education, the teacher is required to assume a number of new roles, including being a collaborator, social worker, classroom manager, counsellor, record keeper, and motivator (Mastropieri & Scruggs, 2000). Such a responsibility comes with many challenges, including the need to make changes to work organization aspects, attitudes and instructional methods (Booth & Ainscow, 1998). In Ghana, it is expected that regular classroom teachers would identify children with potential learning difficulties. Where required, teachers are expected to refer them for formal assessment to be carried out at one of three assessment centres. Finally, classroom teachers having received some training during initial teacher training are expected to recognize special learning needs, devise strategies to provide meaningful instruction to such students and support the development and implementation of IEPs for such students in their classrooms.

Teacher Training for Special Education

Historically, training of teachers for special education began in 1965 with the training of teachers for children with hearing impairment. In 1975 the Presbyterian Training College in Akropong-Akwapim began training teachers with regard to teach children with a visual impairment. The College of Special Education was established in 1985 and offered a two-year certificate programme that combined ordinary teacher training with intensive special education preparation. The college trained teachers to support students with visual, hearing, speech and language, and intellectual impairments. In 1992, the College of Special Education was amalgamated with two other specialist colleges at Winneba and Kumasi to for the University of Education Winneba.

This brief history of special education teacher training indicates that prior to the 1990s, teacher training for special education occurred mainly at the College of Special Education. However, from 1989, efforts were made to expand special needs knowledge, with the introduction of special education content into initial teacher training colleges. In 2004, the Teacher Training Colleges were upgraded from certificate to diploma-awarding institutions and called Colleges of Education. Further, during the establishment of the CBR, a pilot training to teach about inclusive education was launched for teachers in the project districts.

Teacher Training for Inclusive Education under CBR

The introduction of the CBR for people with disabilities in 1992 also envisioned the training of peripatetic teachers for inclusive education in schools within the pilot districts. The SED of GES played a key role in the CBR in terms of trialling inclusive education in 10 and later 20 pilot districts. Under the CBR programme, all districts were required to implement the inclusive education programmes and were provided with at least one peripatetic teacher (PPT). At the start of the CBR programme, eighteen peripatetic teachers from the ten districts (where the inclusive education initiative was launched) attended a two-month training workshop on special needs education. The UNESCO *Teachers' Resource Pack (RP) on Special Needs in the Classroom* (1993) was used as a resource book for this workshop, and adopted by the MoE as the main resource material for training of teachers for special needs education in Ghana. Following the initial workshop, UNESCO carried out three more one week workshops on special needs education in 1993 for four head-teachers (principals), eight regular teachers from four regular schools, eighteen peripatetic teachers and three officers from the SED. Later, other rounds of training were organized for a total of 150 educators including district directors of education, peripatetic teachers and regular classroom teachers from the districts implementing inclusion (Ofori-Addo et al., 1999).

The MoE adopted a train-the-trainer approach for the inclusive education teacher training programme, whereby teachers who received the initial training were required to train other teachers in the respective districts. A resource team of eight peripatetic teachers was set up to provide subsequent training for peripatetic teachers and new teachers in the districts implementing inclusion. In 1994, the district directors of education in another 10 new districts were obligated to provide training in the methodology of the *Resource Pack* to teachers in their districts. However, it soon became evident that in-service teacher training for a demanding undertaking such as inclusion was perhaps unlikely to provide the needed skills to the majority of teachers. This resulted in the MoE initiating The Pilot Action Research Project (PARP), which sought to re-invigorate the earlier attempt to special needs education training into the curriculum of pre-service teacher training colleges (Ofori-Addo et al., 1999).

The Pilot Action Research Project began in November 1994 with a two-week course facilitated by a UNESCO team for a variety of personnel of the MoE. Participants included 20 tutors from ten teacher training colleges, 20 regular teachers from pilot schools affiliated to these training colleges and 10 officers from the different departments of the Ghana Education Service (including Teacher Education and Special Education Departments). Tutors from the teacher training colleges (who had undergone the training) were required to incorporate the content of the special needs methodology advocated by the Resource Pack into the curriculum of teacher training beginning in 1995 (Ofori-Addo et al., 1999). Teacher trainees from such teacher training colleges were therefore afforded the opportunity (from the beginning of 1995) to learn more about special needs education methods in order to meet the needs of students with disabilities in inclusive classrooms.

Current Teacher Training Regime

Only two universities (University of Cape Coast and University of Education Winneba) provide teacher training including special education in Ghana. The bulk of teachers who teach in special schools are trained in Colleges of Education (formally called Teacher Training Colleges). The current structure of basic teacher training in Ghana is designed to provide a three-year pre-service Diploma in Basic Education, which is divided into Program A and B to prepare teachers for teaching in primary and junior secondary schools, respectively. The Colleges of Education practice what is called the *In-In-Out-Program*. The first two years of teacher training are devoted to learning content knowledge in: mathematics, English, science, vocational skills, social studies, music and dance, religion and moral education, physical education, Ghanaian language and educational studies. In essence, the trainees are taught subject content knowledge sufficient for them to be able to teach those subjects. They also learn the pedagogy associated with different subject areas including introduction to special education or teaching students with special needs. In the third year of training student teachers undertake supervised teaching practice in schools. All Colleges of Education have since 1990, included special education into their curriculum. In the last 5 years, the content has been enhanced with the publication of a custom book on special needs for teacher training colleges. The curriculum of the Colleges of Education now includes enhanced special education content (Fobih, 2008). An analysis of the teacher training curriculum shows that inclusive education is given special attention. During the second year of the 3-year training programme, content and competencies related to inclusive education are taught with the framework of a theme called *Educating the Individual with Special Needs*. The content of *Educating the Individual with Special Needs* focuses on causes of various conditions and the different categories of special needs such as students with visual and hearing impairment, physical and behaviour disorders, gifted/talented children and intellectual impairment. It also focuses on instructional strategies that can be used to support such students in special schools and inclusive settings. However, given the short nature of the course, not all areas are adequately covered and much of the research in Ghana shows that teacher complain about inadequate special education knowledge and skills.

In-service Programmes

In-service training sessions have also been organized for teachers at national, regional and districts levels by the GES, including the SED and some NGOs such as the USAID, Volunteer Services Overseas (VSO), Sight Savers International (SSI) and more recently Visio International from the Netherlands, which collaborated with the SED to train Special Education resource teachers. The most recent and much broader initiative with respect to addressing quality of teacher training is the collaborative work between the GES's Teacher Education Division, USAID, and the two teacher training universities (University of Cape Coast and the University of Education) that led to improved special needs content in the teacher training curriculum for pre- and in-service training programmes. An important outcome of this work is a book, which is now used as a training resource for teachers across the country.

PERSPECTIVE ON THE PROGRESS OF SPECIAL EDUCATION IN GHANA

The area of Special education has made great progress in the last decade with the passing of the Disability Act of 2006 and the recently proposed policy on inclusive education. The focus of special education provision is to cater to the needs of those with sensory impairment. Students with physical disabilities are generally educated in the mainstream (MoE, 2008). It is also evident that no formal special education services are offered specifically to students with Learning Disabilities (GES, 2004; MoE, 2008). Many inclusive schools are progressively being established and their development is detailed under inclusive schools.

Special Schools

The broad spectrum of special school provisions includes boarding and day options. The provision of boarding and day special schools is quite limited as these schools are few and therefore are not accessible to children who live far from the towns where such schools are located. As of 2008 the SED of GES managed the following schools:

- 13 segregated special boarding basic education schools for the hearing impaired.
- 2 segregated special boarding basic education schools for the visually impaired.
- 3 units for the visually impaired.
- 12 segregated special boarding schools for the intellectually impaired.
- 23 units for intellectually impaired.
- 3 segregated special boarding secondary/technical/vocational schools for the hearing impaired.
- 4 integrated special secondary schools for the visually impaired.
- 3 integrated teacher training colleges for students with disability.

Table 3 shows the special education school enrolment in 2008.

Table 3. Special Education School Enrolments (2008).

Enrolment	Male	Female	Total
Basic level	2,006	1,442	3,498
Second cycle level	148	66	214
Teacher training colleges	26	15	41
Technical/vocational	181	114	293
Special classes	643	401	1,044

Source: MoE (2008).

Table 4.   Special and Inclusive Schools.

Special and Inclusive schools	Number
Special schools for hearing impairment	15
Special schools for visual impairment	2
Special schools for deaf-blind	1
Special schools for students with intellectual disability	11
Unit schools for students with intellectual disability	25
Unit school for visual impairment	4
Integrated senior high school for	6
Inclusive schools for basic education	3
Inclusive schools for colleges of education	3

Current Provisions

Current data from the SED of the GES, displayed in Table 4 indicate that the following provisions are available to students with special needs in 2012–2013.

The table is evidence that provisions for students with special needs are increasing in number and breadth to meet the growing demands. The effort of government has been geared towards not only setting up schools but also increasing educational access through the building unit schools to serve students with special needs. Several international NOGs and Governmental organizations have supported the drive to provide infrastructure, training and resources. In terms of infrastructure development to increase school access, the most notable government effort has been through the FCUBE programme and the work of the Ghana Education Trust Fund. In this regard the German Technical Co-operation (GTZ) (re-named German Agency for International Co-operation in 2011) supported the GES SED to establish 23 special units and also new classrooms blocks in mainstream schools in different regions of Ghana to assist the inclusion of students with intellectual disabilities. In addition, the Government has been active in developing Technical/Vocational Training streams for students with special needs. Presently, more than 15 schools at primary and secondary level run Technical/Vocational Training courses.

Inclusive Education

The further development of inclusive education is hinged on Ghana's ratification of the provisions of the Salamanca Statement (UNESCO, 1994), the

Dakar 2000 recommendations (UNESCO, 2000) and meeting the Education for All Goals (UNESCO, 1990). As a result, there is a vision and an expectation that by 2015 all mainstream schools will be inclusive in their approach (Ministry of Education [MoE], 2011a, 2011b). Although there has been big expansion in the number of inclusive schools to over 900, the GES states that only 6 of these schools can be said to be well established.

Inclusive schools are set up with variations in terms of special classes and resource rooms in regular schools, and the use of support teachers in regular classes. The GES and the SED has developed six models for implementing inclusive education (SED, 2011). The SED outlines the different models as follows:

Model 1: involves integrating students with low vision and blindness in mainstream schools with the support an itinerant peripatetic teacher.

Model 2: is a unique model involving the education of students with visual impairment (Blind) within special schools for the Deaf. Upon mastery of the some requisite skills the students are moved to mainstream schools.

Model 3: involves the provision of special units for children with Intellectual Disability within mainstream schools.

Model 4: are inclusive schools with resource teachers. These schools aim for full inclusion. The resource teachers collaborate with the regular teachers and work with students.

Model 5: involves mainstream schools that use inclusive approaches but without resource teacher support. Such schools use regular classroom teachers who implement inclusive teaching interventions in order to provide the quality teaching that benefit the learning of all students including those with learning difficulties. It is one of the models aiming for full inclusion.

Model 6: provides hostels for pupils with low vision and blindness that live far away from mainstream schools that can serve their needs. The students are given critical skills that allow them to be moved to mainstream schools (SED, 2011).

Additionally Government is endeavouring to provide qualified teachers and other resources to service the schools. For example resource teachers have been posted to inclusive schools since 2008 to support learning of students with mild disabilities and learning difficulties. Also cooperation with several international philanthropic as well as disability focused organizations such as Sight Savers, VSO, and USAID has led to the injection of teaching resources into the some special schools. For example VSO

Table 5. Model of Educational Provision for Students with Special Needs in Ghana.

Basic Education		
Mainstream Schools	*Inclusive Schools*	*Special Schools*
(Special Units)	Inclusive Education	Special Education
Full Inclusive Education		*Special Education*

provided resources and training for teachers in 2006/2007 when it set up demonstration inclusive schools. Further, the Global e-Schools and Communities Initiative (GeSCI) provide training to teachers and assist Ghana with some assistive technology equipment to enhance teaching and learning for students with special needs (Hooker, 2008).

The future direction for Special and Inclusive Education are yet unclear as the new policy is yet to be finalized. However, Fobih (2008), proposed at the International Conference on Education held in Geneva in 2008 under the title *Inclusive Education: the Way of the Future,* education of students with special needs will follow the pattern of special schools, mainstream schools with special units and inclusive schools with and without resource teachers. The last two will be seeking to achieve full inclusion. Thus by 2015, the model will be as shown in Table 5.

CHALLENGES OF SPECIAL EDUCATION IN GHANA

Ghana has made significant progress in making provisions for access to education and to improve quality education for students with special needs. However, school structures and quality of instruction in these schools have many challenges related to: access, resources, teacher training and teaching quality. These aspects are discussed in more detail below.

Access

In terms of access to services, earlier conclusions of Kuyini (1998), Ofori-Addo et al. (1999), and O'Toole et al. (1996) blamed limited access to schools and rehabilitation on service/school location, parental poverty and resourcing. In line with the view that general poverty and resource constraints were resulting in limited services for students with disabilities, O'Toole et al. (1996) and Ofori-Addo et al. (1999) asked a critical question;

'... how high a priority is it to provide education for a child with a disability?' Currently, there remains the problem of geographic spread of schools. Many schools are still located in urban areas, which mean that families in rural areas have to send their children to schools far away from home and find the resources to pay for their accommodation. There are also the psychological issues of separation at a very young age from family and local community. Recent research on special units for students with Intellectual disabilities in mainstream schools also shows that there are issues with achieving meaningful inclusion (Kuyini, 2014). For example, the special units form part of the inclusive education Model 3 which involves the provision of special units for children who are intellectually impaired within mainstream schools (SED, 2011), however, many of the schools are not providing the academic and social interactional opportunities to allow these students to be integrated (Kuyini, 2014).

Resourcing

The problem of access is linked to resourcing. In general, resourcing education in Ghana is a huge problem despite the Government increasing educational spending to about 25% since 2008 (World Bank, 2010). In 2005, Capitation Grants were introduced as part of the new education reforms to absorb user-fees at the elementary not secondary level in order to increase access, retention, and completion (MoE, 2006). The premise underlying the Capitation Grant was that it would remove the burden on households to pay fees for basic education, especially poor children whose access to education has been constricted by these fees (Akyeampong, 2011). For special schools, resourcing is a greater problem because special schools have additional activities and materials required for teaching which are not adequately budgeted on an annual basis. One can therefore conclude that despite the inception of the Capitation Grants, the question posed by O'Toole et al. (1996) and Ofori-Addo et al. (1999) remains a useful question. In the current climate some special schools are unable to meet their basic cost on a sustainable basis because they don't receive even basic government funding to keep them afloat. For instance, in 2013, there have been reports of philanthropists coming to the rescue of two special schools, which were going to be evicted from rented premises. Such incidents completely align with the notion that the government is neglecting the special education sector even though both the national constitution and the FCUBE programme have promised access to education for all children.

Making the situation worse, many parent groups have been unable to support the schools where their wards are in attendance and this accentuates the fact that diminished parental capacity is contributing to limited educational access for children with disabilities.

Resources for Inclusive Education

The effect of limited teaching resources and supplies (Obi, Mamah, & Avoke, 2007) also continues to be a challenge for schools. Teachers have voiced huge concerns about inclusive education owing to resource constraints (Gyimah, Sugden, & Pearson, 2008; Kuyini & Desai, 2007, 2008; Obeng, 2007). Regular classrooms teachers require additional resources (teaching materials) as well as the support of teacher assistants to implement inclusive teaching in the generally large classrooms, average 50 students in many schools. Such resources are however, unavailable and this reality led Hooker (2008) to recommend a systemic approach to inclusive education, with a consistent commitment of resources and stability of personnel in order to realize the stated Governments objectives by 2015. However, this asking is doubtful in current Ghanaian context with limited resources and lack of political perseverance on the part of Government. The failure of government to commit resources is not new and it is known to have impacted upon the sustainability of past programmes such as the CBR programme in the 1990s. Another example is that although the GeSCI supported the Ghana Education Service's (GES) with assistive technologies for special educational needs in 2007–2008, there are no clear policy initiatives to support or maintain the assistive technology resources in schools for special needs. Thus, there is no guarantee that any meaningful support for students included in regular schools will be achieved into the future.

Further, although The Persons with Disability Act (715) of 2006 has made laudable provisions for increased educational access, the main provisions in relation to access and ensuring that technical and vocational schools include sign language and Braille reading and writing into their curriculum are unlikely to be achieved. In this regard, one of the key strategies of inclusive education is to ensure 'equitable educational opportunities' and maximize opportunities for students with 'non-severe special education needs' to be included into mainstream schools by 2015. The main challenge is budgetary allocation for the so-called none essential aspects of government, which includes the services to people with disabilities. These are never seen as priorities and the National Council on Disability has observed that the budget for implementing the education strategy policy is showing large funding gaps that might not be met by 2015 or even beyond. Secondly, while it is very important to ensure that children with disabilities are admitted to schools, the most critical issue in Ghana at this stage is not the refusal to admit children with disabilities to school. Rather, it is the inability of schools and the lack of effort on the part of teachers to address their learning needs, due in part to inadequate knowledge and skills and the lack of resources (Kuyini & Desai, 2007, 2008). One of such areas is the need to have technical and vocational schools that would include sign language and Braille reading and writing into their curriculum. At the moment, this is not happening because schools don't have resources (human and material) to effect these recommendations.

Problem with Policy Making

Public policy making in Ghana is characterized by problems of process and implementation. In terms of process, it has been criticized as being exclusionary and elitist; with inconsistencies in the selection and prosecution of policy priorities as government alternate between political parties of different ideologies; and an unstable political environment in which the authoritative allocation of values for society is made. In respect of implementation, there are issues with what is called implementation deficits caused by the lack of resources and the inability of government to build an efficient and effective coordination and communication network among all the individuals and agencies involved in putting the policy into effect (Kuyini, Alhassan, & Mahama, 2011). In a developing country like Ghana, such a scenario can have severe consequences for service delivery and impact negatively on service users.

In addition to the problem of policy making, there is concern that the government's approach to establishing inclusive education since the 1990s, has been quite piece-meal and ineffective. In relation to this piece-meal approach, Hooker (2007, 2008) noted that Ghana's rather ad hoc approach to inclusive education does not augur well for achieving the vision of inclusion in line with the EFA and Millennium Development Goals agenda. Hooker, like Peters (2004), Kuyini and Desai (2007) recommends that

A policy framework and legislative support at the national level must be in place as a necessary prerequisite to access and equal participation in IE programs. [She observes further that] Countries that have passed legislation and adopted IE policies, with systematic monitoring, backed-up by enforcement are most positively positioned to enact IE policy. Successful countries have coupled these strategies with comprehensive education (knowledge dissemination) and awareness training directed at all levels of the system, recognizing that national policy is of little value if it isn't enacted in school and in the classrooms. (p. 12)

Another issue with inclusive education policy is the lack specificity in the many initiatives as well as the Disability Act to guide implementation. For example the Persons with Disability Act (Act 715) of 2006 talks about the rights of Persons with Disabilities to services such as education and rehabilitation, but it is not specific about how students with special needs with be included into regular school classrooms. Further, the recently appointed National Disability Council is yet to initiate discussions about what priority areas of the inclusive education process should be tackled in order to ensure that other segments of the inclusive policy intents can be given attention. On the basis of these limited actions in relation to inclusive schooling, it is going to take some time before broad policy intents are translated into service realities for many students with special learning needs in Ghana.

Issues with Policy Implementation

Implementing policies with regard to people with disabilities is a big challenge in Ghana. For example, after piloting the CBR programme in the 1990s the government indicated its willingness to transfer responsibility to local government agencies. However, no resources were provided and despite efforts by disability advocacy groups the programme was starved of funding and it collapsed (Kuyini et al., 2011). Another example of implementation problems relates to the Persons with Disability Act of 2006. Since the passage of the act seven years ago, the government has been unable to fund the implementation of the law. It will be interesting to note that even simple requirements such as making public buildings accessible to all people with disabilities by 2016 are yet to take hold and therefore, unlikely to be achieved. There is also no evidence that the Government is committed to providing the needed resources within the budgetary processes to support broad scale implementation with regard to services.

In terms of inclusive education implementation in Ghana, there are obvious problems with teacher training, knowledge and skills, teacher attitudes, teaching quality and resources. Also, there are barriers associated with school personnel and social attitudes, however, despite the persuasive arguments by writers such as Agbenyega (2007), Ocloo et al. (2002), and

Kuyini et al. (2011) who have highlighted the negative effects of traditional beliefs and stigmatizing attitudes to the provision of educational services to students with disabilities, these issues have not impacted the actual actions or inactions of government to provide such services in the first place. Thus, while traditional beliefs and attitudes are contributory implementation bottlenecks, the limited priority given to such services by government is more damaging.

Teacher Training and Quality of Instruction in Inclusive Classrooms

Inclusive education practices in Ghana shows that teachers hold relatively positive attitudes towards including students with disabilities/special needs in regular school classrooms, however, over the last 10 years, many studies have reported that teachers have limited knowledge of inclusive education and the instructional skills needed for supporting such students (Agbenyega, 2007; Casely-Hayford, 2002; Gyimah et al., 2008; Kuyini & Desai, 2007, 2008). This limited knowledge and skills among teachers has been attributed to inadequate initial training, limited in-service training opportunities for teachers, and shortage of qualified general and special educators (Agbenyega & Deku, 2011, Ghana Education Service [GES], 2008; Sayed, Akyeampong, & Ampiah, 2000).

Teacher training programmes in Ghana have aimed to increase teachers' repertoire of knowledge and skills to improve on the quality of instruction for all students as reiterated by the 2007 education reform (Government of Ghana, 2007a, 2007b). However, it appears that the training institutions are not providing enough content and practical knowledge to meet teachers' needs. As Agbenyega and Deku (2011) observed, 'teacher training is still framed within colonial-culturally blended pedagogical practice and that the pedagogical archetypes in practice in current teacher training institutions and schools lack the complexity of teaching required in inclusive classrooms' (p. 20). Also, studies by Obi et al. (2007) and Casely-Hayford (2002) found that regular teachers did not receive adequate training to handle children with special needs and therefore lacked confidence to implement inclusion in schools. Such an outcome led Johnstone (2010) to conclude that since regular teachers lack the knowledge and skills to implement inclusive teaching practices for children with special learning needs, more special education teachers are needed in schools to support regular teachers in their efforts to implement inclusion in classroom.

In an address to the teachers at an in-service session on 24 March 2010, Madam Victoria Opoku, Director in charge of Secondary Education at the Ghana Education Service Head-office corroborated research findings (Agbenyega, 2007, Avoke, 2002; Gyimah et al., 2008; Kuyini & Desai, 2007) on the limited teacher knowledge and skills and the poor quality of instruction in schools. The Director admitted that despite in-service training programmes and other extra classes, the performance of secondary students in recent times was at its lowest. This was indicative of the problems with quality of instruction for even the most capable students and greater concerns of students with special needs in inclusive classrooms.

The above aside, there are still problems related to the appropriateness of educational programmes designed to meet the needs of students with disabilities (GES, 2010, Kuyini & Desai, 2008). More crucial to meeting the needs of students with disabilities therefore was the provision of appropriate educational programmes within regular education settings. Over a decade ago, The National Disability Policy document (Government of Ghana, 2000) lamented the reality that educational programmes in regular schools do not often take the special needs of children with disabilities into account, and this was hampering the process of integrating children with disabilities into mainstream schools. This limited educational participation further reinforced the need for conscious effort in pursuing effective measures to provide rehabilitation, educational and other services to persons with disabilities. In pursuance of the objective of increasing access to services including education, both the 1992 Constitution of Ghana and the National Disability Policy Document (Government of Ghana, 2000, 2006) called for awareness creation on disabilities, and the provision of adequate educational and social services for people with disabilities. These calls have resulted in the creation of more special schools, unit and inclusive schools. However, the reality on the ground today still shows a huge discrepancy between needs and available services and resources.

Although the new Ghana Education Reform 2007 made provisions for addressing these inadequacies, the World Bank (2010) reported that teaching quality and educational and curriculum access is still a huge problem across the Ghanaian education sector. Kuyini and Desai (2008) found in a study of instruction in inclusive classrooms that teachers demonstrated more generic teaching practices and few adaptive teaching practices designed to meet the individual needs of students with disabilities. Indeed teachers were found not to be providing the individual support to students with disabilities in the generally overcrowded classrooms to allow them to achieve meaningful educational outcomes (Kuyini & Desai, 2008). Given these realities Agbenyega and Deku (2011) concluded that current pedago-gical practices are prescriptive, mechanistic, and do not value student diver-sity and different learning styles. Agbenyega and Deku recommended that 'Teacher training institutions in Ghana need to design inspiring pre-service and in-service programmes that engage learners in problem-based learning communities, transforming their understanding and experience of learning, teaching and inclusive practice...inspire transformational learning in stu-dent teachers by structuring learning opportunities and experiences that respond to the student's home culture ...' (p. 21). Such training will empower students to become critical thinkers while creating teachers that will adequately value and celebrate diversity, and difference.

Another dimension in relation to quality of teaching in inclusive class-rooms has to do with high teacher attrition in Ghana (Cobbold, 2006). For some time now, many teachers have been leaving the system to join other sectors of the economy due to low incomes in the teaching sector. This trend implies that the aim of government to train teachers to meet expand-ing education demand is therefore rendered more difficult to attain. In respect of inclusive teacher skills, this often means that pre and in-service training is being provided to teachers who are unlikely to stay in the system long enough to exert positive influences on student outcomes. In other words, students with special needs are less likely to receive adequate sup-port in regular classrooms and correspondingly are more likely to achieve significantly lower school outcomes than their peers.

CONCLUSIONS

Special Education in Ghana has progressed from an activity confined to Christian Missions in the early part of the 20th century to one, which the government of Ghana considers an essential component of the education system. The creation of units for special education has helped the develop-ment of policies and programmes to advance and address the essential needs of students with disabilities. The Education Strategic Plan (ESP) of the Ministry of Education has adopted inclusive education as the main pol-icy to inform the future direction of special education and this has culmi-nated in the progressive expansion of inclusive schools with the aim of achieving national coverage by 2015. While it is evident now that this goal is unlikely to be achieved due to the slow pace of establishing more inclu-sive schools, it is worth noting the effort that Ghana has made to improve on educational provisions for students with special needs.

REFERENCES

Agbenyega, J. (2007). Examining teachers' concerns and attitudes to inclusive education in Ghana. *International Journal of Whole Schooling*, *3*(1), 41–56.

Agbenyega, J., & Deku, P. (2011). Building new identities in teacher preparation for inclusive education in Ghana. *Current Issues in Education*, *14*(1), 4–36. Retrieved from http://cie.asu.edu/

Akyeampong, K. (2011). *(Re)assessing the impact of school capitation grants on education access in Ghana*. CREATE Pathways to Access Research Monograph, No. 71. Center for International Education, University of Sussex, UK.

Anson-Yevu, V. C. (1988). *A case study of special education in Ghana*. UNESCO. Retrieved from http://unesdoc.unesco.org/images/0009/000944/094448eb.pdf. Accessed on August 18, 2013.

Avoke, M. (2001). Some historical perspectives in the development of special education in Ghana. *European Journal of Special Needs Education*, *16*(1), 29–40.

Avoke, M. (2002). Models of disability in the labeling and attitudinal discourse in Ghana. *Disability and Society*, *17*(7), 769–777.

Booth, T., & Ainscow, M. (Eds.). (1998). *From them to us: An international study of inclusion in education*. London, UK: Routledge.

Casely-Hayford, L. (2002). *Ghana education sector review: General education, gender and the disadvantaged*. Accra, Ghana: Ministry of Education.

Cobbold, C. (2006). Attracting and retaining rural teachers in Ghana: The premise and promise of a district sponsorship scheme. *Journal of Education for Teaching*, *32*(4), 453–469.

Education of All Handicapped Children Act. (1975). P.L. 94-141.

Fobih, D. K. (2008, November 25–28). Inclusive education: The way of the future, Ghana. Paper presented at international conference on education, 48th session. Retrieved from http://www.ibe.unesco.org/fileadmin/user_upload/Policy_Dialogue/48th_ICE/Messages/ghana_MIN08.pdf. Accessed on March 20, 2013.

Ghana Education Service (GES). (2004). Annual Report 2004. Accra, Ghana.

Ghana Education Service. (GES). (2005). *Special education needs policy framework*. Accra, Ghana: Ghana Government Publication.

Ghana Education Service. (GES). (2006). *Education strategic plan*. Accra, Ghana: Ghana Government Publication.

Ghana Education Service. (GES). (2008). *Many teachers untrained in Northern Region*. Retrieved from www.Ghanaweb.com. Accessed on July 16, 2009.

Ghana Education Service. (GES). (2010). *Education sector performance report, 2010*. Ghana Ministry of Education. Retrieved from http://www.google.com.au/url?sa=t&rct=j&q=&esrc=s&source=web&cd=10&ved=0CHsQFjAJ&url=http%3A%2F%2Fwww.idpfoundation.org%2FGhana%2520MoE%2520Ed%2520Performance%2520Report%25202010.pdf&ei=cLroULO-FbG8iAeTz4C4BA&usg=AFQjCNH4IzQBeIIrKIkyZmnZMiIq-eNX2g&bvm=bv.1355534169,d.aGc. Accessed on November 13, 2011.

Government of Ghana. (1961). *Education Act of 1961*. Accra, Ghana: Parliament of Ghana.

Government of Ghana. (2000). *National disability policy document*. Accra, Ghana: Parliament of Ghana.

Government of Ghana. (2006). *Persons with Disability Act (Act 715)*. Accra, Ghana: Parliament of Ghana.

Government of Ghana. (2007a). *Ghana Education Reform 2007*. Retrieved from http://www.ghana.gov.gh/index.php/governance/ministries/331-ministry-of-education. Accessed on May 2, 2009.

Government of Ghana. (2007b). *Ghana Education Reform 2007*. Retrieved from http://www.ghana.gov.gh/ghana/ghana_education_reform_2007.jsp. Accessed on May 2, 2009.

Gyimah, E. K., Sugden, D., & Pearson, S. (2008). Teacher education and inclusion in Ghana: An investigation into the emotional reactions of inclusion of Ghanaian mainstream teachers. *Support for Learning, 23*(2), 71–79.

Helander, E., Mendis, P., & Nelson, G. (1989). *Training in the community for persons with disabilities* (4th ed.). Geneva, Switzerland: World Health Organization.

Hooker, M. (2007). *GeSCI and the inclusive education agenda in Ghana: A question of 'diversification' or 'leverage'?* Retrieved from http://www.gesci.org/old/files/docman/IEiGhana-DiversificationLeverageFinal.pdf. Accessed on November 13, 2012.

Hooker, M. (2008). *Concept note: Developing a model for inclusive education and assistive technology appropriate for teaching and learning contexts in developing countries*. Retrieved from http://www.gesci.org/old/files/docman/model_ie_at.pdf. Accessed on November 13, 2012.

Jaffer, R., & Jaffer, R. (1990). The WHO-CBR approach – programme or ideology: Lessons from experience in Punjab, Pakistan. *International Journal of Mental Health, 20*(2), 61–75.

Johnstone, C. J. (2010). Inclusive education policy implementation: Implications for teacher workforce development in Trinidad and Tobago. *International Journal of Special Education, 25*(3), 33–42.

Korsah, M. (1983). Development of rehabilitation in Ghana. In K. Marfo, S. Walker, & B. Charles (Eds.), *Education and rehabilitation of the disabled in Africa: Towards improved services* (Vol. 1, pp. 60–81). Edmonton, Canada: Centre for International Education and Development, University of Alberta.

Kunc, N. (1992). The need to belong: Rediscovering Maslow's hierarchy of needs. In R. Villa, J. Thousand, W. Stainback, & S. Stainback (Eds.), *Restructuring for caring and effective education* (pp. 25–39). Baltimore, MD: Brookes.

Kuyini, A. A. B. (1998). *The Ghana community-based rehabilitation programme: An outsider assessment of programme implementation and functioning in Northern Ghana*. Unpublished M. Phil thesis, University of Cape Coast, Ghana.

Kuyini, A. B. (2014). Exploring teaching practices in special units for students with intellectual disability in Ghana. *Journal of Research in Special Education Needs*. Forthcoming.

Kuyini, A. B., Alhassan, A. R., & Mahama, F. K. (2011). The Ghana community-based rehabilitation program for people with disabilities: What happened at the end of foreign donor support? *Journal of Social Work in Disability & Rehabilitation, 10*(4), 247–267.

Kuyini, A. B., & Desai, I. (2007). Principals' and teachers' attitudes toward and knowledge of inclusive education as predictors of effective inclusive teaching practices in Ghana. *Journal of Research in Special Educational Needs, 7*(2), 104–113.

Kuyini, A. B., & Desai, I. (2008). Providing instruction to students with special needs in inclusive classrooms in Ghana: Issues and challenges. *International Journal of Whole Schooling, 4*(1), 1–39.

Mamlin, N. (1999). Despite best intentions: When inclusion fails. *The Journal of Special Education, 33*, 36–49.

Mastropieri, M., & Scruggs, T. (2000). *The inclusive classroom: Strategies for effective Instruction.* Boston, MA: Prentice Hall, Inc.

Ministry of Education (MoE). (2003). *Education strategic plan 2003–2015.* Accra, Ghana: Ministry of Education.

Ministry of Education (MoE). (2008). Annual Report, MoE. Accra, Ghana: Ministry of Education.

Ministry of Education (MoE). (2011a). *Education strategic plan 2010 to 2020: Policies, strategies, delivery, finance* (Vol. 1). Accra, Ghana: Ministry of Education.

Ministry of Education (MoE). (2011b). *Education strategic plan 2010 to 2020: Strategies and work programme* (Vol. 2). Accra, Ghana: Ministry of Education.

Ministry of Education, Ghana. (1996). *National Education report: Submitted to the 45th Session, international conference on Education, Geneva.* Retrieved from http://www.ibe.unesco.org/international/databanks/dossiers/rghana.htm

Ministry of Employment and Social Welfare (MESW). (1998). *SUNEPED report.* Accra, Ghana: The Navrongo Health Research Centre.

Ministry of Employment and Social Welfare (MESW). (2000). *National disability policy document, MESW.* Accra, Ghana: Ministry of Employment and Social Welfare.

Obeng, C. (2007). Teachers views on the teaching of children with disabilities in Ghanaian classrooms. *International Journal of Special Education, 22*(1), 96–102.

Obi, F., Mamah, V., & Avoke, K. (2007). Inclusive education in an emerging country: The state of teacher preparedness in Ghana. *Journal of International Special Needs, 10,* 31–39.

Ocloo, M. A., Hayford, S., Agbeke, W. K., Gadagbui, G., Avoke, M., & Boison, C. I. (2002). *Foundations in special education: The Ghanaian perspective.* Cape Coast, Ghana: Nyakod Printing Works.

Ofori-Addo, L. (1994). The community-based rehabilitation programme in Ghana: Examples of good practice in special needs education and community-based programmes (pp. 24–33). Paris: UNESCO.

Ofori-Addo, L., Worgbeyi, N., & Tay, K. (1999). *Inclusive education in Ghana: A report for the Ghana government, ministry of employment and social welfare.* Accra, Ghana: Government of Ghana.

O'Toole, B. (1987). Community-based rehabilitation (CBR) problems and possibilities. In J. Thorburn, & K. Marfo (Eds.). (1990), *Practical approaches to childhood disability in developing countries: Insights from research* (pp. 45–73). Tampa, FL: Global Age Publishing.

O'Toole, B. (1989). The development and evaluation of a community-based rehabilitation programme in Guyana. In J. Thorburn, & K. Marfo (Eds.) (1990), *Practical approaches to childhood disability in developing countries: Insights from research* (pp. 74–99). Tampa, FL: Global Age Publishing.

O'Toole, B. (1990). 'Step by step': A community-based rehabilitation programme with disabled children in Guyana. *Prospects, 25*(2), 311–319.

O'Toole, B., Hofslett, K., Bupuru, K. A., Ofori-Addo, L., & Kotoku, G. (1996). *Ghana community-based rehabilitation (CBR): Participatory evaluation.* Accra, Ghana: Ghana Publishing Corporation.

Peters, S. (2004). *Inclusive education: A strategy for all children.* Accra, Ghana: World Bank.

Sayed, Y., Akyeampong, K., & Ampiah, J. G. (2000). Partnership and participation in whole school development in Ghana. *Education through Partnership, 4*(2), 40–51.

Special Education Division. (2011). *Initiatives in implementation of inclusive education descriptive models*. Accra, Ghana: Ghana Education Service.

Special Education Division (SED). (2013). *Inclusive education policy* (Unpublished).

UNESCO. (1988). *Consultation on special education in Ghana*. Accra, Ghana: UNESCO.

UNESCO. (1990). *World declaration on education for all and framework for action to meet basic learning needs*. Paris, France: UNESCO.

UNESCO. (1993). *The teacher education resource pack on special needs in the classroom*. Accra, Ghana: UNESCO.

UNESCO. (1994). *The Salamanca statement and framework for action on special needs education: Access and quality*. Paris, France: United Nations.

UNESCO. (2000). *The Dakar framework for action*. Paris, France: UNESCO.

United Nations. (1989). *Convention on the rights of the child*. New York, NY: United Nations.

United Nations. (1993). *Standard rules on the equalization of opportunities for people with disabilities*. New York, NY: United Nations.

United Nations. (2006). *World programme of actions concerning disabled persons. The division for social policy and development of the United Nations (UN) Secretariat*. New York, NY: United Nations.

Walker, S., Marfo, K., & Charles, B. (Eds.). (1986). *Childhood disabilities in developing countries: Issues in habilation and special education* (2nd ed.). New York, NY: Praeger.

Wolfensberger, W. (1972). *The principle of normalization in human services*. Toronto, Canada: National Institute on Mental Retardation.

World Bank. (2010). *Education in Ghana: Improving equity, efficiency and accountability of education service delivery*. Retrieved from http://africaknowledgelab.worldbank.org/akl/node/145. Accessed on November 5, 2010.

World Bank. (2012). *School enrollment, primary (% net)*. Retrieved from http://data.worldbank.org/indicator/SE.PRM.NENR. Accessed on April 25, 2013.

World Health Organization. (2006). *Disability and rehabilitation: WHO action plan 2006–2011*. Geneva, Switzerland: WHO.

PART IV
THE MIDDLE EAST

PART 13
THE MIDDLE EAST

SPECIAL EDUCATION TODAY IN ISRAEL

Hagit Ari-Am and Thomas P. Gumpel

ABSTRACT

This chapter describes the current state of special education in Israel as well as what the future holds with possible solutions to improve services for individuals with disabilities. Israel is a very complex society and, as such, the educational system is very complex as well. The development of the special education system in Israel will be described as well as the current policies. In addition, different service delivery models will be explained. Inclusionary practices in Israel will be discussed as well as the prevalence and incidence rates of different disabilities in Israel and how they have changed over time. Finally, different strategies and models for implementation of services will be described and the importance of teacher training to meet student needs will be highlighted.

The Israeli education system in general, and the special education system, in particular, face complex challenges. Israel is a complex society, fractured into different sectors where each sector pushes its own agenda and attempts to dictate government policy. Israel is also an immigrant country with

Special Education International Perspectives: Practices Across the Globe
Advances in Special Education, Volume 28, 473–504
ISSN: 0270-4013/doi:10.1108/S0270-401320140000028022

a large indigenous population and is engaged in an ongoing political, national, and military conflict with enemies from without and competing national narratives from within. It would be inconceivable that these monumental stresses would not impact on society's greatest instrument of socialization and homogenization: the educational system. In all countries, the provision of special services to children with special educational needs is a civil and human rights issue, and so these fractures in Israeli society are also amplified in the special educational system. As we shall see, this small country faces a series of challenges which are unique to the Israeli context, as well as other challenges which are common to other ethnically diverse nations.

The State of Israel is a small country (20,770 sq. km.) and is slightly smaller than New Jersey, with a primarily industrial and service oriented economy (96.5%). The population of 8 million is composed of two primary ethnic groups: 75.3% Jewish and 20.7% Israeli-Palestinians (also called Israeli-Arabs[1]) who are either Muslims or Christians; Druze and Bedouins are two ethnic groups subsumed within the Arab sector. Four primary religions are represented in the country: Jewish (75.3%), Muslim (17.2% — predominately Sunni Muslim), Christian (2%), and Druze (1.7%) (Central Bureau of Statistics, 2012b). In this rich ethnic mosaic, the Jewish population can be roughly divided into four groups: secular, traditional (keeps some sort of Jewish traditions and holidays and would be considered "reform" or "conservative" Judaism in North America), religious (would be considered "orthodox" Judaism in North America, men are noticeably visible by the knitted yarmulke), and the ultra-orthodox (who live in separate communities, often known as "Hassidic Jews" in North America, men are noticeably visible by their black suits, hats, and beards). The Jewish population is also divided into *Ashkenazi* (of European descent) and *Sephardic* (also called *Mizrahim* and are of Middle Eastern descent) Jews. The ultra-orthodox are divided into countless subgroups, some *Ashkenazi* and some *Sephardic* (Gumpel, 2011).

SPECIAL EDUCATION IN ISRAEL

The birth of the Israeli special education system can be divided into three historical periods: (a) developments which took place during the period when Ottoman Syria (1516—1918, which included Palestine) was ruled by the Ottoman Empire (1453—1918) and was divided into three primary provinces or *sanjaks* (*Sanjak* of Jerusalem, *Sanjak* of Balqa, *Sanjak* of Acre); the *Sanjak of Jerusalem* was exposed to increased European influence since the cessation of hostilities in the Crimean War (1853–1856), as Ottoman Syria was forced to allow European powers to purchase land and assume rights in the Holy Land; (b) the period following the end of the First World War in which the United Kingdom assumed control of Palestine as a British Mandate (1918–1948) and during which political Zionism, which called for the establishment of a Jewish state as the national (or binational) and secular homeland of the Jewish people; and (c) the period since the establishment of the modern State of Israel in 1948.

The first special education institutions in Palestine (the term to define the pre-state entity) were established early in the 20th century, during the Ottoman Period, mainly by physicians who received funding from organizations and philanthropists. The Jewish Institute for the Blind was established in Jerusalem in 1902, by Nachum Natanzon, a philanthropist and by Abraham Mozes Lontsz who lost his sight as a young man and later published the first Hebrew books in Braille. Concurrently, the Arab Organization for the Welfare of the Blind was established in Jerusalem, by Sobhi El-Dajani, a member of a family of physicians, who was blind himself and directed the institute with his wife and received support from the British government. At roughly the same time, two other institutes for visually impaired Arab students were also founded in Ramallah (for girls) and in Beit-G'an, in the northern part of the country (Sadeh, 2003).

The trend to develop special educational frameworks for sensory impaired children continued during the period of the British Mandate: in 1932 the first school for deaf and hearing impaired children was opened in Jerusalem through the support of the Alliance Israélite Universelle. The school, which is still in operation, has always served both Jewish and Arab children. Concurrently, Dr. Mordechai Birchiyahu, began to work with and teach "difficult to educate" and "nervous" children in the new city of Tel Aviv. Birchiyahu also established an institution for children with intellectual disabilities (ID), with the support of the head of the local educational department at the time, Shoshana Persitz, in 1929; "*Netzah Israel*" was active for 60 years (until 1989, Sachs, Levian, & Weiszkopf, 1992; Sadeh, 2003). In 1939, another school was established in Jerusalem: the David Yellin School served children with various disabilities.

Massive migration along with the United Nations declaration of November 29, 1947, changed Palestine forever by creating a de jure Jewish state through demographic transformation, land acquisition, development of a separate Jewish economy, and the development of separate social, political, economic, and educational institutions (Farsoun & Zacharia, 1977). The shift in balance from an unimportant backwater province of the Ottoman empire, consisting only of a handful of impoverished groups of Jews in the late 19th and early 20th century, to a fledgling modern nation with a clear Europeanized majority created a European style hegemony in all cultural and national institutions which was, of course, reflected in the structure and goals of the educational system of the time.

EDUCATIONAL POLICY IN ISRAEL

Following the establishment of the State of Israel, in 1948, the educational system grew rapidly. A major challenge in becoming a viable and stable Jewish state was the need to recreate a Jewish majority in Palestine where none had existed for 2,000 years. During this time, the seeds of today's primary and basic dilemmas of modern Israeli society were sown, issues whose trajectories are still visible today. Since achieving independence, the country's leaders have repeatedly declared that a primary goal of the educational system has been to reduce socioeconomic gaps between different segments of the population on an inter-ethnic (i.e., Jewish vs. Arab allocations in education) and an intra-ethnic (*Ashkenizim* vs. *Mizrachim*, secular vs. religious) level. These "gaps" exist on a myriad of economic, cultural, and legal levels (Gumpel, 2011). For instance, marked differences are evident in demographic comparisons between Jewish and Arab citizens. Israeli-Palestinian families are larger than their Jewish compatriots (in 2010, 11% of Israeli-Palestinian families had more than five children vs. only 3% of Jewish households, Meyers – JDC – Brookdale Institute, 2012). Likewise, poverty rates between the two groups differ: in 2012, 53% of Israeli-Palestinian families, and 66% of Israeli-Palestinian children lived in poverty versus 14% and 24%, respectively, for the Jewish population. Disability rates also differ between the two groups. In 2012 the prevalence rates for severe disabilities among children was 5% for Israeli-Palestinian and 3% for Jewish children (Meyers – JDC – Brookdale Institute, 2012).

Aside from the declarative nature of these intentions, educational policy has rarely been discussed on a systemic level (Shmueli, 2003). Disparity in educational performance also exists between the primary Jewish groups and between Jews and Arabs (OECD, 2009). For instance, in 2011, 70.4% of all Jewish high schools students were eligible for their high school matriculation diploma, as compared to a 52.5% rate for Arab high school students; these numbers have remained fairly stable since 1995 (Central Bureau of Statistics, 2012b) and are even more disturbing in Jerusalem, the capital. Despite an 8% dropout rate among youth in West Jerusalem, the dropout rate in occupied East Jerusalem[2] approaches 50% (Wargen, 2006).

In 1960 there were 353 special education schools in Israel and only one of them was Arab. Over the succeeding decades, Israel has witnessed a continued reduction of segregated special education schools in the Jewish education system with a concomitant increase of special schools in Arab education (Central Bureau of Statistics, 2012b). Due to a myriad of reasons too numerous to explore here, educational expenditures in the Arab sectors in Israel have trailed those in the Jewish sectors. Figure 1 shows the disparities in the provision of special educational frameworks for these two groups. Despite the fact that Jewish educational institutions were historically funded more than those of non-Jewish groups, funding and resource gaps have been slowly closing since the 1980s. Even though these gaps are being reduced, Israeli-Palestinian children are still underserved; whereas in 2011 the ratio of special education schools for each Jewish child was 1:7,692, for Israeli-Palestinian it was 1:8,695 (Central Bureau of Statistics, 2012a).

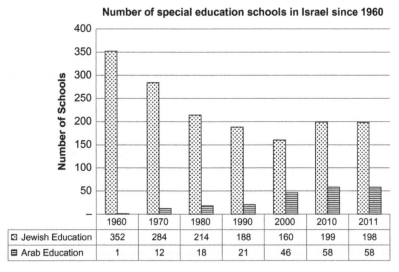

Number of special education schools in Israel since 1960

	1960	1970	1980	1990	2000	2010	2011
▣ Jewish Education	352	284	214	188	160	199	198
⊟ Arab Education	1	12	18	21	46	58	58

Fig. 1. Number of Special Education Schools for Jewish and Israeli-Palestinian Children from 1960 to 2011.

The Israeli educational system is controlled by a strong central bureaucracy located in Jerusalem and is run by the Ministry of Education (MoE) (Gumpel, 2011), which has undergone substantial changes over the last 65 years. The special education system is directed from the ministry via the Division of Special Education (DSE). As a result of the complicated political reality in Israel, educational policy is subservient to different, often conflicting, political and demographical considerations (Avissar, Moshe, & Licht, 2013) as frequent political changes make it difficult to formulate long-term policies. For example, a recent reform to set a clear "strategic plan" was made by the MoE in 2011 where three major goals and 11 operational targets were outlined (e.g., enhancing Zionist ideology along with Jewish, democratic, and social values, reducing violence and creating a positive school atmosphere, improving educational achievements, reducing achievement gaps between different demographic groups, improving teacher' status, and encouraging efficacy in the system). The following year, in 2012, one more major aim was added in a declared intention to strengthen schools' ability to include students with different special educational needs and abilities and to reduce referrals to special education settings (the so-called "The 12th Target − Inclusion" mandate, Avissar et al., 2013).

Inclusionary Practices

The special education system in Israel has historically been dominated by neurologists, neuropsychologists, pediatricians, and psychologists working in a medical and pathology-based categorical model of impairment where all children receiving special education services are divided into 12 different eligibility categories based on their primary disability (Gumpel, 2011). Historically, the first step in changing the policy toward educating students with special needs was the establishment of a ministerial panel of experts to reconsider the definition of a child with special needs and the purpose of special education (known as the "Cohen-Raz Committee," 1976[3] in Ronen, 1982). The committee recommended, for the first time in Israel, that a student would be placed in a special school not only because of his or her disability, but also by his or her special needs and level of functioning (Marom, Bar-Siman Tov, Karon, & Koren, 2006). Despite the panel's recommendations, discussion of integration and inclusion only began to gain momentum following legislation of the 1988 Special Education Law (SEL) and the implementation of the law in the early 1990s, as many children who previously received services in segregated settings began to receive services within the general education framework (Avissar & Layser, 2000; Comptroller's Office, 2001; Gumpel, 2011; Margalit, 1999). Like much of Israeli society, special education procedures prior to the passage of the SEL of 1988 ("Special Education Law of 4758," Knesset, 1988) were based on an informal and personal form of negotiation between the educational system, the child's family, and the Ministry of Education (Gumpel, 1996). Services were provided under the more general auspices of the Compulsory Education Law of 1949 and the State Education Law of 1953. Today, over 30 years after its passage, the SEL of 1988 remains the foundation of Israeli special education and marks a turning point in the provision of special education services to children and adolescents with special needs. As a result of the SEL, the special educational system has slowly shifted to a more inclusionary system with a set of bureaucratic safeguards to ensure that all children receive a quality education.

Currently, the MoE has adopted three models of inclusionary special education: (a) the individual inclusion of students within general education classes and kindergartens where the majority of learners do not have learning disabilities (LDs); (b) self-contained classes within general education schools where the students have identified multiple LDs as well as Emotional and Behavioral Disorders (EBD), Autism Spectrum Disorders (ASD), and mild ID; and (c) inclusionary classes, with a limited number of special needs students and two teachers (a primary "homeroom" teacher and a special education teacher) who work both together and separately (this model is not common, and exists primarily in kindergartens). Despite these guidelines, the number of inclusionary placements has gotten smaller over the last decade, with a fairly consistent downward trend in inclusionary placements (see Fig. 2).

Prevalence and Incident Rates

In the 2011–2012 academic year, there were 2,576,900 children in Israel; approximately 75% were Jewish and 25% Israeli-Palestinians. For all students, 330,000 (12.8%) children had identified disabilities or chronic diseases, according to estimations of the National Council for the Child (NCC) (Zionit & Ben-Arie, 2012). In that same year, 203,200 children (7.9%) were identified by the MoE as having special educational needs, 64.5% were included in general educational settings, 18.6% studied in self-contained classes within general education schools, and 16.9% of them studied in segregated schools. Table 1 shows prevalence rates of ten

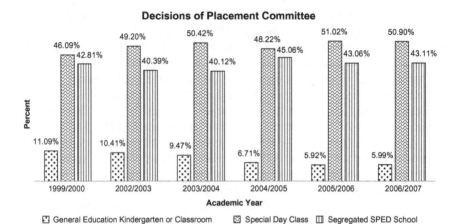

Fig. 2. Decisions of Placement Committees, 1999–2000 through 2006–2007 Academic Years.

primary disability categories in the three types of special educational placements: inclusionary classrooms, special day classes in general education schools, and segregated special education schools (Zionit & Ben-Arie, 2012). LD is the largest category of students and accounts for 51.4% of all students with special needs; however, this number refers only to students who are identified as presenting with complex or multiple LDs, and are supported by special education services (most "mild" LDs are never formally identified through special education placement committees). Students with LDs are also the largest group in inclusionary and self-contained classes. Other categories of special needs students are those with EBD at 7.6%, developmental delays (10.8%), and language delays (6%); for both of these two groups, 70% of identified children receive services in early childhood settings (Zionit & Ben-Arie, 2012).

Table 1 also clearly shows that educational placements in Israel are guided by a categorical system where inclusionary resources are available depending on the student's diagnostic category as opposed to his or her individual functional level. General education placements are implemented primarily among children with LDs where 70.5% of these students are included in general education settings, similar to the placement of students with developmental (72.4%) or language (70.5%) delays. Slightly more than a half of students with EBD are included (56%), and less than a half (44.8%) of students with cerebral palsy/severe physical handicaps are

Table 1. Frequencies of Selected Disability Groups Receiving Services from the Ministry of Education in the 2009–2010 Academic Year, Listed in Order of Prevalence.

	Absolute Number	% Special Schools	% Special Day Class	% Inclusion
LD	106,021	4.8	24.7	70.5
Developmental delay	22,401	23.0	4.6	72.4
EBD	15,825	25.3	18.7	56.0
Language disorders (delay)	12,540	29.6	2.8	67.6
ASD	6,876	42.3	29.0	28.7
Hearing impairment	4,349	15.7	19.0	65.3
Significant physical handicaps	2,806	51.1	4.1	44.8
Moderate/Severe ID	2,766	93.6	6.4	0.0
Psychiatric disorders	2,270	65.0	2.7	32.3
Visual impairment	1,102	15.5	0.0	84.5
Medically fragile	741	0.0	0.0	100.0

Source: Zionit, Berman, and Ben-Arie (2009).

included. Nearly a third of students with psychiatric disorders (32.3%), and ASD (28.7%) are included individually in general educational settings.

CHANGES IN RATES OF DISABILITIES

Figure 3 shows the prevalence rates of selected disabilities since 2006 (the first year that the Central Bureau of Statistics published detailed data on each disability) cross-tabulated with type of placement. While in 2012 nearly 8% of Israeli students were defined as students with special needs, six years earlier only 5.5% were identified as such. The total increase of students in the educational system was of 1.2 during this period, while the increase in the number of special education students was of 1.74.

Three different types of prevalence increases are evident since 2006. First, certain disability groups have kept pace with growth rate of the general education system (moderate and profound ID, sensory impairments, and physical disabilities). A second trend is evident in categories which have almost doubled their size relative to the general educational trends (i.e., LD, EBD, and psychiatric disorders). For instance, the number of students with diagnosed LDs or psychiatric disorders has increased by 92%

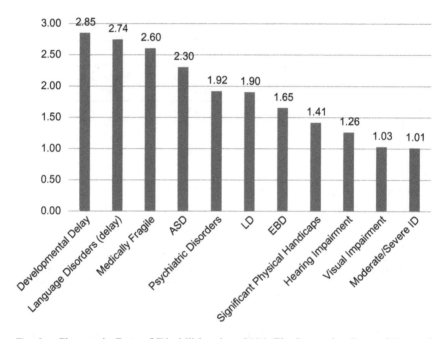

Fig. 3. Changes in Rate of Disabilities since 2006. The Increasing Rate of General
Education = 1.21, Overall Increase of Special Education = 1.74.

and 90%, respectively, during this same period. The third data trend
includes those disability groups whose identification and placement in the
special education system has increased to a much larger extent: at times
over 200% growth (mild IDs and developmental delays, ASD and language
disorders, and medically fragile children). This extreme growth is well
illustrated by the change rates of two separate categories which increased
dramatically over the last several years: ASD and LD.

CASE STUDY: CHANGES IN PREVALENCE OF
STUDENTS DIAGNOSED WITH AUTISTIC
SPECTRUM DISORDER

Currently, due to significant methodological differences across studies,
there is no agreement between Israeli authorities and researchers regarding
the prevalence of ASD in Israel. A report published in 2010 (Tseva, 2012)

in order to estimate the incidence of ASD in Israel and to correlate prevalence rates and other demographic variables, shows a dramatic increase between the 1980s and 2004. The increase was recorded in all populations in Israel, yet most pronounced in the Jewish populations (due to apparent under-diagnosis in other ethnic groups). Among the latter, rates increased from 1.2 per 1,000 among children born in 1986–1987 to more than 3.6 per 1,000 in 2003. The study database included two Israeli national registries: The Israeli Ministry of Social Affairs, which is the official agency responsible for welfare of individuals with autism in Israel and the Israeli Central Bureau of Statistics (CBS), as a source of annual numbers of live births and on infant mortality (defined as death during the first 12 months, between 1986 and 2005), stratified by gender and ethnicity (Gal, Abiri, Reichenberg, Gabis, & Gross, 2012). The increase in prevalence rates showed a strong gender effect. Among males, the average rate increased from 2.3 per 1,000 in 1986–1990 to 5.1 per 1,000 in 2000–2004, while among girls a modest increase was seen from an average of 0.53 per 1,000 in 1986–1990 to 1.0 per 1,000 in 2000–2004; the male to female ratio gradually increased during the study period from 4.8:1 in 1986–1990 to 6.5:1 in 2000–2004. Another recent Israeli study examined physician records rather than governmental reports or educational sources of ASD, in order to calculate the prevalence and incidence of ASD over seven years (Davidovitch, Hemo, Manning-Courtney, & Fombonne, 2012). All children in this report were registered in one of the Israel health maintenance organizations (HMO) which provide services to approximately 25% of Israeli population.[4] In 2010 the prevalence of children diagnosed with ASD was 4.8 per 1,000; boys were 7.8 per 1,000 and girls were 1.6 per 1,000 (corresponding to a male:female ratio of 5.2:1). The study found a significantly lower prevalence of ASD for low SES group as compared to other income groups. Further, prevalence was lower for both Israeli-Arabs (1.2 per 1,000) and ultra-orthodox Jews (2.6 per 1,000) as compared to the rest of the population (Davidovitch et al., 2012).

Generally, despite a significant increase in the last two decades, prevalence rates in Israel are lower as compared to US figures. One possible explanation is that the lower reported prevalence is related to more strict diagnostic criteria in Israel: children younger than six years of age are evaluated at local community Child Developmental Centers where a diagnosis is provided by a multidisciplinary team consisting of at least two specialists with different backgrounds (e.g., a child psychologist and a specialist in pediatric neurology and development) and are conducted over several meetings. Currently, Ministry of Health regulations rely on DSM-IV criteria for ASD; however, new regulations are currently being rewritten to apply DSM-5 criteria. For children older than six years of age, who are not referred to a Child Developmental Center, new health regulations (established in 2008) require that an ASD diagnosis be made only after two separate evaluations (one from a specialist in pediatric neurology and development, and the other from a clinical pediatric psychologist). Physicians and psychologists are required to delineate how each child's symptoms match the DSM-IV criteria (Davidovitch et al., 2012).

According to the MoE, there were 2,990 students with ASD in the educational system in the 2006–2007 academic year, while eight years later, the total number of ASD students increased by 318% to 9,524 (see Fig. 4). When considering the placements of students diagnosed with ASD during these years (see Fig. 5), one can see the increase of individual inclusion and placements from slightly over one-tenth in 2006–2007 to almost one-third in 2011–2012. A small reduction of students in special schools is apparent between 2006 and 2007, 30.7% to 2010–2011, 24.2%, and a sharp increase in 2011–2012. This increase is, apparently, artificial and a product of

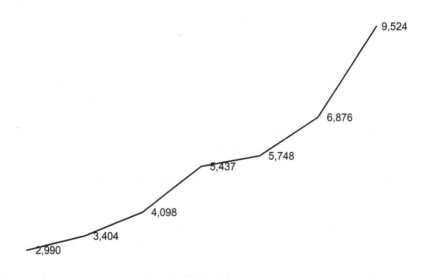

2006–2007 2007–2008 2008–2009 2009–2010 2010–2011 2011–2012 2013–2014

Fig. 4. Total Number of Students Defined as ASD by MOE, between 2006 and 2012.

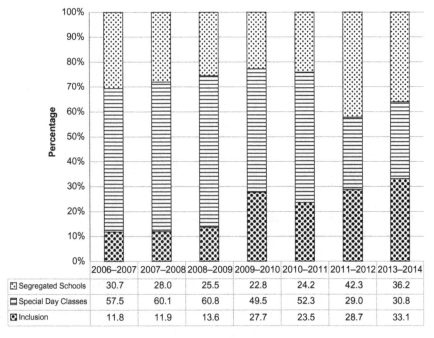

	2006–2007	2007–2008	2008–2009	2009–2010	2010–2011	2011–2012	2013–2014
▣ Segregated Schools	30.7	28.0	25.5	22.8	24.2	42.3	36.2
▢ Special Day Classes	57.5	60.1	60.8	49.5	52.3	29.0	30.8
▣ Inclusion	11.8	11.9	13.6	27.7	23.5	28.7	33.1

Fig. 5. Percentages of Students with ASD in Different Settings between 2006 and 2014.

changes in the way data are currently collected. Following a correction, the percentage of ASD students in special schools reduced to 23.6%, while placement in special classes remains quite stable at 47%.

PROMINENT EDUCATIONAL INTERVENTIONS

DSE guidelines specify that (a) every student is entitled to his or her education and participation in his or her community; (b) every student is entitled to access to resources which will promote self-realization and the development of talents and skills in order to develop skills; (c) every student and his or her family must be involved in planning current and life-long instructional goals; (d) the educational system must respect differences among students with disabilities; and (e) teachers must be committed to cooperative educational processes and professional standards (Avissar & Bav, 2010; Pen & Tal, 2006).

Services are provided in three main frameworks, special kindergartens and schools, self-contained classes, and individual inclusion in general education schools. Individualized Educational Programs (IEPs) for every student with special needs are mandated by the Special Education Law of 1988 and its revision of 2002. The MoE differentiates between IEPs for students in enrolled in segregated schools or self-contained classes (*Tala* or תל"א) and the IEP of individually included students (*Techi* or תח"י), although they are similar in their components. The *Tala* must include a statement of the present educational performance, strengths, and educational goals in all principal academic areas: cognitive, educational, behavioral-emotional, sensory-motor, communication, and life skills. Instructional goals must be set for all relevant areas and a delineation of educational services must be provided (Director General – Ministry of Education, 7/1998) and educational staff are encouraged to invite the parents in order to solicit their input. It is "highly recommended" that the completed IEP will be delivered to the parents during the beginning and ending of the academic year, the teacher must evaluate progress and report to parents. As in the *Tala*, the *Techi* must contain statements of the present educational performance, list strengths and weaknesses, define the responsibilities of each staff member, and specify which educational services are to be provided (if the student is receiving assistance from a paraeducator, his or her role must also be specified). Unlike the *Tala*, however, instructional goals should be based on the general education curricula, and include the expected assignments for the students; students and their parents must be invited to the planning phase and receive a copy prior to the beginning and end of each academic year (Director General – Ministry of Education, 11/2007; Instructions Chapter D1 for Special Education Law, 4763 [Correction number 7 for Special Education Law, 1988], 2002).

EDUCATIONAL PLAN IN SEGREGATED SCHOOLS

In the late 1990s the director of the DSE convened a steering committee for planning a program for adolescents in segregated schools. The results were summarized in a series of guidelines based on a model of quality of life (Reiter, 1999), emphasizing feelings of well-being, opportunities for positive social involvement, and opportunities to achieve personal growth where individual perceptions and values – the subjective views of the person – are recognized as a key facet of quality of life (Schalock et al., 2002). These guidelines outline four domains: social education, career education; independent living in the community, and citizenship education through the use of computers. Initially, the program was designated for students with ID only; however, it has been widely implemented by all special education schools nationwide (Avissar & Bav, 2010; LEV-21, 2009).

Core Curriculum

Until the mid-1980s, the DSE viewed the general education curriculum only as a general framework, allowing teachers to adapt contents and methods. In the mid-1980s, the DSE started to plan a core curriculum along with the Curriculum Planning and Development Division in the MoE, and although cooperation was initially minimal, over time the curriculum became more systematic (Avissar & Bav, 2010). Following passage of the SEL in 1988, professional committees were also set to develop special education curricula in subjects such as mathematics, language, history, science, and physical education. In 2005, the MoE published a core curriculum for elementary schools (general and special education) and defined mandatory content to be mastered by every student in order to develop as productive citizens, able to function both cognitively and emotionally as productive adults based on learning skills and social values (Director General – Ministry of Education, 11/2005). Following the general curriculum, the DSE differentiated between individual inclusion in general education settings and segregated schools, where there is more operational freedom to adopt and adapt appropriate content. All special education schools are required to apply the Core Curriculum for special education. Schools can develop or adopt additional subjects according to their own policies and ideologies (Tal & Leshem, 2007).

Strategies for Accommodations

Three types of accommodations are recognized by the MoE: *Adaptations* – changes in the presentation of the educational material, including enlargement of written material, presenting the material with additional supports and classroom amplification systems; *Modifications* – changes in the contents of the educational program, such as a reduction of part of the material; and *Alternatives* — adding a unique subject requirement for the students (Tal & Leshem, 2007). Accommodations are the most frequent method employed in general education schools, including adding supplemental time, using a calculator, extended formulae page, or allowing oral answers.

RESPONSE TO INTERVENTION

Response to Intervention (RtI) is "the practice of providing high-quality instruction and interventions matched to student needs, monitoring progress frequently to make decisions about changes in instruction or goals, and applying child response data to important educational decisions" (Batsche et al., 2005). RtI models are typically composed of a minimum of the following components: (a) a continuum of evidence-based services available to all students, from universal interventions and procedures to intensive and individualized interventions; (b) decision points to determine if students are performing significantly below the level of their peers; (c) ongoing monitoring of student progress; (d) employment of more intensive or alternative interventions when students do not improve; and (e) evaluation for special education services if students do not respond to intervention instruction (Fairbanks, Sugai, Guardino, & Lathrop, 2007). In the multitier RtI model, the form of academic intervention changes at each tier, becoming more intensive as a student ascends across tiers. Increasing intensity is achieved by using more teacher-centered, systematic, and explicit instruction, conducting it more frequently, adding to its duration, creating smaller and more homogenous student groupings, or relying on instructors with greater expertise (Fuchs & Fuchs, 2006; Lipka, 2013). There are several examples of programs applying principles of RtI in Israel. Some RtI programs were developed by the MoE, and others were developed in teacher training programs and are implemented in schools with the approval of the MoE. For example, the "Safra Model" was developed in Haifa University and is applied both in Hebrew and Arabic in elementary, middle, and high schools. The program includes teacher training in the first tier and intervention with the students in the second tier, using computerized monitoring of students' progress. Efficacy research indicates a significant improvement of basic and advanced reading and writing processes as well as higher student motivation (Lipka, 2013). Another example is the "ELA" program (an acronym in Hebrew for "Detection, Diagnosis,

Learning, and Assessment") implemented among secondary schools and based on mapping tools to identify students with difficulties. Mapping commences at the beginning of each academic year with the administration of a diagnostic language test. When students with difficulties are identified, they receive support in multi-language subjects, like history and literature, within small groups, usually by cooperative learning strategies (Lipka, 2013). A third program is "I Can Succeed" (in Hebrew — EYAL), which is meant to promote students with learning disabilities' academic and emotional development and prevent dropout. It is a three-year program in secondary schools under the auspices of the MoE, local municipalities, the National Insurance Institute, and teacher training programs specializing in LDs. Data are collected in the first year to identify at-risk students, and during all three years of high school students participate in weekly meetings with an educational case-manager and learn educational and personal skills (Lipka, 2013).

The operational principles of the "The 12th Target — Inclusion" (described above) are similar to those of RtI: monitoring all students and identifying those with difficulties, preparing an IEP for every student who experiences difficulties, monitoring progress and adjusting intervention, parental involvement during the entire process and the use of counselor and psychologist resources. Specific guidelines were published for preschool to elementary, middle, and high school (Ministry of Education, 2012, 2013). In preschool, for example, a professional team will be deployed at every local authority and will include the teacher, educational psychologists, preschool counselors, occupational therapists, speech therapists, and behavior analysts. The team will coordinate with the local superintendent and the director of the local municipality kindergarten department. There are also dates for monitoring progress and training educational teams and other professionals. Every school must develop a multidisciplinary team to lead the process and organize the plan as well as a training program for the educational staff, build a functional profile of every student with difficulties, intervention plans based on individual or small learning groups, accommodations and adaptations to be implemented in classes, assessment and data collection. When the interdisciplinary school team considers submitting a child's dossier to the special education placement committee, they must first consult with the local professional committee and validate that all in-school possibilities have been exhausted (Ministry of Education, 2012, 2013). As this program was first implemented in the 2012–2013 academic year, no data are currently available regarding program efficacy.

THE INCLUSION PLAN

Mandated inclusion plans are guided by three main principles: differential services in accordance with individual needs, placement in a general educational facility based on the principle of the "least restrictive environment," and organizational flexibility in service delivery (Avissar, 2012). The plan details four categories of supports. The first category involves teaching and learning, supplemental teaching and special services, including remedial teaching (language, mathematics, and learning strategies), ancillary professionals (creative arts therapists, occupational therapists, speech therapists, and physical therapists), and expert teachers (for applied behavior analysis, ABA, didactic diagnostics, for visually impaired students or hearing impaired students). The second category involves accommodations and adaptations (adapting the curriculum for the student by a special education teacher), technical supports (i.e., hearing devices), and organizational supports. The third category is a combination of teaching and accommodations, such as teaching in a special environment (care center or study center), teaching within specialized facilities or teaching in a cooperative inclusionary model with both general and special teachers in the same class (usually kindergarten). The fourth support method is the provision of individual assistance by a "paraeducator." These ancillary support personnel are only a part of the overall plan and are allocated to specific low frequency populations (ASD, psychiatric disorders, cerebral palsy and physical handicaps, moderate intellectual or developmental disability, visually impaired and blindness, and medically fragile). Support is not automatic by student diagnosis and requires an assessment of the student's level of functioning. Levels of paraeducational support may cover between 5 and 30 hours a week, reassessed on a yearly basis. Paraeducators are employed by the local municipality who contributes 30% of their salaries (the MoE covers the remaining 70%) and typically earn minimum wage (the only employment requirement is 12 years of schooling) (Director General — Ministry of Education, 11/2007).

INTERVENTIONS FOR MAINSTREAMING STUDENTS

Matya — Organizational Resources

Following the "Margalit Report" of 2000 and the 2002 "Revision of the Special Education Law," community resource organizations were established, called *Matya*. *Matyaot* (plural) are organizational entities in each municipality by which educational, and specifically inclusion oriented, resources are organized and allocated. The *Matya* structure allows for the funding of school based and itinerant teachers specializing in a wide variety of specialized skills, from behavioral specialists and consultants, to diagnosticians, and other ancillary services (Gumpel, 2011). Since the establishment of the *Matyaot*, they have become dominant in mediating the relationship between the MoE, the field, and local authorities. Key features include: (a) the ability to act and be an extension of the local educational authority superintendent; (b) flexibility and responsiveness to changing needs; (c) proximity to the field and familiarity with the unique characteristics of the students in order to allow the adjustment necessary assistance; (d) the ability to recruit personnel, to pool resources and transfer them according to changing needs; (e) high-level organizational ability to assist special education schools in performing their tasks, allowing them to devote more time to educational interventions; and (f) the ability to specialize in methods and special care areas needed to include students into general education settings (Director General − Ministry of Education, 12/2010).

Special Issues: Accessibility of Educational Institutes

The accessibility chapter of the Equal Rights for People with Disabilities Law (1998) was passed by the Knesset (Parliament) in 2005. This chapter requires that public places and services must be made accessible, including schools (Bizchut, 2010). However, the Minister of Education published regulations regarding accessibility and access to schools in order to facilitate individual inclusion only in 2011 (despite the fact that the law stated the regulations must be met no later than 2006). According to the MoE, 4,000 classes are now accessible for deaf and hearing impaired students (out of 31,753 or 12.6% all classrooms nationwide). The number of accessible classrooms exceeds the number of children who are deaf or hearing impaired (O. Halpern, personal communication, February 6, 2014). Regulations specify the actual accommodations required by any institution with a student or parent with disabilities, including physical or sensory disabilities (Ministry of Education, 2011). Unfortunately, the educational institution is made accessible only when a student enrolls, a procedure which may take time to complete. In addition, the law requires accessibility only of the entrance, the central area, the specific class where the child is

enrolled and the nearby restroom; other public areas like the library and
the schoolyard may remain inaccessible (Bizchut, 2010).

Blind and Visually Impaired Students

The population of blind and visually impaired students is one of the smallest among special needs populations in the country, 0.53% of all special
needs students. The majority of students with visual impairments are
included in general education settings (85%). Every school district has
a "specialized *Matya*" for educating students with visual impairment,
which is responsible for providing optimal and professional interventions
(Director General – Ministry of Education, 12/2010). Each blind or
visually impaired student is entitled to have the individual support of an
itinerant specialized teacher. Students with visual impairments are entitled
to a paraeducator, according to their level of functioning and independence. There is an increasing use of assistive technologies for students with
visual impairments, such as the "Technological Set for Visually Impaired
Students" which includes: a laptop, a closed circuit television camera connected to the laptop, and software to enlarge material and distance. The set
is usually given to older students who can properly use it and benefit from
its possibilities (Shabat, 2011). There are other resources for blind and
visually impaired people in Israel, such as the Learning Center for the
Blind at the Hebrew University of Jerusalem and the library for the blind
which prints books in Braille and records audio files for students (as well as
other populations who need this services, such as students with LDs).

Students with ASD

The sustained increase in the number of children diagnosed with ASD glob-
ally, as well as in Israel, requires the MoE to address the educational needs
of these children in the least restrictive environment. In recent years, children with ASD are identified at younger ages and at higher rates, and their
clinical management is becoming more intensive, proactive, comprehensive,
and consequently, also more expensive. The Israeli health system bases
most of its services on public organizations and is based on a national
socialized medical model which emphasizes early intervention and prevention. "Well Baby Clinics" and "Family Health Clinics" exist in every community in Israel and are completely free; "Well Baby Clinics" begin their

proactive interventions with every pregnant woman and provide pre- and post-natal care for all babies during the first few years of life. In Israel, all families receive a governmental stipend upon the birth of a baby. This stipend is used as a highly effective incentive for visiting a "Well Baby Clinic" within the first weeks of life. Further, the "National Insurance Institute Act" defines eligibility of children with specific developmental disabilities (ASD among them), for extended health services. Funding of up to three individualized treatments per week is given up until age 18 for all children diagnosed with ASD. Additional treatments may be funded by the Ministries of Health, Education, or Labor, according to the child's age and educational setting. In addition, access to a pediatrician or nurse is unrestricted, most medications are funded with a co-payment of no more than 15%, and some specific ASD treatments are covered (Raz, Lerner-Geva, Leon, Chodick, & Gabis, 2013). From the age of six months to three years, children with ASD are eligible for early preschool special education, including at least 10 hours of individualized treatments per week, all funded by the Ministry of Labor and Social services. After age three, children are eligible for special education in preschool, kindergarten, or a school setting, funded by the MoE. However, if parents or educators opt for integration in general education settings, eligibility for treatments is more limited. Home-based programs and many educational interventions are not reimbursed; they are fully paid for by parents. Gaps in public service availability and eligibility along with medical recommendations for an intensive treatment paradigm may encourage utilization of private health services, and have significant economic and social implications (Raz et al., 2013). A recent study conducted in Israel found that despite the National Insurance Institute coverage, there is a high out-of-pocket expenditure of approximately 21% of the yearly combined family income for one child and so represents a serious economic burden (Raz et al., 2013).

Early intervention in ASD is most often provided in community center-based autism-specific early intervention preschools, using one of the main approaches in the field – ABA, DIR-Floortime, or TEACCH, or a combination of methods. Intervention teams usually include program supervisors, trained therapists, speech and language pathologists, occupational therapists, special education preschool teachers, and educational psychologists (Zachor & Ben-Itzchak, 2010; Zachor, Ben-Itzchak, Rabinovich, & Lahat, 2007). In a study conducted in Israel which compared two early intervention approaches for ASD, the students who received an ABA intervention showed significantly greater improvements than a matched group of students who received conventional educational treatments (Zachor et al., 2007). Alternatively, a more recent study did not find major differences between the two interventions, and in the group of less severe autism symptoms, there was a minor preference to a more eclectic approach (Zachor & Ben-Itzchak, 2010).

Inclusion of Students with ASD
Inclusion of students diagnosed with ASD is part of the Inclusion Plan for low frequency special needs populations, according to the SEL, the 2002 Revision, and MoE regulations. However, disparities are apparent between the inclusion of students with ASD vis-à-vis other populations; these differences are often due to strong parent organizations and support groups of these specific populations. In order to ensure quality inclusion, many families take a primary role in including their children with ASD, either by hiring professionals as program supervisors and "inclusion coordinators" (to differentiate their function from paraeducators) or by surreptitiously (and illegally) supplementing the paraeducator's salary, or paying an extra payment per working hour and privately adding extra work hours. Of course, these courses of action are dependent on family socioeconomic levels, and so are problematic. In schools, an inclusion advisor is a professional responsible for designing the inclusion programs, presenting them to the families and the education system and guiding the inclusion coordinators who work directly with the student in the educational environment. The inclusion advisor usually meets with the inclusion coordinators on a weekly basis in order to solve ongoing problems. As part of the effort to promote individual inclusion, special courses for coordinators are offered by the major parents' organization in Israel (Eldar, Talmor, & Wolf-Zukerman, 2010). De facto, many parents hire the assistants (or inclusion coordinators) privately and the system usually turns a blind eye.

Matyaot have ASD specialists who regularly visit the inclusive settings, some on a weekly basis, other less frequently. *Matyaot* also have continuing education programs for inclusive teachers and ancillary staff in designing and implementing social skills training for students with ASD. Some of the social groups are composed of included students only and others are mixed groups of students with ASD and typically developing peers. In the last decade, various courses and training programs of special interventions and treatments of children with ASD have been provided by Israeli universities, teaching colleges, and other institutions resulting in more professionals providing assistance and care for children with ASD, either in the formal educational system, healthcare centers, or in private settings with families and children.

TEACHER TRAINING

The development of a quality educational system is due to a large extent on the quality of the teachers who work in that system. Therefore, increasing teachers' professionalism is a recurrent and central theme in the Israeli education system. This growing awareness of the importance of teacher training as a means for promoting learning outcomes and school effectiveness has led to the appointment of several national committees to investigate new ways in the training, preparation, accreditation, and compensation of teachers (Gumpel & Nir, 2005).

The "National Committee for Examining Teachers' Status and the Status of Teaching Profession" (also known as the "Etzioni Committee") was established by the MoE in 1979 in order to improve the quality of teacher education and to address the need for measures to strengthen teaching as a profession as well as teachers' professional status. Among suggested measures was the provision of merit benefits to excellent teachers, an increase in the teacher's professional autonomy, an extension of demands for the teacher's continual professional development and academic level, and the enforcement of strict supervision of novice teachers including internship and licensure requirements (Etzioni, 1981; Ministry of Education – Culture and Sport, 2004). Fifteen years later (1994) another national committee was appointed to explore the issues related to the preparation and training of teachers in Israel ("The Committee for the Reform of Matriculation Examinations," also known as the Ben-Pertz Committee). This committee described the deterioration of the teaching profession and teacher status despite previous efforts and emphasized five main issues in its report: (a) the allocation of teacher colleges to train teachers and to award teaching diplomas with a BA or a BEd degree; (b) the examination of the geographic dispersion of the teacher training institutions and an examination of ways to increase collaboration as a means for promoting efficiency; (c) the raising of academic entrance requirements for those applying to teacher training colleges and the improvement of candidate selection; (d) the provision of incentives for outstanding student teachers; and (e) the provision of a teaching license from the MoE to those holding an academic degree and a teaching certificate after they complete their internship. These recommendations were adopted by the MoE and were also deployed at the university level for those seeking a secondary education teaching diploma at the university level (Gumpel & Nir, 2005; Hoffman & Niderland, 2010; Knesset, 2003).

A few years later, in 2005, the government established a "National Task Force to Promote Education in Israel" (known as the "Dovrat Committee") in order to recommend major and inclusive reforms in the education in Israel. In the section dealing with the diminishing status of teachers in the country, the committee emphasized the demand to treat teaching like every other profession, with the addition of more work hours at school and the implementation of means for gauging success in reaching educational milestones (Hoffman & Niderland, 2010). Although the committee's reforms were never actually implemented due to opposition from the two powerful national teachers unions, parts of the recommendations were later incorporated into agreements between the government and unions in 2007 leading to current reforms in the educational system – "New Horizon" (*Ofek Hadash*, or אופק חדש, for elementary schools) and "Courage to Change" (*Oz Latmura* or עוז לתמורה, for secondary schools) (Hoffman & Niderland, 2010).

Despite all of these attempts at reform, in Israel as in much of the western world, approximately 50% of new teachers leave the profession during their first five years of employment due to low salaries, long hours, lack of institutional support (Gavish, 2002), and pervasive school violence. In addition, according to a recent study, novice teachers in Israel experience high levels of burnout as early as the beginning of their first year of teaching, due to three main variables: a lack of appreciation and professional recognition from students, a lack of appreciation and professional recognition from public, and a lack of a collaborative and supportive work environment (Gavish & Friedman, 2010).

Another government committee tasked with reforming teacher training was convened by the Israeli Council for Higher Education: "The Committee for Establishing Guiding Principles for Teacher Training in Higher Education in Israel" (also known as the "Ariav Committee," 2006). A major recommendation by the committee was the national implementation of the requirement of at least an undergraduate degree in education (BA or BEd) and a teacher license as a condition for employment. Prior to these recommendations (since before the founding of the State of Israel), employment was not infrequently granted to teachers with a high school diploma and a teacher's license who were trained in a teacher's college (akin to Normal Schools in the United States or École Normale in France). Requiring an undergraduate degree also necessitated a change in the structure and personnel in many teaching colleges in the country. Whereas, previously, instructors in these teaching colleges could include experienced teachers (without undergraduate degrees), a shift began where all teacher training personnel must possess at least a graduate degree. Over the last decade, many teacher colleges have begun to offer MA or MEd degrees, and so the Israeli Council for Higher Education now requires that all faculty members have a PhD in their area of specialty.

Currently, there are 5 teacher training departments in Israeli universities and 23 teacher colleges (11 secular, 9 Jewish-religious, and 3 in Arab education). About 22,000 undergraduates studied education in 2012, 20% of them specializing in special education, an overall increase of 4.5% from the previous year (Ya'acov, 2012). Nearly 3,500 graduate students were enrolled studied during this same year, a yearly increase of 11%. Figure 6 shows the recent changes in Jewish and Arab primary teaching personnel over the last decade and highlight some important differences between the two groups (Central Bureau of Statistics, 2012b). For both groups, most teachers are women; however, more male teachers work in the Arab sector. Generally, both groups show a marked increase in the number of teachers with undergraduate degrees; this is most pronounced among Jewish teachers, who also lead in the number of teachers with graduate and postgraduate degrees. Further, the population of teachers has gotten older during this decade, as fewer younger teachers enter the school work force.

In the second decade of this century, teacher training in Israel is in the midst of fundamental reforms. The first phase is characterized by undergraduate baccalaureate studies, coupled with practicum during studies, and one year of induction, followed by two more years of internships, during which time the novice receives guidance and support from both an experienced teacher and a group at their teaching college or university. The school principal is responsible to evaluate the novice's work before acceptance as a permanent teacher eligible for tenure. The second phase of these reforms relates to ongoing in-service training throughout the teacher's professional employment (Zilbershtrum, 2013). In 2009, the MoE published provisions for professional development of all teachers, including special education teachers and ancillary staff.

A NEW FRAMEWORK FOR TEACHER TRAINING

The purpose of the framework is to improve teacher quality and professionalism by developing new and attractive professional possibilities, to set more stringent acceptance criteria for teacher training, to emphasize the importance of practical experience, to enhance the relationship between

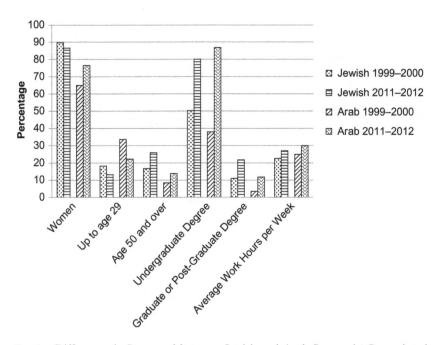

Fig. 6. Differences in Personnel between Jewish and Arab Sectors in General and Special Primary Education.

theory and practice, and to set uniform required core subjects (allowing for variability and uniqueness according to each school's educational vision). The "Ariav Committee" recommended core studies which include three main parts: content area, studies in educational foundations (pedagogy, teaching methods, research, field work, philosophical foundations, cognitive-emotional-social development, theories of teaching and learning, organization and evaluation methods, ethnic and cultural differences, and students with special needs), and compulsory studies in English, the Hebrew or Arabic, culture and citizenship, and technology skills (Ariav et al., 2006). Special education students teachers are required to master these core subjects as well as a special education specialization, either for children aged 6–21 years (usually all children with special needs and all type of placements, and in the last year students can specialize in one disability or category of disabilities) or focus on specific disabilities in preschool, elementary, or secondary school. Some of the teacher training colleges offer specific specialization in specific disabilities, such as LD,

ASD, or EBD and all students in special education have one or two days of field experience each week for every year of their training. Field work includes observations, interviews with the staff, and actual teaching, with the support of both the college tutor and the staff within their class. Graduating students receive a Teaching Certificate from their college and a BEd; however, they must also be licensed (certification from MoE) after two years of successful internships. Recent data of the Central Bureau of Statistics (2010 in Ma'agan, 2013) reveals that 60% of graduated Jewish students and 67% of graduated Arab students begin their internship and more than 23% of Jewish primary teachers and 18% of Arab primary teachers leave the profession after first year of teaching (Ma'agan, 2013).

Narrative research about students' motives for studying special education reveals that many of them choose the profession from individual motives, some have LDs themselves, others have a family member with special educational needs and have had successful life experiences (e.g., volunteering or during their compulsory military service). Often, they are motivated to improve the educational system and make it more responsive for students and most of them perceive the special education system as more significant and challenging than the general education system (Lavian, 2013). Despite their sense of idealism and a belief in their willingness and ability to work hard, special education teachers, mainly teachers in special day classes, experience professional burnout at the same levels of general education teachers; however special education teachers who work in inclusionary settings, often with small groups of students, appear to be at a lower risk for burnout (Lavian, 2012).

CONCLUSION

It appears that the DSE promulgates a comprehensive and coherent policy in accordance with special education goals and policies and is responsive to field-based needs. However, it is unclear as to what extent these plans are currently implemented (Avissar & Bav, 2010). General education teachers in Israel often do not use accommodations or modifications in their instructional methods for students with special needs, despite acknowledging their benefits and need. For example, in a study of general and special education teachers in general education settings, it was apparent that teachers did not cooperate with other professionals at school to solve problems or to share responsibility in classroom management. Special education teachers, on the other hand, reported limited yet inefficient cooperation with parents, despite official exhortations to cooperate and develop partnerships (Layser & Ben-Yehuda, 1999). Similar findings regarding this gap between the ideal and reality was found in another study of general education teachers, who rarely used instructional accommodations for students with special educational needs, despite positive attitudes and opinions regarding these accommodations (Almog & Shechtman, 2004).

NOTES

1. In this chapter we use the term Palestinian to describe ethnic Palestinians (as opposed to Druze and Bedouins), a sector of the Arab minority of Israel, and citizens of the State. In its current usage, the term *does not refer* to those Palestinians living in the Occupied Territories or Gaza Strip (areas captured by Israel in the 1967 war, also known as the Six Day War); these non-Israeli Palestinians do not hold Israeli citizenship and do not receive services from the Israeli Ministry of Education.

2. The term East Jerusalem refers to part of the city annexed by Jordan in 1948 after the Israeli War of Independence and then again by Israel in 1980, following the 1967 or "Six Day War." The Israeli annexation of East Jerusalem is not recognized by any other country in the world, nor by the United Nations. The 1980 Israeli annexation annexed only the land; Arab residents were not granted citizenship or equal rights commensurate with citizenship.

3. Israeli government ministries often convene panels of experts in order to clarify and develop policy recommendations. These committees are often named after their Chair.

4. Israel has a mandatory national healthcare system in which all citizens are free to choose between four HMO, each providing equivalent medical services. All citizens are covered from "cradle to grave."

REFERENCES

Almog, O., & Shechtman, Z. (2004). Teachers' instructional behavior towards students with special needs in regular classes and their relationship to student's performance [in Hebrew]. *Issues in Special Education and Rehabilitation, 19*, 79–94.

Ariav, T., Olshtain, E., Alon, B., Back, S., Grienfeld, N., & Libman, Z. (2006). *Committee for guidelines for teacher education: Report on programs in higher education institutions in Israel.* Jerusalem, Israel: Council for Higher Education [in Hebrew].

Avissar, G. (2012). Inclusive education in Israel from a curriculum perspective: An exploratory study. *European Journal of Special Needs Education, 27*(1), 35–49.

Avissar, G., & Bav, T. (2010). תהליכים ומגמות בתכנון לימודים בישראל לתלמידים עם מוגבלויות [Process and trends in educational planning for students with disabilities in Israel] [in Hebrew]. *Theory and Practice in Educational Planning, Ministry of Education, 21*, 141–167.

Avissar, G., & Layser, Y. (2000). Evaluating values in special education as change in education [in Hebrew]. *Halacha veMa'ashe b'Tichnun Limudim, 15*, 97–124.

Avissar, G., Moshe, A., & Licht, P. (2013). "These are basic democratic values": The perceptions of policy makers in the ministry of education with regard to inclusion. In G. Avissar & S. Reiter (Eds.), *Inclusiveness: From theory to practice* (pp. 25–48). Haifa, Israel: AHVA Publishers.

Batsche, G., Elliot, J., Graden, J. L., Grimes, J., Kovaleski, J. F., & Prasse, D. (2005). *Response to intervention: Policy considerations and implementation.* Alexandria, VA: National Association of State Directors of Special Education.

Bizchut. (2010). *The accessibility to education in Israel – General data file* [in Hebrew]. Bizchut – The Israel Human Rights Center for People with Disabilities.

Central Bureau of Statistics. (2012a). *8.29. Students with special needs in secondary education by type of disability and type of setting, 2007/08, 7.* Retrieved from http://www.cbs.gov. il/reader/shnaton/templ_shnaton.html?num_tab = st08_29&CYear = 2012. Accessed on July 3, 2012.

Central Bureau of Statistics. (2012b). *Statistical abstract of Israel 2012, selected data from the new Israel statistical abstract No. 63-2012.* Jerusalem, Israel: Central Bureau of Statistics.

Comptroller's Office. (2001). *State comptroller's annual report.* Jerusalem, Israel: Government Press.

Davidovitch, M., Hemo, B., Manning-Courtney, P., & Fombonne, E. (2012). Prevalence and incidence of autism spectrum disorder in an Israeli population. *Journal of Autism and Developmental Disorders, 43*(4), 1–9.

Director General – Ministry of Education. (1998, July). *Individual educational program (IEP) for students in special education settings.* Jerusalem, Israel: Ministry of Education and Science Press.

Director General – Ministry of Education. (2005, November). *3*(A), Director General's regulations: The core curriculum for primary education. Jerusalem, Israel: Ministry of Education and Science Press.

Director General – Ministry of Education. (2007, November). *3*(d), Director General's regulations: Inclusion plan in regular education and the treatment of children with special needs in regular education. Jerusalem, Israel: Ministry of Education and Science Press.

Director General – Ministry of Education. (2010, December). *4*(A), Director General's regulations: Matya – Local organizational resources for implementation of the special education law and expertizing Matyas of visually impaired students. Jerusalem, Israel: Ministry of Education.

Eldar, E., Talmor, R., & Wolf-Zukesrman, T. (2010). Successes and difficulties in the individual inclusion of children with autism spectrum disorder (ASD) in the eyes of their coordinators. *International Journal of Inclusive Education, 14*(1), 97–114.

Etzioni, A. (1981). Report of the national committee which examined the statues of the teacher and the teaching profession [in Hebrew]. *Hed Hachinuch, 53*(18), 7–17.

Fairbanks, S., Sugai, G., Guardino, D., & Lathrop, M. (2007). Response to intervention: Examining classroom behavior support in second grade. *Exceptional Children, 73*(3), 288–310.

Farsoun, S. K., & Zacharia, C. (1977). *Palestine and the Palestinians.* Boulder, CO: Westview Press.

Fuchs, D., & Fuchs, L. S. (2006). Introduction to response to intervention: What, why, and how valid is it? *Reading Research Quarterly, 41*(1), 93–99.

Gal, G., Abiri, L., Reichenberg, A., Gabis, L., & Gross, R. (2012). Time trends in reported autism spectrum disorders in Israel, 1986–2005. *Journal of Autism and Developmental Disorders, 42*(3), 428–431.

Gavish, B. (2002). *The gap between role expectations and actual role perception for beginning teachers during their first year of teaching.* Jerusalem, Israel: The Hebrew University of Jerusalem.

Gavish, B., & Friedman, I. A. (2010). Novice teachers' experience of teaching: A dynamic aspect of burnout. *Social Psychology of Education, 13*(2), 141–167.

Gumpel, T. P. (1996). Special education law in Israel. *Journal of Special Education, 29*(4), 457–468.

Gumpel, T. P. (2011). One step forward, two steps backward: Special education in Israel. In M. Winzer & K. Mazuek (Eds.), *International practices in special education: Debates and challenges* (pp. 151–170). Washington, DC: Gallaudet University Press Publishers.

Gumpel, T. P., & Nir, A. E. (2005). The Israeli educational system: Blending dreams with constraints. In K. Mazurek & M. A. Winzer (Eds.), *Schooling around the world: Debates, challenges and practices* (pp. 149–167). Boston, MA: Allyn & Bacon.

Hoffman, A., & Niderland, D. (2010). Teachers' image in the mirror of teachers training, 1970–2006 [in Hebrew]. *Dapim, 49*, 43–86.

Instructions Chapter D1 for Special Education Law, 4763 [Correction number 7 for Special Education Law, 1988]. (2002).

Knesset. (2003). *Center for research and information: Background document for discussion of teacher preparation in Israel and the structure of the curricula in teacher training institutions.* Jerusalem, Israel: Knesset Printing Office.

Lavian, R. H. (2012). The impact of organizational climate on burnout among homeroom teachers and special education teachers (full classes/individual pupils) in mainstream schools. *Teachers and Teaching, 18*(2), 233–247.

Lavian, R. H. (2013). "You and I will change the world": Student teachers' motives for choosing special education. *World Journal of Education, 3*(4), 10–25.

Layser, Y., & Ben-Yehuda, S. (1999). The challenge of inclusion: Applying intervention programs by general and special education teachers [in Hebrew]. *Issues in Special Education and Rehabilitation, 14*(2), 17–29.

LEV-21. (2009). *LEV-21 – "Towards adulthood", curriculum for adolescents and adults between the ages of 16–21 in special education* [in Hebrew]. Ministry of Education, Curriculum Division, Jerusalem, Israel.

Lipka, O. (2013). The response to intervention (RTI) model: Components and implications for teaching and learning. In G. Avissar & S. Reiter (Eds.), *Inclusiveness: From theory to practice* (pp. 161–188). Haifa, Israel: AHVA Publishers.

Ma'agan, D. (2013). *Reform "Ofek Chadash": Did the reform improve the attraction of teaching profession and student achievement?* [in Hebrew]. 29th annual conference, Israel Economic Committee. Retrieved from http://www.cbs.gov.il/www/presentations/educ_4_0613.pdf

Margalit, M. (1999). *Report on the actualization of the abilities of students with learning disabilities.* Jerusalem, Israel: Minister of Education and Science.

Marom, M., Bar-Siman Tov, K., Karon, A., & Koren, P. (2006). *Inclusion of children with special needs in the regular educational system.* Jerusalem: Myers – JDC – Brookdale Institute.

Meyers – JDC – Brookdale Institute. (2012, March). *The Arab population in Israel: Facts and figures 2012.* Jerusalem: Author.

Ministry of Education. (2011). *Regulations for equal rights to people with disabilities: Individual accessibility accommodations for a student and a parent.* Jerusalem, Israel: Ministry of Education.

Ministry of Education. (2012). *The inclusion book: Investigating perceptions and their implementation in the inclusion process.* Jerusalem, Israel: Ministry of Education, Pedagogical Administration.

Ministry of Education. (2013). *Support model for the expansion of inclusion capacity and advancement of students in educational institutions* [in Hebrew]. Jerusalem, Israel: Ministry of Education.

Ministry of Education – Culture and Sport. (2004). *The pedagogical administration: The division of elementary schools.* Jerusalem, Israel: Ministry of Education – Culture and Sport.

OECD. (2009). *OECD economic surveys: Israel 2009* (Vol. 2009). Paris: OECD Publishing.

Pen, R., & Tal, D. (2006). Environment designs around the principles of "quality of life" and "universal design" summons a platform of addressing any person without labeling [in Hebrew]. *Eureka: Teaching Science and Technology in Primary Schools, 22,* 1–6.

Raz, R., Lerner-Geva, L., Leon, O., Chodick, G., & Gabis, L. V. (2013). A survey of out-of-pocket expenditures for children with autism spectrum disorder in Israel. *Journal of Autism and Developmental Disorders, 43,* 2295–2302.

Reiter, S. (1999). Special needs students' quality of life, in light of expansion the principle of normalization [in Hebrew]. *Issues in Special Education and Rehabilitation, 14*(2), 61–69.

Ronen, C. (1982). *Introductory chapters in special education* [in Hebrew]. Tel Aviv: Otsar Hamore.

Sachs, S., Levian, M., & Weiszkopf, N. (1992). *Introduction to special education* [in Hebrew] (Vol. Unit 1). Tel Aviv, Israel: Open University.

Sadeh, S. (2003). *Special education in Israel: Pre-state period. Historical documentation of special education* [in Hebrew]. Tel Aviv, Israel: Special Education Division, Ministry of Education.

Schalock, R. L., Brown, I., Brown, R., Cummins, R. A., Felce, D., Matikka, L. ... Parmenter, T. (2002). Conceptualization, measurement, and application of quality of life for persons with intellectual disabilities: Report of an international panel of experts. *Mental Retardation, 40*(6), 457–470.

Shabat, Y. (2011). An assisting technology – For what? [in Hebrew]. *Field of Vision ("Sde Reiya"), 3,* 2–4.

Shmueli, E. (2003). Forming factors of educational policy in Israel. *Studies in Educational Administration and Organization, 27,* 7–36.

Special Education Law of 4758, Knesset. (1988).

Tal, D., & Leshem, D. (2007). *Curriculum for students with special needs.* Jerusalem, Israel: The Division of Special Education, Ministry of Education.

Tseva, Y. (Ed.). (2012). *A review of public services* [in Hebrew]. Jerusalem: Ministry of Social Affairs and Social Services.

Wargen, Y. (2006). *Education in East Jerusalem* (p. 15). Jerusalem: Knesset Center for Research and Information.

Ya'acov, S. (2012). Training teachers in Israel: Who needs the retraining plan? [in Hebrew]. *Kav HaHinuch, 586,* 1–3.

Zachor, D. A., & Ben-Itzchak, E. (2010). Treatment approach, autism severity and intervention outcomes in young children. *Research in Autism Spectrum Disorders, 4*(3), 425–432. doi:10.1016/j.rasd.2009.10.013

Zachor, D. A., Ben-Itzchak, E., Rabinovich, A.-L., & Lahat, E. (2007). Change in autism core symptoms with intervention. *Research in Autism Spectrum Disorders, 1*(4), 304–317. doi:10.1016/j.rasd.2006.12.001

Zilbershtrum, S. (2013). The policy of the division of internship and teaching entry [in Hebrew]. In S. Shimoni & A. Avinadav-Unger (Eds.), *The sequence: Training, specialization and professional development of teachers – Policy, theory and practice* (pp. 95–100). Tel Aviv: Mofet.

Zionit, Y., & Ben-Arie, A. (2012). 2012 ילדים בישראל *[Children in Israel, 2012]* [in Hebrew]. Jerusalem, Israel: The Israel National Council for the Child.

Zionit, Y., Berman, T., & Ben-Arie, A. (2009). 2009 ילדים בישראל *[Children in Israel 2009]* [in Hebrew]. Jerusalem, Israel: The Israel National Council for the Child.

SPECIAL EDUCATION TODAY IN THE KINGDOM OF SAUDI ARABIA

Turki A. Alquraini

ABSTRACT

The purpose of this chapter is to provide a comprehensive view of special education in the Kingdom of Saudi Arabia. The chapter starts with the origins and attitudes of the Saudi citizens regarding persons with special needs. Next the chapter examines trends in legislation and litigation pertaining to persons who are disabled which led to the government's passage of Regulations of Special Education Programs and Institutes (RSEPI) in 2001. The RSEPI regulations were modeled after the United States 1997 Individuals with Disabilities Education Act (IDEA). Included in the discussion of the RSEPI is a delineation of the Disability Code which is comprised of 16 articles. The author also provides information on prominent educational intervention employed in the Kingdom as well details about the preparation of paraprofessionals and special education teachers. The chapter concludes with the special education progress that has occurred since the passage of RSEPI.

Special Education International Perspectives: Practices Across the Globe
Advances in Special Education, Volume 28, 505–528
ISSN: 0270-4013/doi:10.1108/S0270-401320140000028023

INTRODUCTION

Special education today in the Kingdom of Saudi Arabia (KSA) has been significantly influenced by a number of factors that include its religious and cultural differences of its citizens as well as its recent formation as a country. KSA is located in the southwest of the Arabian Peninsula. This country is partially bordered in the east by Bahrain, the United Arab Emirates, and Qatar, and in the north by Jordan, Iraq, and Kuwait (Alquraini, 2010). King Abdul-Aziz al Saud and a small group of men established this country in 1932. After this date, the Saudi government considered the improvement of several fields, including healthcare, the economy, and the education system. As part of its educational system improvement, KSA established the Ministry of Education which regulates the free education services for all Saudi students. Right now, there are 26,934 schools that serve almost 5 million students (boys and girls) from kindergarten to the high school level with almost a half-million teachers (men and women) (Ministry of Education, 2012). This Ministry of Education has to take into consideration the KSA religious and cultural aspects in the education of the Saudi students; therefore, there are separate boys' and girls' schools. This ministry is also responsible for establishing education building codes and architectural requirements, certifying and hiring teachers, setting standards for teacher degrees, providing workshops and in-services training for teachers, and developing the general curriculum (Alquraini, 2010). Additionally, this ministry provides special education services for students with disabilities, especially those who have mild to moderate disabilities from the ages of 6 to 18 years. In the following sections, readers will be provided with a more comprehensive and detailed information to understand special education today in Saudi Arabia after its recent formation as a country. It includes the following sections: origins and attitudes, prevalence and incident rates, trends in legislation and litigation, prominent education interventions, preparation for special education personnel, and the overall progress that KSA has made in establishing inclusive special education services.

ORIGINS AND ATTITUDES

In KSA, there are religious and cultural aspects that differentiate it dramatically at times from Western countries and contexts. For instance,

Saudi society values are inherently affected by the Islamic religion, which is based on the Qur'an and the Sunnah of the Prophet Muhammad. These long established society values, in some cases, view disability as punishment for a person because he or she or his or her family has done something wrong in the form of a "sin" toward Allah (God) or another individual in society. This value may lead to derision and ridicule of a person/family that has a child with a disability. Another view toward disability, according to Saudi values, is that having a child with a disability serves as a test from Allah for either the person or his or her family to see if they will be patient in order to enter Paradise, the holy place prepared by Allah for those who follow the rules of the Qur'an and the Sunnah. This view toward disability in KSA leads most Saudi citizens to believe that individuals with disabilities are dependent on other people, are entrenched in a low quality of life, and are helpless (Al-Gain & Al-Abddulwahab, 2002). Unfortunately, this latter view can cause Saudi citizens to consider people with disabilities as objects of ridicule and may prevent and exclude them from participating in any type of typical community or social activity. The effect of holding these values and views leads to different attitudes toward people with disabilities which can have an effect on their education and treatment. Some of these attitudes are discussed later.

Several studies have examined the attitudes toward people with disabilities in KSA. For example, Al-Abdulwahab and Al-Gain (2003) examined the attitudes of 130 healthcare professionals regarding people with physical disabilities. Their research pointed out that the majority of healthcare professionals had positive attitudes toward people with physical disability. From this finding, the researchers postulated that the values of Saudi culture apparently had little effect on healthcare professionals' attitudes toward people with physical disabilities. Another attitude investigation about people with physical disabilities was carried out by Al-Demadi and Al-Shinawi (1989), who examined the attitudes of 458 college students with different undergraduate majors at King Saud University toward people with physical disabilities. The authors investigated the attitudes of the students based on three independent variables: gender, educational level, and major. The researchers found that students with a special education major had more positive attitudes than other students in other college majors. Further, it was reported that there were no differences in the attitudes among sophomores, juniors, and seniors toward people with physical disabilities, and that male students had more positive attitudes toward individuals with physical disabilities than females.

Another study was conducted by Al-Muslat (1987), who examined the attitudes of 420 teachers, 115 principals, and 52 supervisors toward people with disabilities, including people with visual impairments, hearing impairments, emotional and behavior disorders, intellectual impairments, and learning disorders. Al-Muslat indicated that the teachers, principals, and supervisors in Saudi Arabia exhibited negative attitudes toward people with emotional and behavior disorders and intellectual impairments but positive attitudes toward people with learning disorders, visual impairments, and hearing impairments.

Another interesting attitude study was carried out by Al-Sartawi (1987), who investigated the attitudes of 252 college students at the College of Education at King Saud University toward people with intellectual impairments. The investigator examined the students attitudes based on college major, level of education, and grade point average (GPA). Al-Sartawi reported that students who majored in special education or physiology had more positive attitudes toward people with intellectual impairments than students who had other college majors. This researcher also indicated that junior students had more positive attitudes than did students in other levels of education. Lastly, the researcher found that the college students with the highest GPAs expressed more positive attitudes toward individuals with intellectual impairments than those students with lower GPAs.

A more inclusive study on attitudes was carried out by Sadek, Mousa, and Sesalem (1986) who explored the attitudes of Saudi citizens toward people with visual impairments. The researchers examined attitudes by age, education level, and gender. The researchers indicated that citizens had positive attitudes toward people with visual impairments, and that there was no difference in their attitudes based on their age or level of education. However, female citizens expressed less positive attitudes than male citizens toward people with visual impairments.

Lastly, another inclusive study was carried out by Al-Marsouqi (1980) who investigated the attitudes of Saudi citizens toward people with hearing impairment, visual impairment, and intellectual impairments. The researcher analyzed citizen's attitudes based on both demographic and independent variables that included gender, contact with individuals with disability, and level of education. This study revealed that Saudi citizens had positive attitudes toward people with hearing impairment and visual impairment; however, they had negative attitudes toward people with intellectual impairments. Additionally, those citizens who had experiences with people with disabilities expressed more positive attitudes than citizens who did not. In contrast from the findings above, female citizens were found to have more positive attitudes toward people with disabilities than male citizens.

The above studies indicate that a variety of variables affect attitudes of Saudi healthcare providers, college students, teachers, principals, school supervisors, and citizens toward people with disabilities. Variables such as college major, gender, age, prior experience, education level, and the specific disability can influence one's attitudes. While long standing KSA cultural and religious differences may have a negative effect on a Saudi citizen's view of an individual with a disability, there is more recent special education literature evidence that reports that many Saudi citizens have a positive view of people with disabilities. Such evidence is an indication that Saudi citizens are becoming more willing to accept individuals whose abilities differ from theirs and participate with them in different life activities.

This growing acceptance and engagement in KSA can be traced historically to the early efforts of families to gain support for special education considerations for their children in the 1950s and 1960s. For example, prior to 1958, most students with disabilities in KSA did not obtain any type of special education services or related services. The majority of these students were supported by their families, who struggled in order to obtain healthcare and other assistance for their children (Al-Ajmi, 2006). In 1954, a few Saudi citizens with visual impairments started to learn the Braille method from someone who came back from Iraq at that time (Al-Mousa, 2008). After that, this group tried to teach this method to more students with visual impairments in schools as well as colleges. Within a short period of time, their efforts paid off in 1959 and 1960, when the Ministry of Education established the first institute for 40 students with visual impairments (Al-Mousa, 2008).

A few years later in 1962, the Ministry of Education established a special education department to serve three categories of students: those with visual, hearing, and intellectual disabilities. The Ministry of Education then established institutes for these three categories across the country where special curriculums were used to educate these students. Students could attend these institutes when they reached public school age. However, in 1997, the philosophy of this special education department changed, which dramatically affected the special education services for students with disabilities. For example, the department started to consider early assessment for students at-risk so that those students with identified disabilities could be provided early remedial intervention. This department also extended its services to include many other types of students with disabilities, such as students with physical, learning, and multiple disabilities, and autism (Al-Mousa, 2008).

With these changes, it became apparent to the Saudi government that there was a lack of appropriate and best practice special education services for students with disabilities. As a means to remedy this situation, the Saudi government made a significant effort to improvement these services. The government requested that personnel from the Special Education Department under the Ministry of Education and some special education faculty at King Saud University, who earned their doctoral degrees from the United States, review the United States' special education policies, including the Individuals with Disabilities Education Act (IDEA, 1997) in the hope of developing a more appropriate special education policy for KSA. Their efforts resulted in the 2001 Regulations of Special Education Programs and Institutes (RSEPI) which introduced the first special education regulations for students with disabilities in KSA (Alquraini, 2013).

The RSEPI identified 10 categories of disability that should be served by the schools: hearing disabilities, visual disabilities, intellectual disabilities, learning disabilities (LD), gifted and talented abilities, autism, multiple disabilities, physical and health impairment, communication disorders, and emotional and behavioral disorders. These categories were based on commonly used special education terms among special education professionals across the globe and the prevailing best practice special education literature.

The RSEPI specifies that students identified as having one of these categories must be assessed by a multidisciplinary team which is housed in each school. Once a student is identified with a disability, he/she will be provided the necessary special education services. This team usually uses formal tools to assess the child with a presumed disability, such as intelligence quotient scales (e.g., Wechsler Intelligence Scales), adaptive behavior scales (e.g., Vineland Adaptive Behavior), and achievement tests (Wechsler Individual Achievement Test). This team might also use other informal scales, such as interviews or observation. Even though this effort to provide appropriate special education services for those students has improved the practice of special education in KSA immensely, these services are still similar to those that were provided in the 1970s in the United States such as the mainstreaming philosophy, self-contained classrooms, resource room placement, placement of students into a classroom by their identified categorical classification (learning disabled, behaviorally and emotionally disordered, intellectual impaired), and the establishment of special schools and centers for children with a specific type of disability (center for the physically impaired).

PREVALENCE AND INCIDENT RATES

According to the Central Department of Statistics and Information Population and Vital Statistics (2011) in KSA, 0.8% of the Saudi population is reported as having disabilities (approximately 17,493,364 people). Also, the number of KSA children born annually with a disability is between 400 and 500. Additionally, the number of people with disabilities by age as reported by this center is as follows: 1% younger than 1 year, 3% from 1 to 4 years, and 4% from age 5 to 80 years and above. The percentage of KSA people with disabilities by gender is 65% males and 35% females. This center reported the number of people with disabilities in KSA by type of disability as follows: 9,522 people with visual impairment, 29,507 people with intellectual disabilities, 21,462 people with multiple disabilities, 5,306 people with psychological disorders, 5,773 people with hearing impairment, 7,067 people with communication disorders, and 44,456 people with physical disabilities. Finally, there are two main factors that might cause disability in KSA: genetic causes associated with consanguinity, and a high rate of car accidents (Al-Gain & Al-Abddulwahab, 2002).

In the community of Saudi schools, there are different prevalence and incident rates of disability. The Ministry of Education has reported that 53,414 disabled students (see Table 1), including those with intellectual disability, deaf and hard of hearing impairment, learning disability, autism, multiple disabilities, and visual impairment, receive special education

Table 1. The Categories and Number of Students with Disabilities Who Are Serviced by Special Education in Public Schools in KSA.

Categories	Students (Male)	Students (Female)	Total
Learning disability	17,842	6,964	24,806
Intellectual disability	13,657	5,932	19,589
Hearing impairment	13,657	1,606	19,589
Visual impairment	1,041	480	1,521
Autism	725	100	825
Multiple disabilities	421	32	453
Total	38,300	15,114	53,414

services in public schools or institutes. Today, 24,806 students (17,842 male and 6,964 female) out of the entire public school-age population between the ages of 6 and 18 years have been identified as having a learning disability. Students classified with a learning disability therefore represent about 46% of the entire school-age disability population. Another major category is students with intellectual disabilities. Today 19,589 students (13,657 male and 5,932 female) receive special education services due to their intellectual impairment. This number represents about 36% of the entire public school-age disability population. Students classified with hearing impairment or as hard of hearing represent approximately 13%, or a total of 6,219 (4,613 male and 1,606 female) students out of the entire school-age disability population. Additionally, 3% (1,521 students: 1,041 male and 480 female) of the entire school-age disability population is considered visually impaired. Students with autism represent 2% of the public school-age disability population with a total of 825 students (725 male and 100 female). Finally, a total of 453 students (421 male and 32 female) with multiple disabilities represent only 1% of the public school-age disability population. Even though these reported numbers are meant to represent the percentage of students with disabilities, special education professionals in KSA question whether these numbers accurately represent the total number of students with disabilities given that the total public school population is 4,904,777 students. Unfortunately, this question cannot be answered for now, since KSA does not have a national study regarding the prevalence and incident rates for all categories of disability at the school-age level.

Additionally, there are some reasons that might affect conducting accurate research regarding the disability issues in Saudi Arabia, including "incidence of consanguineous marriage, the high incidence of car accidents, and the fact that some families feel ashamed about having a child with a disability, as a result, they tend to avoid participation in such research" (Al-Gain & Al-Abddulwahab, 2002, p. 2).

TRENDS IN LEGISLATION AND LITIGATION

Since the early 1990s, the Ministry of Education has considered how to improve the special education services for students with disabilities by establishing rules that protect the rights of these students. In 2001, the Special Education Department in the Ministry of Education established the RSEPI, after extensive collaboration with other agencies, such as the Special Education Department at King Saud University, as well as taking into consideration the US special education policies, including IDEA (1997) and Alquraini (2013). In essence, the RSEPI is modeled after the US's IDEA and its major elements are delineated below.

Major Elements of the RSEPI

The RSEPI includes 11 parts that present critical education provisions to adequately serve special education students and their families (Ministry of Education, 2002). Part One delineates the important definitions used in this legislation so that teachers, administrators, supervisors, parts, mental health professionals, and other service providers can easily communicate essential aspects to one another. For instance, it defines the concepts of "disability," "least restrictive environment," "transition services," "multi-disciplinary team," "IEPs," "special education teacher," "resource room," and other aspects of providing education services to special education students (Alquraini, 2013).

In Part Two, the primary goals of special education services are presented. For example, these services should be provided for students with disabilities to meet their unique needs and support them in obtaining the necessary skills that will assist them in living independently and integrating appropriately into society. These goals can be achieved through different procedures such as: (a) determining the needs of students with disabilities through early detection process; (b) providing a free and appropriate special education and related services that meet their needs; (c) specifying these services to the students with disabilities within their IEPs; (d) taking advantage of scientific research to improve the services of special education; and (e) raising awareness about the disability among the members of society by discussing the causes of the disability and the ways to reduce it (Alquraini, 2013).

Part Three presents the foundations of special education in KSA in 28 subsections that discuss important concepts concerning the rights of students with disabilities to acquire appropriate education. This part emphasizes that students with disabilities should be educated in general education and that IEP teams should make decisions regarding the placement of students with disabilities, taking into consideration a continuum of alternative placements.

Furthermore, in Part Four, the characteristics of the 10 categories of disabilities discussed previously (hearing impairment, visual impairment, intellectual disabilities, LD, gifted and talented abilities, autism, multiple disabilities, physical and health impairment, communication disorders, and emotional and behavioral disorders) are explained. Also, it defines the procedures of the assessment for each disability in each category (Alquraini, 2013).

Part Five presents the transition services available for students with disabilities in KSA. It indicates that the main goal of transition services is assisting these students to prepare in moving from one environment to another. Further, this part emphasizes that transition services should be provided for the student when he or she needs them as part of his or her IEPs. Additionally, it defines the types of transition services that might be provided, such as those that assist these students in moving across different levels of education (e.g., preschool to elementary). Finally, Part Five emphasizes that the transition services should be provided for the students with disabilities at an early stage (Alquraini, 2013).

Part Six describes in a comprehensive manner the tasks and responsibilities for professionals (e.g., teachers, principals, and service providers) who work with students with disabilities, either in public schools or special schools. The responsibilities of the agencies for the school districts and the schools regarding these students and their families are determined in Part Seven of the RSEPI. This is a critical aspect because these agencies are responsible for providing a free and appropriate education for students with disabilities. In addition, these agencies must provide awareness programs for the families of these students that will increase their knowledge regarding different issues accompanying disability. Lastly, these agencies are to encourage these families to be involved in different activities, such as participating in short- and long-term planning and providing IEPs for their children (Alquraini, 2013).

Part Eight includes specific procedures of assessment and evaluation for students to determine if they are eligible for special education services. For example, this part indicates the definition, goals, and procedures associated with assessment and the composition of the multidisciplinary team (e.g., the special education teacher, general education teacher, parents, and others). It defines the steps of assessment that should be considered by the schools to determine the eligibility for special education services: (a) obtaining consent from the parents before diagnosis of the child; (b) gathering preliminary information on the status of the child who might need special education services; (c) referral of the child for further assessment procedures if needed; (d) and assessment of the child's needs in different areas by the multidisciplinary team (Alquraini, 2013).

Part Nine delineates the individual education program (IEP) that should be provided for each student who is eligible for special education services. This part defines the importance of the IEP for students with a disability and specifies that the IEP is a unique approach that should be considered to meet the individual curriculum needs of each student and appropriate special education and related services which must be incorporated into the student's school day. Further, it explains the essential considerations of the IEP such as the requirement that it be jointly developed by the multidisciplinary team and the student's family; aspects that should be included in the IEP (general information about the student, the current performance of the student, special education and related services that the student might need, the professionals who are participating in its delivery). Finally, this part mandates that the student must participate in the IEP and the requirement that the IEP should be evaluated annually to determine whether or not its goals have been met (Alquraini, 2013).

The evaluation process for students with disabilities is explained in Part Ten. It describes the definition and goal of the evaluation process (e.g., to determine the current performance of the student). In addition, Part Ten defines significant aspects that should be considered by the multidisciplinary team such as appropriate assessment devises and tests for evaluating each type of disability (e.g., when evaluating a student with possible intellectual impairment, the multiple disciplinary team should consider three assessment devises to measure the student's current intellectual, adaptive functioning, and academic level). Lastly, Part Eleven explains general rules for schools and school districts, such as the fact that only the Special Education Department is responsible for the interpretation of the RSEPI (Alquraini, 2013).

Disability Code

The Disability Code was passed by the Saudi government in 2000. It includes 16 articles that present different issues regarding disability. For instance, Article One of this legislation describes the term of disability as described by the Prince Salman Center for Disability Research (2004), namely,

> A person with a disability is one who is totally or partially disabled with respect to his/her bodily, material, mental, communicative, academic or psychological capabilities, to the extent that it compromises the ability of that person to meet his/her normal needs as compared to his/her non-disabled counterparts. (p. 5)

Based on Article One, a student with a special need could be eligible under one of nine categories of disability, namely: visual disability, hearing disability, cognitive disability, physical disability, LD, speech and language impairments, behavioral problems, developmental delay, and multiple disabilities (Prince Salman Center for Disability Research, 2004). A provision of this article further requires government and private agencies to assist eligible people under the Disability Code in welfare, habilitation, health, education, training and rehabilitation, employment, complementary services, and other areas (Prince Salman Center for Disability Research, 2004).

Article Two of the Disability Code specifies that people with disabilities should have access to free and appropriate services in the areas of health, education, training and habilitation services, employment, social programs, and public services through public or governmental agencies. More specifically, it defines the main issues that should be considered by services providers in these areas. For instance, in the health area, this legislation requires service providers in the healthcare field to provide medical as well as habilitation services in the early stages of disability for both the person with a disability and his or her family and to improve the healthcare for people with disabilities while taking into consideration the current approach to healthcare; health service providers (e.g., nurses) are also expected to have an adequate level of training to be able to provide high quality health-care services for people with disabilities (Prince Salman Center for Disability Research, 2004).

Specific to the education area, the Disability Code requires a free and appropriate education for all people with disabilities regardless of their educational stage (e.g., preschool, general, vocational, and higher education). Under the Disability Code, training and habilitation services should be provided by vocational and social habilitation centers for individuals with disabilities in KSA as required by the labor law (Prince Salman Center for Disability Research, 2004).

In the employment area, this legislation indicates that people with disabilities have the right to get jobs that might assist them in discovering their personal capabilities and allow them to earn income just like other individuals in society. It also requires all agencies either governmental or private that have 25 employees or more to employ 4% of their workforce from categories of people with disabilities and give them equal job growth opportunity in the employment environment similar to those of nondisabled workers (Prince Salman Center for Disability Research, 2004).

The Disability Code also emphasizes that people with disabilities should participate in all of the social programs that guarantee them the right and opportunity to fully integrate with other people in society without discrimination based on their disabilities. Also, it requires that public services should be facilitated and accessible for all people with disabilities in terms of public transportations, technology, and other services. Finally, under this legislation most people with disabilities can get benefits, such as:

• Persons with disabilities get 50% off of their tickets through all public transportation.
• Persons with disabilities are provided all types of care, including treatment and medicines free of charge.
• Persons will disabilities are provided job support on an equal basis as other people without disabilities.
• Persons will disabilities are provided parking spaces for their cars.
• Persons with disabilities, as well as their families, are provided with financial assistance.

These legislations, particularly Disability Code legislation, guarantee the right for all people with disabilities to receive free and appropriate services in terms of health, education, training and habilitation services, employment, social programs, and public services. They also work to protect against any type of discrimination.

To summarize, the RSEPI and the Disability Code support the right of children with disabilities to obtain a free and appropriate education by considering many issues that guarantee this right. The RSEPI requires schools to educate their students with disabilities in a general education setting to the maximum extent, taking into account a continuum of alternative placements. Further, the RSEPI requires that special education services (e.g., IEPs, related services, transition services, and others) should be carried out with students with disabilities in the real world to discourage isolation and segregation while increasing opportunities for acceptance and tolerance by other nondisabled citizens (Alquraini, 2013).

PROMINENT EDUCATIONAL INTERVENTION

The KSA special education services and intervention are in a developing and formative stage, similar to the commencement of special education policies and practices that were initiated in the United States during the late 1960s and early 1970s (Marza, 2002). Due to their current stage of development, provisions and best practices of appropriate education for students with disabilities are lacking in the following areas.

Education Setting

Even though the RSEPI requires schools to allow students with disabilities, including students with moderate and severe disabilities, to receive their education with typically developing peers in regular classrooms to the maximum extent of their abilities, this has not been practiced with students with disabilities in KSA. In other words, students with disabilities still receive their education separately in special schools, private institutions, and self-contained classrooms within the school. Positively, students with LD are educated in general education classrooms with their typically developing peers, with some support from special education services such as resource rooms (Al-Ahmadi, 2009; Al-Mousa, Al-Sartawi, Al-Adbuljabar, Al-Batal, & Al-Husain, 2006). LD students follow the general education curriculum. Meanwhile, students with intellectual disabilities receive their education in self-contained classrooms within public schools, sharing some non-curricular activities with their typically developing peers (Al-Mousa et al., 2006). These students follow the special education curriculum designed by the Ministry of Education, which is different than the general curriculum that is provided to their typically developing peers. Students with autism, multiple disabilities, and visual and hearing impairments are educated in special schools which does not allow to them to interact with their typically developing peers.

Procedures to Determine Eligibility for Special Education Services

Unfortunately, in KSA the diagnosis and assessment processes to determine the eligibility of students for special education and related services are still not free of shortcomings. First off, the assessment process for children does not begin early enough to successfully determine disabilities. This process usually starts when the child goes to school, so the schools and other agencies do not provide early intervention for preschool children with disabilities and their families (Alquraini, 2010). Additionally, most of the special education institutes, as well as public schools, lack a multidisciplinary team and reliable and valid assessment scales to carry out intellectual, adaptive, achievement, and behavioral evaluations that are appropriate for the cultural standards of KSA (Al-Nahdi, 2007). Lacking an appropriate multidisciplinary team, assessment procedures for children with mild to moderate disabilities are non-team based. Therefore, in most cases, the schools' psychologists define students' eligibility for special education service based on a student's IQ scores and teacher observation. In time, the overall assessment and diagnostic procedures will be reassessed and revised to achieve a truly reflective practice in KSA but for now misdiagnosis and inappropriate diagnosis may occur.

Providing Individual Education Programs

The RSEPI requires schools to provide an IEP for each student with a disability and it has become one of the most important educational services provided for each child. However, little historical research has examined IEPs for students with disabilities in Saudi Arabia but recently researchers (Al-Herz, 2008) have begun to shed light on this vital provision of the law. For example, Al-Herz (2008) examined achievement of IEP goals and related difficulties in programs and special education institutes in Riyadh, Saudi Arabia. This researcher found that special education teachers successfully determine the important elements of IEPs in terms of the student's weaknesses and strengths, annual goals and short-term objectives, and needs requiring specially designed instruction. However, this study concluded that some obstacles impede the provision of effective and appropriate IEPs, such as the lack of efficient multidisciplinary teams members (including the special education teacher, the child's previous teachers, the parents of the child, and other members as needed) to formulate short- and long-term IEP goals. Also, the study indicated that the IEPs did not address the student's needs based on their current individual strengths and weaknesses (Al-Herz, 2008). Lastly, Al-Herz pointed out those families in the study did not participate effectively with other school staff in determining the needs of their children, or in the preparation and implementation of IEPs.

The above study points out significant deficit issues regarding the provision of establishing appropriate individual education programs. Not having team members establish a student's IEP based upon their current strengths and weaknesses is problematic because many times IEPs and short- and long-term goals are written by special education teachers without participation of the parents and other service providers (Al-Herz, 2008). This leads to the classroom special education teacher being solely responsible for IEPs for up to 15 students with disabilities in the class. Unfortunately, this situation makes it difficult for the teacher to pay individual attention to each student needs. To summarize, although students with mild to moderate disabilities have received appropriate education, more effort is needed to truly individualize the services received.

Related Services for Students with Disabilities

The RSEPI states that in order for students with special education needs to receive maximum benefit from their special educational programs, related services such as physical therapy, occupational therapy, speech–language, and counseling services must be provided (Ministry of Education, 2002). A number of researchers (Al-Otaibi & Al-Sartawi, 2009; Alquraini, 2007; Al-Sartawi & Grageah, 2010; Al-Wabli, 1996; Hanafi, 2008) have examined the feasibility of related services and their importance for students with disabilities in special education institutes or centers and public schools. For instance, Al-Wabli (1996) examined the feasibility of related services and their importance in special institutes for students with intellectual disabilities. This researcher found that speech–language pathologists, school counselors, psychologists, and social workers were available in these special institutes examined but occupational therapy and physical therapy services were lacking at times.

Following the above line of investigation, Alquraini (2007) examined the feasibility and effectiveness of related services for students with intellectual disabilities in public schools. According to this researcher, the most readily available related services were transportation, speech and language therapy, psychological services, school counseling, and school health services. On the other hand, social work service, occupational, and physical therapy services were available infrequently for these students. A similar study was conducted by Hanafi (2008), who examined the viability of related services for students with hearing disabilities in public schools. The researcher indicated that health and medical services were more available for these students; however, social worker and rehabilitation services were not available. Al-Otaibi and Al-Sartawi (2009) investigated the feasibility of related services for students with multiple disabilities in special education centers and institutes. The researchers reported that the special education centers and institutes lacked health, medical, and physical therapy services. Finally, Al-Sartawi and Grageah (2010) examined the feasibility of related services for students with autism in special education centers. These researchers concluded that there were shortcomings in the provision of related services for students with autism in terms of speech and language therapy, psychological, school counseling, and social worker services.

In summary, although KSA students with a variety of disabilities, who attend public schools or special education centers and institutes, receive some related services other services that they need are unavailable. This is likely due to a lack of professionals who specialize in these fields, or because professionals with these foci (e.g., physical and occupational therapy) are often employed in hospitals instead of schools due where they receive greater salaries (Alquraini, 2007). That being said, there are some private agencies such as Sultan Bin Abdulaziz Humanitarian City that do provide these services. Unfortunately, parents must pay for these services, since the RSEPI does not require schools or schools districts to pay for private agencies to provide these services. In conclusion, students with disabilities in KSA public schools, special education centers and institutes receive some related services but for those students that need a professional with a specific focus (e.g., physical therapy) their special needs go unmeet.

Transition Services

The RSEPI requires that transition services be provided for students with disabilities. According to the RSEPI, transition services are intended to prepare the student with disabilities to move from one environment or stage to another (Ministry of Education, 2002). Additionally, this legislation emphasizes that transition services should be provided for the student when he or she needs them as part of his/her IEP. The RSEPI defines the types of transition services that may be provided in order to assist students to move to different levels of education (e.g., preschool to elementary, high school to higher education, or employment settings) (Ministry of Education, 2002). Finally, the RSEPI indicates that transition services should be provided for students with disabilities at an early stage without defining that age. For instance, it states that when the student is 16 years or younger, he or she should receive transition services when necessary. Despite this fact, transition services have not always been completely carried out for students with disabilities (Almuaqel, 2006). This was demonstrated by Almuaqel (2006) in a study which examined the perceptions of parents, special education teachers, and rehabilitation counselors for students with intellectual delays regarding these students' individualized transitional plans. Finally, even though transition services are mandated by the RSEPI, to the best of this researcher's knowledge, there is no published research addressing transition services for students with disabilities in KSA.

PREPARATION OF SPECIAL EDUCATION PERSONNEL

Paraprofessionals

In KSA, the public schools lack paraprofessionals who can be supportive of both teachers and students in different ways (e.g., that assist the teachers in adapting and modifying curricular activities). It is becoming critical that the Ministry of Education consider ways to increase the number of paraprofessionals that can be trained and hired to assist public school teachers and students with disabilities. This author recommends that this can be accomplished by employing people who have at least a high school diploma and have passed a specific test that determines whether they are qualified for the job. Once they are qualified for the role of a paraprofessional, they can be trained via in-service workshops regarding the specific roles that need to be carried out. This training would then be followed up with on the job training and supervision.

Teacher Preparation

In KSA, there are 24 university special education departments that prepare special education teachers based on a category (e.g., learning disabled, hearing impaired) of students that they will work with. Some of these departments prepare their teachers to work with three main categories of disability (intellectual disability, learning disability, and hearing impartment). Other departments prepare their teachers to work with students with autism, communication disorders, and behavioral disorders. There is only one university department that prepares teachers to work with students with multiple disabilities and provide early intervention for children with disabilities. Most of the university departments have general programs in special education that provide general special education coursework (e.g., educating students with disabilities in public schools, inclusive education, introduction of special education, etc.) and a special program that focuses on specific disabilities such as intellectual disabilities (e.g., teaching methods for students with intellectual disabilities, an introduction to intellectual disability). There is only one special education department at King Saud University that has been accredited by the National Council for Accreditation of Teacher Education (NCATE). All college students in teacher training programs complete three and a half years of coursework and a practicum of one semester. After successfully completing the above requirements, the students participate in day-to-day teaching of students with disabilities in self-continued classes, institutes, or a resource room. After successfully completing their day-to-day training, they become certified as a special education teacher and can seek employment as a special education teacher. Special education teachers are encouraged to get a graduate degree at one of four university special education departments that provide a master's degree in special education based on a category of disability.

PROGRESS OF SPECIAL EDUCATION SERVICES IN SAUDI ARABIA

Despite the problematic issues addressed above regarding special education services in KSA, the services have improved. This improvement has occurred in educating students with mild and moderate disabilities in the least restrictive environment, such as general classrooms or self-contained classrooms in public schools, with some opportunities to participate with their typically developing peers in nonacademic activities. An emerging agenda is to improve the education of students with moderate to severe disabilities, including those with autism and multiple disabilities. Also there has been more interest in the past few years in adding students with attention deficit hyperactivity disorder (ADHD) and emotional and behavioral disorders to meet their special needs. Financial and governmental support will be sought to increase the number of professionals who can participate in related, transition, vocational, and multidisciplinary team services. It is obvious that individuals with disabilities who acquire maximum benefit from their special educational programs will be better prepared to transfer from their school environment to a community environment and be less dependent on others on a daily life long basis.

Even though, there are 24 university special education departments that prepare special education teachers in KSA, these departments do not always provide the best knowledge base and teaching technique skills required to assist the teachers to work in inclusive classrooms, to provide effective transition services, and to use assistive technologies. Therefore, it is recommended that these department curriculums be revised and reoriented so that general and special education teachers are taught to work together in a collaborate manner to educate students with disabilities who are placed in an inclusive classroom. This reoriented curriculum can be enhanced by classroom teachers' use of available assistive technology.

The RSEPI and public school programs for students with LD highlight the right for people with disabilities to obtain free appropriate education services as well as other services such as: healthcare, training and habilitation, employment development, and social programs. However, in the real world, these rights have not been fully granted to individuals with disabilities in KSA. Today in KSA, there are different types of discrimination that people with disabilities still face related to accessing education, employment, and social services. Additionally, females with disabilities are still suffering from discrimination based on gender bias and prejudice similar to nondisabled females. The following section discusses the above issues in more detail and makes appropriate recommendations and suggestions that policymakers, educators, and other professionals might consider to improve the quality of life and promote equal rights for individuals with disabilities in the Saudi society.

Although the code of disability legislation underlined the rights of individuals with disabilities, these individuals still struggle with some issues regarding employment in terms of their hours worked, workplace safety and security, and negative attitudes from employers toward hiring people with disabilities. The Ministry of Labor is now trying to solve these issues by creating laws that protect the rights of these individuals in getting appropriate jobs and fair work conditions.

As KSA continues its dramatic period of improvement, changes in special education services will occur rapidly (Al-Quraini, 2012). The following suggestions might be considered to improve special education services in KSA. First, policymakers should review existing legislation related to students with disabilities and evaluate each laws' relevance to worldwide current trends in providing best practice special education services. This review should take into consideration successful policy experiences such as IDEA (1997) in the United States. More specifically the review should evaluate major tenets for providing a free appropriate education for individuals with special needs in terms of the following:

(A) *Least Restrictive Environment* (LRE): This term should be clarified in the RSEPI to mean that the appropriate place to educate students with disabilities is in a general education setting to the maximum extent possible; however, when the level or severity of disability does not allow for the student to be the placed in this setting, the continuum of alternative placement options should be considered, including the general classroom, the special education classroom, special schools, home instruction, or instruction in hospitals and institutions.

(B) *Procedural Safeguards*: Under this regulation, an amendment to the RSEPI should be made for identifying procedures (procedural safeguards) that guarantee the rights of parents or guardians of children with severe disabilities regarding settling education disputes. This part should outline procedures that assist students with disabilities to be educated using special education services. For example, parents or guardians should receive a written letter that informs them about any procedures that might be conducted by the schools with their children regarding educational placement. This letter should be sent by the school to the parents with sufficient notice (Yell, 2006). This letter also ought to explain clearly the description of the action, reasons for this action, and the further procedures that might be conducted with the student.

RSEPI must also mandate that the parent has the right to discuss any educational placement pertaining to their child made by the school that requires further procedures. There are some times when parents disagree with the decision made by the schools about educational placement. Therefore, another agency should be involved in solving this disagreement. For instance, the school districts might establish an *office of hearing* in each school district that aims to facilitate a problem between the schools or service providers and the parents (Yell, 2006).

Additionally, when the parents of the student cannot solve the dilemma with the school or school district, further procedures might be considered in terms of taking the issue to the local court in each city or the Supreme Court (the highest level of court in KSA). The final decisions of the courts should be reported and published in a specific database that might assist policymakers and researchers in developing special education policy regarding placement in the general education setting for students with severe disabilities in KSA.

(C) *Responsibility for Implementation*: A regulation that should be considered in the amendment to the RSEPI is the name of the agency or department that has responsibility for the implementation of this legislation. This part should also identify responsibility to enforce the implementation of the RSEPI. For example, the Special Education Department should have the power and responsibility to monitor and enforce special education services, particularly educating students with disabilities in the LRE under this legislation.

(D) *Developing an Effective System of Accountability*: The main reason behind many of the problems with the implementation of the RSEPI in Saudi Arabia is a system accountability absence to enforce the requirements of this legislation in the real world. Therefore, it is highly recommended that an effective monitoring system needs to be put in place to assist the Special Education Department in Saudi Arabia in investigating whether the requirements of the RSEPI have been carried out for students with disabilities, particularly educating students with disabilities in the LRE.

The main goals of this system would be enforcing and monitoring these requirements, and ensuring continued improvement in educational outcomes for children with disabilities who are eligible for special education and related services. The main features of this system should be explained in terms of the aspects of accountability, the role of the agency that has responsibility for accountability of the RSEPI, and main steps or procedural safeguards that might be considered to make sure that school districts and the service providers follow these regulations. Additionally, the Ministry of Education should annually evaluate the quality of special education services and present a report that explains these services to public agencies. This report might assist these agencies in providing effective best practice services, and helping them improve their provision of special education services to students with disabilities. Another suggestion is to address critical elements of successful inclusion, such as accommodation and instructional modifications of general curriculum, and collaborations. Furthermore, the stakeholders' perspectives toward inclusion should be examined through more research to determine the best ways to enhance their perspectives of how to be more supportive of students in a general education setting. Procedures to determine eligibility for special education services should be based on the findings of a multidisciplinary team as well as the other issues discussed above. Finally, schools should consider providing related services in support of their IEPs, particularly occupational, physical, and speech–language therapy.

REFERENCES

Al-Abdulwahab, S. S., & Al-Gain, S. I. (2003). Attitudes of Saudi health care professionals toward people with physical disabilities. *Asia Pacific Disability Rehabilitation Journal, 14*(1), 63–70.

Al-Ahmadi, N.A. (2009). *Teachers' perspectives and attitudes towards integrating students with learning disabilities in regular Saudi public schools.* Unpublished doctoral dissertation. Retrieved from http://etd.ohiolink.edu

Al-Quraini, T. (2012). Factors that are related to teachers' perspectives towards inclusive education of students with severe intellectual disabilities in Riyadh, Saudi Arabia. *Journal of Research in Special Education Needs.* Retrieved from http://onlinelibrary.wiley.com/doi/10.1111/j.1471-3802.2011.01220.x/abstract

Al-Ajmi, N. S. (2006). *The Kingdom of Saudi Arabia: Administrators' and special education teachers' perceptions regarding the use of functional behavior assessment for students with mental retardation.* Unpublished doctoral dissertation, University of Wisconsin-Madison, Madison, WI.

Al-Demadi, A., & Al-Shinawi, M. (1989). Types of attitudes toward people with physical disability among students in King Saud University. *Journal of College Education, 4*(2), 40–62.

Al-Gain, S. I., & Al-Abddulwahab, S. S. (2002). Issues and obstacles in disability research in Saudi Arabia. *Asia Pacific Disability Rehabilitation Journal, 13*(1), 45–49.

Al-Herz, M. M. (2008). *Achievement of goals of the individualized education program (IEP) for students with mental retardation and related difficulties.* Master's thesis. Retrieved from http://www.dr-banderalotabi.com/new/admin/uploads/2/dov17-5.pdf

Al-Marsouqi, H. A. (1980). A facet theory analysis of attitudes toward handicapped individuals in Saudi Arabia. *Dissertations Abstracts International: Section C, Education, 41*(9), 8726431A.

Al-Mousa, N. A. (2008). *Development process of special education in the Kingdom of Saudi Arabia: From segregation to integration.* Dubai, United Arab Emirates: Dar Alqlam Co.

Al-Mousa, N. A., Al-Sartawi, Z. A., Al-Adbuljabar, A. M., Al-Batal, Z. M., & Al-Husain, A. S. (2006). *The national study to evaluate the experiment of the Kingdom of Saudi Arabia in mainstreaming children with special educational needs in public education schools.* Retrieved from http://www.se.gov.sa/Inclusion.aspx

Almuaqel, A. (2006). *Perception of parents, education teachers, and rehabilitation counselors of the individualized transition plan (ITP) for students with cognitive delay.* Unpublished doctoral dissertation, University of Idaho, Idaho, Moscow.

Al-Muslat, Z. A. (1987). Educators' attitudes toward the handicapped in Saudi Arabia. *Dissertations Abstracts International: Section C, Education, 48*(11), 264781A.

Al-Nahdi, G. H. (2007). *The application of the procedures and standards of assessment and diagnosis in mental education institutes and programs as regards Regulatory Principles of Special Education Institutes and Programs in Saudi Arabia.* Master's thesis. Retrieved from http://faculty.ksu.edu.sa/alnahdi/DocLib/Forms/AllItems.aspx

Al-Otaibi, B., & Al-Sartawi, Z. A. (2009). *Related services that are needed for the students with multiple disabilities and their families in Saudi Arabia.* Retrieved from http://www.drbanderalotabi.com/new/1/pdf

Alquraini, T. A. (2007). *Feasibility and effectiveness of related services that are provided to the students with mental retardation in public schools.* Master's thesis. Retrieved from http://www.drbanderalotaibi.com/new/admin/uploads/2/5.pdf

Alquraini, T. A. (2010). Special education in Saudi Arabia: Challenges, perspectives, future possibilities. *International Journal of Special Education, 25*(3), 139–147.

Alquraini, T. A. (2013). Legislative rules for students with disabilities in the United States and Saudi Arabia: A comparative study. *International Interdisciplinary Journal of Education, 2*(6), 601–624.

Al-Sartawi, A. M. (1987). Attitudes of students at college of education in King Saud University toward people with mental retardation. *Journal of College Education, 2*(7), 112–127.

Al-Sartawi, Z., & Grageah, S. (2010). The provision of the related services for children with autism and their families. *Journal of College of Education,* Ain Shamas University, *2*(40), 210–225.

Al-Wabli, A. M. (1996). Related services that are provided for students with mental retardation in special education institutes in Saudi Arabia. *Journal of Education, 20*(3), 191–232.

Central Department of Statistics and Information Population and Vital Statistics. (2011). *Population and housing characteristics in the Kingdom of Saudi Arabia.* Retrieved from http://www.cdsi.gov.sa/pdf/demograph1428.pdf

Hanafi, A. (2008, June). Actual related services for students with hearing disability in Saudi Arabia. Paper presented at the first scientific conference of mental health in the College of Education, University of Banha, Egypt. Retrieved from http://faculty.ksa.edu.sa/70443/Pages/cv.aspx

Individuals with Disabilities Education Act of 1997. (1997). Pub. L No.105-17, 111, Stat. 37.

Marza, H. M. (2002). *The effects of early intervention, home-based, family-centered, support programs on six Saudi Arabian mothers with premature infants: The application of interactive simulation strategies.* Unpublished doctoral dissertation, University of Maryland, College Park, MD.

Ministry of Education of Saudi Arabia. (2002). *Regulations of special education programs and institutes of Saudi Arabia.* Retrieved from http://www.se.gov.sa/rules/se_rules/index htm

Ministry of Education of Saudi Arabia. (2012). *General directors of special education.* Retrieved from http://www.se.gov.sa/hi/

Prince Salman Center for Disability Research. (2004). *Kingdom of Saudi Arabia provision code for persons with disabilities.* Riyadh, Saudi Arabia: Prince Salman Center for Disability Research.

Sadek, F. M., Mousa, F. A., & Sesalem, K. S. (1986). Attitudes of Saudi Arabian society toward people with blindness. *Journal of College Education, 3*(6), 51–77.

Yell, M. L. (2006). *The law and special education* (2nd ed.). Columbus, OH: Prentice Hall Publishers.

SPECIAL EDUCATION TODAY IN TURKEY

Macid Ayhan Melekoğlu

ABSTRACT

As a result of human right movements, the importance of special needs of individuals with disabilities has become more prominent in many countries in the world. Hence, endeavors of people with disabilities, their family members, and advocates to seek accessible communities and equal opportunities for education, as well as, job placement have been widely accepted as human rights for individuals with disabilities. Consequently, establishing barrier-free environments and inclusive societies for people with disabilities have become important indicators of social development of countries. Besides, since education is considered as a fundamental human right, the importance of providing special education for children with disabilities has been recently realized by many nations (United Nations. (2006). World programme of action concerning disabled persons. *New York, NY: United Nations). Turkey is one of those countries that have quite recently started to invest in special education services for its citizens with disabilities. This chapter focuses on the development, as well as the current state of special education in Turkey. Included in this development are the following sections: origins of Turkish special education, prevalence and incident rates, trends in laws and regulations,*

Special Education International Perspectives: Practices Across the Globe
Advances in Special Education, Volume 28, 529–557
Copyright © 2014 by Emerald Group Publishing Limited
All rights of reproduction in any form reserved
ISSN: 0270-4013/doi:10.1108/S0270-401320140000028024

educational interventions, working with families, teacher preparation,
progress that has been made, and special education challenges that exist.

INTRODUCTION

Turkey, known as the Republic of Turkey, is located in Western Asia. It is
also known as the bridge between Europe and Asia which makes it a country of geostrategic importance. The actual area of Turkey is 814,578 square
kilometers, of which 790,200 are in Asia and 24,378 are located in Europe.
According to Turkey's most recent census, the country's population is
nearly 75 million (Turkish Statistical Institute, 2012). The vast majority of
citizens are Muslims. The country's official language is Turkish. The country is a founding member of the Organization for Economic Co-operation
and Development (OECD), and Group of 20 (G-20) major economies.
Furthermore, Turkey has the world's 15th gross domestic product (GDP)
(World Bank, 2012). In addition, Turkey is a candidate country for the
European Union (EU) membership following the Helsinki European
Council.

Turkey is a republic based on secular, democratic, and pluralistic principles. The Turkish Republic was established in 1923 by Mustafa Kemal
Atatürk, and has a parliamentary system of government that constitution-
ally protects personal rights and freedoms. As a result, Turkey has the divisions of power that one would expect: judicial, legislative, and executive.
The Constitution of the Republic of Turkey (1982) is the supreme law of
the country. In terms of educational structure, "formal education" and
"informal education" are two main parts of the Turkish education system.
The typical education that citizens are exposed to is in school environments
defined as formal education and based on specific ages. Educational
environments that provide early childhood, primary, secondary, or higher
education are classified as formal education. However, there are informal
education environments which consist of academic and nonacademic
education and vocational training workshops and centers available for
people who have never received formal education, dropped out of school at
any level, or graduated from an informal school system. Additionally, all
Turkey educational activities are governed by two institutions, the Ministry
of National Education (MEB, Milli Eğitim Bakanlığı) and the Higher
Education Council (YÖK, Yükseköğretim Kurulu). All public and private
institutions that provide education, including special education, from early

childhood to secondary level operate under the responsibility and control of the MEB, while all higher education institutions are controlled by the YÖK (Melekoğlu, Cakiroglu, & Malmgren, 2009).

ORIGINS OF SPECIAL EDUCATION

The Republic of Turkey is a considerably young country which was established in 1920; however, Turkish people have existed in history for centuries. In fact, when some individuals with intellectual disabilities were exiled or burned in Western countries during the Middle Ages, there were healing centers established in the lands of Turkish people. Especially after accepting the religion of Islam, Turkish people placed strong emphasis on human health and provided free access to hospitals for individuals in Turkish countries such as Seljuks of Anatolia and the Ottoman Empire (Baykoç-Dönmez & Şahin, 2011). In terms of provision of special education, gifted and talented children were systematically selected and educated in the Enderun School (Enderun Mektebi) which was founded in 1455 by Fatih Sultan Mehmed, the Sultan of that time, and served during the era of the Ottoman Empire (Melekoğlu et al., 2009). Furthermore, conscious and systematic special education services for children with disabilities started in 1889, for children with hearing impairments in a school that was established as a part of the Istanbul Trade School under the leadership of Mister Grati (Grati Efendi) who was a citizen of Austria and principal of the school. After one year, another section was opened in the school for students with visual impairments. This special education school served students with disabilities for 30 years and was shut down in 1919 (Akçamete, 1998; Akkök, 2000; Baykoç-Dönmez & Şahin, 2011; Cavkaytar & Diken, 2012; Eripek, 2012).

Right after the official establishment of the Republic of Turkey, after the collapse of the Ottoman Empire, a private association started a special education school called the "School for Deaf-Mute and Blind" for children with hearing impairments and visual impairments in Izmir in 1921. The school was turned over to the Ministry of Health and Social Aid in 1924 and continued to provide services until 1950. Since the provision of special education services was considered the responsibility of the Ministry of Health and Social Aid at that time, special education schools and institutions were functioning under the management of that ministry until 1950. Afterwards, special education became a duty of the MEB and the

"School for Deaf-Mute and Blind" was transferred to this ministry in 1951. In the meantime, to improve participation of blind people into the society, the first blind union, called Altınokta Körler Derneği (Six Dots Foundation for the Blind), was established under the leadership of Associate Professor Mitat Enç in 1950 (Akçamete, 1998; Baykoç-Dönmez & Şahin, 2011; Şahin, 2005). Professor Enç, who had a visual impairment, was an important pioneer in the field of special education because of his endeavors in the development of university special education programs and his service at the MEB. In the current era, the National Conference of Special Education is organized each year in remembrance of Associate Professor Mitat Enç and the 23rd National Conference of Special Education was held in Bolu Abant İzzet Baysal University in 2013 (http://oek2013.ibu.edu.tr).

As a recently established country, Turkey started to exhibit striking and critical developments in the field of special education after 1950. First of all, the transfer of responsibility for special education from the Ministry of Health and Social Aid to the MEB reflected the government's interest in making education of individuals with disabilities a major issue of education rather than a health-related issue. Starting in 1950, special education services were carried out by a branch office of the General Directory of Elementary. In addition, a systematic teacher training structure was initiated at the Gazi Education Institute in Ankara by forming the Department of Special Education in 1952. Also, the section of the "School for Deaf-Mute and Blind" for children with visual impairments was moved to a building that is currently known as the Estimesgut Orphanage in Ankara, the capital of Turkey, in 1951 and then, relocated to a building at the Gazi Education Institute in 1952. The Department of Special Education at the Gazi Education Institute admitted 40 students to train as the first special education specialists of the country. However, after two years of training students, the department was shut down in 1955 (Şahin, 2005).

However, schools continued to be opened for children with visual and hearing impairments, and a selection procedure was developed for children with intellectual disabilities which allowed them to participate in the education system as well. The first psychology clinic, which is currently called the Guidance and Research Center (RAM, Rehberlik ve Araştırma Merkezi), was formed in Ankara in 1955 to evaluate educable children with intellectual disabilities, examine other students with special needs, and provide guidance for these students. Consequently, a special education classroom was formed for children with intellectual disabilities in the Ankara Kazıkiçi

Bostanları Primary School in 1955 (Şahin, 2005). Soon after, additional special education classrooms were established for students with intellectual disabilities in the Yeni Turan and Hıdırlıktepe Primary Schools in Ankara in 1955. Eventually, these classrooms became the first examples of incorporating the special education classroom model in regular education schools (Baykoç-Dönmez & Şahin, 2011).

In 1957, the Children in Need of Protection Law (No. 6972) was enacted, and article 22 of the law indicates that the MEB was required to provide necessary precautions for children with special education needs who were considered children in need of protection. Also, the rights of individuals with disabilities to receive special education were secured in the amended 1961 Constitution by article 50 which states that the government must take necessary precautions for individuals with special education needs to make them beneficial to the society.

In 1961, another law important to the development of special education was enacted, namely, the Elementary and Education Law (No. 222). This law officially indicated the special education needs of children with disabilities required compulsory education age by mentioning that children who are at the compulsory education age and have disabilities due to intellectual, orthopedic, mental, and social deficits need to be provided special education (Akkök, 2000; Baykoç-Dönmez & Şahin, 2011). Of note in the development of the above laws and article 50 was the advocacy influence of The Blind Union, Altı Nokta Körler Derneği (Six Dots Foundation for the Blind), which stressed the need for inclusion provisions regarding individuals. In addition, the Blind Union developed and implemented the first workshop day shelter system for individuals with disabilities in Turkey (Şahin, 2005).

Initial steps for the education of gifted education occurred in the 1956 Education of Gifted Children in the Fine Arts Law (No. 6660). This law stated that the government was responsible for the education of gifted children in the fine arts. Due to a lack of gifted educational resources, gifted children were sent abroad to receive the necessary education for 17 years. While this law is still in force, the government stopped sending these children after 17 years of implementation (Şahin, 2005). Starting in the 1963–1964 school year, gifted students were selected from primary schools in Ankara and Istanbul and educated in separate special education classrooms with a special curriculum. However, this educational practice ended in 1968. A few years later, another attempt was initiated to provide gifted classrooms to meet the skills of gifted students in primary schools but those attempts were stopped in 1972 (Şahin, 2005).

The importance of special education in Turkey became even more evident in 1980, when MEB directed the Department of General Directorate of Elementary Education to make special education services a division rather than a branch. Soon after this, Turkey's first special education law, namely, the Children with Special Education Needs Law (No. 2916) was enacted in 1983. This law was supported by many constituted special education regulations and provisions. In fact, the Turkey Constitution was amended in 1982 to include special education provisions that are still in force today such as article 42 that states the Constitution is responsible for taking necessary precautions for individuals with special education needs to make them beneficial to the society (Akçamete, 1998; Baykoç-Dönmez & Şahin, 2011; Vuran & Ünlü, 2012).

Although endeavors for training special education specialists were interrupted in the 1950s, many educators including first graduates of the Department of Special Education at Gazi Education Institute contributed to the development of special education in Turkey. These educators trained many special education teachers for the field, disseminated various special education implementations in the education system, and made significant contributions to the establishment of national politics on special education. These educators include the pioneering university work of Associate Professor Mithat Enç, Professor Yahya Özsoy, and Professor Doğan Çağlar, who helped establish college special education programs, as well as MEB professionals, Şaban Dede and Hasan Karatepe, who made great contribution to the developments of the national special education system.

After the innovative and pioneering efforts of the above individuals, other universities established special education programs in Turkey with the help of many talented professors. For example, Professor Şule Bilir helped constitute the Division of Special Education under the Department of Child Development at the prestigious Hacettepe University, in Ankara in 1978. This special education division has been a leading division in training academicians, child development specialists, and teachers in the field of special education in Turkey for many years. Also, Professor Ayşegül Ataman and Professor Ümit Davaslıgil are well-known pioneers, who made great contributions in the area of special education in the Turkish education system (Baykoç-Dönmez & Şahin, 2011).

By the 1990s, the development of special education gained further momentum due to the increased number of trained personnel, an increase in conducted studies, and a fury of published research papers in Turkey. For instance in 1965, there were only 55 associate degree graduates, three master's graduates, and one doctoral graduate in the field of special education. This number increased to 625 teacher certificate holders, 187 bachelors graduates, 66 master's graduates, 16 doctoral graduates, 2 assistant professors, 6 associate professors, and 5 professors in 1990 (Baykoç-Dönmez & Şahin, 2011).

Furthermore, Köksal Toptan, who was the Minister of MEB between 1991 and 1993, put great emphasis on special education and the country's most comprehensive works were carried out during this period. These works resulted in the targeted employment of workers in special education, the securing of employee rights for individuals with disabilities, and a vast improvement in the quality and quantity of special education institutions. In addition, necessary tools and materials were developed and provided for special education practices and new implementations were started in the field of special education. Also, a new service, namely, the General Directorate of Special Education, Guidance and Advisory Services was established in the Central Ministry Organization in 1992 (Akçamete, 1998; Baykoç-Dönmez & Şahin, 2011). Further, Professor Necate Baykoç-Dönmez, who was an academician in Hacettepe University, was appointed as the general director of the above service between 1992 and 1995, and she initiated many reforms in the field of special education in Turkey.

The above aspects had an effect on the acceptance and value of inclusion practices in Turkey. This was evident when the MEB accepted inclusion practices as an important concept for special education. The ministry supported the dissemination of information about the importance of inclusion for students with disabilities into regular education in schools across the country. In essence, inclusion practices were viewed as a means to nourish awareness in the society and promote consciousness for the needs of people with disabilities. The importance of this practice was further enhanced when the Turkish government proclaimed 1993 as the Year of Special Education (Akkök, 2001). It is noteworthy that only a few years after this proclamation, the 1997 Special Education Regulation Law (No. 573), which is currently in force, was enacted. Due to this law, the number of private special education and rehabilitation centers (özel özel eğitim ve rehabilitasyon merkezleri) escalated because the government started to pay the special education, rehabilitation, and therapy services expenses provided by these centers (Baykoç-Dönmez & Şahin, 2011; Vuran & Ünlü, 2012). Lastly, based on the law, the MEB enacted the Special Education Services Regulation in 2006 which delineated current definitions of special education categories and terms (Diken & Batu, 2010). These MEB categorical definitions of exceptionality (Çuhadar, 2012; MEB, 2006) follow. An individual with an *intellectual disability* (zihinsel yetersizliği olan birey) is defined as one who has an IQ score at least two standard deviations below 100, and limited performance or deficiencies in conceptual, social, and practical adjustment skills, and who manifests those characteristics during the development period before the age of 18 years. In addition, individuals with intellectual disabilities are classified into four categories: mild intellectual disabilities (hafif düzeyde zihinsel yetersizlik), moderate intellectual disabilities (orta düzeyde zihinsel yetersizlik), severe intellectual disabilities (ağır düzeyde zihinsel yetersizlik), and very severe intellectual disabilities (çok ağır düzeyde zihinsel yetersizlik). An individual with *multiple disabilities* (birden fazla yetersizliği olan birey) is a person with disabilities in more than one domain. A person with *attention deficit and hyperactivity disorder* (dikkat eksikliği ve hiperaktivite bozukluğu olan birey) is defined as one who shows attention deficit, over activity, hyperactivity, and impulsivity characteristics that are not appropriate for one's age and developmental level in at least two contexts for a minimum of six months before the age of 7 years. An individual with *speech and language disorders* (dil ve konuşma güçlüğü olan birey) is depicted as a person who displays problems in the use of speech, acquisition of speech, and communication. A person with *emotional and behavioral disorders* (duygusal ve davranış bozukluğu olan birey) is defined as one who manifests emotional reactions and behaviors that vary significantly from the social and cultural norms. An individual with a *visual impairment* (görme yetersizliği olan birey) is a person who has partial or total loss of vision. Whereas, a person with a *hearing impairment* (işitme yetersizliği olan birey) is one who experiences problems with acquisition of speech, use of speech, and communication due to partial or total loss of hearing sensitivity. An individual with *orthopedic disability* (ortopedik yetersizliği olan birey) is person with movement deficiencies due to dysfunction in muscular, skeleton, and joint systems as a result of disease, accident, and genetic problems. A person with *autism* (otistik birey) is an individual with significant deficiencies in social interaction, verbal and nonverbal communications, and interest and activities. An individual with a *specific learning disability* (özel öğrenme güçlüğü olan birey) is one who experiences academic difficulties, which emerge in one or more knowledge acquisition processes such as understanding and using written or oral language, listening, speaking, reading, spelling, concentrating, attention, or performing mathematical operations. There is separate special education category for a person with cerebral palsy. A person with *cerebral palsy* (serebral palsili birey) has disabilities in motor skills that are connected to dysfunctions in muscular and nervous systems due to pre-, peri-, or postnatal brain damage. An individual with *chronic health problems* (süreğen hastalığı olan birey) is a person with health problems that require continuous or long time nursing and treatment. Lastly, a *gifted individual* (üstün yetenekli birey) is a person who shows high level performance in intelligence, creativity, art, sports, leadership capacity, or specific academic domains compared to his/her peers.

An examination of Turkey's special education literature reveals that definitions of special education categories can include those based upon the Special Education Services Regulation (MEB, 2006) and definitions from the US's special education literature that is incorporated in the Individuals with Disabilities Education Improvement Act (IDEA, 2004), the Diagnostic and Statistical Manual of Mental Disorders (DSM) (American Psychiatric Association, 2004), and US text books (see Akçamete, 2009; Ataman, 2005; Baykoç, 2011; Diken, 2010a, 2010b; Rotatori, Obiakor, & Bakken, 2011; Sucuoğlu & Kargın, 2010). In fact, many laws and regulations related to special education in Turkey have been deeply influenced by US laws and regulations about special education such as the least restrictive environment (LRE) and individualized education programs (IEPs).

PREVALENCE AND INCIDENT OF STUDENTS WITH SPECIAL NEEDS

In terms of the number of students in special education, Turkey publishes overall statistics for special education annually. There is no official publication of the number of students in each special education category (Cakiroglu & Melekoğlu, 2013). However, the official publication includes the number of students in separate and inclusive school settings. According to the National Statistics there were 32,180 students with special needs in formal school system in the 2002–2003 school year in Turkey (MEB, 2003). This number has increased to 220,649 in the 2012–2013 school year (MEB, 2013). In the current education system, approximately 7% of all children with special needs are included in formal and informal education settings in Turkey (Baykoç-Dönmez, 2011). In fact, a steady increase in the number of students with special needs in formal education system was reported when the annual statistical reports were analyzed (see Table 1) by Cakiroglu and Melekoğlu (2013). These researchers used a linear regression analysis to determine the extent to which there is a linear relationship between school years and the total number of students with special needs for each school year. The regression analysis indicated a significant increase in the number of students with special needs from 2002–2003 to

Table 1.   Students with Special Needs in Formal Education in Turkey.

School Year	Total Number of Students in Formal Education	Total Number of Students with Special Needs in Formal Education	Percentage of Students with Special Needs in Formal Education System
2002–2003	13,686,616	32,180	0.023
2003–2004	13,852,429	19,447	0.014
2004–2005	14,039,609	61,127	0.044
2005–2006	14,482,335	68,967	0.047
2006–2007	14,874,496	78,743	0.053
2007–2008	14,817,654	89,703	0.061
2008–2009	15,351,849	88,931	0.058
2009–2010	16,137,436	120,111	0.074
2010–2011	16,845,528	141,248	0.084
2011–2012	16,905,143	199,513	1.180
2012–2013	17,234,452	220,649	1.280

2012–2013 ($R^2 = 0.895$, $F[1,10] = 86,513$, $p < 0.000$). This model accounted for 89.5% of variance in the increase, and the researchers reported that the school year was a significant predictor variable that had a significant impact on the increase in the numbers of students with special needs ($\beta = 0.952$, $p < 0.000$). These findings show that the increase in the numbers of students with special needs in formal education has been statistically significant over the last decade in Turkey (Cakiroglu & Melekoğlu, 2013).

When the number of students in segregated school settings was examined in the 2012–2013 school year, results show the following distribution by exceptionality: 1,006 early childhood education students; 3,577 students with hearing impairment; 1,406 students with visual impairments; 642 students with orthopedic disabilities; 2,658 students with mild intellectual disabilities; 14,427 students with moderate and severe intellectual disabilities including autism; and 68 students with adaptation problems (including emotional and behavioral disorders).

In addition to those students with disabilities who are enrolled in formal schooling, there were students with special needs that are educated in informal schools. Currently, 31,376 students are categorized as receiving informal education. Of this number, 11,268 are gifted students enrolled in 66 after regular school Science and Arts Centers. In addition, 20,108 students with disabilities received informal education in 152 private special education schools in the 2012–2013 school year according to the MEB (2013).

Inclusion practices are also widely accepted in Turkey's education system. However, the official publication of national enrollment statistics

Table 2. Students with Special Needs in Inclusive Classrooms in Turkey (by MEB).

School Year	Elementary School Level			Secondary School Level			Total Number of Students in Inclusion
	Male n (%)	Female n (%)	Total	Male n (%)	Female n (%)	Total	
2004–2005	24,634 (61.5)	15,416 (38.5)	40,050	–	–	–	40,050
2005–2006	27,706 (61.6)	17,239 (38.4)	44,945	761 (51.8)	707 (48.2)	1,468	46,413
2006–2007	27,725 (61.4)	17,429 (38.6)	45,154	813 (52.1)	749 (47.9)	1,562	46,716
2007–2008	34,293 (61.4)	21,547 (38.6)	55,840	–	–	–	55,840
2008–2009	15,450 (32.3)	32,417 (67.7)	47,867	1,443 (54.2)	1,220 (45.8)	2,663	50,530
2009–2010	23,064 (32.4)	48,078 (67.6)	71,142	2,854 (56.4)	2,208 (43.6)	5,062	76,204
2010–2011	27,444 (32.4)	57,136 (67.6)	84,580	4,816 (61.9)	2,959 (38.1)	7,775	92,355
2011–2012	84,309 (61.1)	53,584 (38.9)	137,893	6,744 (62.1)	4,116 (37.9)	10,860	148,753
2012–2013	89,852 (61.1)	57,196 (38.9)	147,048	8,777 (61.6)	5,470 (38.4)	14,247	161,295

Note: "–" indicates absence of data.

related to inclusive education includes only overall numbers. Data for inclusion education has been available since the 2004–2005 school year but only at the elementary level. There were 40,050 students with special needs in inclusive settings in the 2004–2005 school year (MEB, 2005). This number increased to 92,355 in the 2010–2011 school year (MEB, 2011a), and then increased to 161,295 in the 2012–2013 school year (MEB, 2013; see Table 2 for details). In terms of the percentage of students with special needs in inclusion among all students in special education, the rate has always been more than half since the 2004–2005 school year and has increased to almost three quarters of all students with special needs during the last two school years. The percentage of students with special needs in inclusion can be examined in Fig. 1.

Although, the officially published national statistics do not include data regarding separate special education categories in Turkey, a secondary data set obtained from the Turkish Ministry of National Education Strategy Department was analyzed to gather statistical details about special education categories in inclusion in Turkey (MEB, 2011b). The raw data about special education statistics was officially requested with a written application by the chapter's author to the MEB for analysis and research purposes. Details about the number of students in each special education category in inclusive classroom between the 2004–2005 and 2010–2011 school years can be found in Table 3.

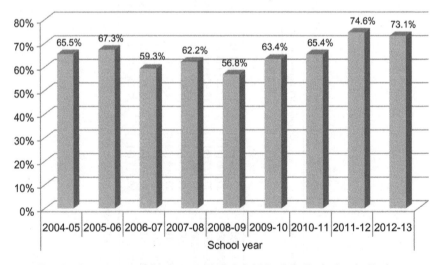

Fig. 1. Percentage of Students with Special Needs in Inclusion in Turkey.

Table 3. Number of Students in Each Special Education Category in Inclusive Classrooms in Turkey.

SE Category	2004–2005	2006–2007		2007–2008	2008–2009		2009–2010		2010–2011	
	E	E	S	E	E	S	E	S	E	S
MD	0	0	0	0	16,487	0	32,006	0	45,430	0
ID	28,110	30,116	359	37,766	11,328	932	20,063	3,494	20,740	5,007
EBD	4,103	2,730	49	3,211	15,153	112	12,912	1,024	12,146	1,795
S/LD	2,088	1,991	78	2,204	1,553	86	1,971	75	2,120	159
HI	1,670	1,792	583	2,324	1,322	645	1,690	255	1,626	392
OD	1,669	2,050	178	2,472	1,083	337	1,346	82	1,374	176
VI	1,459	1,179	246	843	362	401	462	92	460	152
A	542	828	9	1,054	318	29	376	14	373	41
LD	0	4,107	60	5,500	220	121	267	24	263	47
G	409	361	0	466	41	0	49	2	48	6

Note: SE = special education; E = elementary school level; S = secondary school level; MD = multiple disabilities; ID = intellectual disabilities; EBD = emotional and behavioral disorders; S/LD = speech and language disorders; HI = hearing impairments; OD = orthopedic disabilities; VI = visual impairments; A = autism; LD = specific learning disabilities; G = gifted.

The results of the data analysis indicate that there has been a steady increase in the number of students with special needs in inclusion education. It is noted that the fastest increasing special education category is multiple disabilities. Further it should be noted that many students with special needs have been diagnosed with a secondary disability over the years, and categories such as learning disabilities, autism, or intellectual disabilities, the number of students has either declined or stayed steady even though the number of students in inclusion has been escalating.

TRENDS IN LAWS AND REGULATIONS IN TURKEY

The Constitution of the Republic of Turkey has included laws and regulations regarding special education for individuals with disabilities since its first enactment in 1926. Special education was first addressed in Turkish Civil Law (No. 743) that was enacted in 1926. This law required parents to raise their children with physical or intellectual disabilities and they would receive appropriate education. In 1961, the Constitution was amended to incorporate rules about people with special needs that was proposed by the Blind Union. The formal regulation about education of individuals with special needs was explained in articles 42, 50, 62 of the Constitution. For the first time, these articles included provisions related to regulations regarding special education services (Şahin, 2005). Then in 1961, The Elementary and Education Law (No. 222) was enacted. This law indicated that all schools and classes must accommodate children with special needs. Additionally, article 12 specified that provision of special education services should be secured for students with intellectual, psychological, physical, emotional, and social disabilities (Senel, 1998).

In addition to the above, a number of laws and regulations that govern issues about employment of people with disabilities have been enacted. For example, regarding employment of people with disabilities, article 50 was enacted in the Employment Law (No. 1475). This law indicates that a business that employs 50 or more employers needs to hire 2% of their workforces from people with disabilities as well as provide appropriate working conditions based on their specific needs (Şahin, 2005).

The Constitution of the Republic of Turkey was amended in 1982, and it currently includes several vital regulations for individuals with disabilities; especially, human rights which address the rights of individuals with special needs. Right after the amendment of the constitution, the first comprehensive law regarding individuals with disabilities was enacted in 1983. This law entitled The Children with Special Education Needs Law (No. 2916) consisted of sections on: definitions, principles, special education institutions, duties about special education, diagnosis, placement, and monitoring of children with special education needs. The law stayed in force until a new law, namely, The Special Education Law was enacted in 1997 (Akçamete, 1998; Baykoç-Dönmez & Şahin, 2011).

The Special Education Law (No. 573) published in The Official Gazette (No. 23011) in 1997. The law's aim is to regulate principles and provisions regarding the rights of persons with disabilities to receive general and vocational education according to the general goals and basic principles of the Turkish National Education System. The law defines diagnostic, special education assessment, and placement processes of special education. In addition, educational principles regarding early childhood, elementary, secondary, higher, and informal education are specified for individuals with special needs. Further, the law delineates educational settings and highlights educational principles about inclusive education. Other issues illustrated by the law include: the active participation of family members in all aspects of their child's special education processes; the importance of contributions of special education organizations to the development of special education policies; the incorporation of special education services into social interaction; and the adaptation processes. In essence, this law provides the basic principles of special education which include that: (a) special education needs to be viewed as an absolutely necessary part of general education; (b) all students with disabilities should receive required special education services regardless of the severity of the disability; (c) early intervention is critically important for better provision of special education services; (d) all students with special needs should have IEPs that meet their specific needs; (e) students with special needs should be placed in least restrictive educational environments with their nondisabled peers; (f) vocational education and rehabilitation services need to be continuous for students with special needs; and (g) education services that are provided in all educational levels for students with special needs should be planned by the relevant institutions (Akçamete, 1998; Akkök, 2000; Baykoç-Dönmez, 2000). These principles are clearly outlined in the law and children with special needs are viewed as being a crucial part of public education. Soon after the law was enacted the number of students in inclusion increased. However, due to financial drawbacks and a shortage of trained professionals in the field of special education, these principles have not been fully adhered to and implemented by the professionals, who provide special education services to children with special needs (Melekoğlu et al., 2009).

Another important development for individuals with disabilities in 1996 was the establishment of the Administration for Disabled People which was connected to the Turkish Prime Ministry. The purpose of this administration is to execute services for individuals with disabilities regularly, effectively, and efficiently by ensuring cooperation and coordination between national and international institutions and organizations; support generation processes of national policies about individuals with disabilities; and identify problems of individuals with disabilities and find solutions for these problems (Akçamete, 1998; Baykoç-Dönmez & Şahin, 2011). This administration was transferred to the Ministry of Family and Social Policies in 2011 and became the General Directorate of Disabled and Elderly Services.

In 2006, the Special Education Services Regulation was enacted by the MEB (2006). This regulation consists of nine parts and provides specific details about provisions of special education services in the Turkish education system. General provisions, educational assessment and placement, special education services board and duties, working procedures, and principles of the special education assessment board, educational practices through inclusion, educational services, institutions, staff, duties, authority and responsibilities, education and training, and miscellaneous and final provisions are parts of the regulation. As mentioned earlier, this regulation includes definitions of many terms, including special education categories, about special education. According to this regulation, the goal of special education includes: (a) educating individuals to perform their roles in the society, establish good relations with others, be able to work in cooperation, adapt to their environments, and be productive and happy citizens; (b) developing basic living skills to live independently in the community and become self-sufficient; and (c) preparing individuals for upper levels of education, business and professional fields, and life in line with the educational needs, capabilities, interests, and abilities by using appropriate educational programs and special methods, personnel, and equipment.

A close examination of the above laws and regulations regarding special education points to a great impact from special education legislations that originated in the United States and the United Kingdom (Akçamete, 1998). In fact, many Turkish legislative acts were modeled after US special education laws such as the IDEA (2004) because a number of influential special education Turkish academicians and special education experts, who completed their graduate studies in special education at universities in the United States, were involved in the formulations of Turkey special education laws. In terms Turkey's special education laws and regulations, the legal infrastructure was vigorously established and enacted by the endeavors of advocates, academicians, and politicians rather than individuals with disabilities and/or their family members. Therefore, the implementations of these laws and regulations are not controlled by people and family members receiving those services. Consequently, even though the quantity of special education services and institutions has quickly increased, the quality of special education services is still not at a desired level in Turkey.

EDUCATIONAL INTERVENTIONS IN TURKEY

As seen in the official Turkey statistics about students with special needs in special education, almost three quarters of students are educated in inclusion classrooms and the rest are placed in segregated schools or classrooms. The 2006 Special Education Services Regulation (MEB, 2006) indicates the importance of inclusion by describing it as a special education practice based on the idea that students with special education needs should be educated with their nondisabled peers in public and private early childhood, elementary, secondary, and adult education institutions that include necessary support services that enhance their educational well-being. In fact, dissemination of inclusion practices has been widely supported in the last decade, and special education and inclusion practices are developing rapidly in the Turkish education system since the enactment of the special education law. Even though inclusion practices are not presently at the desired level of quality, dissemination information about inclusive education is embraced as an important educational policy (Diken & Batu, 2010; Melekoğlu, 2013; Melekoğlu et al., 2009; Sucuoğlu & Kargın, 2010). However, studies about inclusion practices in Turkey have been limited to: investigation of opinions and suggestions of teachers regarding inclusion of children with intellectual disabilities; the impact of inclusion practices on children with intellectual disabilities; and factors influencing social acceptance of children with intellectual disabilities by their normally developing peers (Diken & Batu, 2010).

While inclusive educational intervention is experienced by the majority of students with disabilities, there are quality primary and middle school educational interventions for students with disabilities who are in self-contained classrooms. For instance, in the 2012–2013 school year, a total of 25,477 students were educated in self-contained classrooms (MEB, 2013). Most of these classrooms are cross-categorical self-contained classrooms while some are non-categorical classrooms. Self-contained classrooms usually consist of students with moderate and/or severe intellectual disabilities, autism, visual impairments, hearing impairments, and multiple disabilities. The number of students in each classroom is usually between 8 and 10 but those numbers can vary depending on the location of the school. Typically, there is one special education teacher in most classrooms.

Meaningful primary and secondary educational intervention is also provided at residential schools for children with visual impairments, hearing impairments, and orthopedic disabilities. Almost all of the students with hearing impairments use hearing aids in their classrooms. Also, students with visual impairments can access brailed educational documents in segregated settings.

Similar to other countries, educational intervention at private special education and rehabilitation centers is widespread in Turkey. Students with disabilities in these placements can receive individual and/or group education and rehabilitation or therapy services. The government covers the expenses of these services for 2–3 hours per week. If families desire additional hours of services, they must pay for it (Vuran & Ünlü, 2012). Families with gifted children receive special education in Science and Arts Centers after their regular education hours. As of the 2012–2013 school year, there are 66 Science and Arts Centers serving 11,268 gifted and talented children (MEB, 2013). Typically, instruction for these students involves exposure to specific academic topics and/or accelerated learning opportunities in various ability domains.

In terms of teaching techniques for students with special needs such as a specific learning disability, there is no special instructional techniques that are universally employed (Özyürek, 2005). This occurs because most general education teachers working in inclusive classroom usually do not receive any educational support in terms of best special education practices and many have little awareness of teaching techniques for students with special needs. In contrast, students with special needs, who are instructed by teachers with special education training, are exposed to quality education. For example, many of these teachers employ best practice special education techniques such as applied behavior analysis (ABA) methods (see Anderson, Marchant, & Somarriba, 2010). Further, the Turkish education system has started discussions about adopting the Response to

Intervention (RTI) model (see Kauffman, Bruce, & Lloyd, 2012) that is employed in the United States.

All special education experts and academicians emphasize the importance of early intervention and prevention programs, and the Special Education Services Regulation has aspects related to early childhood special education. However, there is no officially practiced and supported early intervention program or prevention system throughout Turkey and there are only a couple of early childhood institutions that provide this service to young children with special needs. Thus, even though the critical importance of early intervention and prevention programs for the success of special education practices are well known, the lack of those programs is a significant deficiency in the special education field in Turkey (Baykoç-Dönmez, 2011; Er-Sabuncuoglu & Diken, 2010).

Another common special education practice, namely, a systematic transition procedure for individuals with disabilities from school to adult life, is not occurring in Turkey. While school placements of individuals with disabilities are coordinated by the RAMs in cooperation with parents/primary carers of these individuals, the transition of students with special needs is not systematically planned. Positively, after their school completion, students with disabilities can attend vocational schools or training centers until age 23 years. After completing their work training in these programs, there is no transition system to place them in a job. The options for adult individuals with disabilities who complete vocational schools or training centers are: living in an adult education institution governed by the General Directorate of Life Long Learning; living with their family members; and living in a care center.

WORKING WITH FAMILIES OF INDIVIDUALS WITH DISABILITIES IN TURKEY

Parents or primary carers of individuals with disabilities have legal rights related to: special education assessment of their children; school placements of their children; and the preparation of individualized education plans for their children. The Special Education Services Regulation (MEB, 2006) stresses the active participation and education of families under the principles of special education. In addition, the regulation indicates that family approval is required for educational assessment and diagnosis of their child. It also emphasizes that the family is an important partner in the cooperation between schools, institutions, and RAMs for efficacy of special education services (MEB, 2006). Since the majority of families of individuals with disabilities are from a low socioeconomic level and have limited education, they are not aware of or do not pursue their legal rights for the education of their children. Further complicating the situation is the fact that most of the families of individuals with disabilities are at a denial or aggression stage rather than an acceptance and adjustment stage in Turkey. Often, these parents are embarrassed to have children with disabilities which interferes with their seeking financial supports or advocating for their children to receive quality special education and become integrated into the society.

Typically, school guidance counselors or teachers work as liaisons with families of children with special needs. For most of the families, their interaction with these experts is limited to participation in parent–teacher conferences and getting periodic information about the annual progress of their children. Such limited interaction becomes problematic because families, who have a child in an inclusive classroom, may encounter resistance or exclusion from families of nondisabled students. Sometimes this negative reaction by parents of nondisabled children leads to their nondisabled students refusing to interact with children who have special needs. Lastly, families are responsible for all stages of special education assessment of their children which can be a problem due to their lack of knowledge about special education.

Studies of families of individuals with disabilities in Turkey have focused on topics such as evaluating the effectiveness of family education programs that are formed to teach a variety of skills to children with special needs; characteristics of families of children with special needs; family education and family guidance; family participation; family anxiety, worries, stress, social support, and resilience levels; family needs; and family attitudes (Meral, 2011).

TEACHERS TRAINING IN SPECIAL EDUCATION

Teacher training in special education in Turkey is a relatively new endeavor. The first attempt for special education teacher training started in the 1952–1953 school year in the Department of Special Education at Gazi Education Institute. This program was open just for primary education teachers with three years of experience. The program involved two years of instruction. Unfortunately, after only two terms of graduating students, the teacher training program ended. This resulted in regular education teachers meeting the special education needs of students until 1980s. These teachers were trained via exposure to in-service training workshops and/or special education certification programs.

A second attempt at formal special education teacher training was initiated by the Educational Sciences Department in the School of Education at Anadolu University in Eskisehir in 1983. This program had its first graduates in the 1986–1987 school year. In 1990, the Department of Special Education was established in the School of Education at Anadolu University. This Department of Special Education has been teaching college students who had an interest in teaching individuals with intellectual disabilities and hearing impairments. Soon afterwards, Gazi University offered special education teacher training programs for college students interested in educating individuals with intellectual disabilities and visually impairments (Akçamete, 1998; Baykoç-Dönmez & Şahin, 2011; Eripek, 2012).

Currently, a four-year undergraduate education is necessary to become a special education teacher in Turkey. Teacher candidates are centrally placed in undergraduate programs based on the results of nationwide higher education exams. Regular teacher candidates are trained by faculty in the Education Department while special education teacher candidates are trained by faculty in the Special Education Department. There are approximately 180 universities in Turkey, and as of the 2013–2014 school year, only 19 of these universities have undergraduate special education departments that offer programs to train special education teachers. Typically, these programs offer training in intellectual disabilities, hearing impairments, visual impairments, and gifted. Almost all offer a program of study in intellectual disabilities because it has the largest special education teacher quota (over 1,500) in the country's central higher education placement.

The undergraduate programs in special education use preset curriculums that are approved by the YÖK. There are required courses in these curriculums and teacher candidates at times need to fulfill field work for some courses. In addition, these programs require students to complete a teaching practicum over two semesters (28 weeks). All special education teacher candidates who successfully complete a program of study with a 2.0 grade point average have the right to work as a special education teacher. While there is no national teacher certification that is necessary to work in public schools, teacher candidates must take a nationwide teacher placement exam. Based on their exam scores and the national quota in appointment periods, teacher candidates are placed by the MEB.

PERSPECTIVE ON THE PROGRESS OF SPECIAL EDUCATION

Although special education is a considered a new field in the Turkish education system, there are positive developments, as well as, problems in educating students with special needs. First of all, there are sufficient numbers of special education teachers in most of the segregated schools and the RAMs but the current quality of education and assessment processes being practiced needs to be improved. Second, inclusion practices have been rapidly disseminated in general education schools but there are almost no support services in the school for children with special needs nor in-service assistance to the teachers of students in inclusive classrooms. These aspects are problematic because many regular education teachers are not trained about inclusion and/or education of individuals with special needs. Therefore, most of the students with special needs do not receive quality education or in some cases, any education. In addition, the majority of teachers of inclusive classrooms are against inclusion practices, and teachers, administrators, nondisabled peers, and their families often manifest negative attitudes toward children with special needs and their families (Melekoğlu, 2013). Given all the above negative aspects, inclusion practices can be harmful for some children with special needs.

In terms of training special education teachers, there are 19 special education departments training special education teachers in universities but most teachers are educated to work with individuals with intellectual disabilities. Due to this, the current supply–demand balance cannot be achieved. While special education department faculty support other education departments by providing special education foundation and/or inclusion courses there are many university educational departments that do not have a special education expert to offer these courses. Therefore, teacher candidates that graduate from these universities are not well equipped concerning special education and inclusion best practices (Melekoğlu, 2013). Also, even when teacher candidates are exposed to special education courses, the courses are taught from a theoretical perspective rather than a practical knowledge base perspective. Positively, special education teacher candidates receive practical knowledge perspectives and working experience about students with special needs in their last year of college. Even then the teacher candidates have a lot to learn as most do not have any school or society contact with students who have special needs prior to entering college.

Another problem with the teacher training system is the categorical approach that special education programs use to training special education teacher candidates. The categorical system does not allow teacher candidates who study under one category, such as intellectual disabilities, to earn a certificate in another category such as hearing impaired. A more efficient approach that is used in many countries would be to train special education teacher candidates using a cross-categorical approach that would allow them to be certified to teach students from different categories. Also, this approach would help to reduce teacher shortages in some areas of special education. Further, university graduate programs do not allow certified regular education teachers (e.g., history, science) to become special education teachers in Turkey. Hopefully as inclusive education increases, universities will allow non-special education teachers to be trained in special education in a master's degree program. Such a change would be very logical for regular education teachers with specialities in say math or science to become certified to teach gifted students in these areas especially at the secondary school level.

Unfortunately, there is almost no official government attempt to improve quality of life, employment training, and living arrangements of individuals with disabilities in Turkey. While vocational schools or training centers provide work training for some individuals with disabilities, the training does not comply with contemporary needs of businesses. There are some nongovernmental organizations and municipalities that work on providing opportunities for individuals with disabilities to acquire employment training and a job placement but they are very limited in scope and often result in job failure due to a lack of on the job training, follow up, or sustainable long-term funding. In terms of living arrangements, individuals with disabilities usually stay with their families or in care centers rather than in independent living settings. There is no community independent living arrangement settings such as group homes that have been established by the government for individuals with disabilities.

Positively, funding educational services and certain life aspects from the government has significantly improved for individuals with disabilities and their families in the last decade. For example, all individuals with disabilities are eligible for monthly disability salary if they meet the official requirements for disability. In addition, if the individual with a disability is in need of care, a family member or someone else who provides care to that person can receive a care salary. Also, the government pays education, rehabilitation, or therapy expenses for persons with a disability if the services are provided by private special education and rehabilitation centers (Akçamete, 1998; Vuran & Ünlü, 2012). Furthermore, all medical expenses of individuals with disabilities are covered by the government. Government reforms in funding education and services for individuals with disabilities has improved considerably, however, more needs to be done especially in the employment domain and the quality control of care services.

SPECIAL EDUCATION CHALLENGES

There are nine challenges that remain in special education today in Turkey. These challenges were identified and discussed by experts in the special education field at a recent conference, namely, the Special Education Search Conference, that was held at Anadolu University in November 2013 (Özel Eğitim Arama Konferansı, 2013). The first identified challenge is to establish a new model of training special education personnel. While there are training programs for special education teachers, there are no program to train paraprofessionals who work in special education schools, institutions, and centers. In addition, the current teacher training model does not respond to the needs of the Turkish education system. Further is the need for special education teacher candidates to be trained in cross-categorical programs.

A second challenge is to resolve the academic personnel shortage needs at universities. In many university special education departments, there are only a couple of academicians with doctoral degrees in special education. Additionally, there are many universities that wish to establish special education departments but they cannot find faculty with graduate degrees in special education. There needs to be more information dissemination about graduate special education program offerings. Due to special education teacher shortages, graduate students in special education should be supported financially to encourage other college students to enter into special education.

A third challenge in special education is establishing effective inclusive education. There should be at least one special education teacher in each school to serve as a support person. Also, paraprofessionals should be allowed to work in inclusive classrooms. Teachers of inclusive classrooms need to be comprehensively trained in effective special education best practices and receive necessary support as required.

A fourth challenge in Turkey is the need for early diagnosis and intervention of young students with special needs. Positively, there have been several studies about the adaptation of early intervention programs in Turkey such as the "Small Steps Early Intervention Program," "Portage Early Education Program," "Behavioral Education Program for Children with Autism," "Responsive Teaching," and "First Step to Success" (Diken, Cavkaytar, Batu, Bozkurt, & Kurtılmaz, 2010; Er-Sabuncuoglu & Diken, 2010; Yıldırım Doğru, 2011) but these programs have not been integrated in the early childhood special education system in Turkey. To accomplish this, there needs to be an official coordination system established between the Ministry of Health, the Ministry of National Education, and the Ministry of Family and Social Politics for early diagnosis and early intervention of children with disabilities. Also, education and rehabilitation centers and schools need to be directed by the government to focus on early intervention and rehabilitation. For this to occur, the MEB needs to establish official procedures, plans, and regulations for early childhood special education and intervention starting at the birth of a child.

The fifth challenge in special education is to develop better family participation and support. Families of children with disabilities should be educated about the child's disability, rights, interventions, educational practices, and related issues as soon as a disability is diagnosed in children. This education procedure should be operated by the government in a systematic and planned way. In addition, active participation of families in all stages of special education should be secured officially, and if necessary, advocates for families should be integrated into the process.

The sixth challenge in special education today in Turkey is the need for job training and placement of individuals with disabilities. Similar to best practice in many developed countries, the government needs to start planning transition to work plans for individuals with disabilities when these students enter their teenage years. These students need exposure to work training and work environments to increase their success in future job placements. To make this a sustainable process, the government should make agreements for job placements and training procedures of individuals who have disabilities with national and local business entities. In addition, the government should promote public and private shelter workshops and require strict and regular controls of these workshops.

The seventh challenge is dealing with the current deficiency in laws and policies about special education. All existing laws and regulations should be revised to address critical comments made by directors of nongovernmental organizations and experts regarding the needs of the Turkish education system (Eripek, 2012). Also, the government should determine functional policies and be accountable for the implementation of those policies.

Dissemination of research-based practices is the eighth challenge in special education in Turkey. The MEB should play an active role in this process and officially create an environment that introduces and promotes research-based practices in special education and requires educators to use those practices in schools. Additionally, the government should provide funding to universities and community researchers for the investigation of effective special education practices.

The ninth challenge existing in special education is the transition of individuals with disabilities to independent living. The government should plan and coordinate the transition process early on, and train experts about the issue and create adequate environments and a support system for smooth transition of individuals with disabilities to independent living.

In summary, special education in Turkey today has come a long ways and is still in the process of development. There are many challenges remaining in special education in Turkey but those challenges are not completely new in the special education field. Many countries have already handled those problems, and Turkey can study these solutions and adapt them according to national needs and expectations. Positively, there is strong governmental support for special education but more determined administrators are needed for resolving the special education challenges listed at the 2013 Special Education Search Conference. Addressing these challenges will go a long way in fulfilling Turkey's comprehensive reform in special education.

REFERENCES

Akçamete, A. G. (2009). *Genel eğitim okullarında özel gereksinimi olan öğrenciler ve özel eğitim.* [*Students with special needs in general education schools and special education.*] Ankara: Kök Yayıncılık [Kok Publication].

Akçamete, G. (1998). Türkiye'de özel eğitim. [Special education in Turkey]. In S. Eripek (Ed.), *Özel eğitim* (pp. 195–208). [*Special education.*] Eskişehir: Anadolu Üniversitesi Yayınları [Anadolu University Publications].

Akkök, F. (2000). Special education research: A Turkish perspective. *Exceptionality: A Special Education Journal, 8*(4), 179–273. doi:10.1207/S15327035EX0804_5

Akkök, F. (2001). The past, present, and future of special education: The Turkish perspective. *Mediterranean Journal of Educational Studies, 6*(2), 15–22.

American Psychiatric Association. (2004). *Diagnostic and statistical manual of mental disorders* (4th ed., text rev.). Washington, DC: Author.

Anderson, D. H., Marchant, M., & Somarriba, N. Y. (2010). Behaviorism works in special education. In F. E. Obiakor, J. P. Bakken, & A. F. Rotatori (Eds.), *Current issues and trends in special education: Identification, assessment, and instruction* (pp. 157–173). Bingley, UK: Emerald Group Publishing Limited.

Ataman, A. (2005). *Özel gereksinimli çocuklar ve özel eğitime giriş.* [*Children with special needs and introduction to special education.*] Ankara: Gündüz Eğitim ve Yayıncılık [Gunduz Education and Publication].

Baykoç, N. (2011). *Özel gereksinimli çocuklar ve özel eğitim.* [*Children with special needs and special education.*] Ankara: Eğiten Kitap [Egiten Book].

Baykoç-Dönmez, N. (2000, July). Special education in Turkey. Paper presented at the meeting of International Special Education Congress (ISEC), Manchester, UK.

Baykoç-Dönmez, N. (2011). Türkiye'de özel eğitim çalışmaları günümüzde yaşanan sorunlar ve çözüm önerileri. [Special education studies in Turkey current problems and proposed solutions]. In N. Baykoç (Ed.), *Özel gereksinimli çocuklar ve özel eğitim* (pp. 535–556). [*Children with special needs and special education.*] Ankara: Eğiten Kitap [Egiten Book].

Baykoç-Dönmez, N., & Şahin, S. (2011). Özel eğitimin tarihi gelişimi [Historical development of special education]. In N. Baykoç (Ed.), *Özel gereksinimli çocuklar ve özel eğitim* (pp. 535–556). [*Children with special needs and special education.*] Ankara: Eğiten Kitap [Egiten Book].

Cakiroglu, O., & Melekoğlu, M. A. (2013). Statistical trends and developments within inclusive education in Turkey. *International Journal of Inclusive Education.* Advance online publication. doi:10.1080/13603116.2013.836573

Cavkaytar, A., & Diken, İ. H. (2012). *Özel eğitim 1: Özel eğitim ve özel eğitim gerektirenler.* [*Special education 1: Special education and those who require special education.*] Ankara: Vize Yayıncılık [Vize Publication].

Children in Need of Protection Law [Korunmaya Muhtaç Çocuklar Hakkında Kanun], Government of Turkey. (1957).

Children with Special Education Needs Law [Özel Eğitime Muhtaç Çocuklar Kanunu], Government of Turkey. (1983).

Constitution of the Republic of Turkey. (1982). Retrieved from http://www.tbmm.gov.tr/anayasa.htm. Accessed on May 20, 2013.

Çuhadar, S. (2012). Özel eğitim süreci [Special education process]. In S. Vuran (Ed.), *Özel eğitim* (pp. 3–30). [*Special education.*] Ankara: Maya Akademi [Maya Academy].

Diken, İ. H. (2010a). *İlköğretimde kaynaştırma.* [*Inclusion in elementary school.*] Ankara: Pegem Akademi [Pegem Academy].

Diken, İ. H. (2010b). *Özel eğitime gereksinimi olan öğrenciler ve özel eğitim.* [*Students with special educational needs and special education.*] Ankara: Pegem Akademi [Pegem Academy].

Diken, İ. H., & Batu, S. (2010). Kaynaştırmaya giriş. [Introduction to inclusion]. In İ. H. Diken (Ed.), *İlköğretimde kaynaştırma* (pp. 1–25). [*Inclusion in elementary school.*] Ankara: Pegem Akademi [Pegem Academy].

Diken, İ. H., Cavkaytar, A., Batu, E. S., Bozkurt, F., & Kurtılmaz, Y. (2010). Effectiveness of the Turkish version of "first step to success program" in preventing antisocial behaviors. *Education and Science, 36*(161), 145–158.

Education of Gifted Children in the Fine Arts Law [Güzel Sanatlarda Fevkalade İstidat Gösteren Çocukların Devlet Tarafından Yetiştirilmesi Hakkında Kanun], Government of Turkey. (1956). Retrieved from http://www.mevzuat.gov.tr/ MevzuatMetin/1.3.6660. pdf. Accessed on May 20, 2013.

Elementary and Education Law [İlköğretim ve Eğitim Kanunu], Government of Turkey. (1961). Retrieved from http://mevzuat.meb.gov.tr/html/24.html. Accessed on May 20, 2013.

Employment Law [İş Kanunu], Government of Turkey. (1971). Retrieved from http://www. mevzuat.gov.tr/MevzuatMetin/1.5.1475.pdf. Accessed on May 20, 2013.

Eripek, S. (2012). Zihinsel yetersizliği olan bireyler ve eğitimleri. [Individuals with intellectual disabilities and education.] Ankara: Eğiten Kitap [Egiten Book].

Er-Sabuncuoglu, M., & Diken, İ. H. (2010). Early childhood ıntervention in Turkey: Current situation, challenges and suggestions. International Journal of Early Childhood Special Education, 2(2), 149−160.

Individuals with Disabilities Education Improvement Act of 2004, U.S.C. § 612 et seq.

Kauffman, J. M., Bruce, A., & Lloyd, J. W. (2012). Response to intervention (RTI) and students with emotional and behavioral disorders. In J. P. Bakken, F. E. Obiakor, & A. F. Rotatori (Eds.), Behavioral disorders: Practice concerns and students with EBD (pp. 107−128). Bingley, UK: Emerald Group Publishing Limited.

Melekoğlu, M. A. (2013). Examining the impact of interaction project with students with special needs on development of positive attitude and awareness of general education teachers towards inclusion. Educational Sciences: Theory & Practice, 13(2), 1053−1077.

Melekoğlu, M. A., Cakiroglu, O., & Malmgren, K. W. (2009). Special education in Turkey. International Journal of Inclusive Education, 13(3), 287−298.

Meral, B. F. (2011). Gelişimsel yetersizliği olan çocuk annelerinin aile yaşam kalitesi algılarının incelenmesi. [Examination of the family quality of life perceptions of mothers who have children with disabilities.] Unpublished doctoral dissertation, Anadolu Üniversitesi [Anadolu University], Eskişehir.

Milli Eğitim Bakanlığı (MEB) [Ministry of National Education]. (2003). Millî Eğitim sayısal veriler 2002−2003 [National education numerical data 2002−2003]. Retrieved from http://sgb.meb.gov.tr/istatistik/ist2002_ 2003.zip. Accessed on February 23, 2012.

Milli Eğitim Bakanlığı (MEB) [Ministry of National Education]. (2005). Milli Eğitim istatistik-leri 2004−2005 [National education statistics 2004−2005]. Retrieved from http://sgb. meb.gov.tr/istatistik/ist2004-2005.rar. Accessed on February 23, 2012.

Milli Eğitim Bakanlığı (MEB) [Ministry of National Education]. (2006). Özel eğitim hizmetleri yönetmeliği. [Regulation of special education services.] Published in the Official Gazette of Republic of Turkey, Issue 26184, May 31, 2006.

Milli Eğitim Bakanlığı (MEB) [Ministry of National Education]. (2011a). Milli Eğitim istatis-tikleri örgün eğitim 2010−2011 [National education statistics formal education 2010−2011]. Retrieved from http://sgb.meb.gov.tr/istatistik/meb_istatistikleri_orgun_ egitim_ 2010_2011.pdf. Accessed on September 6, 2011.

Milli Eğitim Bakanlığı (MEB) [Ministry of National Education]. (2011b). Özel eğitimle ilgili istatistiki bilgiler. [Statistical information about special education.] Obtained from the Ministry of National Education Strategy Development Presidency on a CD as an attachment to the official document dated September 30, 2011 and numbered 6543.

Milli Eğitim Bakanlığı (MEB) [Ministry of National Education]. (2013). Milli Eğitim istatistik-leri örgün eğitim 2012−2013 [National education statistics formal education 2012−2013]. Retrieved from http://sgb.meb.gov.tr/istatistik/meb_istatistikleri_orgun_egitim_2012_ 2013.pdf. Accessed on May 12, 2013.

Özel Eğitim Arama Konferansı [Special Education Search Conference]. (2013). *Anadolu Üniversitesi özel eğitim arama konferansı raporu, 16–17 Kasım 2013.* [*Anadolu University special education search conference report, 16–17 November 2013.*] Arama Araştırma Organizasyon Danışmanlığı [Search Research Organization Counseling], Anadolu Üniversitesi, Eskişehir [Anadolu University, Eskisehir].

Özyürek, M. (2005). Öğrenme güçlüğü gösteren çocuklar. [Children with learning disabilities]. In A. Ataman (Ed.), *Özel gereksinimli çocuklar ve özel eğitime giriş* (pp. 215–228). [*Children with special needs and introduction to special education.*] Ankara: Gündüz Eğitim ve Yayıncılık [Gunduz Education and Publication].

Rotatori, A. F., Obiakor, F. E., & Bakken, J. P. (Eds.). (2011). *History of special education.* Bingley, UK: Emerald Group Publishing Limited.

Şahin, S. (2005). Özel eğitimin tarihçesi. [History of special education]. In A. Ataman (Ed.), *Özel gereksinimli çocuklar ve özel eğitime giriş* (pp. 49–70). [*Children with special needs and introduction to special education.*] Ankara: Gündüz Eğitim ve Yayıncılık [Gunduz Education and Publication].

Senel, H. G. (1998). Special education in Turkey. *European Journal of Special Needs Education, 13*(3), 254–261.

Special Education Law [Özel Eğitim Hakkında Kanun Hükmünde Kararname], Government of Turkey. (1997). Retrieved from http://orgm.meb.gov.tr/meb_iys_ dosyalar/2012_10/10111011_ozel_egitim_kanun_hukmunda_kararname.pdf. Accessed on May 20, 2013.

Sucuoğlu, B., & Kargın, T. (2010). *İlköğretim'de kaynaştırma uygulamaları.* [*Inclusion practices in elementary schools.*] Ankara: Kök Yayıncılık [Kok Publication].

Turkish Civil Law [Türk Kanunu Medenisi], Government of Turkey. (1926).

Turkish Statistical Institute. (2012). *Population and development indicators.* Retrieved from http://www.turkstat.gov.tr/PreTablo.do?tb_id=39& ust_id=11. Accessed on April 12, 2011.

Vuran, S., & Ünlü, E. (2012). Türkiye'de özel gereksinimli çocukların eğitimi ile ilgili örgütlenme ve mevzuat. [Organization and legislation about education of students with special needs in Turkey]. In S. Vuran (Ed.), *Özel eğitim* (pp. 57–80). [*Special education.*] Ankara: Maya Akademi [Maya Academy].

World Bank. (2012). *World development indicators database. Gross domestic product 2010.* Retrieved from http://siteresources.worldbank.org/ DATASTATISTICS/Resources/GDP.pdf. Accessed on April 12, 2012.

Yıldırım Doğru, S. S. (2011). Erken çocuklukta özel eğitim. [Early childhood special education]. In S. S. Yıldırım Doğru, & N. Durmuşoğlu Saltalı (Eds.), *Erken çocukluk döneminde özel eğitim* (pp. 37–102). [*Special education in early childhood.*] Ankara: Maya Akademi [Maya Academy].

PART V
SOUTH ASIA

PART 4
SOUTH ASIA

SPECIAL EDUCATION TODAY IN INDIA

Ajay Das and Rina Shah

ABSTRACT

Similar to Western countries, the early origins of special education in India started with Christian missionaries and nongovernmental agencies which stressed a charity model of serving populations such as the visually, hearing, and cognitively impaired. However after its independence from Great Britain in 1947, the Indian government became more involved in providing educational, rehabilitation, and social services. Thus over the past four decades, India has moved gradually toward an inclusive education model. This chapter discusses the implementation of such a model related to the prevalence and incidence rates of disability in India as well as working within family environments that often involve three to four generations. Also included are challenges that an inclusive education system faces in India, namely, a high level of poverty, appropriate teacher preparation of special education teachers, a lack of binding national laws concerned with inclusive education, a dual governmental administration for special education services, and citizen's and special education professionals strong concern about whether inclusive education practices can be carried out.

Special Education International Perspectives: Practices Across the Globe
Advances in Special Education, Volume 28, 561–581
Copyright © 2014 by Emerald Group Publishing Limited
All rights of reproduction in any form reserved
ISSN: 0270-4013/doi:10.1108/S0270-401320140000028025

INTRODUCTION

Historically, persons with disabilities in India have enjoyed coexistence with the general mass, though at different times, their treatment and attitudes toward them varied but they were never excluded from society by confinement in institutions. Rather, they lived with their families. As far as education was concerned, even the *Gurukula Ashram* (educational institutes) promoted the basic educational principles of special education, for example, ascertaining the abilities and needs of each pupil, individualization of teaching targets and methods to match their skills and interests, and preparing them to meet the social expectations of their prospective interests. The famous epic of *Mahabharta* is evidence that King Dhritrashtra was the king of all India although he was visually impaired.

ORIGINS OF SPECIAL EDUCATION

However, during more recent times, systematic efforts took place in providing educational and vocational opportunities to individuals with disabilities in India. Starting with Christian missionaries in the 1880s, the charity model became part of the special schools they established (Alur, 2002). For instance, formal educational institutions were established for the blind in 1887, for the deaf in 1888, and for mentally deficient in 1934 (Misra, 2000). After these early establishments in the late 19th century or early 20th century, a growth was seen in the establishment of these institutions in the later half of the 20th century. After independence from Great Britain in 1947, there was a systematic development of special education in India that saw the establishment of 81 schools between 1960 and 1975. By 1979, the number of special education centers was 150. With the establishment of the National Institute for the Mentally Handicapped (NIMH) in 1986 and others soon after, the availability of trained personnel and suitable models of service made the growth of special schools for children with disabilities very significant.

PREVALENCE OF DISABILITY IN INDIA

According to a UNICEF Report on the Status of Disability in India (2000), there were around 30 million children that had some form of disability. Another report, the sixth All-India Educational Survey reported that of India's 2,000 million school aged children (6–14 years), 20 million require special needs education (Rehabilitation Council of India (RCI), 2000). Although these numbers show a large discrepancy, it is clear that there are a large number of students with special needs that require appropriate educational services. Recognizing the large number of special needs population and regional disparities, the Government of India (GoI) initiated policy reforms and strategies for special needs and inclusive education. The educational system in India has witnessed many changes after the coveted independence from Great Britain in 1947. The post freedom era together with the economic and social development policies in the last four decades have contributed substantially to bringing about an evolution in the overall educational system in India through legislative measures as well as social welfare activities.

GOVERNMENT'S EFFORTS IN PROVIDING SERVICES

The efforts of the GoI over the last four decades have been toward providing a comprehensive range of services for the education of children with disabilities. In particular, inclusive education has been the focus of delivery of instruction to the students with disabilities in the country. In considering the educational provisions made for students with special educational needs in India, Jha (2002) states that while the agenda for inclusion in the West is concentrated mainly on the inclusion of students with physical and intellectual disabilities and those whose learning difficulties are due largely to emotional and behavioral factors, in India the focus extends beyond such groups. They also include children who are educationally deprived due to social and economic reasons, for example, street children, girls in rural areas, children belonging to scheduled castes and scheduled tribes, as well as various minorities and groups from diverse social, cultural, and linguistic backgrounds. According to Jha, all these children are considered to have special needs. He argues that what is called "special needs" in Britain would be considered the "normal needs" of a large minority of children in India. Hence, the terminology, which has its origins in the medical world of diagnosing the disability in the West, cannot explain the educational deprivation of large numbers of children in the developing countries (Jha, 2002, p. 67).

PROMOTING INCLUSIVE EDUCATION IN INDIA

The remainder of the chapter focuses on the significant strides made by the GoI toward promoting inclusive education in its national legislation and policies in the recent decades. Some key initiatives in each decade in the last four decades are discussed to illustrate the development of special education services for students with special needs in India.

The 1960s

The Indian Education Commission, widely known as the Kothari Commission (Kothari, 1966), was the first statutory body which highlighted the issue of children with disabilities in the Plan of Action in 1964 (Alur, 2002; Puri & Abraham, 2004). It made strong recommendations for including children with disabilities into regular schools. Elaborating on the allocation of funds for handicapped children, the commission proposed that:

> The Ministry of Education should allocate the necessary funds and NCERT should establish a cell for the study of handicapped children. The principal function of the cell would be to keep in touch with the research that is being done in the country and abroad and to prepare material for teachers. (Kothari Commission, 1966, p. 124)

The Commission emphasized that (a) the education of children with disabilities should be "an inseparable part of the general education system" (Azad, 1996, p. 4) and (b) it should be organized, not merely on humanitarian grounds, but also on grounds of utility (Azad, 1996; Puri & Abraham, 2004). Moreover, the Commission set specific targets for four categories of disability to be achieved by 1986: education for about 15 percent of the blind, the deaf, and orthopedically handicapped and 5 percent of the mentally retarded (Panda, 1996; RCI, 2000). In addition, the Commission strongly proposed inclusive education as a model for the delivery of educational services emphasizing that not only was it cost-effective but would also enhance mutual understanding between children with and without disabilities (Panda, 1996; Puri & Abraham, 2004). However, it was apparent that not much had been achieved in realizing the targets set by the commission (Azad, 1996); despite the fact that subsequent to the Kothari Commission recommendations, the 1968 National Education Policy was formulated, which had suggested: (a) the expansion of educational facilities for children with physical and mental disabilities; and (b) to develop integrated program to enable children with disabilities to study in regular schools (Jha, 2002).

The 1970s

The Ministry of Welfare launched the scheme for Integrated Education for Disabled Children (IEDC) to overcome some of the difficulties faced by the special education system in the country, particularly, limited coverage and a lack of qualified and trained teachers (Dasgupta, 2002). The Central Government provided 50 percent financial assistance to the State Governments for the implementation of the IEDC in regular schools.

The objectives of the IEDC included the retention of children with disabilities in the regular school system, preschool training for children with disabilities, and counseling for parents. One hundred percent financial assistance was offered by the central government to: (i) provide facilities for children with disabilities for books and stationery, uniform, transport allowance, readers' allowance for blind children, and boarding and lodging charges for these children residing in hostels; (ii) setting up of resource rooms; (iii) resource teacher support in the ratio of 1:8 in respect of all disabled children except those with locomotor disabilities; (iv) survey for identification of disabled children and their assessment; (v) purchase and production of instructional material; (vi) training and orientation of resource teachers and school administrators; and (vii) salary of persons working in an IEDC Cell at the state level to implement and monitor the program.

Until 1990, the scheme was implemented in 14 states. In 1999, the Ministry of Information and Broadcasting reported that the scheme was being implemented in 26 states and union territories benefiting over 53,000 students enrolled in 14,905 schools. It has been noted that among all the states, Kerala has shown significant progress in implementing this scheme where 4,487 schools were implementing IEDC and serving 12,961 children (Puri & Abraham, 2004).

The overall lack of success of this scheme was attributed to a lack of coordination among various departments toward its implementation (Azad, 1996; Pandey & Advani, 1997). Furthermore, issues such as nonavailability of trained and experienced teachers; lack of orientation among school staff on the difficulties of children with disabilities and their educational needs; and nonavailability of equipment and educational materials were stated as major contributory factors in the failure of the program in Maharashtra (Rane, 1983). Consequently, in 1992, the IEDC scheme was revised to overcome some of its limitations. Under the revised scheme, schools involved in the inclusion of students with disabilities were entitled to 100 percent assistance and a full funding provision was made for non-government organizations to implement the scheme.

The 1980s

The IEDC scheme was followed by the seminal year of International Year for the Disabled Persons (IYDP) in 1981. The United Nations established that all countries should frame legislation for people with disabilities and that was the major thrust of the year. India was one of the first signatories to the resolution proclaiming the year 1981 as the "International Year for the Disabled Persons." India demonstrated its commitment toward people with disabilities by endorsing the objectives proposed in the resolutions of the United Nations General Assembly (RCI, 2000). In response to the United Nations initiatives, the GoI enacted a series of legislations and policies to advance integrated education in the country (RCI, 2000).

The GoI in its Sixth Five-Year Plan (1980–1985) considered inclusive education for children with disabilities as a priority. Subsequent increased funding for inclusive education and supplementary policies, legislation, and programs indicate the government's dedication in this sphere. In particular, the provision of inclusive education as an integral part of the education system by the GoI is reflected in the National Policy of Education (NPE) (Ministry of Human Resource Development, 1986) and Project Integrated Education for the Disabled (PIED) (Ministry of Human Resource Development, 1987).

The 1986 NPE was a major initiative of the GoI toward inclusive education for students with disabilities (RCI, 2000). It envisaged a meaningful partnership between the union and states (National Council of Educational Research and Training (NCERT), 2000). The policy outlined specific steps "to integrate the physically and mentally handicapped with the general community as equal partners, to prepare them for normal growth and to face life with courage and confidence" (Ministry of Human Resource Development, 1986). The NPE, under its all-encompassing objective of "Equal Education Opportunity," proposed the following measures for the education of children with disabilities: (i) "wherever it is feasible, the education of children with motor handicaps and other mild handicaps will be common with others; (ii) special schools with hostels will be provided, as far as possible at district headquarters, for severely handicapped children; (iii) adequate arrangements will be made to give vocational training to the disabled; (iv) teachers' training programs will be reoriented, in particular for teachers of primary classes, to deal with special difficulties of handicapped children, by including a compulsory special education component in preservice training of general teachers (Dasgupta, 2002); and (v) voluntary effort for the education of the disabled will be encouraged in every possible manner" (Jha, 2002, pp. 93–94).

The NPE highlighted various issues in relation to children with disabilities, such as, the magnitude of the problem, the approaches to service delivery, the scheme of human and material resources, and nature of linkages between various agencies, in special education, which created the platform for serving children with disabilities as well as highlighted "education as the right of the disabled child" (RCI, 2000).

NCERT, following the guidelines of NPE 1986 and with the assistance of UNICEF and the Ministry of Human Resource Development (MHRD), launched PIED for children with disabilities to strengthen the implementation of the IEDC scheme (Dasgupta, 2002). However, this project did not include children with intellectual impairment within its scope (RCI, 2000). This project was undertaken in 10 states/union territories of Haryana, Madhya Pradesh, Maharashtra, Mizoram, Nagaland, Orissa, Rajasthan, and Delhi. Ten blocks were selected in each state/union territory on the basis of "composite area" approach, to ensure appropriate coverage. Each of these blocks constituted as a "project area" and all the schools in that block were required to implement integrated education programs. Furthermore, the idea for clustering schools in the specified project area was to share facilities: instructional materials, instrumental aids, specialized equipment, resource teachers and medical, psychological and social support personnel. One of PIED's main objectives was to improve access for children with disabilities within their own environments and neighborhoods (Alur, 2002). A major component of this project was the training of regular classroom teachers to work with students with disabilities. The teacher training programs were provided at three levels:

Level I: All primary school teachers in the project area underwent orientation training for the duration of one week;

Level II: Ten percent of the teachers participated in an intensive six-week training to equip them to handle children with a disability; and

Level III: Eight to ten teachers from each block completed a one-year multi-category training program provided by the colleges of NCERT. These teachers were subsequently placed in each project area to function as resource teachers for a cluster of schools (Dasgupta, 2002; Jha, 2002).

According to Azad (1996), PIED, resulted in both regular school teachers and students becoming more receptive toward students with disabilities. Azad added that over 9,000 teachers received training to implement integrated education programs. The success of the PIED project led to an increased commitment by the Department of Education to integrate students with disabilities (Jangira & Ahuja, 1993). An external evaluation of this project in 1994 showed that, not only the enrollment of children with disabilities increased noticeably, but also the retention rate among children with disabilities was higher (approximately 95 percent) than the nondisabled children in the PIED blocks (Dasgupta, 2002; Jha, 2002). In addition, results of the project showed that the achievement of children with disabilities was found to be at par with children without disabilities in both scholastic and non-scholastic activities in schools (Alur & Rioux, 2004; Jha, 2002; RCI, 2000).

The 1990s

During this period, the GoI spurred various projects, schemes, and legislations to reinforce inclusion programs. Some of the initiatives were: the National Policy of Education-Plan of Action (NPE-POA) (1990–1992); the District Primary Education Programme (DPEP) (Ministry of Human Resource Development, 1994); and perhaps the most significant of these initiatives was the passage of the landmark legislation, The Persons with Disabilities Act of 1995.

NPE (1986) was revised in 1992 and is referred to as the NPE-POA (Ministry of Human Resource Development, 1992). The revised act resulted from criticism of the 1986 NPE, namely, due to its lack of commitment to the universalization of elementary education for all children, especially for those with disabilities (Jangira & Ahuja, 1993). In contrast, the 1992 NPE-POA reemphasized the principle of integration by stating that those children who may be enrolled in a special school for the acquisition of daily living skills, plus curriculum skills, communication skills, and basic academic skills should be subsequently integrated in regular schools (Dasgupta, 2002). In addition, all basic education projects, such as, nonformal education, adult education, vocational education, and teacher education schemes, which are funded by the central government, should adhere to the principle of integration (Ministry of Human Resource Development, 1992). Two important features pertaining to training issues in the NPE-POA (1992) were: (i) it focused on the need for incorporating a module on the education of children with disabilities as an integral component in training for educational planners and administrators; and (ii) it upgraded teacher education, especially for primary school teachers by introducing the "concept of teacher accountability" to the students, their parents, the community, and to their profession as part of teacher training programs. Furthermore, a resolution was made to set up District Institute of Education and Training (DIET) to provide preservice and in-service education to regular school teachers to enhance their skills to meet the needs of students with disabilities in their classrooms. The NPE-POA made an impressive commitment for universal enrollment by the end of the Ninth Five-Year Plan (1997–2002) for children who could be educated in regular primary schools and those who required being educated in special schools or special classes in regular schools (Ministry of Human Resource Development, 1992, p. 18). This administrative initiative further highlighted the GoI's commitment to integrated education.

The DPEP, a centrally sponsored scheme, was launched in 1994, with the ultimate goal of achieving universal education. This program laid a special emphasis on the integration of children with mild to moderate disabilities in line with the world trends. The DPEP is noteworthy because it was the first time that primary education had been delinked from the state (Alur, 2002). The DPEP in 1994–1995 with financial support from the World Bank, the European Community, and the United Kingdom's Overseas Development Agency, UNICEF, and the Government of the Netherlands and the GoI became one of the largest programs of the GoI in terms of funding. Approximately 40 billion rupees were budgeted to fund this program in 149 districts, in 14 states.

The multiple components of the DPEP were: (i) environment building, development of innovative designs for primary schools, and removal of architectural barriers in existing schools; (ii) the development of teaching-learning materials and research; (iii) provision for regular in-service teacher training conducted by the DIET and the State Council of Educational Research and Training (SCERT); (iv) activities related to community mobilization; (v) provision for early detection, functional assessment, the use of specialized aids and appliances, and the implementation of individualized educational plans; and (vi) resource support at block/district level with regards to availability of funding for educational aids and appliances as well as placement of a program officer at the DPEP district project office.

In addition, nonformal/alternate schooling incorporating a flexible curriculum, informal evaluation criteria, and flexible timings would be promoted (Alur, 2002). Furthermore, an advisory resource group would be formed at the state and national level to guide the overall efforts as well as to provide technical and academic support to integrated education under DPEP (Dasgupta, 2002). The other significant components of this program were its emphasis to: (i) actively promote the different government agencies and nongovernmental organizations (NGOs) at various levels to work in synchronization; (ii) to keep a track of student enrollment, retention, drop-outs, and gender-wise specifications through case-studies and statistical records to be compiled annually; and (iii) start primary schools in every village to address the issues of out-of school children and early marriages (Alur, 2002). An evaluation of the DPEP indicated that innovative and practical interventions introduced by the DPEP significantly improved access and retention, as well as quality of education of all students (World Bank, 1997).

In the last decade of the millennium, the turning point in the educational provisions for children with disabilities in India was brought about by the enactment of the landmark legislation titled, The Persons with Disabilities (Equal Opportunities, Protection of Rights, and Full Participation) Act of 1995 (Ministry of Law Justice and Company Affairs, 1996). The aforementioned Act was ratified to give effect to the proclamation on the full participation and equality of people with disabilities in the Asian and Pacific region to which India was a signatory at the meeting to launch the Asian and Pacific Decade of Disabled Persons 1993—2002 convened by the Economic and Social Commission for Asia and Pacific (ESCAP) held at Beijing on December 1—5, 1992. This Act, passed by the Indian parliament seeks, *inter alia*, to create a conducive environment in the country to facilitate equal participation and giving an opportunity to the disabled to join the mainstream and contribute to the process of nation building. An essential aspect of the legislation according to a number of authors (Kulakarni, 2000; Rao, 2000) was the emphasis it placed on the inclusion of students with disabilities into regular schools. For the first time, the inclusion of students with disabilities in regular schools entered the realm of Indian jurisdiction. Consequently, one of the essential features of this Act is that discrimination specifically against persons with disabilities came under the purview of law through grievance redressed machinery established at the central and state levels.

With regard to education, it called upon the three tiers of government, namely, national, state/union territories, and local governments to promote inclusive education. The Act charged upon these governments to ensure that all children with disabilities had access to a "free and appropriate" education until the age of 18 years. Concurrently, the Act entailed that local bodies, NGOs, and all others involved with the education of children with disabilities, would be responsible for implementing its various provisions (Dasgupta, 2002). In addition, Chapter five of the Act articulated the need for establishing open schools and universities and nonformal/alternative education with the aim of facilitating education for students with disabilities. It also emphasized teacher training programs, adaptation of curriculum materials, reform of the examination system, and the promotion of research (Dasgupta, 2002).

In addition, for the purpose of effective implementation of the legislation, coordination committees were established at the national and state levels and headed by the commissioners appointed at the central and state level. The role of the Chief Commissioner, who holds important statutory functionary, includes coordinating the work of the State Commissioners, for persons with disabilities, monitoring utilization of funds disbursed by the Central Government, and taking appropriate action to safeguard rights and facilities made available to persons with disabilities (Ministry of Information and Broadcasting, 2004). Furthermore, the commissioners possess the powers to intervene legally for deprivation or violation of the rights of the disabled, including matters of equal opportunity in education (Jha, 2002). The GoI in its Ninth Five-Year Plan (1997–2002) earmarked billion rupees specifically for the provision of integrated education (Ministry of Information and Broadcasting, 2000) in order to expand educational opportunities for children with disabilities in the country.

The National Trust Act was established as a statutory body under the Ministry of Social Justice and Empowerment set up under the "National Trust for the Welfare of Persons with Autism, Cerebral Palsy, Mental Retardation and Multiple Disabilities" Act (Ministry of Law Justice and Company Affairs, 1999). This Act further strengthened the PWD Act of 1995 and had provisions for students with autism, intellectual impairment, and cerebral palsy.

The 2000s

A number of significant initiatives have taken place in the last decade that further strengthened inclusion movement in India. Some of these initiatives included: *Sarva Siksha Abhiyan* (Ministry of Human Resource Development, 2000), The Action Plan for Inclusion in Education of Children and Youth with Disabilities (Ministry of Human Resource Development, 2005), National Policy for Persons with Disabilities (Ministry of Social Justice and Empowerment, 2006), and Inclusive Education of the Disabled at Secondary Stage (Ministry of Human Resource Development, 2009a). Detailed information on these initiatives follows.

The Centrally Sponsored Scheme of *Sarva Shiksha Abhiyan* (Education for All movement) (SSA), which was implemented in 2000, set time-bound targets for the achievement of Universal Elementary Education (UEE) by 2010. With a premise of "zero rejection," the program provided support for the inclusion of children with disabilities in regular schools at the elementary level. SSA provided an assistance of rupees, namely, 1,200 per special needs child per annum. This money was allocated toward assistive devices, materials in alternative learning formats, and anything else that would assist children with disabilities to be included in mainstream classrooms. Under the scheme, over 2 million children with disabilities were identified and over 1.5 million children with disabilities in the age group 6–14 years were enrolled in regular schools. Under SSA, a continuum of educational options, learning aids and tools, mobility assistance, support services, etc. were made available to students with disabilities. This included education through an open learning system and open schools, alternative schooling, distance education, special schools, wherever necessary home-based education, itinerant teacher model, remedial teaching, part time classes, Community Based Rehabilitation (CBR), and vocational education. Alur and Rioux (2004) however argue that the implementation of SSA was adversely affected due to the inadequate disbursement of financial assistance.

The Action Plan for Inclusion in Education of Children and Youth with Disabilities was an ambitious plan that was introduced by the Government to promote the inclusion of students with disabilities in mainstream schools. Under this plan, the first level of intervention was offered through the Integrated Child Development Services (ICDS) program. This program aimed to reach out to all children aged 0–6 years, and it trained *anganwadi* workers to detect disabilities in children at an early stage. In addition, this plan included a number of specific objectives including the following: (a) providing home-based learning for persons with severe, multiple, and intellectual disability, (b) modifying physical infrastructure and teaching methodologies to meet the needs of all children including children with special needs, and (c) providing training to preservice teachers about inclusion concepts by including a module on inclusion in their preservice teacher preparation programs and offering professional development opportunities to existing teachers.

The National Policy for Persons with Disabilities (2006) recognized that persons with disabilities are valuable human resource for the country and sought to create an environment that provided them with equal opportunities, protection of their rights, and full participation in society. The focus of the policy included prevention of disabilities, rehabilitation measures, and physical rehabilitation strategies. More specifically it involved (a) early detection and intervention, (b) counseling and medical rehabilitation, (c) the use of assistive devices, (d) development of rehabilitation professionals, (e) education for persons with disabilities, (f) economic rehabilitation of persons with disabilities, (g) serving women and children with disabilities, (h) creating barrier free environment, (i) issuing disability certificates, (j) providing social security, (k) the promotion of NGOs, (l) carrying out research, (m) sports, recreation, and cultural life, (n) making amendments and existing acts dealing with the PWDs.

SSA specifically supported inclusion of children with special needs at the early childhood education and elementary education level and Inclusive Education for the Disabled at the Secondary Stage (IEDSS) was introduced to provide assistance to students with special needs at secondary level. The scheme for IEDSS was therefore envisaged to enable adolescents with disabilities to have access to secondary education and to improve their enrollment, retention, and achievement in the general education system. Under the scheme every school was proposed to be made "disabled-friendly." IEDSS especially aimed to identify students with disabilities at the secondary stage, provide 3,000 rupees per child per annum for instructional materials, and set up model schools in every state to develop replicable practices in inclusive education.

Right of Children to Free and Compulsory Education (RTE) Act (Ministry of Human Resource Development, 2009b) proposed free and compulsory education to all children aged between 6 and 14 years. Also, the Act made it binding that all public and private schools reserve 25 percent of their classroom seats for children from "disadvantaged sections." Section 3 of the law stated that "disadvantaged sections" cover children with disabilities as specified under the PDA. In 2012, a bill was passed by the parliament of India to amend the Act. This bill allowed children with autism, cerebral palsy, intellectual impairment, and multiple disabilities the benefit of choosing to study from home. The bill emphasized that the "home schooling option" should not become an instrument for schools not wanting to take these children in classrooms.

CURRENT CHALLENGES FOR INCLUSIVE EDUCATION IN INDIA

The movement toward inclusive education has become a major focus in recent education reform in India. In spite of the government's efforts in the last four decades, less than 1 percent of children with disabilities are educated in inclusive setting (The Hindu, 2013). India's unique problems and characteristics such as poverty, the absence of a binding law for inclusive education, a lack of resources, and its unique cultural and social background are daunting obstacles to the inclusion of children with disabilities into the regular education setting.

A high level of poverty in India has been a real challenge for the implementation of inclusive education. In spite of recent economic developments, poverty is rampant in India. World Bank reports that as much as 400 million people in India are living in poverty, that is, living on less than 82 pence a day (The Telegraph, 2013). According to the most recent report published in *Business Standard* on January 21, 2014, per capita income in India stands at Rupees 68,748 per year which is equivalent to about $1,087. This is significantly below even with developing countries' standards. The principal causes of disability — inadequate nutrition, faulty childbearing practices, infections from diseases, and accidents — are products of poverty and insufficient human services. Thus, the risk of impairment is much greater for the children of the poverty-stricken. The birth of an impaired child or the occurrence of disability in the family, often places additional demands on the limited resources of the family and strains its morale, thrusting it deeper into the morass of poverty. Poverty is also an obstacle to the improvement in educational opportunities for children with disabilities in India. Karna (1999) points out that a large number of children with disabilities live in families where family income is significantly below the poverty level. Many of these children become a part of the child labor force not due to choice but out of compulsion to meet the basic needs of their family. For the majority of these children and their families, subsistence takes precedence to education as they have an immediate need for food and shelter. This notion severely restricts educational opportunities for a vast majority of children let alone children with disabilities.

Another significant challenge for the successful implementation of inclusive education in India is the lack of binding laws. There have been several legislations such as PWD Act, RTE Act, and others that have been passed in India which focus on inclusive education. However, in absence of binding clauses such as "zero reject," "least restrictive environment," "due process," and others included in the Individuals with Disabilities Education Improvement Act (IDEIA) which was passed by the United States Congress in 2004, the provisions made in the PWD Act and others did not yield the required outcome in terms of creating equitable educational opportunities for children with disabilities in India. In absence of binding laws, the legislations passed in India emphasizing inclusive education remains nothing but a hollow and empty promise.

The lack of resources has been a major hurdle in the implementation of inclusive education in India. A number of authors including Alur (2002), Bhatnagar and Das (2013), and Das, Gichuru, and Singh (2013) pointed out that constraints of resources have been a major barrier in the implementation of inclusion programs in India and therefore, it should be a matter of priority. Alur (2002) further asserts that "Policy without funding is no policy at all" (p. 25). Jangira (2002) argued that the inclusion education plan can only be successful if the GoI allocates resources based on prevalence of special educational needs. The Working Group Report on Elementary Education and Literacy under the 12th Five-Year Plan (2012−2017) made a number of recommendations to address the resource crunch for inclusive education which included the following: support for inclusive education to be provided at the rate of Rupees 3,000 per year for every child with special needs and 1,000 of these Rupees will be made available for resource teachers; provision of aids and appliances will be provided as needed; and that their will be training of regular school teachers.

Another reason for non-realization of the inclusion endeavor in India could be the dual administration of special education in the country. While special schools fall under the administration of Ministry of Social Welfare, inclusive education is the responsibility of the Department of Education in the Ministry of Human Resource Development (Jangira, 2002). In addition, inclusive education to be effective requires the coordination between different sectors of operations, namely, the welfare sector, the women and child development sector, and the health sector. However, there is no co-coordinating system in place either at the central, state, district, or subdistrict levels which hold up the inclusion process at the school level (Jangira, 2002). Furthermore, there is no appropriate regulatory framework to monitor and enforce accountability for the successful implementation of inclusive education programs at all levels (Alur, 2002; Jangira, 2002).

Another important challenge is teacher concerns and a lack of supportive attitudes for inclusive education in India. The available research on teacher attitudes and concerns in India indicate that while many general education teachers philosophically support inclusion, most have strong concerns about their ability to implement it successfully (Bhatnagar & Das, 2013; Das, Kuyini, & Desai, 2013; Shah, 2005). For instance, studies have shown that most general education teachers question their ability to teach students with disabilities, and some doubt they will be provided with the resources and support necessary for the programs (Bhatnagar, 2006; Shah,

2005). Another similar challenge is a lack of trained work force to effectively meet the needs of children with disabilities. A number of researchers have highlighted that the regular school teachers in India have reported not receiving appropriate training in special education instructional methods (e.g., Das, 2001; Jangria, Singh, & Yadav, 1995; Shah, Das, Desai, & Tiwari, 2014). It is rather unfair to ask these teachers to do something that they have not been trained in.

WORKING WITH FAMILIES OF CHILDREN WITH DISABILITIES IN INDIA

Understanding family structure in India is important in the context of delivering services to children with disabilities. The traditional "Western" notion of family as having a nuclear structure does not apply to Indian families which may include three or four generations of family members living under one roof. Both joint and nuclear families exist in almost equal proportions in India, but reflect some geographic variations in family structure. In the southern part of India, about 60 percent of the families are nuclear, whereas this proportion is 42 percent in the northern part of the country. The joint family system is, however, shrinking due to industrialization, urbanization, increased mobility, and influence from the Western world (Pinto & Sahur, 2001). Professionals need to be aware of role functions of family members while communicating with them. For example, while men typically assume primary role in key decision making process involving financial and outside home-related aspects, women assume primary role in day-to-day household tasks and implementation of any intervention at home. Professionals, therefore, must adjust their communication accordingly while communicating with family members. Another aspect that needs professionals' attention is the changing nature of family in India. While even until a decade ago, majority of the family used to have one member (typically men) who was the primary breadwinner for the family, in the last decade this notion has changed drastically due to increased industrialization and urbanization. This has also resulted in increased number of nuclear families in India. While grandparents or other family members took care of the disabled child earlier, this support system is slowly fading away and exerting increased pressure on the families that have a child with disabilities. In addition, families of children with disabilities in India still have to deal with the stigma associated with disability.

This is more prevalent in rural areas. For this reason, inclusive education is a preferred option for many parents in spite of receiving minimal services, in most instances, from the school where their children attend. In the last decade or so, however, mass media has played a significant role in developing awareness among people and reducing the stigma attached with disability.

TEACHER PREPARATION

While teacher preparation in special education has witnessed a major change in the last two decades in India, it is still lagging behind to meet the demands of increased number of teachers in the country. In order to meet with the demands of special education teachers in the country, the GoI had set up national institutes on various disabilities in the 1980s (e.g., NIMH, National Institute for the Visually Handicapped (NIVH)). These national institutes and their regional centers in various parts of the country became instrumental in offering bachelor's degree or diploma courses in special education. For example, the NIMH started offering a Bachelor's degree course in Mental Retardation (BMR) as early as 1987. Other national institutes started such initiatives as well. The range of courses offered by these institutions and other universities grew rapidly over a period of time. Currently the course offerings include certificate courses that may last for three months to doctoral degree in special education and allied fields. In addition to aiding with the manpower development in the country, these national institutes played a key role in conducting research in special education and developing pedagogy unique to India. The GoI also formed an autonomous body, RCI in 1993 by passing RCI Act in 1992 to regulate the special education and rehabilitation course offered by government agencies and NGOs. RCI has been instrumental in ensuring program quality offered by the teacher training institutions. It regulates and monitors services rendered to persons with disabilities and standardizes syllabi. It also maintains a Central Rehabilitation Register of all qualified professionals and personnel working in the field of Rehabilitation and Special Education in India. According to the latest information obtained from the RCI website, there are 60 different categories of courses offered in special education and allied fields in the country. These courses are both offered through regular as well as distance mode.

With regard to the inclusion of children with disabilities and meeting their unique needs in that setting, a number of researchers have highlighted a lack of preparation among regular teachers in India. For example, Das (2001) conducted a survey of 310 primary and 130 secondary regular school teachers in Delhi and reported that a vast majority of these teachers had never received any training in working with children with special needs. These teachers were nonetheless charged with meeting the needs of all children in their classrooms that were already overcrowded and under resourced. Bhatnagar (2006) and Shah (2005) raised similar concerns regarding teachers' lack of preparation for inclusive education.

CONCLUSION

India appears to be at the crossroads with the implementation of inclusive education. On one hand, the Indian government has demonstrated its determination by implementing a number of policies, programs, and legislations for inclusion in the last four decades; while on the other it faces a number of unique challenges that limits its successful implementation. Policy makers need to address these challenges appropriately to make inclusive education a reality for millions of children with disabilities in India. While research (Singal, 2005; Singal & Rouse, 2003) on inclusive education in India is limited, external research can be evaluated and adopted to meet the unique socio-cultural-educational traditions of India. Similarly, specialized services can be sought from those professionals who have extensive experiences with the implementation of inclusive education in other contexts and an understanding of Indian scenario as well.

REFERENCES

Alur, M. (2002). Introduction: The social construct of disability. In S. Hearty & M. Alur (Eds.), *Education and children with special needs* (pp. 21–22). New Delhi: Sage.

Alur, M., & Rioux, M. (2004). *Included! An exploration of six early education pilot projects for children with disabilities in India*. Mumbai: The Spastics Society of India. UNICEF, Canadian International Development Agency, and The Spastics Society of India.

Azad, Y. A. (1996). *Integration of disabled in common schools: A survey-study of IEDC in the country*. New Delhi: National Council of Educational Research and Training.

Bhatnagar, N. (2006). *Attitudes and concerns of Indian teachers towards integrated education*. Unpublished doctoral dissertation, Victoria University.

Bhatnagar, N., & Das, A. K. (2013). Attitudes of secondary school teachers towards inclusive education in New Delhi, India. *Journal of Research in Special Educational Needs*. doi:10.1111/1471-3802.12016

Business Standard. (2014). India's per capita income rises to Rs. 5,729 per month. Business Standard. Retrieved from http://www.business-standard.com/article/economy-policy/ india-s-per-capita-income-rises-to-rs-5-729-per-month-113020700995_1.html. Accessed on January 21.

Das, A. K. (2001). *Perceived training needs of regular and secondary school teachers to implement inclusive education programs in Delhi, India.* Unpublished doctoral dissertation, The University of Melbourne.

Das, A. K., Gichuru, M., & Singh, A. (2013). Implementing inclusive education in Delhi, India: Regular school teachers' preferences for professional development delivery modes. *Professional Development in Education, 39*(5), 698–711.

Das, A. K., Kuyini, A. B., & Desai, I. P. (2013). Inclusive education in India: Are the teachers prepared? *International Journal of Special Education,* 28(1), 27–36.

Dasgupta, P. R. (2002). Education for the disabled. In S. Hegarty & M. Alur (Eds.), *Education and children with special needs* (pp. 41–50). New Delhi: Sage.

Individuals with Disabilities Education Improvement Act. (2004). *Public Law No. 108-446.* United States Congress.

Jangira, N. K. (2002). Special education needs of children and young adults: An unfinished agenda. In S. Hegarty & M. Alur (Eds.), *Education and children with special needs* (pp. 67–76). New Delhi: Sage.

Jangira, N. K., & Ahuja, A. (1993). Special education in India. *Asia Appraiser, 23*(October–December), 6–12.

Jangira, N. K., Singh, A., & Yadav, S. K. (1995). Teacher policy, training needs and perceived status of teachers. *Indian Educational Review, 30*(1), 113–122.

Jha, M. M. (2002). *School without walls: Inclusive education for all.* Oxford: Heinemann.

Karna, G. N. (1999). *United nations and rights of disabled persons: A study in Indian perspective.* New Delhi: A.P.H. Publishing Corporation.

Kothari, O. S. (Kothari Commission Report, 1966). *Report of the Indian education commission 1964–1966.* New Delhi: Ministry of Education.

Kulakarni, V. R. (2000). *Thinking care.* Retrieved from cbrnet@vsnl.com. Accessed on March 17.

Ministry of Human Resource Development. (1986). *National policy on education.* New Delhi: Department of Education, Government of India.

Ministry of Human Resource Development. (1987). *Project integrated education for the disabled.* New Delhi: Department of Education, Government of India.

Ministry of Human Resource Development. (1992). *National policy on education.* New Delhi: Department of Education, Government of India.

Ministry of Human Resource Development. (1994). *DPEP guidelines.* New Delhi: Department of Education, Government of India.

Ministry of Human Resource Development. (2000). *Sarva Shiksha Abhiyan: A programme for the universalization of inclusive education.* New Delhi: Department of School Education & Literacy, Government of India.

Ministry of Human Resource Development. (2005). *The action plan for inclusion in education of children and youth with disabilities.* New Delhi: Department of Education, Government of India.

Ministry of Human Resource Development. (2009a). *Inclusive education of the disabled at secondary stage.* New Delhi: Department of School Education and Literacy.

Ministry of Human Resource Development. (2009b). *Right of Children to Free and Compulsory Education (RTE) Act.* New Delhi: Government of India.

Ministry of Information and Broadcasting. (2000). *India 2000: A reference annual.* New Delhi: Publication Division.

Ministry of Information and Broadcasting. (2004). *India 2004: A reference annual.* New Delhi: Publication Division.

Ministry of Law Justice and Company Affairs. (1996). *The Persons with Disabilities (Equal Opportunities, Protection of Rights and Full Participation) Act, 1995.* New Delhi: Government of India.

Ministry of Law Justice and Company Affairs. (1999). *The National Trust for the Welfare of Persons with Autism, Cerebral Palsy, Mental Retardation and Multiple Disabilities Act.* New Delhi: Government of India.

Ministry of Social Justice and Empowerment. (2006). *National policy for persons with disabilities.* New Delhi: Government of India.

Misra, A. (2000). Special education in India. In C. R. Reynolds & E. Fletcher-Janzen (Eds.), *Encyclopedia of special education* (pp. 86–97). New York, NY: Wiley.

NCERT. (2000, July 4–5). *UNESCO-NCERT need assessment workshop for Asia Pacific region.* International Centre for Special Needs Education. Department of Education of Groups with Special Needs, National Council of Educational Research and Training, New Delhi.

Panda, K. C. (1996). Research in special education. *Indian Educational Review, 31*(2), 1–15.

Pandey, R. S., & Advani, L. (1997). *Perspectives in disability and rehabilitation.* New Delhi: Vikas Publishing House Pvt. Ltd.

Pinto, P. E., & Sahur, N. (2001). *Working with people with disabilities: An Indian perspective.* Center for International Rehabilitation Research Information & Exchange. Retrieved from http://cirrie.buffalo.edu/culture/monographs/india/#copyright. Accessed on January 19, 2014.

Puri, M., & Abraham, G. (2004). *Handbook of inclusive education for educators, administrators, and planners.* New Delhi: Sage.

Rane, A. (1983). *An evaluation of the scheme of integrated education for handicapped children based on a study of the working of scheme in Maharashtra.* Mumbai: Unit for Child and Youth Research, Tata Institute of Social Sciences.

Rao, I. (2000). *A comparative study of UN rules and Indian disability act 1995.* Retrieved from cbrnet@vsnl.com. Accessed on March 17.

Rehabilitation Council of India (RCI). (2000). *Status of disability.* New Delhi: Rehabilitation Council of India.

Shah, R. (2005). *Concerns of Indian educators in integrated education.* Unpublished doctoral dissertation, University of Pune.

Shah, R., Das, A. K., Desai, I. P., & Tiwari, A. (2014). Teachers' concerns about inclusive education in Ahmedabad, India. *Journal of Research in Special Educational Needs.* doi:10.1111/1471-3802.12054

Singal, N. (2005). Mapping the field of inclusive education: A review of the Indian literature. *International Journal of Inclusive Education, 9*(4), 331–350.

Singal, N., & Rouse, M. (2003). "We do inclusion": Practitioner perspectives in some "inclusive schools" in India. *Perspectives in Education, Special Issue: The Inclusion/Exclusion Debate in South Africa and Developing Countries, 21*(3), 85–98.

The Hindu. (2013). *Report says enrolment of disabled children in govt. schools under 1%. The Hindu.* Retrieved from http://www.thehindu.com/news/national/report-says-enrolment-of-disabled-children-in-govt-schools-under-1/article5519483.ece. Accessed on January 4, 2014.

The Telegraph. (2013). India has one third of world's poorest, says World Bank. *The Telegraph*. Retrieved from http://www.telegraph.co.uk/news/worldnews/asia/india/10003228/India-has-one-third-of-worlds-poorest-says-World-Bank.html. Accessed on January 20, 2014.

UNICEF. (2000). Examples of inclusive education India. The United Nations Children's Fund Regional Office for South Asia, 2003.

World Bank. (1997). *World development report*. New York, NY: Oxford University Press.

SPECIAL EDUCATION TODAY IN BANGLADESH

Md. Saiful Malak

ABSTRACT

This chapter provides a comprehensive description of special education in Bangladesh. It begins with the early origins of special education and then proceeds with definitions of and prevalence of current disabilities in Bangladesh. This section is followed by governmental policies and legislation related to the right to education for all students with disabilities. Next, educational intervention methods are delineated along with a description of governmental special schools and teacher training and preparation of special educational professions. Early intervention practices and working with families is also discussed. The chapter ends with the progress that Bangladesh has made and the challenges that remain.

INTRODUCTION

As one of the most densely populated countries of the world, Bangladesh is distinct in terms of its language liberation, religious values, and customs. With a population of over 164 million, this country has made significant

Special Education International Perspectives: Practices Across the Globe
Advances in Special Education, Volume 28, 583–620
ISSN: 0270-4013/doi:10.1108/S0270-401320140000028026

progress toward achieving the Education for All (EFA) goals during the
past decade (World Bank, 2008). The net enrollment rate at primary level
has increased from 87.2% in 2005 to 98.7% in 2012 (Directorate of
Primary Education [DPE], 2012). The gross and net enrollment rates are
increasing steadily (Miles, Fefoame, Mulligan, & Haque, 2012). However,
the perspective of education for students with disabilities provides a different story. Only 4% of an estimated 1.6 million school-going age children
with disabilities attend a range of schools including nonformal, special,
integrated, and inclusive settings (Disability Rights Watch Group
Bangladesh, 2009, p. 4). Interestingly, the literature suggests that
Bangladesh has enacted a good number of policies and legislation regarding educational placement of children with disabilities (Ahsan & Burnip,
2007; Ahsan & Mullick, 2013). Moreover this country is a signatory of
world's most prominent treaties including United Nations Conventions on
the Rights of Persons with Disabilities — 2006 (Ahsan, Sharma, &
Deppeler, 2012) in which education of children with disabilities is to be
implemented through inclusive education. Therefore, it is necessary to
understand the situation of children with disabilities that might be a concern to the Department of Education in Bangladesh. Based on descriptive
review, this chapter critically analyzes the development, progress, and challenges of special education in the context of Bangladesh. More importantly,
it explores the prospects of inclusion of students with disabilities into
regular education.

ORIGIN OF SPECIAL EDUCATION IN BANGLADESH

The origin of special education in Bangladesh seems to have been limited
to the discipline of psychology. As a separate discipline, psychology was
taught in very few institutes during the 1960s. A group of psychologists
formed Bangladesh Psychological Association (BPA) in 1970. Gradually, a
wing of BPA started growing interest in clinical psychology which turned
into Bangladesh Mental Health Association in early 1980s. During
1970s—1980s, Professor Sultana Sarwatara Zaman with her dynamic initiative formed an organization named Society for the Care and Education of
the Mentally Retarded — Bangladesh (SCEMRB), for the welfare of children and young adults with mental retardation. The organization comprised of a group of professionals, social workers, and parents of mentally
retarded children, when most of the people of this country had diminutive

knowledge and concept about social and educational aspects for this segment of population. With the advent of time, the terminology to address children with mental retardation have revolutionized that led later to rename the organization as the Society for the Welfare of Intellectually Disabled — Bangladesh (SWID-BD). Presently, SWID has approximately 51 branches all over Bangladesh (Rahman, 2011).

As a pioneer in the arena of special education, Professor Zaman devoted a lot of time and contribution to uphold the status of children with intellectual disability through raising mass awareness on disability, when there were misconceptions and superstitions about disability issues among most of the communities in Bangladesh (Kibria, 2005; Miles & Hossain, 1999). With time this self-motivated professor along with her associates has realized the necessity to expand her activities in a broader perspective. These expansions led the way to establish a similar organization with new innovations (Zaman & Munir, 1992). Giving emphasis on teacher preparation and research on special education, Professor Zaman established the "Bangladesh Protibondhi (disabled) Foundation (BPF)" in 1984 (Zaman & Munir, 1992) through which she continued her interest on the care, education, and research for children and young adults with intellectual disability in Bangladesh. Her continuous interest, advocacy, and work on teacher development helped develop courses and degree programs for special education teachers (Rahman, 2011). In the early 1990s, the Institute of Education and Research (IER) at the University of Dhaka revised its teacher education curriculum and established the Department of Special Education within the preview of the institute. A number of degrees in special education, including Diploma in Education (Dip-in-Ed), Bachelor of Education (BEd)-Honors, and Master of Education (MEd) with specialization in intellectual disability, hearing impairment, and visual impairment were started at the University of Dhaka. Further, after the establishment of the Department of Special Education, the scope of conducting small scale research on special education and disability studies was formally created at the University of Dhaka. As a result, various research works and psychological assessment services in the late 1990s led to the development of psychometric assessment tools and technologies in the context of Bangladesh (Rahman, 2011).

The decades of 1990s and 2000s were remarkable in the field of special education in the context of Bangladesh (Miles et al., 2012) for several reasons. First, the establishment of the Department of Special Education had created the opportunity for prospective teachers to be skilled in teaching children with disabilities. A good number of people, mostly parents of children with disabilities, showed their interests in opening special schools. Accordingly, several special schools were established in city areas and parental interests on sending their children with disabilities to special schools significantly increased. During the mid-1990s, several pressure groups (e.g., Parent Association, Special Teacher Association) were formed and special education had widely been recognized in the nongovernment sector in Bangladesh. Second, the growing interest of special education in nongovernment organizations (NGOs) had gradually been recognized by the Government of Bangladesh (GoB) and a National Policy on Disability was formed in 1995. This policy was the first initiative by GoB on disability in the context of Bangladesh. Since 1995, various pressure groups were involved in advocacy with different levels of GoB toward getting a complete legislation regarding persons with disabilities. Finally, in 2001, the people of Bangladesh received their first legislation entitled "Bangladesh Persons with Disability Act, 2001." As a result, education for children with disabilities has become obligatory to the GoB and special education has been included in the government's reform agendas.

DEFINITION OF DISABILITY

There are variations in terminologies used in the area of disability among academics, human right activists, NGO professionals, and government officials working on disability issues. According to Bangladesh Persons with Disability Act, 2001 (Ministry of Social Welfare [MoSW], 2001), "disability" is defined by the GoB as follows:

> Disability means any person who is physically crippled either congenitally or as result of disease or being a victim of accident, or due to improper or maltreatment or for any other reasons became physically incapacitated or mentally imbalanced, and as a result of such crippledness or mental impairedness, has become incapacitated, either partially or fully; and is unable to lead a normal life. (MoSW, 2001, p. 5)

Over the past decade, this definition has widely been criticized by academics and human right activists as they tend to view that disability has been seen through the lens of Medical Model (e.g., see Kibria, 2005; Šiška & Habib, 2013). Although the majority of the stakeholders, including social workers, academics, human right activists, and the persons with disabilities themselves are more likely to consider disability from the perspective Social Model, their consideration seems to have little impact on the GoB's initiatives regarding disability (National Forum of Organizations Working with

Disabled [NFOWD], 2009). Various pressure groups, in collaboration with NFOWD, continued to work with the GoB with an intention to revise the Bangladesh Persons with Disability Welfare (BPDW) Act, 2001. Consequently after a decade a relatively more comprehensive definition of disability with its various types has been provided by the GoB through the most recent legislation called "Rights and Protection of Persons with Disabilities Act, 2013" (MoSW, 2013). Under this Act, disability is defined as follows which seems to capture more social aspects than medical condition:

> "Disability" means any person who, by any reason acquires long-term or short term physical, mental, developmental or sensory problem that might create a negative attitude and environmental barrier for that individual and which can lead an individual not to achieve his equal rights to have an independent and effective participation in the society. (MoSW, 2013, p. 3)

TYPES OF DISABILITY

There has been a little change in the types of disability between 2001 and 2013 (Table 1). Autism and deaf-blindness have been added, cerebral palsy has been separated from physical impairment, and a distinction between mental illness and intellectual disability has been established through the Rights and Protection of Persons with Disabilities Act, 2013.

Table 1. Types of Person with Disabilities.

2001: Bangladesh Persons with Disability Welfare Act	2013: Rights and Protection of Persons with Disabilities Act
—	Autism
Physical handicap	Physical disability
—	Mental illness leading to disability
Visual impairment	Visual disability
Speech impairment	Speech disability
Mental disability	Intellectual disability
Hearing impairment	Hearing disability
—	Deaf-blindness
—	Cerebral palsy
Multiple disabilities	Multiple disabilities

PREVALENCE OF DISABILITY

Over the past several decades, the prevalence of persons with special needs in Bangladesh has been an issue of debate due to lack of national statistics. The Bangladesh Bureau of statistics (BBS) is the only responsible organization to provide national data about the population of Bangladesh. It runs the national census called population and housing census (PHC) every decade. There is no provision of gathering data nationally about the population rather than the PHC. Persons with disabilities had always been ignored during the first, second, and third censuses which took place in 1974 (could not take place in 1971 due to liberation war), 1981, and 1991 respectively. The disability population issue was planned to be addressed for the first time in the 4th census in 2001. However, the result created a huge contradiction about the number of persons with disability identified. Persons with disabilities counted in the 4th census were 0.6% of the total population (National Foundation of Disabled Development (NFDD), 2013, p. 105) which seems to be a faulty estimation.

The national census scheduled in the early part of 2011 was planned to address the above issue in a detailed manner. This census was supposed to give the GoB a detailed statistics on persons with disabilities, disaggregated by: the 14 types of disability; age; gender; ethnic origin; and urban/rural strata. It was anticipated that this census would give an opportunity to address further statistics on their progress toward accessing rights issues.

Organizations working for persons with disabilities have rejected the findings of the 5th PHC-2011, saying that it undercounted the people belonging to this group. According to the census findings launched, 1.4% of the total population belongs to people with disabilities. The number of people with disabilities has been cited as 2,016,612 (NFDD, 2013, p. 105) which was far below the 2011 estimation of Household Income Expenditure Survey of the BBS that reported people with disability at 9.07% (BBS, 2011). It is widely claimed that the questionnaires used for the census could only identify those individuals who had severe disabilities that were visible to all. Most recently, Action AID Bangladesh (AAB) conducted a number of baseline surveys in various locations in Bangladesh. Based on AAB, Ahsan (2013, p. 3) reported that the overall prevalence rates of disability is around 14.4%. Even through there is no accurate statistics on the number of children and adults with disabilities in Bangladesh, most people rely on the data found in various sources that suggest that 10% of the people in Bangladesh have disabilities (United Nations, 2006; World Health Organization [WHO], 2006).

Disability Type and Prevalence

Since there is no reliable national data of persons with disabilities in Bangladesh, the prevalence of disability according to type is less likely to be shown. However, within the context of Bangladesh, there a number of sources which could provide an impression about how the prevalence would look like based on the type of disability. For example, a study jointly conducted by the DPE and Center for Services and Information on Disability (CSID) (2002) to explore the education status of children with disabilities in 12 districts in 6 divisions of Bangladesh collected data from 360 children with disabilities. This study reported that among the participants the majority (50%) had physical disability which was followed by speech and hearing impairment (16%), intellectual disability (13%), visual impairment (9%), multiple disabilities (9%), and other (3%) developmental disabilities (Fig. 1).

Japan International Cooperation Agency (JICA, 2002) conducted a study on 2,559,222 children with disabilities aged between 3 and 10 years. This study reported that physical disabilities showed the highest incidence (41.5%) followed by visual impairments (19.7%), speech and hearing impairment (19.6%), intellectual disabilities (7.4%), cerebral palsy (7%), multiple disabilities (3.4%), and mental illness (1.4%) (JICA, 2002, p. 47). Lastly, a recent Primary School Census 2010 conducted by the DPE (2011) identified 83,023 children having disabilities. The census also showed that the type of children with disabilities enrolled in primary education are visually impaired (12,455), hearing impaired (5,541), intellectually

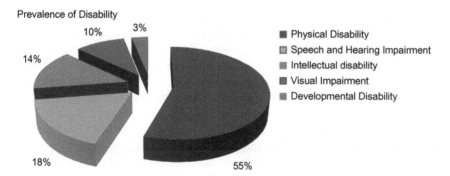

Fig. 1. Prevalence According to Type of Disability.

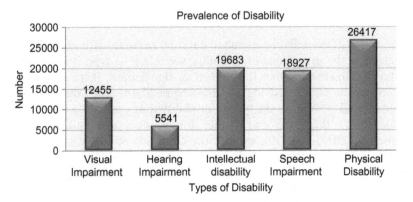

Fig. 2. Disability Prevalence in Primary Education.

challenged (19,683), speech problem (18,927), and physically challenged (26,417) (Fig. 2).

This is important to note none of the studies mentioned above included children with autism as separate type of disability although it is said that there has been a significant increase in the number of children with autism in recent years in Bangladesh.

POLICY AND LEGISLATION

During the past three decades, disability has been treated as a charitable issue in Bangladesh. The Department of Education, which comprises the Ministry of Primary and Mass Education (MoPME) and Ministry of Education (MoE), is responsible to provide education for all children across the country. However, "the education of children with disabilities, as well as issues related to disability, is under the purview of the MoSW, and thus looked upon as a charity or welfare, not as a human rights issue" (Munir & Zaman, 2009, p. 292). Therefore, the right of persons with disabilities in Bangladesh seems to remain segregated from mainstream policy though it is protected by the constitution.

The need for education for all children, regardless of any special circumstances, has been echoed from the birth of this country through its constitution in 1972. Articles 17 and 28 of the constitution clearly articulated how the state should provide education to all children without making any discrimination.

[Article 28 (3)]: No citizen shall, on grounds only of religion, race, caste, sex or place of birth be subjected to any disability, liability, restriction or condition with regard to access to any place of public entertainment or resort, or admission to any educational institution. (Ministry of Law Justice and Parliamentary Affairs [MoLJPA], 2000, p. 5)

[Article 17 (a)] ... establishing a uniform, mass oriented and universal system of education and extending free and compulsory education to all children to such stage as may be determined by law. (MoLJPA, 2000, p. 8)

Despite the strong constitutional ground, lack of knowledge and awareness regarding disability remains one of key challenges to enacting a complete legislation for persons with disabilities in Bangladesh. As mentioned earlier, there is a large group of NGOs working for persons with disabilities across the country. NFOWD, claiming to be the parent organization of those NGOs, is considered as one of the vital advocacy groups providing the government with comprehensive guidelines necessary for persons with disabilities (Miles et al., 2012).

Working in collaboration with the government, local NGOs, and academic groups (University academics and researchers), NFOWD and other organizations have prioritized efforts to promote persons with disabilities through various activities including organizing national seminars and symposiums, celebrating National and International Days for persons with disabilities, and providing legislative support for persons with disabilities. Due to increasing exposer and supports of various advocacy groups to the government, the GoB has enacted the very first policy called the "National Policy on Persons with Disabilities" in 1995. Since 1995, there has been an increased emphasis on enacting a comprehensive legislation for persons with disabilities. Additionally, over the past 20 years, Bangladesh has been keen to show positive attitudes toward various international declarations, conventions, and commitments regarding persons with disabilities. Like many other countries around the world, Bangladesh has agreed with the declaration of *Education for All* (*EFA*) (UNESCO, 1990), *the Salamanca Statement and Framework for Action on Special Needs Education* (UNESCO, 1994), and *the Dakar Framework for Action* (UNESCO, 2000). Agreeing with all the international treaties, Bangladesh has committed to address education for children with disabilities within the existing education system.

After three decades of continuous advocacy of various pressure groups and significant influence of several international treaties, the GoB enacted its first legislation regarding persons with disabilities in 2001. Although there were numerous gaps in terms of terminologies and definitions of the BPDW Act, 2001, it has opened the door of establishing rights of persons with disabilities in the context of Bangladesh. The following section describes major policies and legislation regarding persons with disabilities enacted in Bangladesh.

Bangladesh Persons with Disability Welfare Act, 2001

BPDW Act covers different aspects of persons with disabilities including definition, education, health care, employment, transport facilities, social security, and so on. Particularly, in education, this Act has been recognized as the very first initiative to ensure education as a legislative right for children with disabilities. The Act postulates:

> Create opportunities for free education to all children with disabilities below 18 years of age and provides them books and equipment free of cost or at low-cost (Part D: 2). (MoSW, 2001)

In the third section, the Act calls for creating opportunity for the children with disability to study in the mainstream education.

> Endeavor to create opportunities for integration of students with disabilities in the usual class-set-up of regular normal schools wherever possible. (MoSW, 2001, p. 12)

Despite having several important guidelines for students with disabilities, the Act itself can be considered as a barrier to inclusive education. First of all, this Act seems to lean on the medical model of disability (Šiška & Habib, 2013). For example, the definition of a person with disabilities is articulated on the basis of clinical feature of the individual. For instance, a person with visual impairment is referred to as "No vision in any single eye or in both eyes, or visual acuity not exceeding 6/60 or 20/200 ..." (MoSW, 2001, p. 5).

Also, Part D (1) of this Act suggests segregated education for children with disabilities

> ... establishment of Specialized Education Institutions to cater to the special needs of the special categories of children with disabilities, to design and develop specialized curriculum and write special text books and to introduce Special Examination System, if situations so demand. (MoSW, 2001, p. 11)

Since the Act has been enacted from medical and charity point of view, it remains weak to articulate equal educational setting for the children with disabilities. It is also noted that this Act has been initiated by the MoSW instead of MoE or Law Justice and Parliamentary Affairs. It implies that disability has been perceived as charity by policy makers (Šiška & Habib, 2013). It can be argued that due to the welfare attitudes toward disability, the education of students with disabilities have not been considered as a right. As a result, inclusive education has not been stated clearly through this Act.

National Education Policy (NEP) 2010

The NEP 2010 (MoE, 2010) was formally approved by the Parliament of Bangladesh in December 2010. It is worthy to mention that NEP 2010 was revised, modified, and finalized from the very first version available in 2000. This policy is another official commitment of the government toward inclusive education. In its foreword, the Minister of Education underscored that ensuring quality education for all children is a fundamental issue (MoE, 2010, p. vi). The NEP 2010 calls for every child to be educated. The NEP highlights the education for diverse learners within its main objectives as follows:

> 07: Eliminate discriminations on grounds of nationality, religion, class and gender; build up an environment that promotes secularism, global-brotherhood, and empathy towards humanity and respect towards human rights.
>
> 22: Bringing all socio-economically disadvantaged children into education including street-children.
>
> 24: Ensuring the rights of all children with disabilities.
>
> MoE, 2010, pp. 1–2

Further, a number of statements described in the NEP 2010 documents relate to quality and inclusive education facets. Table 2 displays the summary of major statements relevant to learners with disabilities for both primary and secondary education sectors.

Despite the fact that the NEP 2010 has mainstreamed the educational rights of children with disabilities, it is likely to create a debate among people working for children with disabilities as none of the policy statements directly uses the term inclusion or inclusive education. Critical analysis of the policy statements suggests that most of the statements are broad and often unclear in indicating specific meaning. The policy comprises a number of sections that underpin education for all children, but it is not clarified in the policy whether children with disabilities will get access to the same school with their regular peers. Instead, in some statements, "special

Table 2.   Key Statements of National Education Policy 2010
Regarding Disability.

Chapter	Themes	Summary of Key Policy Statements
2	Preprimary and Primary Education	Ensure equal opportunities for all kinds of disabled and underprivileged children
4	Secondary Education	Alleviate discriminations among various socioeconomic, ethnic, and socially disadvantaged children
18	Education for challenged learners (special education)	• Include handicapped students in the mainstream education • Provide special education to acutely handicapped children with physical or mental disability
24	Teachers' Training	• Increase teachers' efficiency in using strategies for educational innovation • Encourage teachers to teach all students irrespective of religion, race, and socioeconomic conditions maintaining equal opportunities • Assist teachers to acquire efficiency to deliver lessons to students from disadvantaged and ethnic community and disabled learners by considering their special (learning) needs

Note: The statements are summarized in case of very long sentences.

education provision" is suggested for the education of the children with special needs. For example, section 18 (7) states – "Separate schools will be established according to special needs and in view of the differential nature of disabilities of the challenged children" (MoE, 2010, p. 43). Some vocabularies clearly contradict with the philosophy of inclusion. For example, in Chapter 18, the words "handicapped," "dumb," etc. are used to describe the children with special needs. This reflects an attitude (of policy makers) that is aligned with segregation rather than inclusion. This is rather contradictory to the notion of inclusive education. Therefore, education reform based on policy statements such as the above may reduce the effective implementation of inclusion at the school level of Bangladesh.

Rights and Protection of Persons with Disabilities Act, 2013

Since 2001, there has been increased emphasis on the revision of the Bangladesh Persons with Disability Welfare Act. Consequently the Rights and Protection of Persons with Disabilities Act, 2013 was enacted as a revised version of the previous Act. Various important sections under the present Act seem to be more comprehensive in terms of definition, clarification, and implementation guideline. A summary of this Act is presented in Table 3.

One of the significant aspects of this Act is that it clearly states that children with disabilities cannot be denied from their enrollment in regular schools (MoSW, 2013). In Article 15, this Act provides a clear description on how people can be aware of the ability and potential of persons with disabilities. It states that "In order to develop positive attitudes towards persons with disabilities from childhood, relevant contents about children with disabilities should be included in the curriculum of all levels of education" (MoSW, 2013, p. 10).

It is claimed that Bangladesh has undertaken a good number of policy initiatives to provide equity and access to education for all children (Ahsan & Burnip, 2007). However, it is important to note that the trend of enacting inclusive (IE) policy and legislation in Bangladesh is mainly based upon the international treaties (Malak, Begum, Habib, Banu, & Roshid,

Table 3. Key Information of Rights and Protection of Persons with Disabilities Act, 2013.

Article	Themes	Summary of Key Policy Statements
1	Detection	• Conduct national survey for collecting data about persons with disabilities • Include necessary instrument in all national level surveys including human census for identification of persons with disabilities • Develop a national database on persons with disabilities
5	Accessibility	Use IT for making textbooks prepared by the National Curriculum and Textbook Board (NCTB) accessible for children with disabilities
9	Education and training	• Provide flexibility in admission to children with disabilities regarding their age • Ensure reasonable accommodation and joyful environment for children with disabilities in order to facilitate inclusive education for all children • Take necessary steps to integrate specialized educational institutes with regular schools
12	Freedom from violence, access to justice, and legal aid	Protect persons with disabilities from any kinds of abuse and violence and provide them with administrative, legal, social, educational, and other necessary support

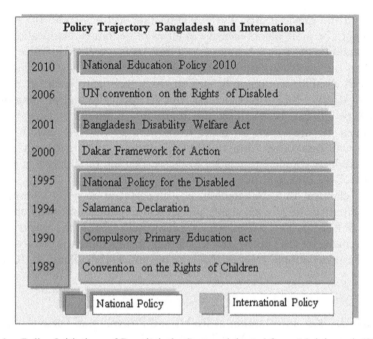

Fig. 3.   Policy Initiatives of Bangladesh. *Source*: Adapted from Malak et al. (2014).

2014). Fig. 3 shows how Bangladesh government endorsed disability-related policy and legislation soon after signing an international treaty.

Fig. 3 shows that IE initiatives in Bangladesh have been embedded in different policy and legislations, including Compulsory Primary Education Act, 1990;National Education Policy for the Disabled, 1995; BPDW Act, 2001; and NEP, 2010.

EDUCATIONAL INTERVENTIONS

Over the period of 1970s–1990s, students with disabilities were segregated from the mainstream education in Bangladesh as disability issues seemed to be less focused on government's main reform agendas. Special schools, though inadequate in number, were the only option for educating students with disabilities. However, in recent years, Bangladesh has become a cosigner of all international treaties regarding education and disabilities such as the Education for All declaration (UNESCO, 1990), the Salamanca Statement and Framework for Action on Special Needs Education (UNESCO, 1994), the Dakar Framework for Action (UNESCO, 2000), and the UN Convention on the Rights of Persons with Disabilities, 2006 in which education for children with disabilities is likely to be provided through an inclusive framework. As a result, inclusive education has been an area of focus for both government and nongovernment agencies.

During the past decade, the GoB has been keen to practice inclusive education through undertaking various programs. Two major programs namely Primary Education Development Program (PEDP) and Teaching Quality Improvement in Secondary Education (TQI-SEP) are considered to be the most important interventions to implement inclusive education in regular schools. The following section describes how inclusive education has been practiced in educational settings through these programs.

Primary Education Development Program

PEDP is an umbrella program of Bangladesh government to enhance primary education. The first program (1997−2003) focused on the gross enrollment rate in primary education. However, the second program (2004−2011) incorporated a specific component on inclusive education to address diversity in the regular school system. The inclusive education component included four specific target groups: gender, children with disabilities, children from ethnic background, and children from vulnerable group (e.g., slum children, refugee children, street children, orphans, children from ultra-poor families) to bring them into regular classrooms. The second PEDP was a massive training program for teachers, head teachers, and local education administrators on inclusive education.

Studies indicated that the second PEDP made important strides forward in terms of inclusion of students with disabilities during its early years (Ahuja & Ibrahim, 2006; Nasreen & Tate, 2007). Under the second PEDP, a formal declaration was made by the DPE that students with disabilities would not be denied enrollment from regular school. This declaration was the first government initiative to provisionally ensure the admission of students with disabilities in regular schools. BANBEIS (2011) has documented the enrollment figures of children with disabilities for six consecutive years (from 2005 to 2010) (see Fig. 4). The figure clearly shows that the number of enrolled children with disabilities has nearly doubled in a five-year duration.

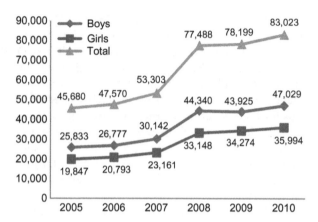

Fig. 4. Trend in Enrollment of Children with Disability at Primary Level.

The baseline survey conducted in 2005 revealed that 45,680 children with disabilities were accommodated in primary schools and among them a significant number of students were with intellectual disabilities (PEDP Completion Report, 2011; DPE, 2011). The enrollment of special needs children increased by 5% each year (DPE, 2010). However, the exact number of school-aged children with disabilities has not been reported yet. While Fig. 4 shows an increased trend in children with disabilities enrollment, the proportion of the total enrollment number of school-aged children with disabilities could not be computed due to the noted gap absences.

The second PEDP provided improved basic education to children in remote areas, and infrastructure facilities (e.g., by providing ramps, modifying classroom furniture to increase the access for children having disabilities). However, recent studies report that infrastructural development has not been reached its set target (DPE, 2012) and teachers have demonstrated disappointments on inadequate classroom facilities for practicing inclusive education (Malak, 2013a).

In addition to improving infrastructure, the role of SMC is consistently suggested as a major support for implementing inclusive education at schools. However, though it is claimed that massive training has been provided by the second PEDP, studies (Malak, 2013b; Mullick, Deppeler, & Sharma, 2012) found that due to the lack of awareness of teachers and school administrators regarding disability, the implementation of inclusive education is facing numerous challenges. In order to address the challenges PEDP has been extended for the third time in 2011. One of the important aims of the third PEDP is to ensure inclusive education practice through empowering school community.

Teaching Quality Improvement in Secondary Education

In order to enhance quality of secondary education, the GoB has undertaken a number of initiatives. TQI-SEP (Directorate of Secondary and Higher Education (DSHE), 2005) was one of the initiatives to address the equity, inclusion, and quality aspects in the secondary education of Bangladesh. This project was jointly funded by the GoB, Asian Development Bank (ADB), and the Canadian International Development Agency (CIDA). It was formally launched in 2005 and closed in 2012. The DSHE worked as the implementing agency (Project Management Unit) under the purview of the MoE along with the project's two partner organizations, namely, the National University and the National Academy for Educational Management (NAEM).

Improving teacher training facilities, strengthening in-service and preservice teacher training, and increasing equitable access and improving community involvement were the key areas of intervention under TQI-SEP (DSHE, 2005). As part of the broader goal of achieving quality secondary education in Bangladesh, the project adopted substantial measures for the implementation of inclusive education. The main goal of the project was strengthening the provisions/opportunities for equitable access of all eligible children (with primary completion) in the secondary classrooms and underpinning their participation in all relevant activities within the school or classroom setting. In believing that teachers play the most important role in enhancing students' learning (ADB, 2004), the project involved strategic planning for teachers to assist them in the development of necessary knowledge and inclusive teaching practices skills that would empower them to create a learner-friendly environment which in turn would allow effective learning for all children regardless of disability, gender, geographical location, and ethnicity (DSHE, 2007).

The above project's philosophy was that teacher professional learning was seen as a comprehensive part of a total inclusive environment. In addition to professional learning opportunities, the project plan included a range of supportive activities to enhance the implementation of inclusive education in a real classroom setting. These supporting activities included the following: improving the physical facilities (to remove the barrier to physical movement), modifying teachers' education curriculum, and introducing continuous professional development (CPD). The project's activities not only strengthened the classroom teacher's skills but enhanced the provisions for inclusive practice.

A number of reform activities were undertaken in TQI-SEP to enhance inclusive practice in the secondary education sector. The major activities of this project included: strengthening school capacity to provide effective learning environment for all children including children with disabilities; inclusive education awareness raising program for head teachers and members of school management committee; awareness raising program for district level officers (District Education Officers, DEO); inclusive education orientation program for teacher educators from Teacher Training Colleges (TTCs) and relevant NGO representatives and professional development programs for secondary in-service teachers. Under TQI-SEP numerous teacher training activities have been performed. Malak et al. (2014) reported that 195,000 teachers have taken the first CPD program which comprised a series of three programs to use participatory and inclusive approaches in the classroom, instead of rote learning. Included in the above teacher training program where 1,650 teachers from three outreach districts.

Despite the above adequate teacher training initiatives, TQI-SEP has been criticized as having little impact of training activities in real settings. Studies by Khan (2012) and Rahaman and Sutherland (2012) demonstrated that secondary teachers in Bangladesh have shown inadequate understanding and a variety of interpretations of the IE concept. According to Khan, teachers' understanding IE is fairly vague and broader rather than focused and specific. As a result, Rahman and Sutherland indicated that teachers do not adequately take the responsibility of facilitating learning for all students including those with disabilities. Khan considered insufficient teacher professional learning opportunities as a dominant negative issue in ways to implement IE at the secondary level. Furthermore, the literature suggests that the lack of good quality professional development is a significant barrier for empowering secondary teachers with inclusive instructional knowledge and skills in Bangladesh (Malak et al., 2014). Evidence suggests that engaging classroom teachers in high quality professional development is an inherent aspect for the effectiveness of inclusive practices (OECD, 2005).

Thus, the TQI-SEP professional development activities have created some awareness or enthusiasm about inclusion among the secondary teachers. However, the practice of inclusion in teachers' classroom instruction is far from completion. Because of this, the first TQI-SEP was extended for another five years in 2012. A major component will be to address inclusive education and gender friendly environment in secondary education classrooms.

Generally, students with disabilities have little access to regular schooling in developing countries. The literature suggests that there is only 1 or 2% of students with disabilities that go to regular schools in South Asian countries (USAID, 2005). Unexceptionally in Bangladesh, access of students with disabilities to regular schooling is negligible. Although the above mentioned interventions, PEDP and TQI-SEP, seem to be an influential effort from the GoB to facilitate inclusive education, it is likely that the majority of students with disabilities are still segregated from nondisabled peers in regular schools. As a result, special education is predominant for children with disabilities in Bangladesh. The following section describes how students with various types of disabilities are taught in the context of Bangladesh:

Special Schools Run by the Government of Bangladesh

Opportunity to attend a special government school for children with disabilities is extremely limited in Bangladesh (USAID, 2005). If fact, there are only 13 government managed special schools in Bangladesh. The schools are for four categories of children with disabilities, namely, visual impairment, hearing impairment, intellectual disability, and autism (NFDD, 2013). The following sections describe these special categorical schools.

Schools for Students with Visual Impairment

There are four schools for students with visual impairment at the primary level with a capacity to serve 500 students. The schools are located in four geographic regions, namely, Dhaka, Rajshahi, Khulna, and Chittagong. Of the total number of students, 180 students are provided residential facilities.

There are 64 government-funded integrated secondary schools for students with visual impairment in 64 districts. A resource teacher, trained in visual impairment, is appointed in every integrated school. While the function of these integrated schools is thoroughly described in government documents, the reality of their functions is unclear.

Schools for Students with Hearing Impairment

There are seven government-sponsored special schools for students with hearing impairment. These schools have a capacity to facilitate special schooling for 700 students of which 180 students receive residential facilities.

Schools for Students with Intellectual Disability

Access of children with intellectual disability to schooling is extremely limited. There is no government school for these children. However, due to continuous advocacy of several NGOs working with children with intellectual disabilities, including the SWID-Bangladesh and BPF, the MoSW introduced an Integrated Special Education Policy, 2009 for providing educational access to children with intellectual disabilities. Under this policy, 48 special schools of SWID-Bangladesh and 7 inclusive schools of BPF have been receiving government fund for their teachers since 2010. A total of 463 teachers from SWID-Bangladesh and 75 teachers from BPF are receiving 100% of their salary on behalf of the government through the MoSW (NFDD, 2013).

Schools for Children with Autism

Autism as a separate category disability has been recognized very recently in the context of Bangladesh. In July 2011, Autism Speaks (an NGO), in collaboration with the GoB and World Health Organization, organized an International Conference on Autism and Developmental Disabilities in Dhaka where over 1,000 delegates from 11 countries attended. This conference has had a huge impact on both government and nongovernment agencies working with disabilities. Consequently, the MoSW, under the NFDD has introduced a resource center for children with autism which provides special education, therapy and referral services, and counseling to autistic children and their parents. A group of experts consisting of psychologist, occupational therapist, and speech and language therapist are working in this center (NFDD, 2013).

Under the patronization of the MoSW, the NFDD has opened the Autistic School in 2011. Autistic children of poor families are entitled to study in this special school free of cost. A group of specially trained teachers have been imparting special education in this school. This government-sponsored school can provide special schooling for up to 50 children with autism (NFDD, 2013).

Schools for Children with Physical Disabilities

There are no specially designed educational services for children who are physically challenged. There are several reasons behind this, including inaccessible buildings, lack of appropriate handicapped toilet facilities, mobility aids such as crutches and wheelchairs, and appropriate curriculum and instructional materials (USAID, 2005).

EDUCATIONAL FACILITIES PROVIDED BY LOCAL NGOs

It is worthwhile to note that apart from the above mentioned government facilities, a good number of NGOs have been working with children with disabilities in Bangladesh. A contemporary report of MoSW shows that there are more than 600 NGOs that work with children with disabilities in 64 districts (MoSW, 2012, p. 78). These NGOs are providing education for children with disabilities in various forms including special education, integrated education, and inclusive education. A few of the reputed NGOs working in the area of education for children with disabilities in Bangladesh include the following: *HI-CARE* provides primary and secondary education for children with hearing impairment and preschooling for 2 to 5-year-old children; *The Baptist Sangha Blind School*, which was established in 1977, works in 64 districts through a variety of activities including vocational training for children with visual impairment, integrated education, computerized Braille book production, residential facilities are available for visually impaired girls and a source of technical assistance for orientation and mobility, Braille translators, special teaching techniques, and vocational training for students with visual impairment; *The Bangladesh Protibondhi Foundation (BPF)*, which was established in 1984, serves children with intellectual disability and children with neurological damage (e.g., cerebral palsy) in eight urban poor subdistricts and runs a special school for children with intellectual disability while providing variety of screening and diagnosis services for young children; *The Center for Rehabilitation of the Paralyzed (CRP)* is widely recognized as a pioneer organization for rehabilitation of persons with physical disability in Bangladesh which runs an inclusive school, established in 1993 mainly for children with cerebral palsy. It also provides training for special education teachers and community-based rehabilitation (CBR) workers; *Autism Welfare Foundation* (*AWF*) is a relatively new NGO founded by a mother of an autistic child, which serves children aged 3–15 years with home-based educational intervention for children and supports high-functioning children who are in mainstream education programs; *Bangladesh Rural Advancement Committee* (*BRAC*) operates 35,000 schools in Bangladesh and provides basic education to young learners through its education pro-gram (World Bank, 2008). Recently, BRAC has started including three children with disabilities in each of its existing schools (Mahbub, 2008). Lastly, there are a number of international organizations which have been playing key roles in Bangladesh to facilitate schooling for children with disabilities such as Plan, Sight Severs, and Action-Aid.

USE OF TECHNOLOGY FOR STUDENTS WITH DISABILITIES

The use of appropriate technology in education could have enormous impact on the learning of children with disabilities. While a variety of assis-tive and educational technologies are recognized as the key elements for pro-moting children with disabilities, the availability of such technologies seems to be minimal in the context of Bangladesh (USAID, 2005). Huq (2005) argued that the government agencies had little understanding of technologi-cal development for children with disabilities. Accordingly, government's effort to arrange assistive and educational technology for children with dis-abilities is less likely to meet the actual demand (USAID, 2005). Generally, it is only those children who have parents with means who can get access technology in Bangladesh. However, there are some NGOs that arrange dif-ferent types of low-cost assistive and educational technology for children with disabilities. For example, HI-CARE provides low-cost hearing aids for children with hearing impairment. There are also quite a few local NGOs which provide low-cost hearing aids for children across the country. Also, Braille materials are provided by Baptist Sangha Blind School. Additionally, learning materials for low vision children are provided by Sight Severs Bangladesh and a low vision laboratory has been established at the University of Dhaka to help preservice special education teachers conduct research on developing low-cost teaching materials within the context of Bangladesh. Also, the Department of Special Education of the University of Dhaka with the financial support from Center for Disability in Development (CDD) has developed a sign language in 2003, called Sign Supported Bangla Language (SSBL). The BPF has played a leading role in developing an Augmentative Communication system for children with intellectual disabilities and for those with cerebral palsy. Several special schools in the capital city of Dhaka are using Augmentative Communication system for improvement of their students. Further, worldwide Applied Behavior Analysis (ABA) is recognized as one of the most effective tools for responding to children with autism and several NGOs including Proyash and AWF have conducted a number of workshops on ABA.

EARLY INTERVENTION PROGRAMS

Early intervention program seems to be a common component for majority of NGOs working in disability in Bangladesh. The primary focus of most of the early intervention programs in the context of Bangladesh is on screening and assessment of disability and referral for services (Sultana, 2010). School- and home-based therapeutic services are also provided by a number of NGOs while a few of them emphasize on preparation for regular schooling as part of their early intervention programs.

Realizing the benefit of early intervention programs in child development, the GoB has included an early intervention component in its comprehensive Early Childhood Care and Development (ECCD) policy in 2012 (Ministry of Women and Children Affairs [MoWCA], 2012). The policy underpins early participation in education for all children irrespective of special needs, ethnicity, and economic status through inclusion. The significant features of this policy are undertaking screening measures for children with disability and providing supports within three years from birth (MoWCA, 2012, p. 16). Since this policy caters inclusive education through early childhood, it is more likely that students as well as their teachers will experience more inclusive culture in regular schools.

WORKING WITH FAMILIES

An effective collaboration between school and home can play a significant role in empowering students with disabilities as well as their parents within the school community (Stanley, 2008). Research suggests that students with disabilities are best served when school and home work together (Sheridan, Bovaird, Glover, Garbacz, & Witte, 2012; Sointu, Savolainen, Lappalainen, & Epstein, 2012). In Bangladesh, school−home relationship (schools working with parents), is one of the less focused areas in education. Accordingly, parents are less likely to appear in the decision making process employed by the schools. Although a number of NGOs are involved in working with families through various programs such as CBR and home-based rehabilitation (USAID, 2005), the state-supported services remained less functional (USAID, 2005). However, in recent years, the GoB seems to underpin community participation in school activities. The third Primary Education Development Program (PEDP-III) is an example where parental involvement has been considered as a means to improving the quality of primary education (DPE, 2013). In its strategy and action plan, PEDP-III has provided a comprehensive guideline on how the existing approaches of parental involvement can be functional. Provisionally, parents of children with disabilities do not have a separate approach to be involved in school activities. Rather they have to take part in the locally developed approaches which are not necessarily considered as ideal approaches. The following section gives a brief of such approaches used to work with families in both government schools and NGOs run schools.

STRATEGIES USED IN GOVERNMENT TO WORK WITH FAMILIES

School Managing Committee (SMC)

SMC is known as a local governing body of the school where a group of parents can directly place their opinion. It is mandatory for every primary and secondary school to have an SMC (DPE, 2009). Generally, an SMC constitutes 12 members including teachers and parents. All the parents of a school elect five members as their representatives in the SMC. Even though the primary aim of SMC is to bridge the gap between parents and teachers, research suggests that due to the lack of awareness about disability, SMC members were found to work against inclusion of students with disabilities (Malak, 2013a; Mullick et al., 2012).

Parent−Teacher Association (PTA)

There is a provision of government that a primary school have a PTA consisting of a group of parents and teachers. Like SMC, PTA is also formed to enhance parental participation in the primary education sector in Bangladesh. However, although a number of steps have been taken to improve governance such as SMC and PTA, the effectiveness of such bodies remains a concern (UNESCO, 2013).

Mothers' Meeting

Mothers' meeting (*MaaShomaabesh* − in Bangla) is a recently developed strategy to encourage parents of children with and without disabilities to be engaged with the school. Since fathers in the context of Bangladeshi families remain busy with income-generating activities, they find little time to participate in programs organized by school. Keeping this in mind, mothers' meeting has been prioritized with a view that parental involvement would be more effective. Mothers of children with and without disabilities are invited every month to attend a meeting where they are informed about the progress of their children. As there is no published work found on mothers' meeting, it is difficult to comment on the impact of this strategy.

School Survey

Within the existing provision of the government primary school, teachers need to visit the families of those children who frequently remain absent from classes. The number of teachers in each primary school in Bangladesh ranges from five to seven. Every month, the teachers provide counseling services to such parents by visiting their homes. In a case study of three rural schools in a Northern district of Bangladesh, Islam (2010) reported that frequent home visit had increased the students' classroom attendance. It is, however, important to note that due to the increased workloads of teachers because of government's inclusive education policy, they get limited time to do home visit (Islam, 2010).

In addition to the above mentioned strategies, the GoB works with the families of children with disabilities through its Social Welfare Department.

In every district, under the Social Service Office, there are several field workers, known as social service workers, who work at grassroots level (NFDD, 2013). The primary responsibility of these field workers is to identify children with disabilities by visiting door to door in subdistrict and provide the families with appropriate guidance and referral services.

STRATEGIES EMPLOYED BY NGOs TO WORK WITH FAMILIES

As mentioned earlier, a number of NGOs work closely with the families of children with disabilities in Bangladesh. For example, Sightsavers Bangladesh has been running CBR programs for children with visual impairments since 2008, and there has been a big change in the empowerment of persons with visual impairment and their families due to the establishment of a strong network (Miles et al., 2012). Also, CBR professionals of BPF conduct door-to-door survey to help identify children with disabilities (USAID, 2005). Community networking is a strategy to serve children with disabilities and their families that has been practiced by several NGOs including NFOWD, Center for Rehabilitation of the Paralyst CRP, CDD, and many other local NGOs. The term "community networking" is conceptualized in the context of Bangladesh as

> Networking for us is about communication and making contact, for example with local MPs, the upazila [sub-district] Chairman, rich people, other NGOs, the social welfare department to secure disability allowances, local bank branches, and hospitals to ask for priority service for disabled people. (Miles et al., 2012, p. 288)

Through building network, children and adults with disabilities as well as their parents in rural Bangladesh have increased their participations in the mainstream community. Accordingly, the social inclusion of persons with disabilities has claimed to be improved significantly in rural Bangladesh (Miles et al., 2012). Home- and center-based approaches have also been practiced by numerous national and local NGOs in Bangladesh (Haque, 2008). Most of these NGOs claiming to employ home- and center-based approaches to work with families of children with disabilities are shown as models of good practice of inclusive education in Bangladesh (see CSID, 2007). Lastly, The CDD has developed a model termed as "community approaches to handicap and disability (CADD)" in Bangladesh. The CADD model is originally a systematic approach to implement CBR more effectively in the community. Based on the positive impact of CADD on disability, a number of NGOs have started using this approach in the rural community (USAID, 2005).

TEACHER TRAINING

Over the past decade, the GoB has been keen to focus on teachers' professional development through preservice and in-service teacher education. As mentioned earlier, a variety of training programs has been conducted with primary and secondary education teachers through PEDP and TQI-SEP programs for preparing teachers to address children with diversity in classrooms. Despite a massive effort for teacher training through different projects, the opportunity of preservice and in-service teachers to develop their teaching skills for accommodating children with disabilities in the government's mainstream professional development program remains limited (Ahsan, Sharma, & Deppeler, 2011; Ahsan et al., 2012; Khan, 2012). In a review, Malak (2013a) has identified the following institutions as responsible for providing training to preservice and in-service teachers regarding children with disabilities in the context of Bangladesh.

GOVERNMENT'S ARRANGEMENT FOR TEACHER TRAINING

National Center of Special Education (NCSE)

The NCSE is the only government training center that prepares special education teachers. It offers a 10-month Diploma course, known as Bachelor of Special Education (BSEd), for in-service and preservice teachers. A school practicum is mandatory requirement of this program. Students undertake their practice teaching in three different special schools adjacent to the NCSE. The primary focus of the course is on special education with a little emphasis on inclusion of students with disabilities.

Primary Training Institute (PTI)

The GoB provides training to primary education teachers through 56 PTIs. Provisionally every novice teacher needs to complete a foundation training called Certificate in Education (C-in-Ed) from PTI. It is important to clarify that most of the novice teachers in primary education in Bangladesh commence teaching without any prior training. For example, a candidate with a minimum qualification (Year-12 Certificate for female and Bachelor for male) can apply for a teaching position in primary school. Education Degree is not required for applying for this position. Therefore, novice teachers who participate in foundation training in PTIs are treated as pre-service teachers.

The critical point is that the entire training program of PTI contains only one chapter focused upon disability. Therefore, although PTIs have potential to prepare novice teachers for inclusive practices, due to the traditional nature of the curriculum, teachers are being deprived of achieving required skills. However, a remarkable change occurred in the training program of PTI which is discussed later under the section of teacher education at University level.

Directorate of Primary Education

The DPE works on behalf of the MoPME for primary education sector. The Inclusive Cell of DPE prepares inclusive education training manuals for Upazila (subdistrict) Education Officers (UEOs). The UEOs then transfer the training to the head teachers and general teachers at the subdistrict level.

Cluster Training Program

Cluster training is one of the innovations of primary education in Bangladesh. Teachers receive a daylong training session once a month in a cluster. A cluster contains 10–12 schools of a subdistrict. Usually education officers at the subdistrict level conduct the cluster training in which teachers are given opportunities to share their experiences and receive feedback on their queries from the education officers. The concept of IE is being integrated in the cluster training program gradually.

Teacher Training College

There are 13 government TTCs in Bangladesh for secondary education teachers. TTCs offer a one-year Diploma in BEd and one-year MEd programs for preservice and in-service teachers. Students of BEd program need to undertake their practice teaching sessions in secondary schools. The TTC curriculum contains a limited unit on disability which seems to be inadequate to prepare secondary education teachers toward teaching students with disabilities.

TEACHER EDUCATION INSTITUTE AT UNIVERSITY LEVEL

Graduate Programs

The IER of the University of Dhaka and Dhaka Teacher Training College under National University provide teacher education programs in both bachelor (four-year) and master's (one-year) levels. The Department of Special Education of IER prepares 20 teacher education students each year with specialization in disability. To gain hands-on training, BEd (Honors) students are placed in regular and special schools for a period of 6 months. Graduates qualified as preservice teachers from these institutes not only teach at the school level but also contribute to the national level as educational consultants.

Undergraduate Program

There has been a remarkable change in the teacher education program for primary teachers in Bangladesh during the past two years. The C-in-Ed course of PTIs has been entirely revised in an 18-month long program, known as "Diploma in Primary Education" (DPEd). The newly developed program has been pilot tested in seven PTIs and necessary adjustments have been made for commencing. The most important aspect of the DPEd program is that it has been accredited by the IER of the University of Dhaka from 2013. This is the first initiative since the birth of this country when the professional development of the entire primary education sector comes under a University. In a radical departure from the previous teacher training program in Bangladesh, the DPEd is grounded in trainees' experiences of school placements. The program focuses on the development of both their professional knowledge and ability to create an enabling classroom environment where lessons are taught in an engaging, interactive, and inclusive manner (IER, 2013). The program is modular in structure, with separate subject knowledge and pedagogy courses in six curriculum subjects, four periods of school experiences during which trainees are taught and assessed in accordance with a newly developed set of professional competences. Also, within the program, the professional studies course acts to unify trainees' practical experience and PTI-based learning with a strong focus on "reflective practice" (IER, 2013). In essence, the DPEd program aims to develop professionally skilled teachers who are able to teach children in a joyful and child friendly environment according to their age and capabilities for their physical, mental, emotional, social, aesthetic, intellectual, and linguistic development, that is, their holistic development (IER, 2013).

Initiatives of Nongovernment Organizations for Teacher Training

The role of NGOs in preparing teachers for inclusive practice seems to be passive (Malak, 2013a). For example, the BRAC is committed to inclusion (Ahuja & Ibrahim, 2006) and currently 28,144 children with disabilities are enrolled at BRAC schools (Mahbub, 2008, p. 34), however, its philosophy, one teacher for one school, sometimes seems to be very challenging to address inclusive practices. Further, the CDD in collaboration with DPE trains primary education teachers for inclusive education and provides training on disability to special education teachers and professionals. While training a huge number of teachers from almost all parts the country, the contemporary research conducted in Bangladesh suggests that teachers' attitudes are less supportive for accommodating students with disabilities in regular schools (Ahsan et al., 2012). Further, teachers demonstrate lack of knowledge on disability (Kibria, 2005; Malak, 2013b) and inclusive pedagogy (Das & Ochiai, 2012). Moreover, research also suggests that Bangladesh teachers have limited knowledge regarding existing policy, laws, and legislation of education for students with disabilities (Khan, 2012).

PROGRESS OF SPECIAL EDUCATION

Bangladesh has made a remarkable progress in educating children with disabilities during the past decade. Policy reform, teacher training, and awareness creation were consistently reported to have a significant impact on the access of children with disabilities to education in Bangladesh (Ahsan & Burnip, 2007; Ahsan & Mullick, 2013; Ahsan et al., 2012). The following section presents the overall achievement of Bangladesh to promote children with disabilities.

EDUCATING STUDENTS WITH DISABILITIES

In policy and legislation context, there has been a significant improvement through which children with disabilities have received their legislative ground for getting enrolled in regular schools (Malak et al., 2014). Education of children with disabilities has been given priority in both primary and secondary education sectors. Due to two major interventions, PEDP and TQI-SEP, there has been significant increase in the enrollment of students with disabilities in regular primary and secondary schools (Ahsan & Mullick, 2013; Das, 2011). Further, the access of students with disabilities to special education has increased. Also, educational participation regarding children with autism has improved noticeably in special education throughout the country (NFDD, 2013). Further, students with disabilities have got access to several basic aspects of education such as extra time in examination and using writers during examination for students with visual impairment and those having cerebral palsy.

TEACHER TRAINING

Training curricula of most of the training institutes have been revised and special and inclusive education issues have been embedded (Ahsan & Mullick, 2013). The issue of disability has been sensitized through CPD with primary and secondary education teachers (Ahsan & Mullick, 2013). In addition, the accreditation of DPEd program by the University of Dhaka will help primary education teachers enhance their teaching efficacy for students with disabilities (IER, 2013).

QUALITY OF LIFE

During the past decade, there has been an increase in disability assessment centers in Bangladesh. While there were only three to five Dhaka-based centers in late 1990s, at present disability assessment centers can be seen in all Divisional cities. Due to the increased awareness of disability in recent years, evidence suggests that misconceptions and superstitions about disability among mass population seem to decrease (NFDD, 2013) and persons with disabilities are more likely to be valued and acknowledged in the society. Furthermore, the use of assistive and educational technologies has improved. Due to improved access to assessment centers, children with disabilities are identified at an early age and are exposed to various technologies based on their needs, such as hearing and visual aids, electric wheelchairs, and white canes which were rare in the past. In order to disseminate services to grassroots level, the government's plans to set up a special unit on disabilities in every government hospital which will help persons enhance their life.

EMPLOYMENT TRAINING

The Employment and Rehabilitation Center for the Physically Handicapped (ERCPH) has been providing vocational training and rehabilitation of speech and hearing impaired as well as persons with physical impairment since 1978. This is the only government run reputed vocational training center for persons with disabilities. In recent years, the center has increased its capacity in terms of human resource, technology, and physical facilities. At present, it has the capacity to accommodate 85 persons in its residential dormitory (NFDD, 2013). Although employment training for students with disabilities seems to be limited in government sector, a number of NGOs including CRP, CDD, BPF, and Underprivileged Children's Education Program (UCEP)-Bangladesh have been training these students through different kinds of vocational education (CSID, 2007; USAID, 2005). The students with disabilities are undergoing training in several areas including engineering work, electronics, plastic processing work, leatherwork, wood carving, sewing-machine operator, and bag and brush making (NFDD, 2013; Nuri, Hoque, Akand, & Waldron, 2012).

FUNDING FROM THE GOVERNMENT

The GoB provides financial support to children and adults with disabilities through the *Jatiyo Protibondhi Unnayan Foundation* (National Foundation for Disabled Development, NFDD) for various purposes including rehabilitation of persons with disabilities, insolvent disability allowance, and a stipend for students with disabilities, and rehabilitation and stipend training for persons with physical impairment. The amount of allowances has increased by 10% during the past five years (NFDD, 2013). Also, the government has established a special arrangement for providing loans to students and adults with disabilities with special offers. Special grants have also been provided through the NFDD to a number of NGOs working in disability since 2002. A total of 380 NGOs have received a total disability grant of Tk. 89,45,000 in the year of 2010−2011 (NFDD, 2013, p. 47).

CHALLENGES TO THE EDUCATION FOR CHILDREN WITH DISABILITIES

Despite the fact that Bangladesh has gained significant progress in ensuring rights of students with disabilities, it is important to acknowledge that there are numerous challenges that need to be addressed. The first and foremost challenge is that there is no actual data about persons with disabilities in Bangladesh. Without having a national statistics it is hard to plan facilities for children with disabilities. Second, there are some issues embedded in the policies and legislations that lead to confusion among the practitioners and teachers about educational placement of students with disabilities. For instance, while inclusive education has been considered as a means of educating students with disabilities, segregation has been underpinned within the same policies. Therefore, a contradiction exists between special education and inclusive education which creates barriers to facilitate education for students with disabilities. Part of this confusion is the conceptual variation or absence of a common language regarding inclusive education (Ainscow, 2005; Ainscow, Booth, & Dyson, 2006; Ainscow & Miles, 2009) which leads to a major barrier to the successful implementation of inclusion. A third challenge is in teacher training about inclusive education because researchers (e.g., see Ahsan, 2013; Ahsan et al., 2011, 2012) have suggested that although teachers hold positive beliefs, they feel less prepared to teach students with disabilities. This may be due to a lack of experiential learning opportunity for preservice teachers in the teacher training institute in Bangladesh (Malak, 2012, 2013a) because these programs tend to focus more on actual classroom perspective rather than emphasize the theoretical aspect of students with disabilities. Another challenge is curriculum flexibility. The NCTB prepares textbooks for primary and secondary students. It is claimed that majority of textbooks prepared by NCTB remain inaccessible for children with disabilities. On the other hand, there is no national curriculum for students with disabilities who are enrolled in special education. A fifth challenge is the lack of awareness and understanding among various stakeholders including teachers, administrator, SMC, community leaders, and the mass population (Kibria, 2005; Foley, 2009). Another challenge is a lack of collaboration among policy makers, teacher trainers, University academics, NGO professionals, and school teachers in the context of Bangladesh. To remedy this, Ahsan and Mullick (2013) emphasize an interagency collaboration to improve inclusion of children with disabilities in mainstream education. Lastly, the MoE in Bangladesh is dealing with a huge shortage of essential resources such as: teachers, educational materials, accessible classrooms, school buildings, funds for primary and secondary education sectors, and provisions to have a teaching assistant or support teacher. One teacher has to manage nearly 70—90 students in a class.

CONCLUDING REMARKS

The national level inclusive and special education policies in Bangladesh are mostly modeled after the international policies. Therefore, it can be hardly expected that the guidelines are underpinned by the inclusion philosophy that fit into the national context. Even within the national context, a noticeable feature of such policies is that they are imposed from the center to periphery (Mullick et al., 2012). This means that teachers and other stakeholders do practice what and how the providers want them to do. Educators have expressed their concerns regarding the increased trend of pursuing top-down and de-contextualized policies where equity is narrowly equated with improved examinations achievements (Ainscow & Goldrick, 2010). Thus, a locally constructed approach of educational placement of children with disabilities is needed in Bangladesh.

REFERENCES

Ahsan, M. T. (2013). *National baseline study for developing a model of inclusive primary education in Bangladesh project based on secondary data*. Dhaka: Plan Bangladesh.
Ahsan, M. T., & Burnip, L. (2007). Inclusive education in Bangladesh. *Australasian Journal of Special Education, 31*(1), 61—71.

Ahsan, M. T., & Mullick, J. (2013). The journey towards inclusive education in Bangladesh: Lessons learned. *Prospects, 43*, 151–164.

Ahsan, M. T., Sharma, U., & Deppeler, J. (2011). Beliefs of pre-service teacher education institutional heads about inclusive education in Bangladesh. *Bangladesh Education Journal, 10*(1), 9–29.

Ahsan, M. T., Sharma, U., & Deppeler, J. (2012). Exploring pre-service teachers' perceived teaching-efficacy, attitudes and concerns about inclusive education in Bangladesh. *International Journal of Whole Schooling, 8*(2), 1–20.

Ahuja, A., & Ibrahim, M. D. (2006). *An assessment of inclusive education in Bangladesh.* Dhaka: UNESCO-Dhaka.

Ainscow, M. (2005). Looking to the future: Towards a common sense of purpose. *Australasian Journal of Special Education, 29*(2), 182–186.

Ainscow, M., Booth, T., & Dyson, A. (2006). *Improving schools, developing inclusion.* Abingdon: Routledge.

Ainscow, M., & Goldrick, S. (2010). Making sure that every child matters: Enhancing equity within education systems. In A. Hargreaves, A. Lieberman, M. Fullan, & D. Hopkins (Eds.), *Second international handbook of educational change* (Vol. 23, pp. 869–882). Netherlands: Springer.

Ainscow, M., & Miles, S. (2009). *Developing inclusive education systems: How can we move policies forward?* Retrieved from http://www.ibe.unesco.org/fileadmin/user_upload/COPs/News_documents/2009/0907Beirut/DevelopingInclusive_Education_Systems.pdf. Accessed on February 10, 2013.

Asian Development Bank. (2004). *Teaching Quality Improvement in Secondary Education Project: Reports and recommendations of the president.* Dhaka: Asian Development Bank.

BANBEIS. (2011). *Basic education data and indicators in Bangladesh.* Retrieved from http://www.lcgbangladesh.org/Education/reports/Basic%20Education%20Data%20and%20Indicators%20in%20Bangladesh%20-%20CAMPE.pdf

BBS. (2011). *Household income expenditure survey.* Dhaka: BBS.

CSID. (2007). *A study report on documentation of good practices on inclusive education in Bangladesh.* Dhaka: Regional Office of South Asia, UNICEF.

Disability Rights Watch Group Bangladesh. (2009). *State of the rights of persons with disabilities in Bangladesh, 2009.* Dhaka: Disability Rights Watch Group Bangladesh.

Das, A. (2011). Inclusion of students with disabilities in mainstream primary education of Bangladesh. *Journal of International Development and Cooperation, 17*(2), 1–10.

Das, A., & Ochiai, T. (2012). Effectiveness of C-in-Ed course for inclusive education: Viewpoint of in-service primary teachers in Southern Bangladesh. *Electronic Journal for Inclusive Education, 2*(10), 23–32.

DPE. (2009). *School managing committee (SMC).* Dhaka: DPE.

DPE. (2010). *Training manual for teacher trainers: Inclusive education.* Dhaka: DPE.

DPE. (2011). *Primary school census 2010.* Dhaka: DPE.

DPE. (2012). *Bangladesh primary education annual sector performance report (ASPR-2012).* Dhaka: DPE.

DPE. (2013). *Bangladesh primary education annual sector performance report (ASPR-2013).* Dhaka, Bangladesh: DPE.

DPE & CSID. (2002). *Educating children in difficult circumstances: Children with disabilities.* Dhaka: CSID.

DSHE. (2005). *Project proposal of teaching quality improvement in secondary education project.* Dhaka, Bangladesh: DSHE.

DSHE. (2007). *Teaching quality improvement: What does TQI do?* Retrieved from http://tqi-sep.gov.bd/about.php. Accessed on July 15, 2009.

Foley, D. (2009). The contextual and cultural barriers to equity and full inclusive participation for people labeled with disabilities in Bangladesh. *Disability Studies Quarterly Winter*, *29*(1). Retrieved from http://dsq-sds.org/article/view/170/170

Huq, S. (2005). Children with disabilities in different circumstances. *Teacher's World: Journal of Education and Research*, *29*(1), 78–88.

Haque, S. (2008). *Bangladesh CBR*. Dhaka: Social assistance and rehabilitation for the physically vulnerable (SARPV). Retrieved from http://www.unesco.org/new/en/dhaka/education/primary-education/

IER. (2013). *The accreditation of Diploma in Primary Education (DPEd) program.* Dhaka: IER, University of Dhaka.

Islam, K. (2010). Challenges of outreach education program in Bangladesh: A case studies. *The Disadvantaged Education*, *1*, 12–15.

JICA. (2002). *Country profile on disability: People's republic of Bangladesh.* Dhaka: JICA.

Khan, T. A. (2012). Secondary school teachers' perceptions of inclusive education in Bangladesh. *Critical Literacy: Theories and Practices*, *6*(2), 102–118.

Kibria, G. (2005). Inclusion education the developing countries: The case study of Bangladesh. *Journal of the International Association of Special Education*, *6*(1), 43–47.

Mahbub, T. (2008). Children's views on inclusion: Inclusive education at a BRAC school – Perspectives from the children. *British Journal of Special Education*, *35*(1), 33–41.

Malak, M. S. (2012). Pre-service special education teachers' preparation for inclusive education in Bangladesh: An action research. *Journal of Education and Practice*, *3*(14), 91–100.

Malak, M. S. (2013a). Inclusive education reform in Bangladesh: Pre-service teachers' responses to include students with special educational needs in regular classrooms. *International Journal of Instruction*, *6*(1), 95–114.

Malak, M. S. (2013b). Inclusive education in Bangladesh: Are pre-service teachers ready to accept students with special educational needs in regular classes? *Disability, CBR and Inclusive Development*, *24*(1), 56–82.

Malak, M. S., Begum, H. A., Habib, M. A., Banu, M. S., & Roshid, M. M. (2014). Inclusive education in Bangladesh: Are the guiding principles aligned with successful practices? In H. Zhang, P. W. K. Chan, & C. Boyle (Eds.), *Equity in education: Fairness and inclusion* (pp. 107–124). Rotterdam, The Netherlands: Sense Publishers.

Miles, M., & Hossain, F. (1999). Rights and disabilities in educational provisions in Pakistan and Bangladesh: Roots, rhetoric, reality. In F. Armstrong & L. Barton (Eds.), *Disability, human rights and education: Cross-cultural perspectives* (pp. 67–86). Buckingham, UK: Open University Press.

Miles, S., Fefoame, G. O., Mulligan, D., & Haque, Z. (2012). Education for diversity: The role of networking in resisting disabled people's marginalisation in Bangladesh. *Compare: A Journal of Comparative and International Education*, *42*(2), 283–302.

Ministry of Education. (2010). *National Education Policy 2010.* Retrieved from http://www.moedu.gov.bd/index.php?option=com_content&task=view&id=338&Itemid=416. Accessed on November 15, 2012.

Ministry of Law Justice and Parliamentary Affairs. (2000). *The constitution of Bangladesh revised.* Dhaka: Government Press. Retrieved from www.parliament.gob.bd/constitution_english/index.htm. Accessed on December 12, 2012.

Ministry of Social Welfare. (2001). *Bangladesh Persons with Disability Welfare Act*. Retrieved from http://www.ilo.org/public/english/region/asro/bangkok/ability/regional_laws_bangla2001.htm. Accessed on October 12, 2012.

Ministry of Social Welfare. (2013). *Rights and protection of persons with disabilities Act-2013*. Dhaka: MoSW.

Ministry of Women and Children Affairs. (2012). *Comprehensive early childhood care and development (ECCD) policy draft*. Retrieved from http://www.mowca.gov.bd/wp-content/uploads/ECCD-Revised-ECCD-Policy

MoPME. (1990). *The compulsory primary education act 1990*. Dhaka: MoPME.

MoSW. (2012). *Bangladesh disability working groups: Government and NGOs*. Dhaka, Bangladesh: Directorate of Social Service.

Mullick, J., Deppeler, J., & Sharma, U. (2012). The leadership practice structure in regular primary schools involved in inclusive education reform in Bangladesh. *The International Journal of Learning, 18*(11), 67−82.

Munir, S. Z., & Zaman, S. S. (2009). Models of inclusion: Bangladesh experience. In M. Alur & V. Timmons (Eds.), *Inclusive education across cultures: Crossing boundaries, sharing ideas* (pp. 290−298). New Delhi: Sage.

Nasreen, M., & Tate, S. (2007). *Social inclusion: Gender and equity in education SWAPs in South Asia. Bangladesh case study*. Kathmandu: UNICEF.

NFDD. (2013). *Desk review on persons with disabilities in Bangladesh*. Dhaka: NFDD.

NFOWD. (2009). *Technical guide on inclusive education for person with disabilities in Bangladesh* (In Bangla). Dhaka: NFOWD.

Nuri, M. R. P., Hoque, M. T., Akand, M. M. K., & Waldron, S. M. (2012). Impact assessment of a vocational training programme for persons with disabilities in Bangladesh. *Disability, CBR and Inclusive Development, 23*(3), 76−89.

OECD. (2005). *Teachers matter: Attracting, developing and retaining effective teachers*. Paris: OECD Publishing.

PEDP Completion Report. (2011). *Bangladesh second primary education development program*. Dhaka, Bangladesh: DPE.

Rahaman, M., & Sutherland, D. (2012). Attitudes and concerns of teacher educators towards inclusive education for children with disabilities in Bangladesh. *Critical Literacy: Theories and Practices, 6*(2), 86−101.

Rahman, M. M. (2011). *Current vital issues for Bangladeshi psychologists, clinical psychologists and other applied psychologists*. Retrieved from http://www.bcps.org.bd/publication/2011/Current%20Vital%20Issues%20for%20Bangladeshi%20Psychologists%20Prof%20M%20Rahman.pdf

Sultana, N. (2010). Early intervention programs for children with disabilities in Bangladesh. *Teacher's World: Journal of Education and Research, 35−36*, 65−72.

Sheridan, S. M., Bovaird, J. A., Glover, T. A., Garbacz, S. A., & Witte, A. (2012). A randomized trial examining the effects of conjoint behavioral consultation and the mediating role of the parent-teacher relationship. *School Psychology Review, 41*(1), 23−46.

Šiška, J., & Habib, A. (2013). Attitudes towards disability and inclusion in Bangladesh: From theory to practice. *International Journal of Inclusive Education* (online first). doi:10.1080/13603116.2011.651820

Sointu, E. T., Savolainen, H., Lappalainen, K., & Epstein, M. H. (2012). Parent, teacher and student cross informant agreement of behavioral and emotional strengths: Students with and without special education support. *Journal of Child and Family Studies, 21*, 682−690.

Stanley, A. (2008). *Types of home-school communication and autistic spectrum disorder: A case study of parents and teachers in two primary schools*. Unpublished doctoral thesis, Faculty of Education, Griffith University. Retrieved from https://www120.secure.grif-fith.edu.au/rch/file/85cc415a-a9c8-12cf-3a3e-25827c09984f/1/Stanley_2010_02Thesis.pdf

UNESCO. (1990). *World declaration on education for all and framework for action to meet basic learning needs*. Paris: UNESCO.

UNESCO. (1994). *Salamanca statement and framework for action on special education needs*. Paris: United Nations.

UNESCO. (2000). *The Dakar framework for action*. Paris: UNESCO.

UNESCO. (2013). *Primary education*. Dhaka: UNESCO Bangladesh.

United Nations. (2006). *World program of action concerning disabled persons*. New York, NY: The Division for Social Policy and Development of the United Nations (UN) Secretariat.

USAID. (2005). *Assessment of educational needs of disabled children in Bangladesh*. Dhaka: USAID.

World Bank. (2008, April). *Education for all in Bangladesh. Where does Bangladesh stand in achieving the EFA Goals by 2015?* Bangladesh Development Series, Paper No. 24. World Bank Office, Dhaka.

World Health Organization. (2006). *Disability and rehabilitation: WHO action plan 2006—2011*. Geneva, Switzerland: WHO.

Zaman, S. S., & Munir, S. Z. (1992). Special education in Bangladesh. *International Journal of Disability, Development and Education*, 39(1), 3—11.

PART VI
AUSTRALASIA

SPECIAL EDUCATION TODAY IN AUSTRALIA

Umesh Sharma

ABSTRACT

This chapter reports the development of special education in Australia. The chapter begins with a discussion of general information about the country. This discussion is important to understand the overall development of special education considering Australia is a young country with a number of events directly influencing educational activities. It then presents some of the key historical milestones in special education in Australia. Information about the relevant legislation and policy reforms that are relevant to people with disabilities is also discussed. Some of the recent national initiatives that have had significant influence for students with disabilities are also discussed. The last part of the chapter delineates challenges that Australia faces related to the education of children with special needs.

UNDERSTANDING THE CONTEXT

Australia is located in the Southern hemisphere. Its land mass consist of 7,692,024 square kilometer and it is the sixth largest country after Russia,

Special Education International Perspectives: Practices Across the Globe
Advances in Special Education, Volume 28, 623−641
Copyright © 2014 by Emerald Group Publishing Limited
ISSN: 0270-4013/doi:10.1108/S0270-401320140000028028

Canada, China, the United States, and Brazil. Australia is the driest continent on Earth with 70% of the population living in coastal areas in eight large cities (Sydney, Melbourne, Brisbane, Perth, Adelaide, Hobart, Canberra, and Darwin) (About Australia, 2014). Australia has six states (Victoria, New South Wales, South Australia, Tasmania, Western Australia, Queensland) and two union territories (Canberra and Northern Territory). Western Australia is the largest state and it is as big as Western Europe. Australia is one of the oldest inhabited continents. Aborigines and Torres Strait Islanders have lived in Australia for over 40,000 years (About Australia, 2014).

The history of modern Australia could be traced back to 1606 when the first European (a Dutch explorer) — Willem Janszoon landed in the western coast of Cape York Peninsula in Queensland (About Australia, 2014). Over the next two centuries Australia was visited by a number of European explorers and traders and it was known as "New Holland." In 1770, Captain James Cook, a British explorer charted east coast of Australia and claimed it under the British Crown. Britain used the newly found continent as a penal colony (About Australia, 2014). In 1788, 11 ships with 1,500 people (half of them convicts) arrived in Australia. The ships arrived in Sydney on January 26 and it is on this day that Australia Day is celebrated each year. In total 160,000 convicts were sent to Australia between 1788 and 1868 (About Australia, 2014). It was in 1901 that Commonwealth of Australia was born under a single constitution.

HISTORY OF SPECIAL EDUCATION IN AUSTRALIA

Early Beginnings

The origins of special education in Australia could be traced back to 1811 when the first public institution for people with intellectual disability was established in New Norfolk in Tasmania (Ashman, 1997). The institution later became part of the Royal Derwent Hospital. It took another 70 years before the first special school was opened for students with disabilities in 1880 (Ashman, 1997). It is important to highlight that some attempts to provide special education services were made by Christian asylums and hospitals prior to the establishment of first special school. Residential schools for people with disabilities were established in the later part of the 1800s. Two such famous facilities were Kew Cottages in Melbourne (in Victoria) and Minda Home in Adelaide (in South Australia). Both of these facilities employed at least one teacher whose primary responsibility was to develop and implement educational programs for the residents (Andrews, Elkins, Berry, & Burge, 1979).

Formal Advances in the 1900s

With the turn of the century and Australia becoming a federation, a renewed emphasis was placed on the education of children with disabilities. Education now became the responsibility of state governments. Each state passed education acts and promoted opening of new special schools. In Victoria, children's cottages were opened at Kew Cottages and the first special school was opened in western part (Moone Ponds) of Melbourne. In 1913, "Bell Street School for Subnormal Children" was opened in Fitzroy, Melbourne. A primary role of the school was to provide services to students who were "educable" (i.e., an IQ of 50−70) (Ashman, 1997). In 1923, Victorian Department of Education began providing a new kind of special education services known as "Opportunity Grades." This could be seen as the first step toward the integration movement in Australia. "Opportunity Grades" were for students who were "educationally backward" (i.e., IQ 71−85) (Ashman, 1997). Opportunity Grades were established in regular schools and involved providing services such as individual instruction in academic areas like literacy and numeracy. In 1929, teachers were provided training to work with students in Opportunity Grades within their schools.

Significant changes took place in the provision of educational services after World War II in Australia largely due to the enactment of educational acts (Ashman, 1997). For example, The Educational Act (Department of Education, 1999) in Western Australia required the Minister to provide appropriate educational services to all school aged children. Such acts in various states improved services for children with mild disabilities. However, children with more severe disabilities continued to be excluded from regular or special schooling (Ashman, 1997). These children were either placed in institutions or they stayed at home with their parents. A significant national initiative addressed this issue of exclusion of children with severe disabilities. For example, in 1981, the Commonwealth Schools Commission released special funds to ensure that all children, including those with severe disabilities, were receiving an appropriate education (Andrews et al., 1979). The release of funds was based on a report that indicated that at least 800 children throughout Australia did not have access to any form of education (Andrews et al., 1979). A large number of these 800 children had a severe or profound disability. The next section delineates more recent developments in special education that were largely influenced by a number of national legislation and policy reforms.

TRENDS IN LEGISLATION, LITIGATION, AND POLICY DEVELOPMENT IN AUSTRALIA

Australia has been proactive in legislating for the rights of people with disabilities for the past 20 years. For example, in 1992, the Commonwealth of Australia passed the Disability Discrimination Act (DDA) (Australasian Legal Information Institute, 2009). Although this Act was not as prescriptive as similar legislation in other countries (e.g., Individuals with Disabilities Education Act [IDEA], 1990) in the United States), it was the first time that Australia made a serious attempt to ensure that the people with disabilities were not discriminated in a range of areas including education. Section 21 of the DDA particularly addressed education of people with a disability. The DDA states:

1. It is unlawful for an educational authority to discriminate against a person on the ground of person's disability:
   (a) by refusing or failing to accept the person's application for admission as a student; or
   (b) in the terms or condition on which it is prepared to admit the person as a student.
2. It is unlawful for an educational authority to discriminate against a student on the ground of student's disability:
   (a) by denying the student access, or limiting the student's access to any benefit provided by the educational authority; or
   (b) be expelling the student;
   (c) or by subjecting the student to any other detriment.
3. It is unlawful for an educational authority to discriminate against a person on the ground of the person's disability:
   (a) by developing curricula or training courses having a content that will either exclude the person from participation, or subject the person to any other detriment; or
   (b) by accrediting curricula or training courses having such content. (Australasian Legal Information Institute, 2009).

There are at least two features of the DDA that are worth further discussion. First, the DDA defines disability very broadly. Not only students with more typical disabilities (e.g., intellectual disability, vision impairment, and hearing impairment) are considered to have a disability but a number of other nontraditional categories of students are also classified as having a disability. For instance, students who do not currently have a disability but likely to develop one in the future (e.g., those who are predisposed to a genetic disorder) are considered to have a disability. Therefore the number of students that could have disability, according to the DDA, may range from 15% to 20%. It should be noted that state and union territories use select categories of children with disability. According to Bureau of Statistic the number of students with disabilities range from as low as 7.4% in Queensland to as high as 11.7% in Tasmania (Australian Bureau of Statistics [ABS], 2010). Differences in ranges of disability may be accounted for due to state and union territories using select categories to certify children as being disabled. Unfortunately, this has created ongoing tension between Commonwealth and State and Union Territory Governments. According to the Commonwealth definition of disability, much larger number of children with a disability are eligible to receive educational services from state governments. However, not all children eligible for services receive necessary services. One such category is students with specific learning disabilities.

Second, the DDA has a clause of "unjustifiable hardship." Educational providers can use this clause in their defense to discriminate against a student with a disability. However, to use this clause schools have to prove that carrying out their obligation to enroll (and provide appropriate education) a student with disability is too hard either in terms of resources required or the safety of the individual and those around the individual.

It is because of such clauses that Australian DDA is often criticized. Lindsay (2004, p. 387) in her analysis of Australian legislation and policies stated that:

> The evidence demonstrates that education policy and practice in Australia incorporate principles of inclusion. However, it is not apparent that the broad and deep objectives of inclusion are reflected in Australia's disability discrimination laws, neither in their drafting nor in their interpretation. The common approach to discrimination laws that prohibits discrimination as defined on the basis of so-called "irrelevant characteristics" is inadequate in the case of disability. Effective inclusion of a student with a disability (ies) may require substantial change, even systemic change. This is not reflected in the legislative language of (reasonable) "accommodation" and "unjustifiable hardship."

To some extent a number of drawbacks (but not all) of the DDA (1992) were addressed when the Education Standards of the DDA were enacted in

2005 (Commonwealth of Australia, 2006). One primary purpose of enacting the Educational Standards was to eliminate discrimination against people with a disability by educational authorities. The standards specify how education and training are to be made accessible to students with disabilities (Commonwealth of Australia, 2006). The standards cover the following areas:

- enrollment;
- participation;
- curriculum development;
- accreditation and delivery;
- student support services; and
- elimination of harassment and victimization.

The Educational Standards also provide detailed guidance about what educational authorities need to do in each of the above areas. The Educational Standards clearly articulate that students with disabilities are entitled to an education on the same basis as their peers without a disability. An implication of this clause is that schools are *now* required to be flexible in their approach in providing educational services to students with a disability. Schools are also required to consult with the student or his or her advocate when determining the educational needs and planning for them.

STATE POLICIES ON EDUCATION OF CHILDREN WITH DISABILITIES

Schooling is compulsory in Australia between the ages of 6 and 15 years (or 17 years in some jurisdictions). There are three educational systems within each jurisdiction that provide educational services to students with disability in Australia. These are public, Catholic, and independent school systems. The public school system is by far the largest one in terms of number of students served. In 2009, 66% of all students attended public schools. All state and union territories jurisdictions have specific policies that target students with disabilities. Most jurisdictions use a two-stage system of determining how students with disabilities be funded. At the first stage, it is determined whether a student is eligible to receive funding under the state disability programs. A categorical approach is used in determining the eligibility (e.g., students with intellectual disability, visual impairment). At the second stage, the extent of support required for the student is determined based on the educational needs of the student. The funding is determined using a needs-based system which requires identification of level of needs across a number of domains: curriculum, receptive language, expressive language, social competence, safety, hygiene, eating and dietary, health care procedures, mobility and positioning, and hand motor skills.

There are slight variations in each of the federal states with regard to eligibility for funding under state disability programs. In the state of Victoria, seven categories of disability are funded and these are: intellectual disability, hearing impairment, vision impairment, mobility impairment, autism spectrum disorder, language and communication impairment, and social emotional impairment. Students with learning disabilities are not funded in Victoria or the state of New South Wales However, such children do receive funding in other states (e.g., South Australia).

In more recent years, a significant emphasis has been placed across all state and union territories to include students with disabilities in mainstream schools. However, there are slight variations in the way inclusion is defined by researchers and policy makers. Van Kraayenoord, Elkins, Palmer, and Rickards (2000) define inclusive education as "the practice of providing for students with a wide range of abilities, backgrounds and aspirations in regular school settings" (p. 9). Foreman (2011, p. 16) states "inclusion is based on the philosophy that schools should, without question, provide for the needs of all children in the community, whatever their background, their ability or their disability." Over the years, Departments of Education have adopted different definitions but with significant overlaps. For example, according to the Department of Education (2006) inclusive education means that all students, regardless of their differences, are part of the school community and can feel that they belong. Access, participation, and achievement of all students, particularly those with disabilities, are at the core of the mandate.

In Western Australia, emphasis is not just on placement but on the delivery of high-quality services (Department of Education, 2013a). The Department states that "Inclusive classroom practice" may occur in "the local school or an Education Support School, Center or Unit. Inclusive classroom practice is not about placement. It is about making sure that children are taught in ways that suits their needs. Inclusive classroom practice is not about where parents choose to enroll their children, but how schools educate all children, including those with diverse needs" (n.p.).

WORKING WITH PARENTS

Parents of children with disabilities in Australia have a right to choose the type of educational placement options that they want for their child. Parents can decide whether their child would attend a regular or special school. Some researchers have looked at parental opinion with regard to the placement options for their child. For example, Elkins, van Kraaayenoord, and Jobling (2003) investigated the attitudes of 354 parents who had a child with a disability in the state of Queensland. The children were attending a range of options from special schools, special classes in regular schools to regular classes in mainstream schools with support from specialist staff. A large number of parents favored inclusion for their child when their child was well supported. Parents also believed that in-service teachers needed more professional development to teach effectively in inclusive classrooms.

Most jurisdictions across Australia recognize the need for active involvement of parents of children with disabilities. There are formal processes to engage parents in the education of their child across Australian schooling systems. For example, in Victoria parents work in close partnership with schools in designing educational plans through Program Support Meetings (Department of Education and Early Childhood Development [DEECD], 2013). The Department is of the view that parents or carers have a holistic understanding of the child and they are in the best position to provide information on the effectiveness of the program (DEECD, 2013). Parents are also well placed for informing educators about strategies that have worked with their child and those that have had limited success. Such information is highly useful when developing educational plans for their child. In order to further support parental involvement in educational planning of their child, several jurisdictions have also provision to engage parent advocates at the time of educational planning meetings. Such advocates make sure that parents are fully supported during the process of educational planning. Parents can appoint a friend or a supportive community member as their advocate. Parent advocates can assist families in a number of ways. They: (a) encourage the sharing of the parents' knowledge, skills, and perceptions about the student with the educational planning group, (b) discuss any difficulties or uncertainties being experienced by the parents when participating in the educational planning meetings, (c) assist the development of a co-operative and collaborative working relationship between the parents and the school community, (d) assist the parents to understand the

Departmental procedures, and (e) link the parents with relevant services and organizations (DEECD, 2013).

PREVALENCE AND INCIDENCE OF STUDENTS WITH DISABILITIES IN AUSTRALIA

The ABS collects national data on people with disabilities using the household component of the Survey of Disability, Aging and Carers (SDAC). In its most recent survey (2010), the Bureau reported that there were 292,600 children with disability who attended schools. This constitutes 8.3% of Australia children aged 5–20 years who attended schools. Children with disability have a variety of options available to attend schools. The options ranged from special schools, special classes in regular schools, and regular schools. At the time of the census, a large proportion of children with disabilities were attending regular schools (65.9%) (ABS, 2010). The remaining children either attended a special class within a regular school (24.3%) or a special school (9.9%) (ABS, 2010). There are slight variations in the proportion of children with disabilities attending regular schools compared to those attending special classes or special schools across jurisdictions. For example, in Queensland 37.3% of children with a disability were attending special classes compared to 13.3% of children with a disability in Western Australia. While one would think that a majority of children with severe or profound disabilities would be enrolled in either special classes or special schools in Australia, in reality, slightly above half of the children with severe or profound disabilities (52%) were enrolled in mainstream classes at the time of the last census.

Dempsey (2011) looked at the trends in number of students with special needs enrolling in Australian schools between 2000 and 2009. He reported that the number of such students has risen from 2.6% in 1996 to 3.5% in 2009. More recent estimates suggest the number is 4.8% of the school age population. This increasing trend is noticed not just in one jurisdiction but across jurisdictions. Furthermore, Dempsey reported that in the State of New South Wales there is a steady and substantial increase in the number of students identified with one or more disabilities. He also reported that the number increased both in regular schools and support classes. Although the number of students with disabilities has increased overall, there is no evidence to say that more students with disabilities are being included in mainstream schools. In fact, the number of students with disabilities in support classes in New South Wales has not decreased. However, students that are most recently identified are more likely to be placed in mainstream school settings (Dempsey, 2011). In the State of Victoria, the number of students accessing support under the state disability program has almost doubled since 2000 (Victorian Auditor General, 2012). The figures below show the number of students in various disability categories in the State of Victoria:

- intellectual disability (13,393 students or 64.1%);
- autism spectrum disorder (4,396 or 21%);
- severe behavior disorder (1,141 or 5.5%);
- physical disability (976 or 4.7%);
- hearing impairment (608 or 2.9%);
- severe language disorder with critical educational needs (263 or 1.3%);
- visual impairment (107 or 0.5%). (Victorian Auditor General, 2012).

It is important to note that while the number of students with disabilities identified as eligible to receive special education funding has doubled, the increases, however, are not spread evenly across the seven categories of disability. The Victorian Auditor General (2012) report states that "From 2000 to 2011 the number of students eligible for intellectual disability support rose by 58 per cent. Since 2000 the number of students qualifying for autism spectrum disorder support rose tenfold − from 325 to 4,396 [and] that from 2008 to 2011 severe behaviour disorder grew by 38.5 per cent whereas physical disability decreased 9.7 per cent over the same period. Increases in the hearing and visual impairment categories were modest" (p. 12). The reasons for the significant rise in the numbers of students identified as having a disability and eligible for special education funding are not known but the significant increases of students in the autism spectrum disorder, intellectual disability, and severe behavior disorder categories have placed enormous pressure on teachers to have the necessary instructional skills and categorical disability knowledge base to ensure that they can provide an appropriate learning environment and educational programs (Victorian Auditor General, 2012).

TEACHER EDUCATION AND SPECIAL EDUCATION

A variety of special education teacher education programs exist across the country. In most cases, teachers first complete a basic degree in teaching and then specialize in special education. A significant shift in the focus of university special education teacher training programs has been noticed the past few years across Australian universities. For example, while the focus of these programs followed a traditional categorical approach, more recently, the programs are following a holistic approach where future educators are being prepared to work with students with a range of special needs rather than a category need. This focus has created some significant challenges due to the range of skills that are necessary to instruct low incidence students with disabilities (Morris & Sharma, 2011). One such challenge involves preparing special education teachers to instruct students with sensory impairments. To instruct these special needs students the teacher must have highly specialized skills (such as Braille, Orientation and Mobility, and sign language). Unfortunately, the number of special education teachers with such highly specialized skills are in short supply across Australia (Gallimore, 2005; Morris & Sharma, 2011). This shortage creates significant barriers in providing quality education to students with sensory impairments. Another challenge is preparing special education teachers at the university level to instruct students with severe and profound disabilities who have unique learning styles and many interfering deficit characteristics (Stephenson, Carter, & Arthur-Kelly, 2011). These challenges are further complicated by surveys that point to the lack of special education qualifications among teachers who instruct special needs students. For instance, in a survey of special education qualifications in the State of New South Wales, 40% of the staff lacked special education qualifications (Thomas, 2009). What is even more concerning is that teachers who do have special education qualifications may not have sufficient in-depth knowledge and their instructional skills were acquired from a typical generalist program (Foreman, Arthur-Kelly, & Pascoe, 2007). Due to their educational backgrounds, they are less likely to be confident in their ability to implement effective practices in their classroom that are composed of students with a broad range of special needs (Foreman et al., 2007).

Similar concerns with regard to shortage of teachers with special educational qualifications were raised in a survey that was undertook by the Victoria Principals' Association of Special Schools (Thomas, 2007). The survey included 81 special schools in Victoria. Approximately half of the schools responded to the survey ($n = 43$). Thomas found that in 15 schools (almost 20% of respondent schools) less than half the staff had special education qualifications and in 43% of responding schools (33 schools) between 50% and 79% of the staff had special education qualifications. What was of significant concern was that a large proportion of older teachers in these schools, who held special education qualifications (70% of principals and 40% of teachers), were likely to retire over the next five years. Thomas summarized the dire results of the survey by stating the following:

> The PASS survey on special education qualifications in Victoria's special schools shows a disturbing scenario for the future. If present trends continue, within the next few years there will be a serious depletion in the numbers of teachers with special education qualifications in the state's specialist schools. There are currently few incentives, other than a desire to work with students with special needs, to compensate teachers for the extra work and money needed to gain additional qualifications in special education. (p. 144)

Considering the large number of students with disabilities are in regular schools, it is important to examine if regular school educators are being adequately prepared for the job. In 2002, the Senate Committee (Commonwealth of Australia, 2002) reported significant concerns regarding the preparation of pre-service teachers to teach students with disabilities. The concerns were raised about significant variations across jurisdictions and within jurisdictions regarding preparation of pre-service teachers. At the time of the enquiry, it was mandatory for all pre-service teachers to complete subjects related to effectively teaching students with disabilities in the states of New South Wales and Western Australia. There were no such requirements in other jurisdictions. The committee cited exemplary practice adopted by the state New South Wales in this regard. It reported that since 1995, all teacher education programs in New South Wales were providing a mandatory component of special education. More specifically, "The department of education provided a contribution to course design, with components being endorsed by the department when they were amended. Any graduate from any of the state's universities which did not have a mandatory component in special education was not employable by the Department of Education and Training. The department repeated its assurance that regular consultation took place between the universities and the department over special education course content, while making the point that universities treated the content in ways they believed to be most appropriate" (Commonwealth of Australia, p. 77). The committee also commended the efforts of state of Western Australia for making significant progress with regard to providing compulsory subjects in special or inclusive education.

The committee recognized that as the challenge of educating students with disabilities, including gifted children with disabilities, is now more common, there must be acknowledgment of this in university education courses. The committee believed that what was current practice in the states of New South Wales and Western Australia should be adopted by other jurisdictions, and urged education departments and other employing authorities to negotiate with universities on the provision of special education units.

Since the publication of the above senate report, a number of state governments have also undertaken reviews of their teacher education programs. For example, the Parliament of Victoria (2005) undertook an Inquiry into the Suitability of Pre-Service Teacher Training in Victoria and found that "new teachers were not 'teacher ready.' Put simply, many new graduates seem to lack practical teaching skills, as opposed to the theoretical foundations required to be an effective teacher" (Parliament of Victoria, p. xviii). The inquiry found that teachers in Victoria lacked skills to work effectively with students with special needs and recommended that "That the Department of Education and Training and the Victorian Institute of Teaching, in consultation with relevant stakeholders, ensure that specific strategies responding to students with special needs are incorporated as a key element of pre-service teacher education" (Parliament of Victoria, p. 129).

A similar enquiry in teacher education in the state of Queensland (Caldwell & Sutton, 2010) found that pre-service teachers were not being adequately prepared to teach students with disabilities and recommended that "all pre-service teachers undertake at least two subjects that build capacity to work with students who have special educational needs or for who, for whatever reasons, fall behind and need special support to catch up. It is understood that those teachers preparing to teach the field generally known as special education will undertake a strand of related studies as part of their degrees" (p. v).

CHALLENGES AND NEW INITIATIVES

This section reports a number of challenges that Australia is currently facing in providing quality education to students with disabilities. The section also reports some of the initiatives that different jurisdictions have undertaken to address some of the challenges.

Who Is Disabled?

One of the fundamental problems that Australia is facing relates to identifying students with disability and determining how much support be provided.

Wu and Komesaroff (2007) presented a comprehensive analysis of this issue. They criticized the use of educational needs questionnaires in determining the level of resources that should be provided to students with disabilities. Their analysis is most relevant to the state of Victoria but similar issues can also be evident in other states. They indicated that schools use educational needs questionnaires to determine the levels of needs in one of the following areas: mobility, fine motor skills, receptive communication, expressive communication, challenging (excess) behavior, safety, hearing, vision, self-care, medical, and cognitive skills. Based on the level of needs, students are then classified as being at one of six levels of educational need from 1 to 6 (higher the level, more severe the needs). Students with mild or moderate learning disabilities (LD) were being sent for assessment in the hope they could access additional resources in mainstream settings. Suddenly, there was a significant increase in the number of students receiving "funding at the lower end of the educational needs spectrum [that] raised problems with the use of the ENQ as a way of determining funding. Funds for students with disabilities were being stretched, with only a small percentage of those identified as having SEN receiving funding support" (Wu & Komesaroff, p. 131). Jenkinson (2001 cited in Wu & Komesaroff, 2007) reported that although a large number of student were being identified as having some form of disability (12–20% of Victorian students), only 2% of these students were considered eligible for special education services. Thus, a large number of students with identified needs were not receiving necessary services. Similar shortfalls in funding were also identified by other researchers in Victoria (Bartak & Fry, 2004) and have raised concerns by both parents and advocates across Australia.

Nationally Consistent Collection of Data: School Students with a Disability

To some extent, the above concern is likely to be addressed with a new initiative that will be implemented by all Australian state and territory governments in 2015. The initiative involves a national collection of data on school students with a disability that is being created by the Department of Education (2013b). The initiative arose due to the lack of national data on the number of students with a disability and the support they required to be educated successfully. The Department of Education emphasized that "The implementation of a nationally consistent approach to collecting data on school students with disability will provide all Australian schools, education authorities and the community with information about:

- how many school students with disability there are;
- where they are; and
- the level of adjustment provided for them to participate in schooling on the same basis as other students." (n.p.)

Additionally, the data collection approach will enable more accurate information to be collected about the number of school students with disability and their levels of need to allow more efficient educational planning and decision making at the national, state and sector levels. This national data will help all Australian schools to better meet their responsibilities under the DDA (1992) and improve support for the learning needs and aspirations of students with disability in all Australian schools. A nationally consistent collection of data would also "provide an evidence base on the national distribution of students with disability and the levels of adjustment they receive. The processes around the national data collection, including the professional learning, have the potential to contribute to a more inclusive schooling system for all Australian students" (Department of Education, 2013b, n.p.).

Inclusion of Students with Disabilities in National Testing

Australia has shown its commitment to provide a world-class curriculum to all students and to promote educational outcomes for all students at the Melbourne Declaration on Educational Goals for Young Australians (Ministerial Council for Education, Early Childhood Development and Youth Affairs [MCEECDYA], 2008). In order to achieve these goals, Australia has taken a number of initiatives. One such initiative includes the development of the National Assessment Program – Literacy and Numeracy (NAPLAN) (Davies, 2012). Since 2008, NAPLAN is mandatory for all Australian students in their birth years 3, 5, 7, and 9. It provides that the students be assessed using common national tests in Reading, Writing, Language Conventions (Spelling, Grammar, and Punctuation), and Numeracy. The Commonwealth of Australia Government has made school funding contingent upon involvement in the program. Each student is benchmarked against national data in different learning domains. The data is publically available on a website My School. This website provides information about each school's performance against national minimum standards, and percentages of students reaching national minimum standards.

Although it is mandated that all students, including those with a disability, be included in national testing under the NAPLAN program, a large number of students with disabilities do not participate in the program (Dempsey & Davies, 2013). It is only recently that this has received attention of researchers who have noticed a significant gap in the policy intent and policy implementation (Cumming, 2012; Dempsey & Davies, 2013). Citing McDonnell, McLaughlin, and Morrison (1997) Dempsey and Davies emphasized that the inclusion of students with disabilities in national and state-wide achievement assessment systems is essential because the absence of such data prevents valid and fair judgments about the effectiveness of educational policies and programs at school, district, or national levels.

Davies (2012) noted that while Australian legislation and policies require equity of opportunity for students with disabilities in all school activities, many students with a disability are not provided with the opportunity to access NAPLAN tests. A large number of students with a disability are excluded from national testing. The reasons for their noninvolvement are not centrally documented or reported (Davies, 2012). This lack of accountability has consequences for a range of stakeholders including students, parents, teachers, and schools. Davies emphasized that the lack of NAPLAN data on the achievement of students with disabilities could easily give the false impression that these students do not exist in the education system which could have significant implications for resourcing of schools. Because of this, Davies recommended that: inclusion of students with disability should be given an urgent priority; all students must have opportunity to learn assessed material; the students be afforded necessary accommodations that do not place them at risk or at significant disadvantages in comparisons to those without a disability; and NAPLAN testing allow testing modifications so that alternative forms of assessment are available to students with special needs.

National Curriculum and Students with Disabilities

Australia is in the process of adopting a National Curriculum for all students. The national curriculum "sets out essential knowledge, understanding, skills and capabilities and provides a national standard for student achievement in core learning areas" (The Australian Curriculum, Assessment and Reporting Authority [ACARA], 2013). ACARA is undertaking a rigorous and robust curriculum development process to produce a high-quality national curriculum. In order to develop the curriculum, opinions from a range of stakeholders (teachers, academics, and parents to business, industry, and community groups) are being sought.

In order to ensure that students with disability receive appropriate curriculum, ACARA (2013) has indicated its commitment by indicating that "All students are entitled to rigorous, relevant and engaging learning programs drawn from a challenging curriculum that addresses their individual learning needs." ACARA (2013) has developed material that can be accessed by schools freely from its website (http://www.australiancurriculum.edu.au/StudentDiversity/Student-diversity-advice) to assist them with the planning of educational adjustments for students with disabilities. The material is intended to:

- help ensure that all students are able to access and participate in the Australian Curriculum;
- provide advice as to how the Australian Curriculum may be used to address the learning needs of all students;
- provide specific advice with regard to meeting the learning needs of students with disability, gifted and talented students, and students for whom English is an additional language or dialect;
- provide examples illustrating how students with diverse needs can access and participate in the Australian Curriculum.

CONCLUSION

Australia is going through a significant phase in providing quality education to students with disabilities. A number of challenges continue to hamper the progress of the country in proving quality education to *all*. Both State and Commonwealth Governments are aware of some of the challenges and continue to implement new initiatives to address the challenges. However, due to political changes at the state and national level, some initiatives gain increased momentum while others are ignored. A much larger challenge that Australia is facing may be the lack of political will to continue to make progress on the educational initiatives started by the previous governments. In essence both sides of the Australia parliament need to recognize that improved educational services and supports for people with disabilities are ultimately going to benefit Australia as a whole not *just* people with disabilities.

REFERENCES

About Australia. (2014). *Australian facts.* Retrieved from http://www.about-australia.com/. Accessed on February 22, 2014.

Andrew, R. J., Elkins, J., Berry, P. B., & Burge, J. A. (1979). *A survey of special education in Australia.* Canberra: Schools Commission.

Ashman, A. F. (1997). Australia. In D. Y. Jung, H. C. Park, A. F. Ashman, C. C. Givner, & T. Ochiai (Eds.), *Integration of students with disabilities into regular schools in Korea, Australia, Japan, and the United States* (pp. 96–157). Ansan City, Korea: Korean Institute for Special Education.

Australasian Legal Information Institute. (2009). Disability Discrimination Act, 1992. Retrieved from http://www.austlii.edu.au/. Accessed on January 31, 2014.

Australian Bureau of Statistics. (2010). *Schools Australia 2000–2009.* Canberra, ACT: Author.

Bartak, L., & Fry, J. (2004). Are students with special needs in mainstream classes adequately supported? Perceptions from teachers in Victoria. *Australian Journal of Learning Disabilities, 9,* 16–21.

Caldwell, B., & Sutton, D. (2010). *Review of teacher education and school induction.* Brisbane: Queensland Department of Education. Retrieved from http://flyingstart.qld.gov.au/SiteCollectionDocuments/review-teacher-education-school-induction-first-full-report.pdf

Commonwealth of Australia. (2002). *Education of students with disabilities.* ACT: Employment, Workplace Relations and Education References Committee.

Commonwealth of Australia. (2006). *Disability standards for education (2005) plus guidance notes.* ACT: Author.

Cumming, J. J. (2012). *Valuing students with impairment: International comparisons of practice in educational accountability.* New York, NY: Springer.

Davies, M. (2012). Accessibility to NAPLAN assessments for students with disabilities: A "fair go". *Australasian Journal of Special Education, 36*(1), 62–78.

Dempsey, I. (2011). Trends in the proportion of students with a disability in Australian schools, 2000–2009. *Journal of Intellectual & Developmental Disability, 36*(2), 144–145.

Dempsey, I., & Davies, M. (2013). National test performance of young Australian children with additional educational needs. *Australian Journal of Education, 57*(1), 5–18.

Department of Education. (1999). *The Education Act of Western Australia.* Retrieved from http://www.austlii.au/au/legis/wa/consol_act/sea1999170/. Accessed on March 11, 2014.

Department of Education. (2006). *Inclusive education.* Retrieved from www.ltag.education.tas.gov.au/focus/inclusiveprac/default.htm. Accessed on May 31, 2006.

Department of Education. (2013a). *Schools plus: Reforming informed practice.* Retrieved from http://www.det.wa.edu.au/schoolsplus/detcms/navigation/parents/?page = 5&tab = Main. Accessed on February 21, 2013.

Department of Education. (2013b). *Nationally consistent collection of data: School students with disability.* Retrieved from http://docs.education.gov.au/system/files/doc/other/attachment_2_-_nationally_consistent_data_collection_-_schools_factsheet.pdf. Accessed on February 22, 2013.

Department of Education and Early Childhood Development (DEECD). (2013). *Student support guidelines.* Melbourne, Victoria: Author. Retrieved from https://www.eduweb.vic.gov.au/edulibrary/public/stuman/wellbeing/2013-SSGGuidlines.pdf

Elkins, J., van Kraayenoord, C. E., & Jobling, A. (2003). Parents' attitudes to inclusion of their children with special needs. *Journal of Research in Special Educational Needs, 3*, 22–29.

Foreman, P. (2011). *Inclusion in action*. Melbourne, Victoria: Cengage Learning.

Foreman, P., Arthur-Kelly, M., & Pascoe, S. (2007). The impact of partner training on the communicative involvement of students with multiple and severe disabilities in special schools. *Journal of Intellectual and Developmental Disability, 32*, 233–247.

Gallimore, D. P. M. (2005). Multiculturalism and students with visual impairments in new south wales, Australia. *Journal of Visual Impairments and Blindness, 99*, 345–354.

Individuals with Disabilities Act of 1990. Pub. L. No. 101–476. 104 Stat. 1142.

Jenkinson, J. C. (2001). *Special education: A matter of choice*. Camberwell, Victoria: ACER Press.

Lindsay, K. (2004). "Asking for the moon"? A critical assessment of Australian disability discrimination laws in promoting inclusion for students with disabilities. *International Journal of Inclusive Education, 8*(4), 373–390.

McDonnell, L. M., McLaughlin, M. J., & Morison, P. (1997). *Educating one and all: Students with disabilities and standards-based reform*. Washington, DC: National Academy Press.

Ministerial Council for Education, Early Childhood Development and Youth Affairs [MCEECDYA]. (2008). *National declaration on the educational goals for young Australians*. Retrieved from http://www.mceecdya.edu.au/verve/_resources/National_Declaration_on_the_ Educational_Goals_for_Young_Australians.pdf. Accessed on January 19, 2014.

Morris, C., & Sharma, U. (2011). Facilitating the inclusion of children with vision impairment: Perspectives of itinerant support teachers. *Australasian Journal of Special Education, 35*(2), 191–203.

Parliament of Victoria. (2005). *Step up, step in, step out: Inquiry into the suitability of pre-service teacher training in Victoria*. Melbourne: Author.

Stephenson, J., Carter, M., & Arthur-Kelly, M. (2011). Professional learning for teachers without special education qualifications working with students with severe disability. *Teacher Education and Special Education, 34*(1), 7–20.

The Australian Curriculum, Assessment and Reporting Authority (ACARA). (2013). *The Australian Curriculum*. Retrieved from http://www.australiancurriculum.edu.au/. Accessed on February 22, 2014.

Thomas, T. (2007). The impending special education qualifications crisis in Victoria. *Australasian Journal of Special Education, 31*(2), 139–145.

Thomas, T. (2009). The age and qualifications of special education staff in Australia. *Australasian Journal of Special Education, 33*, 109–116.

van Kraayenoord, C., Elkins, J., Palmer, C., & Rickards, F. (2000). *Literacy, numeracy and students with disabilities — The literature review* (Vol. 2). Canberra: Department of Education, Training and Youth Affairs.

Victorian Auditor General. (2012). *Programs for students with special learning needs*. Melbourne: Author.

Wu, C. C., & Komesaroff, L. (2007). An emperor with no clothes? Inclusive education in Victoria. *Australasian Journal of Special Education, 31*(2), 129–137.

SPECIAL EDUCATION TODAY IN NEW ZEALAND

Garry Hornby

ABSTRACT

This chapter considers the development and current state of special education in New Zealand. The chapter provides a critique of current policies and practices regarding special and inclusive education for children with special educational needs and disabilities (SEND). It describes how New Zealand has followed similar patterns to other developed countries with regard to how special education facilities and specialist teacher training have evolved, and how the trend towards inclusive education has progressed. It points out that New Zealand has gone further in the inclusion of children with SEND within mainstream schools than most developed countries and that, at the same time, there has been less development of provision for children with SEND in mainstream schools. That has led to a situation where many children with SEND, who are in the lowest 20% of achievers, are not getting the specialist help that they need. As a result New Zealand has one of the largest gaps between high achieving and low achieving children in the developed world.

Special Education International Perspectives: Practices Across the Globe
Advances in Special Education, Volume 28, 643–660
Copyright © 2014 by Emerald Group Publishing Limited
ISSN: 0270-4013/doi:10.1108/S0270-401320140000028029

INTRODUCTION

Origins of Special Education

The first special education facilities in New Zealand to open were the Sumner Institute for the Deaf in 1880 in Christchurch, followed by the Jubilee Institute for the Blind in 1891 in Auckland (Mitchell & Singh, 1987). These were followed by a special school for backward boys in Otago in 1908 and a primary school special class for backward children in Auckland in 1917. (The term backward was used to describe children with a moderate level of learning difficulties.)

A special school for children with severe intellectual disability opened in Auckland in 1931 while special schools for children with physical disabilities emerged later with the Wilson Home for Crippled Children opening in Auckland in 1937 and special schools for children with cerebral palsy opening in Christchurch and Dunedin in 1949.

In 1960, the first residential special school for maladjusted children (those with social, emotional and behavioural difficulties) was opened in Auckland, and a class for hearing impaired pupils began in a primary school in Wellington. In 1962 special classes for backward children at secondary schools were opened in Auckland and Wellington and in 1965 a class for visually impaired pupils began in a secondary school in Auckland.

In 1971 a class for children with physical disabilities began at an Auckland primary school and in 1973 special groups for children with disabilities were established in selected kindergartens in the main centres.

So by the 1970s the pattern was set with many special classes at primary, intermediate and secondary schools for children with moderate learning difficulties, and a few such classes for children with sensory or physical disabilities. There were special schools for children with severe intellectual disabilities, and special groups for children with disabilities in selected kindergartens, in all the major metropolitan centres. There were also five residential special schools for children with social, emotional and behavioural difficulties, two of which enroled children who had moderate learning difficulties. There was one residential special school for children with visual impairment and two for children with hearing impairment, both of which had a few associated resource classes in mainstream schools.

Alongside the evolution of this special education infrastructure, various support services also developed. A key component of this was the Department of Education Psychological Service that was staffed by New Zealand trained educational psychologists from 1960 onwards (Winterbourn, 1974).

Educational psychologists conducted observations and assessments of children with special educational needs and disabilities (SEND) and provided guidance to pre-schools and schools on programmes to address their learning and behavioural difficulties. These psychologists were assigned a geographical area within which they provided services to pre-schools, special schools and classes, and mainstream schools, as well as to parents and families of children with SEND.

During the 1980s, special education provision in New Zealand was at its pinnacle. At the same time, special education practice was being influenced by key overseas developments, namely the *Education of All Handicapped Children Act* in the United States (1975) and the *Warnock Report on Special Educational Needs* in the United Kingdom (DES, 1978). These developments resulted in a comprehensive special education system that had a clear vision and a strong sense of its mission, which was to provide effective education for all children with SEND whether they were in mainstream schools or in special education facilities. However, after around 100 years of incremental improvements in this SEND system, the late 1980s saw the beginning of the decline of special education provision in New Zealand.

There were three main reasons for this. First, the New Zealand government in 1986 brought about a change that established self-managing schools. This led to a major reduction in the national infrastructure for managing education in mainstream schools and special education facilities for children with SEND. This meant that the new Ministry of Education (MoE) had much reduced influence over special education practice. Second, the impact of an inclusive education philosophy and the critique of special classes in the United States led to policies promoting the integration of increasing numbers of children into mainstream schools, particularly those with moderate learning difficulties. Third, the change from special class provision to a consultant model for children with moderate learning difficulties accelerated the closure of special classes for this group in mainstream schools. This change began during the late 1970s when the Guidance and Learning Unit (GLU) model was trialled. It involved having teachers appointed to a primary school special class who worked mainly as consultants to classroom teachers while these children remained in mainstream classes. During the 1980s, the GLU model morphed into a support team approach, and then in the 1990s into a consultant model with Resource Teachers of Learning and Behaviour (RTLB) working with groups of schools to support children with moderate learning and behavioural difficulties in mainstream classrooms (Thomson, Brown, Jones, & Manins, 2000).

The RTLB service replaced the special classes, so that today in New Zealand there are now over 900 RTLB and no special classes in primary, intermediate or secondary schools for children with moderate learning and behavioural difficulties. In essence, children with moderate learning difficulties and behavioural difficulties who would have been in special classes in the past are now all in mainstream schools.

Another type of special education facility to be closed was the special groups for children with disabilities which were established in selected kindergartens in all the major metropolitan centres. With these closings, only 28 day special schools for children with severe disabilities remain, many of which have satellite classes in local mainstream schools. There also remain six residential special schools. One was closed at the end of 2012 and others are under threat of closure by the MoE.

Over this same period, there was an important change in the role of educational psychologists when they went from working within a group of educational psychologist colleagues in Psychological Service centres to working with other professionals including speech therapists, occupational therapists and visiting teachers in the newly created Special Education Service (SES) in 1989. This change was made in order to enable better coordination of support services for children with SEND. However, it meant that educational psychologists went from a management structure consisting of senior psychologist colleagues, to one in which SES centres were typically managed by members of staff, who were not psychologists. This has changed the professional culture within which educational psychologists work. For example, one consequence of the new management structure is that the typical model for service provision has become the 'case' model rather than the 'patch' model which was typical in Psychological Service days. The patch model was one in which educational psychologists were assigned a geographical area in which they provided services to schools and families and therefore could work proactively as well as reactively. In contrast, the current case model constrains them to work mainly reactively, with few opportunities to work proactively, thereby preventing many problems from occurring. In addition, educational psychologists are now required to work with only the 2% of children with the highest level of SEND. So they no longer work with children experiencing mild or moderate learning difficulties that make up the 20% tail of underachievement in New Zealand schools, who are now the responsibility of RTLB. These changes in the model for service provision has resulted in there being few opportunities for educational psychologists to work more systemically in order to help schools to improve their SEND provision.

Special Education Training

The first recorded training courses for special education personnel in New Zealand were for teachers of backward children and speech therapists in 1940 (Mitchell & Singh, 1987). This was followed by training courses for teachers of the deaf in 1943 and for school psychologists in 1946 (Winterbourn, 1974). In 1960, a two-year full-time training course for educational psychologists was started in Auckland and this was followed by other courses being established in Dunedin and Wellington. A major step forward was the opening in 1974 of one-year full-time training courses, in both Christchurch and Auckland, for teachers of children with intellectual and physical disabilities. A one-year training course for teachers of children with visual impairment was added in 1984 in Auckland to complement the above courses and also the one-year courses for teachers of children with hearing impairments, in Auckland and Christchurch. All special education training courses were aimed at qualified teachers who had several years of experience teaching in mainstream schools as well as typically some experience of teaching in special schools or special classes.

So by the mid-1980s, New Zealand had full-time postgraduate training courses for key personnel working in the special education field, including educational psychologists and specialist teachers. However, during the 1990s when self-managing schools were being established within a 'market forces' driven philosophy in education, central coordination of special education was markedly reduced and full-time training courses came under pressure and began to close. Today, there are no full-time training courses for specialist teachers. These have now been replaced by part-time, mainly on-line courses. The part-time courses have been developed and taught by faculty at Massey and Canterbury Universities. Teachers enroled in these courses have their university fees paid and they study one or two days per week over a two-year period. The advantages of these courses over previous centre-based ones include accessibility for teachers from all over New Zealand and the opportunity to make full use of on-line learning. The major disadvantage is that face-to-face contact is limited to two one-week contact courses in each of the two years which makes the inclusion of some aspects difficult, for example, learning the skills necessary to implement interventions such as cooperative learning as well as those necessary for the development of counselling and consultation skills.

As noted above, a two-year full-time training course for educational psychologists was established at Auckland University in 1960 and this was followed by other courses at Otago and Victoria Universities

(Winterbourn, 1974). Entry to the course was following the completion of master's degree papers in educational psychology. The first year of the course was university-based training in assessment and intervention and the second year was an internship, based in a Psychological Service centre, completing a range of cases and intervention projects. However, the two-year full-time training courses for educational psychologists, which were operating at Auckland, Victoria and Otago Universities in the 1970s and 1980s, all closed down during the 1990s. The only training course for educational psychologists available in New Zealand for around 10 years was the part-time distance education course offered by Massey University. Recently Victoria University has begun to offer a two-year training course for educational psychologists. But as a consequence of the limited training available in the last decade there is now a shortage of qualified educational psychologists in New Zealand.

Educational Influences

An early special educational pioneer and reformer was Dr Clarence Beeby, who completed a doctorate in psychology, lectured at Canterbury University and became the first director of the New Zealand Council of Educational Research. His most important influence came when he moved to the Department of Education where he became the Director of Education. He served in this capacity for more than 20 years in the 1940s and 1950s. Dr Beeby reformed the previously formal, examination-ridden New Zealand education system. Under his guidance, schools became more pupil centred and the curriculum was geared to the broad needs of the community. He provided a vision for the New Zealand education system, as often quoted below.

> The Government's objective, broadly expressed, is that all persons, whatever their ability, rich or poor, whether they live in town or country, have a right as citizens to a free education of the kind for which they are best fitted and to the fullest extent of their powers. (Beeby, 1992)

Another influential special education pioneer was Ralph Winterbourn, who like Beeby lectured at Canterbury University and conducted the first major study of special education in New Zealand (Winterbourn, 1944). In this study, Winterbourn (1944) examined the special education that was provided for children with moderate learning difficulties in special classes, which he repeated in the 1960s and again in the 1970s. Winterbourn also established training courses for educational psychologists and provided an influential framework for understanding the coordination of guidance and support services for working with children with SEND (Winterbourn, 1974).

Following the pioneering work of Beeby (1992) and Winterbourn (1974), a series of special education texts emerged over the subsequent years. The first of these books *Issues in New Zealand Special Education* was edited by Havill and Mitchell (1972) who were both based at Waikato University. Their book contains chapters on special education provisions for children with different types of disability, as well as on guidance services and issues of concern at that time. The second book *Mental Retardation in New Zealand*, which was edited by Singh and Wilton (1985), focused on the education and care of children and young people with severe intellectual disabilities in New Zealand. The third book *Exceptional Children in New Zealand* was edited by Mitchell and Singh (1987). This book followed a similar pattern to the Havill and Mitchell (1972) book but with greater emphasis on current issues. The fourth book *Learners with Special Needs in Aotearoa/New Zealand* was edited by Fraser, Moltzen, and Ryba (1995). This book has chapters on different types of special needs children, special education policies and systems, and partnerships in special education. The second edition of this book (Fraser, Moltzen, & Ryba, 2000) follows a similar format but introduces and delineates inclusive education philosophy, practices and parameters for use with special needs children. The third edition of the book (Fraser, Moltzen, & Ryba, 2005) covers similar ground as the previous edition but expands upon the advance of inclusive education for special needs children. Readers delving into these seven books are provided a fascinating insight into the debates, issues and trends in the field of special and inclusive education in New Zealand over the past 40 years.

Prevalence and Incidence

Since there are no national statistics on the numbers of children with SEND, the best way to estimate this is by noting the percentage of pupils being educated in special education provisions, such as special schools and special classes, as compared with those educated in mainstream classrooms.

In 1971, it was estimated that just over 2% of the school population were being educated in special schools and classes (Havill & Mitchell, 1972). Whereas, in 2013, the proportion of the school population being educated in special schools and classes is estimated to be just less than 1%. New Zealand's proportion of just less than 1% compares with Finland's of around 8% (Takala, Pirttimaa, & Törmänen, 2009). So it may be that New Zealand has the lowest proportion of children who are educated in special education provisions in the developed world and now has one of most inclusive education systems in the world, with less than 1% of children educated in residential schools, special schools or special classes in mainstream schools.

Trends in Legislation

In 1989, the New Zealand government passed an Education Act which established a legal right for all children to attend their local mainstream school from age 5 to 19 years. A few years later, in 1996 the MoE introduced a policy called Special Education 2000 (SE2000) which was intended to bring about mainstreaming for all children, that is the inclusion of all children with SEND in mainstream schools. The primary aim of SE2000 was to bring about a, 'world class inclusive education system' (MoE, 1996). However, as Coleman (2011) points out, SE2000 was about the funding of SEND provision rather than providing policy for professional practice. Coleman states that the SE2000 framework is seriously flawed and that children with SEND would be better served by a needs-based rather than a category-based funding system. For example, the SE2000 framework provides separate funding for the 1% of children with severe intellectual disabilities and another 1% for children with high levels of social, emotional and behavioural difficulties. So these two groups are serviced by different sets of professionals, whereas in reality their special needs will encompass both learning and behavioural difficulties. Therefore, professionals such as educational psychologists assigned to deal with children with severe intellectual disabilities also need to address their behavioural issues and other professionals assigned to deal with children with high levels of social and emotional difficulties also need to address their learning needs.

So it is not surprising that Wylie (2000) in her major review of SE2000 and New Zealand SEND provision, concluded that, '... the division of the policy into a number of separate initiatives and funding pools has made it hard to offer students, parents and schools the seamless integrated service which works best for students with special needs' (Wylie, 2000, p. 8). Another example of this is that, whereas SE2000 caters to children with high and very high needs, it does not provide specific funding for students with moderate levels of learning or academic problems, such as those with moderate learning difficulties or specific learning difficulties, such as dyslexia, who need long-term support, and who will be in mainstream schools following the mainly academic New Zealand national curriculum for their entire school lives (Coleman, 2011).

The 1989 Education Act also established self-managing schools, so that New Zealand now has one of the most devolved education systems in the world, with individual schools governed by Boards of Trustees made up mainly of parents. The MoE provides policy guidelines for schools but in most cases these are not mandatory, so schools develop their own policies and practices, including those for children with SEND. The major requirement on schools from the MoE regarding children with SEND is a very general one, that schools identify students with special needs and develop and implement teaching and learning strategies to address these needs (MoE, 2009).

The current policy on education for children with SEND is entitled, *Success for All — Every School, Every Child* (MoE, 2010a). This policy presents a vision of a fully inclusive education system in which all schools have the resources and skills required to provide an environment where learners with SEND are welcomed and thrive. The objective is for children to have the option of attending their local school and have confidence in the knowledge that they will experience positive attitudes, skilled teachers and a supportive environment. The policy's primary aim is to create a fully inclusive education system where parents can have confidence that all children, including those with SEND will receive a quality education. In 2010, a report from the Education Review Office (ERO) found that 50% of schools surveyed demonstrated *mostly* inclusive practices, 30% *some* inclusive practices and 20% *few* inclusive practices. These percentages are consistent with the MoE aims to achieve the goal of *all* schools demonstrating *some* or *mostly* inclusive practices by 2014.

However, when policy and practice regarding inclusive education for children with SEND in New Zealand is compared with that from other countries, such as the United States and England, two differences are clear. First, New Zealand policy for inclusive education has been more radical than that in most countries, with an espoused goal of educating *all* children with SEND in mainstream schools. The impact of this policy is evidenced by the smaller percentage of children with SEND in special schools and special classes than is the case in other countries. The second difference is that when the actual practice of providing for children with

SEND in mainstream schools is compared with that in England and the United States, glaring deficiencies in the New Zealand system become apparent.

Perspective on the Progress of Special and Inclusive Education

Major weaknesses in SEND provision are outlined below in order to highlight the disparity between the rhetoric and reality of special and inclusive education in New Zealand.

No Specific Legislation for Children with SEND

There is no specific education legislation in New Zealand regarding children with SEND. The 1989 Education Act which established self-managing schools, as well as the legal right for all children to attend their local mainstream schools from age 5 to 19 years, does provide that a child whose special needs cannot be met in a mainstream school should, with agreement of the parents, be enroled in a special school, class or clinic. But this is as far as it goes (Varnham, 2002).

This is in stark contrast with the 1996 Education Act in England and the Individuals with Disabilities Education Act (IDEA) (1997) in the United States. These are both examples of specific legislation on children with SEND that set out statutory responsibilities for schools regarding provision for children with SEND. For example, the IDEA specifies six principles for the education of children with SEND (Salend, 2011). First, *zero reject*, which requires that the education system cannot exclude students with special needs or disabilities and must provide special education services when needed. Second, *non-discriminatory evaluation*, which requires that children are evaluated fairly and that parents receive guidelines about special education and related services available. Third, *free and appropriate education*, which requires schools to put in place Individualized Education Programmes (IEPs) for all children identified as having special educational needs. Fourth, *least restrictive environment*, which requires schools to educate children with peers of the same age to the maximum extent appropriate. Fifth, *procedural due process*, which includes safeguards for children and their parents including the right to sue if the other principles are not carried out. Six, *family and student participation*, which requires that parents and students are fully involved in designing and delivering programmes. These principles provide children with SEND and their families in the United

States with a virtual guarantee of an appropriate education. Since legislation for SEND with statutory responsibilities is lacking in New Zealand and schools are self-governing, what schools provide for children with SEND varies widely between schools and ranges from the excellent to the woefully inadequate. However, there is no means of redress for parents who are not satisfied with what a school provides for their child with SEND, except to enrol the child at another school.

No Statutory Guidelines for Schools Regarding SEND

In New Zealand there are no statutory guidelines for schools regarding SEND children that schools must follow. Guidelines on many SEND issues are provided by the MoE, but schools can choose whether or not to take heed of these. This is in stark contrast with the requirements specified in the IDEA in the United States, outlined above, and the detailed statutory guidance for schools provided within the Code of Practice for Special Educational Needs (DfES, 2001) in England. This Code sets out detailed guidelines for the procedures that must be followed and the resources that must be provided for children with SEND and their families. This includes a three-stage process for assessing and planning interventions for addressing SEND. The third stage of this process requires that a 'statement' of SEND be produced that specifies the programmes and resources that are mandated to be provided for the child. Also mandated is the need to take into account the child's views and those of the parents throughout the three-stage process. In contrast, since statutory guidelines are absent in New Zealand, provision for children with SEND varies widely. In some cases it is excellent but in many cases it is inadequate.

No Requirement to Have SENCOs or SEND Committees

The establishment of Special Educational Needs Coordinators (SENCOs) in all New Zealand Schools, with a time allocation of least 0.2 full time equivalent in primary schools and 0.4 full time equivalent in secondary schools, was recommended in the Wylie Report (2000) on special education but was never implemented by the MoE. As a result, schools may have staff assigned to this role but typically limited time allocation is made for them to carry out the requirements of this job. Typically, the SENCO role is added to the responsibilities of school principals, deputy principals or other senior staff. Unfortunately, these professionals often have limited or no time allocation to carry out the necessary tasks. More problematic is that many of these named SENCOs have limited training in the SEND field.

No Requirement for SENCO Training
For New Zealand schools that do have SENCOs identified there is no requirement for them to have qualifications on SEND or to undergo training once they are assigned this role. This is in contrast to England where training is compulsory for SENCOs. Relevant training on SEND is available at most New Zealand universities but this needs to be undertaken at the teachers' own expense and in their own time, so currently, few of them take up these opportunities. In practice, many of the staff named as SENCOs in schools do not have the training or experience with SEND to effectively carry out the SENCO role.

No Requirement for Individual Education Plans
While comprehensive guidance on Individual Education Plans (IEPs) is provided to schools (MoE, 2011), individual schools decide which children will have IEPs, the format and content of IEPs, and the extent to which parents are involved. Therefore, whether students with SEND have IEPs or not varies widely between schools and IEP procedures are often inadequate, particularly with regard to the effective involvement of parents (Hornby & Witte, 2010).

No Statutory Training for Mainstream Teachers on SEND
Until 2011 there was no requirement on institutions offering teacher education to include training on teaching students with SEND. Recently, the Tertiary Education Commission (TEC, 2011) specified the SEND content of teacher education by providing an appendix to the graduating teacher standards that sets out the knowledge and skills on SEND that teachers need to become competent in. This is a major step forward, but it will take several years to implement. A small-scale survey of school principals has found that they are keen to see the new SEND content included in teacher education programmes, but philosophical and implementation issues raised by the academics who are supposed to deliver this content suggest that it will not be a straightforward task (Hornby & Sutherland, 2014). Meanwhile, the vast majority of practicing mainstream school teachers have had minimal or no training on teaching students with SEND. Also, there is no requirement for New Zealand teachers, once qualified, to undertake continuing professional development, like there is in other countries such as England, Australia, and the United States. In addition, it is only a minority of teachers who take up opportunities for professional development regarding SEND that are available.

No Statutory School/Educational Psychologist Involvement
As noted earlier, in New Zealand, educational psychologists are based in MoE Special Education Services along with other staff such as speech/language therapists. Typically, they operate using a case allocation model. Within this model, they work mainly in a reactive rather than a proactive model of service provision (Hornby, 2010). This means that, rather than helping schools develop effective practices for all children, including those with SEND, they are constrained to work with the 2% of children with the most severe learning and behavioural difficulties. They may be involved in IEPs if they are invited by schools or parents, otherwise they have no mandated involvement. In contrast, in England and the United States educational or school psychologist's input is mandated in assessment and programme planning for children identified as having moderate to severe levels of SEND.

No School Counsellors or Social Workers in Elementary and Middle Schools
New Zealand schools do not have school counsellors in primary or intermediate schools, but there are guidance counsellors in high schools. Social workers are not based in schools, but schools do have access to social workers who serve several schools. Thus, although the majority of SEND and mental health issues emerge during the primary and middle school years, children in New Zealand have limited access to professionals who can provide specialist help with mental health issues until they reach secondary schools, by which time these problems may have become entrenched. This is particularly important for children with SEND as they have a higher rate of mental health problems than other children (Atkinson & Hornby, 2002).

No Parent Partnership Services
There are no SEND services equivalent to the parent partnership services that play a key role in providing support and guidance to parents of children with SEND in a country such as England. This is unfortunate because parent partnership services offer information, advice and support to parents and carers who have a child or young person with special educational needs or a disability. Furthermore, such services offer confidential and impartial help with such things as: communicating with the child's school or pre-school setting; providing information about what schools can do to support children with SEND; preparing parents for meetings with school staff; providing mediation to help ensure children with SEND get the education they need; providing guidance on choosing

a school for a child with SEND; providing details of local and national voluntary organizations that offer support to parents; supporting parents during school-based and other assessment processes; helping parents learn about the SEND services and support they and their children are entitled to; and helping parents to meet other parents who are in a similar situation. In England each local education authority has a parent partnership service and there is a National Parent Partnership Network which supports and promotes the work of Parent Partnership Services across the country. Similar services are available in the United States with school districts employing staff typically called parent involvement coordinators who fulfil a similar role to that of the parent partnership services in England. Since services such as these are not available in New Zealand, parents of children with SEND typically find it difficult to obtain the guidance and support they need to ensure an appropriate education for their children.

No Coherent Policy about Inclusive Education
Although 99% of children are educated in mainstream schools, New Zealand still has 6 residential special schools and 28 day special schools. Many of the special schools have satellite classes in mainstream schools and some have special classes in several mainstream schools. A few mainstream schools still have special units or classes, including some in the main centres. However, many special classes have been shut down in the last 20 years and special schools have been under threat of elimination due to MoE policy on inclusion. Interestingly, in a recent National Review of Special Education (MoE, 2010b) the future of special schools was considered with four options for special schools, one of which was closure of all special schools. Only 1% of submissions agreed with closing special schools while 99% were in favour of keeping special schools. However, this has not stopped a vocal minority who are calling for their closure. For example, a group calling themselves the 'Inclusive Education Action Group' (http://www.ieag.org.nz/) has been lobbying the government to further the inclusion agenda and close special schools.

Recent government policy in New Zealand has focused on ensuring that all schools are 'fully inclusive' (MoE, 2010a). The policy notes that special schools will continue to exist but does not clarify what their role will be. In essence, the government appears to be supporting a continuum of provision for SEND but exactly what this involves is not made clear. Because New Zealand has no specific legislation on provision for children with SEND and therefore no statutory guidance for schools, the lack of a coherent policy on inclusive education for children with SEND leaves schools to develop practices based on their interpretation of the non-statutory guidance provided by the MoE. The lack of a clear coherent policy has resulted in a wide variation in the type and quality of the procedures and practices employed by schools that serve students with SEND. This wide variation in procedures and practices is likely to be the case for some time to come.

Another consequence of the lack of specific legislation on the education of children with SEND is that there is no protection for the special education facilities that have been established. So when new Ministers of Education are looking for areas in which to make cuts in their budgets, such facilities are particularly vulnerable. One area that has come under the spotlight in New Zealand in recent times is the provision for children with severe social, emotional and behavioural difficulties. This is a very challenging area of special education that has been the subject of three research studies conducted in New Zealand over the past few years (Hornby & Evans, 2013; Hornby & Witte, 2008a, 2008b; Townsend & Wilton, 2006). But it has recently become very topical with the closure of one of only four residential schools for children with severe social, emotional and behavioural difficulties and the threatened closure of another.

CHALLENGES FOR THE FUTURE

It is clear from the above discussion of perspectives on the progress of special and inclusive education that New Zealand must improve educational provisions for children with SEND, most of who fall in the lowest 20% or so of our school achievers, by addressing weaknesses in New Zealand's current provision for children with SEND. These would include

- Having specific legislation focusing on children with disabilities and special educational needs, like that in the United States, which sets out the rights of children with SEND and their parents, and the responsibilities of the education system to meet their needs.
- Having a Code of Practice for meeting special educational needs, as in England, setting out what schools must provide, such as a staged or tiered approach to intervention, like that in Response to Intervention used in the United States, as well as IEPs for children with moderate and severe levels of special needs.

- Having schools implement a tiered system of intervention to identify up to 30% of children with the lowest levels of achievement in their first year of schooling and target them for additional specialist teaching and support, as they do in Finland. The implementation of this tiered system of intervention could be specified in the Code of Practice for SEND and monitored by the ERO.
- Having trained SENCOs in all New Zealand schools, with specified time allowances to carry out this role, as is mandatory in the England.
- Having mainstream school teachers who have had training on teaching children with disabilities and special educational needs as part of their initial teacher training and also as part of mandatory ongoing professional development.
- Having well trained staff and coordinated support services, including resource teachers, educational psychologists and others, working within effective, proactive models of service delivery to provide assistance to schools in catering effectively for children with SEND.
- Having a parent partnership service in order to help parents of children with SEND to obtain the guidance and support they need to ensure an appropriate and effective education for their children.

Implementing the above changes would bring about substantial improvements in New Zealand's educational provision for children with SEND and in the achievement levels of the lowest 20% of school achievers. These changes would significantly reduce the long tail of underachievement that has been highlighted by international surveys (e.g., PISA, 2006), thereby raising overall achievement levels for New Zealand children. It would also help to achieve the espoused MoE goal of bringing about a 'world class inclusive education system' as well as Beeby's aim of providing for all New Zealand children an, 'education *of the kind for which they are best fitted and to the fullest extent of their powers*' (Beeby, 1992).

REFERENCES

Atkinson, M., & Hornby, G. (2002). *Mental health handbook for schools*. London: Routledge Falmer.

Beeby, C. E. (1992). *The biography of an idea*. Wellington, NZ: New Zealand Council for Educational Research.

Coleman, P. (2011). Special Education 2000 policy: Our leaky home? *Kairaranga, 12*(1), 10–22.

DES. (1978). *Special educational needs (The Warnock Report)*. London: Department of Education and Science.

DfES. (2001). *Special educational needs: Code of practice*. Annesley, England: Department for Education and Skills.

Education of All Handicapped Children Act. (P.L. 94–142). (1975). (20 U.S.C., 1978). Washington, DC.

Education Review Office. (2010). *Including students with high needs*. Wellington, NZ: Ministry of Education.

Fraser, D., Moltzen, R., & Ryba, K. (Eds.). (1995). *Learners with special needs in Aotearoa/ New Zealand*. Palmerston North, NZ: Dunmore Press.

Fraser, D., Moltzen, R., & Ryba, K. (Eds.). (2000). *Learners with special needs in Aotearoa/ New Zealand* (2nd ed.). Palmerston North, NZ: Dunmore Press.

Fraser, D., Moltzen, R., & Ryba, K. (Eds.). (2005). *Learners with special needs in Aotearoa/ New Zealand* (3rd ed.). Southbank Victoria, NZ: Thompson/Dunmore Press.

Havill, S. J. & Mitchell, D. R. (Eds.). (1972). *Issues in New Zealand special education*. Auckland, NZ: Hodder and Stoughton.

Hornby, G. (2010). The demise of educational psychology in New Zealand: A personal view. *Psychology Aotearoa, 2*(1), 26–30.

Hornby, G., & Evans, W. H. (2013). Including students with significant social, emotional and behavioral difficulties in mainstream school settings. In P. Garner, J. Kauffman, & J. Elliott (Eds.), *The SAGE handbook of emotional and behavioral difficulties* (2nd ed., pp. 335–347). London: Sage.

Hornby, G., & Sutherland, D. (2014). School principals' views of teaching standards for inclusive education in New Zealand. In P. Jones (Ed.), *Bringing insider perspectives into inclusive teacher learning: Potentials and challenges for educational professionals* (pp. 47–56). Abingdon, England: Routledge.

Hornby, G., & Witte, C. (2008a). Follow-up study of ex-students of a residential school for children with emotional and behavioral difficulties in New Zealand. *Emotional and Behavioral Difficulties, 13*(2), 79–93.

Hornby, G., & Witte, C. (2008b). *Looking back on school* – Views of their education of adult graduates of a residential special school for children with emotional and behavioral difficulties. *British Journal of Special Education, 35*(2), 102–107.

Hornby, G., & Witte, C. (2010). Parent involvement in rural elementary schools in New Zealand: A survey. *Journal of Child and Family Studies, 19*(6), 771–777.

Individuals with Disabilities Education Act. (1997). (Pub. L. No. 105-17, & 111, Stat 37, U.S.C.). Washington, DC.

Mitchell, D. R., & Singh, N. N. (Eds.). (1987). *Exceptional children in New Zealand*. Palmerston North, NZ: Dunmore Press.

MoE. (1996). *Special Education 2000 policy*. Wellington, NZ: Ministry of Education.

MoE. (2009). *National administration guidelines*. Retrieved from http://www.minedu.govt.nz/ NZEducation/EducationPolicies/Schools/

MoE. (2010a). *Success for all: Every school, every child*. Wellington, NZ: Ministry of Education.

MoE. (2010b). *Review of special education*. Wellington, NZ: Ministry of Education.

MoE. (2011). *Collaboration for success: Individual education plans*. Wellington, NZ: Learning Media.

PISA. (2006). *Programme for International Student Assessment: 2006 results*. Paris, France: OECD. Retrieved from http://www.oecd.org/edu/school/programmeforinternational studentassessmentpisa/pisa2006results.htm

Salend, S. J. (2011). *Creating inclusive classrooms: Effective and reflective practices* (7th ed.). Boston, MA: Pearson.

Singh, N. N., & Wilton, K. M. (Eds.). (1985). *Mental retardation in New Zealand.* Christchurch, NZ: Whitcoulls.

Takala, M., Pirttimaa, R., & Törmänen, M. (2009). Inclusive special education: The role of special education teachers in Finland. *British Journal of Special Education, 36*(3), 162–172.

TEC. (2011). *Graduating teacher standards: Aotearoa New Zealand: Appendix 2.2 special (inclusive) education.* Wellington, NZ: Tertiary Education Commission.

Thomson, C., Brown, D., Jones, E., & Manins, E. (2000). The development of resource teachers in New Zealand: A quarter century of paradigm change. *New Zealand Annual Review of Education, 9*, 23–42.

Townsend, M., & Wilton, K. (2006). Effects of attendance at a New Zealand residential school for students with emotional-behavioral difficulties: The views of former students and their parents. *Australasian Journal of Special Education, 30*(2), 126–145.

Varnham, S. (2002). Current developments in New Zealand: Special education 2000 and Daniels v. the Attorney-General: Equality of access to education for children with special needs in New Zealand. *Education and the Law, 14*(4), 283–300.

Winterbourn, R. (1944). *Educating backward children in New Zealand.* Wellington, NZ: New Zealand Council for Educational Research.

Winterbourn, R. (1974). *Guidance services in New Zealand education.* Wellington, NZ: New Zealand Council for Educational Research.

Wylie, C. (2000). *Picking up the pieces: Review of special education.* Wellington, NZ: New Zealand Council for Educational Research.

PART VII
FAR EAST

PART III
FAR EAST

SPECIAL EDUCATION TODAY IN CHINA

Mian Wang and Yajing Feng

ABSTRACT

Special education in China has lagged behind regular education for many years, however, the past few decades, the government has made considerable efforts to develop and improve the special education system. While the citizens of China have had a generic moral interest in disability since ancient times, the development of special education schools did not occur until American and European missionaries started schools for the visually and hearing impaired in the 19th century. The next major influence in the development of the special education system occurred with China's Cultural Revolution in 1978. Interestingly, there is not any exclusive legislation on special education but in the 1980s, the government started Learning in Regular Classrooms (LRC), which is China's version of inclusion. LRC has progressed rapidly the past two decades; however, the quality of instruction is low due to a lack of specialists, a shortage of personnel, inadequate funding, and limited technology as well as other barriers that are delineated in the chapter. The chapter emphasizes the government's recent efforts in in-service teacher training, the preparation of preservice teachers, working with families, developing community rehabilitation training programs, and implementing

Special Education International Perspectives: Practices Across the Globe
Advances in Special Education, Volume 28, 663–688
Copyright © 2014 by Emerald Group Publishing Limited
All rights of reproduction in any form reserved
ISSN: 0270-4013/doi:10.1108/S0270-401320140000028030

evidence-based practices. Special education in China today is at a good place but it has quite a way from the ideal situation.

INTRODUCTION

As one of the fastest economically growing nations in the world over the last two decades, China has become a primary contributor to the global economy. Enormous changes along with such glamour of economic growth and prosperity have struck dramatically this world's most populous country socially and politically on almost every aspect. However, as a sharp contrast to the image of an emerging economic giant, China is still shy away from having an advanced progressive education system of equality that can ensure education rights for all children, especially those with disabilities. Special education in China, a so-called "step child" of the whole Chinese education system, is at a new crossroad for development and reform.

The earliest idea about disability in China can be traced back to ancient time when Chinese people began to notice the existence of people with obvious disabilities (Deng, Poon-Mcbrayer, & Farnsworth, 2001; Piao, 1992). In a quite vague fashion, Confucius introduces the idea of equally treating people with exceptionality with respect and dignity in his writing of Liji (Book of Rites) in the early Chun Qiu period (770–476 BC), which is the first recording of people with disabilities in Chinese ancient literature. Despite this generic moral call for sympathy toward people with disabilities, there was no formal social support and education system to support people with disabilities at the time, and people with disabilities remained at the lowest social status in the hierarchic feudal system over the long Chinese history. It was not until the late 19th century that the embryo of special education was developed in China with the assistance of American and European missionaries (Deng et al., 2001).

EARLY INCEPTION OF CHINA'S SPECIAL EDUCATION AND ITS DEVELOPMENT

Since the late 19th century, a number of special education schools for children especially with sensory disabilities were established by American and European missionaries in China. The first school for the blind in China was established in 1874 by William Moore, a Scottish Presbyterian pastor.

In 1887, American missionaries Charles and Annetta Mills started the first school for blind and deaf students in Dengzhou, Shandong. Braille and sign language were introduced to China at that time, and students with visual and hearing impairments benefited from learning basic and religious knowledge and life skills through formal school education (Epstein, 1988; Yang & Wang, 1994).

The first special education school founded by Chinese people was actually in the early 20th century when an industrialist and philanthropist, Zhang Jian, established a special school for blind and deaf students in Nantong, Jiangsu, in 1916. This special school emphasized vocational training and learning of general ad basic knowledge (Yu & Zhang, 1994).

The first Chinese government-run special education school, the Nanjing Municipal School for the Blind and Deaf, was established in 1927. The school provided junior and senior high school level education as well as vocational training to students. In addition, a number of private special schools, including teacher training schools, were established. By the end of 1948 before the Communist Party came into the power, there were a total of 42 special schools in China serving more than 2,000 students with visual and hearing impairments. However, education for children with intellectual disability or other disabilities was not available.

The foundation of the People's Republic of China in 1949 brought fundamental changes to education in the country, and as a result all private schools were taken over by the government and merged into the public education system (Ellsworth & Zhang, 2007). Ever since then, special education became part of government-supported affairs and the Chinese government took advantage of the Socialist system to build many special education schools in a relatively short period of time. By 1960, there were 479 special education schools enrolling 26,701 students with disabilities in China. The special education system was deeply influenced by the Soviet Union model (Editorial Department of Year-Book of Education, 1984). Another notable achievement was the establishment of the first special education school for children with intellectual disabilities in Dalian, Liaoning, in 1959 (Ye & Piao, 1995).

CHINA'S SPECIAL EDUCATION IN THE REFORM AND OPEN POLICY ERA

After the Cultural Revolution, the Chinese government reopened its door to the West in 1978. Along with the dramatic changes that occurred in the economic, social, and political arena, special education in China embraced a new development. Under the Reform and Open Policy, special education scholars and practitioners had opportunities to gain information and learn practical skills from other developed countries, especially the United States and some European countries. Although a separate special education system was still predominant, the principles and practices of mainstreaming and inclusion began to gain influence in Chinese special education starting in the late 1980s. These practices were labeled *Learning in Regular Classroom* (LRC). Essentially, LRC is China's version of inclusion, and has some fundamental differences from the inclusion models that are practiced in Western countries such as the United States and the United Kingdom. The LRC practice has led to huge changes in special education in China because it enrolled more children with disabilities into the general education system. In addition to LRC, laws and regulations were also enacted in the 1980s that led to the result of better safeguarding education rights of all children with disabilities. More specifically, two landmark laws were passed (Gu, 1993; Xiao, 1996), namely, the *Compulsory Education Law of People's Republic of China* (National People's Congress of People's Republic of China, 1986) and the *Law on the Protection of Persons with Disabilities of People's Republic of China* (National People's Congress of People's Republic of China, 1990). The impetus behind these laws lead to more governmental special education regulations and guideline concerned with the following aspects: teacher preparation, inclusive education, early intervention, curriculum, diagnosis and classification, instructional education plans, and financial support.

In today's China, more and more students with disabilities are educated in regular schools in resource classrooms with additional supports. Also, more and more special education schools are actively involved in outreach efforts to identify, classify, and certify children with disabilities from rural and economically distressed communities. According to a 2012 Ministry of Education in China (2013) educational statistics report, there are 1,853 special education schools, 178,998 special education students, and 43,697 special education teachers. In addition, the report indicates that there are 199,753 students with disabilities learning in regular schools, which accounts for 52.7% of all students with disabilities attending schools (Ministry of Education in China, 2013). Given China's large population which is more than a billion people, there is still a long way to go in identifying, classifying, and serving students with special education needs in China as well as providing provisions and policies in the areas of legal safeguards, teacher preparation, resources, and so on forth that will ensure appropriate education for these students. While the growth of special education had slow progress and even stagnation in the 1960s and 1970s, China has exhibited a steady and progressive growth since the 1990s.

DEFINITION, PREVALENCE, AND INCIDENCE

Definition

China does not have a national governmental special education law that specifies definitive categories of students with disabilities However, within China, there are several different definition systems that are associated with more generic disability and special education laws and regulations. For example, the reauthorized *Compulsory Education Law* (National People's Congress, 2006) mandates that "special classes and schools should be built exclusively for children with visual and hearing impairments as well as with intellectual disabilities." This newly reauthorized law also mandates services to students with severe problem behaviors including juvenile delinquents with special education needs. This latter provision is one of the main additions to the 1986 Compulsory Education Law. Also, the *Law on the Protection of Persons with Disabilities* (LPPD), which was first issued in 1990 and revised in 2008 (National People's Congress, 2008), defines an individual with a disability as one who has abnormalities or loss of a certain organ in anatomical structure or a psychological or physiological dysfunction, which results in either a partial or entire loss of the ability to perform an activity in normal circumstances. This law further specifies disabilities in eight categories: visual impairment, hearing impairment, speech disability, physical disabilities, intellectual disability, mental disorders, multiple disabilities, and other disabilities.

Utilizing the above disability laws and acts, a group of 12 disability experts, who were led by the *Chinese Ministry of Civil Affairs* and *China Disabled Person's Foundation* (CDPF), initiated a project to develop the first disability classification and diagnosis system in China. The project experts sought information from numerous associations of people with disabilities, family members of individuals with disabilities, and clinical practitioners. In consultation with the *Ministry of Human Resources and Social Security* and the *Ministry of Public Security* and with the endorsement of many other government administrations, the experts published the *Chinese Disability Classification and Diagnosis Criteria* (CDCDC) in April 2011.

This criterion system covers the seven disability categories mentioned above in the LPPD except for "other disabilities." The CDCDC lays a solid foundation for clinicians, physicians, and disability professionals in the identification, diagnosis, classification, and evaluation of an individual with a disability in China. Unfortunately, this new classification system has not brought immediate impact on the special education system.

The Chinese government still has the main responsibility for educating students with intellectual, visual, and hearing impairments as well as students with problem behaviors that are covered by the *Compulsory Education Law*. To date, the education rights of children with severe physical and intellectual disabilities, autism spectrum disorders, cerebral palsy, and multiple disabilities are only mentioned briefly and vaguely in several regulations, such as the *Suggestions on Accelerating the Development of Special Education in China* (China's State Council, 2009) and *Suggestions on the Improvement of Service for People with Disabilities* (China's State Council, 2008). In special education practice, children and youth with other disabilities and severe disabilities, who lack self-help skills to participate in schools and classrooms, are likely to be excluded from school education or extensively underserved (The Office of National Sample Survey of People with Disabilities, 1988). In addition to the latter, children with other kinds of disabilities (e.g., learning disabilities) are left out from the Chinese laws and regulations.

Prevalence and Incidence

In 2006, a comprehensive National Sample Survey on People with Disabilities was conducted in China (China's Disabled Persons Federation, 2006). Based on a national sample of 161,479 people surveyed, it was reported that by estimate there are 82.96 million people with different kinds of disabilities in China. This figure accounts for 6.34% of the whole Chinese population. Table 1 displays China's prevalence and incidence of disability in numbers and percentages. It is noted that physical disability and hearing impairments are the most prevalent and that intellectual disability and speech and language impairments are the least prevalent.

A comparison of the 2006 results with a 1987 national sample survey indicates that the incidence of people with disabilities in China has increased significantly. Interestingly, the prevalence of persons with physical disabilities has gone up ostensibly while the prevalence of persons with intellectual disabilities has decreased significantly. To some extent, the decrease in persons with intellectual disabilities was influenced by the lower IQ cut off score used in 2006 to classify persons with intellectual disabilities. In terms of the distribution of disabilities by age (see Table 2) almost half (45.20%) of all people with disabilities are over 65 years while the proportion of children with disabilities from birth to 14 years old is only 4.66%.

Interestingly, the incident of disability for school-age children (i.e., 6–14 years old, an age range covered by the *Compulsory Education Law*), reveal a surprising low figure (2.46 million children) (CDPF, 2006). As shown in Table 3, children with intellectual disability are the most prevalent group (30.89%), followed closely by those with multiple disabilities (30.49%) suggesting a substantially different distribution of disability when compared with the entire population. Surprisingly, children with mental disorders (2.44%) account for the least proportion of the population with disabilities even when compared to traditionally low incidence special education populations such as those with visual impairments (5.28%) and those with hearing impairments (4.47%).

Table 1. Prevalence of People with Disabilities in China (National Sample Survey of People with Disabilities, 2006).

Disability Category	Number (Million)	Percentage
Physical disability	24.12	29.07
Hearing impairments	20.04	24.16
Multiple disabilities	13.52	16.30
Visual impairments	12.33	14.86
Mental disorders	6.14	7.40
Intellectual disability	5.54	6.68
Speech impairments	1.27	1.53
Total	82.96	100

Table 2. Prevalence and Incidence of Chinese People with Disabilities by Age (National Sample Survey of People with Disabilities, 2006).

Age	Number (Million)	Percentage
0–14	3.87	4.66
15–59	34.93	42.10
60–64	6.61	8.04
65 and above	37.55	45.20
Total	82.96	100

Table 3. Prevalence of Students with Disabilities (between Age 6 and 14) in China (National Sample Survey of People with Disabilities, 2006).

Disability Category	Number (Million)	Percentage
Physical disabilities	0.48	19.51
Hearing impairment	0.11	4.47
Multiple disabilities	0.75	30.49
Visual impairment	0.13	5.28
Mental disorders	0.06	2.44
Intellectual disability	0.76	30.89
Speech disability	0.17	6.91
Total	2.46	100

TRENDS IN LEGISLATION AND LITIGATION

Unlike the United States and other developed countries that typically have exclusive legislations in special education (e.g., U.S. special education law, Individuals with Disability Education Act [IDEA]), there are no exclusive laws on special education provisions existing in China. However, there are a couple of more generic laws such as the 2006 *Compulsory Education Law* and the 2008 LPPD which offer very loosely defined protections and provisions with respect to the rights of education, work, social integration, and living for individuals with disabilities. Because of this situation, many Chinese special education professionals have called for a national policy debate on the significance of establishing an exclusive Chinese special education law to ensure the educational rights and quality of special education provisions for children with disabilities (Wang, 2007). Currently, there are no clear signs for any immediate policy initiatives from government administrative agencies or any proposals of legislative bills and actions despite growing attention to the debate surrounding the necessity and significance of developing specific special education legislations and regulations. Therefore, as a basis to understanding special education today in China, the following section reviews a few existing common laws that are closely related to special education provisions as well as some noteworthy legislation trends.

Major Chinese Disability Laws and Noticeable Trends

As mentioned before, *The Compulsory Education Law* in 2006 and 2008 LPPD are the two most powerful laws related to special education in

China. The reauthorized *Compulsory Education Law* of 2006 includes five clauses offering special education provisions. First, it mandates that all children at the age of 6 years, regardless of gender, ethnicity, or race, are entitled to receiving 9 years of compulsory education in schools. Second, the law states that special education schools and classes shall be established exclusively for children with visual or hearing impairments and intellectual disabilities. Furthermore, regular schools shall accept children with disabilities who are able to adapt to learning in regular classrooms, and the classes need to have equipped facilities that can accommodate children's special needs while providing training to teachers and other school personnel to better work with children with special needs. Third, extra bonus pay is a mandatory fringe benefit to all teachers who work with children with disabilities in special schools, classes, and learning in regular classes (LRC) of regular schools. In addition, for teachers working in rural or economically impoverished areas, there is another kind of government offered bonus pay. Fourth, the per capita government funding for students with disabilities shall be higher than that of normally developing students in regular schools. Lastly, the law mandates that there shall be no rejection of school-age children with disabilities in any kinds of schools, including special education schools and regular schools. In the occurrence of any rejection case, there shall be punitive consequences for school administrators in charge of school admission.

In summary, despite the nature of a general national education law, the reauthorized *Compulsory Education Law* (2006) reveals a legislation trend that emphasizes the enforcement of a zero reject principle of school admission for children with disabilities under the circumstances of lack of exclusive special education legislations. Further, the law provides for enhanced funding for special education (for both students with disabilities and special educators). Lastly, the law specifies necessary classroom equipment and resources for the education of students with special needs.

The LPPD, which was issued originally in 1990, is a legislative milestone in the China's disability and special education field because it is the first law that stipulates exclusively the rights of children with disabilities for rehabilitation, education, vocation, social life, and other legal rights. This law also gives rise to specific regulations that promote prevention, early diagnosis and appropriate assessment and evaluation, and treatment of persons with a disability. Since its reauthorization in 2008, more specific provisions were stipulated related to the improvement of the quality of inclusive education for students with disabilities in compulsory education schools. In addition, LPPD stresses that vocational training centers and higher education institutions should enhance their admission and accessibility aspects for students with disabilities and highlight the importance of teacher education and professional training for special education professionals.

Compared to *the Compulsory Education Law*, LPPD is more comprehensive and involves almost all aspects of life for children with disabilities. Although *the Compulsory Education Law* and LPPD have laid a solid foundation for the provisions of appropriate education to all children with disabilities in China, they both fall short on ensuring comprehensive rights for children with disabilities since the provisions are relatively narrow and limited and the statutes are too brief and imprecise which leaves too much room for different interpretations.

Another important legal component document for China's special education is the *Regulations on the Education of Persons with Disabilities* (REPD) (State Council of China, 1994). REPD focuses on nine specific special education sections that include: general provisions; preschool education; compulsory education; vocational education; secondary education and above; teachers; official funding and financial support; rewards and punishments; and supplementary provisions. In 2013, a draft of REPD reauthorization was under public and expert review. Compared to the 1994 version, the new REPD (State Council of China, 2013) draft has shown some dramatic changes in both structure and contents. For instance, it has six sections including: general provisions, special education in regular schools, special education in special schools, special education teachers, assurance and supervision, and legal responsibilities. More importantly, the new REPD displays a clear trend that puts an intensifying emphasis on the implementation of inclusive education in all schools and early childhood education in China.

However, Wang (2007) indicated that when the above Chinese education and disability laws and regulations are compared to more sophisticated special education laws in such countries as the United States and the United Kingdom, limitations and weakness are quite obvious due to their lack of exclusive provisions and nonexistence of enforceable mechanism to effectively execute the statutes. Further, China's education and disability laws appear to use lots of rhetorical language that is often too vague to be useful regarding executive process and accountability. At this writing, China needs a more comprehensive and exclusive special education law that lays a sophisticated, evidence-based foundation for addressing critical special education issues that include the following: definition and identification of disability; accurate diagnosis; effective early intervention; access to regular schools; best practice inclusive education instruction; exemplary teacher qualities and qualifications; research-based adaptive and functional curricula; meaningful evaluation of students' progress and outcomes; specific funding; and students and parents' legal rights (Deng & Zhou, 2005; Pang, 2009).

Litigation and Court Cases about Disability Rights

In China, people with disabilities rarely choose to stand up and fight for their own rights legally due to their traditional cultural value and belief of obedience and compliance to authority and a pervasive social climate of stereotypical or discriminative attitudes toward people with disabilities. Many citizens either lack awareness of their rights or have concerns about their rights but are afraid of fighting for them publicly (Jiang, 2011). Litigations by families of children with disabilities against school authority are extremely rare if they exist at all in China. Chinese citizens live in a social and cultural context where parents regard schools and teachers as professional authorities as such they tend to believe and pay respect to professionals who in their belief can make the best decisions for their children's education. Although parents' responsibility for ensuring their children's right to receive compulsory education is mentioned in some Chinese laws and regulations, the provisions are not elaborated specifically and thus are impractical (Liu, 2011). After an extensive literature search on disability litigation cases in China, the authors found only a few cases which are discussed in the next section.

One case concerned a person with a physical disability who was wheel chair bound. One day when he went to a bank to open a bank account, he was unable to enter the bank because of no accessible ramp for his wheel chair. He sued the bank and the government agencies that sponsored the bank building for not providing necessary accommodations – accessible ramp in public settings. Unfortunately, he lost the case because the court ruled that there is no specific law or regulation mandating accessible facilities in commercial buildings (Jiang, 2011). Due to publicity and hearsay, the case had a positive impact because more people with disabilities came to realize their rights and were willing to fight to protect their rights. There were a few other similar litigations involving law suits against train services for not offering accessible seats on the train for riders with disabilities and an another suit against the city metro services for denying discount tickets to people with disabilities (*Chengdu Business Daily*, 2009; Luan & Li, 2011).

EDUCATIONAL INTERVENTIONS AND SERVICES

Education interventions and services are provided to school-age children and youth with disabilities through a two-track system in China. In the Kindergarten thru-9 grade public school system, students with disabilities are educated in either segregated special education schools or regular schools through LRC models. For young children with disabilities, early intervention services are sporadic and are often targeted to special populations such as children with visual or hearing impairments (Deng et al., 2001). Positively, recent developments have focused on private kindergartens that are accepting and providing services for children with intellectual disabilities and private early intervention centers founded by parents of children with autism spectrum disorders to provide interventions for their children as well as parent training (Zhang, Wang, Xu, & Ju, in press).

Unlike many developed countries where special education schools are either no longer in existence or in the minority, special education schools in China are regarded as the backbone of the whole special education system. China has three kinds of special education schools that are funded and administered by China's Ministry of Education. They are the *Schools for the Blind and Visually Impaired*, the *Schools for the Deaf and Hearing Impaired*, and the *Schools for Children with Intellectual Disabilities* (Gu, 2007). A 2012 survey reported that there are 1,853 special education schools in China of which 32 are schools for students with visual impairments, 456 are schools for students with hearing impairments, 408 are schools for students with intellectual impairments, and 957 schools for students with a variety of disabilities (Ministry of Education in China, 2013).

LRC is China's version of inclusion. It started in the 1980s as a practical solution for allowing a large number of children with disabilities, who had no regional special schools or programs to attend, go to community regular schools to receive education (Chen, 1996). Over the years, LRC continued to evolve due to increasing legal and political supports. Today in China, LRC has become a major special education service system provider for children with disabilities, especially those with mild and moderate special education needs (McCabe, 2003). In fact, recent special education enrollment statistics show that more than half of students with disabilities attending schools are educated in regular schools via LRC (Ministry of Education in China, 2013). As for LRC practices, instructional resource classrooms are employed extensively especially in regular schools in large metropolis such as Beijing and Shanghai (Li & Zhang, 2008). Because of the emerging LRC practice, today special education schools are beginning to serve as resource centers for regular school teachers to be trained to instruct students with disabilities in their classrooms.

However, research seems to suggest that the quality of LRC instructional practices is relatively low due to: a lack of specialists; a shortage of personnel; inadequate funding; and limited technology (Qian & Jiang, 2004; Qing, Liu, Yang, & He, 2005; Xiao, 2005). Lastly, another form of China's special education service is the limited use of self-contained classes within regular schools. In the 2012 school year, there were only 448 special classrooms attached to primary schools and 25 attached to high schools across the whole country (Ministry of Education in China, 2013).

Vocational education for students with disabilities often begins after students finish their 9-year compulsory education. But some special education schools provide vocational education in their training programs. According to China's Disabled Persons' Federation (China's Disabled Persons Federation [CDPF], 2012) data, there were 152 secondary vocational training programs serving 10,442 students nationwide in 2012. The vocational training programs are highly skill oriented and skills of training are very specific to trainees with disabilities. For example, students with visual impairments are often trained in physical therapy (e.g., acupuncture and massage) and/or musical skills (Xu, 2012). In addition, most programs are highly focused on the training of practical life and work skills.

Higher education services and supports for students with disabilities began in the 1980s. With the provisions of 1990 LPPD, some universities started to admit academically capable students with disabilities who were able to pass their entrance exams (Deng et al., 2001). Currently, China has 17 higher education colleges that enroll 4,000 students with disabilities (Ding, 2013). Despite the good progress being made in higher education services and supports for students with disabilities in China, both quantity and quality of services are under question (Yu, Wang, & Chen, 2010). Furthermore, only limited opportunities exist for students with disabilities to study certain majors at selected institutions (Qu, Zhao, & Xiao, 2007).

In addition to public and private school education services and supports, community-based rehabilitation services are implemented independently and play an important role in the whole special education service and support system for people with disabilities (Tang & Cong, 2003). Under the guidance of the Developmental Guidelines of the 9th Five-year Plan for People with Disabilities (State Council of China, 1996), community-based rehabilitation services have spread across China increasingly between 1996 and 2005. According to the CDPF data (2007), 1,086 counties and 621 cities provide community-based rehabilitation services and supports for people with disabilities in 2005. While this is a positive aspect, these services and supports place more rehabilitative emphasis on health and medical welfare services rather than educational, vocational, and psychological interventions.

WORKING WITH FAMILIES OF CHILDREN WITH DISABILITIES

Research on Chinese families of children with disabilities is limited, however, recently researchers have reported a number of findings (Liu, Lambert, & Lambert, 2007; Tsang, Tam, Chan, & Cheung, 2003; Wang, Michaels, & Day, 2011; Zhang & Li, 2005). Wang et al. (2011) investigated the coping strategies to stress between Chinese and Western parents of children with severe disabilities, intellectual disabilities, and autism spectrum disorders. Their findings indicate similar levels of high stress among the Chinese and Western parents. However, Chinese parents tended to perceive higher levels of stress due to pessimism. Tsang et al. (2003) investigated coping styles and emotional feelings of Chinese parents related to raising a child with a disability. These researchers reported that stigma exists about mental illness in the Chinese culture, and many families feel ashamed about having a child with a disability, thinking that mental illness is the punishment for parents' behavior, particularly, the mother's behavior. Zhang and Li (2005) surveyed 200 parents of children with intellectual disabilities to investigate their stress level and influencing factors. The researcher reported there was no gender effect between fathers and mothers on stress level. However, parents of children in different grades differ significantly on stress levels and that parents' stress is correlated highly with their coping strategies, quality of life, and children's behavior.

As for parents' perceived needs and support related to raising a child with a disability, Wang and Michaels (2009) noted that Chinese families of children with severe disabilities perceived the need for more community services, information, and family/social support. Further, Wang and Michaels indicated that families of children with autism spectrum disorders tended to report greater needs for information and supports than those parents of children with intellectual disabilities or physical disabilities. With respect to supports for families of children with disabilities, there is almost no systematic and comprehensive service and support system for parents of children with disabilities in China (Wang et al., 2011).

There are only a few semigovernmental organizations and nonprofit programs that aim at reducing parents' stress and anxiety toward raising children with disabilities and/or training them in parental management skills to work with their children more effectively. China Disabled Persons Foundation (CDPF) is a semigovernmental organization that has established successfully two large parent organizational support groups. One group is for parents, relatives, and friends of people with intellectual disabilities and another is for people with mental illness and disorders. CDPF offers a platform for parents, relatives, and friends of people with disabilities to share information and their experiences with each other, work together to support families in need, improve educational quality, and protect parents' legal rights through advocacy.

There are semigovernmental parent organizations funded by the Chinese governments to train parents of children with disabilities related to improving the quality of education and rehabilitation for their children. For example, some local and regional governments in Shanxi have started to pilot Parent School Models to integrate different resources such as medical services, and community and professional services for children with disabilities. Another type of informal family support organization is parent to parent support.

In China today, there is an increasing number of intervention programs and centers initiated by parents of children with disabilities. Parents in these programs and centers unite together to seek professional assistance, public funding, welfare, and other kinds of resources for their children with disabilities. A well respected program, which was established in 2012, is Beijing Rong Ai Rong Le Organization of Persons with Intellectual Disabilities. It is a nongovernmental organization (NGO) for people with intellectual disabilities that advocates for their rights to increase available services and assists and supports their families. Similar to all types of family or parent organizations, their partnership with the local school system is challenging and at times troubling.

TEACHERS AND TRAINING IN SPECIAL EDUCATION

Since teacher quality has been regarded as one of the most significant determinants of the effectiveness of special education services, it makes the improvement of teacher quality a priority for the country. In 2012, there were 43,697 full-time special education teachers serving 378,751 students with disabilities in special education schools (Ministry of Education in China, 2013). However, research findings indicate that more than three quarters of special education schools have a shortage of qualified teachers and thus an intense demand for special education teachers and professionals exist (Wang, 2012). Due to this shortage, teacher preparation and professional training has become a central issue of Chinese special education.

Preservice Teacher Preparation

For a long period before the 1980s, special education teachers were mainly trained based on unsystematic approaches such as observation and coaching (Deng & Harris, 2008). The first special education teacher preparation program was the Teacher Education College of Zhaodong. It was established in 1981 and was followed by Nanjing Special Education Teacher Education College in 1984. After these two college programs, many other teacher education colleges followed (Wang & Gu, 2001). The early teacher education programs were 2-year college credential programs, and it was not until the 1990s that teacher college programs elevated to 3 or 4 years higher education institutions. It is estimated that thus far there are more than 50 public universities offering special education teacher preparation programs in China, and most of which were established after 2000 (Wang, 2012). There are two levels of degree programs for teacher preparation at the undergraduate level, namely, a 3-year associate degree and 4-year bachelor level degree. For graduate level special education teacher preparation, there are only a dozen master's degree programs and three doctoral degree granting programs in the entire country.

The overall objectives of teacher preparation programs vary according to the aforementioned two-level preparation systems. For instance, research universities, which are administered directly by the Chinese Ministry of Education such as the Beijing Normal University and East China Normal University, often set their goal of preparing special education professionals who can apply innovative strategies in their teaching activities. The goal of institutions with a 3-year associate degree programs is to prepare students with practical skills to work in special education schools.

In most special education teacher preparation programs, students are required to take three kinds of curricula: general curriculum, basic subject curriculum, and professional curriculum. With a focus on equipping students with a broad knowledge base, *general curriculum* typically includes English, computer sciences, military knowledge, physical exercises, or sports (Li, 2012). The *basic subject curriculum* includes required course work in educational theories, psychology, instructional strategy, and curriculum design. The *professional curriculum* typically includes course work concerned with characteristics of students with different kinds of disabilities and instructional methods, Braille and sign language, and research methods in special education. In addition to the above curriculum course work, a certain number of field-based practicum hours in special education schools are required for the degrees (Wang, 2012).

In-Service Special Education Teachers' Professional Development

In-service training is an important means for special education teachers to continuously improve the quality of their professional practices after entering the profession. Research shows that only 30.9% of Chinese special education teachers received their first degree from special education teacher programs and only 21.8% have a terminal special education degree after their first nonspecial education degree (Wang, 2012). Because of this lack of adequate and specific preservice preparations, in-service training for many special education teachers in China is necessary to make them more effective teachers.

In-service professional training for special education teachers is often more focused yet flexible to meet professional development needs of special education teachers. Because many special education teachers do not graduate with a special education degree, it is critical to offer them some systematic professional training on: instructional strategies, effective behavioral management interventions, assessment and evaluation procedures, the development of individual educational plans, and communication skills to work with families. The primary focus of in-service professional training is to enhance special education teachers' problem solving skills. A secondary focus of in-service professional training is to offer special education teachers great opportunities to learn and keep up with the current research and evidence-based practices in the field which can enhance and improve their instruction.

Like many developing countries, China faces a severe problem of special education teacher shortage both in quantity and quality (Wang, Wang, Zhu, Feng, & Zhao, 2012). Although inclusive education practices are increasingly promoted in China, there is a dire reality that there are not enough highly qualified special education teachers in special education and regular schools who are knowledgeable about utilizing the best inclusive educational practices. This shortage of highly trained teachers is partly due to the dearth of special education graduate training programs. It is strongly recommended by the authors that both preservice and in-service preparation and training programs need to be reformed to meet the rapid growth of students with special needs who are being placed increasingly into inclusive education programs. If special education undergraduate and graduate training programs at comprehensive universities are not reformed and allowed to embrace research evidence and best practices, the special education needs of the students will not be met.

PERSPECTIVE ON THE PROGRESS OF SPECIAL EDUCATION

China's special education has made great strides over the last two or three decades (Zhang et al., in press). The progress of special education in China has manifested in two main areas: (1) positive progressive changes in special education legislations and policy and (2) steady expansion and improvement of special education services and supports. Despite the lack of a specific special education law, Chinese legislations and policies on special education have continually evolved in a positive direction. Some of the new laws also have adopted broader classification system of disability categories changing its coverage from three types of disabilities to eight types of disabilities, for example, in the reauthorized LPPD. Numerous reauthorized statutes (e.g., *Compulsory Education Law* and LPPD) have uniformly laid emphasis on the values and principles of antidiscrimination and equality. When China became a signatory nation of the United Nations Convention on Rights for Individuals with Disabilities in 2008, it signaled the Chinese government's attitude and determination in pursuing better protections of rights of individuals with disabilities. New government regulations (e.g., the draft reauthorization of the *Regulations on the Education of People with Disabilities*, 2013) have made explicit mandates in supporting the principle of zero reject regarding school admission of children with disabilities. Also, stronger governmental and political policies to development and advance special education are evident on the Chinese federal and local governments' actions in increasing special education funding. With a goal of spending

4% of annual Gross Domestic Products (GDP) on education, the Chinese government has made a dramatic increase in its investment in special education. For example, last year a dozen Chinese universities received a special fund from the central government ranging from 10 to15 million dollars to build new teacher training centers. Hopefully, China's recent special education legislations will continue to provide steady forward looking progressive policies and resources that will strengthen special education for students with disabilities for years to come.

Likewise, special education services in China have undergone steady growth and expansion in terms of the size of service systems and the number of students with disabilities being served since the 1980s. There has been a steady increase in the number of special education schools built over the years allowing more students with severe special needs to be educated. Also, there has been significant increases in the enrollment of students with moderate and mild disabilities in regular schools through LRC where they receive inclusive education. For example, compared with 292 special education schools in 1978, there were 1,853 special education schools at the end of 2012. Although the increase of special education schools does not seem to be in line with the international trend of reducing segregated special education schools and promoting inclusive education, special education schools in China still play a unique role in educating many Chinese students with disabilities who cannot go to regular schools for various reasons. Considering the reality and current situations in China, special education schools and inclusion (e.g., LRC) in general education schools will continue to coexist for a certain period of time to address the relatively low enrollment rate of students with disabilities especially in rural areas. The authors are optimistic that China's recent progress in special education will eventually lead to and ensure the compulsory education rights of children with disabilities.

Lastly, China's recent rapid progress in special education teacher training is extremely encouraging. Despite an existing shortage of teacher education programs that can prepare qualified special education teachers, there has been a steady increase in the number of special education teachers today as compared to a decade ago. This is the result of China's funding of higher education to train more highly qualified special education teachers in a variety of institutions. In essence, both quantity and quality issues in special education teacher training programs have gained the attention of the Chinese government and educational authorities, and the government views this area as a national priority for the improvement of special education in China.

REMAINING CHALLENGES FOR CHINA'S SPECIAL EDUCATION

As China's special education attempts to rapidly grow in order to meet the needs of a large underserved population of children with disabilities, there are a great number of challenges. Researchers have summarized a wide array of challenges at both macro and micro levels (Ellsworth & Zhang, 2007; Kritzer, 2011; McCabe, 2003; McLoughlin, Zhou, & Clark, 2005; Zhang et al., in press). Chief among those challenges identified are: access to special education, a lack of exclusive special education law, more professional/teacher training, best practices curriculum development and instructional strategies (e.g., whole-class teaching model), development of an accurate assessment system for diagnosis, effective student progress monitoring, meaningful evaluation of learning outcomes, expansion of early intervention, effective inclusion practices, public awareness about disabilities and special education, increased special education funding, state of the art vocational and higher education for students with disabilities, sufficient classroom and instructional resources, special teacher challenges (e.g., big class size and heavier teaching load), reformed special education teacher training, more access to transportation, the need to increase instructional technology, and consumer friendly parental advocacy. This long list of identified challenges presents Chinese special education challenges at both micro and macro levels including ecological and/or contextual challenges (e.g., societal attitude, public awareness) (Ellsworth & Zhang, 2007). In the section that follows three major areas of challenges surrounding school system are delineated, namely, policy and system barriers, lack of resources and support system (qualified professionals), and lack of evidence-based practices in special education.

Policy and Systems Barriers

The first set of school system challenges involves legislations and policies and related system barriers that impact special education. An examination of legislation in the United States or the United Kingdom reveals that these counties have highly specific and comprehensive special education laws. However, China's legislation related to special education policies and regulations is neither detailed, nor comprehensive and exclusive which becomes a source of many special education problems in China. For example, in

China's generic disability and education laws, there are no clearly defined disability identification and classification mechanisms, no specified range of services that children with disabilities are entitled to, and no legal consequences specified for schools if they violate the rights of children with disabilities and/or families. Due to these aspects, there is no clear regulatory or executive mechanism existing for enforcing implementation of statutes related to special education system and practices. Thus, a system barrier exits which prevents the full and meaningful education of students with special education needs. This system barrier correlates with access to the right to education for hundreds of thousands of Chinese children with disabilities (especially those with severe needs and/or from rural and remote areas). Further, it interferes with the development of any formal special education system channel which could provide a remedy and enforceable provisions to educate all children with disabilities.

Resources and Support System

China's special education system is severely challenged due to a lack of resources (e.g., school materials, funding, buildings, supplies, technology) and a support system (e.g., human capital – teachers and other professionals). Lack of funding, which is the result of poor laws and policies, becomes a strong risk factor in providing effective special education practices. Also, it leads to large class size and heavier workloads for teachers which negatively challenge them to offer effective instruction for their students with disabilities. According to McLoughlin et al. (2005), the combination of large class size, inadequate technology support, and a lack of professional supports to special and regular education teachers makes inclusive education practices extremely hard to implement if not impossible to take place in regular schools.

Teachers are the core of human power in special education. However in China, there is still a significant gap between the supply and demand for special education teachers due to the increasing number of students with disabilities that have been certified for services in LRC and the need to staff the newly built special education schools. Another complicating aspect is the lack of preservice teacher training in special education that general education teachers are exposed to during their higher education degree programs. In-service programs for general education teachers has increased, however, it remains inadequate. All of the above illustrates the need to reform teacher education for special and general education teachers at the university levels. In addition, the significant increase in students with disabilities receiving services has also created a need for support professionals such as physical therapists, occupational therapists, speech pathologists, and school psychologists. Filling this need is challenged due to the few profession support training programs at China's higher education institutions.

Evidence-Based Special Education Practices

Teachers in special education are left in a position where they will inevitably encounter practical and technical challenges related to effectively implementing inclusive education due to: a lack of behavioral management skills, inadequate evidence-based instructional strategies, and invalid assessment and evaluation procedures. China's teachers have a limited exposure to established research literature in evidence-based instructional practices or are trained in outdated course work. Unfortunately, this creates weak special education practices which manifest itself in early childhood, vocational, and higher education instruction for people with disabilities. China's special education system needs to develop a special educational service continuum for children with disabilities at different age stage. More emphasis should be placed on early childhood education which may lead to the remediation of learning and social difficulties. In addition, students with disabilities need to be exposed to vocational training during their early teenage years to enhance their job skills. Lastly, for students with disabilities that have the potential to participate in higher education, they need expanded instructional experiences in self-advocacy, time management skills, study skills, note taking, mastery of technological innovations, and independent life skills so that they are prepared to be successful at universities.

CONCLUSION

In conclusion, this chapter has painted a portrait of China's special education through describing its origin, evolution, and progress from a legal, family, and service aspect as well as discussing issues and challenges. Despite a short and disrupted history, special education has gradually evolved over a century, particularly in the last three decades. Although steady progresses are made, special education in China still has a long way to go as it has to face a myriad of challenges and meet the growing needs of the largest disability population in the world.

REFERENCES

Chen, Y. Y. (1996). Making special education compulsory and inclusive in China. *Cambridge Journal of Education, 26*(1), 47–58.

Chengdu Business Daily. (2009). Disabled people sue minister of railways because of lack of seats for the disabled. Chengdu Business Daily. November 2. Retrieved from http:// gongyi.sohu.com/20091102/n267889988.shtml

China's Disabled Persons Federation. (2006). *2006 nian di er ci quan guo can ji ren chou yang diao cha zhu yao shu ju gong bao (di er hao)*. [*Report of main findings of the second national sample survey on people with disabilities in China in 2006 (1st)*.] Retrieved from http://www.gov.cn/fwxx/cjr/content_1311943.htm

China's Disabled Persons Federation. (2007). *2006 nian di er ci quan guo can ji ren chou yang diao cha zhu yao shu ju gong bao (di yi hao)*. [*Report of main findings of the second national sample survey on people with disabilities in China in 2006 (2nd)*.] Retrieved from http://www.gov.cn/fwxx/cjr/content_1308385.htm

China's Disabled Persons Federation. (2012). *2012 nian zhong guo can ji ren shi ye fa zhan tong ji gong bao*. [*Statistics of services for people with disabilities in China in 2012*.] Retrieved from http://www.cdpf.org.cn/ggtz/content/2013-03/26/content_30440283.htm

China's State Council. (2008). *Guan yu cu jin can ji ren shi ye fa zhan de yi jian*. [*Suggestions on the improvement of services for people with disabilities*.] Retrieved from http://www.gov. cn/gongbao/content/2008/content_987906.htm

China's State Council. (2009). *Guan yu jin yi bu jia kuai te shu jiao yu fa zhan de yi jian*. [*Suggestions on accelerating the development of special education in China*.] Retrieved from http://www.gov.cn/zwgk/2009-05/08/content_1308951.htm

Deng, M., & Harris, K. (2008). Meeting the needs of students with disabilities in general education classrooms in China. *Teacher Education and Special Education, 31*(3), 195–207.

Deng, M., Poon-Mcbrayer, K. F., & Farnsworth, E. B. (2001). The development of special education in China: A sociocultural review. *Remedial and Special Education, 22*(5), 288–298.

Deng, M., & Zhou, H. Y. (2005). Advocacy on the legislation of special education law in China. *Special Education in China, 7*, 3–6.

Ding, X. Z. (2013). Challenges and countermeasures in vocational education for people with disabilities. *University Education, 5*, 27–29.

Editorial Department of Year-Book of Education. (1984). *Year-book of education in China 1949–1981*. Beijing: Encyclopedia of China Publishing House.

Ellsworth, N. J., & Zhang, C. (2007). Progress and challenges in China's special education development: Observations, reflections, and recommendations. *Remedial and Special Education, 28*(1), 58–64.

Epstein, I. (1988). Special education provisions in the People's Republic of China. *Comparative Education, 24*, 365–375.

Gu, D. (2007). Analysis of special education provisions in the reauthorization of the compulsory education law. *Chinese Journal of Special Education, 5*, 9–12.

Gu, D. Q. (1993). Teshu jiaoyu lifa de fazhan. [Changing of legislation on special education in China]. *Te Shu Jiao Yu Van Jiie, 1*, 1–9.

Jiang, Y. (2011). *Strategic litigation as a trigger to enforce human rights in China: From the perspective of rights of the disabled.* Master's thesis, Central European University, Budapest, Hungary. Retrieved from http://www.etd.ceu.hu/2012/jiang_yitong.pdf

Kritzer, J. B. (2011). Special education in China. *Eastern Education Journal, 40*(1), 57–63.

Li, H. C. (2012). A study about the status of the general educational curriculum provision of Chinese universities. *Fudan Education Forum, 2*(4), 21–27.

Li, N., & Zhang, F. (2008). A research on the resource room program of learning in the regular classroom in Shanghai. *Chinese Journal of Special Education, 10*, 66–72.

Liu, J. Q. (2011). On parents' obligation to protect disabled children's right to receive compulsory education. *Chinese Journal of Special Education, 6*, 3–7.

Liu, M., Lambert, C. E., & Lambert, V. A. (2007). Caregiver burden and coping patterns of Chinese parents of a child with a mental illness. *International Journal of Mental Health Nursing, 16*, 86–95.

Luan, Q. P., & Li, J. v. (2011, August). Shenzhen Metro Corporation, Shenzhen Futian District People's Court.

McCabe, H. (2003). The beginnings of inclusion in the People's Republic of China. *Research & Practice for Persons with Severe Disabilities, 28*(1), 16–22.

McLoughlin, C. S., Zhou, Z., & Clark, E. (2005). Reflections on the development and status of contemporary special education services in China. *Psychology in the Schools, 42*, 273–283.

Ministry of Education in China. (2013). *2013 nian Quan guo jiao yu shi ye fa zhan tong ji gong bao. [Basic statistics of education in 2013.]* Retrieved from http://www.moe.gov.cn/publicfiles/business/htmlfiles/moe/s7567/201308/156428.html

National People's Congress of People's Republic of China. (1986). *Zhong hua ren min gong he guo yi wu jiao yu fa. [Compulsory Education Law of People's Republic of China.]* Retrieved from http://www.moe.gov.cn/publicfiles/business/htmlfiles/moe/moe_619/200606/15687.html

National People's Congress of People's Republic of China. (1990). *Zhong hua ren min gong he guo can ji ren bao zhang fa. [Protection for people with disabilities law of People's Republic of China.]* Retrieved from http://www.cdpf.org.cn/zcfg/content/2007-11/29/content_30316065.htm

National People's Congress. (2006). *Yi wu jiao yu fa. [Compulsory education law.]* Retrieved from http://www.law-lib.com/law/law_view.asp?id = 163284

National People's Congress. (2008). *Can ji ren bao zhang fa. [Law on the protection of persons with disabilities.]* Retrieved from http://www.chinanews.com/gj/kong/news/2008/04-24/1231112.shtml

Pang, Y. (2009). A review of China's special education law and its impact on the living standards of individuals with disabilities in China. Paper presented at the 18th Annual Conference of the Global Awareness Society International, May.

Piao, Y. X. (1992). Woguo gudai dui canji ren de taidu. [Characteristics of and attitudes toward disability in ancient China]. *Xiandai Te Shu Jiao Yu, 1*, 34–35.

Qian, L., & Jiang, X. (2004). An investigation report on current situation of the development of mainstreaming in China. *Chinese Journal of Special Education, 5*, 1–5.

Qing, S., Liu, Z., Yang, X., & He, E. (2005). Probe into the supporting system and assessment of mainstreaming on children with disabilities in the country. *Chinese Journal of Special Education, 10*, 68–72.

Qu, X. L., Zhao, B., & Xiao, Y. (2007). Higher education for people with disabilities in China. *Jiaoshi Bolan, 12*, 41–42.

State Council of China. (1994). *Zhong guo can ji ren jiao yu tiao li.* [*Regulations on the education of persons with disabilities of People's Republic of China.*] Retrieved from http://www.cdpf.org.cn/zcfg/content/2001-11/06/content_30316064.htm

State Council of China. (1996). *Zhong guo can ji ren shi ye jiu wu fa zhan gang yao.* [*Developmental guidelines of the 9th five-year plan for people with disabilities.*] Retrieved from http://www.cdpf.org.cn/zcfg/content/2001-11/06/content_30317548.htm

State Council of China. (2013). *The reauthorization of regulations on the education of people with disabilities* [draft]. Retrieved from http://www.chinalaw.gov.cn/article/cazjgg/201302/20130200384148.shtml

Tang, B. Y., & Cong, X. F. (2003). A study on present situation problem and measures of domestic community-based rehabilitation. *Journal of Dezhou University, 19*(1), 17–20.

The Office of National Sample Survey of People with Disabilities. (1988). *Handbook of disabled persons in China.* Beijing: Dizhen Publishing.

Tsang, H. W. H., Tam, P. K. C., Chan, F., & Cheung, W. M. (2003). Stigmatizing attitudes towards individuals with mental illness in Hong Kong: Implications for their recovery. *Journal of Community Psychology, 31*(4), 383–396.

United Nations Convention of the Rights for Individuals with Disabilities. (2008). New York, NY: United Nations.

Wang, H. P. (2007). A study on the necessity and feasibility of special education legislation. *Special Education in China, 7*, 3–6.

Wang, P., & Michaels, C. A. (2009). Chinese families of children with severe disabilities: Family needs and available support. *Research & Practice for Persons with Severe Disabilities, 34*(2), 21–32.

Wang, P. S., Michaels, C. A., & Day, M. S. (2011). Stresses and coping strategies of Chinese families with children with autism and other developmental disabilities. *Journal of Autism and Developmental Disorders, 41*(6), 783–795.

Wang, Y. (2012). *Special education teacher preparation in China.* Beijing: Beijing Normal University Press.

Wang, Y., & Gu, D. Q. (2001). The system of main curricula of special teacher preparation education programs of normal universities in the 21st century. *Research in Special Education, 2*, 3.

Wang, Y., Wang, Z., Zhu, N., Feng, Y., & Zhao, L. (2012). A Survey of special education schools' faculty team structure and demands. *Chinese Journal of Special Education, 11*, 3–8.

Xiao, F. (1996). *Teshu ertong xinli yu jiaoyu.* [*Psychology and education for special children.*] Beijing: Huaxia Press.

Xiao, F. (2005). Mainstreaming in China: History, actuality, perspectives. *Chinese Journal of Special Education, 3*, 3–7.

Xu, B. (2012). Vocational education for the disabled: Problems and strategies. *Journal of Zhejiang Normal University, 37*(6), 95–99.

Yang, H. L., & Wang, H. B. (1994). Special education in China. *The Journal of Special Education, 28*, 93–105.

Ye, L. Y., & Piao, Y. X. (1995). *Te shu jiaoyu xue*. [*The study of special education*.] Fujan: Xiamen.

Yu, L., & Zhang, D. (1994). Shi lun zhangjian te shu jiaoyu sixiang tixi. zhong de zhiye jiaoyu guan. [An analysis of Zhang Jian's vocational education ideology in developing special education]. *Xiandai Te Shu Jiao Yu, 2,* 9–11.

Yu, S. H., Wang, J. Y., & Chen, J. (2010). Current situation of higher education of disabled people in China and reflection on development. *Theory Research, 3,* 109–111.

Zhang, D., Wang, M., Xu, Y., & Ju, S. (in press). Special education in China. In X. Li (Ed.), *Education in China: Cultural influences, global perspectives and social challenges* (pp. 30–47). New York, NY: Nova Scientific Publishers.

Zhang, F. J., & Li, J. (2005). Stress parents of children with mental retardation and relevant factors. *Psychological Science, 28*(2), 347–350.

SPECIAL EDUCATION TODAY IN THAILAND

Kullaya Kosuwan, Yuwadee Viriyangkura and Mark E. Swerdlik

ABSTRACT

The field of special education in Thailand is still in its infancy. This chapter provides a retrospect on special education in Thailand reflecting societal attitudes toward people with disabilities from the past to present. It also provides a list of factors impacting this population and members of the community who are involved with their lives. Special education law, definitions of various disability categories, types of educational settings, as well as issues and challenges in the field are discussed. A critical analysis of special education teacher preparation is also provided. Finally, recommendations and conclusions are offered.

HISTORY OF DISABILITIES IN THAILAND

Although people with disabilities have lived in Thailand as long as in other countries, their treatment in the past has been a mystery because no historical records were found regarding lives of and services provided

Special Education International Perspectives: Practices Across the Globe
Advances in Special Education, Volume 28, 689–721
Copyright © 2014 by Emerald Group Publishing Limited
All rights of reproduction in any form reserved ı
ISSN: 0270-4013/doi:10.1108/S0270-401320140000028027

for this population. Searching the literature for "history of disabilities in Thailand" only yielded the history of the field of disabilities and special education in the United States and Europe. An explanation for why there is no record of these people as if they did not exist can be attributed to several reasons.

First, a large majority of people in Thailand (94.6%) are Buddhists (National Statistical Office of Thailand [NSO], 2013a), which has a tremendous influence on the lives of people with disabilities and societal attitudes toward various types of disabilities and the people who possess them. Buddhists believe in Karma which refers to the cause and effect cycle that actions in the past are passed on to what is happening today. Disabilities are believed to be a result of sins that parents or persons with disabilities themselves committed in previous lives or as part of their own past. Although this attitude is less prevalent today, a majority of Thai people still believe that parents of individuals with disabilities or those individuals themselves are "paying back" to whomever they owed. Because parents were ashamed of "their sins," it was unlikely that disabilities were openly discussed or accurate records kept (Thammarak, 2013).

Second, individuals with disabilities were likely perceived as "not able" and, therefore, unimportant. Being asked whether they recalled having contact with or even observing people with disabilities when they were young, the elderly in Thailand (i.e., in their 80s) said individuals with disabilities wandered around their communities but admitted that their memories were blurred because they did not pay much attention to those people with disabilities. They knew that people with disabilities were fed and assisted by their families with all daily life activities, but those individuals never had an opportunity to participate in family or community events (e.g., weddings or religious celebrations) due to difficulty "controlling" themselves and the shame felt by their parents. There were instances when people with disabilities were seen at special events (e.g., temple fairs) alone where many would beg for money, but they never attended schools prior to the 1940s. In some cases, adults with intellectual disabilities were locked or chained at home to prevent self-injury or harm to others or were treated in psychiatric hospitals as they were viewed as having mental illnesses (Dheandhanoo, 1992).

Third, Thai society has never valued data in making decisions. Historical records are difficult to locate not only related to people with disabilities, but also in the field of special education. It is, therefore, not surprising that the lives of people with disabilities were not recorded (Onkoaksoong, 1984; Punlee, Wongwan, Nildam, & Intapanya, 1973).

Early Efforts Prior to Special Education Legislation

The oldest evidence of individuals with disabilities appearing in an official record was the *Compulsory Education Acts* (1935). The acts "allowed" children and youth with physical and mental disabilities as well as children who lived in poverty to opt out from normal compulsory education. This supported the anecdotes of the Thai elderly and explained why students with disabilities were never observed at school. This "exemption" continued until 1980. Although, at the first glance, it seemed convenient for parents, children with disabilities, and children who lived in poverty; government officials later realized that this opt-out did not benefit those children, their parents, nor the country as a whole in the long run (Srinakharinwirot University, 2013). This led to an awareness of the need for education for people with disabilities resulted from contributions from several individuals in the late 1930s. One of them was Genevieve Caulfield.

Genevieve Caulfield who was an American English teacher with a visual impairment visited Thailand and learned that children who were blind received neither financial support nor an education. She went back to the United States and raised money for her mission in Thailand. Returning to Thailand in 1938, Caulfield worked with a small group of Thai educators to develop Thai Braille characters. It was noted that "this was contemplated to be a great success as Thai language has 44 alphabets, 32 vowels, and 4 tonal marks which as much more than 26 English alphabets" (School for the Blind, 2013, para. 4). Caulfield rented a small house in Bangkok to set up a classroom for children with low vision and blindness. The classroom developed into the *Foundation for the Blind in Thailand* (FBTQ, 2013) in the following year (1939) with support from donors. Resigning after World War II, Caulfield asked sisters and Salesian priests to continue her work. She also founded schools for the blind in Chiangmai (in the North of Thailand) and Vietnam in 1956. The Foundation for the Blind in Thailand (currently known as the *Foundation for the Blind in Thailand under the Royal Patronage of H.M. the Queen*) founded the *School for the Blind*, contributing to students with visual impairments appearing more in the public. Later, this project was expanded into more schools for the blind in the North (Chiangmai), the Northeast (Khonkaen), and the South (Suratthani; FBTQ, 2013).

The Ministry of Education (MOE) recognized the need for special education and started a demonstration project in 1951 to educate slow learners who could not keep up with their classmates academically, students with sensory impairments, physical disabilities, and chronic illness

(Nakhon Ratchasima Rajabhat University, 2011). This movement has never been linked to Caulfield's work, but it is reasonable to assume that it was influenced by the Foundation for the Blind. Other significant changes also took place in the 1950s. In 1954, a self-contained classroom for students with hearing loss developed into the first *School for the Deaf* in Thailand (Setsatian, 2013). In 1956, with the support from the Foundation for the Blind in Thailand, high school students with blindness were included in general classrooms at St. Gabriel's School, a well-known private school in Bangkok (Srinakharinwirot University, 2013). One year later, the MOE initiated a pilot project to integrate students who were considered slow learners into seven Bangkok Metropolitan public schools.

The *Foundation for the Welfare of the Crippled* was established in 1954 and, two years later, received support from the Royal Patronage of H.R.H. the Princess Mother. The foundation provided educational services at Siriraj Hospital for children with physical disabilities and chronic illness caused by polio or meningitis and were originally taught by physician and nurse volunteers. Later, in 1958, the Special Education Division under the Department of General Education, MOE, sent itinerant teachers to provide an educational program for in-patient children where there were 17−25 students from preschool to college level (Nakhon Ratchasima Rajabhat University, 2011). In 1961, the *School for Children with Physical Disabilities* was established, and later it was named after H.R.H. the Princess Mother, *Srisangwan School* (Srisangwan School, 2013; Table 1).

Table 1. Years of Important Events.

Year	Important event
1939	Foundation for the Blind in Thailand was established.
1951	The MOE set up the first special education classroom for slow learners and students with sensory impairments, physical disabilities, and chronic illnesses.
1954	School for the Deaf (Setsatian School) was founded.
1956	St. Gabriel's School allowed students with visual impairments to participate in general education classrooms, and those became the first inclusive classrooms in Thailand.
1959	The first disability survey in Thailand was conducted by World Health Organization.
1960	The Hospital for the Mentally Retarded (Rajanukul Institute) was founded.
1961	School for Children with Physical Disabilities (Srisangwan School) was established.
1980	Division of Special Education was the first government unit directly responsible for special education in Thailand.

Related to intellectual disability, services emerged because of domestic and international influences. In the 1950s, Professor Phon Sangsingkaew, a physician and Director of Somdet Chaopraya Hospital (a psychiatric hospital), suggested that people with intellectual disabilities were not mentally ill and should be treated accordingly. He went on to support Dr. Roschong Dhasananchalee, a psychiatrist, for a training course in the area of intellectual disabilities in the United Kingdom in 1953. In 1959, the research team of the World Health Organization (WHO), collaborated with the Ministry of Public Health, surveyed incidence of intellectual disability in Thailand, and reported that 1% of Thai population had intellectual disabilities of various levels of severity (Komkris, 1989; Kosuwan, 2010). Based on this finding, the Thai government became aware of people with intellectual disabilities and attempted to provide more services for this population.

Upon his return, in 1960, Dr. Dhasananchalee established the *Hospital for the Mentally Retarded* and became its first director. The hospital has since provided diagnostic, treatment, and rehabilitation services for these individuals. In addition to the medical services, the hospital has also provided special education services for school-aged children with mild and moderate intellectual disabilities in the *Rajanukul Special School*. Renamed as *Rajanukul Institute* in 2001, the hospital has remained to this day the first and most well-known hospital for multidisciplinary services for individuals with intellectual disabilities (Komkris, 1989; Rajanukul, 2013).

Another important organization involved in the area of intellectual disability in Thailand is the *Foundation for the Welfare of the Mentally Retarded of Thailand under the Royal Patronage of Her Majesty the Queen* established in 1962 by a group of interested citizens led by Prince Prem Purachatra's wife (Mom[1] Ngarmchit Purachatra). This foundation has provided services for individuals with intellectual disabilities through community-based early childhood centers, schools, and vocational training centers in Bangkok, the North, the Northeast, and the South of Thailand (FMRTH, 2013).

The field of disability studies became established in 1980, and the MOE assigned the *Division of Special Education*, under the Primary Education Department, to administer the provision of education to children with disabilities and children from disadvantaged backgrounds. In 1998, the Division of Special Education was divided into the *Division of Education for Individuals with Disabilities* (DEID) and the *Division of Education for Individuals from Disadvantaged Background* (BSE, 2011). Despite the DEID being directly responsible for people with disabilities, no legislation existed to mandate appropriate education for this population.

Finally in 2003, there was a structural reform of the MOE by combining three departments including the Office of National Primary Education Commission, Department of Primary Education, and Department of Curriculum and Instruction Development into the *Office of the Basic Education Commission* (OBEC). The MOE also combined the DEID and the Division of Education for Individuals from Disadvantaged Background into the *Bureau of Special Education* (BSE, 2011).

The Royal Family and the Field of Disabilities

In addition to services provided by the government, the royal family has also played a key role in the field of disabilities in Thailand. For instance, with support from *H.R.H. the Princess Mother Srinagarindra*, Siriraj Hospital launched a rehabilitation project to provide services for children with physical disabilities from disadvantaged backgrounds (Nakhon Ratchasima Rajabhat University, 2011). *Her Majesty Queen Sirikit* has also supported several foundations such as the *Foundation for the Blind in Thailand under the Royal Patronage of H.M. the Queen* (FBTQ, 2013) and the *Foundation for the Welfare of the Mentally Retarded of Thailand under the Royal Patronage of H.M. the Queen* (FMRTH, 2013). The *School for the Deaf* has been supported by *His Royal Highness Crown Prince Maha Vajiralongkorn* since 2002 and is currently known as *Setsatian School for the Deaf under the Royal Patronage of His Royal Highness Crown Prince Maha Vajiralongkorn* (Setsatian, 2013).

The involvement of the royal family with the field of disabilities was even more prominent when Khun *Poom Jensen* moved to Thailand with his mother, *Her Royal Highness Princess Ubolratana Rajakanya*, in 2001. Raised in the United States and having lived a few years in Thailand, Khun Poom, diagnosed with autism, could fully participate in daily living activities valued by the population without disabilities. Autism has received attention from all parties across the nation, and Khun Poom's story brought great hope to Thai parents that children with autism could learn and contribute to society. Sadly, he was one of the victims of tsunami in Khao Lak, Phang Nga province in 2004. In 2005 after his death, Princess Ubolratana established the *Khun Poom Foundation* to provide financial support for educational purposes to low SES children who have autism or intellectual disabilities (Khun Poom Foundation, 2013). Generous support from the royal family has been, and continues to be, one of the most significant pillars of support of the field of disabilities in Thailand.

Individuals with Disabilities and Laws

Although there have been a number of constitutional laws since 1932, the rights of Thai citizens with disabilities such as equal access to public services was not part of constitutional law until an amendment in 1997 (NEP, 2013a). According to that constitutional law (1997), individuals with disabilities have rights to access and benefit from social welfare, public utilities, as well as other appropriate support from the government in order to be as independent as possible and attain the highest quality of life.

In fact, medical and vocational supports and services as well as accommodations related to government procedures and legal services in case of a lawsuit were mandated in the *Rehabilitation of Disabled Persons Act,* B.E. 2534 (1991) before the constitutional law (1997). The act mandated that Thai citizens who were registered as individuals with disabilities must receive an appropriate education, given access to participate in community activities, as well as securing necessary assistive technology and other services appropriate for people with disabilities (Roonjareon, 2013). Although mandated by law, a number of children with disabilities in some geographical areas of Thailand were denied access to public education in the 1990s because the emphasis of this act was access to community activities and providing financial support, not education (Chandrakasem Rajabhat University, 2013).

The Era of Mandated Special Education

After the *Rehabilitation of Disabled Persons Act,* B.E. 2534 (1991), education for people with disabilities was legislated again in the *National Education Act,* B.E. 2542 (1999; MOE, 2013). Even though the *National Education Act,* B.E. 2542 (1999) was not an official special education law, it was one of the most prominent education laws that led to special education in Thailand for several reasons. The act caused the MOE to announce the year 1999 as "The Year of Education for People with Disabilities," and that launch had a profound impact on the field of special education. The slogan "Every person with a disability must have access to education" gave a signal to all educational institutions that the "Zero-Reject" policy must be in place (but this was not fully implemented in reality). Although this policy did not include a mandate for all schools to implement, it was an initial move to provide education for children with disabilities in general education schools. There were gradual increases in the number of schools that offered to include children with disabilities particularly in self-contained classrooms.

The MOE also heavily advocated that institutions of higher education increase the number and quality of special educators. In that particular year, the Ministry of Finance provided an extra allowance for special educators who met specific criteria. Most importantly, the act led to Thailand's first official special education law in 2008 (Chulalongkorn University, 2012). The *National Education Act*, B.E. 2542 (1999) yielded significant benefits to the field of special education.

Special education appeared, for the first time, in Thailand's constitutional law in 2007. The new constitutional law mandates that, "Every Thai citizen must have equal access to free, quality education for at least 12 years in one's life. The government must provide assistance to those who live in poverty, come from disadvantage backgrounds, or have disabilities to have equal access to education" (NEP, 2013b, p. 13). This constitutional law was another law that led to Thailand's first official special education law, the *Persons with Disabilities Education Act*, B.E. 2551 (BSE, 2012). The Thai special education law was also influenced by American special education law (i.e., the *Individuals with Disabilities Education and Improvement Act* or IDEA, 2004) and the United Nations General Assembly's *Declaration of Human Rights* in 1948 (Chulalongkorn University, 2012)

The *Persons with Disabilities Education Act*, B.E. 2551 (2008) mandated that individuals with disabilities must have rights to receive free education, assistive technology, and other educational support from birth or since one's diagnosis throughout their lives. Each individual has rights to select services, settings, systems, and types of education according to one's abilities, interests, skills, and special needs. Also, education provided must reach national standards, have quality assurance, and match individuals' special needs. Special educators, educational institutions that serve students with special needs, and research projects focusing on improving special education will receive financial support. Individualized Education Plans, appropriate types of instruction, environment, and other educational support are required. Schools must not deny students with disabilities (NEP, 2013c).

DISABILITY CATEGORIES

To provide an appropriate education to students with disabilities, the BSE organized disabilities into nine categories and defined each disability category as follows (MUA, 2013).

1. *Visual Impairment* includes low vision (a vision between 20/70 and 20/200 after correction) and blindness (a vision of 20/200 or more after correction and those who cannot sense light).
2. *Hearing Impairment* includes hard of hearing (hearing loss between 26 and 90 decibels) and deaf (hearing loss at 90 decibels and above).
3. *Intellectual Disability* is defined as having below average intellectual functioning and deficits in two out of 10 adaptive skills before age of 18. The 10 adaptive skills include communication, self-care, home living, social skills, community use, self-direction, functional academics, work, leisure, and health and safety.
4. *Physical, Mobility, or Health Impairment* is defined as (a) losing or having problems with parts of body, bones, muscles that cause difficulties in movement, or (b) having a chronic illness that requires long-term health care and becomes an obstacle to education.
5. *Learning Disabilities* includes brain dysfunctions that cause difficulties in learning one or more academic skills (e.g., reading, writing, mathematics) despite normal IQ.
6. *Speech and Language Disorders* includes problems in producing sounds (e.g., distortion, abnormal speed or rhythm) and/or problems in expressive or receptive language (i.e., oral, written, or other forms).
7. *Emotional and Behavioral Disorders* is defined as markedly and continuously deviant behaviors caused by mental illness or brain dysfunctions (e.g., schizophrenia, depression, dementia).
8. *Autism* is caused by brain dysfunction and results in multiple impairments in language and social development, social interaction, and restricted behaviors or interests. The age of onset is before 30 months.
9. *Multiple Disabilities* is defined as having more than one disability.

Despite these definitions, some teachers and administrators still cannot use these categories in their real-life practice due to lack of knowledge of disabilities and special education.

TYPES OF EDUCATIONAL SETTINGS

Several governmental units are responsible for the education of individuals with disabilities between 3 and 18 years of age. The OBEC has provided inclusive education in selected public schools throughout Thailand. The BSE's responsibility covers 43 special education schools, 63 provincial and 13 regional special education centers, and 25 social welfare schools. The

Department of Non-Formal Education (NFE) also provides education to individuals with disabilities who cannot attend schools (BSE, 2012). Additionally, there are students with disabilities in inclusive private schools, schools under the control of the Ministry of Interior, and educational institutions under the control of the Ministry of Public Health. Details are provided below.

Inclusive Public Schools

In 2011, 242,888 students in the nine disability categories were educated in 18,370 inclusive public schools nationwide. Educational services in those schools, however, vary depending on school administrators' policy. The term "inclusive school" is unclear whether it provides full-time inclusion (i.e., students were instructed the full day in general education classrooms), part-time inclusion (i.e., students with disabilities spend most of their day in general classrooms but were pulled out for a few hours for small group or individualized instruction in a resource room), or full-time segregation (i.e., students were instructed in separate self-contained classrooms in general education schools). In addition, no definitive guidelines exist as to who should receive education in which type of setting. In most cases, final decisions are made solely by school administrators and are dependent on the inclusive options a particular school can offer. In some cases, the personal relationships between special education teachers and general education teachers also play a part in students' placement.

Although most parents desired their children with disabilities to be included in classrooms of same-aged peers regardless of their degree of participation in typical community activities, it is unlikely for those children with more significant disabilities to be included in general education classrooms. This is due to a number of factors. First, general education teachers have limited knowledge and skills in dealing with children with special needs. Second, those teachers are unable to provide accommodations and modify instructional content and curricula taught in general education classrooms. Third, typical classrooms are large (i.e., approximately 35–45 students taught by a teacher) and so, even though general educators may want to comply with the special education law, they are reluctant to have students who need extensive support in their classrooms.

From the authors' experience, most inclusive schools have only one or two special education teachers instructing in self-contained classrooms or resource rooms, and some of these special education teachers were hired by the regional or provincial special education centers, not the schools. For some schools that enroll only a few students with diagnosed disabilities, it would be more likely that the school would not employ a special education teacher. If this is the case, the students with disabilities remain in general education classrooms with their same-aged peers, but this may represent only "physical inclusion" and may not represent an appropriate education for those students.

Although the authors have had opportunities to observe general education teachers who adapted and modified the curricula and lessons, teaching strategies (e.g., hands-on activities instead of lectures or implemented peer tutoring), and evaluation processes (e.g., more time for tests or reading test questions to a student), adaptations and modifications for students with special needs in general classrooms are uncommon in Thailand. Moreover, most general education teachers are unfamiliar with assistive technology (e.g., FM device to amplify sounds for students with hearing impairments or Braille for students with visual impairments) because assistive technology is considered the responsibility of the special educator and the student. These examples provide an illustration of how general education teachers would struggle when they have students with disabilities enrolled in their classrooms without the support of a trained special educator.

Although the MOE has provided numerous special education training courses to enable general education teachers to work effectively with students with disabilities in general education classrooms, this approach has not been as effective as anticipated. Recently, scholars in the field of special education have articulated advantages of inclusive over segregated education, but a majority of people in the Thai society still believe that a stand-alone special education school is the best option for individuals with disabilities because of lack of school personnel's expertise in working with this population (Rattanasakorn, 2007).

Special Education Schools

Thailand has established 43 special education schools in 35 provinces including 20 Schools for the Deaf, 19 schools for students with intellectual disabilities, two Schools for the Blind, and two schools for students with physical and/or health impairments (Wipattanaporn, 2014). The numbers of students in each disability category classified by type of school are presented in Table 2. These special education schools serve students in Grades K-12. Since most of these special schools were located far from the centers

Table 2. Number of Students with Disabilities Classified by Type of
Educational Setting in 2011.

Disability	Inclusive School/ Classroom[a]	Self-Contained Classroom	Special School[a]	Special Education Center[a]
VI	3,980	N/A	311	1,233
HI	1,692	N/A	5,159	1,260
ID	18,102	N/A	7,139	11,077
P&H	7,890	N/A	489	11,533
LD	183,398	N/A	N/A	26,748
S&L	4,359	N/A	N/A	1,032
EBD	6,280	N/A	N/A	900
Autism	3,863	106[b]	N/A	4,961
MD	13,324	N/A	N/A	5,302
Total	242,888	N/A	13,098	64,046

Notes: VI = Visual Impairment; HI = Hearing Impairment; ID = Intellectual Disability;
P&H = Physical, Mobility, or Health Impairment; LD = Learning Disabilities; S&L = Speech
and Language Disorders; EBD = Emotional and Behavioral Disorders; MD = Multiple
Disabilities.
[a]Source: BSE (2012).
[b]C. Chantayanon (personal communication, October 20, 2013).

of towns, it is likely that transportation represents a major obstacle for
students with disabilities and their families coming from homes to schools.
Therefore, all special education schools are residential to address the problem of the lack of public transportation (Viriyangkura, 2010), although
most of them also educate local day students.

As their names imply, each school was established to serve students
with a specific disability. In reality, however, these special education schools
also enroll students with other disabilities. For example, in 2003,
Lopburipanyanukul School (a special school for persons with intellectual
disability in Lopburi province) had 148 students with intellectual disabilities, 154 students with hearing impairments, 9 students with physical disabilities, and 7 students with autism. The following year (2004), the school
served 166 students with intellectual disabilities, 121 students with hearing
impairments, 10 students with physical disabilities, 13 students with autism,
and 7 students with specific learning disabilities. Currently, this special
school has 266 students with intellectual disabilities, 41 students with autism, and 5 students with physical disabilities (Lopburipanyanukul, 2013).

Curricula used in schools for persons with intellectual disabilities have
recently been changed from eight subject areas taught in general education

schools to a functional curriculum to suit these students' needs. Schools for the blind and for the deaf, however, try to prepare their students who are at an age-appropriate level functioning for being educated in general education schools. Despite the difference of the curricula, self-help skills (e.g., dressing, grooming, health care, household chores) are the foci of the curricula. Instructional strategies employed in this type of school typically focus on task analysis, shaping, chaining, reinforcement, and typical teaching methods. At present, most special schools have made efforts to develop programs to prepare adolescents for their careers and their transition to adult lives, but these efforts have not been as successful.

Special Education Centers

Special education centers were established in every province for several purposes. The primary purposes of each center are to provide early intervention services to young children with disabilities, to prepare young children with disabilities for both general education and special education schools depending on their level of abilities, and to educate individuals with disabilities in hospitals or at home (Wipattanaporn, 2014). Responsibilities of these special education centers are also to support teachers in general education schools to provide an appropriate education to children with disabilities (e.g., establish inclusive classrooms or resource rooms and teach educators how to write an individualized education program) as well as to support parents of children with special needs. The special education center network includes 13 regional special education centers and 63 provincial special education centers (BSE, 2012).

In handling a variety of functions, special education centers use different strategies dependent on the age, type, and degree of severity of disability, as well as needs of individual children and families. Because professionals employed by special education centers work with various organizations, effective communication and a high degree of cooperation represent key factors in their success. Although special education centers have similar goals and objectives, the effectiveness of their services are heavily based on their director's policy and leadership skills.

Non-Formal Education

The Department of NFE was developed to serve individuals who wanted to receive education but could not participate in formal classes for several reasons. Provided in homes or hospitals, NFE services include programs in Grades 1–12 and vocational programs taught by NFE teachers from the MOE, teachers from private organizations, and volunteer teachers from nonprofit organizations (Dhammaviteekul, 2009; Wipattanaporn, 2014). The BSE (2012) reported that 3,559 individuals with disabilities were educated in Grades 1–12; 3,223 in vocational programs; 2,051 in Sustainable Community programs; and 3,266 in recreational and other services programs.

Educational Institutions Outside the MOE

In addition to the schools and the special education centers administered by the MOE, there are a number of institutions that provide educational services to children and youth with disabilities. Schools under the administrative control of the city of Bangkok are an example of public schools under the Ministry of Interior. A few special education schools are attached to hospitals (e.g., Rajanukul School for children with intellectual disabilities), and so are under the administrative control of the Ministry of Public Health. There are 16 private special education schools and 644 private inclusive schools in Thailand. Moreover, six special education centers were founded and managed by departments of special education in Rajabhat Universities (BSE, 2012; Wipattanaporn, 2014). These educational institutions have different policies and practices when working with children with special needs.

CONCERNS AND CHALLENGES IN SPECIAL EDUCATION

The field of special education in Thailand is still in its beginning stages, so comparing special education in Thailand to well-established systems in Western countries would inevitably lead to a lengthy list of concerns and challenges. Due to limited space, however, we present only selected issues that require serious attention from everyone associated with the field of special education.

Lack or Excess of Data

Thailand has never been a data-driven society. Searching for data in any field of study, in hard copy or digital format, is a challenge. Some useful data were never retained, some data were relocated without prior notification or a link provided, and some data were removed from their sources for no apparent reason. For instance, the MOE deleted a document *Special Education Strategic Plans 2012–2017* (BSE, 2012) from its website at the end of 2012. A report on the performance of special education teachers (Chulalongkorn University, 2012) was removed from The Teachers Council of Thailand website in July 2013. Moreover, decisions related to keeping data have been arbitrary.

Some educational statistics reported in the field do not align. For example, the OBEC (2013a) reported that 66,330 students with disabilities were included in Grades K-12 in 2012, but the MOE (2013) reported 237,779 students in inclusive schools in 2012 and the BSE (2012) reported 242,888 students in inclusive schools in 2011. Lack of consistency in data collection can be attributed to several possible reasons. One explanation is the fact that special education is new and considered unimportant. Key responsible organizations (e.g., NSO), therefore, did not keep records related to the population with disabilities as compared to the general population. Additionally, organizations collecting data have worked independently which represents another explanation. When collaboration between agencies did not exist, data reflected only small parts of the picture rather than the whole.

On the other hand, there were a number of educational organizations that provided all of the statistics and personal information (e.g., name, age, disability, ID card number, school name, parents' names, home address, and telephone number) for students with disabilities in a particular school or district for public access. A fine line exists between "too little" and "too much" data for public consumption, and this represents another issue that should receive attention in the field.

Individuals with Disabilities Not Enrolled in School

In 2005, the literacy rate in Thai population was 93% (MOE, 2005). Despite the plan to increase the rate to 95% in 2012 (Thairath, July 3, 2009), Thailand's literacy rate has not increased. The general population rate was significantly higher than the rate for those with disabilities. The NSO reported that among 1.5 million people with disabilities at ages 5 years and above, 22.40% never attended school, and 57.60% did not complete sixth grade level. Whereas those in the general population did not attend schools because they did not have financial support (37%) or they were responsible for earning a major portion of income for their families (39%), 65% of people with disabilities did not attend school because their disabilities were "too severe" to receive education (NSO, 2013b, 2013c).

Several reasons for the lack of attendance of those with disabilities include that their parents did not value education for their children, or they may live a distance from school prohibiting attendance. A number of parents, however, reported that they wanted their children to attend school, but school administrators or administrative teachers refused to accept these children because the schools lacked qualified personnel to teach them. Those schools also suggested parents have their children attend another school that "could educate them" (Manager Online, July 6, 2013; Rattanasakorn, 2007). Although this denial of services was illegal, one must consider several factors such as a lack of special education teachers available in such schools. In addition, special education teachers are employed in only leading inclusive schools designated by the OBEC. Further, despite various special education training programs for general education teachers, trainees were too small in number and, without administrators and colleagues' support, these trainees could not implement what they learned. It is, therefore, not unexpected that many schools in Thailand would be uncomfortable accepting students with special needs. The question remains, however, how do schools continue to deny school-aged children with special needs services mandated by law without penalty from the MOE.

After a number of petitions on behalf of parents of children with disabilities were filed, the BSE Director announced in the media that the *Persons with Disabilities Education Act*, B.E. 2551 (2008) would prevent the "schools' denial" (Daily News, December 17, 2007). As mentioned earlier, children and youth with disabilities are still rejected by public schools (TJIC, 2013). The MOE also attempted to increase the quality and quantity of special education teachers by issuing policies regarding special education programs. These policies were aimed to support (and push) higher education institutions throughout the country to increase program quality and raise the capacity to increase the number of special education personnel produced. The results, however, as discussed in the next section, were unsuccessful.

Lack of High Quality Individualized Education Programs

A large majority of, if not every, special educators in Thailand learned that students with disabilities require individualized education programs (IEPs).

Writing IEPs is a skill taught in all preservice programs and as part of continuing professional development offered by the OBEC and the BSE. Further, special educators receive an extra allowance after they have submitted IEPs to the BSE to reflect the number of students with disabilities they are serving each semester. Despite these possible explanations, a number of educators teach their students with disabilities without an IEP. Moreover, a number of teachers have low expectations related to the abilities of their students with disabilities, and therefore the content and methods used are often inappropriate for the students' ages and ability levels. Some students had IEPs, but the documents did not serve the purposes for which they were designed (e.g., teachers did not seek agreement from parents for services, IEPs were written by individual teachers rather than the team, and IEPs of students in the same class were almost identical).

There are several possible reasons for IEPs not being developed for individuals with disabilities. First, some teachers admitted they did not know how to write IEPs and to provide services consistent with the IEP (Chulalongkorn University, 2012). Second, IEPs in many schools are developed by individual general or special educators, not IEP teams. Therefore, the documents are developed based on one person's knowledge. Third, school administrators often do not check or verify the IEPs. Fourth, the BSE does not have an appropriate evaluation system in place. Finally and perhaps most importantly, parents of students with disabilities do not understand the meaning of an IEP and did not see the value of this document. Parents, therefore, approve "whatever" teachers prepare for them. Although the OBEC and the BSE have provided training to special educators throughout the country, education authorities would not know whether IEPs submitted by teachers accurately reflected each student unless parents were actively engaged in the IEP process.

Lack of Preparation for the Post-School Life

Transitions represent a particularly critical juncture in the lives of high school students with disabilities because they are moving from childhood to adulthood with decreasing support along with higher societal expectations for independence. The transition planning process including developing individualized transition plans, however, is not common practice regardless of educational level (e.g., preschool to elementary school and high school to postsecondary education or employment). As a result, most students with disabilities and their families must redo the educational planning process each time there is a move to a new school, to the next phase of life, or even to the next grade with a new teacher.

Special education schools represent an educational setting that utilizes Individualized Transition Plans (ITPs) for students with disabilities for educational planning. However, ITPs typically do not take into account the needs of the individuals with disabilities and their families. Instead, the ITP development process includes having the student's teachers choose from a "menu of careers" for their students. Many of these careers are unrealistic for individuals with disabilities. For example, a special school provides training for a student with disability in agriculture when in fact his family does not own a piece of land. In Thailand, a large number of students with disabilities graduate with no idea of what to do next. Many remain at home after graduation and this situation is exacerbated in inclusive schools because their students are assumed, just like their peers, to continue postsecondary education. As a result, ITPs are not being developed for these students.

It is not surprising that, in 2012, 74.3% of individuals over the age of 15 with disabilities were unemployed (NSO, 2013d). Out of that group, individuals ages 25–59 and youth ages 15–24 years old represented a substantial portion (19.90 and 4.5% accordingly) that were unemployed. Furthermore, the NSO reported that among the 25% of the employed group, 18% worked in agriculture, fishery, and other low-paid jobs. In addition, no records exist reporting which disability groups are employed and which are not. It is possible that the most employed individuals are those with learning disabilities and mild physical disabilities, whereas a majority of people with intellectual disability, sensory impairments, and multiple disabilities remain unemployed, but we do not know.

Problem of Accurate Monitoring Systems

Special educators working in general education schools are formally supervised and monitored by school level administrators and educational supervisors (special education) located in each geographical area of Thailand. There is, however, a lack of supervisors providing support and consultation for general education teachers who give instruction to children with special needs in inclusive classrooms. To solve this issue, educational supervisors in other areas received brief training courses in special education to provide special education supervision to those general education teachers. With a lack of a rigorous monitoring system and an absence in special education knowledge and skills of some educational supervisors, the centralized MOE would be unaware of any problems and teachers were not supported.

Although Thai parents view teachers as authority figures and are "good followers," there are instances that small groups of local families have submitted petitions to the MOE claiming that the education of their children with disabilities was not at no cost to them. Also, they complained that their children were denied admission by schools, or schools "falsely used" their children's names to secure special education financial support. Unfortunately, the impact of this parent advocacy has not been strong enough to lead to changes in these special education practices that are occurring nationwide (Thairath, January 18, 2013).

Historically, there were situations in which parents monitored the teaching by themselves based on their child's development. It is also the case, however, that many parents fear the consequences of providing negative reports of their child's teachers. These consequences can range from their child being ignored to being mistreated.

Lack of Strong Parent Movement and Advocacy

Even though a teaching career is not as attractive to a new generation of Thai young adults as it was in the past (Manager Online, April 26, 2013), teachers generally remain well respected as experts and authoritative figures by parents. There are occasionally some parents of children with disabilities who possess effective communication skills and could advocate effectively for their children, but most Thai parents would never "go against" the teachers' opinions.

Chulalongkorn University (2012) conducted a study of the field of special education and reported that parents and guardians were dissatisfied with the special education services and educational supports (e.g., assistive technology) their children were receiving. Additionally, participating parents and guardians reported that special educators did not possess adequate knowledge and skills. This view was consistent with the self-perceptions of participating special educators who noted, for example, that they did not possess the skills to provide an inclusive education, develop an IEP, and/or address the behavioral problems of their students.

More recently, there are several parent groups and disability associations in Thailand. Although all of these groups are slowly moving the field forward, similarly to other developed countries, the most powerful group represents parents of children with autism. The *Association of Parents of*

Thai Persons with Autism (AU Thai) has developed a network of parents in 76 provinces nationwide and demanded the MOE provide "parallel classrooms" which refer to self-contained classrooms for students with moderate and severe autism located in the same school of their typically developing peers (C. Chantayanon, personal communication, October 20, 2013). According to the AU-Thai's document, however, the future of these classrooms is uncertain as the funding for teachers' salaries is dependent on the governmental budget which varies on a year-to-year basis. This parent advocacy group also strongly influenced policy makers and special education legislation in Thailand.

Parents of children with disabilities are also employing social networks (e.g., Facebook) to communicate and share information among themselves and as a means to provide support to members. A limitation of this communication medium, however, is that only parents from middle- to high-class families have access to information technology, while many parents who reside in rural areas do not have access to the Internet and depend on their local government (e.g., Subdistrict Administrative Organization), school administrators and teachers, and informal communication with neighbors to provide them with information and support.

SPECIAL EDUCATION TEACHER PREPARATION

Over 40 years ago, the MOE contracted with *Suan Dusit Teachers' College* to create a demonstration program to educate young children with hearing impairments, and the program developed into the first bachelor's degree program in special education in 1970 (Nakhon Ratchasima Rajabhat University, 2011). Prior to 2004, a bachelor's level preparation program in special education and other specialty areas required three and a half years of course work and one semester of field experience. Critics of the quality of teachers including special educators, however, caused the MOE to extend the field experience from a semester to a year resulting in an increase in the time to degree completion from four to five years (MUA, 2011). Compared to 4-year bachelor programs in other fields and 6-year bachelor programs in medical specialties, however, these 5-year bachelor programs in special education did not attract the same high quality (e.g., having high GPAs) high school students.

Recently, the MOE announced a double-major program policy that requires special education preparation programs to pair with another education major (e.g., language arts, mathematics, or science) with the expectation that these teachers will be able to provide instruction for typically developing students as well as those with special needs in general education settings. A group of teacher educators argued that the longer field experience and the "hybrid special education" program would solve only a part of the quality problem. It is because most courses in these preparation programs still focus more on general disability information and theories of instructional strategies but less on the relevant hands-on and field experiences. Therefore, instead of addressing critical issues in the field by increasing the quality and quantity of pedagogy courses and field experiences provided for future special educators, the MOE is adding more pressure on teacher preparation programs through these recent policies.

Teacher Shortage

Currently, Thailand has 14 higher education institutions including large universities in major cities and Rajabhat Universities (previously known as community teachers' colleges) that offer bachelor's (nine institutions), master's (six institutions), and doctoral (two institutions) special education preparation programs (MUA, 2013). Each program, however, is limited in the number of future special educators it can prepare each year (approximately 20−50 undergraduate students and 10−20 master's level students annually; Arrayawinyoo, 2001; MUA, 2013). Based on these enrollment limitations, the shortage of special educators remains a critical issue in the field (Chulalongkorn University, 2012).

Based on the statistics presented in Table 2, Thailand has over 300,000 students with disabilities educated in various settings. This 300,000 does not include nearly 200,000 other individuals with disabilities who have never received formal schooling (NSO, 2013c). Although the OBEC (2013b) reported that 2,154 special education teachers were qualified for extra allowance from the MOE in 2012 (Manager Online, December 4, 2012), the number of teachers working in each type of educational setting such as a special education school or an inclusive school was unknown. Assuming an appropriate ratio of teachers to students with disabilities of 1:5, Thailand would need 60,000 special education teachers for the 300,000 students with disabilities currently being educated nationwide. These statistics underscore that the special educator shortage in Thailand is severe.

Lack of Knowledge and Skills

As noted earlier, special education teachers have reported that they lack special education knowledge and skills in providing instruction in inclusive classrooms; writing IEPs; teaching functional skills in addition to academics; handling severe behavioral problems; evaluating student performance; and transitioning their students to other related services and/or new schools (Chulalongkorn University, 2012).

These problems led to an issue which has never been raised in Thailand, special education teachers' burnout. In addition to lack of knowledge and skills, a large number of teachers left the field because they had too many students enrolled in their classrooms; struggled with providing the intensive support that a number of students require; or had extra assigned administrative tasks leaving them less time for their direct instructional responsibilities. Other challenges identified for those in the field of education, including special educators, relates to the heavy demands for paperwork leaving less time for planning and teaching (Manager Online, April 26, 2013).

Lack of Resources

Unlike the United States where authors and their publishers are eager to market special education resources (e.g., textbooks) due to the high demand in the field, Thailand has only a few authors and no publishers who specialize in special education materials because "photocopied editions" are less expensive and publishing special education textbooks are unprofitable. High quality special education textbooks and other related materials written exclusively for special educators working in Thailand are rare. Consequently, students trained to be special educators depend solely on instructor lectures with instructors themselves possessing different levels of knowledge and skills related specifically to special education. Most textbooks currently in use are written only for the authors' classes (e.g., Yodkhampang, 2004) or to satisfy professor tenure requirements. Future and current special educators have not had high quality resources to draw upon during their preservice education or for their continuing professional development.

OTHER FACTORS BEYOND SPECIAL EDUCATION

In Thailand, there are a number of other factors that more indirectly impact the field of special education and individuals with disabilities. Only some of these factors are discussed below.

Numerous Administrative Organizations Creating Confusion

In 1994, the Ministry of Public Health (MOPH, 2013) classified disabilities into five categories: Visual Impairments, Communication and Hearing Impairments, Physical and Mobility Problems, Mental or Behavioral Disorders, and Intellectual or Learning Disabilities. These five categories, however, were not found as helpful by the MOE for individualized education programming. Therefore, the MOE recategorized the various disabilities into an expanded nine category system by (1) dividing Communication and Hearing Impairments into Hearing Impairments and Speech and Language Disorders, (2) dividing Intellectual or Learning Disabilities into Intellectual Disability and Learning Disabilities, and (3) adding Autism and Multiple Disabilities (Kitdham, 2013). The Ministry of Social Development and Human Security (MSO, 2013) also uses its own seven disability categorical system which includes Visual Impairments, Hearing Impairments and Communication Disorders, Mobility or Physical Disabilities, Mental or Behavioral Disorders, Intellectual Disability, Learning Disabilities, and Autism. These differences in classification systems has created confusion for educators, parents, and individuals with disabilities themselves, and have become an obstacle for insuring a "seamless transition" in the provision of services for individuals with disabilities from preschool to school through adult services.

Clearly, the lives of people with disabilities in Thailand are impacted by three major governmental agencies including the Ministry of Public Health, the Ministry of Social Development and Human Security, and the MOE. Every baby and young child receives medical services and a disability diagnosis from personnel representing the Ministry of Public Health which includes pediatricians, psychiatrists, and psychologists. Parents of children with special needs who want to receive support and services from the government are required to "register" their children as "people with disabilities." A "medical report" from a representative of the Ministry of Public Heath represents required documentation in order to secure a "disability identification card" which is necessary for children and adults to access health, special education, and adult services.

Disability registration represents another controversy in the field of special education in Thailand. The NSO (2013b) reported that, out of 1,871,860 people with disabilities in 2007, only 20% actually had a disability identification card. This low percentage can be attributed to individuals with less severe disabilities (63%), individuals whose parents did not want

them to be associated with potential stigmatization (15.44%) discussed earlier in this chapter, and individuals who themselves or their parents were
unaware of the need for disability registration (15.26%).

Formal versus Natural Support

In Thailand, it is difficult to determine whether formal support provided by
the government or natural support coming from families and the community at large has a more significant impact on the lives of people with disabilities. As noted earlier, a large majority of the Thai population are
Buddhists, and Buddhism stresses *natural support* to individuals with disabilities and their families. Although the Thai population generally believes
people with disabilities and their families are paying back for past deeds,
neighbors and other community members are almost always empathetic
and supportive of these families. This natural or informal support from
family and community members may in turn compensate for a lack of
formal support from the government for families in rural areas.
Unfortunately, most of the support that is characterized by empathy based
on moral authority focus on "survival" rather than education or future
development of the individual with a disability (NEP, 2013d; Thammarak,
2013).

Transportation represents another example of a factor impacting the
lives of individuals with disabilities. Children with disabilities tend to
have more medical appointments than children without disabilities.
Public transportation, however, is available only in municipal areas, and
this prevents these children from accessing available formal medical
supports. It is more common that neighbors offer rides to and from hospitals to these families, particularly in emergencies. Another example
relates to the provision of support in daily living activities. Many
families of people with disabilities in rural areas of Thailand live in poverty, and it is even more challenging in single parent families. In many of
these families, there are instances that a parent is ill, cannot work, has
limited funds, and cannot cook for the family. In these situations, one or
more neighbors always take action in one way or another to assist. One
neighbor may give the family a small amount of money to one of the
children to buy food for the family or share their own food while
another neighbor may offer respite care, so the parent can rest
(Viriyangkura, 2010).

Personal Outcomes Measurement

In the United States, personal outcomes for individuals with disabilities are measured in three areas including independent living, education, and employment. Government authorities in Thailand have used identical areas to assess outcomes. However, definitions and the relative emphasis of each area differ. For most Thai professionals, the concept of *independent living* refers to only basic human needs such as dressing and undressing, eating, cleaning oneself, toileting, and communicating needs. Independent living does not include higher level actions that are related to independent functioning such as moving around the community, speaking up for oneself, protecting oneself from danger or exploitation. *Education* typically refers to formal education from preschool to high school levels, whereas other types of education are ignored such as vocational programs and training courses provided post-high school or recreation classes. Education also emphasizes physical inclusion without a consideration of meaningful participation in class activities or social engagement. *Employment* represents another index of an important personal outcome. Most Thai people, however, do not believe that people with disabilities could contribute to society.

The perception that individuals with disabilities cannot engage in activities "normal people" do reflects low societal expectations. As is widely known, possessing low expectations may be reflected in their families doing everything for them, or teachers limiting how much they are taught; and this contributes to restricting their development. There are a number of documented cases in which high school students with disabilities were taught and found to be reading at the 6th grade level, although they had the potential to learn more. In addition to limiting opportunities to learn for individuals with disabilities, low expectations held for them by those with whom they interact leads individuals with disabilities to believe they have little control over their own life (an external locus of control), and self-fulfilling prophecy of low expectations contributing to eventual limited development.

Self-Determination

Although self-determination represents a major issue in special education in the United States, this concept does not exist in Thailand and was only occasionally alluded to in the literature. Jeerapornchai (2010) recently developed a program to enhance self-determination of students with mild intellectual disabilities in Grades 4–6. Unfortunately, the program focused only on decision-making skills that represent only one of many components of self-determination. Additionally, Jeerapornchai's research results were interesting in that participating students earned only 19 out of 40 points (47.50%) before the intervention. Participating students with mild disabilities and attending general education schools exhibited weak decision-making skills.

Kosuwan (2012) also developed a training program to introduce the concept of self-determination and teaching strategies teachers could use to encourage students with intellectual disabilities to develop self-determination. Before the training program, the researcher measured the self-determination skills of 145 students with intellectual disabilities in Grades 9 and 12 as well as self-perception on self-determination of 330 special educators in special education schools in Thailand. The findings revealed that students possessed low levels of self-determination, although teachers reported that they had some knowledge of self-determination. Other than this study, the concept of self-determination has not been researched in Thailand. It is important, however, that this construct receive attention from policy makers, administrators, and practitioners in the field.

Quality of Life

Quality of life (QOL) has been considered one of the most important constructs in terms of its impact on one's life. QOL for the population with disabilities in Thailand, however, is loosely defined as there is a lack of consensus on its definition. According to Schalock (2004), QOL refers to a set of factors reflecting personal well-being. QOL can be measured through a variety of indicators such as interpersonal relationships, social inclusion, personal development, physical well-being, self-determination, material well-being, emotional well-being, and the rights possessed by the individual. An example of this lack of a clear definition of QOL includes the National Office for Empowerment of Persons with Disability (NEP) whose responsibility is to focus on improving the QOL of people with disabilities in Thailand. According to the the *Persons with Disabilities' Quality of Life Promotion Act*, B.E. 2550 (2007) issued by the NEP, the promotion and improving QOL means "rehabilitating, providing welfare, promoting human rights, advocating, encouraging independent living to help this population live equally as a population without disabilities, live with dignity, fully and effectively participate in society in accessible environment" (Thai Lawyer Center, 2013, p. 1).

Bangkok Metropolitan city government, however, defines the term differently in its strategic plan to improve the QOL of people with disabilities. QOL is defined as "a perception of an individual on physical, mental, emotional, social, and environmental aspects of one's life and ability to respond to one's needs" (Bangkok Metropolitan, 2013, p. 7). Disability Support Services at Chiangmai Rajabhat University conducted a study on the QOL of college students with special needs, and only six areas were studied including food and nutrition, living arrangement, health, basic services, safety in life and property, and disability support services (DSS, December 3, 2012). Due to the different definitions mentioned above, it can be concluded that the QOL construct in Thailand needs further study and development.

RECOMMENDATIONS

Thailand has made progress in the field of special education over the past 20 years, but much work remains to more effectively meet the needs of individuals with disabilities. This opinion reflects the perspective of professionals who are familiar with special education in both Western countries and Thailand and is not meant to be critical of those familiar with the field only in Thailand. What follows is a list of recommendations that are intended to lead to the provision of more effective special education services for those with disabilities. These recommendations are based on the analysis of the current status of special education in Thailand provided earlier in this chapter.

Educate and Support Families

Because teacher performance should be continuously monitored, parents and families need to be educated and empowered. Parents and other family members of individuals with disabilities should also become more knowledgeable about their children's disability, their care and characteristics of an effective special education program, as well as their children's rights. Parents should also be empowered to serve as their children's advocates, particularly developing effective communication skills to interact with teachers, administrators, and other professionals as well as learning strategies to report abuses without negative ramifications.

Equip and Encourage Special Educators

Although the MOE provides numerous training programs for special education as well as general education teachers each year, the quality of these
programs should be assessed. Studies have confirmed that "one-shot" training does not work (e.g., Harwell, 2003). Rather, a long-term plan is needed
to provide continuing education to special educators. In order to study the
quality of training, a set of measurements such as pre- and post-training
examinations, hands-on activities, observation in classrooms via face-to-
face, video-taping, or videoconferencing should be in place to be selected
from in order to eventually improve training programs.

Building learning communities within schools, creating mentoring programs, developing programs to provide special education technical assistance should be considered as well as strategies to reduce teachers'
administrative workloads. Completing paperwork and attending meetings
also represent activities that take time away from teaching. Neither exclusively measuring student performance on standardized tests nor the extent
of teacher compliance with policies and processes through document review
are sufficient as measures of the effectiveness of special education services
provided. Instead, instructional effectiveness must be evaluated based on a
combination of criteria that are designed to maximize student learning.

To encourage special educators to provide appropriate educational services to students with disabilities, the MOE chose to use a financial incentive. Special funding allowances represent an effective motivator, but they
are only one of many possible support strategies for special educators.
Nonmonetary strategies should be used such as awards to recognize
high performing special education teachers or productive working conditions (e.g., support from colleagues and administrators) that retain good
special educators in the field.

*Ensure High Quality IEPs – Curriculum, Strategies,
and Evaluation*

Every student with special needs requires an IEP. By having an IEP, the
child is assured an appropriate curriculum (e.g., content to learn and progress at his own pace), appropriate instructional strategies (e.g., which
instructional methods work best for this child), and appropriate evaluation
(e.g., how to measure what the child has learned). Everyone involved with
the child should participate in IEP process. Parents should become

knowledgeable about and advocate for an IEP for their child. Most importantly, they must understand that an IEP is not only possible but desirable. Special education teachers should devote more time and efforts on IEP development and communicating with parents, other professionals, and students themselves if appropriate. School administrators should attend IEP meetings and ensure that the documents are prepared consistent with recommended practices. Finally, the MOE should enforce policies related to IEP development.

Improve Teacher Education

Thailand desperately needs more qualified special educators. Institutions of higher education should expand their special education programs to produce more students. In addition to increasing the supply of special education teachers, the quality of their preparation must also be addressed. Related to increasing the quality of the training of special educators, faculty members should be encouraged to expand their knowledge and skills in the area of special education. Efforts should also be directed toward retaining effective teachers. Teacher educators should also be encouraged to produce more special education resources (e.g., textbooks) in order to expand the knowledge base in the field. To achieve these goals, institutions of higher education must support their faculty through such means as grants for continuing education, incentives for writing, and encouraging their efforts in publishing textbooks and online media. At the same time, the MOE must also support these efforts. Finally, and most importantly, long-term policies to improve teacher quality should be developed.

Encourage Collaboration

Collaboration is critical for the success of students and teachers. Special educators need to work with general education teachers and other professionals. When students move to the next grade, special educators and general educators in both grades need to collaborate. Also, transitioning between services or moving into the different phases of their lives, students benefit from collaboration among responsible agencies under the three ministries in planning their services. With effective communication and collaboration, individuals with different roles and responsibilities and agencies would work as a team toward the same goal. They should also communicate with each other to align data and policies. This collaboration would produce increased and more accurate communication in the field.

Seek Long-Term Policy

Thailand has had 15 Ministers of Education in the past 16 years (Thaipublica, January 24, 2014). Frequent changes at this level have had a significant impact on policy and educational services for individuals with disabilities. To improve the quality of education for individuals with disabilities, education policies should be less influenced by political parties and politicians and more by needs in the field. This change would lead to more stability in policies and services for this vulnerable population of Thai citizens.

CONCLUSIONS

The field of special education in Thailand began in the late 1930s, and progress has been made over the last 80 years. Despite a number of improvements, the field of special education in this country still needs significant changes that require efforts from everyone involved to improve the quality of services and the lives of people with disabilities. Expanding the knowledge base, resources, teacher preservice education and retention, parent education and empowerment, effective monitoring systems, and long-term policies need continuous work. At the same time, Thai citizens must be educated to develop more positive attitudes toward disabilities in general and individuals who live with them.

NOTE

1. Mom is a title for a common woman who got married with a royal family member.

REFERENCES

Arrayawinyoo, P. (2001). *An estimation of special education teachers demand.* Retrieved from http://www.thaiedresearch.org/thaied/index.php?q=thaied_results&-table=thaied_results&-action=browse&-cursor=401&-skip=390&-limit=30&-mode=list&-sort=title+asc&-recordid=thaied_results%3Fid%3D6079

Bangkok Metropolitan. (2013). *Development of quality of life of individuals with disabilities plan (2010–2011)*. Retrieved from http://203.155.220.230/info/Plan/Planacc53_54/plana53_54.pdf

BSE. (2011). *History*. Retrieved from http://special.obec.go.th/history_sss/thai.html

BSE. (2012). *Development of education for individuals with disabilities plan (2012–2016)*. Retrieved from http://special.obec.go.th/download/19.9.55_Pland.pdf

Chandrakasem Rajabhat University. (2013). *Thailand's basic education*. Retrieved from http://arit.chandra.ac.th/edu/Patiroob/education4.html

Chulalongkorn University. (2012). *A study on professional autonomy in teaching*. Retrieved from http://www.ksp.or.th/ksp2009/upload/ksp_kuru_research/files/2935-9862.pdf

Daily News. (2007, December 17). *The new law forbids schools' denial of children with disabilities*. Retrieved from http://news.sanook.com/education/1/education_224731.php

Dhammaviteekul, A. (2009). *Non-formal education*. Retrieved from http://panchalee.wordpress.com/2009/05/17/non-formaleducation/

Dheandhanoo, C. (1992). The progress of Rajanukul hospital within 30 years. *Rajanukul Journal, 7*(1), 8–21.

DSS. (2012, December 3). *Re: Asking for comments on research: Quality of life of students with disabilities at Chiangmai Rajabhat University (Facebook DSS group)*. Retrieved from https://www.facebook.com/download/355925877837033/_ART_ART%20ART__%201-2.docx

FBTQ. (2013). *About us*. Retrieved from http://www.blind.or.th/en/about-us

FMRTH. (2013). *About us*. Retrieved from http://www.fmrth.com/about_us.php

Harwell, S. H. (2003). *Teacher professional development: It's not an event, it's a process*. Retrieved from http://www.cord.org/uploadedfiles/harwellpaper.pdf

IDEA. (2004). *Individuals with disabilities education and improvement act (2004)*. Retrieved from http://idea.ed.gov

Jeerapornchai, P. (2010). *Developing a program to enhance self-determination on making decision skills of grades 4–6 students with intellectual disabilities*. Doctoral dissertation, Srinakharinwirot University. Retrieved from http://thesis.swu.ac.th/swudis/Spe_Ed/Panichaka_J.pdf

Khun Poom Foundation. (2013). *Khun Poom Foundation*. Retrieved from http://www.give.asia/charity/khun_poom_foundation

Kitdham, P. (2013). *Types of disability*. Retrieved from http://sichon.wu.ac.th/file/pt-shh-20110120-171550-LGxcP.pdf

Komkris, V. (1989). Medical care of children with mental retardation to social integration. *The 16th World Congress of Rehabilitation International, 14*, 591–633.

Kosuwan, K. (2010). *Intellectual disabilities*. Nonthaburi, Thailand: Sahamit.

Kosuwan, K. (2012). *The efficacy of teacher training program for enhancing knowledge and positive attitudes toward teaching self-determination to students with intellectual disabilities in special schools*. Retrieved from http://educms.pn.psu.ac.th/edujn/include/getdoc.php?id=584&article=212&mode=pdf

Lopburipanyanukul. (2013). *History of Lopburipanyanukul School*. Retrieved from http://www.lopburipanya.com/index.php?option=com_content&view=article&id=50&Itemid=29

Manager Online. (2012, December 4). *The government approved an extra allowance for special educators*. Retrieved from http://www.manager.co.th/qol/viewnews.aspx?NewsID=9550000147674

Manager Online. (2013, April 26). *Policy of the Ministry of Education resulted lower quality of education*. Retrieved from http://www.manager.co.th/Home/ViewNews.aspx?NewsID=9560000050418

Manager Online. (2013, July 6). *List of inclusive schools*. Retrieved from http://www.manager.co.th/family/ViewNews.aspx?NewsID=9540000082682

MOE. (2005). *Population 6 years of age and over by literacy, age group, sex and area: 2005*. Retrieved from http://www.google.com/url?sa=t&rct=j&q=&esrc=s&source=web&cd=1&ved=0CCsQFjAA&url=http%3A%2F%2Fwww.moe.go.th%2Fdata_stat%2F Download_Excel%2FOutsourceData%2FLiteracyRate2548.xls&ei=vaXcUr3cC4e1i Qec0IBQ&usg=AFQjCNF6XlaotGN9fmXFItvMGWxcNCmy9w&sig2=wgpWjIxhi 7hdPAb3e6Fddg&bvm=bv.59568121,d.aGc

MOE. (2013). *National education act 1999*. Retrieved from http://www.moe.go.th/main2/plan/p-r-b42-01.htm#4

MOPH. (2013). *People with disabilities rehabilitation act (1994)*. Retrieved from http://www.moph.go.th/ops/minister_06/Office2/disable%20law.pdf

MSO. (2013). *Summary of social statistics 2013*. Retrieved from http://www.m-society.go.th/edoc_detail.php?edocid=778

MUA. (2011). *Current teacher education program*. Retrieved from http://www.mua.go.th/pr_ web/udom_mua/data/392.pdf

MUA. (2013). *Royal Thai government gazette (June 8, 2009): Type and criteria for individuals with disabilities in education*. Retrieved from http://www.mua.go.th/users/he-commis-sion/doc/law/ministry%20law/1-42%20handicap%20MoE.pdf

Nakhon Ratchasima Rajabhat University. (2011). *General information on inclusive education*. Retrieved from www.nrru.ac.th/web/special_edu/1-1.html#top

National Education Act, B.E. 2542. (1999). Retrieved from http://planipolis.iiep.unesco.org/upload/Thailand/Thailand_Education_Act_1999.pdf

NEP. (2013a). *Thailand Constitutional Law (1997)*. Retrieved from http://nep.go.th/sites/default/files/files/law/6.pdf

NEP. (2013b). *Thailand Constitutional Law (2007)*. Retrieved from http://nep.go.th/sites/default/files/files/law/2_1.pdf

NEP. (2013c). *Education for individuals with disabilities act (2008)*. Retrieved from http://nep.go.th/sites/default/files/files/law/38.pdf

NEP. (2013d). *Concept of disabilities*. Retrieved from www.nep.go.th/upload/modResearch/file_4_tn-27-182.pdf

NSO. (2013a). *The 2011 key statistics of Thailand: Social and cultural aspects*. Retrieved from http://service.nso.go.th/nso/nsopublish/themes/files/soc-culPocket.pdf

NSO. (2013b). *Number of people with disabilities by disability registration*. Retrieved from http://service.nso.go.th/nso/nso_center/project/table/files/S-disable/2550/000/00_ S-disable_2550_000_000000_03200.xls

NSO. (2013c). *Number of persons with disabilities aged 5–30 years not attending school*. Retrieved from http://service.nso.go.th/nso/nso_center/project/table/files/S-disable/2550/000/00_S-disable_2550_000_000000_00400.xls

NSO. (2013d). *Number of persons with disabilities aged 15 years and over who do not work*. Retrieved from http://service.nso.go.th/nso/nso_center/project/table/files/S-disable/2550/000/00_S-disable_2550_000_000000_01100.xls

OBEC. (2013a). *Educational statistics report 2013*. Retrieved from http://www.bopp-obec.info/home/?page_id=5993

OBEC. (2013b). *Number of special education teachers in special education settings (2011).* Retrieved from http://doc.obec.go.th/web/report/sum2_other1.php

Onkoaksoong, C. (1984). *Exceptional children psychology.* Bangkok, Thailand: Karnsasana Printing.

Persons with Disabilities' Quality of Life Promotion Act, B.E. 2550. (2007). Retrieved from http://www.ilo.org/wcmsp5/groups/public/@ed_emp/@ifp_skills/documents/publication/wcms_112307.pdf

Punlee, P., Wongwan, S., Nildam, A., & Intapanya, U. (1973). *Special education in Thailand.* Unpublished document, Prasarnmit College of Education.

Rajanukul. (2013). *About us.* Retrieved from http://www.rajanukul.com/eng/index.php?mode=about&submode=about&group=1

Rattanasakorn, S. (2007). *Education for all: Inclusion for children with special needs.* Retrieved from http://www.myfirstbrain.com/teacher_view.aspx?ID=68821

Rehabilitation of Disabled Persons Act, B.E. 2534. (1991). Retrieved from http://thailaws.com/law/t_laws/tlaw0245.pdf

Roonjareon, S. (2013). *Special education law.* Retrieved from http://edoffice.kku.ac.th/research/files/108926-8-3-LAW.pdf

Schalock, R. L. (2004). The concept of quality of life: What we know and do not know. *Journal of Intellectual Disability Research, 48*(3), 203–216.

School for the Blind. (2013). *Hall of fame.* Retrieved from http://www.blind.or.th/en/about-us/hall-of-fame

Setsatian. (2013). *History.* Retrieved from http://www.setsatian.ac.th

Srinakharinwirot University. (2013). *Special education.* Retrieved from http://specialed.edu.swu.ac.th/

Srisangwan School. (2013). *Srisangwan School history.* Retrieved from http://swn.ac.th/home1.html

Thai Lawyer Center. (2013). *Enhancing and developing quality of life of individuals with disabilities act (2007).* Retrieved from www.thailandlawyercenter.com/index.php?lay=show&ac=article&Id=538975829&Ntype=19

Thaipublica. (2014, January 24). *When Thailand has had 15 Ministers of Education within 16 years.* Retrieved from http://thaipublica.org/2014/01/the-performance-period-of-the-minister-of-education/

Thairath. (2009, July 3). *Thailand's year of reading.* Retrieved from http://www.thairath.co.th/content/edu/24503

Thairath. (2013, January 18). *Parents protested the director of Nakhonratchsima special education center.* Retrieved from http://www.thairath.co.th/content/edu/321061

Thammarak, T. (2013). *Karma: Effects of causes.* Retrieved from http://torthammarak.wordpress.com/author/happybookcm/

TJIC. (2013). *Over 400,000 children with disabilities are out of school.* Retrieved from http://www.tcijthai.com/tcijthai/view.php?ids=3318

Viriyangkura, Y. (2010). *Family life of young adults with severe intellectual disabilities in the central region of Thailand.* Master thesis, Srinakharinwirot University. Retrieved from http://thesis.swu.ac.th/swuthesis/Spe_Ed/Yuwadee_V.pdf

Wipattanaporn, C. (2014). *Special education in Thailand.* Retrieved from http://www.ser01.com/page/special%20ed%20thai.htm

Yodkhampang, S. (2004). *Teaching children with special needs.* Chiangmai, Thailand: Chiangmai Rajabhat University.